אגרת הקודש

THE STEINSALTZ TANYA

Iggeret HaKodesh

VOLUME IV

THE MAGERMAN EDITION

THE STEINSALTZ TANYA

IGGERET HAKODESH
1–17

COMMENTARY & TRANSLATION BY

RABBI ADIN EVEN-ISRAEL STEINSALTZ

Steinsaltz Center

Maggid Books

The Steinsaltz Tanya:
Iggeret HaKodesh 1–17, Volume 4
First edition, 2024

Maggid Books
An imprint of Koren Publishers Jerusalem Ltd.

POB 8531, New Milford, CT 06776-8531, USA
& POB 4044, Jerusalem 9104001, Israel
www.maggidbooks.com

This book was published in cooperation with
the Israeli Institute for Talmudic Publications.

We acknowledge with gratitude the generous support of
Terri and Stephen Geifman, *who made possible an earlier edition of this commentary.*

Steinsaltz Center is the parent organization of institutions
established by Rabbi Adin Even-Israel Steinsaltz
POB 45187, Jerusalem 91450 ISRAEL
Telephone: +972 2 646 0900, Fax +972 2 624 9454
www.steinsaltz-center.org

Cover design by Tani Bayer

ISBN 978-1-59264-587-9, hardcover

Printed and bound in the United States

Executive Director, Steinsaltz Center
Rabbi Meni Even-Israel

Editor-in-Chief
Rabbi Jason Rappoport

Translators
Zev Bannet
Noam Harris
Yaacov David Shulman
Oritt Sinclair

Editors
Suri Brand, Senior Editor
Noam Harris
Debbie Ismailoff
Rabbi Zalman Margolin
Yaacov Dovid Shulman
Rabbi Michael Siev

Proofreader
Shlomo Liberman

Hebrew Proofreader
Avichai Gamdani

Hebrew Edition Editors
Rabbi Meir Hanegbi, Senior Editor
Rabbi Hillel Mondshein
Rabbi David Brokner

Hebrew Vocalization
Rabbi Hillel Mondshein

Technical Staff
Adena Frazer
Adina Mann
Avi Steinhart

Dedicated to

my wife, **Debra**,

and my children,
Elijah, **Zachary**, **Sydney**, and **Lexie**.

May this new translation of the Tanya,
along with the commentary from Rabbi Steinsaltz (*z"l*),
bring us closer to hasidic teaching and
help us connect with the mystical meaning
behind the Torah.

May all the children of Israel use
the Tanya's knowledge and wisdom
to work together to hasten the coming of Mashiaḥ.

David M. Magerman

ספר התניא מלמד אותנו שהנפש האלוקית מסורה כל כולה לקב"ה והיא מבחינה זו חסרת אנוכיות או תחושת ישות. הנפש הבהמית לעומת זאת מרוכזת בעצמה ומסורה לקיומה הנפרד.

לפיכך לימד אותנו האדמו"ר האמצעי שכאשר שני יהודים לומדים או משוחחים בענייני עבודת ה׳ הרי אלו שתי נשמות אלוקיות כנגד נפש בהמית אחת. הנפש הבהמית לא מצטרפת עם חבירתה משום שכאמור היא מסורה לעצמה אבל הנפשות האלוקיות מצטרפות יחד בלי כל חציצה או הבדל.

(מתוך: "היום יום" כ׳ לטבת)

לזכות
משה ליב בן זיסל שיחי׳ לאיוש"ט
שולמית בת זהרה שתחי׳ לאיוש"ט

The *Tanya* teaches us that the divine soul is fully devoted to G-d, and therefore it is selfless. By contrast, the animal soul is selfish, devoted only to maintaining its own existence.

The Mitteler Rebbe, Rabbi Dovber of Lubavitch, taught that when two Jews learn or discuss matters pertaining to service of God, there are two divine souls against one animal soul. The animal soul thinks only of itself and will not attach itself to the animal soul of the other. But the two divine souls are joined together with no division or barrier.

(Cited from *HaYom Yom*, 20 Tevet)

In the merit of
MOSHE LEIB BEN ZISEL
SHULAMIT BAT ZOHARA

A blessing from the Lubavitcher Rebbe, Rabbi Menaḥem Mendel Schneerson, dated 21 Av 5721 (August 3, 1961), viewing with favor Rabbi Steinsaltz's project of writing a short commentary, with longer explanations, on the *Tanya* in a style accessible to the contemporary reader:

(ושאלות ותשובות – כהמצורף למכתבו) בעניינים המובאים בתניא, כן ביאור קצר או גם ארוך, ובסגנונו, ערוכים בלשון בני דורנו...

בברכה לבשו"ט

In December 2012, the final volume of the Hebrew edition of *The Steinsaltz Tanya* was published. That year, at a hasidic gathering, Rabbi Adin Steinsaltz shared why he wrote the book. He explained that Rabbi Shneur Zalman of Liadi, the author of the *Tanya,* had poured his entire soul, his love and awe, his soul-wrenching oneness with God into that concise book, into pages that obscured his immense spirit so well. Through his commentary, Rabbi Steinsaltz strove to reveal to us this spirit, that powerful fire just barely contained by the words of the *Tanya.*

And he certainly succeeded. Yet he failed to mask his own burning spirit, his own love, awe, and closeness to God, as he had attempted to do his entire life.

The publication of this English edition of *The Steinsaltz Tanya* is the fulfillment of Rabbi Steinsaltz's vision to make the teachings of the *Tanya* accessible to every single individual. At the height of the preparations for this edition, our teacher Rabbi Adin Even-Israel passed away.

In this book, one learns how the life of the tzaddik lives on in this world, in those who learn his works. It is through those students who are open to receiving his teachings and are inspired to build upon his words that his light remains with us. We pray that this commentary of Rabbi Steinsaltz will introduce many generations of Jews to the world of the *Tanya* and to the path of authentic devotion to God.

May it serve to elevate his soul.

Contents

For the Hebrew Tanya Vilna edition, open from the Hebrew side of the book.

אִגֶּרֶת הַקֹּדֶשׁ

Iggeret HaKodesh

The Holy Epistle

Preface to *Iggeret HaKodesh*

Iggeret HaKodesh, or "The Holy Epistle," is the fourth section of the *Tanya*. It is not a treatise in the usual sense of the word, with a beginning, middle, and end. Rather, it is a collection of epistles that the author of the *Tanya* addressed to groups of his hasidim on various occasions regarding a variety of topics.[1] Each epistle was written as an independent unit without reference to the others. Nevertheless, it is clear that they have been thoughtfully arranged, not chronologically but thematically. Wherever possible, these thematic connections are noted in the introductions to the epistles.

The common denominator between these epistles is that they are letters from a Rebbe to his hasidim. As such, they open with verses from the Torah or sayings from the Sages, as well as various hasidic teachings, and then proceed to discuss a specific topic – the purpose for which the letter was written.[2] These teachings are significant in that they represent Torah teachings that the author of the *Tanya* wrote himself in his own words. Moreover, the teachings are applied to particular circumstances in the life of the hasidim.

Since the author of the *Tanya* wrote these epistles in his own hand,

1. It would seem that this section should have been more aptly titled *Iggerot HaKodesh,* "Holy Epistles," in the plural. Perhaps it was given its present title to align with the title of the previous section, *Iggeret HaTeshuva.*
2. At times, if the author of the *Tanya* had a message for his hasidim that he did not wish to publicize, he did not write it down but transmitted it orally through the emissary who delivered these epistles. See *Sefer HaKen* by Rabbi Ḥayyim Lieberman.

they are considered sacrosanct, an essential part of his Torah teachings. In light of this, in 1814 *Iggeret HaKodesh* was published by his sons as an inseparable part of the *Tanya*, which is more broadly considered a foundational hasidic work.

In preparing these epistles for publication, salutations, valedictions, dates, and place names were generally excluded unless these details were essential to understanding the letter's main message.[3] Despite these elisions, the unique character of each epistle has been preserved, both with regard to the intended recipients, indicating whether they were part of the inner circle of the author's hasidim or a broader group, and with regard to the content. This might comprise the elucidation of deep concepts in hasidic thought, an impassioned plea to give charity, or a request that the hasidim take on a certain mode of conduct required of them at that time.

The topics under discussion cover a broad spectrum, encompassing all areas of Jewish life: Torah study, prayer, and mitzvot. Some epistles relate to specific issues affecting the lives of the hasidim, such as those impacting their relationship with their Rebbe or those involving their opponents. Some speak of special occasions, such as the author of the *Tanya*'s release from prison on 19 Kislev or the passing away of a tzaddik. But the topic that recurs most often is the mitzva of giving charity.

The Jewish community, and the hasidic community in particular, was impoverished, and the giving of charity was vital to its survival. This was especially the case for those who had emigrated to the Land of Israel, whom the hasidim living outside the Holy Land had undertaken to support. But precisely because of the widespread poverty, this was a mitzva that was extremely difficult to fulfill. The author of the *Tanya* demanded of his hasidim substantial donations, and not just from discretionary funds but from income they needed for their own survival. To this end, the epistles state that giving charity is not only about helping a person in need, but rather it has a profound impact on the benefactor, even more than on the recipient.

Moreover, since these epistles were written by a Rebbe, and a Rebbe

---

3. The epistles were arranged by the author of the *Tanya*'s sons, who apparently lacked access to the author's original letters but rather were able to obtain only copies. See the approbation to the Shklov edition of the *Tanya* (1814).

does not occupy himself only with his followers' material well-being but also with their spiritual well-being, the letters explain how giving charity, and performing charitable acts in general, constitutes the innermost and most precious expression of a person's essence. This awakens God's benevolence at the loftiest levels so that He bestows on the giver of charity a life of both material and spiritual prosperity.

Epistle 1

ALTHOUGH THIS LETTER, THE FIRST IN THIS COMPILATION known as *Iggeret HaKodesh,* opens by referring to a particular event, it addresses general topics in the service of God that apply at any time and in any place: the essence of Torah, faith and prayer, and the dynamic between them.[1] To set the background for these concepts, in the letter's opening and particularly at its conclusion, the author of the *Tanya* requests of his students, not something abstract, but rather that which relates to the order of prayer in the synagogue, its schedule, and the choosing of a prayer leader. The analytical portion of the letter also focuses primarily on the order of public prayer and even touches on the concept of the service of prayer of every individual.

פּוֹתְחִין בִּבְרָכָה לְבָרֵךְ וּלְהוֹדוֹת לַה׳ כִּי טוֹב.

We begin with a benediction, to bless and give thanks to God, for He is good.

3 Av

7 Av (leap year)

In line with letters of this kind, the author of the *Tanya* opens with poetic words comprised of passages from the *Tanakh* and the Sages.[2] Afterward, he returns to his signature style.

1. See *Sefer HaMa'amarim* (5708), p. 170, which states that this letter was actually not written at a single point in time but rather at various times that span the formative years of the Chabad hasidic movement under the leadership of Rabbi Shneur Zalman of Liadi, the author of the *Tanya.*
2. The expression "to give thanks to God, for He is good" appears many times in *Tanakh.* See, e.g., Jer. 33:11 and Ps. 106:1. The phrase is an expression of gratitude for good tidings. See Rashi, Gen. 24:52.

שְׁמוּעָה טוֹבָה שָׁמְעָה וַתְּחִי נַפְשִׁי, אֵין טוֹב אֶלָּא תּוֹרָה (אבות פרק ו משנה ג),

My soul has heard good tidings and has been revived, and "'good' means nothing but Torah" (Mishna *Avot* 6:3).

This expression of gratitude refers to the "good tidings" regarding Torah study, which is that it enlivens the soul.

תּוֹרַת ה׳ תְּמִימָה, זוֹ הַשְׁלָמַת כָּל הַשַּׁ״ס כּוּלּוֹ

Moreover, God's Torah is perfect, restoring the soul. I **refer to the completion of all of Talmud in its entirety**

By using the Hebrew word *temima*, perfect, to describe the Torah,[3] a word that also connotes that which is whole or complete, the author of the *Tanya* hints at the completion of the entire Talmud. To this day, it is customary among Chabad hasidim to learn the entire Talmud every year, beginning from the nineteenth of Kislev until the nineteenth of Kislev of the next year. The tractates are divided among the hasidim, each one resolving to complete the tractate that he most resonates with and that is within his capacity to study so that the entire Talmud may be completed once every year. ☞

THE COMPLETION OF THE TALMUD

☞ The completion of the Talmud is scheduled for 19 Kislev since it is the "New Year" for Chabad hasidim. This is a day of celebration, the date on which the author of the *Tanya*, Rabbi Shneur Zalman of Liadi, was released from incarceration (see *Iggerot Kodesh* by the fifth Lubavitcher Rebbe, Rabbi Sholom Dovber Schneerson, vol. 2, p. 98). This part of the letter was written, however, before the incarceration and redemption on 19 Kislev, and the custom to complete the Talmud in one year was already being practiced in some communities. When Rabbi Shneur Zalman was incarcerated, his followers resolved to increase their Torah study, and when he was released from prison on the nineteenth of Kislev, the hasidim decided to commemorate this event by beginning and ending the cycle of Talmud study on this day, the day that he was released from prison, the day of liberation, the day of redemption.

3. Based on Ps. 19:8.

בְּרוֹב עֲיָירוֹת וּמִנְיָנִים מֵאַנְשֵׁי שְׁלוֹמֵנוּ.

in most towns and congregations of our community of hasidim.

As these lines show, there were already entire towns of hasidim in those times in the region where the author of the *Tanya* was living. "Congregations of our community" refers to towns that, though not entirely hasidic, had hasidic congregations.

הוֹדָאָה עַל הֶעָבָר וּבַקָּשָׁה עַל הֶעָתִיד.

I express **gratitude for the past and a plea for the future.**

The author of the *Tanya* expresses his gratitude for their completing the Talmud in the past year and makes an appeal for the future: that they accomplish the same the next year and every year thereafter.

כֹּה יִתֵּן וְכֹה יוֹסִיף ה׳, לְאַמֵּץ לִבָּם בַּגִּבּוֹרִים, מִדֵּי שָׁנָה בְּשָׁנָה בִּגְבוּרָה שֶׁל תּוֹרָה. וּלְהוֹדִיעַ לִבְנֵי אָדָם גְּבוּרָתָהּ שֶׁל תּוֹרָה שֶׁבְּעַל פֶּה וְכֹחָהּ עוֹז.

May God thus continue to grant and increase their ability to complete the study of the Talmud, **strengthening their hearts among the mighty with the might of Torah from year to year and informing mankind of the strength of the Oral Torah and its great power.**

Just as God gave the hasidim the energy to complete the Talmud this year, so may He grant them the strength to complete it in the future with even greater fortitude. The author of the *Tanya* specifies the quality of might in relation to the Oral Torah since this aspect of the Torah is aligned with the side of *Gevura*, the attribute of restraint.[4] The Oral Torah constricts and delimits the Written Torah within the parameters of the reality of this world. It also gives power and strength to those who study it to overcome the barriers of the concealment and physicality inherent in this world and in the body while experiencing divine illumination without being nullified or burned by it.[5]

4. *Zohar* 3:257a; see also *Etz Ḥayyim* 35:83.
5. See *Torah Or* 66a; *Likkutei Amarim*, chap. 36.

פֵּירֵשׁ שְׁלֹמֹה הַמֶּלֶךְ עָלָיו הַשָּׁלוֹם: "חֲגְרָה בְעוֹז מָתְנֶיהָ כו'" (משלי לא, יז).

King Solomon, may he rest in peace, explained, "She girds her loins with might…" (Prov. 31:17).

The chapter from which this verse is taken describes the woman of valor, extolling the virtues of the Jewish woman. While this can be taken at face value, its mystical underpinnings open up an entirely different dimension.

The woman of valor is a metaphor for all of reality, for the *sefira* of *Malkhut* (Kingship), for the congregation of Israel, and for the unique holy soul of every individual Jew. In this light, the verse can be understood on a new level. "Might" refers to the Torah, as the Sages affirm: "There is no might besides the Torah."[6] But it is not clear what the "loins" of the Torah refer to, and therefore the author of the *Tanya* goes on to explain this expression in the verse.

'מָתְנַיִם' הֵם בְּחִינַת דָּבָר הַמַּעֲמִיד כָּל הַגּוּף עִם הָרֹאשׁ הַנִּצָּב וְעוֹמֵד עֲלֵיהֶם, וְהֵם הַמּוֹלִיכִים וּמְבִיאִים אוֹתוֹ לִמְחוֹז חֶפְצוֹ.

The loins are the aspect of the body **that supports the entire body, including the head, which is perched** atop the body, **positioned above** the loins. **It is** the loins **that carry** the body **and bring it to its desired destination.**

The loins are what we call the pelvic region, which includes the two legs that emerge from it. The pelvis has two functions: First, it provides stability for the body since it is where the body's weight is centered, and second, it gives the body the ability to move from one place to another. While the head, the center of awareness and cognition, and the heart, the emotional focal point, are loftier, they are incapable of standing alone without the support of the pelvis and unable to move from one place to another without the legs.

וּכְמוֹ שֶׁהוּא בְּגַשְׁמִיּוּת הַגּוּף, כָּךְ הוּא בִּבְחִינַת רוּחָנִיּוּת הַנֶּפֶשׁ הָאֱלֹהִית.

Just as it is with regard to the physical anatomy **of the body, so it is with the spiritual structure of the divine soul.**

6. *Sifrei*, Deut. 32:2, *Shir HaShirim Rabba* 2:10; *Zohar* 2:58a.

The physical structure of man reflects his spiritual composition.[7] A person's spiritual faculties are his spiritual limbs, metaphysical mirrors of his corporeal limbs. There is, then, a spiritual faculty that fills the role of the hips within one's soul, that supports one's conscious essence (the head) and his emotions (the body), enabling him to function without losing his composure and sense of self.

הָאֱמוּנָה הָאֲמִיתִּית בַּה' אֶחָד, The loins of the soul are **true faith in the one God,**

The spiritual faculty called the loins of the soul is the power of faith. Before the author of the *Tanya* goes on to explain how faith, like the loins, holds up the rest of the soul's faculties, he says a few words about faith. The faith that he is talking about, the faith that one's entire spiritual structure stands upon, must be true faith in the one God.

True faith is distinguished in two ways. The first is to believe in that which is true. Some people may harbor faith in that which is false. The second is to truly believe; one's faith must be genuine and palpable. These two facets of faith do not necessarily go hand in hand. A person once asked a rabbi, "Why are heretics so successful?" The rabbi answered, "Because they truly practice their falsity, while we superficially practice our truth." ☞

TRUE FAITH

☞ For faith to be true, it must be defined and specific. This is not the common concept of faith that people refer to today. Faith is what people call that indefinable feeling for the inexplicable. When they feel they have no choice, no other way to relate to something they think is true, they say that they believe. This is how people educate children about values, with that same general vagueness that does not directly explain anything. What kind of values are they? Faith in what? How does this faith relate to me?

Therefore, the author of the *Tanya* emphasizes that the faith he is talking about must be true and real, not just a vague sentiment but rather a defined system of belief that a person lives by, that is integral to his being. It is true faith because it contains particular content, because it is directed toward defined goals. Although that content is rationally incomprehensible, inexplicable, and unprovable, it is rooted in the soul in a very deep and real way and paves a clear road of commitment before the believer.

In his introduction to *Sha'ar HaYiḥud Ve-*

7. See the introduction to *Tikkunei Zohar* 17a.

Moreover, the content of this faith must be in the one God. While faith is a spiritual faculty that transcends rationale, it is built on the basis of a particular cognitive recognition. This logic encompasses the assertion of God's oneness in detail, as will now be explained.

אֵין סוֹף בָּרוּךְ הוּא, דְּאִיהוּ מְמַלֵּא כָּל עָלְמִין וְסוֹבֵב כָּל עָלְמִין,

***Ein Sof*, blessed be He, who fills all worlds and encompasses all worlds,**

Asserting God's oneness means affirming that He exists within everything and beyond everything and that nothing exists outside His oneness. Other sources explain that this perspective of God's unity, that He fills and surrounds every aspect of reality, is actually the definition of faith.[8] The mitzva to believe in God does not entail abstractly believing that He exists. His existence can and must be understood, known, and even felt, with whatever degree of clarity a person can cultivate, just as a person senses the reality of His soul. The mitzva of faith relates not only to God's existence but to His essence: that it fills all worlds and encompasses all worlds. ☞

Ha'emuna, the author of the *Tanya* explains the proverb "Train the lad in accordance with his way; even when he grows old, he will not turn from it" (Prov. 22:6). The education of a small child must obviously begin with simple wording that is "according to his way." Yet it is crucial to transmit true content so that "even when he grows old, he will not turn from it." When a person depicts God to a young child, he may describe the imagery of an old man giving out candies from his abode in Heaven. This is certainly "according to his way" since it is an image the child can easily comprehend. But when the child grows older, he will stop believing it. When a person thinks that faith in God means believing in a giant with a white beard who is out there somewhere, at a certain point he stops believing in it. Rightfully so, not only because a rational person does not believe in such a thing, but also because it is downright forbidden to believe it (see Rambam, *Mishneh Torah, Sefer HaMadda, Hilkhot Yesodei HaTorah* 1:5). Therefore, the author of the *Tanya* emphasizes that one must relate accurate concepts even to children, only using appropriate wording so that no matter what a person's level, his comprehension and resonance with those concepts will be genuine.

BELIEVING THAT GOD FILLS AND SURROUNDS ALL WORLDS

☞ God's absolutely incomprehensible essence is described with phrases such as "He who fills all worlds and surrounds all worlds," "*Ein Sof*, blessed be He," and "the

8. See *Derekh Mitzvotekha, Mitzvat Ha'amanat Elokut.*

וְלֵית אֲתָר פָּנוּי מִינֵּיהּ, לְמַעְלָה עַד אֵין קֵץ, וּלְמַטָּה עַד אֵין תַּכְלִית,

and there is no space void of Him, in the boundless heights and never-ending depths,

The dimension of space in both the spiritual and physical realms has six poles: the four directions, above, and below. God fills each direction, and the infinite light is drawn from the highest of heights to the lowest of depths throughout the progressive descent of the Divine from the source above to the lowest world below. ☞

וְכֵן לְד׳ סִטְרִין, בִּבְחִינַת אֵין סוֹף מַמָּשׁ.

including the four directions, in an absolutely infinite manner.

Lord, He is the God" (see *Derekh Mitzvotekha, Mitzvat Aḥdut Hashem*). The same thread runs through all these expressions: the combination of two opposites, two ways that we can grasp and discuss God.

On the one hand, He fills all. He is the innermost dimension of every iota of reality, permeating everything. On the other hand, He encompasses all. He is the farthest, most distant, and hidden dimension of life, like a circle that surrounds, neither touching nor relating to anything at all. The expression "*Ein Sof*, blessed be He" expresses this dichotomy. On the one hand, God is *Ein Sof*, infinite, like the mathematical expression for that which cannot be measured or defined. On the other hand, He is "blessed." The Hebrew word for blessed, *barukh*, etymologically means to draw down and implies drawing close the transcendent Divine into this reality (see *Or HaTorah*, vol. 3, s.v. "*lehavin inyan haberakhot*").

Many hasidic discourses grapple with the reconciliation of these two aspects of God. Their main point is that the mutual existence of these two facets of the Divine is rationally inexplicable, and therefore belief in both these truths constitutes authentic faith in God.

BOUNDLESS HEIGHTS AND NEVER-ENDING DEPTHS

☞ What meaning does up and down have in the context of the light of *Ein Sof*? The line between up and down in the spiritual realm is determined by the order of progression. "Up" means greater revelation, and "down" means greater concealment. God's infinite essence is manifest in both directions but in different ways. "Up" signifies His ability to endlessly manifest Himself, while "down" expresses His ability to conceal and delimit Himself to an infinite degree. His power to illuminate and His power to conceal are equally endless.

Elsewhere, these two facets of *Ein Sof* are referred to as the power of limitlessness and the power of limit (see *Hemshekh Samekh Vav*, p.188). They serve as the source of the distinction between the light that encompasses all worlds and the light that fills all worlds.

Divine reality fills all the dimensions of space with infinitude. There is no vacant space, no molecule of reality that is impermeable to Him. As the liturgy known as *Shir HaYiḥud* declares, "There is no space empty or devoid of You."

וְכֵן בִּבְחִינַת שָׁנָה וָנֶפֶשׁ, כַּנּוֹדָע. **The same applies to the dimensions of year and soul, as is known.**

Reality consists of three basic dimensions: world, year, and soul, which correspond to existence as it manifests within space, time, and human beings.[9] True faith is believing that God's infinite essence fills all three dimensions. "Year" proverbially refers to time, including its abstract spiritual form: the facilitator of change. God fills it, from its beginning until its end, past, present, and the future. There is no time devoid of Him.

"Soul" refers to the conscious reality that is aware and senses the vitality that exists within time and space. In our world, we are the aware souls, while in a higher realm, the angels are the beings that perceive. Higher yet are the sentient beings called seraphim and so on. In every world, at all times, the souls in reality are permeated with pure divine light.

True faith, then, is knowing that on the one hand "there is no space devoid of Him," that every atom of the universe is absolutely permeated with the Divine Presence so that there is no separation between reality and Him in any way, shape, or form. He who believes that God exists in a particular place, while other places are not privy to God's presence and control, does not have true faith.

On the other hand, true faith must also include the belief that God is infinitely distant and separate, as it says, "This knowledge is too wondrous for me."[10] In view of this, the definition of faith is the basic awareness of God's existence as absolutely separate, beyond us, while simultaneously He is intimately close. He is the "Holy One, blessed be He": "holy" because He is unfathomably distant, and "blessed" because infinitely close.[11]

---

9. See *Sefer Yetzira* 3:6.

10. Ps. 139:6.

11. In hasidic teachings, the term for blessed, *barukh*, implies drawing down the infinite divine light into our selves and into objects, such as food.

הִנֵּה אֱמוּנָה זוֹ נִקְרֵאת בְּשֵׁם בְּחִינַת 'מָתְנַיִם', דָּבָר הַמַּעֲמִיד וּמְקַיֵּים אֶת הָרֹאשׁ, הוּא הַשֵּׂכֶל הַמִּתְבּוֹנֵן וּמַעֲמִיק דַּעַת

This faith is referred to by the term "loins," that which serve to support and uphold the head, which is the intellect that contemplates and deeply ponders

Once there is a foundation of faith, the next stage follows, that of the rationale of the intellect. The intellect contemplates and analyzes, delving in to inquire: What does this mean for me? What is its central axis?

Faith itself serves as the bedrock for every logical idea and feeling and establishes one's whole personhood. Faith constitutes an organic perception of reality, seeing things at their essence. It is not an analytic faculty that organizes and arranges ideas but rather a general outlook that informs a person how he experiences reality itself. When presented with particular concepts, it is faith that enlightens the person as to what is right and what is wrong. While this certainty is not rational nor scientifically provable, it serves as the foreground for all his thoughts and enables his entire rational functioning and being, from which stems all the faculties of the soul.

This is why the author of the *Tanya* places an emphasis on the intellect. The main, conscious spiritual work happens in the head through one's ability to think and contemplate rationally.

בִּגְדוּלַּת אֵין סוֹף בָּרוּךְ הוּא, בִּבְחִינַת 'עוֹלָם שָׁנָה נֶפֶשׁ',

the greatness of *Ein Sof*, blessed be He, in the dimensions of world, year, and soul

There are two facets to this contemplation. The first is contemplation of God's infinite greatness, of His vast distance and separateness. This contemplation evokes the sense of God's might and how that immense, almost oceanic power expresses itself in each of the dimensions of "world, year, and soul." To do this, one should consciously contemplate the infinite nature of space, the infinite aspect of time, and the infinite power of the soul. Afterward, he can attempt to stretch his mind even further to ruminate on the essence of the infinite in relation to the confines of those dimensions.

וּבְרוֹב חַסְדּוֹ וְנִפְלְאוֹתָיו עִמָּנוּ לִהְיוֹת עַם קְרוֹבוֹ, וּלְדָבְקָה בּוֹ מַמָּשׁ.

and God's **abounding kindness and His wonders** that He performs **with us,** allowing us **to be a people near to Him and to literally cleave to Him.**

The other subject of contemplation that the author of the *Tanya* suggests is not the abstract concept of God's exalted loftiness but rather the aspect of His closeness,[12] that the infinitely exalted God creates a personal relationship with each and every one of us, certainly a colossal kindness and wonder. This is true not only of the past, throughout our whole national history, but even within the details of every individual's present are revelations of His kindness and wonders.

כַּנּוֹדָע מִמַּאֲמַר "יָפָה שָׁעָה אַחַת בִּתְשׁוּבָה וּמַעֲשִׂים טוֹבִים בָּעוֹלָם הַזֶּה מִכָּל חַיֵּי עוֹלָם הַבָּא" (אבות פרק ד משנה יז),

This is **known from the** Sages' **statement "One hour of repentance and good deeds in this world is more precious than an entire lifetime in the World to Come"** (Mishna *Avot* 4:17),

This axiom from the Sages expresses this very idea of a person's intimate closeness to God against the backdrop of His infinity. The reference here to life in the World to Come refers to life in the Garden of Eden after death. Edenic experience is a very high level of spiritual experience. Every person, commensurate with his spiritual standing and deeds, has his own World to Come, his own level of divine revelation that his soul experiences after it is divested from all its bonds to the materiality of this world.

There are, in truth, levels upon levels of revelation, endless progressive phases of bonding with the supernal wisdom and delighting in the radiance of the Divine Presence to which a soul can aspire when it is divested of its ties to this material world. The gradations of the World to Come not only vary from person to person, but each individual may have countless rungs of revelation to climb in his own portion of the World to Come.[13]

"All the life of the World to Come," then, refers to all the levels of the

12. Based on Ps. 148:14.

13. See epistle 17.

World to Come. The Mishna is telling us that every movement toward repentance, every good deed, is loftier, deeper, and more powerful than all the achievements, levels, and potential for attachment to the Divine that one could attain in the World to Come.

שֶׁהוּא רַק זִיו וְהֶאָרָה מִבְּחִינָה הַנִּקְרֵאת שְׁכִינָה, "הַשּׁוֹכֵן" כו' (ויקרא טז, טז).

which is but a glimmer and illumination of the level called *Shekhina,* Divine Presence, whose name is derived from the verse **"that dwells** [*hashokhen*] with them…" (Lev. 16:16).

The Divine Presence is but a glimmer of the totality of God's essence, the manifestation of the Divine that has been clothed within the confines and parameters of reality, enlivening every minutia in existence.[14] Yet the World to Come in its entirety is merely an illumination of the Godly revelation experienced in this world called the Divine Presence.

וְנִבְרָא בְּיוּ"ד אַחַת מִשְּׁמוֹ יִתְבָּרֵךְ כו'.

The Word to Come **was created with the single** letter *yod* **of God's name and so on,**

The Sages point out that the name of God that appears in the verse "For God the Lord is an everlasting rock" (Isa. 26:4) is spelled *yod-heh.*[15] They explain that the Hebrew word for "everlasting," *olamim,* literally means "worlds," and the Hebrew word for "rock" that is used in the verse, *tzur,* shares root letters with the word *yatzar,* created. The verse may then read, "God created the [two] worlds [this world and the World to Come] with the letters *yod* and *heh.*"

A name is a particular manner of manifestation that reflects the relationship between the self and the outside world. The name of *Havaya,* which is the name that refers to the divine essence itself, is the name through which God enlivens all the worlds. More specifically, God used the *yod* from the name of *Havaya* to create the World to Come.

---

14. See also *Sifra, Bemidbar* 1; *Raya Meheimna* 3:255b.

15. *Menaḥot* 29b; Jerusalem Talmud, *Ḥagiga* 2:1; *Bereshit Rabba* 12:10.

The smallest letter in the Hebrew alphabet, the *yod* resembles nothing more than a point and is the embodiment of the most minimal degree of independent existence that one could fathom. It follows that the World to Come is nothing but a glimmer of the smallest letter of God's name, a mere spark of the divine light. The essence of the World to Come can be summed up as the most reduced experience of God's name, of the divine essence, that the soul can receive commensurate with its spiritual capacity at that time.

אֲבָל תְּשׁוּבָה וּמַעֲשִׂים טוֹבִים מְקָרְבִין יִשְׂרָאֵל לַאֲבִיהֶם שֶׁבַּשָּׁמַיִם מַמָּשׁ, לְמַהוּתוֹ וְעַצְמוּתוֹ כִּבְיָכוֹל, בְּחִינַת אֵין סוֹף מַמָּשׁ,

but repentance and good deeds bring the Jewish people close to their actual Father in Heaven, to His essence and being, as it were, the level of *Ein Sof* itself,

Repentance and good deeds are not merely instruments through which a person acquires the World to Come. The Torah study and mitzvot that a person performs in his daily life are in and of themselves points of contact with God's infinite essence,[16] opportunities for a genuine connection with God Himself. The closeness attained in the performance of a mitzva is not just a feeling of spiritual positivity from a faint glimmer of the divine light but literal attachment to God's actual infinite essence. ☞☞

CLEAVING TO GOD THROUGH TORAH AND MITZVOT

☞ The Talmud divulges that a deeper layer of the word *anokhi*, the first word of the Ten Commandments, emerges by reading it as an acronym: *Ana nafshi ketavit yehavit*, which means, "I Myself wrote and gave" (*Shabbat* 105a). The simple meaning of this is "I wrote [the Torah] Myself, and I am giving it to you." A deeper understanding is brought in the name of the Ba'al Shem Tov, who reads it as "I have articulated My essence in writing and am giving it to you [through the Torah]" (see *Degel Maḥaneh Efrayim, Ki Tisa*, s.v. "*pesel*"). This implies that the Torah is more

16. Repentance and good deeds are relevant only in this world: mitzvot, because they consist entirely of action in the material realm, and repentance, because the pivotal moment of transformation and change can happen only in our lower world. See *Likkutei Torah*, Lev. 75c.

than a revelation of the Divine. It is literally divine essence. One who engages in Torah study and the performance of mitzvot is fusing with the very essence of the Divine. When a person performs mitzvot, he is not holding an instrument that connects him with God, but rather forges contact directly with God (see *Likkutei Amarim*, chap. 14).

ILLUSORY ATTACHMENT

☞ Attachment to God and the experience of attachment are not necessarily synonymous. A person may feel close to God, while in reality his connection is imagined. On the flip side, a person can have a true attachment to God without a remarkable experience of it. The difference between this world and the World to Come depends on this distinction, on the experience versus the thing itself (even without the experience). In the World to Come, "one hour of tranquility is more precious than an entire lifetime in this world" (Mishna *Avot* 4:17), because it is a world of being, of experience alone, in which we feel and experience the results of our actions in this world. The degree of experience that the soul encounters in the World to Come is infinitely greater than its experience in this world because it is no longer limited to the confines and parameters of the body and its corporeal faculties. Therefore, the experience of the World to Come manifests through other-worldly dimensions and is unfathomably more powerful than the sum total of all the conceivable experiences of this world. Yet still, this world, which is the foreground for performing mitzvot, offers the opportunity for actual attachment to God. Therefore, "one hour of repentance and good deeds in this world is more precious is than an entire lifetime in the World to Come."

The fusion that we can achieve with God Himself in this world is due to "God's abounding kindness and His wonders that He performs with us," as the author of the *Tanya* points out above. Imagine a father and his young child. The father wants to connect in some way with the child, but the distance is too great. They are on totally different wavelengths, unable to relate to each other on a cognitive and emotional level. The only way that the father can forge a connection with his child is through an action: He can extend his hand to his child. The child does not understand at all who the father is and what their connection entails, yet when he takes hold of the hand outstretched to him, he literally connects himself to his father.

The *Zohar* calls the Torah and the mitzvot the "limbs of the King" (*Tikkunei Zohar* 74a). When God gave us the Torah, He gave us His hand, as it were. Every time a person performs a mitzva or studies Torah, he takes hold of God's proverbial hand and fosters a quintessential connection with God Himself, a bond one would not be able to forge in any other way.

A hand that reaches out to bridge an unbridgeable gap is a wondrous phenomenon that only God Himself can accomplish, from above to below. No matter how much a person is driven toward good, he cannot operate beyond his own parameters. Any attachment to God that he is privileged to attain is a product of "God's abounding kindness and His wonders that He performs with us."

וּכְמוֹ שֶׁכָּתוּב: "הוֹדוֹ עַל אֶרֶץ וְשָׁמָיִם וַיָּרֶם קֶרֶן לְעַמּוֹ כו'" (תהלים קמא, יג-יד),

as it is written, "For His name alone is exalted, **His glory across earth and heaven; He raises a horn for His people...**" (Ps. 148:13–14), for His people cleave to God's very essence.

This virtue of Torah study and mitzvot is expressed by this verse, which signifies that God is so exalted and singularly separate from all the revealed worlds that merely the glory and illumination from His name alone is sufficient to enliven and sustain all of reality. Yet, despite His unimaginable exalted essence, He raises a beam of His divine essence to His nation of Israel through the Torah and mitzvot so that they may literally cleave to Him.[17]

"אֲשֶׁר קִדְּשָׁנוּ בְּמִצְוֹתָיו כו'",

Similarly, in the blessings recited upon the performance of a mitzva, we address God **"who has sanctified us with His commandments and commanded us...."**

God imbues us with holiness through our performance of mitzvot, elevating us to His holy essence, which far transcends the aspect of His being called "His glory" that shines throughout the heavenly spheres and the entire universe. The whole purpose of the mitzvot is to forge a connection with the Divine. The word *mitzva* itself is etymologically connected to the word *tzavta,* which means connection.[18] The wording of the blessing recited upon performing a mitzva, "who has sanctified us with His commandments," conveys that not only did we receive the commandments in order to perform them, but every commandment kindles the light of holiness within its doer. It hoists a person beyond

---

17. The word *keren* used in the verse, translated as "horn," also connotes the essence of a thing. See *Pardes Rimmonim, Sha'ar Arkhei HaKinuyim,* s.v. "*keren*"; *Raya Meheimna,* Lev. 24:2.

18. See *Likkutei Torah,* Lev. 45c; *Pri Etz Ḥayyim, Sha'ar HaLulavm,* chap. 3; *Derekh Ḥayyim, Sha'ar HaTefilla* 52:2; *Sefer HaMa'amarim* (5698), p. 52; *Likkutei Siḥot,* vol. 7, p. 30.

the realm of corporeal man and into the dimension of the sacred, the inner sphere of the Divine.

וְ״כַּמַּיִם הַפָּנִים כו׳״ (משלי כז, כט). **"As water reflects a face** to the face, so does the heart of a person to a person" (Prov. 27:19).

When a person gazes into water, it reflects back to him the same expression that he shows it. The Sages say that the heart is like water. When a person thinks about how another person feels toward him, those same feelings are evoked in his own heart. The same is true when a person contemplates God's immeasurable, infinite greatness on the one hand and His outstanding closeness on the other. When a person ponders how God is absolutely separate from anything physical yet provides us with bread to eat and clothes to wear, how He is totally beyond our finite world yet endows us with the most wondrous gift of attachment to Him by imbuing us with holiness through His mitzvot, offering us His outstretched hand through each one, inviting us to approach Him, to literally be with Him, at that moment a corresponding feeling of love burgeons forth, "as water reflects a face to the face," and the person wells up with desire to draw close to God.[19]

לְהוֹלִיד מִתְּבוּנָה זוֹ דְּחִילוּ וּרְחִימוּ Similarly, **such contemplation serves to generate fear and love** of God,

This reflective contemplation that encompasses both facets of our relationship to the Divine, the loftiness and the closeness, creates a bifurcation of emotion. Fear is the feeling that stems from the realization of God's exaltedness and distance, while love arises from feeling how close God is and the desire to bond with Him. ☞

CONTEMPLATION ENGENDERS EMOTION

☞ Contemplation is not necessarily relegated to the practice of great people, as many would imagine. Every person contemplates; the difference lies in the object of the contemplation. No emotion can develop in a significant way without contemplation. When a person gets angry, he must have contemplated the issue

19. See also *Likkutei Amarim*, chap. 49.

שִׂכְלִיִּים אוֹ טִבְעִיִּים, whether **intellectual or innate,**

There are actually two types of love and fear, though the author of the *Tanya* does not elaborate on them here but only gives them a mention. Intellectual love and fear are engendered from intellectual awareness. The deeper and wider one's awareness, the more the emotions will develop.

On the flip side, innate love and fear are not created from conscious awareness and are not even bound to it in the same way. Consciousness merely opens a gate for the innate love or fear to burst outward. While these emotions are woven into the fabric of a person's soul, they are lying latent deep within, unable to manifest on their own in this world of obscurity and concealment. Contemplation, in this context, unleashes that emotion.

This natural love can also be released in ways other than intellectual contemplation. A person can hear a song that makes his heart brim

beforehand. He may react to someone who mistreats him, but he does not get angry. It is only after ruminating on what was done to him (*How dare he? What an insult!*) that he snaps and grows more and more angry. Likewise, if a person contemplates the greatness of God "who sanctified us with His commandments," and thinks deeply about it, over and over, depicting the reality of this truth in his mind more and more clearly, he will undoubtedly awaken an emotional connection to the Divine within himself.

To contemplate God's greatness, one does not need an extraordinary mind nor an exceptional spiritual ability. All one needs is to be invested in it. There were once hasidim, simple people, who hardly knew how to learn Ḥumash with Rashi, but when it came to the teachings of Hasidism, that which touched upon the depths of their being, they arrived at an understanding and an ability to meditate at extremely high levels.

A story in *Tanna deVei Eliyahu* illustrates this point:

> Elijah met a hunter and asked him, "Why don't you study Torah?"
>
> "My parents never taught me," he answered.
>
> Elijah then asked, "And who taught you to hunt?"
>
> "God did," the hunter replied.

When a person wants something, when he feels that he has no choice, that the issue at hand touches on the depth of his soul, he will do whatever it takes. He will tap into the necessary skills and seek out the advice he needs to achieve it. He will discover skills he never imagined he had. People prefer to contemplate all kinds of things other than the greatness of the Divine because it is easier and they feel that other topics are more relevant to their day-to-day life. But once a person prioritizes accordingly and is ready to invest the effort, he too can contemplate the greatness of God's infinity and generate love and fear of God within him.

with love or tremble with fear. The lyrics of the song may not even directly relate to the feeling that arises in the heart of the listener, yet they penetrate the depth of a person's soul, opening a channel to a more subtle, holy divine love or fear.

לִהְיוֹת בְּחִינַת "צָעַק לִבָּם אֶל ה'" (איכה ב, יח) **אוֹ בְּחִינַת רִשְׁפֵּי אֵשׁ וְשַׁלְהֶבֶת עַזָּה** (שיר השירים ח, ו)**, בִּבְחִינַת 'רָצוֹא', וְאַחַר כָּךְ בִּבְחִינַת 'שׁוֹב'.**

giving rise to the level of love that can be described as **"Their hearts cried to the Lord"** (Lam. 2:18), due to their feeling of distance from God, **or the level** described as **sparks of fire, a great conflagration** (see Song 8:6), which is characterized by **an advance followed by a retreat.**

These are the two essential movements of life, like the beating of the heart, like inhaling and exhaling, outward and inward, advancing and retreating, running and returning.[20] Love and fear beat to the rhythm of advance and retreat as well. Love is generally the movement of drawing close, of desire and yearning to leave one's place to run to the beloved. The height of love of God is yearning to leave the world to just be with God. Yet afterward, if the awakening was real, that feeling manifests itself in another way, in retreat. One is struck with the awareness of who it is before whom he is standing, that one is in the presence of the Divine. This awareness engenders fear and trembling and results in retreat and distance, in returning to the place where one originally stood.

לִהְיוֹת פַּחַד ה' בְּלִבּוֹ, וְלִיבוֹשׁ מִגְּדוּלָּתוֹ כו'.

The retreat is the outcome of **when there is fear of God in one's heart and when one feels ashamed before** God's **greatness, and so on.**

Retreat entails a feeling of shame, of smallness compared to God, as in the verse "For who is it whose heart dared to approach Me?" (Jer. 20:21). ☞

THE TRUE TEST OF SERVING GOD

☞ The bond of love and fear, of running and returning, advance and retreat, is a crucial element of serving God (see *Ba'al Shem Tov al HaTorah, Parashat Noaḥ*) and,

20. See Ezek. 1:14; *Ḥagiga* 13b; *Sefer Yetzira* 1:4; *Likkutei Amarim*, chap. 41.

וְהוּא בְּחִינַת "שְׂמֹאל דּוֹחָה",

This fear and shame comes from **the left side** that **pushes away,**

This is followed by the "right hand that draws close."[21] The right hand is the symbol of love, the embodiment of the attribute of *Ḥesed* and the desire to be close, while the left is the side of distancing, the attribute of *Gevura,* the expression of one's awareness of God's exaltedness and the subsequent feeling of fear that necessarily follows coming close.[22]

כְּמוֹ שֶׁכָּתוּב בְּמַתַּן תּוֹרָה: "וַיַּרְא הָעָם וַיָּנוּעוּ וַיַּעַמְדוּ מֵרָחוֹק כו'" (שמות כ, יח).

as it is written regarding the giving of the Torah, "The people saw, and trembled, and stood at a distance..." (Ex. 20:15).

During the revelation of the giving of the Torah, the nation responded with that same movement of advance and retreat. On the one hand, they were propelled forward, drawn like magnets to God's supernal infinite being. Yet, upon encountering that intimidating sight, intense fear sent them recoiling backward.

וְהֵן בְּחִינַת הַזְּרוֹעוֹת וְהַגּוּף שֶׁבַּנֶּפֶשׁ.

These feelings of love and fear **are the arms and the body of the soul.**

The *Tikkunei Zohar* explains that love and fear, the attributes of *Ḥesed* and *Gevura,* are the right and left arms of the soul's faculties. The attribute of *Tiferet,* compassion, which is the synthesis of love and fear,

in a certain sense, of thriving in the interpersonal realm as well. There was a sage who would say that fear without love is senseless trepidation while love without fear is debauchery. The feeling of love, if real, is directed toward God. It is not a nebulous emotion that has no connection to anything. Of necessity, it encompasses an awareness of the Divine, of God's greatness. In view of this, one of the litmus tests of true love of God is that fear follows it. It cannot be that one feels such love of God and does not then feel the fear. A person does not feel both emotions at the same time, but one is constantly moving from one to another, alternating between them, advancing and retreating, running and returning.

21. See *Sota* 47a; *Sanhedrin* 107b.

22. Introduction to *Tikkunei Zohar* 17a.

comprises the "body," or torso, of the soul's faculties.[23] As previously mentioned, the aspect of the soul represented by the head is the faculty of thought and contemplation, which gives power and direction to the arms. The aspect that corresponds to the hips, faith, upholds them all. When there is a weakness in faith, a person lacks content on which to contemplate and necessarily lacks love and fear. But when a person has faith that penetrates the depths of his soul, he has something to contemplate and can arrive at the emotions of love and fear. ☞

This concludes the first part of the letter, which stands, in a certain sense, on its own. It actually comprised one letter in the early years of the author of the *Tanya*'s leadership, as corroborated by the sixth Lubavitcher Rebbe, Rabbi Yosef Yitzḥak Schneerson. This section discussed the cultivation of the faculties of the soul – the head, body, and arms, which correspond to the intellect and the emotions that are engendered by it – all of which are supported by the hips, the power of faith. The author of the *Tanya* explained how faith is that point of absolute certainty in

FAITH: ITS BEGINNING EMBEDDED IN ITS END

☞ Faith ostensibly exists in the lowest level of the soul, lower than conscious awareness, lower than the emotions. Yet, as explained elsewhere, "its beginning is embedded in its end" (*Sefer Yetzira* 1:6). There is a connection between that which transcends rational comprehension and that which lies beneath one's emotional radar. Something inherently lofty and inconceivable by the rational mind can be grasped in the soul's depths in a way that does not demand specific emotional or conscious articulation.

Faith itself is imperceivable. If a person feels that faith burns within him, it is not the faith itself that burns but rather the awareness and emotion that it generates. The reality of faith does not depend on whether it can be proven by logical inference or clearly depicted. On the contrary, rational awareness depends on the foundation of faith.

Faith is like the feet: A person cannot move or progress without it. One cannot walk on his head; he cannot get anywhere with just his cognitive abilities. The Mishna in *Pirkei Avot* (3:9, 17) echoes this idea, warning that one's wisdom should not outweigh one's deeds. The same is true regarding someone whose wisdom exceeds his faith. The more a person thinks abstractly, even on the highest levels, even if he were to arrive at some emotional experience, it will not spark true change or spiritual growth. One's ideas must touch on his center of faith for tangible transformation to take place on any spiritual plane.

23. Introduction to *Tikkunei Zohar* 17a.

God's existence and underlies a person's understanding and emotions. While the intellect is higher, responsible for cultivating a conceptual relationship with God through contemplation and emotional connection, something that is required of a person in his service of God, the contemplation and emotional connection are, at the end of the day, outgrowths of the soul's experiences. The nucleus of faith, on the other hand, is the essential foundation upon which all these faculties must stand and move. Without faith, one has no framework in which to interpret the soul's experiences and cultivate them through contemplation and emotion to develop one's relationship with God.

The author of the *Tanya* now addresses how to develop and fortify one's faith.

4 Av / 8 Av (leap year)

אַךְ מִי הוּא הַנּוֹתֵן כֹּחַ וָעוֹז לִבְחִינַת מָתְנַיִם לְהַעֲמִיד וּלְקַיֵּים הָרֹאשׁ וְהַזְּרוֹעוֹת?

But what gives the loins the ability and strength to support and uphold the head and the arms?

It is faith that enables all of one's spiritual, intellectual, and emotional work. The question is, where does faith get its strength from?

The problem is that we neither know how to reach the realm of faith nor how particular content becomes a matter of faith. We are only aware of its secondary aspects, its peripheral substructures, its outgrowths, but we are not cognizant of its essence or root. We know something about the attributes, how to develop and cultivate them. We know what to contemplate. Yet when it comes to strengthening faith, we are not clear on the mechanism.

While we do not have obvious, direct paths to develop and increase faith, we do have practices that are more indirect, that we might call *segulot*. There is "food" that nourishes faith, that, though illogical (much like faith itself), can be used to strengthen faith.

הוּא עֵסֶק וְלִימּוּד הֲלָכוֹת בַּתּוֹרָה שֶׁבְּעַל פֶּה,

It is the occupation with and study of the laws in the Oral Torah,

When a person studies *halakha* in the Oral Torah, whether it is the laws of *ketubot* (marriage contracts) in the *Mishneh Torah* of Rambam or the laws of forbidden mixtures, which clarify such *halakhot* as the status of a spoon used to eat dairy that fell into a pot that is used for cooking meat, one reveals and strengthens his faith.

שֶׁהִיא בְּחִינַת גִּילּוּי רָצוֹן הָעֶלְיוֹן, **which is the revelation of the supernal will,**

This strengthening of faith does not come about as a direct result of knowing the *halakhot*. There is no obvious connection between this study and faith in God. Furthermore, faith is essentially incomprehensible and cannot be strengthened by intellectual contemplation alone. It is only because the Oral Torah is a distillation of the will of God that its study has the power to strengthen one's faith. ☞☞

THE SUPERNAL WILL OF GOD

☞ *Halakha*, the delineation of what, when, and how to perform the service of God as explained in the Oral Torah, is the revelation of God's will. Essentially, *halakha* is the stipulation of what God wants. This revelation of the divine will, expressed as detailed instructions for the way to conduct ourselves, is independent of any underlying explanation. It is simply how God wants it. While there are layers of insight to be unearthed behind every *halakha* in the Torah, they are all of secondary importance to the action itself.

In other words, since it is the *halakha*, we search for the reason behind it, but it is not essential to our application of it. Our approach to science resembles this approach to mitzvot. We explain natural phenomena by starting with certain facts, certain principles. Even in the field of mathematics, which is entirely a human creation, as it were, there are certain basic givens, like natural numbers, that we accept without any explanation as fact. While the world is a physical reality that God created, and science a collection of its governing laws and principles, the Torah is a revelation of spiritual reality, and *halakha* constitutes the simple laws and principles by which God governs it.

THE ORAL TORAH: THE REVELATION OF GOD'S WILL

☞ The author of the *Tanya* specifically refers to the study of the *halakhot* of the Oral Torah as the manifestation of God's supernal will because the revelation of divine will becomes manifest as practical action only through the Oral Torah. One cannot thoroughly decipher the divine will from the Written Torah in all its detail. It is impossible to know exactly what God wants us to do from the Written Torah alone. It is only through the Oral Torah, and sometimes only through literally hearing the laws from the mouth of a Torah scholar, that the revelation of God's will reaches perfection, becoming clarified to the extent that enables us to actually carry it out.

דְּאוֹרַיְיתָא מֵחָכְמָה הִיא דְּנָפְקַת אֲבָל מְקוֹרָהּ וְשָׁרְשָׁהּ הִיא לְמַעְלָה מַעְלָה מִבְּחִינַת חָכְמָה, וְהוּא הַנִּקְרָא בְּשֵׁם "רָצוֹן הָעֶלְיוֹן בָּרוּךְ הוּא",

for although the Torah is derived from the *sefira* **of *Ḥokhma*** (Wisdom), **its source and root is far higher than the level of *Ḥokhma*. It is** from the level **called** "God's **supernal will, blessed be He,**"

God's will corresponds to the *sefira* of *Keter* (Crown), which transcends the level of wisdom and the intellect: Before wisdom and understanding comes the initial will. The author of the *Tanya* is conveying that the Oral Torah is rooted in the level of the supernal will, from *Keter*. Yet elsewhere it is explained that the root of the Torah lies in *Ḥokhma*.[24] While it is true that the Torah, especially the Oral Torah, is expressed in rational form so that it is the attribute of *Ḥokhma* that is applied for apprehending Torah concepts and the way they interact, the root of the Torah is the expression of God's will. The supernal will far transcends not only every degree of human wisdom and rational understanding, but it also lies far beyond the power of the essence of divine *Ḥokhma* itself. ☞

THE WILL BEYOND ALL WILLS

☞ The expression "God's will" is a loose translation of the phrase used here by the author of the *Tanya*. Its literal translation is "supernal will," and when this term is used in relation to the Torah, it belies a deeper layer of meaning: Not only is it God's will, but it is the highest, deepest, and most primal facet of His will.

God created a world that contains many realities. The existence of some of these realities is conditional (such as that which hinges on Israel's acceptance and fulfillment of the Torah), while others are sustained by God as a cog in the great entirety of creation (see *Tanna deVei Eliyahu Rabba* 1). Encompassed in this is that which does not seem to serve an express purpose, including the presence of evil. It is impossible to say that God does not desire these phenomena. Otherwise they would not exist at all. But the type of desire that God has for them is different. They are part of the system, part of the necessary context for sustaining and operating that which God truly wants to remain in existence.

Torah, in this sense, is the supernal will, that which God truly desires, the highest, deepest will that lies at the core of all other desires, so that that in every level through which the Torah manifests, it expresses the inner will within it.

24. *Zohar* 2:85a, 121a.

וּכְמוֹ שֶׁכָּתוּב: "כַּצִּנָּה רָצוֹן תַּעְטְרֶנּוּ" (תהלים ה, יג), כַּעֲטָרָה שֶׁהִיא עַל הַמּוֹחִין שֶׁבָּרֹאשׁ.

as it is written, "For it is You who blesses the righteous man, Lord, **surrounding him with favor, like a shield"** (Ps. 5:13). The word used for "surrounding," *tatrenu,* is **related to the word *atara,*** crown, **which** sits **above the brain that is in the head.**

The word for "favor," *ratzon,* used in the verse can also be rendered as "will." The will, which transcends *Ḥokhma* is like a crown that sits upon the head. The word for crown, *atara,* which also denotes "surrounding," refers not only to that which sits above but also to the dimension that lies beyond and separate from the soul's cognitive and emotional realm. This is the will, the *ratzon*: It crowns and encompasses the soul from without. It is not an internal faculty that lends insight and apprehension but rather a power that comes from beyond. We sense its existence, yet we are incapable of understanding or defining it.

When a person performs a mitzva or studies *halakha* from the Oral Torah, he connects with that supernal will that surrounds and encompasses all of reality yet also penetrates and nourishes it on a deep, subconscious level. Therefore, the act of studying the Oral Torah or fulfilling a mitzva activates the soul's deep, unconscious levels, such as the soul's faculty of faith.

וְכַנּוֹדָע מִמַּה שֶּׁפֵּרְשׁוּ עַל פָּסוּק: "אֵשֶׁת חַיִל עֲטֶרֶת בַּעְלָהּ" (משלי יב, ד).

This is also **known from the** Sages' **explanation of the verse "A woman of valor is the crown of her husband"** (Prov. 12:4).

The woman of valor is an analogy for the Oral Torah, which corresponds to the attribute of *Bina* (Understanding).[25] "Her husband" refers to the Written Torah, which corresponds to *Ḥokhma. Ḥokhma* influences *Bina,* yet from a certain standpoint, *Bina,* or the Oral Torah, is higher than *Ḥokhma,* the Written Torah, because it is the revelation of God's

25. See epistle 29; see also *Zohar* 2:85a. The *Zohar* there indicates that the Oral Torah can also correspond to the *sefira* of *Malkhut.* See also *Torah Or* 1c, 6c; *Likkutei Torah,* discourses on *Sukkot* 80a.

supernal will, which is rooted in a higher realm than *Ḥokhma*. From this angle, the Oral Torah is the "crown of her husband,"[26] higher than "her husband," *Ḥokhma*, the Written Torah, and having an influence on it. In this vein, this verse is also understood as prophetic insight into the future, when in all the worlds that which now receives will give.[27]

The *halakhot* of the Oral Torah are thus the expression of God's will that transcends *Ḥokhma*. Yet they are manifest in their application on a level lower than *Ḥokhma*. Unlike the wisdom of mystical Torah teachings that we essentially are incapable of understanding,[28] we are meant to understand *halakha*, the laws that instruct us what to do, in a way that enables us to perform it. ☞

CONNECTING ON THE PRACTICAL LEVEL THROUGH THE ORAL TORAH

☞ The intrinsic problem with the service of God, on every level and in every arena, is the issue of connection. When we are standing before God, we are facing the infinite. The gap between us and Him is unbridgeable, no matter how many steps we take. The only one who can bridge the gap is God Himself. He must extend His hand to us. Only He can offer that possibility. Yet even when He does so, when He communicates with us, we can apprehend and connect with Him only at the end stage, on the level of the bottom line, the action.

Consider the following metaphor. Two people who speak different languages face each other. One person must relay a message urgently to the other. He needs to tell him, "Move over to the right! You are about to be run over!" He could explain this with his most eloquent terminology and explanations, yet the other will not understand. But if he makes a motion with his hand, signaling that the other should move and he moves, clearly he got the message. Communication was established; connection was achieved. This is the significance of the Oral Torah. It successfully clarifies the point, that we are supposed to do this and not that. This is the goal of learning *halakha*, the "crown of Torah": It forges a direct connection to the Divine that cuts through all the rifts of lack of comprehension and miscommunication between us and God.

The crown thus embodies the concept of "the beginning is embedded in the end" by manifesting both the point of inception and the point of completion. The summary of practical *halakha* is both the final conclusion of the abstract debate and the very starting point of God's supernal will. This

26. *Megilla* 28b; see also epistle 29.

27. Giving is a masculine aspect, while receiving is characterized as a feminine attribute. See also *Torah Or*, s.v. "*vayigash elav Yehuda*"; *Likkutei Torah*, Song 48b.

28. From this idea stems the expression "The remnants of the supernal wisdom is Torah" (*Bereshit Rabba* 44). The aspects of Torah that we can grasp are only "remnants" that have fallen from divine wisdom.

וְ"כָל הַשּׁוֹנֶה הֲלָכוֹת בְּכָל יוֹם כו'" (נדה עג, א).

The Sages have also taught that "**anyone who studies *halakhot* every day** is guaranteed that he is destined for the World to Come" (*Nidda* 73a).

This idea, that "the woman of valor is the crown of her husband," will ultimately come to fruition only in the time to come. When it comes to the study of *halakha*, God's will is manifest through action, yet the divine rationale behind it remains utterly concealed. The level of *Keter*, which constitutes the divine will, fuses with the level of action yet bypasses the level of *Ḥokhma*, the level of wisdom, of cognitive awareness. One who studies *halakhot* will understand what he must do and act accordingly, but he does not see or feel the Divine there. That is simply the reality of this world. Yet anyone who studies *halakhot* creates vessels and soul garments through which he will be able to receive reward for his mitzva actions in the future, so that he will apprehend the divine illumination that underlies these actions, in the World to Come.

וְזֶהוּ "חָגְרָה בְעוֹז מָתְנֶיהָ" (משלי לא, יז), **אֵין עוֹז אֶלָּא תּוֹרָה שֶׁהִיא נוֹתֶנֶת כֹּחַ וָעוֹז**

This is the meaning of the verse "**She girds her loins with might** and strengthens her arms" (Prov. 31:17). "**Might" means nothing but Torah,**

is why the woman of valor is called the "crown of her husband." This connection between *Malkhut*, Kingship (the final *sefira* and level), and *Keter*, Crown (the first *sefira* and level), is direct. It circumvents neural pathways and limitations, evading the obstacles that the rational mind attempts to present. This connection is pure and free of any distortion that man's intellect may cause, in whatever form it would take.

The Ba'al Shem Tov (some say it was the Vilna Gaon) asked regarding the verse "The Torah of the Lord is perfect" (Ps. 19:8): In what way is it perfect? His answer: Because no one blemished it (see *Degel Maḥaneh Efrayim, Parashat Ha'azinu*; *Kol Mevaser*, vol. 1, *Parashat Toledot*). The Torah is perfect because it transcends all levels; it is beyond all realms. It is the *Keter* of the world, God's supernal will that is beyond everything. It passes through the world, unbreakable and indivisible, a whole package. This explains why it can reach the lowest conceivable levels intact. Likewise, within the soul, the faculty of faith is on the level of *Keter*, transcending the upper reaches of the intellect. At the same time, it touches a point beneath the radar of the emotions so that, like the Torah, it remains perfect and unblemished.

לִבְחִינַת מָתְנַיִם, הַחֲגוּרִים וּמְלוּבָּשִׁים בָּהּ

which gives the "loins," or the faculty of faith in the soul, **which are girded and clothed within it, the ability and might**

We know that strength refers to Torah based on the verse "The Lord gives strength to His people" (Ps. 29:11).[29] By studying the *halakhot* of the Oral Torah, the embodiment of might, a person strengthens the faith within his soul, even if his wisdom, love, or fear do not increase.

לְחַזֵּק וּלְאַמֵּץ זְרוֹעוֹתֶיהָ, הֵן דְּחִילוּ וּרְחִימוּ שִׂכְלִיִּים אוֹ טִבְעִיִּים,

to strengthen and support the soul's **arms, which are fear and love** of God, **whether intellectual or innate,**

The principle is that no matter their origin, whether they develop through cognitive awareness or they are rooted in one's innate love and fear, one cannot develop enduring emotions of love and fear without the foundation of faith. One must accept things as they are before one can develop an emotional response or cognitive attitude toward them.

כָּל חַד לְפוּם שִׁיעוּרָא דִילֵיהּ.

every individual according to his capacity.

Love and fear are very individual. One person's love is not like the next, neither in degree nor in type, neither in the way it is aroused nor in the way it is expressed.

(וְעַל הַעֲמָדַת וְקִיּוּם בְּחִינַת הָרֹאשׁ שֶׁבַּנֶּפֶשׁ, הוּא הַשֵּׂכֶל הַמִּתְבּוֹנֵן כו', אָמַר: "טָעֲמָה כִּי טוֹב סַחְרָהּ" כו' [משלי לא, יח]

(Regarding the support and upholding of the soul's head, the intellect that contemplates and so on, it is written, "She perceives that her merchandise is good…" [Prov. 31:18],

The author of the *Tanya* has primarily been discussing the "arms" of the soul, love, and fear. Here the author comments that the aforementioned concepts apply to the "head" as well. The verse he quotes follows the

29. *Sifrei, VeZot HaBerakha* 2; *Shir HaShirim Rabba* 1:23, 2:12; *Midrash Tanḥuma, Bemidbar* 3.

other verse he just quoted, "She girds her loins with strength," and hints at the stage that comes after a person strengthens his spiritual loins through the study of *halakha*.

The Hebrew word for "perceives" in the verse is *ta'ama,* which literally means "tastes" but can also mean "reasons." The perception mentioned in this verse refers to rational comprehension, as in the verse "Taste [i.e., comprehend] and see that the Lord is good" (Ps. 34:9).[30] Through consciously connecting and relating to an event or concept, a person is privy to the sound reasoning behind it. Faith itself has no sense of rationale because it transcends reason and knowledge. Only when a person can perceive the rationale and the root of a given idea or experience will he taste the pleasure in it.

(וּמְבוֹאָר בְּמָקוֹם אַחֵר.) **which is explained elsewhere.)**

This letter primarily focuses on the strengthening of the "arms," on love and fear of God, during prayer, the service of the heart. The concept of strengthening the "head," the soul's intellect, is explained elsewhere.

From this point onward, the letter delves into the applicable, practical aspects of the concepts discussed herein. The purpose of the ideas explained in these letters, and in a certain sense in every hasidic discourse, is that they should be applied and not remain in the theoretical realm or be reduced to emotional surges that do not manifest in action. Rather, they should be practiced, deeply activating one's soul in his day-to-day life, whether during prayer, while performing mitzvot, or when facing the vicissitudes of life in general. Now, after having built the theoretical framework, the author of the *Tanya* outlines its practical application.

אַךְ עֵת וּזְמַן הַחִיזּוּק וְאִימּוּץ הַזְּרוֹעוֹת וְהָרֹאשׁ הִיא שְׁעַת תְּפִלַּת הַשַּׁחַר, שֶׁהִיא שְׁעַת רַחֲמִים וְעֵת רָצוֹן הָעֶלְיוֹן לְמַעְלָה.

In fact, the occasion and time for strengthening and fortifying the arms and the head is during the morning prayers, which is a time of mercy and a time when the supernal will is revealed above.

30. See *Metzudat Tzion* there.

Each part of the day has its own unique characteristics.[31] The morning is most characterized by *Ḥesed* and the revelation of divine favor.[32] As explained above, the revelation of God's will strengthens faith in the soul, which establishes and fortifies the "arms," love and fear of God, and the "head," the awareness and contemplation of God. This time of day, when the gates of Heaven are opened, is therefore the time for prayer through which one draws down the influence of *Ḥesed* and the supernal will. As a result of this revelation of the divine will, these faculties of the soul will be strengthened and cultivated so that one will be fortified to serve God throughout the day.

The author of the *Tanya* explained above that in order to strengthen the "loins," or the faith within one's soul, one should be committed to learning the *halakhot* of the Oral Torah. This connection is not direct or obvious. When a person engages in this study, he builds the appropriate spiritual infrastructure and creates a fitting environment for his spiritual growth. To actually activate this, however, to unleash an internal effusion of love and fear, a person must pray, not only reciting the words but intensely engaging in the spiritual work of prayer.

וְלָזֹאת אוֹתָהּ אֲבַקֵּשׁ מִמְּבַקְשֵׁי ה׳:

Therefore, this is what I request of those who seek God:

The request that the author of the *Tanya* makes here is directed at those who seek to be close to God, who truly desire to pray and to strengthen their faith and love and fear of God.

יָבִינוּ וְיַשְׂכִּילוּ יַחְדָּיו, וְלִהְיוֹת לְזִכָּרוֹן בֵּין עֵינֵיהֶם כָּל מַה שֶּׁכָּתַבְתִּי אֲלֵיהֶם אֶשְׁתָּקַד בִּכְלָל, וּבִפְרָט מֵעִנְיַן כַּוָּנַת

that **they understand and contemplate together and constantly bear in mind everything I wrote to them last year in general, and** what

31. See *Likkutei Amarim,* chap. 41; see also the introduction to *Olat Tamid, Sha'ar HaKavanot, Keriat Shema.*

32. As the verse states, "Abraham awoke early in the morning" (Gen. 22:3). Abraham was the paradigm of the attribute of *Ḥesed,* and so he formulated the prayer service in the morning, the time most characterized by *Ḥesed*. See *Sha'ar HaKavanot, Birkot HaShaḥar*. See *Berakhot* 26b; *Zohar* 1:72a.

הַתְּפִלָּה מֵעוּמְקָא דְלִבָּא. **I wrote regarding concentration during prayer from the depths of the heart in particular.**

This refers to another letter that appears in this book as well.[33] In that letter, the author of the *Tanya* outlines general ordinances and directives that relate to communal prayer. Here, when he says "in general," he refers to the hasidic community as a whole, that they should contemplate these ideas together in groups. With the words "prayer from the depths of the heart in particular," he is urging the individual to ensure that his prayer is not insincere but rather deeply personal.

יוֹם יוֹם יִדְרְשׁוּן ה׳ **Day after day they should seek God**

Using language from the prophet Isaiah, "Day after day they seek Me" (Isa. 58:2), the author of the *Tanya* appeals to his hasidim not to suffice with the level of relationship that they have with God. Rather, let them harness the power of their daily prayers to truly seek out God by searching for that which is hidden and asking that the Divine, which is concealed from us, should become perceptible and palpable.

בְּכָל לִבָּם וּבְכָל נַפְשָׁם. **with all their heart and all their soul.**

This wording echoes the words of the *Shema* and comes along with their manifold layers of meaning. "With all their heart" implies investing all of one's heartfelt desires and love, and "with all their soul" means with all the faculties of one's soul and the willingness to sacrifice one's soul, as the Sages say, "Even if [God] takes your soul" (*Berakhot* 61b).

וְנַפְשָׁם תִּשְׁתַּפֵּךְ כַּמַּיִם נוֹכַח פְּנֵי ה׳. וּכְמַאֲמַר רַבּוֹתֵינוּ ז״ל בְּ״סִפְרֵי״ (דברים ו, ה): עַד מִיצּוּי הַנֶּפֶשׁ כו׳. **They should pour out their souls like water before God. As the Rabbis state in *Sifrei* (Deut. 6:5), "To the extent of wringing out the soul...."**

33. It seems that this refers to the letter that begins, "You shall surely rebuke," at the end of *Kuntres Aharon*.

A person must do this inner work until he is able to pour out his heart like water before God.[34] When he prays, he must harness all the energies of his soul until he cannot eke out any more, as the *Sifrei* comments on the words "with all of your soul."[35] A person must exhaust his soul of all its energy, of every ounce of spiritual vigor that draws, excites, and enlivens him, like a person drains a vessel of the liquid within it, until the soul becomes stripped of all its faculties, and its essence becomes manifest and pours out like water before God. ☞

5 Av / 9 Av (leap year)

וְעַתָּה הַפַּעַם הִנְנִי יוֹסִיף שֵׁנִית יָדִי, בְּתוֹסֶפֶת בֵּיאוּר וּבַקָּשָׁה כְּפוּלָה, שְׁטוּחָה וּפְרוּשָׂה לִפְנֵי כָּל אַנְשֵׁי שְׁלוֹמִים, הַקְּרוֹבִים

Now once more I put forth my hand a second time, with additional explanation and a twofold request, extended and put forth before all the members of our community, those near and far,

THE WRINGING OF THE SOUL

☞ Some understand this phrase in terms of the image of a barrel that is filled with liquid to the extent that it can no longer hold any more. When only a little more is added, the liquid overflows. While it is the liquid itself that emerges from the barrel in this analogy, it is the sheer force of the quantity in the barrel that pushes it out. This is how prayer should be. Even if a person feels only a very subtle spiritual sensation, it is coming from the overall power and essence of the soul.

There were (and probably still are) hasidim who would pray like this. Some of them exhibited their exertion, excitement, and closeness to the Divine, and others kept it all beneath the surface, not even extending the length of their prayers a significant amount. People would say that although the Kotzker Rebbe did not pray a lengthy prayer, it would take him some time until he began recognizing people again after praying. The work of the "wringing of the soul" would leave the soul empty of everything it possessed. All the associations, assumptions, and identity it had before prayer no longer exist. All were offered up in the experience of the individual who was in the presence of God, and building them anew took time.

---

34. Based on I Sam. 1:29; Lam. 2:19.

35. The *Sifrei* comments there, "Even if it means giving up your soul," as it is written, "For we are killed all day long for You" (Ps. 44:23). Rabbi Shimon ben Menasya asks, "How is it possible for a person to be killed all day long?" He goes on to explain: "Rather, God considers the merit of the righteous as though they gave up their lives for God every day." Shimon ben Azzai says, "'With all of your soul' [means to] love God to the extent of wringing out the soul." See also *Bereshit Rabba* 92.

וְהָרְחוֹקִים, לְקַיֵּים עֲלֵיהֶם שֶׁכָּל יְמֵי הַחוֹל לֹא יֵרְדוּ לִפְנֵי הַתֵּיבָה הַבַּעֲלֵי עֲסָקִים שֶׁאֵין לָהֶם פְּנַאי כָּל כָּךְ.

to take upon themselves that on all weekdays businessmen should not lead the prayers, for they do not have much time to devote to prayer.

Here begins the third section of the letter, which was written at a later time, when the hasidic movement had grown and had become more established around the author of the *Tanya*. A need arose to formulate specific practices and ordinances, and the first of these related to communal prayer.

The author of the *Tanya* knew that it is impossible for a person with limited time to forget everything and immerse himself in the service of prayer with a composed mind. Although there were certainly hasidim who were capable of doing this, devotees who were able to pray as if they had all the time in the world even though they would be imminently delving into business matters and money concerns, this was surely not a common phenomenon. Most people need a great deal of time to attain a mindset of intense connection, a luxury that businessmen do not have.

רַק אוֹתָם שֶׁיֵּשׁ לָהֶם פְּנַאי

Only those who have time,

Those who do not run a business or occupy high-pressure positions can clear space in their souls and free themselves of commonplace matters. The service of prayer that the author of the *Tanya* expects of his hasidim demands more time than simply mouthing the words of prayer. He instructs them to give sufficient time to each word, to allow themselves the mental space to contemplate each one, and imbue them with the light of the hasidic teachings that they learned. They must strive to tap into the depths of their souls, to truly feel and be free to ascend from the mundane concerns of daily living to contemplate and immerse themselves in matters of the Divine, all through the daily morning prayer.

אוֹ הַמְלַמְּדִים אוֹ הַסְּמוּכִים עַל שׁוּלְחַן אֲבִיהֶם,

whether teachers or those who are supported financially **by their father,**

Teachers are included here since elementary-school classes started later in the morning, so they could devote time to their prayers. In addition, those supported by their parents could devote all their time to the study of Torah rather than dedicating some of their time to earning a livelihood and also had more time to spend in prayer.

שֶׁיְּכוֹלִים לְהַאֲרִיךְ בִּתְפִלַּת הַשַּׁחַר עֶרֶךְ שָׁעָה וּמֶחֱצָה לְפָחוֹת כָּל יְמוֹת הַחוֹל, מֵהֶם יִהְיֶה הַיּוֹרֵד לִפְנֵי הַתֵּיבָה עַל פִּי הַגּוֹרָל אוֹ עַל פִּי רִיצּוּי הָרוֹב, וְהוּא יֶאֱסוֹף אֵלָיו בִּסְבִיב לוֹ כָּל הַסְּמוּכִים עַל שׁוּלְחַן אֲבִיהֶם אוֹ מְלַמְּדִים שֶׁיּוּכְלוּ לְהַאֲרִיךְ כָּמוֹהוּ.

who can devote at least about an hour and half to the morning prayers every weekday, one of them should lead the prayers, selected **by a lot or by consent of the majority.** The designated leader **should gather around him all those who are supported by their father or the teachers, who can spend as much time** on the prayers **as he can.**

The leader of the prayer service should be someone accepted by most of the congregation,[36] but unlike the custom in other places, where the person who leads the prayers is the one who is most in a rush, or where the entire congregation prays in order to accommodate those who are in a hurry, so that those who want to pray slowly have to essentially pray on their own, the author of the *Tanya* proposes that it is precisely those who are not pressed for time, who can set aside plenty of time for prayer, should be considered the main part of the quorum, while the rest should be peripheral.

In general, there is a certain basic assumption at play here regarding the foundation of the community, what it considers important and what is secondary. Setting the norm for the correct way to choose the prayer leader highlights the community's values. The community is undoubtedly composed of a plethora of people of all types, each with his own unique place in it, but the axis upon which the whole community stands must be the service of God, and all must recognize this and find their place accordingly. ☞

---

36. *Shulḥan Arukh, Oraḥ Ḥayyim* 53:22. The concept of devoting an hour and a half to morning prayers is based on *Zohar* I:62b and commentaries there. See also *Mevo She'arim* 2b, 9b.

בְּבַל יְשׁוּנֶּה, נָא וְנָא. **This arrangement should not be altered, I beg and beseech you.**

The author of the *Tanya* uses this double language of "I beg and beseech you" to strengthen the intensity of his request.[37] It is hard to institute a custom and ensure that people will not change it when it is contrary to the accepted custom. Therefore, the author of the *Tanya* poses his request using strong language: "I beg and beseech you."

אַךְ בְּשַׁבָּתוֹת וְיָמִים טוֹבִים, שֶׁגַּם כָּל בַּעֲלֵי עֲסָקִים יֵשׁ לָהֶם פְּנַאי וּשְׁעַת הַכּוֹשֶׁר לְהַאֲרִיךְ בִּתְפִלָּתָם בְּכַוָּונַת לִבָּם וְנַפְשָׁם לַה׳, וְאַדְּרַבָּה, עֲלֵיהֶם מוּטָל בְּיֶתֶר שְׂאֵת וְיֶתֶר עָז. **However, on the Sabbath and the festivals, when all the businessmen also have the time and opportunity to pray at length to God with the concentration of their hearts and souls, their responsibility is, on the contrary, much greater.**

Why do the people who are busy working throughout the week have a greater responsibility to pray at length on the Sabbath and festivals than those who spend all week devoted to Torah study and prayer?

כְּמוֹ שֶׁכָּתוּב בְּשׁוּלְחָן עָרוּךְ אוֹרַח חַיִּים (סימן רצ), וּכְמוֹ שֶׁכָּתוּב בְּתוֹרַת מֹשֶׁה: "שֵׁשֶׁת יָמִים תַּעֲבוֹד כו׳, וְיוֹם **As it states in *Shulḥan Arukh, Oraḥ Ḥayyim* (290), and as it is written in the Torah of Moses, "Six days**

THE OTHER ROOM

☞ It was customary in Chabad synagogues to build an extra room where certain hasidim would pray, separate from the main quorum. This prayer was performed with immense mindfulness, sometimes not only for an hour and a half but four or five hours every day. These hasidim would engage in a deeply personal prayer with serious contemplation, offering up all their souls' energies. The presence of a prayer group like this created a model for the entire community of how a person should pray: The prayer should not entail simply fulfilling one's obligation so that he would be free to eat breakfast, but rather should infuse one's entire relationship with God with meaningful content and living significance.

37. This language was common among sages in those times. See, e.g., *Ya'arot Devash* by Rabbi Yehonatan Eibeshitz and *She'eilot U'Teshuvot Ya'avetz* by Rabbi Yaakov of Emden.

הַשְּׁבִיעִי שַׁבָּת לַה׳ אֱלֹהֶיךָ״ (שמות כ, ט-י) דַּיְיקָא כּוּלּוֹ לַה׳.

you shall work…and the seventh day is Sabbath for the Lord your God" (Ex. 20:9–10), **specifying** that the day should be devoted **entirely to God.**

The author of the *Tanya* cites the *Shulḥan Arukh* to bolster his assertion that the Sabbath is a day when working men, who did not have the opportunity to devote all their weekdays to the study of Torah and prayer, should study more than Torah scholars who study all week long.

The Sabbath is the culmination of the weekdays and is nourished from them.[38] In light of this, the heights to which one's prayers ascend on the Sabbath hinges on the weekdays. Yet when a person who was occupied with mundane concerns during the week prays on the Sabbath with sincere intention and at length, he can elevate his prayers to even loftier heights, like a light that emerges from darkness.[39]

וְלָזֹאת גַּם הֵם יֵרְדוּ לִפְנֵי הַתֵּיבָה בְּשַׁבָּת וְיוֹם טוֹב, עַל פִּי הַגּוֹרָל אוֹ בִּרְיצּוּי הָרוֹב, כְּמוֹ שֶׁכָּתַבְתִּי אֶשְׁתָּקַד.

Therefore, they too should lead the services on the Sabbath and festivals, by a lot or by consent of the majority, as I wrote last year.

When a person who sits and studies Torah during the week steps into the Sabbath, he does not change his routine to a significant degree. Conversely, when a person who works throughout the week, immersed in worldly matters, enters the Sabbath, he undergoes both a drastic change and brings something new with him from his workweek. During his weekly dealings with the mundane world, he met holy sparks that the one who sat and studied Torah did not encounter. These sparks come from imperfect realities that seek to be redeemed. When they encountered this businessman, they attached themselves to him and made him their messenger to elevate them to the realm of holiness. These sparks say to him, as it were, "You were with us and dealt with us. Now you must take us with you to elevate us and redeem us from the *kelippot*, the forces of impurity." It is therefore the businessman

38. As the Sages taught, "He who works before the Sabbath eats on the Sabbath" (*Avoda Zara* 3a).

39. See *Likkutei Siḥot*, vol. 30, p. 139.

who should pray on the Sabbath or festival, since he must elevate and redeem the sparks.

Furthermore, the roots of those sparks lie in the world of *tohu,* which is higher than the person who is elevating them. When a person comes to pray as an emissary for those sparks, he receives power from them, like a prayer leader who receives power to pray from the congregation for whom he is praying. They are not only sending him to pray for them, but they are giving him the power to do so.

וּכְגוֹן דָּא צָרִיךְ לְאוֹדוֹעֵי שֶׁבְּדַעְתִּי, אִם יִרְצֶה ה׳, לִשְׁלוֹחַ לְכָל הַמִּנְיָנִים מְרַגְּלִים בַּסֵּתֶר, לֵידַע וּלְהוֹדִיעַ כָּל מִי שֶׁאֶפְשָׁר לוֹ וְכָל מִי שֶׁיֵּשׁ לוֹ פְּנַאי לְהַאֲרִיךְ וּלְעַיֵּין בַּתְּפִלָּה, וּמִתְעַצֵּל - יִהְיֶה נִידּוֹן בְּרִיחוּק מָקוֹם, לִהְיוֹת נִדְחֶה בִּשְׁתֵּי יָדַיִם בְּבוֹאוֹ לְפֹה לִשְׁמוֹעַ ׳דִּבְרֵי אֱלֹקִים חַיִּים׳.

Moreover, be notified that I intend, God willing, to send covert observers to all the congregations to identify and notify me about anyone who is able and anyone who has time to pray at length and in depth yet is lazy and refrains from doing so. Any such person **will be punished by disassociation, being pushed away with two hands when he comes here to hear the words of the living God.**

The "words of the living God" was a description for the Rebbe's hasidic teachings. Since this person is not implementing the hasidic teachings that he heard from the Rebbe, he does not deserve to hear them.

וּמִכְּלַל לָאו אַתָּה שׁוֹמֵעַ הֵן, וְלַשּׁוֹמְעִים יוּנְעַם, וְתָבֹא עֲלֵיהֶם בִּרְכַּת טוֹב, וְאֵין טוֹב אֶלָּא תוֹרָה וכו׳.

From the negative you can infer the positive. May it be pleasant for those who adhere to this message, **and may blessings of good come upon them, and "'good' means nothing but Torah…."**

The author of the *Tanya* does not leave it at that, but "from the negative you can infer the positive."[40] The author of the *Tanya* promises that whoever invests substantial time in the service of prayer and relates seriously to the hasidic discourses that he has heard will be privileged

40. A principle quoted from *Nedarim* 11a.

to acquire further hasidic teachings, or, as the author puts it, "the words of the living God."

The author of the *Tanya* concludes as he began, stating that "good" is synonymous with the Torah. He began with gratitude for the conclusion of the study of the entire Talmud, a study that strengthens a person's faith, and concludes with a blessing directed at one who implements the lessons he has learned from hasidic teachings in his prayer service. By doing this, his newly strengthened faith supports the "head" and "arms," promoting the conscious awareness of the Divine and the love and fear of God.

There are two distinctive components of this letter: The first is analytical and abstract, and the second is about implementation. While the practical portion has been omitted from most of the letters in this book, it is included here because it pertains to times and places other than the context in which the letter was written. The importance of praying slowly with focused intent and the reality of workingmen versus those who have more time for spiritual endeavors still exists today all over the world. But the main reason this section is included here is that it is crucial to bridge the lofty concepts that the letter addresses, the concepts of Torah study, prayer, and faith, with everyday life. They cannot remain theoretical without implementation in one's daily routine.

This letter accentuates the centrality of faith in a person's life. It addresses the way in which one can strengthen his faith through studying the action-based mitzvot of the Oral Torah and the power of staunch faith when infused into prayer to establish and sustain the head and the arms, which are the faculties of awareness and emotion. These connections, of Torah and prayer to faith, are not obvious, direct causal connections but rather have a mystical effect beneath the surface.

Faith itself is subconscious and even imperceptible. It serves as the base, the background and the framework, that positions and sustains the entire conscious structure of the soul's faculties. In light of this, it is important to articulate the practical application of these ideas. Without practical implementation, they are meaningless. In hasidic discourses that guide a person step by step toward apprehension and emotion, it is not necessary to speak about the implementation of the ideas, because they speak for themselves, automatically effecting change in the person who studies these teachings. Then there are discourses like this letter, where the concepts are impossible to internalize in and of themselves, and there is no way to intuit how the study of the Oral Torah leads to "girding the loins," which then "strengthens the arms," except through implementing them.

Epistle 2

THIS LETTER IS PART OF A SEQUENCE OF LETTERS THAT were written around the same time in honor of the same event: the author of the *Tanya*'s release from prison on 19 Kislev in the year 1798.[1] This letter, written for a wide hasidic audience, carries with it an overarching message pertinent to hasidim in every generation: how a hasid should respond when he personally experiences the revelation of God's kindness, whether physical or spiritual, not only in a momentous event or supernatural experience, but even every day. A true hasid must recognize that even the more modest gifts that he receives from God are manifestations of divine kindness intended directly for him.

אַחַר בִּיאָתוֹ מִפֶּטֶרְבּוּרְג The following letter was penned by the author **after his arrival from Saint Petersburg.**

This was the place of Rabbi Shneur Zalman's incarceration, interrogation, and debate, followed by his ultimate release. "After Petersburg" became a hasidic concept that signifies the era following his imprisonment, which was characterized by a significant increase in the revelation and expansion of hasidic teachings and ushered in the coalescence of the unique path of Chabad Hasidism. ☞

THE INCARCERATION

☞ Rabbi Shneur Zalman's imprisonment was related to the opposition to Hasidism that was rampant at the time. The opposition was extremely challenging, perhaps

1. The book *Beit Rebbe* mentions two other letters, one to Rabbi Levi Yitzḥak of Berditchev and one to Rabbi Barukh of Medzibozh. This letter is of a general nature intended for the wider hasidic audience, particularly the hasidim of the author of the *Tanya*.

6 Av
10 Av (leap year)

"קָטֹנְתִּי מִכֹּל הַחֲסָדִים וּמִכָּל וכו'" (בראשית לב, י).

Jacob said, **"I am unworthy of all the kindnesses and of all** the truth that You have performed for Your servant..." (Gen. 32:10).

because it was well meant and those who opposed Hasidism did so for the sake of Heaven. When a fight is fueled by personal interests, people can compromise, but when they are fighting over ideology, there is no room for compromise. The death in 1797 of the Vilna Gaon, who galvanized the opposition, not only failed to weaken the controversy but fueled it, increasing its intensity, until people even resorted to informing on hasidim to the Russian authorities. While it was only individuals who took this action, and the leaders of the opposition did not support this move, it demonstrates the intensity of the hatred and insult people felt, that they would use such ammunition against fellow Jews.

The situation was complicated due to several reasons. Hasidim were accused of giving assistance, financial and otherwise, to the Turks, Russia's enemy on its southern border. This accusation was given substance because of the presence of emissaries who came to Russia to collect funds for those living in the Land of Israel, which was under the authority of the Ottoman Empire (see *Iggeret HaKodesh*, epistles 17, 21). The opposition also accused the hasidim of the theological crime of starting a new religion, which in czarist Russia was considered illegal. Due to this allegation, the author of the *Tanya*'s sentence was not just political but theological, based on the assertion that the new religion of Hasidism was a total divergence from authentic Judaism. One way that the author of the *Tanya* responded was to write a defense of Hasidism (which was published in *Kerem Chabad*, vol. 4, and more recently in Rabbi Yehoshua Mondshine's *HaMa'asar HaRishon* [The First Imprisonment]).

In view of this, the sentence was not against Rabbi Shneur Zalman of Liadi the individual but against Hasidism as a movement and as an ideal. This was apparent not only by the allegations that were aimed against the hasidic movement in general but also by the intended results. If successful, it was almost certain that the Russian government that ruled over the majority of the Jews of Eastern Europe at the time would itself attempt to uproot the hasidic movement. The acquittal of the author of the *Tanya*, then, had a universal impact, signifying the liberation of Hasidism, a victory over its naysayers, and its emergence from the suppression of bitter enemies from within and without.

The acquittal and release of the author of the *Tanya* proved to be a watershed moment in the history of Hasidism. From that moment onward, the controversy against it weakened and never again attained the same degree of intensity. There were still many people who were not counted among the hasidim, of course, and Jewish leaders were not completely accepting of the ideology, but the active war, the attempt to extricate Hasidism from the Jewish people, ceased. The nineteenth of Kislev, or Yod Tet Kislev, as it has come to be called, is therefore, from a historical standpoint, a day of redemption, the day when a new path of Hasidism was forged. This day received its nickname – the "Day of Redemption" or the "New Year of Hasidism" – from a famous letter written by the fifth Lubavitcher Rebbe, Rabbi Sholom

Since the author of the *Tanya*'s release occurred during the week when *Parashat Vayishlaḥ* is read, he opens with a verse from the weekly Torah portion upon which the entire letter is built.[2] These words were uttered by Jacob as a prayer when he was returning to the Land of Israel from Ḥaran before his encounter with Esau. Rashi asks, "Why was Jacob afraid? Didn't God promise him, both when he left the Land of Israel and upon leaving Ḥaran, 'Behold, I am with you; I will keep you wherever you go' (Gen. 28:15)?" Rashi answers that Jacob was worried that perhaps his merits had decreased, that he had "become unworthy" due to the kindness and truth that God had shown him. Since the scale of his debts and merits had shifted after he had received the promise due to the immense kindnesses that God had performed for him, he was concerned that God's promise was no longer in effect.

The author of the *Tanya* will explore this idea in a broader scope as a

Dovber Schneerson (see *Iggerot Kodesh*, vol. 1, p. 98). It is celebrated as a day when Hasidism began to progressively expand while its opposition progressively waned. Those who are not hasidim are no longer "opponents" but rather relate to Hasidism respectfully as one of the bonified sectors of the Jewish people.

This controversy had an internal dimension as well, one that touched on such questions as to what extent it is permissible to publicize and reveal the hasidic approach among Jewish communities without differentiating between tzaddikim and scholars, between simple Jews and even totally ignorant ones. Is this generation equipped to receive these revelations? Will these teachings serve as instruments for ascension and elevation, or will they ultimately do more damage than good because the place and the time are not ripe for them? These questions, which not only the opponents grappled with, but the hasidim as well, were genuine challenges that at that time did not find simple answers. The earthly verdict acquitting Rabbi Shneur Zalman of Liadi reflected the heavenly judgment and was understood as a heavenly stamp of approval endorsing the hasidic approach.

One could only imagine how elevated the energy was among the hasidim "after the author's arrival from Saint Petersburg." It was against this backdrop that the author of the *Tanya* wrote this letter. Intended for the greater hasidic community, the letter cautions its reader not to take advantage of the victory by harming those who inflicted the suffering. Be wary of intensifying the fight but rather, on the contrary, try to mitigate it with behavior that is above and beyond the letter of the law, in line with the verse "A gentle response assuages fury" (Prov. 15:1).

---

2. Based on a discourse by the author of the *Tanya* that a person should "live with the times," meaning that one should live in consonance with the weekly Torah portion.

general instruction for every person on how to act when God showers him with immense kindness and truth.[3] Each and every one of us, the children of Jacob, must respond similarly, and be humbled by all the kindnesses God bestows on us.

פֵּירוּשׁ, שֶׁבְּכָל חֶסֶד וְחֶסֶד שֶׁהַקָּדוֹשׁ בָּרוּךְ הוּא עוֹשֶׂה לָאָדָם צָרִיךְ לִהְיוֹת שְׁפַל רוּחַ בִּמְאֹד,

This means that with every single kindness that the Holy One, blessed be He, does for a person, one must become exceedingly humble,

A person's response to the kindnesses that God performs for him must be a feeling of humility. The more divine kindness he receives, the smaller he should feel. The problem is that human nature is exactly the opposite. When he is in a good place, not only is he in a better mood, but he also considers himself superior and more important. Often, when a person does well in business, he begins to think that he is extremely intelligent and God-fearing. Success and status in one area cause him to feel a sense of superiority in other areas of life, even though this assumption is entirely illogical.

The mystical explanation of this phenomenon is that the essence of the *sefira* of *Ḥesed* (Kindness) aligns with greatness and embodies the quality of expansion.[4] When a person becomes the recipient of greatness and liberation from a given confinement, he may translate this feeling into self-importance and self-aggrandizement.

כִּי חֶסֶד דְּרוֹעָא יְמִינָא,

for kindness is called **the right arm.**

3. The author of the *Tanya* actually did not include the continuation of the verse, "because of all the truth that You have performed for Your servant," in his citation because truth refers to what one deserves according to his merits, and he did not want to imply that he deserved any of God's goodness. Therefore, he included only the word "kindness." See *Likkutei Siḥot*, vol. 15, p. 82.

4. In kabbalistic teachings, the quality of greatness is an aspect of *Ḥesed*. See *Sha'ar HaYiḥud VeHa'emuna*, chap. 2; *Pardes Rimmonim, Sha'ar Arkhei HaKinuyim*, s.v. "*gedula*."

Ḥesed is all about giving. In the configuration of a person's soul, the *sefira* of *Ḥesed* corresponds to the right arm, which gives, acting from the inside out.[5] By contrast, the *sefira* of *Gevura* is the power of contraction and convergence inward, like the left arm that opposes the right, modifying and containing the right hand's outward movement.

"וִימִינוֹ תְּחַבְּקֵנִי" (שיר השירים ב, ו),

as it is written, **"And his right hand embraces me"** (Song 2:6),

God's right hand signifies His attribute of *Ḥesed*. When God gifts a person with a show of His *Ḥesed*, it is as if He is embracing him, drawing him close.

שֶׁהִיא בְּחִינַת קִרְבַת אֱלֹהִים מַמָּשׁ, בְּיֶתֶר שְׂאֵת מִלְּפָנִים.

referring to actual closeness to God to a greater degree than before.

The revelation of divine *Ḥesed* to an individual is an embrace, which brings two parties closer than they were before. This does not mean that they were far from each other, but whatever distance they were from each other, now they are closer. There has been a movement of drawing close.

וְכָל הַקָּרוֹב אֶל ה׳ בְּיֶתֶר שְׂאֵת וְהַגְבֵּהַּ לְמַעְלָה מַעְלָה, צָרִיךְ לִהְיוֹת יוֹתֵר שְׁפַל רוּחַ לְמַטָּה מַטָּה,

Whoever has a greater degree of closeness to God and is raised to lofty heights must be more humble, lowering himself **to the lowest depths,**

How should a person respond to true closeness with God? The more God's kindness elevates a person and brings him close, the more he must lower himself so that he can receive this kindness and experience this connection so that he might preserve it.

Closeness to God is not necessarily mutual. When God draws a person close, this does not necessarily cause the person to be close to Him. For example, there is a relationship described in Jeremiah with the words "For they have turned their back to Me and not their face"

---

5. See introduction to *Tikkunei Zohar* 17a.

(Jer. 2:27).[6] Two people could be standing right next to each other, and one of them does not want closeness, so he turns around. The first person is standing as close as he can to the other, but the other person has created the greatest conceivable distance by turning his back on his comrade. In this sense, when God draws a person close to him, the person needs to make sure to also position himself for closeness. This is not easy. If God elevates a person, and the person views it superficially and not in a deep, internal way, it is as if he is turning his back on God and using the greatness he has merited merely to blow up his ego. This distances him from God to the ultimate degree, preventing him from any real closeness to God.

כְּמוֹ שֶׁכָּתוּב: ״מֵרָחוֹק ה׳ נִרְאָה לִי״ (ירמיה לא, ב).

as it is written, "The Lord appeared to me from afar" (Jer. 31:2).

It is particularly when a person feels distant that God appears to him: "If I ascend to heaven, You are there; if I lie down in the netherworld, You are here" (Ps. 139:8). "If I ascend to heaven," if I feel like I have ascended to a high realm, like I am great and superior, "You are there," distant and concealed. Yet "if I lie down in the netherworld," when I feel that I have descended to the depths, when I have humbled myself, "You are here."

For a person to merit seeing God, he must know that he is far, that he is nothing, because only then can God appear to him. But when he feels great and important, he will see less and less of the Divine, until he will cease to perceive God's presence at all.

By way of analogy, when a person looks at a tall mountain from afar, it seems small. Yet the more he draws close, the bigger the mountain appears and the smaller he feels next to it. A person who stands next to the mountain and still feels big should doubt whether he is truly close to it, or perhaps it is not a mountain at all.

וְכַנּוֹדַע, ׳דְּכוֹלָּא קַמֵּיהּ דַּוְוקָא, כְּלָא חֲשִׁיב׳ (הקדמת זהר יא, ב). וְאִם כֵּן,

As it is known, "Everything before Him is considered nothingness"

6. See *Likkutei Torah*, Lev. 26d.

כֹּל שֶׁהוּא קַמֵּיהּ יוֹתֵר, הוּא יוֹתֵר כְּלֹא וְאַיִן וְאֶפֶס.

(Introduction to *Zohar* 11b), specifically emphasizing "before Him." **If so, the more one is "before Him," the more he is like absolute nothingness.**

The concepts of close and far in relation to God, who is everywhere, must be understood in the context of inside and outside, revealed and hidden, as explained elsewhere.[7] The more a person is "before God," the closer he feels to Him, the smaller he is, the more he is nothing. The feeling of smallness is a result of his closeness to God. Conversely, the closer a person can get to God depends on the degree to which he can nullify his sense of self. ☞

THE CLOSER WE ARE, THE SMALLER WE ARE

☞ Why is it that a prerequisite to being close to God is to be truly humble? To understand this, the broader concepts of *yesh* and *ayin* must be understood. How do we define existence versus nothingness? As explained in other places, this question does not have an unequivocal answer. It depends from which angle we look. As limited, physical creatures, we feel that we exist and have substance, that we are the frame of reference for the experience of reality, the center of existence, while the Divine, which in relation to us is ungraspable, feels like nothing.

When we think about what is tangible to us, we generally think of that which can be perceived with our senses, especially with our sense of touch. The sense of touch is the most powerful of senses; it gives us the certainty that something actually exists more than all the other senses. Therefore, the less something can be touched, the less we regard it as existing. From this standpoint, God, who totally evades our attempts at direct or indirect comprehension, is as nothing to us. The truth is, however, that from God's perspective, as it were, He is the only actual reality, and everything else is negligible and considered absolute nothingness.

Our perception of existence, of something real, depends on its degree of permanence. The more something is established in the world, the more it tangibly exists. The path of the Milky Way exists in a more stable way than planet Earth because it exists beyond the space-time realm of Earth. On the other hand, planet Earth is more real than a man-made building.

There is a verse that refers to "his days like a passing shadow" (Ps. 144:4), and the midrash adds, "If only like the shadow of a wall, if only like the shadow of a tree, but rather like the shadow of a flying bird" (*Bereshit Rabba* 96:2). Shade is inherently a temporary reality, and our existence is not only like a shadow, but like the shadow of

7. See, e.g., *Likkutei Torah* 68a.

וְזוֹ הִיא בְּחִינַת יָמִין שֶׁבִּקְדוּשָּׁה וְ"חֶסֶד לְאַבְרָהָם" (מיכה ז, כ), שֶׁאָמַר: "אָנֹכִי עָפָר וָאֵפֶר" (בראשית יח, כז).

This is the right side **of holiness and the "kindness of Abraham"** (Mic. 7:20), **who said, "I am dust and ashes"** (Gen. 18:27).

When God's right hand, which draws a person close, causes him to feel small in his own estimation, it is called "the right side of holiness." The paradigm of holy kindness and right-handedness is Abraham, who was a chariot for the divine attribute of *Ḥesed* since he humbled himself until he felt that he was mere dust and ashes. ☞

וְזוֹ הִיא גַּם כֵּן מִדָּתוֹ שֶׁל יַעֲקֹב.

This is also the attribute of Jacob.

The more Jacob received in the way of divine kindness, the closer he was brought to God, the smaller he felt, as he said, "I am unworthy of

something that is fleeting. Only God Himself constitutes absolute, unchanging eternality. He is therefore the only one who actually exists, and we are the nothingness (Rambam, *Mishneh Torah, Sefer HaMadda, Hilkhot Yesodei HaTorah* 1:1–3).

There is, then, an essential contradiction between our existence and God's existence. Wherever we are, God is not, and where we are not, there is God. In other words, the stronger our perception of our existence, the more we perceive that we have substance, that we are the tangible reality, the farther God is. He becomes less real. The opposite is also true: The more palpable His reality, the more our reality becomes less real, more ephemeral and insignificant, in the face of His reality.

The person who achieved the greatest degree of closeness to God was Moses, and the verse attests, "And the man Moses was very humble, more than any person on the face of the earth" (Num. 12:3). His humility was commensurate with his closeness to God. That humility was not manifest by what he said or thought about himself compared to other people but rather in his deeply internal perspective of the nature of his essence. In actuality, he knew very well that he was great in comparison to others, yet he also believed that if another person had received his abilities and opportunities, that person would surely be greater than him. His humility, then, was born of a sense of his self in comparison to God. He understood very clearly that one is absolute nothingness before God. If he could perceive his own being as nothingness, then he could feel the presence of the Divine as a tangible reality.

What emerges from this bifurcated lens is that the two sides cannot mutually exist. God says about the arrogant person, "He and I cannot live together in the world" (*Sota* 5a; *Eiruvin* 15b). If God is great, then man is necessarily small and negligible. If a person is great, then God is necessarily small and ungraspable within that person's world.

all the kindnesses and of all the truth that You have performed for Your servant" (Gen. 32:10).[8]

There is a conceptual leap here, because Jacob is not explicitly referring to spiritual kindnesses, about the revelation of God and mystical closeness, but rather about the divine kindness that is manifest in material things, in "bread to eat and a garment to wear" (Gen. 28:20). But this only fine-tunes the point, that God's kindness, even when manifest in physical objects, is still a test for man: Will he now think of himself as greater or lesser? If he has become greater in truth, then his frame of reference has also grown, so that his status, assets, intelligence, and character traits seem much less significant in his own estimation. When a person merits closeness to God, he becomes privy to a larger frame of reference in which he becomes smaller. The more he receives kindnesses from God, the smaller he feels.

וּבְזֹאת הִתְנַצֵּל עַל יִרְאָתוֹ מִפְּנֵי עֵשָׂו, וְלֹא דַי לוֹ בְּהַבְטָחָתוֹ: "וְהִנֵּה אָנֹכִי עִמָּךְ כו'" (בראשית כח, טו). מִפְּנֵי הֱיוֹת קָטָן יַעֲקֹב בִּמְאֹד מְאֹד בְּעֵינָיו, מֵחֲמַת רִיבּוּי הַחֲסָדִים: "כִּי בְמַקְלִי כו'" (בראשית לב, י), וְאֵינוֹ

This is how he justified his fear of Esau, and this is why **he did not suffice with** God's **promise "And, behold, I am with you; I will keep you wherever you go"** (Gen. 28:15). **Since Jacob was exceedingly small in his** own **eyes due to the many acts**

DUST AND ASHES

☞ When did Abraham say these words? After God said to him, "Shall I conceal from Abraham that which I am doing? And Abraham shall become a great and mighty nation..." (Gen. 18:17–18). God gave Abraham the greatest compliment, making him a confidant. No one else in the world needed to know, but Abraham did. He drew him close to share with him and only him, as opposed to the rest of the world. Yet instead of feeling superior, instead of feeling greater than everyone else, Abraham declared, "I am dust and ashes."

8. Jacob's inclusion of truth in his prayer signifies his self-abnegation, not just due to "all the kindnesses," but also to "all the truth," which refers to the Torah (*Sefer HaMa'amarim Melukat*, vol. 5, p. 100).

רָאוּי וּכְדַאי כְּלָל לְהִנָּצֵל כו'.

of kindness God had performed for him, as it is written, **"For with my staff** I crossed this Jordan, and now I have become two camps" (Gen. 32:10), he considered himself **entirely unworthy and undeserving to be saved, and so on.**

Jacob surmised that when he crossed the Jordan River on his way to Ḥaran twenty years before, he had only his staff and nothing else. He was alone and being pursued. "And now I have become two camps" – now he had a large family and great wealth. Yet instead of feeling greater and more entitled, he declared, "I am unworthy of all the kindnesses." You did so many kindnesses for me, God, and You brought me so close, yet I do not deserve any of it.

וּכְמַאֲמַר רַבּוֹתֵינוּ זַ"ל (ברכות ד, א): "שֶׁמָּא יִגְרוֹם הַחֵטְא", שֶׁנִּדְמֶה בְּעֵינָיו שֶׁחָטָא.

This is **in accordance with the Rabbis' statement** "Jacob was concerned **lest a transgression would cause** God to revoke His promise" (*Berakhot* 4a), **because it seemed to him that he had sinned.**

This was not a new feeling stemming from a recent sin that Jacob though he had committed but rather the sharpness of his own internal critique. The more a person grows in holiness, the more he demands of himself. What he would not have considered a sin in the past, he now considered a transgression.

It is recounted that during *Tashlikh*, a prayer said on the afternoon of Rosh HaShana where one metaphorically casts his sins into a body of water, the students used to follow the Lubavitcher Rebbe and collect the sins he was discarding, because for them his sins were considered mitzvot. ☞

מַה שֶּׁאֵין כֵּן בְּזֶה לְעוּמַּת זֶה,

This is not the case with the unholy **counterpart** to divine kindness,

This expression, "unholy counterpart," conveys the parallel between the infrastructure of the world of holiness and the other side, that which opposes the sacred, not only in general but in every detail.[9] The pattern of *kelippa*, the force of impurity, only echoes the pattern of holiness because *kelippa* does not have any authentic vitality in and of itself; it is but a shell, a shadow of the side of holiness.

הוּא יִשְׁמָעֵאל, חֶסֶד דִּקְלִיפָּה. כָּל שֶׁהַחֶסֶד גָּדוֹל, הוּא הוֹלֵךְ וְגָדֵל בְּגוֹבַהּ וְגַסּוּת הָרוּחַ וְרוֹחַב לִבּוֹ.

which is Ishmael, who represents ***Ḥesed* of *kelippa*.** In the realm of *kelippa*, **the greater the kindness, the more** the recipient's **arrogance, pride, and sense of entitlement increases.**

Abraham embodies the holy aspect of *Ḥesed*, while Ishmael, Abraham's son, embodies the *Ḥesed* of *kelippa*. When the kindness a person receives makes him feel entitled to even more, this is the *Ḥesed* of *kelippa*. It is not necessarily a different category of *Ḥesed*. It shares the same source as holy *Ḥesed*, yet becomes distorted by its recipient. Just as kindness can be an instrument for blessing, growth, and holiness, it can also be

SIN IN HIS OWN EYES

☞ We can analyze the subtlety of the wording of the *Tanya*: "It seemed to him that he had sinned." This is not an objective standard that can be applied to other people, only to Jacob in his present situation. Consider the following analogy: There are black spots on the sun that shine brighter than several full moons combined. If they were on the moon, they would be "light spots," but on the sun they appear black.

Similarly, the more a person grows, the more illuminated he becomes, the more his stains become painful and noticeable. The feeling of self-satisfaction is characteristic of young children – and of people who are immature at any age. The more a person grows and learns, in whatever field, the more he realizes how much he does not know.

As he grows, a person may regret not only his sins but his mitzvot as well, and his feelings of remorse regarding his mitzvot may even be more intense. He may feel that everything holy that he has done until today, in every arena of life, is also connected to the other side. Sins have clear and objective parameters, and the way of repentance is open to him, allowing him to fix what he has done. This does not apply to mitzvot. The parameters, the embellishments, and the intentions behind the performance of an ideal mitzva are much more obscure, and the feeling that "it seemed to him that he had sinned" may be more severe regarding mitzvot.

9. See *Torah Or*, Gen. 26d.

destructive and damaging to its recipient. If in response to the kindness a person receives he grows larger in his own eyes, if his appetite grows bigger and bigger, then sooner or later he will lose everything.

It is clear from this that not only are challenging times a test, but so are times of plenty and benevolence. Even when a person is the recipient of open kindness from above, a sense of importance and entitlement will cause all the goodness to revert to *kelippa*.

וְלָזֹאת בָּאתִי מִן הַמּוֹדִיעִים מוֹדָעָה רַבָּה לִכְלָלוּת אַנְשֵׁי שְׁלוֹמֵנוּ, עַל רִיבּוּי הַחֲסָדִים אֲשֶׁר הִגְדִּיל ה׳ לַעֲשׂוֹת עִמָּנוּ, לֶאֱחוֹז בְּמִדּוֹתָיו שֶׁל יַעֲקֹב,

Accordingly, I am hereby making a momentous announcement to all the members of our community about the many acts of kindness that God has magnanimously done for us: Adopt the attributes of Jacob,

In light of the first part of this letter, the entreaty takes on a different tone and scope. The letter does not just outline good attributes versus bad ones or delineate whether it is permitted to take revenge against the opponents of Hasidism. These concepts relate to the soul's quintessential response to God's goodness and the serious ramifications of it. Every person needs to realize that the magnitude of the kindness that God has performed for the hasidim in general and Hasidism as a movement is a personal test: Will one succeed in retaining his essence as a Jew and embody the attributes of Jacob, who was humbled from all the kindnesses God performed for him?

"שְׁאָר עַמּוֹ" (ישעיה יא, יא) וּ"שְׁאֵרִית יִשְׂרָאֵל" (ירמיה ו, ט), שֶׁמֵּשִׂים עַצְמוֹ כְּשִׁירַיִים וּמוֹתָרוֹת מַמָּשׁ, שֶׁאֵין בּוֹ שׁוּם צוֹרֶךְ.

for we are known as **"the remnant of His people"** (Isa. 11:11) **and "the remnant of Israel"** (Jer. 6:9), referring to a person **who regards himself as a remainder and truly dispensable, with no use at all.**

The explanation for this appellation of the Jewish people is mentioned in several places in the Talmud.[10] This is the litmus test of true closeness to God: The receiver sees himself as small, unimportant, and even dispensable.

10. See *Megilla* 15b; *Sanhedrin* 111b.

לְבִלְתִּי רוּם לְבָבָם מֵאֲחֵיהֶם כו׳, וְלֹא לְהַרְחִיב עֲלֵיהֶם פֶּה אוֹ לִשְׁרוֹק עֲלֵיהֶם חַס וְשָׁלוֹם. הַס מִלְּהַזְכִּיר, בְּאַזְהָרָה נוֹרָאָה. רַק לְהַשְׁפִּיל רוּחָם וְלִבָּם בְּמִדַּת אֱמֶת לְיַעֲקֹב

They should not feel superior to their brethren, and so on, and they should not jeer at them or whistle at them derisively, **God forbid.** This is a **strict warning: Mention nothing** to the opponents. **Rather, they should lower their spirits and hearts,** adopting **Jacob's attribute of truth**

The author of the *Tanya* warns the hasidim not to be arrogant and humiliate the opponents of Hasidism, despite the greatly tempting opportunity to act as their superiors and crush them now that Hasidism has the upper hand after his release. He is not implying that the other side was right; the hasidim suffered from brutal, unjustified persecution. But now that the hasidim had won, the author does not just present this conduct as good advice or general words of morality but rather as a practical instruction that includes a strict warning not to stray from it.

The reference to "Jacob's attribute of truth"[11] means that this is not a demand for particular external behavior, but rather it should be felt deep within as well. Moreover, one who is not capable of this conduct does not belong to the community of Chabad hasidim.[12]

מִפְּנֵי כָּל אָדָם בִּנְמִיכוּת רוּחַ, "וּמַעֲנֶה רַךְ מֵשִׁיב חֵימָה" (משלי טו, א), "וְרוּחַ נְכֵאָה כו׳" (משלי יז, כב). וְכוּלֵּי הַאי וְאוּלַי יִתֵּן ה׳ בְּלֵב אֲחֵיהֶם, "כַּמַּיִם הַפָּנִים וגו׳" (משלי כז, יט).

before every person, with humility, with **"a gentle response** that **assuages fury"** (Prov. 15:1) and with a **"depressed spirit…"** (Prov. 17:22). **Through all this, perhaps God will put** a similar response **in the hearts of their brethren, "As water reflects a face** to the face…" (Prov. 27:19).

11. Based on Mic. 7:20.

12. The fourth Lubavitcher Rebbe, Rabbi Shmuel Schneerson, commented that if the author of the *Tanya* had not added the words "Jacob's attribute of truth," another fifty thousand hasidim would have joined him. See *Likkutei Dibburim* 2:44a; *HaYom Yom*, 10 Av.

Even if one does all the above, humbling oneself and behaving toward the opponent with a lowly spirit, it is not guaranteed that they will respond in kind. The author of the *Tanya* is cautioning his followers against using the opponents' response as a condition for their own behavior. This advice is not a tactic or even a strategy for making peace with others but rather a deep, personal test of faith, a path that one should walk in his service of God. This is the right way to act, the way of Jacob's attribute of truth.

In any event, the author of the *Tanya* adds, "perhaps" this will be beneficial and effect change in the other side. A person's nature compels him to feel for his friend what his friend feels for him. Expressing love for another person awakens that same feeling in the other. This is not a guarantee, but nevertheless it "assuages fury." It extinguishes the flame of the dispute. It creates a possibility, an opening, a "perhaps."

This letter is meant not only to prevent the joy and celebration at the author of the *Tanya*'s release from incarceration from turning into gloom, but it demands much more than that: not to take advantage of the victory by seeking to crush his opponents. This instruction reflects the author of the *Tanya*'s underlying intent throughout the dispute, both when being pursued and when he gained the upper hand: not to intensify the fight, to mitigate extreme emotion as much as possible, and to lower the tone of the disputes, debates, and dialogues. In line with this intention, the author of the *Tanya* made many attempts to organize discussions and even a face-to-face debate with the Vilna Gaon, but due to reasons that are unclear, it did not end up happening.[13]

But the crux of the letter is certainly its deeper, analytical portion, which does not just address a superficial, time-sensitive issue about that event but rather poses a question that every person must ask himself, wherein he honestly questions the degree to which he lives with "Jacob's truth" in the face of God's kindness. God's kindness presents man

13. It is told that in the year 1774 the author of the *Tanya* traveled with Rabbi Menaḥem Mendel of Vitebsk to meet with the Vilna Gaon, but the Vilna Gaon did not grant them an audience (*HaYom Yom, Roshei Perakim MiToledot Rabbeinu HaZaken*).

with a test: What will grow in that moment? The recipient's personal feeling of self or the point of holiness within? Does this *Ḥesed* create a *kelippa* and impediment to holiness, or does it create an instrument for connection with the Divine, a medium for holiness that receives and effuses holy *Ḥesed*?

Epistle 3

THIS LETTER IS ONE OF MANY THAT FOCUSES ON INSPIRING people to give charity. From the sheer number of letters on this topic, it is clear that the demand on the hasidim to give charity was not an easy one. This was not an appeal for a penny or two so that a person could feel that he gave the minimum to fulfill his obligation, but rather it was expected that a person donate large sums, amounting to a significant portion of his income. Most of the hasidim addressed by this letter were not wealthy, which meant that giving such amounts of charity demanded not only giving up extras but significantly scaling down their daily living expenses.

As explained in the introduction, all the letters included in this section of the *Tanya* contain a deeper layer that speaks to hasidim wherever and whenever they may live, beyond the context of the time and place in which this letter was written. This letter explores the inner significance of action-based mitzvot in general and the mitzva of charity in particular.

7 Av

11 Av (leap year)

"וַיִּלְבַּשׁ צְדָקָה כַּשִּׁרְיוֹן וְכוֹבַע יְשׁוּעָה בְּרֹאשׁוֹ" (ישעיה נט, יז), וְדָרְשׁוּ רַבּוֹתֵינוּ זַ"ל: "מַה שִּׁרְיוֹן זֶה, כָּל קְלִיפָּה וּקְלִיפָּה מִצְטָרֶפֶת לְשִׁרְיוֹן גָּדוֹל, אַף צְדָקָה, כָּל פְּרוּטָה וּפְרוּטָה מִצְטָרֶפֶת לְחֶשְׁבּוֹן גָּדוֹל" (בבא בתרא ט, ב).

It is written, **"He donned charity like armor and a helmet of salvation on His head"** (Isa. 59:17). **Our Rabbis commented, "Just as** with regard to **this coat of mail, each and every scale** of which it is fashioned **combines to form one large coat of mail, so too** with regard to **charity, each and every penny** that one gives **combines to** form **a great sum"** (*Bava Batra* 9b).

This coat of armor described by the Talmud was a type of armor made up of scales of iron. Such armor, common from biblical times, was used by the Roman army. It was generally made of hide and covered by row after row of overlapping metal discs that looked like fish scales.[1] This type of armor gave its wearer the flexibility of movement that a solid coat of armor could not.

פֵּירוּשׁ, שֶׁהַשִּׁרְיוֹן עָשׂוּי קַשְׂקַשִּׂים עַל נְקָבִים, וְהֵם מְגִינִּים שֶׁלֹּא יִכָּנֵס חֵץ בַּנְּקָבִים, וְכָכָה הוּא מַעֲשֵׂה הַצְּדָקָה.

This means that the coat of mail is made of scales covering gaps and providing protection so that an arrow does not penetrate the gaps, and so it is with the act of charity.

The first level of this analogy is visual. The scales of the armor look like rows of coins. Just as the scales combine to form a complete coat of armor, the pennies given for charity combine with each other to amount to a "great sum," not just in quantity, but also in their essential nature: Together they form a new creation; they become a complete coat of mail. Every scale is necessary for the armor's ultimate purpose. If some are missing, then the entire garment is defective and cannot fulfill its function properly.

The same can be said of charity. Just as the scales in a coat of armor cover any gaps, protecting the vulnerable spots underneath, every coin contributed for charity protects the "holes" in the spiritual garment created by mitzvot, as will be explained below.

וּבֵיאוּר הָעִנְיָן, כִּי גְּדוֹלָה צְדָקָה מִכָּל הַמִּצְוֹת,

The explanation of the matter is as follows: Charity is greater than all the other **mitzvot,**

There is an aspect of charity that transcends all the other action-based mitzvot. This category of the commandments is practical and performed in the material world through manipulating and changing some physical object. This imbues the mitzva item with significance that transcends the confines of the physical world. ☞

1. See I Sam. 17:5, and Rashi ad loc.

שֶׁמֵּהֶן נַעֲשִׂים לְבוּשִׁים לְהַנְּשָׁמָה. **from which garments are formed for the soul.**

In addition to the main effect that a mitzva has in the higher worlds, an effect that is concealed from us, the mitzva acts upon its doer as well: It creates a spiritual garment. Like a physical garment, a spiritual garment envelops a person yet does not bind to his internal faculties. He has no intellectual or emotional connection to the essence of the

MITZVOT IN THE WORLD OF ACTION

☞ For the most part, a mitzva is virtually inconsequential in the dimension in which it is performed. Its significance is revealed only in other, higher realms. In this world, most mitzvot seem like arbitrary actions. Donning *tefillin* or shaking the *lulav* has no real effect in this lower dimension. Their true power manifests itself somewhere else, in a realm beyond our world.

Imagine a command center that controls an intricate and extensive network of powerful machines. In a room filled with buttons and switches sits a man whose job it is to operate them according to very specific instructions: Press button A, pull lever B, wait for something to move, and then flip switch C. The essential act of pushing the button or flipping the switch is negligible compared to the effect that the button or switch activates. A person can sit at his desk, push a small button, and send a command to an aircraft that initiates a world war.

Our world is like a control center, and *halakha* is the manual that tells us how to operate the network: Move the *etrog* from right to left at such-and-such time, build a *sukka*, don *tefillin* in the morning.... If one observed a person's actions in the control room, they would seem meaningless because their principal effect occurs in another dimension.

In our dimension, the effect of the small mitzva gestures we do is almost imperceptible. A person who only considers observable changes in this realm sees a fraction of their value and power, and sometimes he sees none at all.

This disconnection between our actions and their effect serves a certain purpose in that it allows us to continue to function. If we were to be aware of the scope and power of our actions, it could be that we would be so overwhelmed that would not be able to perform them at all.

There is a famous analogy that illustrates this well: A great artist crafted the king's crown. When he was almost finished and ready to affix the most precious gemstone to the tip of the crown, in precisely the right place and angle, his hands shook. He understood too well the immense significance and weight of the responsibility of this act to the point that he was unable to perform it. He hired a simple day laborer who did not grasp the enormity of the task and said to him, "Put this stone here, at this angle." And he did it.

This lack of understanding, of sensitivity to the ramifications of our actions, enables us to function, but also poses a danger and impediment. One who does not tremble at the sanctity of a mitzva also does not recoil from the severity of a sin.

mitzva. He can only tap into its external manifestation, its operating instructions that allow him to perform it, while the essence of the mitzva intrinsically lies beyond his apprehension.

Elsewhere, the author of the *Tanya* explained how the mitzvot are garments compared to the Torah, which serves as nourishment for the soul.[2] Like food that enters a person and becomes part of his body, the Torah that a person studies and apprehends enters him and becomes integrated into his soul's intellectual and emotional faculties. By contrast, a mitzva serves as a garment, in the sense that when one performs it, one enters it, yet it does not enter him. The person receives from it only the properties it offers as a garment.

We can understand this facet of the concept of garment by comparing it to speech. Speech serves as a garment for thought. Thought is revealed through the medium of speech (it can also, by the same token, be revealed through action). The speech does not add any content to the original thought. It does not penetrate its very essence, while thought permeates the speech and is revealed to the listener through the garment of the spoken word. Granted, speech can influence thought, yet not in a direct way so that it affects its essential core, but rather indirectly, wherein the thought takes on another dimension, as it were, beyond that which it possessed when it was only a thought.[3]

Similarly, when a person performs a mitzva, when he dons a *tallit* or *tefillin*, separates tithes or hangs a *mezuza*, the mitzva act does not change him intrinsically, making him a smarter or better person. The Sages taught that mitzvot were not given for pleasure;[4] that is, the fulfillment of the mitzva itself does not provide any direct, tangible pleasure or benefits, neither physical nor spiritual. Rather, a person becomes enveloped by the mitzva that he is performing at that moment. Even if he does not feel it at the time, he belongs at that moment to another reality, exalted and separate, a reality that he can only gain access to through the garment of the mitzva. ☞

2. See *Sha'ar HaYiḥud VeHa'emuna*, chap. 5; Ps. 40:9.
3. See epistle 5, where this idea is explained at length.
4. *Eiruvin* 31a, *Rosh HaShana* 28b.

הַנִּמְשָׁכִים מֵאוֹר אֵין סוֹף בָּרוּךְ הוּא מִבְּחִינַת "סוֹבֵב כָּל עָלְמִין" (כַּמְבוֹאָר הַפֵּירוּשׁ 'מְמַלֵּא כָּל עָלְמִין' וְ'סוֹבֵב כָּל עָלְמִין' בְּלִקּוּטֵי אֲמָרִים, עַיֵּין שָׁם),

These garments are **drawn from the light of *Ein Sof*, blessed be He, from** the light that **encompasses all worlds. (The meaning of** the light that **fills all worlds and encompasses all worlds is explained in *Likkutei Amarim*** [chap. 48]; **see there.)**

Although the garments of the mitzvot become attached to physical actions, they are drawn from far beyond all the worlds, from the encompassing light of *Ein Sof*, which surrounds the worlds like a garment. Just as the light encompasses, so does the mitzva encompass.

There are various types of divine illumination. One is called the light that "fills all worlds," which gives life to all the worlds from within, like the light of the soul that is manifest within the body to give it vitality. The other is the light that "encompasses all worlds." This light does not manifest within the world but rather surrounds it in its entirety and its every detail, like a framework that holds its very existence. ☞

THE MITZVA OF TORAH STUDY

☞ The mitzva of Torah study is an exception to the rule. While it does share some of the garment characteristics of other mitzvot, it necessitates a certain degree of understanding and internalization. If a person does not understand the content that he is studying, he does not fulfill the mitzva of Torah study as fully as possible (see *Hilkhot Talmud Torah* 2:13 by the author of the *Tanya*). Therefore, a person does not just externally wear the Torah study in which he has engaged but internalizes it as well (see also *Likkutei Amarim*, chap. 5). This does not apply to the other mitzvot, wherein a person's emotional and intellectual engagement, whether faint or intense, is not a component of the mitzva's essence but rather is generated from the love and awe that he feels from the power of that simple act.

THE ENCOMPASSING LIGHT

☞ At its essence, the Divine certainly exists beyond the worlds that it created. It preexisted them and will remain in existence after them. This aspect of the Divine transcends the reality of the worlds. It does not manifest within them and cannot be grasped by them. This is the encompassing light.

This expression conjures up a huge circle that surrounds the world. Like a circle, it has no beginning and no end, no up nor down. Within it, there is no difference be-

בְּאִתְעָרוּתָא דִלְתַתָּא

The transcendent light is drawn to the soul **through an awakening from below,**

One of the basic principles in the dynamic between the higher and the lower worlds, between man and God, is that an awakening from above occurs through an awakening from below. The drawing down of an illumination from above to the worlds below depends on a spiritual awakening ascending from below. This principle lies at the bedrock of a person's entire divine service, giving meaning and power to everything he does and for which he prays down here below.

הִיא מִצְוַת ה׳ וּרְצוֹן הָעֶלְיוֹן בָּרוּךְ הוּא.

which constitutes the fulfillment of **God's command and His supernal will.**

Lying at the core of every mitzva is God's directive: "Perform My will." The essence of the divine will, like the will of a person, intrinsically transcends all human understanding, even though it can be interpreted in various rational ways. The will inherently corresponds to the level of encompassing all worlds because it defies any real attempt at comprehension. The connection that is forged through the fulfillment of a mitzva touches on the aspect of the Divine that lies beyond all the worlds, the divine will, the level known as the *sefira* of *Keter*. It is only through a mitzva that such a link can be formed. In fact, the word *mitzva* etymologically comes from the word *tzavta,* which means connection.

וְעִיקַּר הַמְשָׁכָה זוֹ מֵאוֹר אֵין סוֹף בָּרוּךְ הוּא, הוּא לְבוּשׁ וְאוֹר

The primary aspect **of this flow from the light of** ***Ein Sof,*** **blessed be He,**

tween big or small, where "He makes equal the small and great" (see *Iggeret HaTeshuva*, chap. 11). Yet one should not make the error of thinking that this light resembles an actual circle that surrounds only from above. This spiritual encompassment of all worlds, the Divine that does not manifest itself within any element of any world, exists below just as it does above, in the micro as in the macro. There is no reality, general or specific, that does not have the divine essence surrounding it, enveloping it, enabling its very existence. This is the light that encompasses all worlds.

מַקִּיף לְיו״ד סְפִירוֹת דַּאֲצִילוּת, בְּרִיאָה, יְצִירָה, עֲשִׂיָּה,

serves as a garment and encompassing light for the ten ***sefirot*** through which the divine light descends into the four worlds of ***Atzilut, Beria, Yetzira,*** and ***Asiya***

The divine light that descends to the worlds garbs itself in the ten *sefirot* in order to interact with the worlds, both when the Divine forms and enlivens existence and when it manifests within it. The ten *sefirot* therefore constitute the Divine as it operates from within the worlds, their inner vitality, similar to the vitality that the soul imparts to the body. Just as there are ten all-encompassing *sefirot* in the world of *Atzilut* that enliven and manifest the entirety of all the subsequent worlds, that give life to all the worlds, so too every world has ten *sefirot* that enliven it in particular.

הַמִּשְׁתַּלְשְׁלוֹת מֵעִילָּה לְעִילָּה, וּמִמַּדְרֵגָה לְמַדְרֵגָה כוּ׳, הַנִּקְרָאוֹת בְּשֵׁם ״מְמַלֵּא כָּל עָלְמִין״.

that devolve through a chain of causality and from level to level, and so on, the *sefirot* **being referred to as** the light that **fills all worlds.**

Like the faculties of the soul through which the light of the soul progressively descends from the level of wisdom to the level of action, so too the divine light progressively descends through the vessels of the ten *sefirot,* down the path of cause and effect, from level to level, from the level of *Ḥokhma* of *Atzilut* all the way down to our lowly physical world. This progressive descent of the divine light and life force into the confines and minutiae of the worlds is called the light that fills all worlds.

A mitzva that a person performs has broad and all-encompassing significance, beyond one's personal involvement with it and the way in which it creates a garment for his individual soul. The primary effect of the mitzva performance is the drawing down of the divine light from the level of encompassing all worlds to the level of the divine inner vitality that fills all worlds.

פֵּירוּשׁ, כִּי אוֹר אֵין סוֹף בָּרוּךְ הוּא, מִתְלַבֵּשׁ וּמֵאִיר בְּתוֹךְ כָּל הִשְׁתַּלְשְׁלוּת הָעֶשֶׂר סְפִירוֹת

This means that the transcendent **light of** ***Ein Sof,*** **blessed be He, is clothed and shines within the entire**

דַּאֲצִילוּת, בְּרִיאָה, יְצִירָה, עֲשִׂיָּה,

progression **of the ten *sefirot*** in each of the four worlds of ***Atzilut, Beria, Yetzira,*** and ***Asiya,***

The encompassing light that transcends all the worlds, then, is the source of the divine light that fills the worlds from within.

וְהוּא הַמַּאֲצִיל הָעֶשֶׂר סְפִירוֹת דַּאֲצִילוּת,

and that transcendent light **is what initiates the emanation of the ten *sefirot* of** the world of ***Atzilut,***

The first and most exalted level of the light that fills all worlds is the emanation of the *sefirot* of the world of *Atzilut.* ☞

הַמִּשְׁתַּלְשְׁלוֹת לִבְרִיאָה יְצִירָה עֲשִׂיָּה

which in turn **progress to** the worlds of ***Beria, Yetzira,*** and ***Asiya***

The ten *sefirot,* along with the divine light that is clothed within them, descend from the level in which they express pure divine essence to lower levels that express the way the Divine interacts with the worlds: to the world of *Beria,* where the existence of intellect and thought are manifest; to the world of *Yetzira,* where emotion and speech are manifest; and to the world of *Asiya,* the world of action and materiality. ☞ ☞

ATZILUT AND BEYOND

☞ While the world of *Atzilut* is mentioned here as the highest world, kabbalistic and hasidic teachings mention levels beyond it. Yet when we discuss meaningful levels in our reality, we do not relate to levels beyond *Atzilut.* For the sake of illustration, consider astronomy. There are things that we know exist, like nebulae, beyond our galaxy, but this knowledge is pure abstraction because there is no direct link between us and their existence. The worlds too, of *Atzilut, Beria, Yetzira,* and a large part of the world of *Asiya,* lie beyond the lives of most people. Most people in the course of their lives do not tap into anything beyond the spiritual world of *Asiya.* On the other hand, our souls do have a degree of structural parallel to all four worlds in the levels of the soul, including the world of *Atzilut* and the worlds that devolve from it (the soul level of *nefesh* corresponds to the world of *Asiya,* the soul level of *ruaḥ* corresponds to the world of *Yetzira,* and so on). In this sense, they constitute the actual spectrum of our existence, though we are for the most part unaware of it, while the realms beyond *Atzilut* are to us like another dimension, utterly set apart and completely theoretical.

עַל יְדֵי צִמְצוּם עָצוּם הַמְבוֹאָר בְּעֵץ חַיִּים (שער א, ענף ב). **through the immense constriction described in *Etz Ḥayyim* (1:2).**

THE FOUR WORLDS

☞ In a very broad sense, there are four principal stages in which the divine light and life force are channeled from the phase of the light of *Ein Sof* to physical matter. These stages constitute the four worlds, *Atzilut, Beria, Yetzira,* and *Asiya*. These worlds, which unfold one from the next, become more and more physical as they descend. The world of *Atzilut*, the highest of them, is hardly a world. It constitutes infinite existence, even though *Atzilut* itself is not *Ein Sof*, the Infinite One. One can say that the world of *Atzilut* is essentially divine manifestation, pure Divine compared to the other created worlds.

The world of *Beria* is the first of the created worlds, the first reality that is not defined as entirely divine but rather as a creation that stems from the Divine, the manifestation of something from nothingness.

The structure of a person's soul is a microcosm of these four worlds. The world of *Atzilut* is the flash point of *Ḥokhma*, the point of nothingness that manifests as the essential soul. The world of *Beria* is the dimension of *Bina*, of lofty, abstract intellectual constructs. The world of *Yetzira* is paralleled by the emotive faculties, such as *Ḥesed* and *Gevura*, kindness and restraint, likes and dislikes, that are formed from the awareness of the surrounding reality. The world of *Asiya* is the realm of the soul's conclusions about life and their implementation in the world.

The four worlds also parallel the garments of the soul. *Atzilut* represents the essence of the soul itself and its attributes, *Beria* is thought, *Yetzira* is speech, and *Asiya* is action. The world of *Asiya* has two facets, the spiritual and the physical. Amid this duality of the physical and spiritual facets of the realm of *Asiya* we human beings live. Our reality, whether we live holy lives or not, is a mixture of physicality and spirituality, like amphibians that live in two worlds as one, moving from materiality to the realm of the spirit and back. If a person merits, he can reach higher worlds (see *Zohar* 2:94b), worlds that are higher, not only in their degree of abstraction, but also in their level of sanctity.

EMANATION AND PROGRESSION

☞ The word that the author of the *Tanya* uses to explain the emergence of the *sefirot* in the world of *Atzilut* is *ma'atzil*, which denotes emanation, yet with regard to the emergence of the *sefirot* in the worlds of *Beria, Yetzira,* and *Asiya*, he uses the word *mishtalshel*, progresses. Progression denotes a transition of causal connection, like links in a chain. One connection leads to another, and the links can be traced back to their origin in a logical manner. Emanation, on the other hand, is a mysterious, unfathomable transition, like from *Ein Sof* to the world of *Atzilut*, and as in the verse "He drew [*vaye'etzal*] from the spirit that was upon him" (Num. 11:25), which describes the transference of content from Moses to the elders in the wilderness that was beyond the fundamental, rational teachings that Moses imparted. It was pure, inscrutable inspiration from Moses's spirit to theirs.

This transition from *Ein Sof* to the world of *Atzilut* came about through an "immense constriction."[5] This was the first constriction from the highest level to the next one, from the infinite to the next, more finite level, the first of the many constrictions that took place in the order of progression.[6] This initial constriction is an inexplicable, one-way transition, with no way of looking back. Causal connections can only be found linking the *sefirot* in *Atzilut* and in the worlds of the created beings, where one level is a reflection of the one above it. But these levels become progressively more obscure as they get further from the source, but unlike the "immense constriction" from *Ein Sof* to *Atzilut*, they always have some discoverable relationship to each other. ☞

וְנִקְרָא אוֹר פְּנִימִי. This **is called inner light.**

The light that remains after the constriction is called "inner light" because it is the light that becomes constricted within the boundaries and limitations of our world. This inner light is the light that manifests

CONSTRICTION VERSUS PROGRESSION

☞ The change engendered by divine constriction is more intense than a causal shift. An ordinary causal relationship between one thing and the next is comprehensible and logical on both sides. One can follow the transition from the cause to the outcome, and trace their connection in reverse, discovering the cause of a given result. But the transmission from one level to another is reminiscent of a translation from one language to another. There is always some content and power lost in the transition, yet a fundamental aspect that is shared between the two remains. The possibility of returning to the source is ever present. Conversely, in the case of the "immense constriction," the translation is one-sided. We know that something exists on the other side, but we cannot see it. It is like the transition from nothingness to existence.

---

5. See also the commentary of the Lubavitcher Rebbe, Rabbi Menaḥem Mendel Schneerson, in *Ma'amar Bati LeGani* (1977), printed in *Sefer HaMa'amarim*, vol. 1, p. 220.

6. This concept is explained as the distinction between the total removal of the divine light that occurred in the first constriction (to create a space for darkness and emptiness) and the diminishment of the divine light that constituted the subsequent constrictions, where the light descends and is further and further from it source so that it becomes progressively dimmed. See *Ma'amar Bati LeGani* (1977); *Hemshekh Ayin Bet*, p. 12.

within the world. It is the Divine at every single level yet filtered through constrictions that do not reveal the quintessential Divine but rather the divine light as it gets refracted through our experiences and reflects back to us a glimmer of its source.

וְעַל יְדֵי קִיּוּם הַמִּצְוֹת נִמְשָׁךְ אוֹר מַקִּיף, הַנִּזְכָּר לְעֵיל, וּמֵאִיר תּוֹךְ הָעֶשֶׂר סְפִירוֹת – דַּאֲצִילוּת בְּרִיאָה יְצִירָה עֲשִׂיָּה – וּמִתְיַיחֵד עִם הָאוֹר פְּנִימִי,

Through the performance of the commandments, the aforementioned encompassing light is drawn down and shines within the ten *sefirot* of *Atzilut, Beria, Yetzira,* and *Asiya* and is united with the inner light,

The performance of a mitzva catapults its doer, not only to a higher world, nor to contact with supernal angels, but to the divine will itself, which is an aspect of the transcendental, inscrutable encompassing light that lies beyond every level and every world. When a person performs the supernal divine will by performing a mitzva within this world, he makes contact between the inner light that progressively descended into his own world and the encompassing light that hovers above and beyond his world, unifying this world and the inner light with the transcendental will.

This is not an absolutely seamless unification. Rather, it is like the union between man and woman who do not become subsumed into a single reality but meet in oneness. It is a meeting that results in the creation of new life. This contact between inner light and encompassing light, then, forges something greater than a projection of light or even a duplication of it. It gives birth to a new creation comprised of both facets together.

וְנִקְרָא 'יִחוּד קוּדְשָׁא בְּרִיךְ הוּא וּשְׁכִינְתֵּיהּ', כְּמוֹ שֶׁנִּתְבָּאֵר בְּמָקוֹם אַחֵר.

which is called the "unification of the Holy One, blessed be He, and His Divine Presence," as explained elsewhere (*Likkutei Amarim*, chap. 41).

"The Holy One, blessed be He," refers to the aspect of God that is totally separate, that transcends all. "His Divine Presence" refers to the inner light that fills all worlds, the divine vitality that resides with us, the source of our life and existence. The unification between them is the unity of God and the Divine Presence, between the Holy One and the life force that enlivens this world, between the light that encompasses all worlds and the light that fills all worlds. ☞

וּמֵהֶאָרָה דְּהֶאָרָה מֵאוֹר מַקִּיף הַנִּזְכָּר לְעֵיל,

From a glimmer of a glimmer of the aforementioned encompassing light,

A mitzva activates a unification between God and the Divine Presence throughout the worlds. Yet, as mentioned at the beginning of the letter, the performance of a mitzva also has a byproduct that affects its doer personally, and that is the creation of a garment for him. This encompassing garment does not reach the individual's soul at all, not even as an illumination. The author of the *Tanya* therefore speaks of a "glimmer of a glimmer," a glimmer of the encompassing light that creates another glimmer that becomes a garment for the soul.

An example of a glimmer of a glimmer is the light of the moon. When the moon reflects the light of the sun, it is an illumination of the sun. When the light of the moon reflects off planet Earth, we receive an illumination of an illumination, a glimmer of a glimmer, from the light source, the sun.

עַל יְדֵי צִמְצוּם רַב, נַעֲשֶׂה לְבוּשׁ לִבְחִינַת 'נֶפֶשׁ' 'רוּחַ' 'נְשָׁמָה' שֶׁל הָאָדָם, בְּגַן עֵדֶן הַתַּחְתּוֹן וְהָעֶלְיוֹן, שֶׁיּוּכְלוּ לֵיהָנוֹת וּלְהַשִּׂיג אֵיזֶה הַשָּׂגָה וְהֶאָרָה מֵאוֹר אֵין סוֹף בָּרוּךְ הוּא, כְּמוֹ שֶׁנִּתְבָּאֵר בְּמָקוֹם אַחֵר.

through a great constriction, a garment is formed for the *nefesh*, *ruaḥ*, and ***neshama* of a person in the lower and higher** planes of the **Garden of Eden, so that they may enjoy and apprehend some** level of **comprehension and glimmer of the light of *Ein Sof*, blessed be He, as explained elsewhere** (epistle 29).

A person's soul garbs itself in the mitzva that he performs. As explained elsewhere,[7] it is this garment, woven throughout his life from the mitz-

7. *Likkutei Amarim*, chaps. 4–5.

vot that he did,[8] that enables him to enjoy the infinite divine glimmer in the Garden of Eden after his lifetime.[9]

It is the illumination of the mitzva that creates an encompassing garment for the soul that does not penetrate the essence of the soul, since the mitzva inherently relates to the encompassing light, which transcends the parameters of the soul and the confines of the world in which we live. This world is not a place where the essence of a mitzva can be revealed, nor is the garment that was created through the performance of the mitzva apparent in this world. Rather, it is manifest in the planes of the Garden of Eden, a realm where a person is in touch with his inner vitality, with tangible delight in the Divine. ☞

THE UNIFICATION OF THE HOLY ONE AND THE DIVINE PRESENCE

☞ When this unification occurs, it is the most powerful moment in the entire existence of all reality. It is a unification that serves as the foundation of our entire service of God. It is prayer and declaration before performing mitzvot, studying Torah, or praying: "For the sake of the unification between the Holy One, blessed be He, and His Divine Presence." This unification happens in many ways and on varying levels, but at its core it is inherently the same thing: a meeting between the world and the sacred, between the divine light in every detail of reality and the infinite, transcendent divine will.

WHAT IS THE GARDEN OF EDEN?

☞ The concepts of this world and the Garden of Eden are not delineated as locations in time and space but rather as spiritual levels. If we are not in the Garden of Eden now, it is because we are not on an Edenic spiritual level. The Garden of Eden is a particular status or level that the soul can attain. If the soul has attained this level, it is in the Garden of Eden; if it has not attained that level, it is not there. This spiritual level demands two elements. The first is being freed from corporeal limitations.

---

8. The *Zohar* calls this garment a "rabbinical robe." See *Zohar* 1:61a, 226b, 247a; see also *Likkutei Torah*, Num. 44b; *Ma'or Einayim*, *Miketz*, Hanukkah discourse; *Etz Ḥayyim* 50:5.

9. The three levels of soul that the author of the *Tanya* mentions parallel three levels in the worlds: this world, the lower realm of the Garden of Eden, and the higher plane of the Garden of Eden, as explained below. See epistle 29; *Likkutei Torah*, Lev. 31a. When a person performs a mitzva, the resultant garment is manifest in the lower Garden of Eden, and through the accompanying proper intent, it is manifest in the upper Garden of Eden (*Torah Or* 53c).

וְזֶה שֶׁאָמְרוּ רַבּוֹתֵינוּ זַ"ל: "שְׂכַר מִצְוָה בְּהַאי עָלְמָא לֵיכָּא" (קידושין לט, ב).

This is the meaning of **our Rabbis' statement "There is no reward for** the performance of **a mitzva in this world"** (*Kiddushin* 39b).

We generally understand this adage as an assertion that we do not receive the reward of a mitzva in this world but rather in the World to Come. Yet here the author of the *Tanya* uses this saying to illustrate how this world is incapable of encompassing the essence of a mitzva and its reward. Reward in this context actually means the revelation of the mitzva, the ability to see and enjoy its full power. This limited world simply does not offer that window. Yet it is only in this world, where we are blind to the infinite value of a mitzva, that it is even possible to perform it. On the other hand, in the next world, where one can see the mitzva's value, we can no longer perform it.

These limitations are not of the physical body in and of itself, but rather limitations imposed on a person due to the partnership between his body and his soul. Due to this dynamic, all his apprehension, sensations, and perceptions of reality are characterized by physical definitions and corporeal associations. Confined by this corporeal lens, a person cannot ascend to the Garden of Eden because the radiance of the Divine Presence that exists there lies totally beyond the perceptive radar of his bodily senses and associations.

Take the following example: When a person with a certain mental handicap hears or sees others talking about particular topics, he is not really there with them. The topics do not speak to him because he cannot relate to them at all, and therefore he is not actually present.

The second element necessary to attain the level of the Garden of Eden is a special sensitivity to holiness. This is not a matter of one's ability to think abstractly or of cognitive prowess, but rather a sensitivity and openness to that which is holy because holiness is particularly manifest in the Garden of Eden.

Furthermore, for a person's soul to be able to discern the divine light of the Garden of Eden, it needs the correct means. The limited, conscious soul does not have the faculties to apprehend the light of *Ein Sof*. This concept is evident in the observable universe as well. Our world is filled with many things that we can perceive only through various instruments. Our visual spectrum, for instance, is extremely limited; we perceive anything beyond purple and red as total darkness. This is also true regarding sound waves. There is an extremely narrow bandwidth of sound waves that we can hear, and beyond it, we hear nothing at all.

But even with these limitations, it is possible to experience that which we do not clearly perceive yet still sense, such as sound waves at certain high pitches that are beyond our scope of audio registry yet are close enough that we are affected to

כִּי בָּעוֹלָם הַזֶּה, הַגַּשְׁמִי וּבַעַל גְּבוּל וְצִמְצוּם רַב וְעָצוּם מְאֹד, אִי אֶפְשָׁר לְהִתְלַבֵּשׁ שׁוּם הֶאָרָה מֵאוֹר אֵין סוֹף בָּרוּךְ הוּא, כִּי אִם עַל יְדֵי יוּ"ד סְפִירוֹת הַנִּקְרָאִים גּוּפָא בַּזֹּהַר הַקָּדוֹשׁ. "חֶסֶד דְּרוֹעָא יְמִינָא וכו' (תקוני זהר יז, א).

This is **because in this physical world, which is subject to extremely great and immense limitation and constriction, it is impossible for any glimmer of the light of *Ein Sof*, blessed be He, to be clothed within this world unless it is through the ten *sefirot*, which the holy *Zohar* refers to as a body,** as in the phrase **"*Ḥesed*** (Kindness) corresponds to **the right arm** of God..." (*Tikkunei Zohar* 17a).

The *Zohar* likens the ten *sefirot* to the limbs of God, as it were: "*Ḥesed* is the right arm, *Gevura* is the left arm, *Tiferet* is the torso, *Netzaḥ* and *Hod* are the two legs...." The body is the physical garment of the soul,

some degree. In these cases, people do not see or hear anything, but they react with an unpleasant sensation. To actually register that which lies beyond our physical spectrum, to bring those stimuli into our realm of perception, we must build an instrument that will convert these frequencies to those we are capable of registering. Today, for example, there are many devices that enable us to hear infrasound or to see infrared or ultraviolet light.

The garment of mitzvot serves as such a medium between a person's soul and the divine light. The soul that is enveloped in a mitzva can sense the Divine, which generally lies beyond the human range of perception.

This garment actually exists now in in this world, but it has no effect here. Like the divine light itself, we do not perceive it. We are surrounded by too much noise that prevents us from hearing the sound of holiness. Only in the quiet and clarity of the Garden of Eden do those silent garments of mitzvot begin to be heard and to illuminate the soul with the divine light. Since the distracting noise is not an issue at the source but rather a limitation of the receiver due to the physicality and limitations of the body in which the soul is confined, the seeming impermeability of these garments is not inevitable.

There were people who "saw their eternality during their lives," meaning that they perceived their portion in the World to Come while alive in this world. A person does not need to die in order to be in the World to Come. He simply must be sensitive enough to sense the light that lies beyond everything. The body is an opaque screen, but it is not hermetically sealed. A person who achieves high levels of refinement and detachment from the noise of this world can, during his lifetime, sense something through that garment. As the saying goes, tzaddikim are not in Garden of Eden, but rather the Garden of Eden is in them (see the Maggid of Mezeritch, *Likkutei Amarim* 262).

through which the soul operates and manifests itself in this world. We walk with our legs, give and take with our arms, think with our brain, and so on. So too God reveals His infinite essence through the ten *sefirot*. They are the body relative to the source of their emanation, which corresponds to the soul of the entirety of the worlds.

לְפִי שֶׁכְּמוֹ שֶׁאֵין עֲרוֹךְ לוֹ לְהַגּוּף הַגַּשְׁמִי לְגַבֵּי הַנְּשָׁמָה, כָּךְ אֵין עֲרוֹךְ כְּלָל לְיוּ"ד סְפִירוֹת דַּאֲצִילוּת לְגַבֵּי הַמַּאֲצִיל הָעֶלְיוֹן אֵין סוֹף בָּרוּךְ הוּא,

The *sefirot* are likened to the body **because just as there is no comparison between the physical body and the soul, there is no comparison at all between the *sefirot* of *Atzilut* and the Supernal Emanator, *Ein Sof*, blessed be He,**

Just as the body cannot truly express the soul, neither its sensitivities nor its perception, and certainly not its essence, so too the entire universe cannot express or associate with the essence of a mitzva. A mitzva is the divine will itself, which encompasses all worlds, transcending all worlds, lying beyond even the world of *Atzilut* and its *sefirot*. Therefore, the reward, the full apprehension and perception of a mitzva, cannot be translated into the terms of even the *sefirot* and spiritual worlds. A mitzva's essence passes through all the worlds, yet the worlds fail to grasp its meaning. Its essence totally evades them. ☞

THE REWARD OF A MITZVA IN THIS WORLD

☞ An assimilated wealthy Jew once gave the Rebbe of Gur, the author of *Ḥiddushei HaRim*, a ride in his carriage. "Rebbe," the wealthy man said, "I have a question. It says in the *Shema*, 'It shall be, if you will heed My commandments…I will provide the rain of your land,' and the converse, 'Beware, lest your heart be seduced… and you will be quickly eradicated….' Yet I transgress all the commandments in the world and I have everything good!"

The Rebbe said to him, "From your words I understand that you have recited the *Shema*."

"Certainly," the wealthy man answered.

"If that is the case, you must understand that everything that you have and ever will have comes from the very tip of your reward for the one time that you recited the *Shema*. As for your sins, that is a different reckoning." (Ostensibly, for these as well, the world is not enough.)

כִּי אֲפִילּוּ חָכְמָה עִילָּאָה, שֶׁהִיא רֵאשִׁיתָן, הִיא בִּבְחִינַת עֲשִׂיָּה גּוּפָנִית לְגַבֵּי אֵין סוֹף בָּרוּךְ הוּא, כְּמוֹ שֶׁנִּתְבָּאֵר בְּלִקּוּטֵי אֲמָרִים.

because even supernal *Ḥokhma,* the first of the *sefirot,* **is considered like physical action compared to *Ein Sof,* blessed be He, as it is written in *Likkutei Amarim*** (chap. 2).

This concept is expressed by a deeper understanding of the verse "With wisdom You have made them all" (Ps. 104:24). This concept is explained in the second chapter *of Likkutei Amarim* and in more detail in *Sha'ar HaYiḥud VeHa'emuna.*[10] It would seem that the verse should say, "With wisdom You have conceptualized them all." Why does the verse say, "You have made them all"?

The answer is that this portrays the vast distance between wisdom and action. The stage of wisdom, the level or *sefira* of *Ḥokhma,* is the inception of all of reality, just as it is the inception of the soul's existence, and the stage of action is the end point, the culmination of the soul's functions and faculties. Yet in relation to God the stage of wisdom is like the stage of action relative to us. God "makes" through wisdom, through the level or *sefira* called *Ḥokhma,* as we would make something with a hammer.

The *sefira* of *Ḥokhma,* then, and certainly the rest of the *sefirot,* are far removed from God, similar to the distance between a person's actions and the essence of his soul. (In truth, the distance is even greater, yet we cannot articulate or conceptualize a larger distance.) Since the mitzvot essentially correspond to the level of *Ein Sof* itself, which encompasses all worlds, it does not have an actual connection to the ten *sefirot* and certainly not to the worlds.

וְאִי לְזֹאת, בְּמַעֲשֵׂה הַצְּדָקָה וּגְמִילוּת חֲסָדִים שֶׁאָדָם אוֹכֵל מִפֵּירוֹתֵיהֶן בָּעוֹלָם הַזֶּה,

Therefore, the act of charity and kind deeds, which are among those mitzvot **that a person** engages in and **enjoys their profits in this world,**

Until now the author of the *Tanya* has been discussing mitzvot in general. Now he returns to his opening statement, "Charity is greater than all the [other] mitzvot," and will go on to explain how, indeed, charity

10. Chap. 9.

is greater. Although the talmudic dictum he quotes above, "There is no reward for [the performance of] a mitzva in this world" refers to mitzvot in general, there are those that have a certain degree of reward and connection to this world as well. They are, in the broadest sense, those mitzvot that do not involve only man's relationship with God but also those that involve relationships with others, which include the mitzvot of charity and acts of kindness toward other people.

The Mishna describes these mitzvot with the words "These are the matters that a person engages in and enjoys their profits in this world, and the principal reward remains for him for the World to Come" (Mishna *Pe'a* 1:1; *Kiddushin* 40a). The implication is that a person merits some reward for these mitzvot during his lifetime. One might say that the essence of these mitzvot are connected in some way to a person's enjoyment and comfort in this world.

One of the mitzvot enumerated by the Mishna there is Torah study. This mitzva demands a person's engagement beyond the realm of action: He must understand what he is studying. If a person does not understand anything of the Torah he studies, he does not fulfill the mitzva;[11] comprehension is a necessary element of the mitzva of Torah study. Conversely, when a person dons *tefillin*, for example, no understanding of it is necessary. Whether or not he grasps the meaning of this mitzva or senses its power does not affect his basic fulfillment of it. A mitzva does not obligate its doer to even engage spiritually, nor does it promise him anything in return: "Mitzvot were not given for benefit" (*Eiruvin* 31a). Therefore, they do not come with any criteria of enjoyment.

Another category of mitzva specified in the Mishna is charity and acts of kindness. While the physical enjoyment of one who performs the mitzva is irrelevant, the recipient's benefit is crucial and defines whether the mitzva was performed or not. It is a mitzva to feed the hungry, but it is not a mitzva to stuff food down the throat of a satiated

11. One must distinguish between study of the Oral Torah and study of the Written Torah. The former necessitates understanding the content, while the mitzva of studying the Written Torah is performed through reciting its holy letters and words even without understanding them. See the author of the Tanya's *Hilkhot Talmud Torah* 2:13; *Likkutei Torah* 5a, citing *Pardes Rimmonim* 27:1.

person. Making peace between two people or between husband and wife is an important mitzva, but one may not interfere with the marital harmony of a couple who are living together happily in an attempt to perform this mitzva.

The nature of these mitzvot lies in the benefit that the recipient receives. Only if he profits from it in a practical way is the mitzva fulfilled. Since the benefits of the mitzva must be manifest in this world in that the recipient reaps benefit from its fulfillment, the benefits to the doer also manifest in this world. At the same time that the recipient benefits, the doer of the mitzva receives an element of the reward of these mitzvot as well.

יֵשׁ נְקָבִים, עַל דֶּרֶךְ מָשָׁל, בַּלְּבוּשׁ הָעֶלְיוֹן, הַמַּקִּיף עַל גּוּפָא, הֵם הַכֵּלִים דְּיוּ״ד סְפִירוֹת, לְהָאִיר מֵהֶם וּלְהַשְׁפִּיעַ אוֹר וְשֶׁפַע,

can be described as causing there **to be gaps, so to speak, in the supernal garment that encompasses the body, which are the vessels of the ten *sefirot*, so that light and life-giving sustenance shine forth and flow from them,** through the *sefirot,* into this world.

The other mitzvot are like a completely intact garment that does not allow anything to pass from the realm beyond this world to a person in this world. Only the mitzvot that fall under the category of acts of kindness have gaps, as it were, in their garments, through which something penetrates, by degree, so that it has an effect in this world as well. ☞

THE BROADER MEANING OF CHARITY

☞ The main purpose of societal mitzvot goes way beyond building a good, just, and more civil society. While every mitzva is inherently a mode of connection to the divine essence that transcends the reality of this world, certain mitzvot have "gaps," meaning that they express themselves in some way in our reality as well. The way that the mitzva of charity serves a social purpose is just one aspect of a larger framework in which supernal sustenance is drawn down to those in need. Charity is a far-reaching action that provides not only money and kindness and empathy on an individual level, but in the cosmic sense as well it sparks a drawing down of the supernal life-giving sustenance from a high place to a lower one. Likewise, just as charity below is not deserved payment but rather a gift, irrespective of the recipient's mer-

מֵחֶסֶד דְּרוֹעָא יְמִינָא אוֹרֶךְ יָמִים בָּעוֹלָם הַזֶּה הַגַּשְׁמִי, וְעוֹשֶׁר וְכָבוֹד מִדְּרוֹעָא שְׂמָאלָא, וְכֵן בְּתִפְאֶרֶת, וְהוֹד וְהָדָר וְחֶדְוָה וכו'.

From ***Ḥesed,*** **the "right arm,"** stem **long life in this physical world, and** similarly **wealth and honor** stem **from the "left arm,"** ***Gevura,*** **and likewise with regard to the** ***sefira*** **of** ***Tiferet,*** **as well as majesty, splendor, gladness, and so on,** which stem from the *sefirot* of *Hod* and *Yesod.*

Something transcendent trickles into this world through the mitzva of charity. This flow from above comes through the ten *sefirot,* which correspond to the limbs of God. Just as a person's soul manifests itself in the material world through the limbs of his body, God is manifest in the world through the unique refraction that each of the *sefirot* offers. For example, through the *sefira* of *Ḥesed,* corresponding to God's right arm, He endows a person with his physical life span. *Gevura* corresponds to God's left arm, from which flows wealth and honor, as the verse states, "Length of days is on its right; on its left is wealth and honor" (Prov. 3:16). In the same vein, the Talmud states, "One who wishes to become wise should face south [which is *Ḥesed*], and [one who wishes] to become wealthy should face north [which is *Gevura*]. Your mnemonic [for this is that in the Temple] the Table [which symbolized blessing and abundance] was in the north, and

it, charity on high engenders the drawing down of sustenance not commensurate with the merit of the recipients.

In this light, the whole existence of the physical and spiritual worlds is one big act of charity. All our prayers are also requests for charity. The Talmud states that very few people in history can be characterized as "hard-hearted, who are far from righteousness" (Isa. 46:12). This refers to people who are sustained by the force of their own merit. The rest of the world, on the other hand, is sustained by God's charity and not because they deserve to exist (see *Berakhot* 17b). In the midst of God benevolently endowing the world and all its inhabitants with the gift of existence, few are so "hard-hearted" that they insist that they deserve what they have.

When we give charity, we participate in God's worldwide philanthropy. Someone who does not give charity blocks the flow. It follows that a person who does not pass money onward cannot ask that it be transferred through him. This is one reason that Jews invest so much effort into giving charity to the extent that they will seek out a poor person, all so that the worldwide charity network will perpetuate.

the Candelabrum [which symbolized the light of wisdom] was in the south [of the Sanctuary]" (*Bava Batra* 25b).[12] The "majesty, splendor, and gladness" that the author of the *Tanya* goes on to mention are manifest through the *sefirot* of *Hod, Netzaḥ,* and *Yesod,* respectively.[13]

The author of the *Tanya* is conveying that when a person performs a mitzva, a hidden stream of divine energy permeates the "gaps" in the encompassing light and descends from the higher worlds through the *sefirot,* ultimately reaching the doer in this lower world where he performed the mitzva.

Until this point, the author of the *Tanya* has discussed the garment created by the mitzva of charity as hinted at in the verse "He donned charity like armor," and the gaps therein. Now he will explore the function of the armor's "scales."

אַךְ כְּדֵי שֶׁלֹּא יִנְקוּ הַחִיצוֹנִים לְמַעְלָה מֵאוֹר וְשֶׁפַע הַמִּשְׁתַּלְשֵׁל וְיוֹרֵד לְמַטָּה מַטָּה עַד עוֹלָם הַזֶּה הַגַּשְׁמִי,

However, to prevent the external forces of impurity **above from drawing sustenance** through these gaps **from the light and flow devolving and descending steadily downward to this physical world,**

This penetration of the encompassing light into the inner realm poses a risk. The immense constriction engendered by the funneling that happens when the light goes through the gaps enables the light to be received in our world, yet the downscaling of this inestimable intensity in this way is also dangerous. When the limitations of distance and gradation are peeled away through the constriction, the light is left unprotected, effectively removing purpose and direction that were programmed into that light at the source. In its unadulterated form, it would be directed only toward good. The constriction strips the divine

12. The Talmud there proves that the south is equated with the right, and north is equated with the left, based on Ps. 89:13.

13. Apparently, the enumeration of the author of the *Tanya* follows *Zohar* 2:98a, cited by the Tzemaḥ Tzedek on Ps. 104:1, which aligns the three terms "splendor," "majesty," and "gladness" with the *sefirot* of *Netzaḥ, Hod,* and *Yesod* respectively. One can also posit that "and so on" refers to *Malkhut,* which encompasses them all (Lubavitcher Rebbe, Rabbi Menaḥem Mendel Schneerson).

light of its destined address, leaving it vulnerable to being aimed at an unholy cause.

The encompassing light invited by the mitzva that a person performs down here is not like a letter sent exclusively to a particular address. It is a divine endowment that opens a new world of possibilities, of boundless *Ḥesed*. The problem is that this *Ḥesed* is undifferentiated. It showers good on everyone, on the righteous and the wicked alike. When the sun shines, it shines on both flowers and trash; when the rain falls, it falls on everyone, on the wise man and the fool. The question thus arises: Who is receiving this divine effluence and are they fit to employ it properly?

All the mitzvot that bear fruit in this world present this problem. They become vulnerable to corruption. Not only may the reward of a mitzva not be allotted in the best way, but it could even become an agent of destruction. ☞

וְכֵן לְמַטָּה, לְהָגֵן עַל הָאָדָם וּלְשָׁמְרוֹ וּלְהַצִּילוֹ מִכָּל דָּבָר רָע, בְּגַשְׁמִיּוּת וּבְרוּחָנִיּוּת,	**and here below as well, in order to shield a person and to guard him and save him from all evil, material and spiritual,**

This macrocosmic scheme of the leaching of evil can happen in one's personal life as well. While a person needs *Ḥesed,* he must also be protected from it, because when it manifests in his life, it is not limited only by that which is good for the person right now. The bestowal of kindness can also be given to him in the manner of a deadly virus, an entity that spreads uncontrollably like unadulterated *Ḥesed*.

THE DANGER INHERENT IN UNADULTERATED *ḤESED*

☞ The problem with giving that does not take into account the worthiness of the receiver is particularly grave when it comes to charity and acts of kindness. Abraham, who was the chariot for the attribute of *Ḥesed*, gave because it was his nature to give. He did not make his giving conditional on the worthiness of the receiver. Yet he was the one who said, "If only Ishmael shall live before You" (Gen. 17:18). He gave to the chosen son and his other son equally (see *Torah Or* 12a, 119b).

Whenever the gates are flung open for gifts to come through, there is the danger that evil will receive the same as good. Instead of making the world into a better place, an endowment of *Ḥesed* could make the world even worse without measures to prevent corruption. Whenever there are no clear distinctions, and the lines between dimensions are blurred, evil leaches from it.

Protection from anything evil must be in the form of the delineation of fences, of walls of armor, that shield the inner realm from outside attacks. This is where the armor's scales play a part.

לָזֹאת חוֹזֵר וּמֵאִיר אוֹר הַמַּקִּיף וְסוֹתֵם הַנֶּקֶב, עַל דֶּרֶךְ מָשָׁל, כִּי הוּא מִבְּחִינַת אֵין סוֹף וְסוֹבֵב כָּל עָלְמִין כַּנִּזְכָּר לְעֵיל.

for this purpose **the encompassing light once again shines and fills the gap, figuratively speaking, for it is from the level of *Ein Sof* and encompasses all worlds, as stated above.**

Let us revisit the metaphor of the coat of mail, made up of scales that protect the gaps in the armor. In the spiritual garment composed of encompassing light engendered by the mitzva of charity, there are gaps through which the light penetrates and unites with the inner light. To protect the inner light from negative forces that would leach its light, the encompassing light of the mitzva is reflected back, filling in the gaps in the garment and thus enveloping and protecting the inner light.

Each hole in the coat of mail has a scale that protects it. Every gap in the encompassing light leaves room for infiltration and needs protection. It is the encompassing light that provides that screen by refracting back to cover it so that the lines between the inner and outer dimensions will not be entirely blurred.

This is the implication of the image of armor and scales, made to be a combination of hard and flexible. The hard parts are closed and protected from every angle ensuring that nothing penetrates. The flexible parts, whose relationship between the outside and inside is not fixed, needs extra protection. This essential protection comes from the encompassing light, not in its manifestation as categorically separate from the inner light but rather as the particularized encompassing light of the particular gap. Through this particularization, it successfully maintains the distinction between the inside and the outside, between the destined address of the divine energy and the unintended forces that attempt to usurp it. ☞

CLOSING THE GAP

☞ If the encompassing light is undifferentiated and intrinsically separate from reality, then it would ostensibly have no association with distinctions between good

וְזֶה שֶׁאָמְרוּ רַבּוֹתֵינוּ ז"ל: מִצְטָרֶפֶת לְחֶשְׁבּוֹן גָּדוֹל דַּיְיקָא,

This is the meaning of **our Rabbis' statement** that every penny that one gives **"combines to** form **a great sum," specifically** emphasizing the word **"great,"**

and evil. Indeed, in a certain sense, this is true. If one's frame of reference is too broad, it does not pick up on the details of various phenomena.

Take, for example, the scope of statistics. In the statistical sphere, all people are equal, numbers in a body of data. That one person holds office while the next is a garbage collector is meaningless. Then there are more particular frames of reference (such as the particularized returning encompassing light), the very existence of which preserves certain parameters.

This dynamic works in many areas. For instance, there are two ways to protect against parasites. The first is to take great care to ensure that nourishment is provided only to those who need it and not others. This approach necessitates restraint on the part of the giver, a delineation of a precise address, specifying a single, exact destination. The other way is to give that which the parasite is intrinsically unable to leach from, not because it does not have access to it but because its own nature prevents it from benefiting from it.

Consider another analogy: There are two ways to transmit a secret piece of information. The first is to whisper it into the ear of the person who needs to hear it. This is a type of restricted giving that enables it to be registered by one sole individual. The second way is that anyone who does not have a certain characteristic or piece of knowledge cannot access the information. For example, when those who must not know the secret do not understand the language in which it is transmitted, then only the one who must know it understands and the who cannot know it does not. It may seem as if the secret is openly revealed. It is not whispered and anyone can hear it. But certain people are prevented from deciphering it due to a lack in preparedness. One can tell a secret to the whole world in this way, shout it out loud for everyone to hear, yet whoever does not have the necessary prerequisite does not understand anything.

There are many such transmissions of secrets that depend on a certain degree of the recipient's previous knowledge. When a person says to his friend, "Meet me on *yom shelishi, Parashat Vayetze,*" there is a large scope of people who are not equipped to understand his meaning.

The divine response to a person who performs the mitzva of charity or acts of kindness does not happen in the first restrictive way, since charity is intrinsically a mitzva of unrestrained giving, opening a window for charity and lovingkindness from above. Therefore, the protection of those "gaps" is of the second variety, that of the encompassing light. This type of shield is not built on externally imposed restriction but rather on an internal mechanism that prevents others from intruding and benefiting from the light of the divine gift.

How? The essential difference between good and evil depends on a person's sense

Just as the scales on a coat of armor join to create one garment, so does each and every penny given for charity combine to form a "great sum."[14] The emphasis on "great" does not just imply the number of coins that a person gave to charity, but also to the inner spiritual essence of the mitzva. Contrary to worldly calculations, which are relatively small, the mitzva of charity adds up in God's calculation, which is a very great sum, indeed.

כִּי "גָּדוֹל ה' וּמְהוּלָּל מְאֹד" (תהלים מח, ב), בְּלִי סוֹף וְתַכְלִית וּגְבוּל [חַס וְשָׁלוֹם].

for it is written, "**The Lord** [*Havaya*] **is great and exceedingly praised**" (Ps. 48:2), implying an **endless** greatness **without any limit or boundary (God forbid).**

of self and the degree of nullification of that self. The inception of evil lies in the ego, where a person's being becomes the center of the world. Why does the Mishna ask, "What is the difference between the students of our ancestor Abraham and the students of the wicked Bilam?" (*Avot* 5:19), and not "What is the difference between Abraham and Bilam?" Because, the difference between Abraham and Bilam was indecipherable. It only emerged in the students who followed them. Only then did it become clear that Bilam was wicked and Abraham was righteous.

Hidden deep within Bilam was a rotten root – "a conceited spirit and a limitless appetite." This inner characteristic only expanded and became manifest more obviously in his students, so that their whole lives were consumed with their sense of self. Conversely, the students of Abraham operated according to a polar-opposite starting point – with the nullification of the self. As Abraham said, "I am but dust and ashes" (Gen. 18:27).

It is this very distinction that delineates who receives the radiance of the encompassing light and who does not. Inherently, only he who nullifies himself and his desires can receive it. Whoever does not fails to be receptive to that light. It is not something that can be contained and absorbed by rectifying one aspect of oneself. That is a characteristic of the inner light. Rather it must encompass the person as a whole and so can reside only in place of one's sense of self in its entirety, in the void left in the wake of self-nullification. In this sense, the flow that comes from the encompassing light prevents the external forces from entering, not because of a sign that says "Entrance Forbidden," but rather because they are intrinsically incapable of receiving the radiance that demands that they stop relating to themselves in external, superficial, egotistical ways.

14. Here the author of the *Tanya* returns to the talmudic statement from *Bava Batra* 9b that he quoted at the beginning of the letter.

This word *me'od,* "exceedingly," is understood elsewhere to imply endless greatness without any limit.[15] "A great sum" is compared to God's greatness, meaning that it is infinitely immense. Since charity is described as a "great sum," it is related to God's boundless greatness. This implies that through charity one draws directly from the light of *Ein Sof,* which encompasses from above, transcending even the highest stage of the order of progression, and it is drawn to the inner light, which is clothed in the ten *sefirot* hinted at in the name of *Havaya,* the name that is used in the verse quoted here.[16] ☞

The coin that amounts to a great sum therefore accomplishes two things: It opens a window to receiving divine abundance and illumi-

A GREAT SUM

☞ It is explained in kabbalistic and hasidic works (*Etz Ḥayyim* 13:5; *Mevo She'arim* 3:2:9; *Likkutei Torah*, Deut. 93a) how certain categories of numbers correspond to the four worlds., based on the way numbers take on different values according to their position and function. Single digits are associated with the world of *Asiya*, tens to *Yetzira*, hundreds to *Beria*, thousands to *Atzilut*, and ten thousand represents the level of *Ein Sof*, which transcends all the worlds (*Likkutei Torah*, Deut. 93a; *Hemshekh Ayin Bet*, vol. 1, p. 58, vol. 2, p. 865). When the author of the *Tanya* states that the pennies contributed to charity combine to amount to "a great sum," he is implying that they amount to the very large figure that is associated with the level of *Ein Sof* and the encompassing light. As the number of coins that a person gives to charity increases, he draws down loftier, more transcendent revelations of God's greatness from the loftiest plane.

The transition from "a small sum" to "a great sum" can be seen, for example, in several places in the High Holy Day prayers. There is the transition from *Av HaRaḥaman*, "Compassionate Father" (from compassion that is singular) a prayer that is recited every day, to *Av HaRaḥamim*, "Father of Compassion" (to compassion that is in the plural, to abundant compassion), which is said during the *Musaf* prayer service of the High Holy Days and during the afternoon Sabbath prayers. The transition from *le'eila*, "exalted," to *le'eila u'le'eila*, "exalted and exalted," said during the *Kaddish* of *Ne'ila* on Yom Kippur is another example. (In many traditions, this phrase is said throughout all the High Holy Days.) These examples express the transition from the small and specific dimension to the great dimension and signify the transformation that happens during those special days when an illumination on the level of *Keter*, the *sefira* that transcends all the *sefirot*, is shining and the encompassing light enters our reality. This is what is called a "great sum."

15. See, e.g., *Torah Or* 39c.

16. The *yod* of the name represents the *sefira* of *Ḥokhma*, the *heh* to *Bina*, the *vav*

nation from the realm of the encompassing light while simultaneously protecting that illumination from being lost.

אַךְ מִי הוּא הַגּוֹרֵם לִירִידַת הָאוֹר וְהַשֶּׁפַע לָעוֹלָם הַזֶּה הַגַּשְׁמִי, מִיּוּ״ד סְפִירוֹת הַנִּקְרָאִים גּוּפָא?

But what causes the descent of the divine **light and flow to this physical world from the ten *sefirot*,** which are **called the "body"?**

8 Av

12 Av (leap year)

Until now the author of the *Tanya* has discussed the descent of the supernal encompassing light to the ten *sefirot* of the world of *Atzilut*. Now he explains the descent of that light into our world.

הוּא הַיִּחוּד הַנִּזְכָּר לְעֵיל,

It is the aforementioned unification of the Holy One, blessed be He, with His Divine Presence,

The illumination that the author of the *Tanya* refers to is not the one drawn into reality to sustain its routine existence through the devolvement of the illumination of the ten *sefirot* from above to below. What he refers to here is an additional illumination from the level of *Ein Sof*, which transcends the *sefirot* and travels through them into this physical world. It is an illumination through which God Himself shines into His world and enters it, as it were. God does not shine this light perpetually but rather as a response to a person who performs a mitzva. It is an illumination that requires something from below to awaken it and draw it down. With the performance of a mitzva, a person causes the supernal, transcendent divine will to manifest in this world. This is called "the unification of the Holy One blessed be He with His Divine Presence."

שֶׁהִיא תּוֹסֶפֶת הֶאָרָה וְהַשְׁפָּעָה, מִבְּחִינַת אוֹר אֵין סוֹף הַמַּאֲצִיל הָעֶלְיוֹן בָּרוּךְ הוּא, בְּיֶתֶר שְׂאֵת עַל הַהֶאָרָה וְהַשְׁפָּעָה שֶׁבִּתְחִילַּת

which is an additional illumination and flow from the light of *Ein Sof*, the supernal Emanator, blessed be He, with greater intensity than the illumination and flow that is drawn

to the six emotive *sefirot* – *Ḥesed, Gevura, Tiferet, Netzaḥ, Hod,* and *Yesod* – and the final *heh* of the name corresponds to *Malkhut*.

הָאֲצִילוּת וְהַהִשְׁתַּלְשְׁלוּת וכו׳.

down from **the beginning of** the emanation from the world of ***Atzilut* and the progression** through all the worlds, **and so on.**

The illumination sparked by the mitzva act is a new radiance in the world that had not been part of it before. It is an addition to the divine light that perpetuates every minutiae of existence. The purpose of this novel light is not to sustain existent reality nor to change anything in the world but rather to birth something new that was not present before. ☞

וְרֵאשִׁית תּוֹסֶפֶת הַהֶאָרָה וְהַהַשְׁפָּעָה הִיא לְרֵאשִׁית הַיּוּ״ד סְפִירוֹת,

The additional illumination and flow is first transmitted **to the first of the ten** ***sefirot*, *Ḥokhma*.**

Ḥokhma is the first of the ten *sefirot*.[17] When the *sefira* of *Ḥokhma* receives the new illumination, a new existence is created that develops and builds as the light descends through the ten *sefirot*.

וְזֶה הוּא: ״וְכוֹבַע יְשׁוּעָה בְּרֹאשׁוֹ״ (ישעיה נט, יז).

This is the meaning of the words **"a helmet of salvation on His head"** from the verse cited at the beginning of the letter (Isa. 59:17).

Until this point, the deeper meaning of "He donned charity like a coat of mail" has been explored. The author of the *Tanya* now explains the continuation of that verse: "and a helmet of salvation on His head."

A NEW CREATION

☞ The law of conservation of energy and mass operates in the physical world and, to a certain extent, in the spiritual world as well. It follows that the universe is a closed system in which we are generally busy moving things from one place to another, transforming energy from one state to the next. Yet through the performance of mitzvot, we break this overarching law of conservation of reality and add something new. In essence, we create a new world. These novel illuminations are essentially brand-new revelations of the Divine within reality.

17. See *Likkutei Amarim*. chap. 35.

The helmet represents the light that transcends the process of progressive descent, like a hat that sits atop one's head, the foremost point from which vitality spreads to his whole being, and like the faculty of wisdom in one's soul, the first and foremost of the soul's faculties.

"יְשׁוּעָה" הוּא מִלְּשׁוֹן "וַיִּשַׁע ה' אֶל הֶבֶל וְאֶל מִנְחָתוֹ".

The word ***yeshua,*** salvation, in the verse **is related to** the word for turn, as in the verse **"And the Lord turned** [*vayisha*] **toward Abel and to his offering"** (Gen. 4:4).

God's "turning" implies His revelation and shining countenance. A "helmet of salvation," therefore, is the revelation of the encompassing light, which rests "on His head," beyond *Ḥokhma,* the inception of the ten *sefirot.*

וְהוּא יְרִידַת הָאוֹר וְהַשְׁפַּע דְּשׁ"ע נְהוֹרִין שֶׁבַּזֹּהַר הַקָּדוֹשׁ (חלק א ד, ב),

This hints at **the descent of the light and flow of the 370 lights** mentioned **in the holy *Zohar*** (1:4b),

This idea is mentioned in several sources,[18] and it can be viewed in the following illustrative way: Something "interesting" happens in the world and God turns, looking at it anew, and through this creates new worlds, new existences.

Imagine that a person creates some sort of innovation and now stands in front of it, but he is disconnected from it, the creator and the creation. Yet sometimes something from within his creation stirs him anew, catches his attention, and deeply resonates with him. The creator turns to involve himself once again with his creation.

This is the essence of every mitzva. It calls God to turn and involve Himself with that person and the world.

וּכְמוֹ שֶׁכָּתוּב: "יָאֵר ה' פָּנָיו אֵלֶיךָ" (במדבר ו, כה),

as it is written, "The Lord shall shine His countenance toward you" (Num. 6:25),

18. *Zohar* 1:4b and the commentary of Rabbi Moshe Zakuto there; introduction to the *Zohar* 4b; see also *Etz Ḥayyim* 13:13–14; *Likkutei Torah,* Deut. 49b.

This verse expresses the divine turning, the shining of God's countenance and light anew into reality. "You" refers to those who are fulfilling the mitzvot and sparking a new illumination that lights up creation. A distant but helpful example would be to imagine a familiar painting that suddenly appears new. The smile on the painted face is suddenly wider. This type of newness, this fresh illumination in the world, is created when a mitzva is performed: God shines His countenance, and the whole world that had previously crystallized in a certain fashion now appears totally new. It literally becomes a different world.

"יָאֵר פָּנָיו אִתָּנוּ סֶלָה" (תהלים סז, ב). "אִתָּנוּ" הוּא עַל יְדֵי מַעֲשֵׂה הַצְּדָקָה.

and **"May He shine His countenance upon us, Selah"** (Ps. 67:2) – that is, God becomes a partner **"with us" through the act of charity.**

God not only shines His countenance "upon us" but "with us" (the word *itanu*, "upon us," in the verse can also be translated as "with us"). When a person gives charity, especially with a beaming countenance,[19] he becomes a partner with God.

וְזֶה הוּא: "זוֹרֵעַ צְדָקוֹת מַצְמִיחַ יְשׁוּעוֹת".

This is the meaning of the phrase recited in the morning prayers **"He sows charity and brings forth salvation."**

When a person gives a coin to charity, he sows a seed from which salvation sprouts. One cannot reap without planting. These words of conclusion parallel the author of the *Tanya*'s opening verse: "He donned charity like a coat of mail and a helmet of salvation on His head."

וְכָכָה יָאֵר ה' פָּנָיו אֲלֵיהֶם, צִדְקָתָם עוֹמֶדֶת לָעַד וְקַרְנָם תָּרוּם בִּישׁוּעַת מַצְמִיחַ קֶרֶן יְשׁוּעָה, צֶמַח צְדָקָה מֵהַכּוֹבַע יְשׁוּעָה הַנִּזְכָּר לְעֵיל.

May God indeed shine His countenance upon you. May your charity stand forever and your horn be raised with the salvation of the One who **springs forth the horn of salvation, a sprouting of charity from the aforementioned "helmet of salvation,"**

19. See *Ketubot* 111a.

The author of the *Tanya* concludes this letter with words of blessing aimed at the recipients of the letter and givers of charity. The end of the letter, like its beginning, is composed of various biblical verses that mention and summarize the main content of the letter.

These concluding words convey that the horn of salvation burgeons forth and ascends, bursting forth from the garment of charity and the helmet of salvation, as discussed in the body of the letter.

כְּנֶפֶשׁ תִּדְרְשֶׁנּוּ. **in accordance with the soul that seeks Him.**

These concluding words sum up everything. The salvation that a person merits is commensurate with his giving of charity. A person receives salvation to the extent that he gives the charity. This is what "in accordance with the soul that seeks Him" implies: to the extent that you turn your heart and soul toward your friend's needs, so you can "seek Him" – you can anticipate salvation and an illuminated countenance from above.

There are two facets to this dynamic. On the one hand, when we perform mitzvot, we imitate God. It is in this vein that the Sages interpret the verse "This is my God and I will glorify Him" (Ex. 15:2) as "Be similar to Him. Just as He is compassionate and merciful, so too should you be compassionate and merciful" (*Shabbat* 133b). We emulate God and, in so doing, strive to actualize the divine image within us.

There is also another facet: When we perform mitzvot, God imitates us, as it were. Our actions create a model of how God will interact with the world afterward.

These are the two layers of "the soul that seeks Him": We receive and give at the same time, emulating God while God is mirroring us. In the way we give, He gives.

The Midrash comments on the verse "Who surpasses Me? I will pay" (Job 41:3) that for a person who does not yet have a house but occupies himself with the mitzva of *mezuza*, or does not have a garment yet prepares *tzitzit*, God makes sure to provide him with what he lacks to enable him to perform that mitzva.[20]

---

20. *Bemidbar Rabba* 14.

When a person ensures that he has a *mezuza*, God ensures that he has a home. When a person makes it his business to donate to children's Torah institutions, God gives him children. The point is that when a person takes the initiative, when he acts above and beyond his obligation in terms of giving, God gives him accordingly, above and beyond this world, shining His countenance on him and recreating his world.

This letter delineates the powerful effects of charity on this world. Aside from its obvious material benefits to the recipient, the giver of charity reaps its rewards even in this world. This is unlike the majority of mitzvot, whose effects and value can be discerned only in the Garden of Eden, where the veil of corporeality is stripped away, allowing the soul to enjoy the illumination of the divine light without the barriers of this world and the body in which it resides.

This is possible because when one performs a mitzva, that mitzva envelops the person like a garment, providing him the ability to apprehend and take pleasure in the divine light once it leaves this world. Yet the garment created by the mitzva of charity is like armor made of scales. The gaps between the scales allow the divine light to shine through while the soul is still in this world. That divine light is drawn to the world through the ten sefirot, the vessels through which God operates in this world. This allows wisdom, wealth, honor, splendor, and other blessings to be drawn down on the person who gave charity and performed the act of kindness.

Epistle 4

AS CAN BE INFERRED FROM ITS CONCLUDING WORDS, this letter was written soon after the author of the *Tanya*'s liberation from prison in 1798 (or perhaps after the liberation in 1801).[1] The letter is among the letters meant to inspire its readers to give charity, whether by supporting the poor and the needy who were commonly found everywhere at that time or by supporting the hasidic community in Israel. The request for donations was addressed toward people who themselves had little resources, and sometimes they themselves were in dire need, making their donations a true sacrifice.

However, these letters from the Rebbe to his students contain a timeless exploration of the inner dimension of this mitzva, granting a window into its sheer power, not just for the receiver but primarily for the giver.

The author of the *Tanya* explains in the cosmic sense how the charity a person gives redeems the Divine Presence from its exile and the Jewish people from amid the nations of the world, and especially how, within every person, it unleashes the love of God that has been concealed and covered. He guides his reader in how to tap into this hidden emotion through the service of prayer.

1. The author of the *Tanya* was incarcerated by the Russian authorities twice. The first time was in 1798, and the day of his release, 19 Kislev, became a day of celebration for all generations to come. The second time, which entailed a lighter and shorter sentence, occurred in 1801, and he was released on Hanukkah.

9 Av
13 Av (leap year)

אֵין יִשְׂרָאֵל נִגְאָלִים אֶלָּא בִּצְדָקָה, שֶׁנֶּאֱמַר: "וְשָׁבֶיהָ בִּצְדָקָה" (ישעיה א, כז). כְּתִיב: "צֶדֶק לְפָנָיו יְהַלֵּךְ" (תהלים פה, יד), וַהֲוָה לֵיהּ לְמֵימַר: יֵלֵךְ. אַךְ הָעִנְיָן, עַל פִּי מַה שֶּׁכָּתוּב: "לְךָ אָמַר לִבִּי בַּקְּשׁוּ פָנָי" (תהלים כז, ח). פֵּירוּשׁ: בַּקְּשׁוּ פְּנִימִית הַלֵּב.

The Jewish people are redeemed only through charity, as the verse states, "Zion will be redeemed with justice, **and its returnees with charity"** (Isa. 1:27). In addition, **it is written, "Justice will go** [*yehalekh*] **before Him"** (Ps. 85:14). **It should have said** ***yelekh*****. The matter** can be understood **based on the verse "For You my heart said: Seek Me"** (Ps. 27:8), **meaning, seek the inner dimension of the heart.**

The author of the *Tanya* opens the letter by quoting a verse that refers to the Jewish people's redemption from captivity and exile through charity.[2] Then, in the way of hasidic discourses, the author of the *Tanya* immediately transitions into a different thread, which will explain the psalmist's word choice, *yehalekh*, which literally means "will cause to go," instead of *yelekh*, "will go," to which he will return toward the end of the letter.

He begins his explanation by quoting yet another verse in which the word *panai*, "me," or more literally, "my face," is usually understood in the context of this verse as referring to God. However, the author of the *Tanya* explains it in a different light. The word *panai* resembles the word *penim* which connotes that which is internal. From this perspective, the verse can be understood as referring to one's heart speaking to a person and urging him, "Seek my innermost dimension." Further on, the author of the *Tanya* will explain what is meant by the innermost dimension of the heart and how it is the pathway to reaching the inner dimension of the Divine.

כִּי הִנֵּה בְּלַהַב יְסוֹד הָאֵשׁ הָאֱלֹקִית שֶׁבַּלֵּב (נוּסָח אַחֵר: הִנֵּה בְּהַלֵּב [יְסוֹד הָאֵשׁ הָאֱלֹקִית שֶׁבַּלֵּב])

For in the flame of the element of divine fire that is in the heart [alternatively: For in the heart (the element of divine fire that is in the heart)],

2. See Rambam, *Mishneh Torah, Sefer Zera'im, Hilkhot Mattenot Aniyim* 10:1; *Shabbat* 139a.

Both versions of this clause state how the flame of divine fire, which manifests as fervor and passion for the Divine, burns in the heart of the divine soul. The heart, in contrast to the mind, expresses the soul's emotions, which are embodied by the spiritual element of fire that ascends upward like flame and is manifest as desire and yearning for the Divine.[3] The element of water, on the other hand, corresponds to the intellectual facet of a person, and serves as the capability to receive and allow things to flow downward into the inner recesses of the soul.

יֵשׁ שְׁתֵּי בְּחִינוֹת: בְּחִינַת חִיצוֹנִיּוּת וּבְחִינַת פְּנִימִיּוּת.

there are two dimensions: the external dimension and the inner dimension.

This does not refer to externality and internality in their standard usage as the difference between what is displayed outward and what is contained inward, like the difference between an action that a person does with intention felt authentically inside and an action performed only so that it will be seen from the outside. This does not even refer to the broader usage as the difference between that which is primary and that which is secondary. Rather, here both the external and internal dimensions of the heart engender genuine emotions, authentic sensations that a person feels. If that is the case, what is the difference between internal and external expression?

'חִיצוֹנִיּוּת הַלֵּב' הִיא הִתְלַהֲבוּת הַמִּתְלַהֶבֶת מִבְּחִינַת הַבִּינָה וְהַדַּעַת בִּגְדוּלַּת ה' אֵין סוֹף בָּרוּךְ הוּא, [לְהִתְבּוֹנֵן] בִּגְדוּלָּתוֹ וּלְהוֹלִיד מִתְּבוּנָה זוֹ אַהֲבָה עַזָּה כְּרִשְׁפֵּי אֵשׁ וכו'.

The external dimension of the heart is the ardor of the heart **that is evoked through the understanding and knowledge of the greatness of God,** ***Ein Sof*****, blessed be He, by contemplating His greatness and generating from this understanding a love** for God **as fierce as sparks of fire, and so on.**

The external facet of the heart is the awakening of emotion engendered by intellectual contemplation and awareness. When a person contem-

3. See *Likkutei Amarim*, chap. 3; *Torah Or*, Gen. 30c; *Sefer HaArakhim*, vol. 1, p. 255.

plates the greatness of God in a way that inspires him personally and has significance for him, he engenders an emotional response within. In other sources, this response is considered the preferred way to attain love and fear of God, called "intellectual love and fear," because awareness transforms a person and moves him from one spiritual state to another. The deeper it is, the deeper and more blazing the emotion engendered from it will be.

The author of the *Tanya* refers to this love, though genuine, as the external dimension of the heart because it is evoked by the intellectual faculties, which are external relative to the heart itself. Furthermore, such contemplation does not happen within the internal dimension of the divine essence, a dimension that the mind cannot grasp, but only through the divine illumination that shines into the world, a manifestation of the divine essence that is external to the divine essence.

This external dimension of the heart has great advantages in that it can be evoked and directed at any time through the immediate spiritual work of a person's will and intellect, but it is limited in its power and scope due to the limitations of the person's consciousness, which serves as its foundation. ☞ ☞

INTELLECT VERSUS EMOTION

☞ The difference between the soul's faculties of the mind and those of the heart, between the intellect and emotion, lies in the distinction between the intellectual element of the soul and its nonrational elements. A person's love or fear is not commensurate with the degree of his understanding. His emotions may even contradict what he knows to be true. Yet clearly there is a strong bond between the mind and the heart, since it is impossible to love or hate, or develop any other emotion, without some degree of awareness and rational understanding of it. The connection between the mind and the heart is embodied by the throat, the limb that connects the head to the heart. But due to the narrowness of this passageway, not everything that a person understands in his mind is felt in his heart.

Not all people are the same in terms of this mind-heart connection. In some, it is strong, while there are those whose mind-heart bond is weaker. One person can understand a concept clearly yet act in total opposition to it, because his heart pulls him in another direction. Another person may not be intellectually smart, but he has a great deal of enthusiasm, because the little that he does understand he feels palpably in his heart.

This happens with children. When a small child comprehends that something is good, he immediately wants it. This is the reason young children do not want to hear scary stories: because they will not be able to sleep afterward. An adult, on the other hand, can hear the story and sleep soundly without any disturbances. As most people age, the barriers between the head and the heart, between what they know and what they feel, increase.

THE WORK OF CONTEMPLATION

☞ A big part of the spiritual work discussed in hasidic teachings (based on the Mishna in *Avot* 1:2 that refers to Torah study, acts of kindness, and prayer) is about working on the bond between the intellect and the emotions. The work of contemplation does not just entail intellectually understanding a particular concept, but revisiting it in order to ponder it, thinking it over until it becomes vibrantly clear, until the emotion of the heart is aroused.

Imagine that one person insulted another. If the latter does not ruminate over "what he did to me," his emotions will not be aroused. If he contemplates what happened, depending on the level of his sensitivity, he will get fired up until he works himself into a rage.

Another example is worry. What makes a person worry? He sits and thinks about what could happen, depicts in his mind all the worst-case scenarios, until he drives himself mad with worry.

Contemplation is not just a practice written about in books for spiritual growth. Every person has the capability to take a topic and to delve into it. When he delves into it and ponders it thoroughly, then he cultivates a certain degree of emotionality toward it.

Perception, then, does not operate according to truth. The question of whether a particular assumption is correct or incorrect is irrelevant when it comes to the emotion that it generates. The determining factor is one's degree of clarity and feeling of (subjective) certainty regarding it. When a person arrives at the perception that a particular thing is an "enticement to the eyes and attractive to apprehend" (see Gen. 3:6), this creates a positive connection that draws him toward that thing. The converse is also true: Presuming that something is repulsive or harmful creates the negative sensation and desire to distance oneself from it. Without a clear perception, neither a connection to something nor an emotional response to it develops. Feelings of love, fear, and compassion need some seed, some basic framework, to relate to in order for the emotion to intensify, grow, and develop. Awareness provides this foundational seed.

The awareness that engenders love of God does not necessarily entail high intellectual profundity. The *Zohar* (1:103b) explains that in the verse "Her husband is renowned at the gates" (Prov. 31:23), "her husband" hints at the soul's "husband," who is God. The Hebrew word for gate, *sha'ar*, has two other meanings as well: to surmise and amount or degree (related to the word *shiur*). The verse can therefore be read as saying that every person knows God according to the unique manner and degree that he surmises God's presence in his heart, which is then commensurate with the degree of love and fear of God that he is able to cultivate.

Not everything that a person surmises in his heart is correct, but whatever he does surmise in his heart is what creates his relationship toward it. Emotion depends on what the heart picks up from this awareness. Even if a person has a deep understanding of something, yet he does not come to forge certainty and clarity in his heart in relation to it, the soul does not respond in kind, nor does the heart generate the corresponding

וּפְנִימִיּוּת הַלֵּב הִיא הַנְּקוּדָּה שֶׁבִּפְנִימִיּוּת הַלֵּב וְעוּמְקָא דְלִיבָּא, שֶׁהִיא לְמַעְלָה מַעְלָה מִבְּחִינַת הַדַּעַת וְהַהִתְבּוֹנְנָה שֶׁיּוּכַל הָאָדָם לְהִתְבּוֹנֵן בְּלִבּוֹ בִּגְדוּלַּת ה׳,

The inner dimension of the heart is the innermost point in the heart, the depth of the heart, which transcends the faculty of knowledge and understanding with which a person may contemplate God's greatness in his heart,

The intellect cannot define or even reach this innermost point of the heart. It is deeper and more fundamental than anything a person can ever apprehend through contemplation. This point is bound to those things that touch on the essence of a person's life, the very existence of his soul.

וּכְמוֹ שֶׁכָּתוּב: "מִמַּעֲמַקִּים קְרָאתִיךָ ה׳" (תהלים קל, א), מֵעוּמְקָא דְלִיבָּא.

as it is written, "Out of the depths I call to You, Lord" (Ps. 130:1) – **from the depths of the heart.**

The author of the *Tanya* interprets this verse, not as referring to a deep, dark place that a person falls into and from which he calls to God, but rather to a person who calls to God "from the depths of his heart." The person calls to God, not from the external and conscious aspect of his soul, but from a deeper source, from the depth of the innermost quintessence of his being. ☞

(וְעַל דֶּרֶךְ מָשָׁל, כְּמוֹ בְּמִילֵּי דְעָלְמָא

(By way of analogy, it is like in matters of this world

emotions. On the other hand, it may be that a person who imagines God as an old man sitting in the heavens will cultivate a greater love and fear from this perception than the one who has read all the philosophical works and can provide several proofs of God's existence and oneness. This is because the latter's understanding did not become tangible for him yet. He has not "surmised" it in his heart.

Stories are told of simple people who did not understand lofty concepts deeply, and the little they grasped, they misunderstood. Yet still, whatever they presumed about God inspired them to love and fear Him on a very high level. In some cases, this is more precious to God than the love and fear of highly intelligent people.

The external and internal dimensions of the heart are not only modes through which the soul relates to the world of holiness, but they come to play in all worldly pursuits as well. The love or hate that a person feels toward some things were cultivated from his more external, conscious faculties, while his relationship to others seems to be rooted much deeper within the soul itself. This reflects these two dimensions of the soul: the inner dimension and the more external dimension.

לִפְעָמִים יֵשׁ עִנְיָן גָּדוֹל מְאֹד מְאֹד שֶׁכָּל חַיּוּת הָאָדָם תָּלוּי בּוֹ, וְנוֹגֵעַ עַד נְקוּדַּת פְּנִימִיּוּת הַלֵּב וְעַד בִּכְלָל,

where there is sometimes an extremely important matter on which a person's entire life depends, and it affects a person to the core, **up to and including the innermost point of the heart,**

The important matter that the author of the *Tanya* refers to is not necessarily significant in an objective sense, but for this particular person it is essential, to the extent that he cannot imagine life without it. This distinction plays itself out when a person must relinquish something that belongs to him. Every person has things that he values, that he thinks are important, but when push comes to shove, he can give them up. Then there are things to which he has a deep connection, not because of any rational reason, but rather because of some inexplicable bond between that thing and the essence of his soul. Those he cannot give up, except through extraordinary effort that entails giving of his very self.

These things vary from person to person. For one person, giving money touches upon this point in his soul, while for another, money is nothing, not because he is wealthy, but because money does not

"OUT OF THE DEPTHS I CALL"

☞ This psalm is recited every day during the Ten Days of Repentance. In order to repent and genuinely return to God, one must reach down into the deepest depths of his being and call out to God from that place, from the deepest and most foundational point of the soul, from the depth of being where he feels the true essence of his existence. When that inner point of truth awakens within, when he knows with absolute certainty that he cannot bear his current state of being anymore, that is where repentance begins (see *Likkutei Torah*, Deut. 62b, s.v. "*mima'amakim*").

touch on the inner dimension of his heart. Rather, there will be other things that he cannot relinquish.

When the inner point is touched, a person forgets all external factors: education, position, and image. When the quintessential self takes over, with one's knowledge or without, this is the aspect called the "innermost point of the heart." This is the meeting point between the self and the soul of the self, between the self and the self within the self, as reflected in its pure essence, beyond all comprehension.

וְגוֹרֵם לוֹ לִפְעָמִים לַעֲשׂוֹת מַעֲשִׂים וּלְדַבֵּר דְּבָרִים שֶׁלֹּא בְּדַעַת כְּלָל.)

sometimes causing him to commit acts and say things that are completely irrational.)

As long as a person is acting with his external faculties, his intellect regains control over his emotions, over the way in which he expresses his desires, and to a certain degree over his personality. He can maintain a critical eye on himself, choosing how he acts. He may enjoy and love what he is doing, but it is all informed by rationale, by what he knows and the way in which he knows it. When something strikes the inner core of a person's heart, on the other hand, he will act irrationally. He will say and do things that evade his censor, and his whole way of relating will not stem from what he understands and knows intellectually but rather from the essence of his being.

When that which a person is able to give up is taken away from him, even if he worked for it for years, he will react with equanimity. While he certainly may fight for what he feels is important, he will ultimately give it up when necessary. By contrast, when something that is bound to the inner dimension of a person's heart is at stake, he acts irrationally, with an explosion of emotions and energies that he does not even know he has since they are rooted in the essence of his being, in a layer so deep that he does not even know it exists.

One time, a car ran over a baby, and the mother, who was small in stature, ran to the car and hoisted it up. By any calculation, she would have been incapable of lifting a car, but when something is bound to the deepest recesses of the heart, such calculations have no relevance.

It is like the difference between a person who gets poked in the finger and someone who gets poked in the nerve. The intense reaction to the direct contact with the nerve is a result of pain that is not external or filtered but directly plugged into the source of the sensation.

וְזֶה לְעוּמַּת זֶה, כָּכָה הוּא מַמָּשׁ בַּעֲבוֹדָה שֶׁבַּלֵּב.

Corresponding to the analogy of the worldly example, **it is exactly the same with regard to the service of the heart.**

Elsewhere, the author of the *Tanya* explains how the innermost point of the heart within every Jew is his connection to God.[4] When a Jew senses that this connection is threatened, he acts in a way that does not seem at all in proportion to what provoked him. Jewish history is replete with stories about people whose lives were not connected in any obvious way to Judaism or to the Jewish community, yet when something struck that inner spiritual nerve, in one way or another, it was as if something burst out of them, and they acted in totally unexpected ways, even to the extent of literally giving up their lives.

וְהַיְינוּ לְפִי שֶׁבְּחִינַת נְקוּדַּת פְּנִימִית הַלֵּב הִיא לְמַעְלָה מִבְּחִינַת הַדַּעַת הַמִּתְפַּשֵּׁט וּמִתְלַבֵּשׁ בַּמִּדּוֹת שֶׁנּוֹלְדוּ מֵחָכְמָה בִּינָה דַּעַת כַּנּוֹדָע,

This is because the innermost point of the heart transcends the faculty of knowledge, which spreads and becomes clothed in the emotive **attributes, which are engendered from** the faculties of **wisdom, understanding,** and **knowledge, as is known.**

The inner and outer dimensions of the heart operate on two different tracks. The workings of the external dimension operate according to an organized track that carries a thought or concept from one spiritual level to the next, starting from the intellect and moving to the emotive attributes. It starts from the top, from the first flash of awareness that is wisdom, which is then analyzed and expanded through the faculty of understanding, and then becomes integrated into one's being through the faculty of knowledge. That knowledge then gives birth to the emotive attributes and informs the soul whether to be attracted to the concept or repulsed by it, evoking

4. *Likkutei Amarim*, chap. 18.

feelings of love or fear. These attributes, which stem from the external, conscious dimension of the heart, can be viewed as the emotional application of knowledge. They are informed by the knowledge and are therefore beneath it.

רַק הִיא בְּחִינַת הֶאָרַת חָכְמָה עֶלְיוֹנָה שֶׁלְּמַעְלָה מֵהַבִּינָה וְהַדַּעַת,

Rather, it takes the form of a ray of supernal *Ḥokhma*, Wisdom, **that transcends the** attributes of ***Bina*,** Understanding, **and *Da'at*,** Knowledge,

By contrast, there is another track, one that the internal dimension of the heart uses to express itself, which does not pass through all the stages of awareness. In contrast to the external dimension of the heart, which can only register the flash of wisdom through the faculties of understanding and knowledge, the inner point of the heart can decipher that pure spark of wisdom directly. ☞

ḤOKHMA BEYOND *BINA*

☞ While *Ḥokhma*, the highest of all the *sefirot*, is considered one of the cognitive *sefirot*, it is not actually rational. It is a point of direct experience without any medium that absorbs a whole array of things, a whole picture of truth, in an instant. This flash of experience, though it is the source of all rational understanding that follows it, is in itself inherently incomprehensible. We can only be aware of its existence and estimate the essence of what it is, but we cannot grasp it. It is only at the level of *Bina* that the intellect is actually manifest, that *Ḥokhma*'s flash of awareness becomes comprehensible. *Bina*, the intellect, is responsible for analyzing and then synthesizing disparate details into cohesive systems. Of course, it does not begin from nothing but rather builds on initial axiomatic input that it receives from *Ḥokhma*.

Bina can also communicate with *Ḥokhma* in what is, in a certain sense, a conscious process. After all the processing we do, we reflect *Bina*'s final conclusion back to *Ḥokhma* in order to get a stamp of truth from *Ḥokhma*. We cannot explain how we know the truth of a particular conclusion, yet that flash of *Ḥokhma* stands as the ultimate test when we strive to verify what we know. When *Ḥokhma* lights up in resonance with our logical deduction, then we know that we are aligned with truth.

Our whole realm of thinking is therefore woven from the complementary, continuous dynamic between *Ḥokhma* and *Bina*, a give and take similar to the process of breathing. It is only because these mutual processes are so fast that we are incapable of analyzing how the initial flash of understanding gets passed along and when precisely it links back up to the source, to *Ḥokhma*.

וּבָהּ מְלוּבָּשׁ וְגָנוּז אוֹר ה׳ מַמָּשׁ, כְּמוֹ שֶׁכָּתוּב: ״ה׳ בְּחָכְמָה וכו׳״ (משלי ג, יט).

and the light of God itself is literally clothed and hidden within this supernal *Ḥokhma,* **as it is written, "The Lord** founded the earth **with wisdom…"** (Prov 3:19).

While the simple understanding of this verse is that it is a praise to God who created the intricately elaborate world with His divine wisdom, the author of the *Tanya* explains it as describing the kabbalistic process of the creation of the world.[5] The first two words describe the very beginning of the process: God is "in *Ḥokhma,*" within the *sefira* of *Ḥokhma.* The divine name used in this verse, the name of *Havaya,* is the name that represents the divine light that fills the vessels of the *sefirot.*[6] This light first enters the *sefira* of *Ḥokhma,* and only through *Ḥokhma* does it shine and manifest in the other *sefirot.*

Just as in the soul the flash of wisdom is the beginning of perception, so too in the macrocosm *Ḥokhma* is the very inception of existence.[7] It is the point that serves as a mediator between the conscious and the subconscious, between nothingness and existence, and therefore it is only through *Ḥokhma* that the light of *Ein Sof* manifests, transcendent of every limit and definition.

וְהִיא הִיא בְּחִינַת נִיצוֹץ אֱלֹקוּת שֶׁבְּכָל נֶפֶשׁ מִיִּשְׂרָאֵל.

This ray of supernal *Ḥokhma,* in which the divine light is clothed, **is the very spark of divinity that is in the soul of every Jew.**

The innermost point in the inner dimension of the heart, which is the essence of the soul, is synonymous with the point of *Ḥokhma* that transcends *Bina* and *Da'at* and all the other *sefirot,* the point of the divine spark that transcends everything. The awakening to divine service from the innermost dimension of the heart therefore stems

5. See also epistle 20; *Likkutei Amarim,* chap. 18 and gloss to chap. 35.

6. See *Torah Or* 10b.

7. This also accords with the *Targum Yerushalmi*'s translation of the first verse of the Torah, "In the beginning, God created…" – "in *Ḥokhma.*"

from the manifestation of the essence of the Divine itself, as it were, which is the divine spark in a person's soul.

10 Av וּמַה שֶּׁאֵין כָּל אָדָם זוֹכֶה לְמַדְרֵגָה זוֹ, לַעֲבוֹדָה שֶׁבַּלֵּב מֵעוּמְקָא דְלִבָּא בִּבְחִינַת פְּנִימִיּוּת,

That not every person merits this level, namely, **the service of the heart from the depths of the heart, the innermost dimension,**

There are levels of divine service that depend on one's comprehension, on one's abilities and effort, yet every person possesses this innermost point at the heart's core.[8] The soul of every Jew, not just of outstanding people, is a portion of God on high. Every individual possesses this Godly spark. If that is the case, why doesn't every person merit serving God in an active and revealed way from this place deep within? ☞

הַיְינוּ לְפִי שֶׁבְּחִינָה זוֹ הִיא אֶצְלוֹ בִּבְחִינַת גָּלוּת וּשְׁבִיָּה.

is because this level is in a state of exile and captivity within a person.

SERVICE THAT ARISES FROM THE DEPTHS

☞ From the verse "He smelled the scent of his garments" (Gen. 27:15), the Midrash (*Yalkut Shimoni, Toledot* 115) extrapolates that the word for garments, *begadav*, is very similar to the word for rebels, *bogdav*. The Midrash goes on to recount that when the gentiles came to destroy the Temple, they were afraid to enter the inner sanctum. They searched until they found a Jewish collaborator who agreed to go in. They tricked him and said, "If you go in, whatever you take will be yours." The Jew entered the inner sanctum and left with the *menora*, the candelabrum made entirely of gold. They said to him, "That is fitting for a caesar! Go back in and take something else." This time the Jew refused and said, "It is enough that I angered my Creator once. I refuse to do it again!" They offered him large amounts of money, and still he refused. They began to beat him, yet he did not relent. Finally, they took him to a torture chamber and put him between two planks of wood studded with sharp iron stakes. He did not relent and bore the torture until he expired and his soul ascended to Heaven.

This Jew, who was willing to collaborate with such wicked people and steal from the inner sanctum, had the strength to withstand the pain of torture in order to avoid angering his Creator further. The question is, where was this strength before, when he first agreed to enter the inner sanctum? Moreover, if everyone possesses such fortitude, why isn't it manifest in everyday life?

8. See also *Likkutei Amarim*, chap. 19.

While this innermost point, this Godly spark, lies at the core of every Jew, it is not openly manifest. The exile and captivity of the sacred inner dimension of the heart is not a matter of superficial parameters, but rather a result of deep, inner blockages in one's animal soul caused by desires and fears that conceal and restrain the inner dimension of the soul, keeping it in captivity. ☞

וְהִיא בְּחִינַת גָּלוּת הַשְּׁכִינָה מַמָּשׁ, **This is literally the exile of the Divine Presence,**

The exile of the Divine Presence is synonymous with the exile of a person's divine spark, which becomes subjugated to the faculties of the animal soul and thus concealed by them. The author of the *Tanya* does not say that the exile of a person's spark is analogous to the exile of the Divine Presence, but that they are "literally" one and the same. Man, after all, is a microcosm,[9] and everything that happens and exists within him is an actual microcosmic reflection of the reality of the broader world.

כִּי הִיא הִיא בְּחִינַת נִיצוֹץ אֱלֹהוּת שֶׁבְּנַפְשׁוֹ הָאֱלֹהִית. **for** the innermost point of the heart **is none other than the spark of divinity within one's divine soul.**

EXILE AND CAPTIVITY

☞ A Jew cannot destroy the divine spark within him, however hard he may try, but he can conceal it, cover it, and deny its existence. This concealment of one's inner essence is called exile.

Exile entails relocation to a foreign place under a foreign government, such as when a person must leave his home against his will and move to a distant place, where he is forced to fulfill other people's desires that contradict his own. While in his inner being, he remains the same person, his self-expression is now totally different. Before, he was his own person, expressing his genuine self, and now he is a captive in a framework that other people have chosen for him, obligated to abide by other people's values and wishes. The inner depths of his heart, the divine spark at his essence, has not changed, for it is immutable. But when it is in exile and captivity, it does not manifest at its essence but rather according to other people's whims, only rarely finding windows to express its true being.

9. See, e.g., in the *Sefer HaIkkarim* 2:21; *Midrash Tanḥuma, Pekudei* 3.

If this spark is in exile within a given person, this signifies that in the broader sphere the Divine Presence is also in exile. This means that the Divine Presence no longer expresses itself, no longer manifests in the world in a clear and revealed way, but rather its influence is manifest in ways that oppose and even negate its very existence.

וְסִבַּת הַגָּלוּת הוּא מַאֲמַר רַבּוֹתֵינוּ ז״ל: ״גָּלוּ לְבָבֶל שְׁכִינָה עִמָּהֶם״ (מגילה כט, א).

The cause of this exile is, as our Rabbis state, that **"they were exiled to Babylonia,** and **the Divine Presence** went **with them"** (*Megilla* 29a).

The exile of the Divine Presence is not just an uprooting of an individual or the Jewish people from their geographic location, but it is primarily a spiritual dislocation. When the Jewish people experience a spiritual descent, the Divine Presence descends there as well. Just as this applies in the macrocosmic scheme of the entire nation and the Divine Presence in general, it also applies to every individual Jew and his personal Divine Presence within, the divine spark within that descends with a person into whatever lowly place of exile he may find himself. In this light, the exile of the Divine Presence is the result of the overall exile of the Jewish people and of the individual exile of the divine soul in each and every Jew.

דְּהַיְינוּ מִפְּנֵי שֶׁהִלְבִּישׁ בְּחִינַת פְּנִימִית נְקוּדַּת לְבָבוֹ בְּזֶה לְעוּמַּת זֶה,

This is because a person **invested the innermost point of his heart in the counterpart** to holiness,

"This corresponding to that"[10] is a common expression describing the dynamic of good and evil, how the framework of good and holiness has an equal and opposite counterpart of evil and impurity. When a person invests in pursuits that parallel yet counteract holiness rather than investing the inner point of one's heart where it is supposed to be, in sacred matters, then he effectively sends his personal Divine Presence, his divine spark within, into exile.

10. Eccles. 7:14; *Ḥagiga* 15a.

דְּהַיְינוּ בִּלְבוּשִׁים צוֹאִים דְּמִילֵּי דְעָלְמָא, וְתַאֲוֹת עוֹלָם הַזֶּה הַנִּקְרָא בְּשֵׁם "בָּבֶל".

namely, in the soiled garments of worldly matters and the desires of this world, which are referred to by the name Babylonia.

This does not necessarily refer to sin but rather to all worldly matters and indulgences in which a person partakes as an end in and of themselves, without any connection to holiness.

When a person invests his desires and thoughts into worldly matters, when he places the external dimension of his heart in "Babylonia,"[11] then the innermost point of his heart will become captive there as well. The inner dimension of his heart, which has the potential to imbue him with all the power and vitality that he could ever dream of, is being employed for superficial and trivial purposes rather than the deeply significant mission for which it was destined.

If a person were to know that the quintessential point of his heart is purely divine, he would be able to accomplish things that far transcend his own capacity. His entire life would be different. But this point is concealed in the external *kelippot*, in murky, soiled garments that conceal the source of their vitality and life force. ☞

THE EXILE OF THE INNERMOST DIMENSION OF THE HEART

☞ The depth of a person's heart can manifest in almost anything. When it is drawn to something and identifies with it, it becomes invested in it and operates as if it were truly an expression of it. This explains how the inner dimension of a person's heart can become invested in food or money, for example.

If this person's homeland, nation, or God gets threatened, he will certainly respond with an emotional, active, and fitting response commensurate with how much he understands and relates to the repercussions of the threat.. But his response will stem from the external dimension of his heart. If, however, you touch his money, his reaction will be more extreme. At that moment, the inner, irrational side of his heart will have been awakened, and he will defend what is his like

11. See the Arizal's *Likkutei Torah, Parashat Ki Tetzei,* which states that "Babylonia" is the *Ḥokhma,* or head, of *kelippa*. See also *Kehillat Yaakov,* s.v. "*Bavel*." One can posit that the reason the author of the *Tanya* emphasizes this concept of Babylonia is because it is the counterpart to the aforementioned supernal *Ḥokhma* that manifests as the inner dimension of the heart.

וְהִיא בְּחִינַת עָרְלָה הַמְכַסָּה עַל הַבְּרִית וּנְקוּדָּה הַפְּנִימִית שֶׁבַּלֵּב.

This state of exile **is** considered like **the foreskin that conceals the covenant** of circumcision in that it conceals **the innermost point of the heart.**

Just as a man's physical body has a foreskin that covers the masculine organ, the place of the covenant of circumcision, there is a foreskin of the heart that covers the innermost point of the heart, a person's

a person defending his life. This is called "exile" and "captivity" of the inner dimension of the heart within materiality. The essential point that lies at the core of his heart still exists. But he has invested it in "soiled garments" of this world. This person now directs that inner point that was intended from its inception to be directed toward the inner sanctum of holiness toward that which is diametrically opposed to his true inner essence.

This perspective of the exile of the Divine Presence and the exile of the inner dimension of the heart recalls various types of mental illness and their treatments. The assumption is that the soul has a fundamental desire that expresses itself in various ways and distortions, sometimes in healthy outlets and sometimes in harmful disorders. One approach to treatment is to show the person the perversion that his desire has become and to reorient him toward his original direction. You say to him, "You think that you want *a* or *b*, but really you want something else entirely." The difference between various psychological and spiritual approaches to healing lies in the presumption of the nature of the person's true desire, the quintessential desire that lies at the core of all his other desires.

Every person has this inner point in his heart in which his divine spark burns. In the depth of his heart, he yearns for only one thing: for God. But this desire goes through a series of distortions and delusions called "exile of the Divine Presence." The fallout is that the inner point of his will that originally wanted God alone now becomes enveloped in other things. The Torah calls this idol worship, or, more literally, "foreign service." Idolatry does not necessarily entail denial of God's existence but rather a transferal from subservience to God to something that is other than God.

The Talmud (*Sanhedrin* 64a) relates how the members of the Great Assembly eliminated the evil inclination to serve idolatry. The hasidim asked: How did they get rid of it? Isn't this inclination an angel? How can a spiritual essence be obliterated? They answered that in truth they did not obliterate it; they just transferred it to another mission (because an angel cannot perform two functions), and now it serves as the evil inclination of money (see *Zohar* 3:332b; *Likkutei Torah*, Num. 62d).

The simple definition of idolatry is the deviation from one's essential will to serve God. Therefore, every deviation, even if it is not an expression of service to another god but a craving for something as mundane as money or power, is considered idolatry and constitutes an expression of the basic psychospiritual corruption called "exile of the Divine Presence."

deep, inner truth, preventing it from manifesting.[12] It is relegated to expressing itself only through the veil of the foreskin. The result of this is that one's innermost yearning will latch onto other people's cravings for various goals and not God's intended vision for the fulfillment of that person's unique soul mission.

וְעַל זֶה נֶאֱמַר: "וּמַלְתֶּם אֵת עָרְלַת לְבַבְכֶם" (דברים י, טז).

Regarding this the verse **states, "Remove the obstruction of your heart"** (Deut. 10:16).

Just as there is a mitzva to circumcise and remove the physical foreskin, every person must remove his spiritual foreskin to reveal the innermost point of his heart. This directive does not imply that a person should cut into his heart, to squelch all feeling and sensation. The intention here is only to remove the *kelippa* that is covering it, to reveal the rawness of one's genuine heart, without any veil.

The foreskin of the heart that we are commanded to remove includes all those things in which the heart is invested that do not have any real, lasting substance in and of themselves. These are things that cause the deviation and distortion of the innermost point of one's heart. On a deeper level, then, the instruction to remove the foreskin of the heart is a directive to free oneself of the concealment of one's most essential self and bring himself to a spiritual redemption.

וְהִנֵּה בְּמִילָה יֵשׁ שְׁנֵי בְּחִינוֹת: מִילָה וּפְרִיעָה, שֶׁהֵן עָרְלָה גַּסָּה וּקְלִיפָּה דַּקָּה. וְכֵן בְּעָרְלַת הַלֵּב יֵשׁ גַּם כֵּן תַּאֲוֹת גַּסּוֹת וְדַקּוֹת: מִילָה וּפְרִיעָה,

There are two stages to the mitzva of **circumcision:** ***mila*****,** excision, **and** ***peria*****,** uncovering, **which** remove **the coarse foreskin and the thin membrane,** respectively. **Similarly, in the foreskin of the heart there are also coarse desires and** more **subtle** ones, requiring ***mila*** **and** ***peria*** respectively,

There are several ways of understanding the subtle distinction between coarse desires and more refined ones. In a general sense, the coarse

12. See Rashi, Deut. 10:16.

desires are those that are clearly bad desires, while the more refined desires are those that are not clearly bad. ☞

COARSE DESIRES AND SUBTLE DESIRES

☞ This distinction parallels another one made elsewhere in the *Tanya* (*Likkutei Amarim*, chaps. 7–8), that of desires characterized by "foreign demons" and desires characterized by "Jewish demons" (see also *Ba'al Shem al HaTorah, Parashat Koraḥ*). Foreign demons are those that tempt a person to transgress obvious Torah infractions, such as murder, adultery, and stealing. It is obvious that anyone who is tempted to commit one of these transgressions is being tempted to sin and to indulge in a "coarse desire." By contrast, Jewish demons are temptations to indulge in that which is technically permitted according to Jewish law, yet still, since it is not a mitzva nor is it being channeled for divine service, but rather as pure, selfish indulgence, it is considered a bad desire. For instance, if a person craves kosher meat purely out of lust for food, this is considered a "Jewish demon" desire. Since it is hard to define these transgressions as such, the desire to indulge in them is much more subtle and complex.

Coarse desires can be expressed in the realm of the permitted as well, when a person craves that which is permitted in a physical and unrefined way. Furthermore, coarse desires are not expressed only in the realm of physicality either. In the spiritual realm as well, a person can desire something in a very uncouth way. There are, therefore, many forms that coarse desires can take: in the realm of the forbidden and in the permitted, in the physical realm and on the spiritual plane.

By contrast, there are subtle desires that are not even actual desires but what we might call propensities. This subtle deviation, which can involve anything, constitutes the lens through which a person views himself and the world, a lens that is distorted by the person's own ego. This selfishness may not express itself in a blatant way, in trampling over weaker people or in wishing ill of others, but rather manifests as a very subtle impulse, a way of relating to others and the world that takes into account only one's own desires and status. This motivation can be expressed in the most beautiful thoughts and actions. A person can be involved in only good things, mitzvot, Torah study, and prayer, yet he may be totally unaware that he is really occupied only with himself.

A person may, for example, be playing the part: He grows a long beard, prays and sways, all because he gets benefit from the impression that this has on others. Then there is a more subtle *kelippa*: a person who is not pretending, but he gets pleasure from his service of God. This pleasure may even be spiritual pleasure, yet be so subtly distorted that a person cannot distinguish between the holiness and the *kelippa*, between the deep, fundamental purpose of it all and its superficial, secondary face.

There is a well-known story about a Kotzker hasid. This hasid never gave other people reproof because, as he put it, there are many sides to rebuke, and even if everything he would say were true, it could be that he would get pleasure from delivering it. He chose, instead, to maintain his silence. When his time came to pass on to the next world, and his loved ones gathered around him, he lifted himself up and said, "Now that I am going to die, and I do not care anymore what people will say and think about me, I can say everything."

ו"מָל וְלֹא פָּרַע כְּאִלּוּ לֹא מָל" (משנה שבת פרק יט משנה ו). מִפְּנֵי שֶׁסּוֹף עֲדַיִין נְקוּדַּת פְּנִימִית הַלֵּב הִיא מְכוּסָּה בִּלְבוּשׁ שַׂק דַּק בִּבְחִינַת גָּלוּת וְשִׁבְיָה.

and "if one circumcised but did not uncover the flesh, **it is as if he had not circumcised"** (Mishna *Shabbat* 19:6), **because ultimately the innermost point of the heart remains concealed in a garment of thin sackcloth, in a state of exile and captivity.**

One of the laws of circumcision is that if a person removes the coarse layer but not the fine layer – *mila* but not *peria* – he did not perform the mitzva.[13] Likewise, even after the removal of several coarse *kelippot,* if the innermost point of the heart is coated with ulterior motives and desires, he is still spiritually uncircumcised. That which puts a person in exile is not quantitative, but qualitative, so that as long as there is still *kelippa,* no matter how thin and subtle, the inner dimension of the heart is still in a state of exile. In essence, the Divine Presence is captive.

There is certainly a difference between a coarse membrane and a fine one, just as there is a difference between a bitter and painful exile and an exile that is not perceptible. In a certain sense, there is a benefit to a harsh and painful exile, since at least the person is aware that he is in exile and wants to be liberated. When a person knows that he is committing a transgression, he wants to resist, while if he is not aware of a subtle transgression that he may be committing, it is harder and more complicated to rectify it. Either way, coarse or subtle, exile is exile. ☞

Everyone gathered close and tilted their ear to hear what he would say, but then he thought to himself, *Seventy years I held myself back, and now, at the last moment, the evil inclination thinks that he will succeed in catching me. I will not speak!* With that, he died.

There are those who add to the story: That is the moment when the evil inclination caught him, because a person like that, at such a powerful moment, could have brought benefit to a lot of people, yet instead he thought only of himself.

THE DIFFERENCE BETWEEN THE JEWISH PEOPLE AND THE WORLD

☞ There is a significant distinction between the circumcision commanded of the Jewish people and gentile circumcision (that which Abraham was command-

13. See also Rambam, *Mishneh Torah, Sefer Ahava, Hilkhot Mila* 2:2.

וְהִנֵּה עַל מִילַת הָעָרְלָה מַמָּשׁ כְּתִיב: "וּמַלְתֶּם אֵת עָרְלַת לְבַבְכֶם" (דברים י, טז) – אַתֶּם בְּעַצְמְכֶם,

Regarding the circumcision of the coarse **foreskin itself, it is written, "Remove the obstruction of your heart"** (Deut. 10:16) – **you yourselves** shall remove it.

In one way or another, every person can fix his attributes and overcome his bad desires, peeling them off his soul. This occurs in the realm of his coarse desires, in which he can clearly distinguish between what is *kelippa* and what is not. Here a person can triumph over problems and rectify blemishes that he recognizes and understands. When he knows that a given desire is forbidden, when he feels that he has a choice, then the slicing is very simple. He knows that he cannot be on two mutually exclusive sides at the same time. He knows that he cannot free his innermost point when he is sunken in this desire. No matter how hard he must work, he is capable of fighting and winning this war.

ed before the giving of the Torah). Gentile circumcision entails *mila* without *peria* (see *Yevamot* 71b), while the Jewish people have this additional element not required of the gentile. One can say that this is the difference between a person who does something just as a symbol, as a mere remembrance and a sign, and a person who is authentic, whose dedication is real. He does not ask himself whether he has carried out his obligation because he technically performed the necessary motions, but whether he truly accomplished what the action was meant to accomplish. Therefore, even though a Jew may have performed an action (the *mila*), as long as a part of the *kelippa* remains intact, as long as the innermost point of the heart has not been uncovered (*peria*), it is as if he was not circumcised at all.

A person who consciously abandons his coarse desires, even his unrefined spiritual desires, yet does not let go of that subtle element of ego in the things he does, cannot attain total revelation of the innermost point of his heart, which is still in exile. A person can consciously relinquish things that other people crave, he could triumph over many superficial, coarse desires, yet that innermost point in his heart will still be caught up in exile. This expresses itself in the most noble, refined desires, even those that seem to be directed toward holiness. When a person wants to do something holy but only for his own purposes, or he is ready to dedicate himself to exalted ends yet still wants to see himself at the center of things, he has not succeeded in revealing the depths of his heart. These desires express subtle manifestations of his will that even the person himself is hard pressed to recognize.

אַךְ לְהָסִיר הַקְּלִיפָּה הַדַּקָּה - זֶהוּ דָּבָר הַקָּשֶׁה עַל הָאָדָם,

But removing the thin membrane is a difficult matter for a person,

The distinction between a thin *kelippa* and holiness is much harder to make and is essentially impossible for the person himself to distinguish. Since this *kelippa* does not have clear parameters, it is very hard to hone in on the place where the severance must be made, where the *kelippa* ends and the person's self begins, and to harness the necessary faculties to remove it. The whole essence of this *kelippa* is the entanglement of the self within it, that element of personal investment that causes the distortion of things for one's own personal gain. When the question of what is right and what is wrong depends on the person's subjective judgment, the solution is ambiguous. On the one hand, a person needs to do this himself, because no one else can assess these subtle, delicate matters from the outside. On the other hand, when a person judges himself, when he is both judge and culprit, he does not have an objective way to evaluate the situation. This *kelippa* hardly ever presents itself as *kelippa*, as actual evil. Entangled in one's every move, it always expresses as an element of holiness, and therefore there is no clear way for a person to discern it, let alone remove it. ☞

וְעַל זֶה נֶאֱמַר בְּבִיאַת הַמָּשִׁיחַ: "וּמָל ה' אֱלֹהֶיךָ אֶת לְבָבְךָ כו'"

and regarding this the verse states about the coming of the Messiah, "The Lord your God will remove the obstruction from your heart...

THE TEST OF THE THIN *KELIPPA*

☞ In the time of the Maggid of Mezeritch, hasidim in a certain place were looking to appoint a rabbi and leader. They asked the Maggid to give them a telltale sign that would indicate whether the candidate was indeed a great person. The Maggid told them to ask him how to rectify the attribute of pride. If he gave them advice, they would know that he was nothing great.

Later, they asked Rabbi Menaḥem Mendel of Vitebsk the question, and he answered, "What can I tell you? I also do not know. A person can come across as a humble, lowly person and actually think that he himself is humble, yet in truth he is full of pride. Another person can be dressed sumptuously and act in a lofty manner and actually be broken and humble inside."

The answer to uncovering these subtle distinctions is that we do not know. the solution is not in man's hands at all.

This implies that the removal of the thin *kelippa* will only happen in the future, in messianic times, when the Divine and its involvement in our lives will be evident far beyond our current perception.

It would seem that there is a contradiction between the verse "Remove the obstruction from your heart," which implies that one should remove the foreskin covering one's heart himself, and the verse "The Lord your God will remove the obstruction from your heart," conveying that God will do so.

The author of the *Tanya* resolves this contradiction by pointing out that circumcision of the heart entails both aspects, *mila* and *peria*. The first verse speaks about *mila*, the part that we must do, and the second verse refers to *peria*, the part that only God can and will do in the future with the coming of the Messiah.

לְאַהֲבָה אֶת ה׳ אֱלֹהֶיךָ בְּכָל לְבָבְךָ וּבְכָל נַפְשְׁךָ לְמַעַן חַיֶּיךָ״ (דברים ל, ו),

to love the Lord your God with all your heart, and with all your soul, for the sake of your life" (Deut. 30:6),

The continuation of the verse tells us that only after the total revelation of the innermost point of the heart, after the *peria* and the removal of the thin *kelippa* membrane, can one attain a strong and deep love of God that flows from this innermost point to the extent that a person feels: This is what it means to be alive.

כְּלוֹמַר, ״לְמַעַן״ כִּי ה׳ לְבַדּוֹ הוּא כָּל חַיֶּיךָ מַמָּשׁ.

meaning, "for the sake" of the absolute recognition **that God alone is literally your whole life.**

The author of the *Tanya* explains that the Torah's usage of the words *lema'an ḥayeḥa*, "for the sake of your life," implies that every person has something that touches on the innermost point of his life, something he cannot give up for anything, because he cannot live without it. Through the revelation that "the Lord your God will remove the obstruction from your heart," a person can tap into this feeling that there is nothing but God. He will arrive at this feeling, not amid the concealment of exile, but in a palpable and real way. This is the personal point of redemption of every individual in which he feels that his love of God is his life, his very definition of the perception of reality.

שֶׁלָּכֵן אַהֲבָה זוֹ הִיא מֵעוּמְקָא דְלִבָּא, מִנְּקוּדָּה פְּנִימִית מַמָּשׁ, כַּנִּזְכָּר לְעֵיל, וּלְמַעְלָה מִבְּחִינַת הַדַּעַת.

This is why this love stems from the depths of the heart, from the innermost point, as stated above, transcending the faculty of knowledge.

As explained above, there is a love that stems from the external dimension of the heart, that is created through cognitive awareness, through knowledge, from that which a person understands and knows. Then there is a deeper love that flows from the depths of a person's heart. The distinction between them does not just manifest itself in matters of holiness. We determine our relationship to certain aspects of our lives, positive or negative, according to our awareness. Then there are other things to which we relate based on the innermost recesses of our heart. These sentiments are not built on a person's understanding nor are they dependent on his conscious awareness or knowledge. Any rational explanations are but cover-ups for the real reason that lies beyond the reaches of his intellect. Just as a healthy person does not need any reason to love himself and that which belongs to him, so too he does not need any additional contemplation when he feels that God is literally his life, the inner depth of his own being.

וְלָכֵן מָשִׁיחַ בָּא בְּהֶיסַּח הַדַּעַת

Therefore, the Messiah will come by means of a diversion of attention

The ultimate redemption and the coming of the Messiah are synonymous with the escape from exile in all its manifestations and levels, which comes along with the revelation of the innermost point of reality, the divine spark. This redemption parallels the revelation of the innermost point of a person's heart and the welling up of that deep, internal emotion that transcends awareness. It is for this reason that the Talmud teaches that the Messiah will come as a result of a diversion of attention.[14] On a deeper level, this refers to a suspension of the faculty of knowledge, because then reality will not be comprised of phenomena that we are familiar with but rather will flow from a

14. *Sanhedrin* 97a.

deeper, hidden source that does not come through knowledge but rather through a suspension of knowledge. ☞

לִכְלָלוּת יִשְׂרָאֵל. **by Israel as a whole.**

Every person can have his own personal redemption in which the innermost point of his heart becomes revealed. This personal redemption does not wait for the end of days. It can come to every person each in his own time. But when we speak about the coming of the Messiah, we refer to a collective redemption, which heralds a transformation for every person forever, not just for a private individual regarding his own private affairs, but for the collective soul of the entire Jewish nation as a whole.

וְהִיא גִּילּוּי בְּחִינַת נְקוּדָּה פְּנִימִית הַכְּלָלִית וִיצִיאַת הַשְּׁכִינָה הַכְּלָלִית מֵהַגָּלוּת וְהַשִּׁבְיָה לָעַד וּלְעוֹלְמֵי עוֹלָמִים.

The revelation of the innermost point in the heart of the collective Jewish people **is the revelation of the innermost point of the totality** of existence **and the exodus of the totality of the Divine Presence from the state of exile and captivity forever and for all of eternity.**

There is a close bond between an individual's personal redemption and that of the entire Jewish people and that of all the worlds. All events,

THE SUSPENSION OF KNOWLEDGE

☞ The phrase *heseḥ da'at*, literally, "suspension of knowledge," or the diversion of one's attention, is generally understood as a moment of distraction and forgetfulness. Here the author of the *Tanya* explains it to mean the lack of the need to engage in one's awareness and knowledge. The messianic era is a time when, as the prophet puts it, "for with actual eyes they will see" (Isa. 52:8). As long as a person does not see something in front of him, he must make calculations about whether it exists. His intellect and knowledge become the active and pivotal factors. But when that thing is staring him in the face, he no longer needs to employ his cognitive faculties.

The coming of the Messiah will happen at a moment of the suspension of awareness. His very revelation will suspend every person's thought processes, because from then on, the divine reality will be a reality that people see with their very own eyes, without the need to examine it with the intellectual faculties that they used to measure what they knew beforehand.

from those recounted in the Torah to major historical events that have become engraved on the collective psyche of the Jewish people, happen at every moment, recurring and becoming etched on the psyche of each and every person. The cycle of descent to Egypt and the subsequent exodus, from exile to redemption, expresses the life cycle of every individual as well. While one's personal redemption is an outcome of a particular revelation that emerges from his unique situation at that time, there will also be a revelation in the collective redemption that the verse describes as "The glory of the Lord will be revealed and all flesh will see together that the mouth of the Lord has spoken" (Isa. 40:5). God is here, in the world, as He was before the creation of the world and as He will be after the world ceases to exist. The difference lies only in our perception. When an individual person sees the revelation of the Divine, this constitutes his personal redemption. When the world sees it, it will constitute the collective redemption of the entire world. ☞ ☞

A GLIMPSE OF THE ULTIMATE REDEMPTION

☞ In *Likkutei Amarim* (chap. 36), the author of the *Tanya* explains that all the revelations that will happen in the future already happened when the Jewish people received the Torah. At Mount Sinai, their eyes were opened, and everyone merited seeing the Divine.

Similarly, at the very beginning of time, God spoke the world into being. These words continue to be spoken for all time and perpetually articulate every detail of reality into existence (see *Sha'ar HaYiḥud VeHa'emuna*, chap. 1). This is also true regarding the word of God in the Torah. The divine words of the Torah are essentially the way that God reveals Himself in the world. The verse attests that at Mount Sinai there was "a great voice that did not cease" (Deut. 5:19). This was the voice of God that did not cease to speak even after we left that mountain. It never ceases, continuing to speak until this day, continuing to reveal its secrets, the secrets of the Divine, though we as a people no longer hear it (see *Ba'al Shem Tov al HaTorah, Parashat Yitro*). The revelation at Mount Sinai was therefore a revelation from on high, a tearing open of the heavens for all to see.

When all of us will regain the ability to hear the word of God in the world and see "that the mouth of the Lord has spoken," this revelation will bring about the absolute exodus of the Divine Presence from exile and captivity. The cycles of exile and redemption will be no more. The entire world will be transformed from now and forever, and there will be an utter and total transformation of reality, an irreversible shift, in which everything will be different from what it was before.

PERSONAL REDEMPTION VERSUS COLLECTIVE REDEMPTION

☞ There is a difference between works of *halakha* and those of Hasidism that seems to be only one of style. Halakhic works uses phrases like "there is a difficulty" and "one

וְכֵן כָּל נִיצוֹץ פְּרָטִי מֵהַשְּׁכִינָה שֶׁבְּנֶפֶשׁ כָּל אֶחָד מִיִּשְׂרָאֵל יוֹצֵאת מֵהַגָּלוּת וְהַשִּׁבְיָה לְפִי שָׁעָה בְּ"חַיֵּי שָׁעָה" זוֹ תְּפִלָּה וַעֲבוֹדָה שֶׁבַּלֵּב. מֵעוּמְקָא דְלִבָּא, מִבְּחִינַת נְקוּדָּה הַפְּנִימִית הַנִּגְלֵית מֵהָעָרְלָה, וְעוֹלֶה לְמַעְלָה לְדָבְקָה בּוֹ בִּתְשׁוּקָה עַזָּה בִּבְחִינַת "לְמַעַן חַיֶּיךָ".

Similarly, each individual spark of the Divine Presence that is in the soul of every Jew leaves the exile and captivity temporarily during the temporal life that is prayer and the service of the heart from the depths of the heart, from the innermost point revealed from behind **the foreskin, and ascends on high to cling to Him with fierce longing, the kind that is "for the sake of your life."**

must question," while hasidic works uses phrasing such as "one must understand." On the surface, the meaning is the same. In both cases, a question is asked and an answer given. Yet the difference is significant. The wording "one must question" reinforces the question itself. The question becomes fixed as a reality: There is an inherent problem here, and it comes with certain solutions. When we come back to the same place, we will encounter the same question, and again it will challenge us, but this time we will know that there is an answer. By contrast, the phrase "one must understand" expresses another type of question and answer in which the answer does not just answer the question but nullifies it entirely, to the extent that after putting forth the answer, there is no longer a question.

For example, when we do not understand the meaning of a particular word, and afterward it is explained to us, the question no longer exists. The question has been refuted, and we will not encounter it again. In this light, a personal redemption is a question and answer of the first type, a question with an answer to follow. There is exile, and we know that there is redemption. We are in Egypt, yet we know that after four hundred years, we will leave. By contrast, the ultimate redemption will bring the concept of exile to a permanent end. After seeing that "the mouth of the Lord has spoken," the question regarding the true purpose of life no longer exists. As long as we sit in darkness, we must expend effort to know where must place our focus. But when we see it blatantly, the question dissolves.

Every personal revelation and redemption leave in their wake aspects of one's being that are still in the dark and have not yet been enlightened. As long as the revelation is not total, it is in a certain sense only superficial. It exists only in a certain slice of reality, while various circumstances cause that innermost point of the heart to be covered again. But at the ultimate redemption, when "God will remove the obstruction from our hearts," when we will see the Divine clearly and plainly, the revelation will be absolute, without any subsequent concealment. It will be an answer that is not followed by a question, redemption without another exile.

Every person can get a taste of the ultimate redemption and release from all *kelippot*, though this personal redemption is only temporary and the soul does not acquire it permanently. This redemption depends on heartfelt prayer, which the Talmud refers to as "temporal life."[15] Such prayer reveals the inner dimension of the heart, freeing it from all its trappings. At that moment, a person identifies fully with the inner dimension of his heart, which is the divine spark within. In the prayerful moment, when a person feels that God is literally his true life, his relationship with God is not with a separate, distant God but rather with a God who is deeply involved in his life, responsible for the inner source of his vitality. This is a glimpse of redemption, a taste of the ultimate redemption, which a person can experience during prayer.

וְהוּא גַּם כֵּן בִּבְחִינַת הֶיסַּח דַּעַת הָאָדָם. כִּי בְּחִינָה זוֹ הִיא לְמַעְלָה מִדַּעַת הָאָדָם וְהִתְבּוֹנְנוּתוֹ בִּגְדוּלַּת ה'.

This too is a suspension of a person's faculty of knowledge, **for this state transcends a person's knowledge and his contemplation of God's greatness.**

There is a level in the service of prayer and mindful contemplation in which one can cultivate love and fear that comes from conscious awareness. But here the author of the *Tanya* refers to a loftier level in which the emotional connection comes from beyond one's conscious intellect, beyond what a person can know and contemplate, a level that is essentially a leap beyond consciousness, a state commensurate with that of the ultimate redemption in messianic times. At this moment, a person stops thinking even about his relationship with God, because he becomes immersed in a state induced by the innermost point of his heart that transcends the cognitive realm. This entails a "suspension of knowledge" since the knowledge, the cognitive awareness, is surpassed to allow for a spiritual awareness that does not stem from any cognitive framework. It is the transcendence of all intellectual structures, of all barriers that separate between the innermost point of one's heart and God. At that moment, the seamless bond between the person and God is unearthed.

---

15. See *Shabbat* 10a, which states that prayer is called "temporal life" as opposed to Torah study, which is called "eternal life." See also *Likkutei Torah*, Deut. 42c.

רַק הִיא בְּחִינַת מַתָּנָה נְתוּנָה מֵאֵת ה' מִן הַשָּׁמַיִם

Rather, it is a gift from Heaven granted by God

When a person invests effort into his prayer, he can tap into internal wellsprings of love and fear of God simply through contemplating with "the exertion of the soul and the exertion of the flesh,"[16] by concentrating all one's thoughts and attention to the exclusion of everything else. But the revelation of the inner dimension of the heart cannot be earned through effort, because it is a gift. A person cannot claim a gift like he demands payment for work. Conversely, a gift does not depend on the work a person does. One does his job and earns his payment, and occasionally, irrespective of what he knows or understands, he gets an hour or a moment, of raw, unfiltered truth that God is literally his very life, that actually there is no other besides Him. At that moment, he experiences redemption.

מֵהֶאָרַת בְּחִינַת פָּנִים הָעֶלְיוֹנִים, כְּמוֹ שֶׁכָּתוּב: "יָאֵר ה' פָּנָיו אֵלֶיךָ" (במדבר ו, כה),

from the illumination of the divine countenance, as it is written, "The Lord shall shine His countenance toward you" (Num. 6:25),

When God suddenly turns to look at you and smiles, that is the gift of God's shining countenance. The revelation of the inner dimension of a person's heart depends on this revelation of the supernal countenance. In prayer, a person works toward encountering this innermost dimension within. He prepares himself to experience the depths of his being, and when God shines His countenance on him, then for that moment the innermost point of his heart awakens and manifests.

וּכְמוֹ שֶׁכָּתוּב: "וּמָל ה' אֱלֹקֶיךָ כו'" (דברים ל, ו).

and as it is written, "The Lord your God will remove the obstruction from your heart…" (Deut. 30:6).

In the time of the future redemption, it will be God Himself who will remove the obstructions from our hearts because of the subtlety and depth that this entails. The same is true during the "temporal life" that

16. See *Likkutei Amarim*, chaps. 30, 42.

is prayer. A person alone is incapable of achieving the extremely lofty experience of uncovering the innermost point of his heart, irrespective of how hard he works for it, yearns for it, and contemplates it. It is only God alone who can reveal that point and grant a person the possibility of truly connecting to it.

אַךְ מוּדַעַת זֹאת כִּי 'אִתְעָרוּתָא דִלְעֵילָּא' הִיא בְּ'אִתְעָרוּתָא דִלְתַתָּא' דַוְקָא,

But it is known that an awakening from above occurs **only through an awakening from below,** 11 Av

Although this illumination is a gift from above, or as the *Zohar* calls it, an "awakening from above," meaning that it is not a reward or natural consequence of a person's level or effort, it does not happen without some connection to what is happening below. A person cannot expect to be privy to this illumination without any preparation on his own part. Even a gift is given, to some degree, in response to a person's level and nature.

בִּבְחִינַת הַעֲלָאַת 'מַיִם נוּקְבִין', כְּמוֹ שֶׁאָמְרוּ רַבּוֹתֵינוּ ז"ל: "אֵין טִפָּה יוֹרֶדֶת מִלְמַעְלָה כו'" (זהר חלק ג רמז, ב).

referred to as **the rise of the feminine waters, as our Rabbis stated, "No drop** of rain **falls from above** without two drops rising from below" (*Zohar* 3:247b).

The kabbalists speak of raindrops that fall from above, referred to as "masculine waters," and the waters that ascend from the abyss below called "feminine waters."[17] When drops of rain fall into the water below, little water droplets splash upward, as it were, to greet the raindrops that are falling from above. This imagery provided by the *Zohar* implies that the water from below reaches up, beckoning the waters from on high to descend. This is how the world works, in both the physical and spiritual dimensions: All giving and influence from above depends on an awakening and receptiveness from below.

These words of the author of the *Tanya* appear in many other

17. See, e.g., *Etz Ḥayyim* 25:2, 29:2. Masculine implies giving, the waters that provide. This is the water that falls from above. The feminine attribute, on the other hand, is receiving. The waters from below receive the rainfall from the heavens.

mystical sources, that "an awakening from above is initiated through an awakening from below." A person can engender an awakening from below through his actions and receptivity, which primes him and the world to merit a divine response from above. ☞

וְלָכֵן צָרִיךְ הָאָדָם לַעֲשׂוֹת בְּעַצְמוֹ תְּחִלַּת מִילָה זוֹ, לְהָסִיר עָרְלַת הַלֵּב וּקְלִיפָּה הַגַּסָּה וְדַקָּה הַמַּלְבִּישׁוֹת וּמְכַסּוֹת עַל בְּחִינַת נְקוּדַּת פְּנִימִית הַלֵּב,

Therefore, a person must perform the first stage **of this circumcision himself, removing the foreskin of the heart and the coarse and thin membranes that clothe and conceal the innermost point of the heart,**

Despite God's promise to collectively circumcise the hearts of the entire Jewish people in the future, and despite the possibility of meriting an awakening from above during prayer that effectively removes the thin foreskin from the inner dimension of the heart, he himself must do everything in his power to remove that covering himself.

שֶׁהִיא בְּחִינַת אַהֲבַת ה' בְּחִינַת 'לְמַעַן חַיֶּיךָ'.

which is the kind of love for God that is "for the sake of your life."

There are various levels and ways in which a person may love God without the revelation of the innermost point of his heart. But when love of God is deep, to the extent that it is his very life, when a person

THE RISKS OF A FREE GIFT

☞ Occasionally people get free *Ḥesed*, though they may not deserve it. They merit a down payment of sorts, an illumination and special awakening that is not commensurate with their level at all. The problem with such an awakening is that a person is not ready for it, so he cannot sustain it. It does not have a lasting effect like an illumination for which a person prepares and reaches up to receive. The purpose of free *Ḥesed* is to grant a person an opportunity, to show him another dimension of reality. A person can live thirty or eighty years in the basement without any clue that there is another floor above his head, that there is a sky out there. Then one day someone up there opens a tiny window, and he sees the sky. He certainly will not retain that lofty vision, but he will keep something, a remnant of the memory. That remnant may inspire him down the road to embark on another journey, yet this time he will prepare himself for it. This is called the rise of the feminine waters.

feels that he has nothing else, that his whole life depends on it, this is the sign that he is connected to that innermost point of his heart. It may still be hidden, but it is certainly there.

שֶׁהִיא בַּגָּלוּת בְּתַאֲווֹת עוֹלָם הַזֶּה, שֶׁהֵם גַּם כֵּן בִּבְחִינַת 'לְמַעַן חַיֶּיךָ' בְּ'זֶה לְעוּמַּת זֶה', כַּנִּזְכָּר לְעֵיל.

That innermost point **is in exile amid the desires of this world, which are also "for the sake your life"** but **in** the impure **spiritual counterpart** to holiness, **as stated above.**

Every person has this intense love that he feels is bound up with the very definition of his life, but it is not expressed as love of God since the innermost point in his heart is held captive to the desires of this world. Everyone has things that he feels is the whole point of his life, those things that he feels he absolutely cannot give up, that without them his whole sense of self will be negated. When that feeling expresses itself in the desires and matters of this world, it is not being invested in love of God.

Every person, then, must extract the innermost point of his heart from other extraneous aspects of life and channel it into the true source of life on the side of holiness. This is the work of removing the foreskin from the heart, work that each person himself must do.

וְהַיְינוּ עַל יְדֵי נְתִינַת הַצְּדָקָה לַה' מִמָּמוֹנוֹ, שֶׁהוּא חַיּוּתוֹ,

This deep love for God may be revealed **by giving charity to God from one's money, which is one's life,**

A person's money constitutes his life, in a certain sense, both in terms of his effort, the degree to which he invests his body and soul in earning money, and because money holds value through which a person can acquire every worldly thing he may desire. When he gives money to charity with pure intentions, he essentially gives up his life for God. Although it is actually the poor person who receives the money, charity is intrinsically an act of giving to God because giving charity implies that the giver does not expect any recompense from anyone. This is what it means to give to God, donating to holiness, pledging one's money to that which is separate and distinct from all worldly matters and his own ego. ☞

וּבִפְרָט מִי שֶׁמְּזוֹנוֹתָיו מְצוּמְצָמִים, וּדְחִיקָא לֵיהּ שַׁעְתָּא טוּבָא שֶׁנּוֹתֵן מֵחַיָּיו מַמָּשׁ,

and particularly one whose income is limited and who is currently very hard pressed, for in that case **one is giving of his very life,**

When money is not important to a person, when he gives what he does not need, it is also considered charity, since he could have bought other things with that money. But this constitutes charity that does not touch upon the innermost point of his life. When a person's economic situation is incredibly pressed, and he himself needs the money that he is giving to charity, not for extras but for basic necessities, then he is literally giving a piece of his very life.

וּבִפְרָטוּת אִם נֶהֱנֶה מִיגִיעַ כַּפָּיו,

and particularly if he is sustained by the toil of his hands,

There is a difference between a person who toiled to earn his money and one who did not have to work so hard. Someone who inherited or received his money as a gift, or through financial assistance, will feel that that money is meant to be spent. A person who worked hard

CHARITY: GIVING TO GOD

☞ The tzaddik Rabbi Simḥa Bunim from Peshisḥa once lodged with one of his hasidim, an upstanding but destitute and tormented person. During his stay, the tzaddik made sure to feed and dress his host and fix his up house so that at least, on the outside, the situation would look better. Before he left, the tzaddik said that he wanted to give his host a gift. He claimed that he wanted to fulfill the mitzva of charity. The man was astonished. "Rebbe," he said, "everything you gave me was not enough?"

"Everything I gave you was for myself," the tzaddik answered. "I could not bear to see a Jew in such dire straits. My heart ached to see your suffering so everything I gave you was in order that I would feel better. Now that my pain has been assuaged, and I have indulged my sense of compassion – now that you have been fed and dressed and have some income – this is the time to give charity."

True charity is charity for God, and if it is not for God, if it fills another need other than charity, it does not constitute the ultimate fulfillment of the mitzva of charity.

to earn his money, investing his blood, sweat, and tears into his work, will feel that it is his very life.

שֶׁאִי אֶפְשָׁר שֶׁלֹּא עָסַק בָּהֶם פְּעָמִים רַבּוֹת בִּבְחִינַת נְקוּדַּת פְּנִימִית הַלֵּב מֵעוּמְקָא דְּלִבָּא, כְּמִנְהַג הָעוֹלָם בְּעִסְקֵיהֶם בְּמַשָּׂא וּמַתָּן וּכְהַאי גַּוְונָא.

for it is impossible that such a person **worked often** with his hands **without the innermost point of the heart, from the depths of the heart, as is the way of the world when** people are **occupied with business and such.**

When a person earns the money himself, he not only invests his time and energy but also his very soul. Whether he worked for it physically and emotionally, or enjoyed spiritual pleasure from the profit, he feels that his life depends on it. This money does not just hold exchange value. Every penny carries with it memories of the heartbreak and agony that accompanied the toil he invested to earn that penny. It is as if it took a piece of his soul. Therefore, when he gives that money to charity, he is literally giving his very life and soul.

וַהֲרֵי עַתָּה הַפַּעַם כְּשֶׁמְּפַזֵּר מִיגִיעוֹ וְנוֹתֵן לַה׳ בְּשִׂמְחָה וּבְטוּב לֵבָב,

Now, at this time, when he disburses the earnings of **his labor and gives to God with joy and a glad heart,**

This is an even higher level: to give without feeling pain over his loss, over the obligation to give, but rather wholeheartedly, with the joy of being able to fulfill the mitzva.

הִנֵּה בָּזֶה פּוֹדֶה נַפְשׁוֹ מִשַּׁחַת.

he thereby redeems his soul from the abyss.

The giving of charity to God is like giving ransom money to redeem one's soul from punishments such as Gehenna.[18]

18. This is in line with the concept "Charity saves from death." See also epistle 21 below.

דְּהַיְינוּ בְּחִינַת נְקוּדַּת פְּנִימִית לְבָבוֹ, שֶׁהָיְתָה בִּבְחִינַת גָּלוּת וּשְׁבִיָּה בְּתוֹךְ הַקְּלִיפָּה גַּסָּה אוֹ דַּקָּה,

This means he redeems **the innermost point of his heart, which was in a state of exile and captivity within the coarse or thin membrane,**

In a deeper sense, when a person gives of his very life, it does not only rectify the external aspects of his soul, its garments and faculties, but it also redeems the essential innermost point of his heart, of his quintessential being.

Although the verse tells us that God will remove the foreskin of the heart, a person himself must make an effort to release his heart from *kelippa*. When a person gives something, money or otherwise, to God, he should, to the best of his ability, disconnect himself from that thing in which he invested his soul and life, that which was until now his very life. He must do whatever he can to redeem his soul.

כְּמוֹ שֶׁכָּתוּב: "מִכָּל מִשְׁמָר נְצוֹר לִבֶּךָ". "מִשְׁמָר" פֵּירוּשׁ בֵּית הָאֲסוּרִים,

as it is written, "Above all else, safeguard [*mishmar*] **your heart"** (Prov. 4:23), where ***mishmar*** **may connote a prison,**

Generally, this verse is understood as a warning to guard one's heart more than one guards anything else.[19] But the author of the *Tanya* extrapolates this verse differently: A person needs to make sure that his heart does not become imprisoned.

There are various types of prisons. There is the prison of the reality of this world, and there prisons built from the desires and yearnings of the animal soul, all of which hold a person's innermost point confined to jail, preventing it from feeling the essence of its divine life force.

וְעַתָּה נִפְדָּה מֵהַחִיצוֹנִים בִּצְדָקָה זוֹ.

and now, the innermost point of the heart **is redeemed from the external forces** of impurity **through** the giving of **this charity.**

When a person gives charity in this way, the inner point of his heart is saved from that which is superficial and secondary to holiness, which includes all the pursuits of this world in which that point of his heart

19. See commentary of *Metzudot* there.

had been held captive. Giving charity is therefore an act that releases one's innermost being from servitude to his ego, from his own selfish desires, and effectively extracts the heart's innermost point from being bound to the transitory affairs of this world.

Generally, the reality is that people's hearts are split, "half for God and half for you."[20] The real question is not which half is bigger, but rather which part is more important. If the division is what is important is for me and what is unimportant I pledge to God, then one's heart is trapped in exile. When a person gives what is important to him to his Creator, even if he has not arrived at total redemption, he nevertheless breaks out of the prison.

וְזֶה גַּם כֵּן לְשׁוֹן פְּרִיעָה, עִנְיַן פְּרִיעַת חוֹב, שֶׁנִּתְחַיֵּיב וְנִשְׁתַּעְבֵּד לַחִיצוֹנִים שֶׁמָּשְׁלוּ בוֹ עַל נְקוּדַּת פְּנִימִיּוּת לְבָבוֹ.

This is another meaning of the word *peria*: **It connotes the repayment of a debt, since one had become beholden and enslaved to the external forces** of impurity **that ruled over him, over the innermost point of his heart.**

As explained above, there are two stages of circumcision: *mila* and *peria*. Both have significance in the context of the circumcision of the heart. The author of the *Tanya* explained one of the deeper meanings of the act of *peria:* removing the thin *kelippa* that covers the innermost point of the heart by giving charity. Here he offers another relevant interpretation of the word *peria*.

Every person creates his own unique angels of destruction,[21] which rule over the innermost point of his heart. A person who subjugated that innermost point to external things becomes indebted, so to speak, to those negative energies of concealment. When he gives charity, it is as if he has repaid his debt and is freed from their hold.

---

20. See *Pesaḥim* 68b; *Beitza* 15b, where Rabbi Yehoshua states that a festival is "half for God and half for you." One should enjoy the festival, eating fine foods and wearing fine clothes, but one should also devote time to prayer and Torah study. The author of the *Tanya* translates this into everyday life, but delineates the "half" that is for God as that which is essential to the person's life.

21. See Mishna *Avot* 4:11.

וְזֶהוּ "וְשָׁבֶיהָ בִּצְדָקָה" (ישעיה א, כז).

This is the meaning of the verse "Zion will be redeemed with justice, **and its returnees with charity**" (Isa. 1:27), quoted at the beginning of the letter.

The basic interpretation of this verse is that in God's righteousness, He will redeem the returnees of Zion. But the author of the *Tanya* reads this verse as saying that God will redeem the captives through charity. Thus the word *shaveha* can mean both returnees and captives, and *tzedaka* connotes both righteousness and charity. ☞

12 Av / 14 Av (leap year)

וְזֶהוּ "צֶדֶק לְפָנָיו יְהַלֵּךְ" (תהלים פה, יד). "לְפָנָיו" הוּא מִלְּשׁוֹן פְּנִימִיּוּת, וְ"יְהַלֵּךְ" הוּא מִלְּשׁוֹן הוֹלָכָה. שֶׁמּוֹלִיךְ אֶת פְּנִימִית הַלֵּב לַה'.

This, then, **is the meaning of "Justice will go before Him"** (Ps. 85:14). The word ***lefanav***, "before Him," **is related to the word *penimiyut***, inner dimension, **and *yehaleḥ***, "will go," **is related to the word *holakha***, to lead, conveying **that** the mitzva of charity, **leads the inner dimension of the heart to God.**

This answers the question posed at the beginning of the epistle: Why did the psalmist use the causative verb *yehalekh* instead of the simple verb form *yelekh*? The former is the causative of the verb, meaning to cause someone or something to go. Here the author of the *Tanya* concludes that the verse therefore can be read as saying that *tzedaka*, which can mean justice but in this interpretation connotes charity, draws the innermost dimension of one's heart to God.

REPAYING THE DEBT

☞ All charity that a person gives, even a mere penny, has value, since he decided that there is something more important than himself. Yet the true power of giving charity is unleashed when a person gives not just what he wants to give or what he is capable of giving, but what he feels that he owes himself and the external forces that he identifies with, that which he feels he cannot live without. When a person takes that which he feels he must have, that which he feels he cannot live without, and gives it to God, he is redeemed from his servitude to all those external forces. When giving reaches the point of pain, when a person breaks his nature, then his giving liberates him. He pays back what he owes the external forces of impurity and goes free.

וְאַחַר כָּךְ יָשִׂים לְדֶרֶךְ ה׳ פְּעָמָיו, **Then one may set his steps on the path of God,**

Until now the author of the *Tanya* focused on the first step: giving of that which represents one's very life. This leads to *peria,* uncovering the innermost point of the heart. This is the first step, akin to Naḥshon from the tribe of Judah jumping into the Red Sea before it split. It is impossible to begin walking if one does not first take the risk of falling. By trustingly jumping into unknown waters, one is privy to their splitting, to the breaking of the frameworks of prior obligations and routines.

When a person finds himself in exile and he feels good and comfortable there, he will never leave if he does not take that leap, if he does not take the first step despite not knowing what will be. Only then "may he set his steps on the path of God." Only then is it possible to begin walking, not only with one's innermost point of his heart, but with all his soul's faculties as well.

This does not mean that a person who gives charity, even in the most authentic way, will immediately experience the heavens opening and see divine visions. It could happen but may not. This letter highlights that without this deeply internal step, the heavens will certainly not open up. This relinquishing of what is truly important to a person's heart will open a door, and it is through this door that he can begin to "set his steps on the path of God."

כְּמוֹ שֶׁכָּתוּב: "וְהָלַכְתָּ בִּדְרָכָיו" (דברים כח, ט), **as it is written, "You shall walk in His ways"** (Deut. 28:9),

Attaining closeness to God is a path that a person must tread. There is no complacency when it comes to service of God. Even when on touches upon that deepest of places within, he must move on to the next stage: to walk in His ways.

"אַחֲרֵי ה׳ אֱלֹהֵיכֶם תֵּלֵכוּ" (דברים יג, ה). and **"You shall follow the Lord your God"** (Deut. 13:5).

This path is not always lit up with the light of God's countenance. It can also be a path that takes a person *aḥarei Hashem,* literally, "behind God," by way of the desert, a way that God may not illuminate. One could be on this path for a day, a year, or an entire lifetime. This is a path that one treads even when he does not see a purpose in what he is doing, even when he does not see or hear anything from the other side, yet nevertheless he walks the path anyway.[22]

בְּכָל מַעֲשֵׂה הַמִּצְוֹת וְתַלְמוּד תּוֹרָה כְּנֶגֶד כּוּלָּן,

This is accomplished **with all** acts of **mitzva performance, and Torah study is equal to them all,**

The author of the *Tanya* here mentions a concept from the Mishna:[23] that Torah study is the equivalent to the performance of all the commandments. A person merits to "follow the Lord your God" when he fulfills all the mitzvot he possibly can during his lifetime and when he studies Torah with every spare moment.

שֶׁכּוּלָּן עוֹלִין לַה׳ עַל יְדֵי פְּנִימִית הַלֵּב, בְּיֶתֶר שְׂאֵת וּמַעְלָה מַעְלָה מֵעֲלִייָתָן לַה׳ עַל יְדֵי חִיצוֹנִית הַלֵּב,

for the mitzvot and Torah study **all ascend to God through the inner dimension of the heart with greater intensity and reach far higher than their ascent through the external dimension of the heart,**

As the author of the *Tanya* explained elsewhere,[24] Torah study and mitzva performance without any accompanying fear and love of God do not ascend at all. The Torah study is still Torah study, the mitzva is still a mitzva, but if they are not performed with heartfelt intention, out of love and fear of God, they do not have as much of an impact. They remain in our world right where they were performed.

Furthermore, when a person walks on the path of God by the force of the love that stems from the innermost point of the heart, his mitzvot

22. See *Likkutei Torah*, Deut. 14d, where it is explained that the concept of *aḥarei Hashem* in the verse, which literally means "behind God," intimates the aspect of *aḥorayim*, the back side, which represents the world as the framework and background for the true purpose of the Creation, the fulfillment of mitzvot. By contemplating how all the worlds are only the back side and a glimmer of the divine light, the love of God is drawn down, which is conveyed by the term for walking, *halikha*. Thus the verse can be explained as saying that one exhibits love for God even when one walks behind Him (or on the back side).

23. *Pe'a* 1:1; see also *Likkutei Amarim*, chap. 37.

24. *Likkutei Amarim*, chaps. 38–41.

and Torah study ascend exponentially higher than if they were spurred by love that stems from the external aspects of the heart. ☞

הַנּוֹלָד מֵהַתְּבוּנָה וְהַדַּעַת לְבַדָּן, בְּלִי הֶאָרַת פָּנִים מִלְמַעְלָה, אֶלָּא בִּבְחִינַת הֶסְתֵּר פָּנִים,

which is engendered by understanding and knowledge alone without God's **shining countenance from above but rather with a concealed countenance,**

The intent of a person who performs the mitzvot with the external dimension of his heart is certainly authentic, but it does not engender the direct sensation of God's countenance shining on him from above. Rather, it stems from a feeling born of one's cognitive perception and

THE VALUE OF A MITZVA

☞ A mitzva is always a mitzva, whether performed with intent or without, even if a person was hardly aware that he performed it. The distinction between good and evil, between a mitzva and a sin, is not subjective but intrinsic. Even if a person does something good by accident, it is still considered a good deed. The difference between one mitzva and the next is in its power, in the extent of its impact. The more one's innermost being is invested in it, the greater its power.

Mitzvot (and transgressions) can be compared to exponential numbers. The exponent does not change the absolute value of the digit; it just increases its power. Similarly, one's intent does not change the absolute value of the mitzva; it simply increases its power to the next level. The deeper one's intent, the higher the mitzva goes and the greater the impact it has in all the worlds.

Above all, the loftiest level is when a person does something with the innermost point of his heart. Then his intent transcends even the highest level of awareness possible, where one's conscious intent can only attain a certain order of magnitude and no more. But when a person invests the deepest recesses of his heart into that which he does, his action ascends beyond any conceivable level.

The Ba'al Shem Tov would paint the following picture: A person who walks around the market all day forgets everything that is holy: God, the Torah, even the fact that he is a Jew. He walks around exhausted and overwhelmed, when suddenly he remembers, *It's time to pray the afternoon prayers!* Then he lets out one big sigh, lamenting his place in the world.

The Ba'al Shem Tov said that the highest heavens tremble from this sigh, since at that moment, he has touched upon the innermost point of his heart, therefore, the value of what he does in that moment is invaluably immense. It could be that he will not understand a word of the prayers that he will recite, yet his prayer will far transcend that of a learned person who understands all the words perfectly with all the meanings attributed to them by the Arizal. The simple intent that flows from the innermost point of his heart, that he infuses into all of his soul, is beyond any conscious perception and knowledge that comes from the external dimension of the heart.

understanding, from a place where God's countenance is concealed from him. When the divine countenance shines on a person, when a person is privy to see the Divine clearly, there is no need for the faculties of understanding and knowledge, for contemplation and reflection. One simply sees, face-to-face. Only when there is a concealed countenance, when a person does not see, does he need to cultivate his perception through intellectual means, through analyses and attainment of knowledge, which does not have access to the inner dimension of the heart to awaken it. Cognitive awareness operates only in the external dimension.

This is the deeper meaning of the verse "Justice [or charity] will go before Him." The type of intent that elevates all of one's Torah study and mitzva performance more than any intent that stems from the external dimension of the heart, is intent that comes from the innermost point of the heart through the giving of charity.

כִּי אֵין הַפָּנִים הָעֶלְיוֹנִים מְאִירִים לְמַטָּה אֶלָּא בְּאִתְעָרוּתָא דִלְתַתָּא, בְּמַעֲשֵׂה הַצְּדָקָה,

for the supernal countenance does not shine below without an awakening from below through an act of charity,

When a person gives charity with all his heart, he breaks the *kelippa* of his ego more than he could with any other mitzva and reveals his innermost point. In this way, he merits the illumination of the divine countenance from above.

הַנִּקְרָא שָׁלוֹם.

which is called peace.

When a person who has money gives to someone who lacks, he equalizes their status, making peace between them. This is one reason that charity is called peace. On a deeper level, charity is called peace because it reveals the intrinsic connection between one who is ostensibly superior and one who is inferior, which negates the disparity between them. At their essence, they are the same, and one is no better than the other.[25] The connection forged by the external dimension of the heart is, at most, a cease-fire, a temporary agreement and partnership of sorts, while the bond forged by the act of charity that awakens the internal dimension of the heart creates true peace.

---

25. See also epistle 12 below.

וְזֶהוּ שֶׁכָּתוּב: "פָּדָה בְשָׁלוֹם נַפְשִׁי" (תהלים נה, יט) 'נַפְשִׁי' דַּיְיקָא.

This is the meaning of the verse "He redeemed my soul unharmed" (Ps. 55:19)**, specifying *nafshi*,** my soul.

The author of the *Tanya* interprets this verse saying, "He redeemed my soul with peace," which refers to charity.[26] The word for soul, *nefesh*, has various implications throughout the Torah. In a general sense, it refers to the soul as opposed to the body, where the soul is the inner dimension of a person. In that sense, one redeems, or reveals, the soul through the act of charity. But the word *nefesh* can also connote the ego, the self.[27] Therefore, the verse implies that charity redeems the giver himself, not the recipient of the charity. One might assume that the verse is saying that when a person gives charity to a poor person, he redeems the poor man, yet the emphasis here is on the giver's soul, that he redeems the depths of his very own soul, the innermost point of his heart.

וְזֶהוּ גַּם כֵּן הַטַּעַם שֶׁנִּקְרָא הַצְּדָקָה שָׁלוֹם, לְפִי שֶׁנַּעֲשֶׂה שָׁלוֹם בֵּין יִשְׂרָאֵל לַאֲבִיהֶם שֶׁבַּשָּׁמַיִם, כְּמַאֲמַר רַבּוֹתֵינוּ ז"ל.

This is also the reason that charity is called peace: because through charity **peace is made between the Jewish people and their Father in Heaven, as our Rabbis stated.**

The act of charity creates an overall peace. As the Sages point out,[28] it creates peace not only between people down below, but also between the souls of Israel and God, since through the power of charity and the unleashing of the innermost point of the heart, the soul ascends from within the world to unite and connect with Him.

דְּהַיְינוּ עַל יְדֵי פִּדְיוֹן נַפְשׁוֹתֵיהֶן, הֵם חֵלֶק ה' מַמָּשׁ, מִידֵי הַחִיצוֹנִים,

This is accomplished **through the redemption of their souls, which are literally a portion of God, from the external forces** of impurity,

A person redeems himself from the captivity and subjugation of evil through taking something that is precious to him and giving it to God.

26. See also *Berakhot* 8a and Rashi there.

27. See, e.g., Isa. 44:20.

28. *Tosefta, Pe'a* 4:20.

At that moment, the soul, which was previously captive and subjugated to other forces, deeply and essentially connects to God.

וּבִפְרָט צִדְקַת אֶרֶץ יִשְׂרָאֵל,

particularly through **charity** given **for the Land of Israel,**

The particular charity on which this letter was focused was charity for the community in the Land of Israel. More specifically, charity was meant for the hasidic settlement led by Rabbi Menaḥem Mendel of Vitebsk, which the author of the *Tanya* hoped to fund and strengthen.

שֶׁהִיא צִדְקַת ה׳ מַמָּשׁ. כְּמוֹ שֶׁכָּתוּב: ״תָּמִיד עֵינֵי ה׳ אֱלֹקֶיךָ בָּהּ״ (דברים יא, יב); ״וְהָיוּ עֵינַי וְלִבִּי שָׁם כָּל הַיָּמִים״ (מלכים א ט, ג).

which is literally God's charity, as it is written regarding the Land of Israel, **"Always the eyes of the Lord your God are upon it"** (Deut. 11:12), **and "My eyes and My heart will be there always"** (I Kings 9:3).

The Land of Israel is special to God in the sense that His essence, represented by His eyes and heart, so to speak, are invested there, in contrast to the other lands, which receive their blessings from the more external aspect of God. This means that charity given to the poor people of the Land of Israel is considered "God's charity."

וְהִיא שֶׁעָמְדָה לָנוּ לִפְדּוֹת חַיֵּי נַפְשֵׁנוּ מֵעֲצַת הַחוֹשְׁבִים לִדְחוֹת פְּעָמֵינוּ,

This is what has stood by us to redeem the life of our souls from the schemes of those who wish to repel our steps,

This statement connects the concepts discussed in the letter to events that were happening in those days: the opposition to Hasidism and the slander and incarceration of the author of the *Tanya*.[29] The author is saying here that the merit of giving charity to the Land of Israel helped

29. As mentioned in previous letters. Moreover, when the author of the Tanya quoted the verse "He redeemed me unharmed," or "He redeemed my soul with peace," he was certainly referencing a part of the famous letter that he wrote to Rabbi Levi Yitzḥak of Berditchev when he was released from prison: "When I read…'He redeemed my soul with peace…,' I went out in peace…." See *Iggerot Kodesh*, letter 38; *Beit Rebbe*, vol. 1, chap. 18.

them in their struggle to establish the path of Hasidism as well and to redeem the inner dimension of Judaism that Hasidism had unearthed.

וְתַעֲמוֹד לָנוּ לָעַד, לָשׂוּם נַפְשֵׁנוּ בְּחַיִּים אֲמִיתִּיִּם מֵחַיֵּי הַחַיִּים, לֵאוֹר בְּאוֹר הַחַיִּים, אֲשֶׁר יָאֵר ה׳ פָּנָיו אִתָּנוּ, סֶלָה. אָמֵן כֵּן יְהִי רָצוֹן.

and it will stand by us forever, to infuse our souls with the true life that stems from the infinite source of life so that we may be enlightened with the light of life that God will shine on us from **His countenance,** ***Sela*. Amen, may this be His will.**

The author of the *Tanya* concludes the letter in the same way he started: with poetic words interspersed with verses from *Tanakh*. The phrase "infuse our souls with the true life that stems from the [infinite] source of life" inspires the reader to strive for a life that is connected to the source, the Giver of the gift of life, which is the only true life, as opposed to living a life in tandem with all kinds of pursuits that are not everlasting and are far from the source and therefore false. In light of this connection, a person merits living a life filled with God's shining countenance.

This epistle, written to the hasidim to inspire them to give charity, explains the deep meaning of the mitzva of charity, not from the perspective of the receiver, but rather from that of the giver. A person's spiritual work is essentially a labor of love. He strives to awaken love of God as the drive that powers his mitzva performance and Torah study, as the force that elevates his divine service and the person's very soul beyond the physical reality in which they were performed.

At its outset, the epistle explored the two aspects of love of God, external and internal. A person can tap into external love through contemplation and knowledge, but the revelation of the innermost point of his heart, is not within a person's reach. In a certain sense , it is only in the hands of Heaven. That being said, when a person does something below that exceeds his conscious faculties, such as giving charity, which literally slices off a piece of his soul, he can awaken the illumination of *Ein Sof* from above and thus reveal the innermost point of his heart and the infinite power invested in his soul.

Epistle 5

THIS LETTER WAS PROBABLY WRITTEN IN 1801 TO THE hasidic community at large to inspire them to give charity. Like the previous letters, it discusses the deeper significance of giving charity, but it expands on foundational concepts in hasidic thought more than previous epistles, concepts such as the nature of the Hebrew letters, human speech, the internal and external dimensions of the divine letters, the relationship between light and vessel, the essence of a name, and the relationship between the name and the thing itself. The author of the *Tanya* applies these concepts to a person's divine service, particularly to his Torah study and acts of kindness, explaining how these mitzvot draw the divine letters of God's name into this world of action.

"וַיַּעַשׂ דָּוִד שֵׁם" (שמואל ב ח, יג).

It is written, **"David made a name"** (II Sam. 8:13).

13 Av / 15 Av (leap year)

The simple meaning of these words imply that David made a name for himself because, as the verse goes on to say, he had demonstrated his might "upon his return from his smiting the Arameans in the Valley of Salt, eighteen thousand men." Here, however, the author of the *Tanya* interprets the verse according to the *Zohar*, connecting it to verses that follow in the same chapter.

וּפֵירֵשׁ בַּזּוֹהַר הַקָּדוֹשׁ: מִשּׁוּם שֶׁנֶּאֱמַר "וַיְהִי דָוִד עוֹשֶׂה מִשְׁפָּט וּצְדָקָה לְכָל עַמּוֹ כוּ'" (שמואל ב שם טו), "בָּכָה ר' שִׁמְעוֹן וְאָמַר: מַאן עָבֵיד שְׁמָא קַדִּישָׁא בְּכָל

The holy *Zohar* explains that this is related to **the verse "And David performed justice and charity for his entire people..."** (II Sam. 8:15), as the *Zohar* states (3:113b), **"Rabbi Shimon**

יוֹמָא? מַאן דְיָהֵיב צְדָקָה לְמִסְכְּנֵי" כו' (זהר ח"ג קיג, ב).

cried and said, 'Who makes the holy name every day? One who gives charity to a pauper....'"

The Hebrew word *asa* can mean both "made" and "performed." The *Zohar*, then, extrapolates that David "made a name" through "performing justice and charity for his entire people."

In light of this, it is not that David made a name for himself but rather that he made a name for God, as it were. The author of the *Tanya* goes on to explore what it means to make a name for God, what is the essence of a name in general, and the connection between making a name and "performing justice and charity." The answers to these questions comprise the contents of this letter.

וְיוּבַן בְּהַקְדִּים מַאֲמַר רַבּוֹתֵינוּ ז"ל עַל פָּסוּק "כִּי בְּיָ"הּ ה' צוּר עוֹלָמִים" (ישעיה כו, ד): בְּהֵ' נִבְרָא עוֹלָם הַזֶּה, בְּיוּ"ד נִבְרָא עוֹלָם הַבָּא (מנחות כט, ב).

This may be understood in light of the Rabbis' statement regarding the verse "For God the Lord is an everlasting rock" (Isa. 26:4). The Rabbis expound that **this world was created with the letter *heh,*** while **the World to Come was created with the letter *yod*** (*Menaḥot* 29b).

The name used for God in this verse is comprised of the letters *yod* and *heh.* The word for rock, *tzur,* is also etymologically connected to the word *yatzar,* to create or fashion, and the word for everlasting, *olamim,* also means "worlds." The Sages thus read this verse saying, "For with the letters *yod* and *heh,* God created worlds." He created this world with the letter *heh,* while the blueprint for the World to Come is the *yod.* ☞

THIS WORLD AND THE NEXT

☞ We are familiar with this world. It is the one in which we live, the reality in which we exist. We know much less about the World to Come. In the simple sense, the World to Come is a world that comes chronologically after this one, yet its nature is a matter of dispute (see Rambam, *Mishneh Torah, Sefer HaMadda, Hilkhot Teshuva* 3:8; Ramban, *Sha'ar HaGemul, Avodat HaKodesh* 2:41–43; see also epistle 17). The various opinions can be broadly categorized according to two approaches, that of Rambam and that of Ramban and the kabbalists.

All agree that the World to Come is a

פֵּירוּשׁ, שֶׁהַתַּעֲנוּג שֶׁמִּתְעַנְּגִים נִשְׁמוֹת הַצַּדִּיקִים וְנֶהֱנִין מִזִּיו הַשְּׁכִינָה

This means that the delight experienced by the souls of the righteous and the pleasure they derive from the radiance of the Divine Presence

Unlike in our world, the radiant splendor of the Divine Presence is openly revealed in the Garden of Eden, a radiance in which the souls who merit being there delight after a lifetime in this world. In the words of the Sages: "The righteous sit with their crowns upon their heads, enjoying the radiance of the Divine Presence" (*Berakhot* 17a).[30] ☞

fundamentally different realm of existence that follows the reality of our world. Not every opinion surmises that the World to Come is entirely spiritual, but all agree that the relationship between the spiritual and the physical therein takes on a whole new meaning, that it is on a different plane.

Defined broadly, the World to Come includes the Garden of Eden. While the realm of the Garden of Eden exists even now and is accessible to spiritually great people, every individual reaches this realm after death. The Garden of Eden can be summed up as the reward and outcome of a person's deeds while he was alive. When the author of the *Tanya* distinguishes here between this world and the next, he associates the Garden of Eden with the World to Come.

The Garden of Eden is not a particular place in the spatial sense so that souls must travel a certain distance to reach it. Rather, it is a place in the abstract sense, a divine revelatory experience in which particular phenomena take place.

We too use spatial terminology when referring to concepts. When we say that a particular idea "does not fit," we do not mean that it does not have enough room to squeeze into a given paradigm, but that it does not conform to our mental space. It does not contain enough of a logical or factual foundation to be accepted into our personal viewpoint. When we relate to the Garden of Eden as a place, we mean that it is such a fundamentally different realm from anything we know that it does not fit into our mental space. It is a particular level of soul reality in which the soul delights in the radiance of the Divine Presence, an experience that far transcends our familiar mindset.

THE REVELATION OF THE DIVINE PRESENCE

☞ There is no place, neither in this world nor in the next, that lacks the Divine Presence. There is no aspect of reality that is totally devoid of divine vitality. But there are differences in the degree to which the divine vitality is revealed. This world is a world in which the Divine Presence is inherently concealed. We see a table, a chair, a wall, but we do not see the radiance of the Divine Presence. Our world is a mate-

30. See also *Avot deRabbi Natan* 1:8; *Midrash Tehillim* 48:3.

הַמֵּאִיר בְּגַן עֵדֶן עֶלְיוֹן וְתַחְתּוֹן **that shines in the higher and lower** planes of the **Garden of Eden**

In a general sense, there are two levels of the Garden of Eden: the higher and the lower planes. Other sources explain that the expression "the higher and lower [planes of the] Garden of Eden" does not imply that there are two levels but rather that there are various levels of the Garden of Eden, one higher than the next.[31] Above the higher level of the Garden of Eden is an even higher edenic realm, and so on and so forth. This is how we understand the talmudic statement "Torah scholars have rest neither in this world nor in the World to Come" (*Berakhot* 64a; *Mo'ed Katan* 29a). Even in the Garden of Eden, Torah scholars ascend from one level to the next in their apprehension of Torah, not just one or two levels but endless levels, to the extent that they do not rest on any given level, because every level has another level above it.

הוּא שֶׁמִּתְעַנְּגִים בְּהַשָּׂגָתָם וְהַשְׂכָּלָתָם שֶׁמַּשְׂכִּילִים וְיוֹדְעִים וּמַשִּׂיגִים **consists of their taking pleasure in their intellectual apprehension** of the divine light. **They perceive, know, and apprehend**

"Intellectual apprehension" in the Garden of Eden indicates a deep apprehension with all the faculties of the intellect: wisdom, indicated by the fact that they "perceive"; understanding, conveyed by the term "apprehend"; and knowledge, intimated by "know." There are levels of apprehension wherein a person knows the details, can repeat the words, yet still does not fully understand. This is common in children but happens with adults as well. A person learns and reviews a piece of information, but when we check to see what he gleans, it turns out

rial one in which our principal experience depends on physicality. Even other, immaterial worlds are not privy to the revelation of the Divine Presence. For example, the Divine Presence is not openly revealed in the metaphysical world of mathematics. The Garden of Eden, on the other hand, is a realm built for the manifestation of the Divine Presence, whose whole purpose is to reveal how the divine essence was actually orchestrating every detail of our lives and each occurrence of this physical world.

31. See epistle 17 below.

that he does not have any idea what he is talking about. When there is no understanding or internal acquisition of the information, there is also no enjoyment of it. He may have other vague emotions associated with the knowledge, but he will only delight in the idea when he has a palpable understanding of it.

אֵיזֶה הַשָּׂגָה בְּאוֹר וְחַיּוּת הַשּׁוֹפֵעַ שָׁם מֵאֵין סוֹף בָּרוּךְ הוּא, בִּבְחִינַת גִּילּוּי לְנִשְׁמָתָם וְרוּחַ בִּינָתָם,

some degree of **apprehension of the light and life force that flows there from *Ein Sof,* blessed be He, as a revelation to their souls and their spirit of understanding**

Even the righteous in the Garden of Eden do not apprehend the full scope of the Divine Presence in all its glory. It is beyond human comprehension, even of that of the greatest tzaddikim. Apprehension in the Garden of Eden is restricted to what the author of the *Tanya* refers to as "some [degree of] apprehension," a limited glimmer tailored to every soul.

לְהָבִין וּלְהַשִּׂיג אֵיזֶה הַשָּׂגָה, כָּל אֶחָד וְאֶחָד לְפִי מַדְרֵגָתוֹ וּלְפִי מַעֲשָׂיו.

so they may understand and apprehend some degree of **apprehension, each one according to his level and according to his deeds.**

One's capacity for comprehension in the Garden of Eden depends on two factors: his spiritual level, which refers to the soul's nature and the degree of its perfection, and his deeds, which are a person's actions and the lifestyle he followed while in this world.

The first criterion implies the level on which the person's soul was created at its inception. Although the quintessential nature of every soul is equal, the extent to which each one reveals itself in nature differs. God creates different people on different levels. The higher the level of the soul, the greater its capacity for apprehension. ☞

THE SOUL'S LEVEL

☞ This begs the question that the Talmud attributed to Job: "Master of the universe, You created the ox with split hooves [making it kosher], and You created the donkey with closed hooves [making it forbidden]; You created the Garden of Eden, and You created Gehenna; and You created righteous people and You created wicked people" (*Bava Batra* 16a). Job is asking, "Why are some people created to be wicked and some are created to be righteous, just as You created some animals to be prohibited and some permitted?"

The author of the *Tanya* explains that this does not mean that God created some people wicked and others righteous. He did not make a stipulation regarding each individual and decide who would be righteous and who wicked. The intent is that each soul has a different capacity to become righteous and attain levels of holiness. Not all people are equal. Every person is born with a unique soul, and just as some are born with musical aptitude or mathematical acuity, there are also those who are born with an aptitude for holiness. Just as not every person who is born with musical sense becomes a famous musician, so too not every person who is born with an inclination for holiness becomes righteous.

The distance between a person's inborn spiritual level and the level he actually attains is what determines how much God delights in him, as it were. Moreover, the illumination that results is itself that person's reward in the World to Come. God makes people different from each other because He wants every person to be unique. He enjoys each one in a special way, different from everyone else who ever lived, lives, or will live.

Along similar lines, the author of the *Tanya* explains the deeper, timeless allusion of Isaac's request to Esau: "Prepare for me tasty food, such as I like" (Gen. 27:4; see *Likkutei Amarim*, chap. 27). The Divine Presence, represented by Isaac, asks this of her children, the Jewish people, represented here by Esau, as a whole and individually. The author points out that the Hebrew word for food, *matamim*, is in the plural, hinting at the two types of food that God enjoys, as it were: sweet and sharp or sour. Sweet food represents people who serve God with love and fear, who study Torah and perform mitzvot. These people bring God sweet delight. The second type refers to people who do not have love and fear of God and barely overcome their desire to sin. When these people serve God, they elevate their doubts, weaknesses, and desires as well. When they regret their wrongdoings, they even elevate their sins.

Take a person who can hardly read the Hebrew alphabet yet at every step overcomes the impediments of his life and fully develops his potential, giving God a deep sense of delight, so to speak. Then there is the person who could have accomplished so much yet failed to do so. God does not delight in this. If God wanted intelligence, he would have created hyperintelligent angels. If He had wanted people to be totally stripped of physicality and serve Him with every ounce of their being, He would have created another billion seraphim. But God wants humans, with all their internal struggles.

God wants something unique from every person that no other person can give Him. From this perspective, the potential delight a person like Moses generates and that of the lowliest person is absolutely equal if each does what God wants him to do. The accomplishment of a simple person who maximizes his potential is commensurate with the perfection attained by the greatest people of all time. People are like colors, like flavors, which contain equal value even though some are more impactful and others less. Each one is a totally unique reality and engenders a unique delight for God.

The Sages state that every tzaddik has his own canopy in the Garden of Eden so

The second parameter that determines a person's level in the Garden of Eden is his deeds during his lifetime. Although the essential power of the mitzvot a person performs in this world far transcends their personal effect on him, they do affect his soul and form spiritual garments around him.[32] The soul arrives in the Garden of Eden with that mitzva garment and through it receives and apprehends the radiant splendor of the Divine Presence.

For the soul, which is a creation, to enjoy the radiance of the Divine Presence, which is divine, it needs a medium that will bridge the gap and translate the holiness of *Ein Sof* into terms that it can grasp. Even after the soul separates from the body, the soul remains individualized, defined, and distinct, and no matter how spiritual and ethereal it is, it is limited by its own confines. The garment of a mitzva serves as the medium through which contact with the Divine is forged. This is what is meant by "according to his deeds": The apprehension and delight of the souls in the Garden of Eden are dependent on the mitzvot and good deeds a person did while alive. ☞

that each will not be burned by his neighbor's canopy (*Bemidbar Rabba* 21:22; *Bava Batra* 75b; see also *Torah Or* 32d; *Likkutei Torah*, Num. 35c). In the Garden of Eden, even more than in this world, every person has his own unique world, his own experience, different from that of every other person. In this world, despite the vast distance between each individual's unique experience of reality, a person can relate to that of another person. In the World to Come, every person gets his own unique World to Come that no one else can penetrate at all.

A MITZVA: THE ULTIMATE CONNECTOR

☞ The word *mitzva* is etymologically connected to *tzavta*, which means connection. Even in this world, the role of a mitzva is to be a vehicle for connection between the human world and the Divine, between limited beings and the infinite (see *Likkutei Torah*, Lev. 35c; *Sefer HaMa'amarim Melukat* 3:72). The difference is that in this world, where we perform the mitzva and forge the connection, we do not experience the divine light from the other side of the divide due to this world's opaqueness and inherent limitations. It is in the World to Come, where we can no longer create those connections, that we get to experience them.

The very obscurity of this world is an essential criterion that makes this world the place in which we perform the mitzvot: If we were to grasp the power of the

32. See *Zohar* 1:66a, 247a, 266a; epistle 3; *Sha'ar HaYiḥud VeHa'emuna*, chap. 5.

וְלָכֵן נִקְרָא עוֹלָם הַבָּא בְּשֵׁם בִּינָה בַּזּוֹהַר הַקָּדוֹשׁ.

Therefore, the World to Come is called *Bina* in the holy *Zohar.*

The Garden of Eden is the place where the soul perceives the Divine. This perception is such that the soul can delight in it. The World to Come is thus the place of *Bina,* of the attribute of understanding, the place where one truly comprehends and delights in this sublime awareness.

וְהַשְׁפָּעָה זוֹ נִמְשֶׁכֶת מִבְּחִינַת חָכְמָה עִילָּאָה, שֶׁהוּא מְקוֹר הַהַשְׂכָּלָה וְהַהַשָּׂגָה, הַנִּקְרָא בְּשֵׁם בִּינָה.

This flow of *Bina* issues forth from the level of supernal *Ḥokhma,* which is the source of the perception and apprehension called *Bina.*

Like the faculties of the soul, *Ḥokhma,* the *sefira* of Wisdom, is the level that precedes *Bina,* Understanding, so that it serves as the source of flow and illumination for *Bina.*

וְהוּא קַדְמוּת הַשֵּׂכֶל, קוֹדֶם שֶׁבָּא לִכְלַל גִּילּוּי הַשָּׂגָה וַהֲבָנָה, רַק עֲדַיִין הוּא בִּבְחִינַת הֶעְלֵם וְהֶסְתֵּר,

Ḥokhma **is the preceding state of the intellect, before it** is developed and **manifests as apprehension and understanding.** At that point, **it is still in a hidden, concealed state**

connection that a mitzva engenders, we would be incinerated. One's corporeal limitations are not capable of containing the light. His soul would not be able to continue existing within the confines of his body. To avoid getting burnt, to be able to perform mitzva after mitzva, one must do so from behind a screen, a barrier that protects him from being blinded by the light.

This echoes the words of the Sages "The reward of a mitzva is not in this world" (*Kiddushin* 39b). The reward of a mitzva, which constitutes the apprehension and experience of one's connection with God, is impossible to apprehend in this world at the moment of the mitzva's performance. This can be compared to metalworkers who must wear a thick mask when engaged in welding. Otherwise, they would be blinded by the glare of the flame. The welder's ability to do his work is dependent on his partial blindness so that he does not entirely see what he is doing. An inherent aspect of our existence in this world depends on a certain lack of awareness of the essential impact of the deeds we perform.

Ḥokhma is the unperceived stage that precedes understanding, like an idea before it becomes articulated as a rational thought. In this raw state, at the inception of comprehension, the intellect cannot be grasped. It is still concealed. But we can occasionally sense something. We can feel the flash of an idea inside us that we cannot wrap our heads around. We grasp only a glimmer of it. This feeling, which is not rational but rather is the very inception of clear comprehension, points to the hidden stage of *Ḥokhma*. ☞

רַק שֶׁמְּעַט, מִזְּעֵיר שָׁם זְעֵיר שָׁם, שׁוֹפֵעַ וְנִמְשָׁךְ מִשָּׁם לִבְחִינַת בִּינָה, לְהָבִין וּלְהַשִּׂיג שֵׂכֶל הַנֶּעְלָם.

but for a minuscule amount, a bit here, a bit there, that flows forth and is channeled from there to the faculty of *Bina,* so that one may understand and comprehend a hidden concept rooted in *Ḥokhma.*

ḤOKHMA VERSUS *BINA*

☞ In our normal cognitive processing process, we generally cannot distinguish between the stage of *Ḥokhma* and that of *Bina*, between that first flash of perception and comprehension. The process is too continuous, too quick, so that the idea that comes to mind is always a composite of both together (see *Zohar* 3:4a). Only on rare occasions, when the process is extremely slow, either because the topic is too heavy or because a person is in a foggy mental state, can one experience the transition between *Ḥokhma* and *Bina*. Then a person is privy to perceiving the flash of wisdom, in which he receives images and unformed ideas that do not yet have meaning. Between that stage and the one that follows, in which these images and ideas are crystallized, they undergo processing and analysis.

In other words, when a person apprehends something, it does not involve pure wisdom or pure understanding, just as there is no individual that is exclusively wise or insightful. The difference between the wise person and the insightful person is the degree to which these two faculties are more prominent in them. A person who lacks one of these stages entirely, so that he either cannot register new information or he is incapable of developing his ideas, most probably has some sort of cognitive disorder.

In the dynamic between *Ḥokhma* and *Bina*, *Ḥokhma* is the seed from which the process of awareness begins, but throughout the thinking process there are still axiomatic points that serve as litmus tests of truth, points of truth that originate from *Ḥokhma*. This is another aspect of the definitive function of *Ḥokhma*: It is the faculty that affirms the verity of a thought.

At the *Bina* stage, one can distinguish, through various cognitive measures, between what is right and what is wrong, but when he arrives at the root of the matter,

The content in *Ḥokhma* is hidden. Only a minuscule measure, like that of a needle point, is drawn down and threshed out through the faculty of *Bina.*[33] ☞

וְלָכֵן נִקְרָא בְּשֵׁם "נְקוּדָא בְּהֵיכָלָא" בַּזּוֹהַר הַקָּדוֹשׁ.

Therefore, *Ḥokhma* is called a "dot in the palace" in the holy *Zohar.*

The *Zohar* explains that *Bina* is the palace and *Ḥokhma* is the point in the palace.[34] *Ḥokhma* itself is a pure point, without any dimensions.

his ultimate assertion of truth, affirming what is real and what is not, must resonate with *Ḥokhma*. This clarity in determining what is right or good, whether in the intellectual arena or otherwise, belongs to the faculty of *Ḥokhma*. The appellation of genius in any field relates to a person's aptitude regarding his faculty of *Ḥokhma*, to his ability to perceive the truth with a bird's-eye view in one sweeping survey.

This is the person who in a split second can recognize a good business deal or a bad one, or the one who can instantly see whether the structure of a formula is correct or not. Of course, there are people in every field whose role it is to analyze these systems and break them down into intelligible units, into terms that everyone can understand. *Ḥokhma*, on the other hand, is inherently passive, and if a person lacks the ability to translate concepts into a comprehensible language, to transmit them from one dimension to another, this genius will remain at the stage of *Ḥokhma*, totally hidden and concealed.

A BIT HERE, A BIT THERE

☞ This unusual phrasing intimates constriction, the way the unformed flash of wisdom is constricted as it is analyzed and brought to light. Yet the phrase indicates that the hidden light of *Ḥokhma* does not undergo just one stage of constriction, on one level or dimension, but rather undergoes several stages of constriction on various levels, "a bit here, a bit there."

One implication of this is that the constriction is not a simple, straightforward devolvement from brilliant flash to concrete idea. Rather, it is a complex process that cannot be traced backward directly to its origin, that cannot be grasped by the faculty of *Bina*. Furthermore, the constriction and sculpting of the light of *Ḥokhma* does not distort or change it, but rather preserves the same relative perfection it possesses in its state of concealment. Throughout all the constriction and reduction, it retains its original pattern, always a ready receptacle to download more and more from its source on the level of paradigmatic *Ḥokhma*.

---

33. This phrase, "a bit here, a bit there," is from Isa. 28:10–13. See also *Likkutei Levi Yitzḥak* on the *Tanya*, p. 36, where this phrase is explained further.

34. See *Likkutei Torah*, Deut. 18b, citing *Zohar* 1:20a, 3:193b; see also *Torah Or* 41a.

It manifests within the palace and within reality as a point of contact, a nexus of congruence between the hidden source of the intellect and the thinking soul. In the process of understanding, where *Bina* is employed, this point progressively expands, shining its light more and more until it fills the palace.

וְזוֹ הִיא תְּמוּנַת יוּ״ד שֶׁל שֵׁם הֲוָיָה בָּרוּךְ הוּא,

This dot is reflected by **the shape of the letter *yod* in the name of *Havaya*,**

The four letters of the name of *Havaya* correspond to the ten *sefirot*.[35] Moreover, the Sages and kabbalists explain that the shape of the written letters expresses their essence.[36] The letter *yod* is closest to the shape of a point (it is actually impossible to draw a quintessential point) and so represents the point of *Ḥokhma*. The tips of the letter *yod*, protrusions that extend from the top and bottom of the letter, are extensions from the point of *Ḥokhma*, representing its ability to connect to other realities, above and below it.

וְנִקְרָא ׳עֵדֶן׳ אֲשֶׁר עָלָיו נֶאֱמַר: ״עַיִן לֹא רָאָתָה כוּ׳״ (ישעיה סד, ג).

and it is called Eden, of which it is said, "No eye has seen…" (Isa. 64:3).

The Garden of Eden has two aspects: garden and Eden, as the verse states, "And a river emerged from Eden to water the garden" (Gen. 2:10). There is Eden, there is a river that flows out of it, and then there is the garden that receives that river. The place where the souls bask in the radiant splendor of the Divine Presence is in the garden, while Eden, the hidden source of the vitality of the garden, is concealed, as the verse attests, "No eye has seen…."[37] Eden is the point of *Ḥokhma*, which is intrinsically incomprehensible. Only its effect, that which flows from it, can be grasped.

Until this point, the author of the *Tanya* has focused on the *yod* of the name of *Havaya* with which the World to Come was created. He

---

35. See *Iggeret HaTeshuva*, chap. 4.

36. See *Shabbat* 104a; *Zohar* 1:3a; *Pardes Rimmonim, Sha'ar HaOtiyot*; see also *Sha'ar HaYiḥud VeHa'emuna*, chap. 12.

37. See also *Berakhot* 32b, 63a.

has also described the relationship between the *yod* and the first *heh* of the name, with the relationship between *Ḥokhma* and *Bina,* also called "father" and "mother," which the *yod* and *heh* represent. Now the author will discuss the second part of the statement from the Midrash quoted above, the *heh* with which this world was created. Meaning, the relationship between the "father" and the "daughter," between *Ḥokhma* and *Malkhut,* between the *yod* and the final *heh* of the name.

וְנִקְרָא "אַבָּא יְסַד בְּרַתָּא" (זהר חלק ג רנו, ב).

Ḥokhma **is also called "the father who founded the daughter"** (*Zohar* 2:256b).

Ḥokhma is described here in terms of its relationship to the daughter, which is the *sefira* of *Malkhut,* which in turn corresponds with the final *heh* of the name of *Havaya.* The expression "the father who founded the daughter" is a kabbalistic rendition of the verse "The Lord founded the earth with wisdom, established the heavens with understanding" (Prov. 3:19). *Ḥokhma,* which is the highest level among the *sefirot,* as well as among the faculties of the soul, connects to the earth, the lowest, most physical level, while *Bina,* which is lower than *Ḥokhma,* corresponds to the heavens, the spiritual world above the earth. Ostensibly, the opposite should be true, yet lofty *Ḥokhma,* which is the origin of the intellect and can be grasped neither by the intellect nor by any conscious faculty of the soul, reveals itself particularly at the lowest level, the level of *Malkhut,* that of the lowly earth. In the soul, *Malkhut* manifests in the words and letters of speech, which emerge from within the soul outward.

To further explain the unique relationship between the father and the daughter, between *Ḥokhma* and *Malkhut,* the author of the *Tanya* delves into a deep and unique explanation of the nature of the Hebrew letters.

פֵּירוּשׁ, כִּי הִנֵּה הִתְהַוּוּת אוֹתִיּוֹת הַדִּבּוּר הַיּוֹצְאוֹת מֵה׳ מוֹצָאוֹת הַפֶּה אֵינָן דָּבָר מוּשְׂכָּל.

The meaning of this is as follows: **The formation of the letters of speech emitted by the five organs of articulation is not an intellectual process.**

The twenty-two letters of the Hebrew alphabet are formed by the five organs of articulation: the throat, the palate, the tongue, the teeth, and the lips. The process by which the letters emerge from their origin, the unique articulation of each one, is not rational. When a person speaks, he is unaware of what he does and why. He does not consciously think to himself that he wants to express certain letters instead of others, through particular organs of articulation versus others.

וְלֹא מוּטְבָּע בְּטֶבַע מוֹצָאוֹת הַלָּלוּ לְהוֹצִיא מִבְטָא הָאוֹתִיּוֹת עַל יְדֵי הַהֶבֶל וְהַקּוֹל הַמַּכֶּה בָּהֶן עַל פִּי דֶּרֶךְ הַטֶּבַע וְלֹא עַל פִּי דֶּרֶךְ הַשֵּׂכֶל.

It is also not inherent in the nature of these five **organs** for them **to articulate the** specific **sound of the letters by means of the breath and the sound that strikes them through** a **natural faculty nor by any intellectual process.**

There is no rational connection between the content of words and the letters that serve to express that content, nor is the expression of the letters a natural phenomenon that is ingrained in the organs of articulation, necessarily causing certain sounds instead of others to be expressed. The low of a cow is inborn in the cow. It creates a certain sound and not any other. A donkey does not sing like a bird, not because it does not want to but because its vocal chords are not made to create bird sounds. Likewise, the five organs of articulation of a human being produce the basic sounds that are natural to the human voice. By contrast, the words and letters that we vocalize and articulate using the organs of articulation do not stem from our hard-wired instruments of speech, but rather depend on our will, which is not confined to any biological principles.

כְּגוֹן הַשְּׂפָתַיִם עַל דֶּרֶךְ מָשָׁל, שֶׁאוֹתִיּוֹת בומ"ף יוֹצְאוֹת מֵהֶן, אֵין הַטֶּבַע וְלֹא הַשֵּׂכֶל נוֹתֵן לִיצִיאַת מִבְטָא אַרְבַּע חֶלְקֵי שִׁינּוּיֵי בִּיטּוּי אוֹתִיּוֹת אֵלּוּ, עַל פִּי שִׁינּוּיֵי תְּנוּעַת הַשְּׂפָתַיִם שֶׁמִּתְנוֹעֲעוֹת בְּהֶבֶל אֶחָד וְקוֹל אֶחָד הַפּוֹגֵעַ בָּהֶן בְּשָׁוֶה.

For example, concerning the lips, from which the letters ***bet, vav, mem,*** **and** ***peh*** **are articulated, neither the nature** of the lips **nor** any conscious decision of **the mind dictates the emission of the sounds of the four different expressions of these letters, in accordance with changes in the movement of the lips, which move by one breath and one voice that strikes them equally.**

The lips form these letters by molding the breath and simple sounds. The basic breath is the same with all the letters and changes only through the movement of the lips as it expresses the letters *bet, vav, mem*, and *peh*. But the shape of the lips as they formulate letters, the particular sound that emerges from the throat and causes the lips to take a particular shape, is neither rational nor physically ingrained.

וְאַדְּרַבָּה, שִׁינּוּי הַתְּנוּעוֹת שֶׁבַּשְּׂפָתַיִם הוּא לְפִי שִׁינּוּי בִּיטּוּי הָאוֹתִיּוֹת שֶׁבִּרְצוֹן הַנֶּפֶשׁ לְבַטֵּא בִּשְׂפָתַיִם כִּרְצוֹנָהּ, לוֹמַר אוֹת ב׳ אוֹ ו׳ אוֹ מ׳ אוֹ פ׳.

On the contrary, the change in the movements of the lips is determined by a change in the pronunciation of the letters that the soul desires to express with the lips according to its will, to pronounce the letter *bet* or *vav* or *mem* or *peh*.

The lips do not receive their direction from a later stage of intellectual processing, or even from an external biological urge. The shape of the letters themselves mirror the letters as they arise in the inner will of one's soul. There, in the inner will of the soul, the letters already exist and are but copied and pasted to the outside world through the mouth's organs of articulation.

וְלֹא לְהֵיפֶךְ, שֶׁיִּהְיֶה רְצוֹן הַנֶּפֶשׁ וְכַוָּונָתָהּ לַעֲשׂוֹת שִׁינּוּי תְּנוּעוֹת הַשְּׂפָתַיִם, כְּמוֹ שֶׁהֵן מִתְנַעְנְעוֹת עַתָּה בְּבִיטּוּיֵי אַרְבַּע אוֹתִיּוֹת אֵלּוּ.

It is **not the other way around, that the soul desires and** consciously **intends to make a change in the movement of the lips as they move now when these four letters are enunciated.**

The soul does not express the letters according to its wishes and intention, but rather the letters are expressed automatically according to internal templates that exist in the origin of the soul. ☞

וְכַנִּרְאֶה בְּחוּשׁ, שֶׁאֵין הַנֶּפֶשׁ מִתְכַּוֶּונֶת וְיוֹדַעַת לְכַוֵּין כְּלָל שִׁינּוּי תְּנוּעוֹת הַשְּׂפָתַיִם בְּשִׁינּוּיִים אֵלּוּ.

It is apparent from experience that the soul does not consciously **intend or even know how to direct a change in the movements of the lips according to these distinctions** between the letters.

THE EXPRESSION OF LETTERS

☞ Our speech is not a mechanical instrument that simply produces the sounds that it is built to make. In wind instruments, for example, the type and structure of the instrument cause the air blown into it to vibrate in a particular way, which determines the sound it produces. If speech worked in this way, the sounds of the letters we utter would be made in accordance with our intentions and thoughts, similar to the way a violin produces sound through the particular manner that the bow brushes against the strings.

Our speech works differently. It is not us who direct the speech but rather it stems from a place that is deeper than our conscious perception. When we speak, we do not think about the mechanics and structure of the formation of the letters. At most, we think about the content of what we are saying, while the letters, the instruments through which the content is conveyed, are formulated automatically. On the one hand, the enunciation of letters is not dictated by our physical linguistic apparatus, yet it is also not a direct outcome of rational thought. The articulation of letters is a creation in and of itself that does not stem from the conscious formation of letters but rather from deep in the subconscious.

There are two different mechanisms involved in the speech process, in the transmission of content from one phase to another, which work together with a certain degree of compatibility. One is the thought behind the content, which can be called the "light" of the concepts, and the other is that which activates the instruments of speech, or the "vessel" that expresses the concepts. These two mechanisms act, not as an outcome of one from the other, but as two distinct parallel operations. While there is certainly a connection between what a person thinks and what he says, it is not a simple, linear progression from thought to the letters of speech so that the speech merely expresses the words formed in thought. The letters of speech are in and of themselves rooted deeper than thought. Not only do the letters receive from the thought process in an almost mechanical fashion, but, as can be occasionally observed, the letters of speech also impact thought and soul, to the extent that even a thought that was not present in one's mind at all suddenly manifest itself in one's words.

This concept are more perceptible in writing than in speech. When a person records his thoughts in writing and compares that which he intended to say and that which he wrote, even in a short note, a discrepancy arises between one's thoughts and what ends up on the page. This applies even more to lengthy pieces of literature. The two, the processes of thought and expression through letters, do not work in complete tandem with each other.

The distinction between them has two facets. On the one hand, there is a certain diminution that results from the transition between one phase to the other. The transition from thought to speech causes some degree of loss of the facts, some level of distortion of the original. When pure thought transitions into the letters of thought, then from the letters of thought to the letters of speech, a process of constriction must take place. At every stage, the pure, unformed mass of content gets a more concrete, yet less faithful, expression.

Every person feels that it is impossible to fully express, in speech or in writ-

The author of the *Tanya* admits that this concept is difficult to understand but observable. A person is not aware of the actions he takes to express the various letters that he employs in his speech and writing, since this mechanism originates from a place deep within, beyond the intellect. He speaks, and the speech seems to activate the mouth, throat, lips, and so on.

וְיוֹתֵר נִרְאֶה כֵּן בְּבִטּוּי הַנְּקוּדּוֹת, שֶׁכְּשֶׁהַנֶּפֶשׁ רְצוֹנָהּ לְהוֹצִיא מִפִּיהָ נְקוּדַּת 'קָמַץ' אֲזַי מִמֵּילָא נִקְמָצִים הַשְּׂפָתַיִם, וּבְ'פַתָּח' נִפְתָּחִים הַשְּׂפָתַיִם, וְלֹא שֶׁרְצוֹן הַנֶּפֶשׁ לִקְמוֹץ וְלֹא לִפְתּוֹחַ כְּלָל וּכְלָל.

This is even more evident in the enunciation of the vowels. When the soul wishes to produce the sound of **the vowel** ***kamatz,*** **the lips automatically constrict, and for the sound of the** ***pataḥ,*** **the lips** automatically **open, and it is not that the soul** consciously **desires to constrict or open** the lips **at all.**

The Ashkenazic pronunciation of the *kamatz* and the *pataḥ* requires this constriction and opening of the lips, respectively. Thus the name of the vowel itself, *kamatz,* literally means to constrict, and *pataḥ* literally means to open.

ing, what he thought in the exact manner that he thought it. But there is another side to the discrepancy between speech and thought. Occasionally, when one tries to capture his thoughts in writing, it becomes clear that the words that emerge on the page are highly superior to his original thought. Sometimes, the difference is subtle; sometimes it is significant. Often a person discovers underpinnings behind what he wrote that were not noticeable in his initial thought. Sometimes the outcome is surprisingly better than what he expected, to the extent that the creator himself is shocked by his own creation.

We see that the speech process is more than a simple linear progression in which the pure, abstract thought progressively gets degraded, losing its subtleties, clarity, and inner content. The second mechanism, the mechanics that produces the speech and writing, operate in an independent way, not in a predictive, linear way: awareness, emotion, thought, speech. Rather, within the seemingly purely mechanical process of speech or writing, something new appears that was imperceptible in the intellect and thought, yet were obviously present in the will and origins of the intellect.

וְאֵין לְהַאֲרִיךְ בְּדָבָר הַפָּשׁוּט וּמוּבָן וּמוּשְׂכָּל לְכָל מַשְׂכִּיל, שֶׁמִּבְטָא הָאוֹתִיּוֹת וְהַנְּקוּדוֹת הוּא לְמַעְלָה מֵהַשֵּׂכֶל הַמּוּשָּׂג וּמוּבָן,

There is no need to go on at length about something so obvious, comprehensible, and sensible to any intelligent person, that the process of **enunciating the letters and the vowels transcends the** realm of **apprehensible, conceivable intellect.**

Other physical actions, such as hand gestures or the operation of machinery, happens according to one's plan. By contrast, when a person speaks and enunciates the letters, he expresses his inner self, his essence, whose source lies beyond the revealed faculties of his soul.

אֶלָּא מִשֵּׂכֶל הַנֶּעְלָם וְקַדְמוּת הַשֵּׂכֶל שֶׁבַּנֶּפֶשׁ הַמְדַבֶּרֶת.

Rather, it stems **from the hidden intellect and the origins of the intellect that is within the speaking soul,**

In conclusion, the root of speech lies in the "hidden intellect" of the soul, which transcends the conscious intellect. This is the point of *Ḥokhma,* the source of speech, which reveals a glimmer of the highest, deepest aspect of the speaker, a facet of his being that far transcends the outermost reaches of his conscious mind.

וְלָכֵן אֵין הַתִּינוֹק יָכוֹל לְדַבֵּר, אַף שֶׁמֵּבִין הַכֹּל.

which is why a small child is unable to speak, even when he understands everything spoken to him.

There is a particular age that a very young child understands that which is spoken to him yet still cannot speak. Although he has something to say and has reached the developmental stage necessary to produce all the sounds of speech and certainly expresses himself in other ways, he still cannot speak. Understanding speech and formulating speech do not necessarily go hand in hand. Formulating speech is its own enigma that stems from a very high level that young children have not yet reached. To attain this level, a child must arrive at a stage of spiritual development that is beyond the technical ability to speak. ☞

Until this point, the author of the *Tanya* has explained the axiom of the Sages regarding the verse "For God the Lord is an everlasting rock," employing the letters *yod* and *heh* to express God's name. The

THE ENIGMA OF SPEECH

☞ Although in a certain sense, speech is very simple, an action that does not have any independent content or meaning in and of itself, there is a mystery to these letters of speech, an element that is so lofty that it is not graspable through the conscious intellect at all.

Speech appears to be nothing more than a mechanical, neutral tool, while thought seems to be the creative engine that reveals the uniqueness of the human being. Yet the primary definition of a human being that distinguishes him from all other creations is "one who speaks." Clearly, speech is not just the mechanical ability to make particular sounds. A parrot too is capable of uttering such sounds, yet its status does not get upgraded to that of speaker. On the other hand, there are animals that, to the extent that we can evaluate them according to their behavior, have a fairly high level of intelligence, yet clearly this intelligence does not find expression in the spoken word.

Obviously there is a certain very defined shift between animal sounds and the concept of speech. The difference between them is more than just two distinct systems of meaningful symbols. The sounds that animals make are inborn, ingrained in their nature. These sounds sometimes convey some symbolic meaning but mostly express emotions. One can posit that the language of animals is a language almost entirely of interjections, almost completely without nouns. Human speech, on the other hand, not only as a medium of communication but as a medium for the expression of content, is a uniquely human act, rooted in a place that is higher than the cognitive process. The definition of humans as speakers, as articulators of symbols, concepts, and terms, is more of a distinguishing feature than their cognitive functioning because speech affiliates man's existence to a higher level than that of the rest of creation.

Clearly, there is a deep significance particularly to words, to the carriers of concepts, the basic symbols of speech. Words are not just instruments for transmitting content. Every word has a particular weight. The word or combination of words encompasses a certain direction of thought. Every so often, new words are even invented to allow for the expression of new content and novel understandings that did not exist before. In a similar vein, George Orwell relates in his book *1984* how to prevent an entire society from thinking "heretical" thoughts: By taking certain words out of the dictionaries and out of usage, the possibility of thinking related thoughts becomes impossible. Even if a person senses that something is not right, he does not have the words to express it, neither to others nor even to himself.

Again and again, it becomes clear how crucial are the words we use. The use of a particular word creates the possibility of thought to the extent that without certain foundational words in a given field, no idea can endure.

Sages learned from this that God created this world with the letter *heh* and the World to Come with the letter *yod*, which corresponds to *Ḥokhma*, which then informs *Bina*. The World to Come is the place of *Bina*, the phase wherein people bask in their apprehension of the radiant splendor of the Divine Presence. This world, on the other hand, created with the letter *heh*, signifies that *Ḥokhma* is embedded within it, since "the father founded the daughter."

Now he will go on to explain what is unique about the influence of *Ḥokhma* specifically in speech, unlike the influence of *Ḥokhma* in *Bina* and in the World to Come. What is this special effect that comes from such a high place and descends so low, into the physical letters of speech? What quality do these letters possess that they stem from such a high and hidden place?

אַךְ הָאוֹתִיּוֹת הֵן בִּבְחִינַת חוֹמֶר וְצוּרָה, הַנִּקְרָא פְּנִימִית וְחִיצוֹנִית.

However, the letters are comprised of matter and form, which are also **referred to as** their **inner and external dimensions.**

Letters, like most things in reality, are comprised of matter and form, which reflect the internality and externality of the letters. Form refers to the inner essence and content of a thing, while matter refers to the external structure, the material mass that takes on the thing's characteristics. A material like wood can take many forms: table, chair, board, or stick. The wood itself is also comprised of form and matter. The form is a composite of characteristics that comprise wood, its hardness, its flexibility and quality, and then there is the matter itself.

A letter, whether spoken or written, also has two facets. It has an extremely lofty aspect, which is what it represents. Letters have meaning, and combining them formulates a meaningful message. Then there is its mechanical framework, how it is actually articulated and in what format it exists, its actual sound, written symbol, and so on. ☞

MATTER AND FORM IN THE LETTERS OF THOUGHT

☞ Other sources discuss "letters of thought," since, not only do we speak with words, but we think in words and defined concepts (see epistle 19; *Likkutei Amarim*, chap. 20; *Sha'ar HaYiḥud VeHa'emuna*, chap. 11). The letters that formulate

כִּי הֲגַם שֶׁמְּקוֹרָן הוּא מִקַּדְמוּת הַשֵּׂכֶל וּרְצוֹן הַנֶּפֶשׁ, זוֹ הִיא בְּחִינַת צוּרַת שִׁינּוּי הַמִּבְטָא שֶׁבְּכ״ב אוֹתִיּוֹת.

Although their source is in the origins of intellect and the soul's will, that applies to **the form, the differences in the enunciation of the twenty-two letters.**

The form of the letters stem from the incomprehensible origins of the intellect. This is the inner, essential facet of the letters that separates them from each other and defines their uniqueness. This characteristic comprises the great wonder that is the mystery of speech. This enigma has the power to reveal intellectual apprehension, but is itself much loftier, being intrinsically incomprehensible.

אֲבָל בְּחִינַת הַחוֹמֶר וְגוּף הִתְהַוּוּתָן, וְהוּא בְּחִינַת חִיצוֹנִיּוּתָן - הוּא הַהֶבֶל הַיּוֹצֵא מֵהַלֵּב, שֶׁמִּמֶּנּוּ מִתְהַוֶּה קוֹל פָּשׁוּט הַיּוֹצֵא מֵהַגָּרוֹן.

But the matter and body of their formation, which is their external dimension, is the breath issuing from the heart, from which a simple sound is formed that emerges from the throat.

The matter of the letters, which bears all the forms of speech, is essentially the simple sound produced from the breath, the exhalation of air, that leaves the throat.

וְאַחַר כָּךְ נֶחְלָק לְכ״ב הֲבָרוֹת וּבִיטּוּי כ״ב אוֹתִיּוֹת, בְּה׳ מוֹצָאוֹת הַיְּדוּעוֹת אחה״ע מֵהַגָּרוֹן, גיכ״ק מֵהַחֵיךְ כו׳.

Then it is divided into twenty-two types of **pronunciation and expression of the twenty-two letters through the five known organs** of articulation: ***alef, ḥet, heh,* and *ayin* through the throat; *gimmel, yod, kaf,* and *kof* through the palate...**

a thought also have form and matter, yet their structure is more refined. Instead of apparatus like vocal chords or lungs, thought uses neuroelectric or neurochemical combinations that create the cognitive process at the physical level. In a deeper sense, there is also differentiation between form and matter in the spiritual world. On the one hand, there are particular templates that concepts fit into and patterns of thinking. On the other hand, there is the inner content that they express.

The movement of air, the basic sound that issues forth through the throat and the vocal cords, is then divided through the five organs of articulation, which each receive the basic sound, the matter of the letters, and formulate them into specific forms. The lips create the sounds of the *bet, vav, mem,* and *peh,* the tongue makes a *dalet, tet, lamed, nun,* and *tav,* and the teeth make *zayin, samekh, tzadi, resh,* and *shin.* The organs of articulation give form to the letter, while the matter of the letter is the sound, the simple breath that emerges from the throat.

וּמִבְטָא הַהֶבֶל הוּא אוֹת ה׳, ״אָתָא קַלִּילָא כו׳״ (פיוט ״אקדמות״),

The breath itself **is uttered by the letter *heh,* "a light letter,** lacking substance" (*Akdamut* liturgy),

The letter *heh* is nothing but exhaled air without the intervention of the organs of articulation, without the obstructions and variations placed on the basic sound of breath issuing forth from throat. Therefore, it is the letter without substance. The rest of the letters are uttered by obstructing that breath in various ways, while the enunciation of the letter *heh* is like the breath itself before it is otherwise articulated.

וְהוּא מְקוֹר הַחוֹמֶר וְגוּף הָאוֹתִיּוֹת טֶרֶם הִתְחַלְּקוּתָן לְכ״ב, וְלָכֵן אָמְרוּ רַבּוֹתֵינוּ ז״ל שֶׁעוֹלָם הַזֶּה נִבְרָא בְּה׳.

which is the source of the matter and body of the letters before they are divided into twenty-two, and therefore the Rabbis said that this world was created with the *heh.*

The sound of the letter *heh* is a basic form, the original form, of all letters, and so it is like the mother and root of all the other letters. This is why the Sages tell us that this world was created with the letter *heh*. This world is called the "world of speech" and speech is comprised of the structures and forms that the sound of the letter *heh* takes. It follows that the initial root of this world is one big breath: the letter *heh.*

וְהִנֵּה הֲגַם שֶׁהִיא ה׳ תַּתָּאָה, ה׳ אַחֲרוֹנָה שֶׁבְּשֵׁם הֲוָיָ״ה, וְרַבּוֹתֵינוּ ז״ל דָּרְשׁוּ זֶה עַל פָּסוּק: ״כִּי בְּיָ״הּ״,

Though this is the lower *heh*, the final *heh* in the name of *Havaya*, whereas the Rabbis taught that "this world was created with the letter *heh*" **based on the verse "For God** [*yod-heh*] **the Lord** is an everlasting rock," implying that the world was created with the first *heh* of the name,

The name of *Havaya* contains two *hehs*, the second and last letters. The first *heh* corresponds to *Bina* and the second to *Malkhut*. The aforementioned explanation of the letter *heh* being the source of the letters of speech refers to the second *heh* of the divine name. Yet the Sages' statement regarding the creation of the world with the letter *heh* of the name refers to the first *heh*, which follows the *yod* and receives vitality from it.

הַיְינוּ לְפִי שֶׁמְּקוֹרָהּ וְרֵאשִׁיתָהּ לָבֹא לִבְחִינַת גִּילּוּי מֵהֶעְלֵם הַיּוּ״ד, הוּא מוּשְׁפָּע וְנִמְשָׁךְ מִבְּחִינַת ה׳ עִילָּאָה.

this is because the source and origin of the final *heh* **progressing to a state of revelation from the concealment of the** ***yod*** **issues forth from the upper** ***heh*****.**

The answer to this question lies in the fact that all the letters of the name of *Havaya* reveal in various ways the primordial point of *Ḥokhma* concealed in the letter *yod*. It is not coincidental that two letters of the name of *Havaya*, the second and the last, are identical. In the teachings of Kabbala, the upper *heh* and the lower *heh* are mother and daughter, *Bina* and *Malkhut*. This implies that the vitality that flows from the *yod* to the final *heh* must pass through the first *heh*. The final *heh* is therefore a reflection and projection of the first.

שֶׁיֵּשׁ לָהּ הִתְפַּשְּׁטוּת אוֹרֶךְ וְרוֹחַב,

The form of the first *heh* **is an expansion** of the *yod* **in length and breadth,**

The four letters that comprise the name of *Havaya* are essentially three different letters, *yod*, *heh*, and *vav*. If one contemplates the shape of the written letters, one will find that the letter *yod* hardly has any dimension at all. It is a simple dot. The letter *vav* has the dimension of length, while the letter *heh* has the dimensions of both length and breadth.

לְהוֹרוֹת עַל בְּחִינַת בִּינָה, שֶׁהִיא הִתְפַּשְּׁטוּת הַשֵּׂכֶל הַנֶּעְלָם בִּבְחִינַת גִּילּוּי וְהַשָּׂגָה בְּהַרְחָבַת הַדַּעַת.

indicating *Bina,* which is the expansion of the hidden intellect into a state of revelation and comprehension, broadened with *Da'at,* Knowledge.

The *yod* is *Ḥokhma,* inherently incomprehensible and impossible to delve into or expand. It has just one graspable or ungraspable point. The first *heh* corresponds to *Bina,* the expansion of the hidden intellect into apprehension and understanding. Then comes a process of revelation and expansion called the expansion of *Da'at.* Expansion into the dimension of *Da'at* entails the spreading out to a realm that is not just intellect but also constitutes a rational connection to the emotional faculties of the soul, to the heart. ☞

וְהַשְׁפָּעָתָהּ מִסְתַּיֶּימֶת בַּלֵּב, וּכְמוֹ שֶׁכָּתוּב בַּתִּיקּוּנִים (יז, א): "בִּינָה לִבָּא וּבָהּ הַלֵּב מֵבִין".

The flow of *Bina* **culminates in the heart, as it is written in *Tikkunei Zohar*** (17a), **"*Bina* is the heart, and with it the heart understands."**

Beyond the mind-heart connection, the concept that "*Bina* is the heart" signifies a fabric of knowing that is more personal, affirming that it is particularly the faculty of *Bina,* as opposed to *Ḥokhma,* that forges the connection. *Bina*'s whole purpose is to reach the heart, to be the heart. This is the test of *Bina,* of whether a person truly

THE NAME OF *HAVAYA* AND THE PROCESS OF BECOMING

☞ The orthographic depiction of the written letters portrays their kabbalistic function: constriction, expansion, drawing down, and further expansion. The letter *yod,* the point, is the epitome of constriction, encompassing everything in one monodimensional, indivisible point. The *heh,* with its dimensions in breadth and length, expresses the movement of expansion and particularization. The letter *vav,* which looks like a line, expresses drawing down and transmission, and the final *heh* expresses another degree of expansion and spreading out.

understands: If one's heart wells up with emotion, then he truly comprehends. ☞

וּמִשָּׁם יוֹצֵא הַהֶבֶל מְקוֹר גִּילּוּי גּוּף הָאוֹתִיּוֹת הַדִּבּוּר הַמִּתְגַּלּוֹת בְּה' מוֹצָאוֹת

From there issues forth the breath, the original manifestation of the body of the letters of speech, which are manifest through the five organs of articulation

The physical dimension mirrors the spiritual: Physical air that comprises the breath emerges from the chest, from the heart, and passes through the mouth's organs of articulation, which sculpt the letters.

מֵהֶעְלֵם הַיּוּ"ד.

from the hidden state within the ***yod.***

This whole process of the formulation of the breath, the basis of the enunciation of the letters, stems from the hidden state of the *yod*, from concealed, supernal *Ḥokhma*. In contrast to the form, the internal dimension, which is bound to the point of *Ḥokhma* (the "father that founded the daughter"), the formulation of the matter, the external

BINA IS THE HEART

☞ The heart can only register *Bina*, not *Ḥokhma* – understanding and insight, not wisdom. *Ḥokhma* alone cannot be manipulated, projected, or applied and so cannot foster emotion. A person may experience the feeling of that flash of revelation created by *Ḥokhma*, but that feeling cannot be expanded upon or broadened. If a person encounters a wild animal, the first thing he registers is an awareness: This is a lion. But if that initial realization is not applied, it will not develop any further. He knows that he is facing a lion, period. Only when the repercussions dawn on him, when he considers that a lion is a dangerous, carnivorous animal that will likely attack him, will that initial point, that flash of awareness, forge an emotion, and only then will he feel frightened.

A person cannot create a relationship with something only by virtue of seeing it in his mind or with his eyes. If he does not understand it to some degree, it is meaningless. The image will pass through him without leaving an impression or manifesting in other faculties of his soul. More material is needed to create an association and to add a volume of meaning. *Ḥokhma* is that pure point of awareness in which all content is contained in one unified essence that cannot be broken down into structures and definitions. By contrast, the expansion of *Bina* allows for the creation of associations and emotions. Therefore, "*Bina* is the heart": It is specifically the effect of *Bina* that touches the heart.

dimension of the letters, emerges from a transitional process: from their hidden state in the *yod* (*Ḥokhma*), through understanding (*Bina*) and heartfelt emotion (the emotive attributes), until they are manifest as the letters of speech. The operations of physical speech resemble this process: The heart's function cultivates the movement of the lungs, which engenders the movement of air, which is the breath that is the source of the body of the letters.

וּתְמוּנַת ה׳ תַּתָּאָה בִּכְתִיבָתָהּ, גַּם כֵּן בְּהִתְפַּשְּׁטוּת אוֹרֶךְ וְרוֹחַב, מוֹרָה עַל הִתְפַּשְּׁטוּת בְּחִינַת מַלְכוּתוֹ יִתְבָּרֵךְ,

Like the first letter *heh,* **the written form of the final *heh,*** which **is also an expansion in length and breadth, indicates the expansion of God's kingship,**

The final *heh* of the name of *Havaya* expresses the attribute of *Malkhut* in that its shape contains both length and breadth, depicting the expansion of the divine illumination from the essence of the *sefirot* in the world *Atzilut* (which, in a general sense, is the level of *Ḥokhma,* the dimensionless point) into the created worlds.

מַלְכוּת כָּל עוֹלָמִים,

the kingship of all the worlds,

Malkhut expands throughout all the worlds in the sense that it sustains and enlivens every facet of every level of all the worlds.[38]

לְמַעְלָה וּלְמַטָּה וּלְד׳ סִטְרִין

above and below and in the four directions

These six directions are the dimensions of both the physical and spiritual worlds. The expansion of *Malkhut* to the six directions is what creates the dimensions of the world, its whole structure and character as we know it.

הַמִּתְפַּשְּׁטוֹת וְנִמְשָׁכוֹת מֵאוֹתִיּוֹת דְּבַר ה׳,

that extend and issue forth from the letters of God's speech,

38. As explained in *Sha'ar HaYiḥud VeHa'emuna,* chap. 7, all the created worlds exist through the divine attribute of *Malkhut,* in general and in all their details.

As the author of the *Tanya* explains in *Sha'ar HaYiḥud VeHa'emuna*, the letters of God's word in the ten utterances of Creation, in their various combinations and transmutations, create all the worlds. It is *Malkhut* and divine speech that creates and sustains all the worlds.

כְּמוֹ שֶׁכָּתוּב בְּקֹהֶלֶת (ח, ד): "בַּאֲשֶׁר דְּבַר מֶלֶךְ שִׁלְטוֹן", כְּמוֹ שֶׁנִּתְבָּאֵר בְּמָקוֹם אַחֵר.

as it is written in Ecclesiastes (8:4), **"Since governance is by the king's word," as explained elsewhere** (*Iggeret HaTeshuva*, chap. 4).

The word *malkhut* literally means governance, and the essence of governance depends on the "king's word," on the ability to disclose and transmit the king's wishes. Governance is not coercion. One can force people to do things on pain of death, but this is not *Malkhut*. The power of *Malkhut* and governance depends on the will and word of the king being performed, not through coercion, but rather through the transmission of the will in a way that those on the outside will resonate with it and be influenced. Governance is therefore an outcome of speech, of communication. When there is no communication, governance cannot happen. A person who cannot forge communication cannot rule. The whole point of governance is a clear and applicable external expression of the inner will. ☞

[וּלְהָבִין מְעַט מִזְּעֵיר עִנְיַן וּמַהוּת אוֹתִיּוֹת הַדִּבּוּר בֶּאֱלֹהוּת,

(With regard to understanding a small fraction of the concept and essence of the letters of divine speech

Here the author of the *Tanya* makes a general parenthetical comment about the analogy of physical speech and letters to divine speech and

SPEECH, *MALKHUT*, AND GOVERNANCE

☞ These are three facets, three different parameters, of the same thing. Speech is communication, governance is the message, and *Malkhut* is the outcome. Governance is the will that emerges outward, speech is the internal instrument of governance, the way in which the inner will emerges to the outside, and *Malkhut*, in the broad sense, is what we call the realm of action, the realm in which everything becomes actualized.

the ten utterances. The problem is not only with the analogy itself but also with its physical details as well: the air that emerges from the lungs, the vocal chords, the mouth's organs of articulation, the lips, the palate, and so on. The question is, how does all this physicality relate to the Divine?

שֶׁאֵין לוֹ דְּמוּת הַגּוּף וְלֹא הַנֶּפֶשׁ חַס וְשָׁלוֹם,

considering **that God has no physical or spiritual form, God forbid,**

How do these physical images apply to God, who does not have any corporeality at all? How can we apply such a physical analogy to the Divine?

The analogy of the articulation of the letters is presented here as a physical metaphor, but the author of the *Tanya* adds a comment to emphasize that divine speech, to which human speech is being compared, is ultimately incomprehensible, since "God has no physical or spiritual form." This is not just about the physicality of the letters, but also about the deeper aspects of the analogy, which are not particularly physical or material. God does not have anything that resembles a body, nor anything that vaguely resembles a soul. Just as it is forbidden for us to describe God in corporeal terms, it is forbidden to describe God as a spiritual entity. Spirituality, like physicality, follows particular principles and obviously cannot be attributed to the Divine. God fits neither into physical nor spiritual parameters since both are constructs of the created world, while the Divine is totally other.

The only justification to speak about God as spiritual is when we define "spiritual" as everything that is not physical. The truth is that we can equally define God as material if we define the word "material" as anything that is not spiritual. Either way, the salient point here is that God has neither a physical nor spiritual form, God forbid.

כְּבָר נִתְבָּאֵר בְּדֶרֶךְ אֲרוּכָּה וּקְצָרָה (בְּלִקּוּטֵי אֲמָרִים, חֵלֶק ב׳ פֶּרֶק י״א וְי״ב עַיֵּין שָׁם).]

it has been explained at length yet concisely [in volume 2 of *Likkutei Amarim*, *Sha'ar HaYiḥud VeHa'emuna,* **chaps. 11 and 12; see there].)**

The phrase "at length yet concisely," or, more literally, "in a long yet short way," echoes the wording that the author of the *Tanya* used in his introduction to *Likkutei Amarim*, which also applies to the second section of the *Tanya*, *Sha'ar HaYiḥud VeHa'emuna*. On the surface, this line seems to be a simple cross-reference to another place where these concepts are explained. Still, the author of the *Tanya* raises the question here and even adds the words "see there," since question is important with regard to the concepts presented in this letter. The author indicates that the reader should delve deeper into the question and study the concepts discussed there since the path to answering this question, the "long yet short way," passes through there. ☞

THE LETTERS OF DIVINE SPEECH

☞ The explanation of the question presented here, how God could be anthropomorphized, stands at the heart of this discussion. Not only in the question of how it is possible to employ these images at all, but also in the question of the limits of these metaphors and the correct way of employing them.

The basic assumption is that despite the immense distance and unfathomable difference between us and God, we do exist in the "image of God" (Gen. 1:27), as the verse states, "From my flesh I will view God" (Job 19:26). Therefore, we have permission to look inside ourselves and perceive therein a reflection of the Divine.

A person relates to the Divine like a symbol is related to its meaning. One is not synonymous with the other, but there is a certain relationship between them, like a mark that a person makes on a paper that expresses something, whether it is a musical note that represents a sound or a number that symbolizes a quantity, weight, or size. The musical note is not the sound, nor is numerical figure the quantity, but the symbol expresses what it symbolizes.

The use of symbols in abstract thought allows us to resonate with content to which we do not have direct access. But this connection is genuine only as long as we know that the symbol and the essence it represents are two different things. There is a risk that due to the extensive use of symbols, one may forget that they are only symbols, not actual realities. One can build ideas using symbols and make an association with symbols, as long as the relationship between the symbols and what they represent is preserved and the distinction between them maintained. Therefore, when we think and speak about symbols, it is important not to view the concepts merely as symbols, as the matter and form of speech in this case, but to attempt to see the connections necessary to follow the concepts through to their abstract truths.

We see that speech is comprised of two layers, matter and form, which correspond to three levels. The first level is the matter that comprises speech, the sound waves of vocal speech or the written letters in writing (which in the analogy of divine speech corresponds to the aspect of the "body" that comprises the reality of the world). The second level are the symbols that point to the essence of speech. They constitute the vessel that contains the abstract content. The third level is the actual content that is expressed through the symbols.

If we were to look at these things in hi-

אַךְ בֵּיאוּר הָעִנְיָן, לָמָּה אָמְרוּ רַבּוֹתֵינוּ זַ״ל שֶׁעוֹלָם הַזֶּה דַּוְקָא נִבְרָא בְּהֵ׳?

Now we must explain why the Rabbis stated that it was specifically this world that was created with the letter ***heh*:**

16 Av
17 Av (leap year)

erarchical order, from above to below, the highest level is that of the fundamental symbolic content, which emanates from the origins of the intellect. The next level is where the content reaches the level of *Bina*, so that the symbols can be organized into a form of expression. The lowest level is the mechanical instruments that express the content that these symbols represent to the outside.

Malkhut, which represents speech, is the lowest level of all of existence in a certain sense, since *Malkhut* can traverse realities. To cultivate a common denominator between realms, the simplest possible medium is needed. One person cannot convey his inner world to another without a medium that can carry his message, that can cross the chasm that separates between him and the other person. This medium must be something incredibly simple, such as a sound or ink blots on paper. On the other hand, there is another level to speech, which is its hidden essence, the system of abstract symbols that stem from a lofty level that transcends the soul.

This model explains the paradox pertaining to practical mitzvot to a certain degree, which is part of the overall paradox of "he who is big is small" (see *Zohar* 3:168a, 185a), that the lowest is actually the highest, that *Malkhut* is *Keter*, where the highest essence operates through physical action. One defining characteristic of speech is that very low forms express lofty symbols, occasionally so lofty that even conscious thought cannot probe their content. The mind can only combine them and relate them to each other. In this sense, the inner meaning of speech is bound to the initial point of all existence. This is the connection referred to as "the father founded the daughter," the point of *Ḥokhma* that creates the reality of *Malkhut.*

This paradox emerges from the intrinsic complexity of speech. Instead of one psychospiritual production line, there are two causal chains that create the essence of a word. One connection is the long and complex chain from *Ḥokhma* to *Bina,* from *Bina* to the emotions, from the emotions to the desire to express, and then actual expression. Every link must be activated for the word to reach the endpoint. The other causal chain is a direct link from pure supernal *Ḥokhma,* from the most initial basic awareness, to the spoken word. Since both connections exist, the spoken word can be the product of the order of progression, yet simultaneously include within it an immense amount of information that is not a product of that progression and appears in the spoken word after having skipped the whole progressive order above it.

Speech includes both facets: supernal *Ḥokhma* hailing from the origins of the intellect and the lowest physical matter. Both comprise the world in the broad sense, as well as the minutiae of our lives. Since the letters are actualized most in this world, and even more, since this world is comprised of the letters that originate in *Ḥokhma*, it is particularly in our world, which is the lowest of them all, that we can touch the point of *Ḥokhma*, the supernal root of all of existence that transcends all the worlds.

Since all the worlds were created with divine speech, from supernal letter combinations, it would make sense to say that all the worlds were created with the letter *heh*. Why did the Sages say that it was particularly this lowest and most physical of all worlds that was created with the *heh*?

הִנֵּה יָדוּעַ לְכָל חַכְמֵי לֵב כִּי רִיבּוּי הָעוֹלָמוֹת וְהַהֵיכָלוֹת אֲשֶׁר אֵין לָהֶם מִסְפָּר,

It is known to all the wisehearted that there are **a multitude of worlds and chambers,** so many **that** they **cannot be counted,**

Until now, the author of the *Tanya* has referred to a general division of the two worlds: this world and the next world, or the physical world and the spiritual world. This distinction is extremely loose and only relates to the simplest perspective of reality. We speak about insects in a similar way. There are hundreds of thousands of species of insects, each different and unique. But since we have nothing to do with them, we are not interested in the differences between them. Most people do not care how many joints a particular species has in its middle leg compared to the number of joints in another species' middle leg. These differences are not meaningful to our everyday lives. To us, they are all just bugs.

This is how we relate to the supernal worlds as well. Since we have nothing to do with them, nor the angels within them, we relate to them as if they are one homogenous entity. Yet occasionally we do need to relate to the infinite multiplicity within them and the unfathomably wide spectrum of variation found therein.

כְּמוֹ שֶׁכָּתוּב: "הֲיֵשׁ מִסְפָּר לִגְדוּדָיו" (איוב כה, ג).

as it is written, "Is there a number to His troops?" (Job 25:3).

The troops of angels parallel what is called the *heikhalot*, or chambers, on high. While both express spiritual realities, the two are not synonymous. "Chamber" relates to a spiritual world or space, while "troop" implies a *nefesh*, the being that populates that spiritual world. The troop or chamber define a backdrop or framework that encompasses a certain number of beings. Such frameworks resemble what we call fields, like the mathematical expression that defines a range of numbers to which specific mathematical laws apply.

וּבְכָל הֵיכָל וּגְדוּד אֶלֶף אַלְפִּין וְרִבּוֹא רִבְבָן מַלְאָכִים.

In each chamber and troop there are **thousands upon thousands and myriads upon myriads of angels.**

Other sources speak of God's countless troops,[39] but even still, in every troop there is a defined number of beings, if vast in number. At the end of the day, a troop is a parameter, a field, which means that the number of creations it contains is necessarily defined and limited. By contrast, the number of possible troops is infinite.

וְכֵן נֶפֶשׁ, רוּחַ, נְשָׁמָה, חַיָּה, יְחִידָה, מַדְרֵגוֹת לְאֵין קֵץ.

Likewise, the soul levels of ***nefesh, ruaḥ, neshama, ḥaya,*** and ***yeḥida*** are each comprised of **unlimited levels,**

There are myriad souls in every world and chamber. Moreover, the soul itself is not one undifferentiated entity but rather is comprised of five consecutive, fundamental levels that span from below to above,[40] from the energy that comes in contact with the physical body to the highest level, which is unified with *Ein Sof.* Every segment of this endless continuum is a complete unit in and of itself.

וּבְכָל עוֹלָם וְהֵיכָלוֹת מֵרִיבּוּי הֵיכָלוֹת שֶׁבַּאֲצִילוּת בְּרִיאָה יְצִירָה.

and there are likewise unlimited levels **in every world and** in all the **chambers among the multitudes of chambers that exist in** the worlds of ***Atzilut, Beria,*** and ***Yetzira.***

These are the spiritual worlds that exist beyond the world of *Asiya,* each containing an infinite multiplicity of beings. ☞

A MULTITUDE OF WORLDS

☞ Even our familiar world, the world of *Asiya*, with its physical and spiritual dimensions, has an unimaginable plurality of detail. The spiritual world of *Asiya* has a *heikhal*, a chamber, that we call music and includes all the facets of the musical di-

39. See *Ḥagiga* 13b.
40. See *Sha'ar HaGilgulim,* Introduction; *Sha'arei Kedusha* 3:2; *Likkutei Amarim,* chap. 2.

הִנֵּה כָּל רִיבּוּיִים אֵלּוּ, רִיבּוּי אַחַר רִיבּוּי עַד אֵין קֵץ מַמָּשׁ - הַכֹּל נִמְשָׁךְ וְנִשְׁפָּע מֵרִיבּוּי צֵירוּפֵי כ״ב אוֹתִיּוֹת דְּבַר ה׳, הַמִּתְחַלְּקוֹת גַּם כֵּן לְצֵירוּפִים רַבִּים עַד אֵין קֵץ וְתַכְלִית מַמָּשׁ,

All these multitudes, multitudes upon multitudes, which are **literally without limit, all issue forth and flow from the myriad combinations of the twenty-two letters** that constitute **the word of God, which are likewise divided into a multitude of sequences, to a literally infinite and endless extent,**

Though each world and realm has a defined boundary, the number of worlds is infinite. All these worlds, be they physical or spiritual, receive their existence and vitality from combinations of the twenty-two letters. Every detail of reality is the manifestation of a different, unique letter permutation.

כְּמוֹ שֶׁכָּתוּב בְּסֵפֶר יְצִירָה (פרק רביעי משנה יב): ״שִׁבְעָה אֲבָנִים בּוֹנוֹת חֲמֵשֶׁת אֲלָפִים וְאַרְבָּעִים בָּתִּים. מִכָּאן וָאֵילָךְ צֵא וַחֲשׁוֹב, מַה שֶּׁאֵין הַפֶּה יָכוֹל לְדַבֵּר״ כו׳.

as stated in *Sefer Yetzira* (4:12): **"Seven stones build five thousand forty houses. From here onward, go ahead and calculate that which the mouth cannot utter…."**

By way of analogy, *Sefer Yetzira* describes the way in which so many combinations are made from the twenty-two letters. It states there, "Two stones build two houses; three [stones], six houses; four [stones] build twenty-four houses; five [stones] build one hundred and twenty houses; six [stones] build seven hundred and twenty houses; seven [stones] build five thousand and forty houses…." The stones are a metaphor for letters, and the houses are words. "Two stones build two houses" indicates that two letters combine into two different

mension. There is also a chamber of mathematics, and so on. This is even more true in the spiritual worlds beyond *Asiya*, in *Yetzira*, *Beria*, *Atzilut*, and beyond.

To illustrate even further, in the scope of the physical world the size of the Earth is less than a particle of dust compared to outer space, and the size of the entire physical universe is smaller than a speck of dust relative to the spiritual worlds above it.

permutations to make two different words. Three letters can combine with each other in six possible ways to create six words. Seven letters can already create up to 5,040 different words, and so on and so forth.

Yet this formula calculates only how many permutations different letters can form together. When letters repeat and appear in different sequences, the number of combinations becomes so immense that it becomes virtually infinite and impossible to calculate to the extent that the mouth cannot express them.[41] ☞

INFINITE PERMUTATIONS

☞ The simple calculation of the *Sefer Yetzira* does not take into account all the layers of permutations in reality. Every letter and every letter combination has meaning and weight beyond the mathematical calculation presented above. There are foundational combinations and secondary combinations; there are direct connections and more distant ones. There is also significance to the sequence of the letters, to their origins and the associations that they have had in the past and will have in the future.

To illustrate, when it comes to certain compounds, it does not matter in which order the chemical formulae are written. There is no difference between NaCl and ClNa. Both are the same compound; their written form is only a matter of convention.

By contrast, there are chemical formulae, especially in organic chemistry, that have significance, not only in the number and amount of chemicals they comprise, but also in their sequence, in the way they are built. Different substances may be comprised of the exact same ingredients, in the same exact ratios, but since their ingredients are arranged differently, this results in two different substances. Moreover, two different substances may be identical in their chemical makeup yet different regarding their past, in the way in which they were created.

Another example: According to the rules of grammar, two words can be identical in form but possess different meanings because they come from two different roots. In this sense, permutations of letters are not arbitrary combinations of strokes and curves. The unique function of every letter, besides being counted among the twenty-two letters, is its unique placement in a given sequence or the way in which it the combination was reached: through exchanges, numerical values, or otherwise.

41. The phrase "that which the mouth cannot utter" appears in the Talmud, in *Shevuot* 20b. The *Sefer Yetzira*'s use of this phrase implies that the letters of speech being discussed do not resemble the letters of human speech. Divine speech cannot be even remotely encapsulated by the analogy of human speech, no less fathomed by the human mind.

וְהֲגַם שֶׁיֵּשׁ בְּמַעֲלוֹת וּמַדְרֵיגוֹת הַמַּלְאָכִים וּנְשָׁמוֹת כַּמָּה וְכַמָּה מִינֵי מַעֲלוֹת וּמַדְרֵיגוֹת חֲלוּקוֹת לְאֵין קֵץ, גָּבוֹהַּ עַל גָּבוֹהַּ,

Though among the degrees and levels of the angels and souls there are many different kinds of degrees and levels, an **unlimited** amount, **one higher than the other,**

When we speak of physical combinations, such as a number of chairs or a number of stones or stars, they can amount to an immense quantity. Yet each individual detail therein exists on the same level, on the same plane of existence. When we speak of spiritual realities, on the other hand, of angels and souls, they are differentiated into myriad entities, not only within the same plane of existence, but in many different layers of existence.

הִנֵּה הַכֹּל נִמְשָׁךְ לְפִי חִילּוּפֵי הַצֵּירוּפִים וְהַתְּמוּרוֹת

they all issue forth according to the substitutions, combinations, and conversions of the letters

As explained in *Sha'ar HaYiḥud VeHa'emuna,* the substituted letters are not the letters in their original form at Creation, but rather the letters of Creation after having undergone substitutions according to particular exchange systems. The original letters of Creation, which are the foundational forces through which the world was created, are the letters that comprise the ten utterances in Genesis. To enliven and sustain every one of the infinite creations in the endless places and times of existence, in both the higher and lower worlds, the original letters from those foundational utterances are substituted, particularized, and recombined.

בְּא״ת ב״ש כו׳ (וּכְמוֹ שֶׁנִּתְבָּאֵר בְּפֶרֶק י״ב).

through the letter-substitution system called ***at-bash*** **and so on (as explained in chapter 12** of *Sha'ar HaYiḥud VeHa'emuna*).

At-bash is one method of letter substitution, where the first letter of the Hebrew alphabet, *alef,* is exchanged with the last letter, *tav*. The second letter, *bet,* is replaced with the second to last letter, *shin,* and so on.

Every method of letter exchange holds different significance. How did a given letter reach its place in a given word? Through which exchange? The answers to these questions begin to shed light on the unique meaning of each new permutation, heaping additional significance on the fundamental significance of each letter on its own.

אַךְ דֶּרֶךְ כְּלָל, הִנֵּה כּוּלָּם בַּעֲלֵי חָכְמָה וְדַעַת,

But in general, beyond the variations and distinctions among them, **all** the angels and souls **possess wisdom and knowledge,**

It may seem that only human beings possess wisdom and knowledge, but the higher worlds also contain sentient, knowledgeable beings.[42]

וְיוֹדְעִים אֶת בּוֹרְאָם,

and they know their Creator,

The awareness of supernal beings is of God. They possess an immediate, unmediated perception of their Creator. ☞

KNOWING THE CREATOR

☞ This knowledge comprises, to some degree, the entirety of these beings' knowledge. Since they belong to lofty worlds that are transparent to the divine vitality that sustains them, they palpably feel it and are clearly aware of it. The existence of the Divine is not a distant idea that they speak of, nor does it come to them as the occasional epiphany, but rather it constitutes the very tangible reality of their lives. On the other hand, in contrast to human beings, these beings are incapable of relating to anything beyond their reality, their source, or their purpose. Although "they know their Creator," they do not know anything else and cannot perceive other facets of reality.

This applies not only to lofty creations that are subsumed in holiness, but also to the various harmful forces. The Talmud asserts that demons never say God's name in vain (*Megilla* 3a). Even though they are harmful, they cause man to commit sins only because that is their purpose, and they are unable to stray from this mission. They are devoted to their holy cause and are therefore unable to utter God's name in vain.

Similarly, the author of the *Tanya* explains elsewhere (*Likkutei Amarim*, chap. 24) that a human being can fall lower than any *kelippa*, than any force of impurity, when he transgresses God's will. Even though the harmful forces misled the person so that he would sin, they themselves

42. See Rambam, *Mishneh Torah, Sefer HaMadda, Hilkhot Yesodei HaTorah*, chaps. 2–3.

מִפְּנֵי הֱיוֹת חַיּוּתָם מִפְּנִימִיּוּת הָאוֹתִיּוֹת הַנִּמְשָׁכוֹת מִבְּחִינַת חָכְמָה עִילָּאָה, וְכַנִּזְכָּר לְעֵיל.

because their life force comes from the inner dimension of the letters, which issue forth from the level of supernal *Ḥokhma*, as stated above.

As explained above, there are two facets to the letters: an inner dimension and an outer dimension, which correspond to their content and form. Letters are physical entities, whether they are visible in their written form, audible as verbal speech, or virtually imperceptible as electromagnetic waves. These are the physical aspects of the letters, their outer dimension.

The inner dimension of the letters is the symbolic meaning behind them. Since the spiritual supernal worlds receive their vitality from the inner dimension of the letters, they do not need to contend with any obstructions posed by the letters' form. Their meaning and significance are transparent. For this reason, there are no opaque barriers between realms in these spiritual worlds. The connection between one level and the next is clear, and there is a clear transmission of messages from one world to the next. Every level and every being in every world can perceive the order of progression, of the transmission of existence from one level to the next. All these spiritual creations are able to clearly perceive the world above it, seeing all the way to the highest levels of existence. ☞

are incapable of transgressing God's will. It is man who possesses something unique, something that is rooted in *Ein Sof*, that allows him to ascend to infinite heights or plummet to infinite depths.

THE PERCEPTION OF THE DIVINE IN THE SPIRITUAL WORLDS

☞ The inner dimension of the letters parallels to a certain degree the realm of thought before it is articulated in the form of speech. There is a seamless connection between words of thought; they are not separated by external garments. The words that exit a person's mouth, on the other hand, often have an intrinsic concealment about them. Words can contradict each other and certainly hide the thought and the inner dimension of thought that was responsible for articulating them. But when a person thinks a thought, or even a fragment of a thought, it is still bound to the internal processes of the soul.

The abstract forms of letters of thought are connected to each other even though they are not identical, or even similar. There are no solid contours separating between them. All of them comprise one

18 Av (leap year)

אַךְ הָעוֹלָם הַזֶּה הַשָּׁפֵל, עִם הַחַיּוּת שֶׁבְּתוֹכוֹ, קָטָן מֵהָכִיל וְלִסְבּוֹל אוֹר וְחַיּוּת מִבְּחִינַת צוּרַת הָאוֹתִיּוֹת וּפְנִימִיּוּתָן, לְהָאִיר וּלְהַשְׁפִּיעַ בּוֹ בְּלִי לְבוּשׁ וְהֶסְתֵּר, כְּמוֹ שֶׁמְּאִירוֹת וּמַשְׁפִּיעוֹת לִנְשָׁמוֹת וּמַלְאָכִים.

But this lowly world, with its life force, is too small to contain and bear the light and life force of the form of the letters and their inner dimension. It is impossible for the inner dimension **to shine and issue forth** the light and life force **within it without any garment or concealment in the same way that they shine and bestow** light and life force **on the souls and angels.**

Since our world is lowly, limited in its ability to contain the light that is beyond it, it cannot directly register the message that the inner dimension of the letters transmits. It struggles to relate to the internal meaning of its own existence and is therefore compelled to use other, superficial forms, reminiscent of a translation.

A person may believe and think that he is connected, but it is all external. He is not connecting with actual spirituality, but rather with what he imagines in his being to be the spiritual realm. By contrast, souls and angels apprehend spirituality in a direct way, in the same way that we know that a table is a table. ☞

fluid field in which everything is connected to each other through a certain degree of causal connection.

Our physical world suffers from a type of disconnection. It seems to end at a certain point, and it appears that the only way to get beyond its outermost boundaries is by leaping. Since there is a disconnect between one world and the next, and there is no direct communication between us and the world above us, faith inherently demands a leap beyond reality's outermost limit, a limit that is impossible to scale by means of direct contemplation.

DIRECT APPREHENSION IN OUR WORLD

☞ There are many examples of things that we are incapable of registering through direct sensory perception and can only access through particular mediums of translation. Our visual faculty, for instance, is limited to specific wavelengths, beyond which we cannot see. If we want to perceive those wavelengths that are outside our visual spectrum, we need an instrument that will translate them into a picture that we are able to perceive. Of course, the translation process itself has inherent points of disconnect and obstruction that make direct transmission of the

רַק הַהֶאָרָה וְהַהַשְׁפָּעָה בָּאָה וְנִשְׁפָּע לָעוֹלָם הַזֶּה מִבְּחִינַת חוֹמֶר וְגוּף הָאוֹתִיּוֹת וְחִיצוֹנִיּוּתָם שֶׁהוּא בְּחִינַת הַ'הֶבֶל' הַמִּתְחַלֵּק לְשִׁבְעָה הֲבָלִים שֶׁבְּקֹהֶלֶת

Rather, the ray and flow of life force **comes and issues forth into this world from the dimension of the substance and body of the letters, their external dimension, which is the breath that is divided into the seven breaths** described **in Ecclesiastes**

Our lower world can register only the external dimension of the letters with which the world was created. The author of the *Tanya* refers to this dimension as the "breath." This is analogous to the exhalation of raw air that emerges from the lungs and passes through the five organs of articulation to form speech. Obviously this breath and the physical letters work in tandem with the symbolic, internal ideas that they carry, but the breath that enables speech is physical matter compared to the symbolic forms therein.

The breath of divine speech can be divided into seven general breaths. The Sages extrapolate these seven breaths from a verse in Ecclesiastes: "Futility of futilities, says Kohelet; futility of futilities, all is futility" (Eccles. 1:2).[43] The Hebrew word for "futility" is *hevel,* which also means breath. The Sages explain that the first appearance of the word *hevel* in the singular refers to one breath, the plural *havalim* hints at two, *hevel havalim* implies six, and the final phrase in the series, *hakol hevel,* makes seven.

message impossible. It must reconstruct and alter the original message in some way.

Another way of describing the limits of human comprehension is in the ability to apprehend something in the abstract. When a person has limited intellectual capability and is unable to understand deep abstract concepts, we must transmit such ideas through analogy and example. While there are people who can understand that adding two fish to two fish equals four fish, they are incapable of comprehending that two plus two equals four. When the idea is transmitted as symbols and numbers, it becomes too abstract. When the message deals with that which is beyond the physical, beyond the confines of this world, it also exists beyond the confines of human comprehension.

43. *Midrash Tehillim* 92; *Zohar* 1:146b, 2:10b.

שֶׁעֲלֵיהֶם הָעוֹלָם עוֹמֵד, כְּמוֹ שֶׁכָּתוּב בַּזּוֹהַר הַקָּדוֹשׁ (חלק א קמו, ב).

upon which the world stands, as stated in the holy ***Zohar*** (1:146b).

In this context, the word *hevel* from the verse in Ecclesiastes is not used as a metaphor for futility, as it is generally understood, but rather as a particular ubiquitous substance that sustains the world. This substance, upon which the materiality of the world stands,[44] is like nothingness, futile, compared to its innermost essence.

וְהוּא מוֹצָא פִּי ה׳ הַמִּתְלַבֵּשׁ בָּעוֹלָם הַזֶּה וְכָל צְבָאָיו לְהַחֲיוֹתָם.

This is the utterance **that emanates from God's mouth, which becomes clothed in this world and all its hosts to give them life.**

That which emanates from God's mouth, the source of divine speech, which is the source of the vitality of the worlds, is the simple breath. This expression, "that emanates from God's mouth," is borrowed from the verse "Man does not live by bread alone; rather, it is by everything that emanates from the mouth of the Lord that man lives" (Deut. 8:3). The Ba'al Shem Tov explains that it is not physical bread that gives a person life but rather that which emanates from God's mouth, the source of divine speech, of the ten utterances of Creation.[45]

וּבְתוֹכוֹ מְלוּבֶּשֶׁת בְּחִינַת צוּרַת אוֹתִיּוֹת הַדִּבּוּר וְהַמַּחֲשָׁבָה,

Within the breath **is clothed the form of the letters of speech and thought,**

Breath is nothing but the matter that enclothes the form, as in the letters of human speech. The form includes all the characteristics that the breath takes on when it expresses the letters, including the deep meaning that they symbolize. The same is true of the letters of thought, which comprise the inner dimension of the letters of speech. Within these letters too lies the form of the letters, their deep symbolic meaning.

---

44. See *Zohar* 1:146b, 2:10b; see also *Likkutei Torah*, Lev. 50d, Num. 12d.

45. *Keter Shem Tov* 18b; *Ba'al Shem Tov al HaTorah*, Deut. 8:3; *Likkutei Torah* of the Arizal, *Parashat Ekev* 96a; see also epistle 25; *Sha'ar HaYiḥud VeHa'emuna*, chap. 1.

מִמִּדּוֹתָיו הַקְּדוֹשׁוֹת, וּרְצוֹנוֹ וְחָכְמָתוֹ וכו׳,

which emanate **from His holy attributes and** from **His will and wisdom and so on,**

Divine speech, like human speech, stems from the emotive attributes. A person thinks and speaks when he has an emotional connection to something. The more a person loves or fears something, the more he thinks and talks about it. These emotive attributes stem from the higher levels in his soul, from his will and wisdom, which in terms of the *sefirot* correspond to *Keter* and *Ḥokhma*.

הַמְיוּחָדוֹת בְּאֵין סוֹף בָּרוּךְ הוּא בְּתַכְלִית.

which are unified with *Ein Sof*, blessed be He, in the ultimate union.

There is an absolute, seamless bond between God and His attributes, which applies to the inner dimension of the letters as well.[46]

In the physical sense, the breath of speech is a puff of air. A breath of air that could, for instance, cause a small wheel to turn. Yet it is not just any breath of air, since the significance of the breath of speech does not lie in its outward function, but rather in its inner purpose. It is an external instrument that transmits inner content. Every one of its oscillations carries with it a letter of speech. Therefore, although the external aspect of speech is totally physical, its inner dimension harbors the symbols of thought that can express love, awareness, and even the inner essence of the speaker.

The author of the *Tanya* now goes on to convey these concepts relating to the inner and outer dimensions of the letters in kabbalistic terminology, which will be meaningful to those who are familiar with these concepts. They can then connect the aforementioned ideas that were formulated in abstract (and to some degree new) language with the realm of kabbalistic concepts. This paves the way for the discovery of additional insights in other contexts.

(וְזֶה שֶׁאָמַר הָאֲרִ״י ז״ל: שֶׁבְּחִינַת חִיצוֹנִיּוּת הַכֵּלִים דְּמַלְכוּת

(This is the meaning of the Arizal's statement that the external dimension

46. As the *Tikkunei Zohar* states, He and His attributes are one." See also epistle 20.

דַּאֲצִילוּת, הַמְרוּמָּזוֹת בְּה׳ שֶׁל שֵׁם הֲוָיָה בָּרוּךְ הוּא, הֵם יָרְדוּ וְנַעֲשׂוּ נְשָׁמָה לְעוֹלַם הָעֲשִׂיָּה.)

of the vessels of *Malkhut* of *Atzilut*, represented by the letter *heh* of God's name of *Havaya*, descended and became a soul for the world of *Asiya*.)

The "external dimension of the vessels of *Malkhut* of *Atzilut*" is what is called here the breath of the letters of divine speech. As the author of the *Tanya* explained, this breath is what enlivens our world. In the language of the Arizal, it creates a soul for the world of *Asiya*.[47]

The illumination of the world of *Atzilut* sustains all the worlds below it: the worlds of *Beria*, *Yetzira*, and *Asiya*. Yet there is a difference between the world of *Atzilut* and other worlds: While the light of quintessential *Ḥokhma* shines in the world of *Atzilut* and permeates it, infusing its every level with vitality, the worlds of *Beria*, *Yetzira*, and *Asiya*, do not receive vitality directly from the level of *Ḥokhma*. Rather, the light of *Ḥokhma* is clothed in something called "the externality of the vessels." In the world of *Beria*, this external vessel is called *Ima*, in the world of *Yetzira* it is called *Zeir Anpin*, and in the world of *Asiya*, it is the *Malkhut* of speech. It follows that the "externality of the vessels" of *Malkhut* in *Atzilut*, which is the breath of divine speech, becomes the soul and life force of the world of *Asiya*.

The divine life force within the worlds is also called *Shekhina*, or Divine Presence.[48] The word *Shekhina* comes from the word *shokhen*, dwells, and refers to the aspect of the Divine that dwells within the worlds and sustains them, like a soul hidden deep within. That the life force of the worlds is called the "externality of the vessels" implies that this life force is not visible or felt tangibly in the worlds but rather is veiled and hidden, obscuring its inner essence so that only its external manifestations, the outcomes of its presence, are evident. Particularly in our world, the world of *Asiya*, the Divine Presence is so hidden that we can hardly sense the life force that vivifies every minutia of reality. We see only the many ways in which it expresses itself – in other words, its vessels. For this reason, the revelation of the Divine Presence in this

47. See *Etz Ḥayyim* 47:2.

48. See epistle 8.

world is extremely rare. Only in the Temple was the Divine Presence clearly revealed to all.[49] Today, only the most spiritually outstanding people are privy to it at certain auspicious times. ☞ ☞

THE EXTERNALITY OF THE VESSELS

☞ Every vessel has a dual nature: its inner aspect, or content, which is the purpose of its existence, and its external aspect, which facilitates the interaction between the vessel and the person who uses it.

The inner dimension of a pot, for example, is its function, the part of it that serves to contain its contents. Every other aspect of it is solely an outer shell. It is not intrinsic to its purpose but is there to serve as a framework for it. Even if we wanted to, we could not create a pot that is purely function, purely receptacle, because for it to exist in reality, its walls need to have substance. This substance is part of its externality, purely there to facilitate the pot's actual purpose. In this sense, the more physical and the more complex the vessel, the smaller its functional parts compared to the grand structure needed to achieve its purpose.

This is also true for abstract "vessels," such as words. Every word and letter has an essential component, an inner content, and an external component that is necessary for the transmission of that content. The more external its external aspect – the further it gets from its source – the more substantial and complex the vessels need to be and the more distant their relationship to the internal content becomes. One can express a big idea in ten words, but for that same idea to be transmitted to a broader, less initiated audience, more words are needed, and those words must be more external and distant from the crux of point. There could be only two truly relevant sentences among the string of words, but to deliver those two sentences, an entire complex structure must be construed. That structure, which is needed to sustain the vessel itself, is called "the external dimension of the vessels."

REVELATION FROM THE EXTERNAL VESSELS

☞ The Divine Presence, the divine life force that is within all things, is everywhere. It also "speaks" through the way in which it sustains every facet of existence. Yet in our world, it needs external avenues of expression. It cannot speak to us face-to-face because we do not understand its native language. It is therefore not revealed but hidden behind the "externality of the vessels."

Still, our world does have two principal avenues through which the Divine Presence can reveal itself: through miracles and through the tzaddikim (see *Sha'ar HaYiḥud VeHa'emuna*, chap. 5). The first happens by forcing matter to appear in a significantly different form. When matter transforms into extraordinary new forms in plain sight, it signifies the revelation of the Divine Presence. This is the definition of a miracle. The second way is when a person becomes transformed, when his eyes are opened and he sees that which is hidden.

49. See epistle 25; *Likkutei Amarim*, chaps. 51–53.

וְכֵן כָּתוּב בַּתִּיקּוּנִים (כג, א) שֶׁהַיּו״ד הוּא בַּאֲצִילוּת כו׳, וְה׳ תַּתָּאָה מְקַנֶּנֶת בַּעֲשִׂיָּה.

Likewise, it is written in *Tikkunei Zohar* (23a) **that the *yod* is in** the world of ***Atzilut* and so forth, and the final *heh* nests in** the world of ***Asiya*.**

Similar concepts are outlined in *Tikkunei Zohar*,[50] which states that each of the four letters of the name of *Havaya* manifests itself in one of the four worlds: the *yod* in the world of *Atzilut,* the first *heh* in the world of *Beria,* the *vav* in the world of *Yetzira,* and the final *heh* in the world of *Asiya*. This means that the final *heh* of the name of *Havaya* enlivens this world. This letter also corresponds to *Malkhut*

The book of Kings records a conversation between Elisha and his servant boy (II Kings 6:16). The boy sees the Aramean army and becomes frightened. Elisha says to him, "Do not fear, as there are more who are with us than who are with them." He then prays that God should open the boy's eyes. God answers the prayer and reveals to the boy that "behold, the mountain was full of horses and chariots of fire." The horses and chariots of fire were not created so that the lad would see them. They were there all along. He just could not see them. This is an example of a revelation of the Divine Presence through the opening of one's eyes, which is a change in a person's nature. This is in contrast to revelation through a miracle, which entails a transformation of nature itself.

Sometimes, both modes occur at the same time, as experienced at Mount Sinai. On the one hand, there was a compulsion of the physical, a change in the nature of the world, when God descended on Mount Sinai. Yet God also "drew us close to Mount Sinai" (as recounted in the Passover Haggada), signifying that a change had happened within the Jewish people, even if it was temporary, allowing them to see beyond their normal spectrum. Only afterward did God alter the nature of the world. That change lasted forever, while the change in the Jewish people was fleeting. This implies that God continues to speak those revelatory words in "a great voice that [does] not cease" (Deut. 5:19) with the same power and truth. We just do not hear it in the same way. There are, however, some people today who can hear the voice of God as clearly as they did at Mount Sinai, while others hear only a heavenly voice, an echo of an echo (see *Degel Maḥaneh Efrayim*).

In general, the reality of the world of *Asiya* is such that the life force is so embedded within it that most people do not see evidence of it at all. The soul of the world, the Divine Presence, is clothed within external vessels, in the matter and body of the letters and their external manifestations, in the breath of divine speech, symbolized by the final *heh* of the name of *Havaya*.

50. See also *Etz Ḥayyim* 42:4, 47:2.

and speech, as mentioned above, and more specifically, the breath and the external dimension of speech. This implies that the most raw and external aspect of divine speech is that which lends vitality to our world.

To summarize the concepts outlined here about divine speech, matter and form, breath and the content that is concealed within it, the worlds are comprised entirely of God's speech. God speaks to the worlds, and this constitutes their very existence. The difference between our world and the higher worlds, between this world and the next, is that while supernal creations residing in the higher worlds hear divine speech and glean something of its meaning, we in this world hear only noise. This is like a person hearing voices, but he cannot decipher their message. He may not even realize that these sounds are voices and therefore does not even attempt to interpret their meaning.

When an illiterate person sees a piece of paper with writing on it, he sees scribbles. He may notice that there is an order to the scribbles, that they are arranged in lines with spaces between them, but that is about all he sees. Generally, children pass this stage when they are three years old. A two-year-old just sees scribbles, while a three-year-old can already understand that these scribbles are expressing something. He does not yet know how to read, but he knows that there is some message being relayed.

Our world registers only the external contours of speech, the body and form of the letters, while the supernal worlds glean something of their inner content, their spiritual essence. Our goal in this world is to discern how the "noise" we hear and the "scribbles" we see are actually the word of God directed straight at us.

After the long explanatory introduction based on the saying of the Sages that this world was created with a *heh* and the World to Come with a *yod*, and the unique exploration of the nature of the Hebrew letters, the author of the *Tanya* returns to the practical message of the letter: to encourage the giving of charity.

17 Av / 19 Av (leap year)

וְהִנֵּה בְּאָדָם הַתַּחְתּוֹן לְמָשָׁל, מִי שֶׁהוּא חָכָם גָּדוֹל לְהַשְׂכִּיל נִפְלְאוֹת חָכְמָה וּמְצַמְצֵם שִׂכְלוֹ

With regard to mortal man, for example, when someone is a great sage, who is able **to perceive the wonders**

וּמַחֲשַׁבְתּוֹ בְּאוֹת אֶחָד מִדִּבּוּרוֹ - הִנֵּה זֶה הוּא צִמְצוּם עָצוּם וִירִידָה גְּדוֹלָה לְחָכְמָתוֹ הַנִּפְלָאָה.

of wisdom, and he constricts his intellect and thought into a single letter of his speech, that constitutes an immense constriction and a great descent for his wondrous wisdom.

When a person is able to apprehend ideas that are beyond most people, and he wants to express the depth and breadth of the lofty concepts that he is capable of apprehending, yet he cannot disclose the full scope of his thoughts but rather must constrict them to express a single point, a word, or a particular letter, that single word or letter is an unfathomable constriction compared to what the person knows. To illustrate this concept further, when a donkey brays, it expresses one sound, and through that one sound, it expresses the majority of its wisdom. Beyond that, it does not have much to say. Yet when an incredibly wise person, brimming with a treasure trove of wisdom, articulates one letter, it is an immense constriction. Instead of his wisdom manifesting in all its breadth and depth, it manifests as only one point.

כָּכָה מַמָּשׁ עַל דֶּרֶךְ מָשָׁל, וְיָתֵר מִזֶּה לְאֵין קֵץ,

So too, figuratively speaking, this is actually analogous, though to an infinitely greater extent,

That the analogy is "actual" means that we as human beings can indeed imagine a parallel in the familiar human realm. Yet it is only "analogous" since the analogy explains only a portion of the dynamic as it actually exists in reality. The difference between a letter of human speech and the power of his thought spans a huge distance, yet it is still conceivable. But when it comes to divine speech, the difference is so unfathomably great that we cannot possibly apprehend it.

הָיָה צִמְצוּם גָּדוֹל עָצוּם וָרַב, כַּאֲשֶׁר בִּדְבַר ה׳ שָׁמַיִם נַעֲשׂוּ בְּשֵׁשֶׁת יְמֵי בְרֵאשִׁית וּבְרוּחַ פִּיו כָּל צְבָאָם. הִיא אוֹת ה׳ שֶׁל שֵׁם הֲוָיָ״ה בָּרוּךְ הוּא, אָתָא קַלִּילָא,

to a great, powerful, and mighty constriction, when the heavens were created by the word of God during the six days of Creation and all their hosts by His breath. That is the letter *heh* of the name of *Havaya*, the "light letter* lacking substance,"

Everything that was created during the six days of Creation, from the higher realms to the lower realms, is nothing but God's breath. That breath constitutes the letter *heh* of the name of *Havaya*. This letter is called a "light letter, lacking substance." It has no specific sound that is articulated by any of the five organs of articulation but rather constitutes pure breath, the exhalation of air. While this breath encompasses the root of all letters, in and of itself it is formless, lacking the substance of even a single letter.

כְּמוֹ שֶׁכָּתוּב: "בְּהִבָּרְאָם" (בראשית ב, ד) - בְּה' בְּרָאָם (מנחות כט, ב).

as it is written, "This is the legacy of the heavens and of the earth **when they were created** [*behibaram*]" (Gen. 2:4). The Rabbis expounded, "Do not read it as *behibaram*, 'when they were created'; rather, read it as **'He made them with the letter *heh* [*beheh bera'am*]'"** (*Menaḥot* 29b).

We need to keep in mind that God's letter *heh* is not like the *heh* expressed by a human being. With extreme effort, a person can extinguish a flame by producing the letter *heh*, while God's articulation of the letter *heh* created all the worlds, with their endless levels. The analogy is meant only to illustrate the common denominator between them: Just as the *heh* that we articulate is but a tiny fraction of what we can say and do, and certainly a negligible degree of who we are, so too the *heh* of God, which is the source of the heavens and earth, is an unfathomably immense constriction and infinitesimally tiny expression of the totality of His divine speech, of what it can express and create, and certainly of His essence.

הִיא מְקוֹר הַתִּשְׁעָה מַאֲמָרוֹת שֶׁנִּמְשְׁכוּ מִמַּאֲמָר רִאשׁוֹן, "בְּרֵאשִׁית", דְּנַמִּי מַאֲמָר הוּא.

The letter *heh* **is the source of the nine utterances** of Creation **that flowed from the first utterance, "in the beginning," which is also one of the utterances.**

The Mishna teaches that the world was created with ten utterances, referring to the ten statements recorded in the first chapter of Genesis.[51]

---

51. *Avot* 5:1; see the commentary of Rabbi Ovadya Bartenura ad loc.; *Bereshit Rabba* 17:1.

The Talmud asks, "But is it not the case that the words 'and God said' appear only nine times in the story of the Creation?"[52] The answer is that the words "in the beginning" in the very first verse comprise one of the utterances.[53]

הִיא בְּחִינַת חָכְמָה הַנִּקְרֵאת 'רֵאשִׁית'. **It is the level of *Ḥokhma*, which is called the beginning.**

According to the mystical teachings, the first utterance, "in the beginning," hints at the *sefira* of *Ḥokhma*, the first *sefira*, which that is called *reshit*, first or beginning.[54] The two concepts are synonymous: Wisdom means beginning. ☞

The signification of the first utterance, "In the beginning…," as *Ḥokhma* appears in the Aramaic translation of the Jerusalem Talmud,

THE BEGINNING IS WISDOM

☞ The relationship between the first utterance and the rest of the utterances parallels the relationship between the *sefira* of *Ḥokhma* and the rest of the *sefirot*. The *sefira* of *Ḥokhma* is the seed, that initial flash of awareness that encompasses all the understanding and knowledge that will develop and manifest from it through the cognitive and emotional processes that follow. Similarly, the utterance "in the beginning" is the first utterance, the foundation, through which the entire world was created, while the utterances that follow only particularize and reveal all that it contains.

Just as a seed contains everything that will result in the full-grown tree, so too the word *bereshit*, "in the beginning," encompasses the entirety of the creation within it. Furthermore, just as the tree does not have the same shape and form as the seed and takes on forms that do not seem to have existed in the seed, creation works in the same way. The difference is not just in size; that at the outset, everything existed as a single point that afterward grew and expanded. That which lies latent in the seed is only a hint, a code of sorts, that directs the development of every detail of the creation. The code in the seed is an embryonic form of expression that must undergo many stages of de-

52. *Rosh HaShana* 32a; *Megilla* 21b.

53. The Talmud explains that although the words "and He said" do not appear there, another verse, "By the word of the Lord were the heavens made" (Ps. 36:6), signifies that the entire creation came into existence through God's word. Thus the entire Creation is encapsulated in that utterance. See also Ramban, Gen. 1:1; Rabbeinu Baḥya, Gen. 1:3; *Avodat HaKodesh*, vol. 4, chaps. 3, 4; *Degel Maḥaneh Efrayim, Beshalaḥ*; *Torah Or* 53a; *Likkutei Torah*, Num. 13a.

54. This is also inferred from the wording of the verse "Wisdom begins with fear of the Lord" (Ps. 111:10).

which renders these first two words of the Torah as "with *Ḥokhma* He created." The simple implication of this is that God used *Ḥokhma* to create the world, just as a person uses a hoe to till the soil. This implies an immense distance between God Himself and *Ḥokhma*. In man, wisdom is an internal faculty that most genuinely expresses his essence, while the concept of "with *Ḥokhma* He created" likens *Ḥokhma* to a physical instrument that expresses nothing of the essence of the one who wields it.

Yet the imagery of *Ḥokhma* as an instrument for the expression of God's will and for God Himself, through which He chooses to manifest Himself to create all the worlds,[55] is significant for the rest of the epistle. The main purpose of our existence and service in this world is to awaken God's will, to arouse His desire to descend and connect to His creative work, to wield His wisdom, so to speak.

אַךְ אָז הָיְתָה הַמְשָׁכָה וִירִידָה זוֹ בְּלִי אִתְעָרוּתָא דִלְתַתָּא כְּלָל, כִּי "אָדָם אַיִן לַעֲבוֹד כו'" (בראשית ב, ה),

But at that time, at the beginning of Creation, **this flow and descent** from *Ḥokhma* **occurred without any awakening from below at all, for "there was no man to till** the ground" (Gen. 2:5),

At the outset of Creation, there was *Ḥokhma*, which then manifest as divine speech. At this stage, there was not yet anyone to awaken God's will from below, and the creation of the world was manifest solely through an awakening from above. God gave Himself, from within Himself, without any connection to others or the needs of others.

velopment, many transitions and causes and effects, until it attains its ultimate defined forms.

While creation cannot invent something new that was not already contained in the seed, each of its elements has a unique and significant growth path, with various factors that cause the seed to sprout a trunk or a branch or fruits. The same is true of all the minutiae of creation: Each must undergo a particular path, certain stages of development, whose origin is contained in the nine particularized utterances of the six days of Creation.

55. Elsewhere it is explained that also this level, that of the will that fuels the initial flash of wisdom, is hinted at in the word *bereshit*, implying that the will, or the level of *Keter*, is above *Ḥokhma*. See *Sefer HaMa'amarim Melukat* 3:164.

רַק כִּי חָפֵץ חֶסֶד הוּא, **but rather** it occurred **only because He desires kindness,**

Generally, love has an object, a target. That object arouses the love, and that arousal from below brings about an awakening of love above toward that object. Yet there is a higher level of this attribute of *Ḥesed,* of love, coined by the early thinkers: "The nature of good is to bestow good." This refers to love that emerges on its own from the bestower of the love, irrespective of the object of his love. This level of supernal *Ḥesed,* of providing for the other without considering the receiver's mental state or life situation, is a level of love that overflows, that must reveal itself, not for any particular reason but only because "He desires kindness."

וְעוֹלָם חֶסֶד יִבָּנֶה. **and the world is built with kindness.**

At its outset, the world was created with *Ḥesed,* as a gift given out of love, not because it was requested by the receiver, not because it was awakened from below, for there was no one in existence to awaken it, but rather as a free gift.[56]

וְזֶהוּ "בְּהִבָּרְאָם", בְּאַבְרָהָם, **This is the meaning of** another interpretation of the verse "This is the legacy of the heavens and of the earth **when they were created** [*behibaram*]": The Rabbis read it as ***be'Avraham,*** through Abraham,

The letters of the word *behibaram* from the verse in Genesis can be rearranged to spell *be'Avraham,* implying that the Creation was in the merit of Abraham.[57] This idea, that the whole universe exists in the merit of a certain individual, appears several times in the teachings of the Sages. The implication is that God created an entire universe, with myriad creations, solely as a background for a single person, and this person justifies the existence of all those creations and worlds.

56. See Ps. 89:3; *Likkutei Torah,* discourses on Rosh HaShana 53d.

57. *Bereshit Rabba* 12:9.

כִּי "חֶסֶד לְאַבְרָהָם כו'" (מיכה ז, כ). **for** "You give **kindness to Abraham...**" (Mic. 7:20).

Abraham was the embodiment of the attribute of kindness. He represents that primordial attribute of divine *Ḥesed*,[58] and Abraham is therefore the tzaddik for whom the entire creation was initiated, as it were. The source of the universe was entirely *Ḥesed* that did not come about from the impetus of the receiver but rather from the giver's desire to do good. This was Abraham's attribute of kindness.[59] Abraham's *Ḥesed* pertains to every person. He does not check whether the receiver is worthy of receiving or how much.

Abraham's giving stemmed from his deep inner need to give and not from the lack of the other. The Midrash describes Abraham sitting at the opening of his tent and he is searching. Perhaps he will find some guest with whom he can perform the mitzva of hospitality. He welcomed in guests, not because they were hungry and knocking at his door, but because he himself suffered from a lack of guests.

A story reminiscent of the story of Abraham is told about the Sanzer Rebbe, Rabbi Ḥayyim Halberstam. The Rebbe never went to sleep without giving all his money away to charity. One day he was lying in bed, and he could not fall asleep. Finally, he called his shamash and said, "Search the house. It seems that there is some money left in the house that is preventing me from sleeping." The shamash indeed found a letter with money enclosed. As soon as he distributed the money, the Rebbe fell asleep.

What prevented the Rebbe from sleeping was not the lack of those in need but rather the money that he had not yet distributed to charity. It was due to a lack in himself, his own need to bestow good, because "the nature of good is to bestow good." This is the attribute that lies at the dawn of creation: *behibaram*.

Now the author of the *Tanya* arrives at the practical culmination of the epistle that connects all the aforementioned abstract concepts to their practical implementation in divine service.

---

58. See *Zohar* 1:264b, which states, "The attribute of *Ḥesed* said, 'As long as Abraham was in the world, I did not need to do my work; Abraham replaced me.'" See also *Sefer HaArakhim* 1, s.v. "*Avraham*."

59. See also *Torah Or* 12a.

20 Av (leap year)

אַךְ אַחַר בְּרִיאַת הָאָדָם, "לְעָבְדָהּ כו'" (בראשית ב, טו),

However, after the creation of man, who was created **"to cultivate it"** (Gen 2:15),

Man's mission "to cultivate it and to keep it" constitutes the whole purpose of his creation, and the creation of man is the objective of the entire creation. From now on, it is only man's work that awakens the original intent and design of creation.

אֲזַי כָּל אִתְעָרוּתָא דִלְעֵילָא, לְעוֹרֵר מִדַּת חֶסֶד עֶלְיוֹן, הוּא בְּאִתְעָרוּתָא דִלְתַתָּא

then any awakening above to awaken the attribute of supernal kindness occurs due to an awakening from below

While the initial impulse to create the world came from God Himself, from the force of His will, the relationship between God and the world became a mutual one. This reciprocal relationship means that everything is connected, that every action we do awakens a response from above.

Practically speaking, virtually every mechanism works within a framework that is based on this type of relationship. Even an ordinary pendulum clock operates through two forces working against each other: the driving force that moves it and the force that regulates and restrains it. The operation of the clock is an expression of the interrelationship between these two forces. Yet there is another aspect that is not related to this system. In order that this clock will begin to work, it must receive an initial impulse that necessarily comes from outside the system. Though a self-sustaining operation kicks in from the second moment onward, that first, singular moment stands alone.

This is how God operates the world. He contributes the initial spark of creation Himself because "He desires kindness" and "the world is built with kindness," yet from then onward, the flow of vitality depends on a mutual relationship between the higher and lower realms: an awakening from below and an awakening from above. ☞

THE SWING OF THE PENDULUM

☞ This dynamic is more complicated in the animate world and even more so among human beings. When it comes to a human being, who has a divine soul and who was the purpose for which the world was created, the question of where this dynamic begins is not so clear. Must the first movement come from above, or can it

Which action below awakens supernal *Ḥesed* above? Since an awakening from above does not manifest due to a sense of lack below, it is not awakened because a person says "I need" or "I don't have." While these expressions can awaken the kindness that preempts a free gift, so to speak, bestowed even on those who are not deserving, they do not spark the power of the primordial *Ḥesed* that issues forth the life force that sustains the world, that supernal desire to endow all *Ḥesed*, including the free gift. Like all the supernal attributes, it is awakened particularly through that which is similar to it. This means that when a person does something in the lower world, he arouses something similar in all the worlds. This is reminiscent of an idea that is taught in the name of the Ba'al Shem Tov regarding the verse "The Lord is your shade [*tzel*] by your right hand" (Ps. 121:5). The word *tzel* also means shadow. The Ba'al Shem Tov points out that a person's shadow mimics his movements: When he lifts his hand, so does his shadow. In the same way, God is like our shadow, reflecting back our actions, as it were. ☞

בִּצְדָקָה וָחֶסֶד שֶׁיִּשְׂרָאֵל עוֹשִׂין בָּעוֹלָם הַזֶּה.

through charity and acts of kindness that the Jewish people perform in this world.

All the blessings and sustenance that God bestows to this lower world, a world that is considered negligible to Him, is a bestowal of charity and kindness. Yet this bestowal of supernal *Ḥesed* is drawn down

also come from below? Furthermore, must the movement from below always be commensurate with the movement from above, like with a pendulum? Or is there a possibility, perhaps even an ideal, that it should come from a higher and deeper place, from that initial point of creation? This too is not clear. Not because we do not understand well enough, but because the answers seem to be beyond our ability to articulate in our minds.

GOD IS YOUR SHADOW

☞ The tzaddik Reb Zusha of Anipoli lived his whole life in intense privation. He once encountered a simple Jew, who was unaware of Reb Zusha's greatness yet saw before him an upstanding, modest, God-fearing yet extremely destitute Jew.

particularly through the acts of charity and kindness that a person does toward others who are poor and lacking. If people would not perform acts of charity and kindness below, even if they would study Torah and be meticulous about fulfilling the other mitzvot, supernal *Ḥesed* would not be drawn down to them from above.

לָכֵן אָמְרוּ רַבּוֹתֵינוּ ז״ל (יבמות קט, ב): כָּל הָאוֹמֵר אֵין לוֹ אֶלָּא תּוֹרָה, בְּלִי גְּמִילוּת חֲסָדִים, אֲפִילוּ תּוֹרָה אֵין לוֹ, אֶלָּא לַעֲסוֹק בַּתּוֹרָה וּבִגְמִילוּת חֲסָדִים.

This is why the Rabbis said (*Yevamot* 109b) that **anyone who says he has nothing other than Torah, without acts of kindness, he does not even have Torah. Rather, one should engage in** both **Torah** study **and acts of kindness.**

Granted, "Torah study is equal to them all" (Mishna *Pe'a* 1:1), and one who studies Torah is exempt from performing any other mitzva that others can do just as well. Yet one who says that he wants to only Torah to the exclusion of all else, asserting that performing acts of kindness is not for him, not only does not merit bestowing kindness on others but does not even retain his Torah study.

Every time he met him, the Jew would slip a few coins in Reb Zusha's *tallit* bag. After a while, this Jew saw that his business had become very successful, and with time, he amassed a large fortune.

One day, this Jew entered the synagogue and noticed that Reb Zusha was not there. He inquired about his whereabouts and learned that Reb Zusha had traveled to his Rebbe. This Jew said to himself, *If I have gained so much by giving charity to the disciple, I will certainly gain so much more by giving to the Rebbe.* Wasting no time, he traveled straight to Reb Zusha's Rebbe, the Maggid of Mezeritch, and gave him a large monetary gift.

Yet this time, the more he gave, the less he succeeded. He went to Reb Zusha in distress and demanded an explanation. Reb Zusha said to him, "It is very simple. Before, you saw an unfortunate Jew, and you did not inquire about who he was or whether he was worthy. You just gave. That is also how God behaved with you. He did not scrutinize you to see who you are and whether you were worthy. He just gave. Now that you have started checking, God is also checking!"

There were people who intentionally were not exacting in their giving of charity and gave to poor people whom they knew were not deserving with the same thing in mind: that God treat them in the same fashion.

כִּי הִנֵּה הֲגַם דְּאוֹרַיְיתָא מֵחָכְמָה נָפְקַת, וּבְאוֹרַיְיתָא מִתְקַיֵּים עָלְמָא, וּבְאִינוּן דְּלָעָאן בָּהּ, כִּי בְּדִבּוּרָם מַמְשִׁיכִים הֶאָרוֹת וְהַשְׁפָּעוֹת (נוּסָּח אַחֵר: וְהַשְׁרָאוֹת) חָכְמָה עִילָּאָה, מְקוֹר הַתּוֹרָה, לִבְחִינַת אוֹתִיּוֹת הַדִּבּוּר שֶׁבָּהֶן נִבְרָא הָעוֹלָם, כְּמַאֲמַר רַבּוֹתֵינוּ ז"ל: "אַל תִּקְרֵי בָּנַיִךְ אֶלָּא בּוֹנָיִךְ" (ברכות סד, א),

Although the Torah stems from the *sefira* of ***Ḥokhma,* and the world is sustained by Torah and those who discuss it, because through their words, they draw down illuminations and sustenance (alternatively: indwellings) from supernal *Ḥokhma,* the source of the Torah, to the letters of speech with which the world was created, as our Rabbis stated, "Do not read your children** [*banayikh*]**, but your builders** [*bonayikh*]" (*Berakhot* 64a),

By articulating the words when studying Torah, Torah scholars channel supernal *Ḥokhma* to the level of speech that created the world.[60] Torah study therefore resembles the creation of the world, which God brought about through the spoken letters and words of His divine *Ḥokhma*. For this reason, Torah scholars are not only called "Your children" but also "Your builders." Through their articulation of the letters and words of the Torah, they construct letters and words that build the world.

הֲרֵי הַמְשָׁכָה זוֹ הִיא בְּחִינַת יְרִידָה גְּדוֹלָה. וְלָזֶה צָרִיךְ לְעוֹרֵר חֶסֶד עֶלְיוֹן,

this flow nevertheless **constitutes a great descent. For this** flow to occur, **it is necessary to awaken supernal *Ḥesed,***

While Torah study engenders an awakening from below, drawing down supernal *Ḥokhma* into the letters of speech that the one studying Torah is articulating, to actually bring it down into the physical world, which entails an unfathomably enormous descent, study alone is not enough. The attribute of supernal *Ḥesed* must also be awakened from below. ☞

60. See *Zohar* 1:47a, 1:77a, 2:85a, 2:121a, 2:200a; *Likkutei Torah*, Deut. 15a.

הַנִּמְשָׁךְ כַּמַּיִם, מִמָּקוֹם גָּבוֹהַּ לְמָקוֹם נָמוּךְ.

which flows, like water, from a high place to a low place

There is a difference between *Ḥesed* and *Ḥokhma. Hokhma* inherently relates to that which is its equivalent. *Ḥokhma* relates to *Ḥokhma,* and *Ḥokhma* does not necessarily or particularly desire to descend from its level. By contrast, the nature of the attribute of *Ḥesed* is to descend from above to below. When a person speaks to his friend of the *Ḥokhma* of the Torah, of Torah wisdom, both of them need to be at approximately the same level. By contrast, kindness may be bestowed on someone who is much lower in level and status.

The classic symbol for *Ḥesed* is water, whose nature is to flow from a high place to a low place. Some things, if placed high up, stay there, but water, if given a path, does not remain. It flows down to a lower place, only stopping once it has descended as low as possible. This is the nature of *Ḥesed,* which gives and keeps on giving. The lowliness of the recipient does not prevent him from receiving *Ḥesed.* On the contrary, the lower and more unfortunate a person is, the greater the mitzva of acting with kindness becomes.

בְּאִתְעָרוּתָא דִּלְתַתָּא בִּצְדָקָה וָחֶסֶד תַּתָּאָה שֶׁמַּמְשִׁיכִים חַיִּים וְחֶסֶד לְהַחֲיוֹת רוּחַ שְׁפָלִים וְנִדְכָּאִים.

with an awakening from below through charity and acts of kindness that draw down life and kindness to revive the spirit of the humble and downtrodden.

THE CREATION OF WORLDS

☞ There is a major difference between human speech and divine speech. When a person transmits an idea from the level of wisdom to that of speech, it is a relatively small descent, entailing the transmission of concepts that are on one level of abstraction to a lower level of abstraction. Both levels are still in the realm of human comprehension. By contrast, the divide that separates divine wisdom from the physical world is unfathomably vast.

Therefore, although a person creates (nonphysical) worlds through his Torah study, even if God were to create worlds in tandem, they would be certainly not a part of the reality of this world. A human being does not have enough of a span between his highest faculty and his lowest, most tangible faculty to draw down *Ḥokhma* to the level of the physical world through his Torah study alone. Modeling God's creative process is not enough to actuate and create material change. Therefore, a person must awaken not only the divine creation and divine speech, but divine *Ḥesed* as well, drawing it down to this world.

When a person sustains the downtrodden in accordance with his means, he awakens God's giving, so that He provides for the downtrodden and needy. ☞

וְזֶהוּ שֶׁכָּתוּב: "אַל יִתְהַלֵּל חָכָם בְּחָכְמָתוֹ כו', כִּי אִם בְּזֹאת יִתְהַלֵּל כו', כִּי אֲנִי ה' עוֹשֶׂה חֶסֶד כו'" (ירמיה ט, כב-כג),

This is the meaning of the verse "Let the wise not glory in his wisdom.... Rather, let the one who glories **glory in this ... for I am the Lord who acts with kindness ..."** (Jer. 9:22–23),

The emphasis is on "*Ḥesed,*" because *Ḥesed* draws down the life of *Ḥokhma*. What is activated in the upper worlds, does not stay there, but rather is drawn down, descends into and affects reality below.

כִּי הַחֶסֶד הוּא הַמַּמְשִׁיךְ חַיֵּי הַחָכְמָה לְמַטָּה, וְאִם לָאו, הֲרֵי נִקְרֵאת חָכְמָתוֹ לְבַדּוֹ

for it is acts of kindness that draws down the vitality of *Ḥokhma*. Otherwise, if one does not engage in acts of kindness in addition to Torah study, his Torah study **is called "His wisdom" alone**

A CYCLE OF *ḤESED*

☞ A person who only studies Torah only creates spiritual worlds, theoretical abstract worlds, in the realm of Torah study, not actual worlds in this reality. This person's Torah study merely awakens God to study Torah, as it were, but it does not arouse God to create worlds. Granted, the Torah is the blueprint of reality, but the Torah itself is on a very high level. On its own, then, Torah study does not create life in our reality below. To bring new life into this world, one must create a cycle of *Ḥesed*, which can be created only when the person himself performs acts of kindness.

Furthermore, someone who only studies Torah, "does not even have Torah," according to the talmudic statement that the author of the *Tanya* quotes above. This implies that the Torah he studies does not reach his soul down here in this world. This type of Torah does not pass from God to the worlds, because it cannot bridge the gap between the Divine and the world. For God's Torah to be man's Torah to some degree, so that a Torah scholar will have true, living contact with the Torah, the Torah must descend to a person's actual world below. If a person does not truly meet the Torah, if he simply analyzes texts and says, "I do not want to perform charity or acts of kindness. I'm only interested in Torah as an abstraction," then God also keeps the Torah to Himself, as it were. What that person is left with is not essentially Torah. For the Torah down below to truly mirror the Torah on high, it must come with acts of kindness.

A person who does not perform acts of kindness does not impact the world below. Yet it remains to be explained why he does not even have his Torah. What aspect of his Torah is blemished?

For a person's Torah to become part of the grand scheme of reality, and more specifically, so that his Torah will serve as a channel of connection between the higher and lower worlds, he must act through it, influencing not only his own being but also the entire world. The giving of charity and the performance of acts of kindness shows that this person is paying attention to others, creating an all-encompassing network of relating to that which is outside of him. If a person studies Torah in a disconnected way, as an isolated experience, then he acquires wisdom of his own, but he is not privy to God's Torah, since Torah is essentially about teaching, about connecting to others. Its name imparts its essence: The word *Torah* is etymologically connected to the word *hora'a*, which means guidance and transmission to the world. As soon as a person disconnects the Torah from all this, it becomes an abstract pursuit, like any other intellectual endeavor.

בְּלִי הַמְשָׁכַת חַיִּים מִמֶּנָּה חַס וְשָׁלוֹם.

without the downward **flow of life from it, God forbid.**

When the Torah is not a living Torah, it is dead. A person who studies Torah in this manner is studying dead letters that do not channel life from above. When one studies Torah without performing acts of kindness, and fails to infuse the world around him with life, God does not infuse life into the Torah he studies.

וּבְזֶה יוּבַן מַה שֶּׁכָּתַב הָאֲרִיזַ"ל, שֶׁיֵּשׁ שְׁנֵי מִינֵי נְשָׁמוֹת בְּיִשְׂרָאֵל, נִשְׁמוֹת תַּלְמִידֵי חֲכָמִים הָעוֹסְקִים בַּתּוֹרָה כָּל יְמֵיהֶם, וְנִשְׁמוֹת בַּעֲלֵי מִצְוֹת הָעוֹסְקִים בִּצְדָקָה וּגְמִילוּת חֲסָדִים.

Based on this, we can understand the Arizal's statement that there are two kinds of souls among the Jewish people: the souls of Torah scholars who study Torah all their days and the souls of those who perform commandments, who engage in charity and acts of kindness. 18 Av

Souls are distinct from one another in various ways. One of the most basic distinctions is between souls that are like heads, whose roles parallel that of the head in relation to the body, and these are the souls of Torah scholars. Then there are souls of the givers of charity and acts of kindness, whose role parallels the other limbs of the body. Both camps serve God, each one doing his part, according to his unique nature.[61] ☞

דְּלִכְאוֹרָה, הֲרֵי גַּם תַּלְמִידֵי חֲכָמִים צְרִיכִים לַעֲסוֹק בִּגְמִילוּת חֲסָדִים, כְּמַאֲמַר רַבּוֹתֵינוּ ז״ל שֶׁ״אֲפִילּוּ תּוֹרָה אֵין לוֹ״.

It would seem that Torah scholars must also engage in acts of kindness, in accordance with the Rabbis' statement that otherwise **"he does not even have Torah."**

Yet this categorization of souls is not so clearcut. The aforementioned axiom of the Sages suggests that if a Torah scholar does not also perform acts of kindness, he does not even have Torah. The implication of this is that not only is the Torah scholar not exempt from playing the role of his comrade, from performing acts of kindness, but if he does not do so, his own mission, that of Torah study, will not endure.

אֶלָּא שֶׁהַתַּלְמִידֵי חֲכָמִים, שֶׁתּוֹרָתָן עִיקָּר וְרוֹב יְמֵיהֶם בָּהּ, וּמִיעוּט יְמֵיהֶם בִּגְמִילוּת חֲסָדִים,

But the Torah scholars, whose Torah study is their primary occupation, on which they spend most of their days, while spending **a minority of their time on acts of kindness,**

The author of the *Tanya* explains that the categorization of Torah scholars versus charity givers is not categorically diametric. It simply

VARIOUS TYPES OF SOULS

☞ One tzaddik likened this concept to units in an army. When a soldier positioned in one unit moves to another unit of his own volition, he must face a court-martial for the crime of desertion. So too a person who is supposed to perform charity yet spends all his time studying Torah, or vice versa, is considered a deserter.

61. To date, we have not found the source of this explanation of the Arizal. But this idea is found in several other places. See, e.g., *Sha'ar Ruaḥ HaKodesh* 4:2; Introduction to *Sha'ar HaGilgulim*.

comes to explain the priority of every person, the main pursuit in which he invests most of his time and energy, what most expresses his role in life.

הִנֵּה פְּעוּלַּת אִתְעָרוּתָם דִּלְתַתָּא, לְעוֹרֵר חֶסֶד עֶלְיוֹן, לְהַמְשִׁיךְ וּלְהוֹרִיד אוֹר אֵין סוֹף הַמְלוּבָּשׁ בְּחָכְמָה עִילָּאָה מְקוֹר תּוֹרַת ה' שֶׁבְּפִיהֶם,

the effect of their awakening from below to awaken supernal *Ḥesed*, to draw forth and bring down the light of *Ein Sof*, which is clothed in supernal *Ḥokhma*, the source of God's Torah that is in their mouths

For one's Torah study to be genuine, and not just an intellectual pursuit, one must draw down through his Torah study the essence of the Divine itself that transcends *Ḥokhma*. This drawing down from such extremely high heights to the world below is, as explained earlier, constitutes the attribute of supernal *Ḥesed* that is awakened through the charity and acts of kindness that a person performs below.

הוּא רַק לְעוֹלַם הַנְּשָׁמוֹת שֶׁבִּבְרִיאָה, עַל יְדֵי עֵסֶק הַתַּלְמוּד, וְלַמַּלְאָכִים שֶׁבִּיצִירָה עַל יְדֵי לִימּוּד הַמִּשְׁנָה.

extends only to the realm of the souls in the world of ***Beria*** **through the study of Talmud and to the angels in** the world of ***Yetzira*** **through the study of Mishna.**

Yet the Torah scholars who engage in acts of kindness a minority of the time do not draw the divine vitality all the way down to our low level of reality. Rather, they bring it down to the beings that inhabit the world of *Beria*, the world of the intellect, who relate to their Creator in an intellectual way. *Beria* therefore corresponds to the realm of intellectual Talmud study, and it is through the study of Talmud that Torah scholars draw the Torah and its vitality down to the world of *Beria*.

The Mishna, on the other hand, is focused on the practical *halakha*, on what is permitted and what is prohibited. This is also the main thrust of the world of *Yetzira*, the world of the attributes and the angels. The power of the Mishna and *halakha* lies in the assertion of opinions that determine one's association with the topic at hand, not just theoretically, but as a tangible sentiment in favor or opposed, which then informs one's actions and choices, much like the emotive attributes, which prompt a person to action.

The Torah scholar's Torah shines in lofty spiritual worlds, in the world of *Beria* (also known as the upper Garden of Eden) and the world of *Yetzira* (also called the lower Garden of Eden), but that light does not penetrate the lower physical world. So too in a person's soul, this Torah illuminates his mind and emotions, but it does not reach and affect his actions.

יַעַן הֱיוֹת חַיּוּת הַנְּשָׁמוֹת וְהַמַּלְאָכִים נִשְׁפָּעוֹת מִצֵּירוּפֵי אוֹתִיּוֹת הַדִּיבּוּר, הִיא תּוֹרָה שֶׁבְּעַל פֶּה, וּמְקוֹר הָאוֹתִיּוֹת הוּא מֵחָכְמָה עִילָּאָה, כַּנִּזְכָּר לְעֵיל.

This is **because the life force of the souls and angels is derived from the combinations of the letters of speech, which is the Oral Torah,** the Talmud and Mishna, **and the source of the letters is from supernal *Ḥokhma*, as stated above.**

The author of the *Tanya* now connects this concept with the idea of the matter and form of the letters that he explained above. The Torah that is expressed in combinations of words and letters, in the form of the letters, is the Oral Torah that Torah scholars study. While the source and matter of the letters, the breath that produces speech, becomes revealed only through the power of supernal *Ḥokhma* itself, which transcends the intellect and the mind's understanding that shines in the worlds of *Beria* and *Yetzira.*

In this light, when the Torah scholar studies Torah, he creates words and combinations of letters. The supernal worlds, that of *Beria* and *Yetzira*, can register the content and message of these letters, as opposed to our world, which cannot relate to the internal content of the letters without the external "matter" that carries the words. The letters that the Torah scholar articulates during his Torah study are therefore meaningful until a certain point, yet are not fully absorbed and do not have an impact on this lowly world. To draw the letters down further, the light must descend from a higher place, as will be explained below.

אַךְ לְהַמְשִׁיךְ וּלְהוֹרִיד הֶאָרָה וְחַיּוּת מִבְּחִינַת הֶבֶל הָעֶלְיוֹן, ה׳ תַּתָּאָה, לָעוֹלָם הַזֶּה הַשָּׁפָל, שֶׁהוּא צִמְצוּם גָּדוֹל בְּיֶתֶר עַז - לֹא דַּי בְּאִתְעָרוּתָא דִּלְתַתָּא שֶׁל תַּלְמִידֵי חֲכָמִים הָעוֹסְקִים מִיעוּט יְמֵיהֶם בִּצְדָקָה וּגְמִילוּת חֲסָדִים,

But to draw forth and bring down the illumination and life force from the level of the supernal breath, the final *heh*, to this lowly world, which entails an immense constriction to an even **greater degree, the awakening of the Torah scholars below who spend a minority of their days on charity and acts of kindness is not enough.**

In order to draw down the light of *Ein Sof* from the level of the supernal breath that constitutes the matter of the letters down to this material world of *Asiya*, the awakening achieved by the Torah scholar, who spends minimal time on charity and acts of kindness, does not have enough power to achieve this.

אֶלָּא עַל יְדֵי אִתְעָרוּתָא דְּבַעֲלֵי מִצְוֹת, הָעוֹסְקִים רוֹב יְמֵיהֶם בִּצְדָקָה וּגְמִילוּת חֲסָדִים (וּכְמוֹ שֶׁכָּתוּב בְּלִקּוּטֵי אֲמָרִים, בְּחֵלֶק א׳ פֶּרֶק ל״ד).

Rather, it occurs **through the awakening of those who perform commandments, who spend most of their days engaged in charity and acts of kindness (as it is written in volume 1 of *Likkutei Amarim*, chapter 34).**

Only those who spend most of their time, energy, and resources on performing acts of kindness, those who express with all their being the physical action of drawing down the flow of vitality all the way to this world, are the ones who draw down the light of the divine will and wisdom into this world. ☞

DRAWING THE LIGHT OF TORAH INTO THE WORLD OF ACTION

☞ There are many examples today that did not exist in earlier times of indecipherable communication. This does not refer only to content that does not cross certain boundaries, but also to actual letters that we are incapable of registering. Today, most information is transmitted through electromagnetic waves in one way or another. We as humans lack the capability to register most of these messages, not

וְלָכֵן נִקְרָאוּ 'תָּמְכֵי אוֹרַיְיתָא'.

Therefore, those who engage in charity and acts of kindness **are called supporters of the Torah.**

The expression "supporters of the Torah" is explained not in the social sense of people who support Torah scholars or Torah institutions, but rather in the sense that they uphold the Torah itself, establishing the Torah within our reality.[62]

וְהֵן בְּחִינוֹת וּמַדְרֵגוֹת נֶצַח וְהוֹד, לִהְיוֹתָן מַמְשִׁיכִין אוֹר הַתּוֹרָה לְמַטָּה לְעוֹלַם הָעֲשִׂיָּה.

They represent **the levels of *Netzaḥ*, and *Hod*, for they draw the light of the Torah down to the world of *Asiya*.**

In kabbalistic terminology, *Netzaḥ* and *Hod* are called the "two legs" that connect the body to the ground.[63] The supporters of the Torah are like the legs of the Torah. The Torah, in this sense, is a superstructure built on a particular substructure, without which the superstructure would not be able to relate to the world, to reality. It would associate only with that which transcends our reality. To pragmatize the Torah,

because we are incapable of understanding their meaning, but because we do not have the tools to register the "matter" of the letters that carries these messages.

The encryption of the letters in radio waves, for instance, is meaningless to us. It passes over us, next to us, and through us without our feeling anything. Similarly, a person who studies Torah creates a major broadcast that reverberates throughout all the worlds. This livestream resounds throughout our world as well, but our world does not necessarily register it. This is not a problem of location, as if the broadcast does not reach our world, as if our coordinates are off the map, but rather it is a reception issue. The instruments of the creations in our world are incapable of picking up those messages, and the letters pass us by as if they did not exist.

The world can be filled with Torah, just as it is filled with the melodies and sounds of all the languages. Yet a person who lacks the proper instrument cannot pick up any of it. We must create a tool that can translate the sound waves of Torah into a language we can perceive. In this sense, Torah scholars create the letters and words that traverse all the worlds, and masters of charity and doers of kindness create the means by which these letters can be registered. They generate the instruments that can translate from a lofty level of reality into terms that are meaningful to us below.

62. See *Zohar* 1:8a, 3:53b, based on Prov. 3:18.

63. Introduction to *Tikkunei Zohar* 17b.

legs for it to stand on must be built. The role of charity givers is therefore an extension of that of Torah scholars. Torah scholars create lights in the upper worlds, while masters of charity draw down that illumination to our world.

וּבָזֶה יוּבַן לָמָּה נִקְרָא הַצְּדָקָה בְּשֵׁם מַעֲשֶׂה, כְּמוֹ שֶׁכָּתוּב: "וְהָיָה מַעֲשֵׂה הַצְּדָקָה שָׁלוֹם" (ישעיה לב, יז), עַל שֵׁם שֶׁפְּעוּלָּתָהּ לְהַמְשִׁיךְ אוֹר ה' לְעוֹלַם הָעֲשִׂיָּה.

Based on this, we can understand why charity is called an act, as it is written, "The act of charity will be peace" (Isa. 32:17). It is so called **because its effect is to draw down God's light to the world of *Asiya*, the world of Action.**

God's light that is in the Torah shines in the worlds of *Beria* and *Yetzira,* but not in the world of *Asiya.* In the world of *Asiya,* the world of Action, God's light is drawn down only through the power of the mitzva of charity. It is for this reason that charity is called "an act of charity." ☞

וְזֶהוּ דִּקְדּוּק לְשׁוֹן זוֹהַר הַקָּדוֹשׁ: "מַאן דְּעָבֵיד שְׁמָא קַדִּישָׁא" (חלק ג קיג, ב), "דְּעָבֵיד" דַּיְיקָא,

This is the meaning of the precise wording of the holy *Zohar* (3:113b) in the expression **"who makes the holy name," specifying "who makes,"**

THE OTHER MITZVOT

☞ In the broader scheme, these concepts apply not only to charity but to all action-based mitzvot. As explained elsewhere in the *Tanya* (*Likkutei Amarim*, chap. 37), all mitzvot are an aspect of the mitzva of charity, a type of act of kindness that God (and man) bestow on the world. When a person takes an etrog and fulfills the mitzva with it, he transforms something that was merely a fruit, a plant like any other, into an object of holiness. Yet the ultimate drawing down of the light and life force to the lowest levels is specifically the mitzva of charity.

The world does not sense or realize the gift of the majority of the mitzvot. One could argue that they do not receive the divine effluence that they engender in the fullest way. By contrast, when a person gives a coin to a poor person or smiles and tells him a joke to brighten his spirits, he becomes the carrier of a mitzva just like the *etrog* that he shakes. The act of kindness that was performed, the money that was received, and the benefit therein are tangible and revealed below just as they are above.

This expression seems strange. What does it mean to "make a name"? The answer is that it parallels the aforementioned explanation of the act of charity, which is that charity is dependent on action and thus it has the power to "make" something happen. Through the act of charity, one brings down the light of the life force to the reality of the world of Action, the world of *Asiya.*

כִּי בְּאִתְעָרוּתָא דִּלְתַתָּא, בִּצְדָקָה וָחֶסֶד תַּתָּאָה, מְעוֹרֵר חֶסֶד עֶלְיוֹן לְהַמְשִׁיךְ אוֹר אֵין סוֹף מִבְּחִינַת חָכְמָה עִילָּאָה. יוּ״ד שֶׁל שֵׁם לְהֵ׳ שֶׁל שֵׁם - בְּחִינַת הַדִּבּוּר וְרוּחַ פִּיו יִתְבָּרֵךְ, כְּדֵי לְהַשְׁפִּיעַ לְעוֹלַם הָעֲשִׂיָּה.

for the awakening below through charity and kindness below awakens supernal *Ḥesed* to draw down the light of *Ein Sof* from the level of supernal *Ḥokhma.* It draws down **the letter *yod* of** God's **name to the letter *heh* of the name,** which is **the speech and breath of His divine utterance, causing it to flow to the world of *Asiya.***

Through the act of charity and kindness that a person bestows on someone who is lower than him, the Divine is awakened above to manifest in the letters of speech and impact all the worlds down to our low world of *Asiya.*

וְעַל דֶּרֶךְ מָשָׁל, לְהַבְדִּיל הַבְדָּלוֹת אֵין קֵץ, כְּמוֹ שֶׁאָדָם אֵינוֹ מְדַבֵּר אֶלָּא לַאֲחֵרִים (וְלֹא כְּשֶׁהוּא בֵּינוֹ לְבֵין עַצְמוֹ),

By way of analogy, though it is infinitely incomparable, it is like a person who does not speak except to others (and not when he is by himself),

The author of the *Tanya* offers this analogy to explain why it is specifically speech and the breath of the divine utterance (which is the "matter" of speech) that comprise the vessel that imparts the life force to all the worlds below.

When a person is by himself, discovering and clarifying who he is, his understanding and his emotions, he uses the medium of thought. But when he turns to another person, he speaks. Speech is the instrument through which a person emerges from himself. Similarly, speech is the vessel through which God creates the world that He is hidden within, the world that seems to be a different reality other than that of the Divine.

וְאָז מְצַמְצֵם שִׂכְלוֹ וּמַחֲשַׁבְתּוֹ בְּדִבּוּרוֹ אֲלֵיהֶם. **and then, when he speaks to them, he constricts his intellect and thoughts.**

In the transition from intellect to speech for the sake of others, an immense constriction must occur from the rationality as it exists in the person's mind to the fraction of it that gets expressed in his speech, that which the listener actually receives. In the referent, the "other" is the physical world of *Asiya* in which God is concealed, and the little that is revealed is the whole reality of this dynamic world that is created with that speech.

וְהַמַּשְׂכִּילִים יָבִינוּ. **The scholars of Kabbala will understand.**

It is unclear what the author of the *Tanya* meant with these concluding words. The Lubavitcher Rebbe, Rabbi Menaḥem Mendel Schneerson, comments that perhaps he was referring to the previous sentence, "By way of analogy…." With this he would be implying that the scholars of Kabbala will glean insight from it into the entire letter, since he does not appear to thoroughly settle all the concepts mentioned therein. Perhaps these concise words hint at the resolution of everything that the author did not expressly articulate in the summation.

At the beginning of the letter, the author of the *Tanya* quotes the verse "David made a name," but he does not clarify what this name is. Later he quotes from the *Zohar*, which states, "Who makes the holy name every day?" How is the holy name made? Through the giving of charity. In the concluding sentence, by way of analogy, he mentions human speech intended for another and not just for oneself.

In hasidic teachings, it is explained that a name is similar to speech in the sense that one's name is not for himself but rather for others to be able to refer to him. Both speech and a person's name share similar functions: Both serve as the vessel and garment that draws one's essence outward. In a deeper sense, with speech God sustains the entire external reality, all the worlds and everything in them. To "make the name," then, means drawing God's name down into our world of *Asiya*, the world of Action. Yet if the concept of speech, or more specifically, the ten utterances, expresses the creation and vitality of the worlds, the concept of name emphasizes the revelation of the Divine that is drawn down to the worlds.[64]

The overall topic of this epistle can be summed up as being about divine speech: how through Torah study the "form" and messages of divine speech are revealed. Yet in order to express the "matter" of divine speech as well, through which the divine speech descends to the world of Action, one must fulfill the mitzva of charity. The charity must be performed not only through those who study Torah, whose acts of kindness are secondary to their Torah study, but in the most serious way, where one invests his entire being in charity, giving his very life and soul to someone else who is lacking and who cannot reciprocate at all. This is the only way that charity arouses supernal *Ḥesed* to literally endow the lower world with the divine light.

Torah study is a type of charity in and of itself, since it offers ways to bring its own content down to the world and to one's soul in an integrated, genuine way. When a person shares Torah, it is as if God Himself articulates those words of Torah,[65] meaning, that He draws it down to the worlds, commensurate with the degree that a person does so. When a person sits and studies on his own, his Torah resonates only with himself. Though he articulates it out loud, there is a still a difference between a person speaking to himself and one speaking to someone else. Even in the realm of thought, there is a difference between the thought that a person thinks to himself and the thought that a person thinks with the intention of transmitting it to others. Intentional thought is steered thinking, meant from the outset for its recipient. This addition of directionality, of relation and compatibility with the other, is itself the whole thrust of the mitzva of charity.

---

64. The hasidic teachings explain that a name points to the essence of a thing. Not to the illumination and revelation that comes from it but to its very self. Therefore, when we refer to God by one of His names in our prayers, we are supposed to keep Him in mind and not His attributes.

65. *Tana deVei Eliyahu Rabba* 18: "When every torah scholar sits, learns and engages in torah, God sits across from him and learns."

One of the unique aspects of the mitzva of charity is that it is not just a mitzva between man and God, but it is also a mitzva that relates to another person as well and so must be performed according to the status and needs of the recipient. Therefore, in the verse "Happy is one who attends to the helpless" (Ps. 41:2), the word for attends, *maskil,* also means one who is intelligent.[66] A person must consider and tailor his giving, and the way in which he gives, according to the level and status of the recipient so that it will not be arbitrary giving but rather giving that is commensurate with the needs of the recipient. Then, through Torah that is accompanied by charity, the Torah descends and manifests in the body of the letters and the words, in our physical world of action. This is what is meant by "David made a name" through "justice and charity," through which the light of God in the Torah, or the name of God, is drawn down in the physical world.

How does one "make" the great name, the name of *Havaya?* When a person reaches the world of *Beria* by studying Torah with lofty intention, he writes the first *heh* of the name. When he merits love and fear, he enters the world of *Yetzira,* and thus writes the letter *vav.* When he gets here, to this world, by performing "justice and charity," acts of charity and kindness, he "makes" the last *heh* of the name, and completes the name entirely, drawing it down to the world of *Asiya.*

---

66. See *Vayikra Rabba* 34:1.

Epistle 6

THE AUTHOR OF THE *TANYA*'S PRACTICAL GOAL IN writing this letter was to inspire the giving of charity in general and particularly to the hasidim living in the Land of Israel.[1] Like most of the letters in this section, it contains a deeper message as well and expounds on the power that charity has on the divine service of the giver. He explores how the reward of charity is the infusion of truth into the giver's love and fear of God. He discusses the character of that truth and the way to acquire it, which is through compassion. He also explains the function of true compassion in the context of divine service and how to cultivate it: through contemplation and especially through charity and acts of kindness.

"זוֹרֵעַ צְדָקָה שֶׂכֶר אֱמֶת" (בְּמִשְׁלֵי יא, יח). פֵּירוּשׁ: שֶׁשְּׂכַר זְרִיעַת הַצְּדָקָה הִיא מִדַּת אֱמֶת.

19 Av / 21 Av (leap year)

It is written, **"The sower of charity has a true reward" (Prov. 11:18). This means that the reward for sowing charity is the attribute of truth.**

It would seem that a reward should be reminiscent of the service performed so that the reward for an act of kindness should be related to kindness, as in the verse "He who pursues charity and kindness will find life, charity, and honor" (Prov. 21:21). Therefore, the author of the *Tanya*'s explanation of this verse attesting that the reward of charity is the attribute of truth begs elucidation.

1. Based on various references made throughout the letter, it was probably written after the printing of the *Tanya* in 1796.

וּכְתִיב: "תִּתֵּן אֱמֶת לְיַעֲקֹב" (מיכה ז, כ), וּשְׁבָחָא דְקוּדְשָׁא בְּרִיךְ הוּא מְסַדֵּר נָבִיא כו׳, כְּמוֹ שֶׁכָּתוּב בַּזֹּהַר הַקָּדוֹשׁ (חלק ג קלא, ב). פֵּירוּשׁ, שֶׁהַקָּדוֹשׁ בָּרוּךְ הוּא הוּא הַנּוֹתֵן מִדַּת אֱמֶת לְיַעֲקֹב.

It is also written, "You will give truth to Jacob" (Mic. 7:20). In this verse, **the prophet speaks the praises of the Holy One, blessed be He, as the holy** ***Zohar*** (3:131b) **states, which means that the Holy One, blessed be He, is the one who gives the attribute of truth to Jacob.**

"You will give truth to Jacob" is not a prayer or request but rather a praise of God, that He gives truth to Jacob. The *Zohar* explains how the verses "Who is God like You … ? You will give truth to Jacob … as You took an oath to our forefathers from days of old" (Mic. 7:18–20) correspond to God's thirteen supernal attributes of mercy.[2] The prophet articulates them just as we mention them in our prayers as a way to praise God, expressing how He runs the world using these attributes of abundant mercy.

These words, "You will give truth to Jacob," also have a deeper implication. Not only is whatever God gives us (Jacob) real and true, but He actually gives the attribute of truth itself to Jacob.

וְצָרִיךְ לְהָבִין - וְכִי אֵין אֱמֶת בְּיַעֲקֹב, חַס וְשָׁלוֹם, עַד שֶׁהַקָּדוֹשׁ בָּרוּךְ הוּא יִתֵּן לוֹ מִלְמַעְלָה?

This **requires explanation: Is there no truth in Jacob, God forbid, until the Holy One, blessed be He, gives it to him from above?**

Why does Jacob need the gift of truth? Doesn't he already have this quality? Doesn't Jacob himself embody the attribute of truth?

The simple understanding of the verse's words, "You will give truth to Jacob, kindness to Abraham …," provides a window into the ways of God. He gives truth to Jacob because that is his attribute and kindness to Abraham because that is his primary quality. God augments each person according to his nature, not endowing him with attributes for which he does not have a predisposition. As another verse says, "And in the hearts of all the wisehearted I have put wisdom"

2. See *Etz Ḥayyim* 13:9; see also *Likkutei Torah,* Deut. 34:2, regarding the discrepancy between Micah's attributes of mercy and those of Moses.

(Ex. 31:6). God imbues additional wisdom into the heart of one who is already wise.

Similarly, we find that "[God] grants wisdom to the wise and knowledge to those who know understanding" (Dan. 2:21). He does not grant wisdom to fools, even though, ostensibly, they need it more, in the same way that money is lent to the rich and not to the poor, because the rich have the ability to repay it.

The author of the *Tanya* will explain this concept in a deeper and more thorough way below. But first he will preface his explanation by exploring the function of the attribute of compassion in divine service, the nature of the attribute of truth, and, finally, the connection that truth and compassion have to charity.

אַךְ הִנֵּה מוּדַעַת זֹאת דְּמִדַּת יַעֲקֹב הִיא מִדַּת רַחֲמָנוּת, **But it is known that the attribute of Jacob is the attribute of compassion,**

The forefathers were not only men but were also spiritual embodiments of particular attributes.[3] Abraham embodied the attribute of *Ḥesed* and love, Isaac personified *Gevura* and fear, and Jacob embodied the attribute of compassion. ☞

COMPASSION, HARMONY, AND TRUTH

☞ Jacob also embodied the attributes of harmony and truth. What is the connection between all these qualities – compassion, harmony, and truth? To understand the connection, we need to understand the essential distinction between the attribute of kindness and compassion. There is a distinct difference between them even though they seem very similar.

Kindness is the outward expression of love, a gift from the lover to the beloved. The lover feels love, and although that love may grow stronger or weaker in response to the beloved, intrinsically it does not depend on the object of the love. Love, rather, depends on the lover. Furthermore, the endowment of kindness depends more on the giver than on the needs of the receiver. Kindness is not endowed on one who needs but rather on one who is loved, even if he does not need it.

By contrast, compassion is always sensitive to the needs of the other. To have compassion on a person, there must be a degree of understanding the other and relating to his situation. Giving from a place of compassion is objectively true since it responds to what is realistically needed. Thus, compassion relates to the attribute of harmony in the forging of harmonious, mutual relationships. It also relates to truth, to relating to the actual needs and reality of another person.

3. See *Torah Or*, beginning of *Toledot*; *Likkutei Torah*, Lev. 17d, 34b.

וַעֲבוֹדַת ה׳ בְּמִדַּת רַחֲמָנוּת הִיא הַבָּאָה מֵהִתְעוֹרְרוּת רַחֲמִים רַבִּים בְּלֵב הָאָדָם עַל נִיצוֹץ אֱלֹקוּת שֶׁבְּנַפְשׁוֹ, הָרְחוֹקָה מֵאוֹר פְּנֵי ה׳, כַּאֲשֶׁר הוֹלֵךְ בְּחֹשֶׁךְ הַבְלֵי עוֹלָם.

and the divine service performed **with the attribute of compassion is** the service **that comes from awakening in a person's heart abundant compassion for the divine spark that is in his soul, which is far from the light of God's countenance while** a person **walks in the darkness of the vanities of the world.**

What does it mean to use compassion in one's service of God? This is more easily understood in the context of the performance of mitzvot. There are mitzvot that one performs out of love and others out of fear, and then there are mitzvot, like charity, that a person performs out of compassion. Yet where does compassion fit in within the context of divine service, in one's relationship with God? Loving God or fearing Him makes sense, but how does one have compassion for Him?

The author of the *Tanya* explains here that having compassion for God means having compassion for the divine spark within man, for the source of man's soul, which is literally a portion of God that descends into a physical body "in the darkness of the vanities of the world." This is the goal: to awaken compassion for that aspect of God within man.

Having compassion for one's soul in this context does not mean having compassion for one's self with which one identifies but rather on the aspect of the Divine within that is drowning in the depths of exile. One metaphor that can help us to visualize this dynamic is of a prince who was taken captive. A prince in captivity certainly deserves compassion, but even more so, it is the king who has lost his heir and the empire from which he hails, who lost their prince, who need compassion. Even if the prince became accustomed to his new life to the extent that he ceases to feel the pain of his situation, and even if he thinks that he is living a tranquil, good life, the compassion for the king and the kingdom does not lessen.

Likewise, compassion in divine service is not compassion for a single individual, for me or someone else, but rather an all-encompassing compassion for the Divine Presence, which is in exile. ☞

According to the teachings of Kabbala, the *sefirot* can be divided into three arrays, and the attribute of compassion characterizes the middle array. This attribute, which is the attribute of the *sefira* of *Tiferet,* extends all the way up to *Keter,* the highest level, and all the way down to *Malkhut,* the lowest.[4] It can extend so far that it can reach a place that other emotions do not reach, awaken, or influence, both on the upper and lower ends of the spectrum. A person may not know his divine spark, may not acknowledge the divine soul within him, but he can still have compassion for it, to commiserate with it because it is stuck in exile. Very few people are successful at making their divine spark their master. With regard to most, it is in captivity, sometimes in a bitter and humiliating exile. When a person thinks about how God is within him, not as a king but as a captive, forced into being with him and his lowly thoughts and repulsive deeds, he feels compassion for Him.

SERVING GOD WITH COMPASSION

☞ Serving God with compassion has benefits over serving God with love and fear, since it does not necessitate any prior emotional relationship or even familiarity with Him at all. As mentioned elsewhere (see, e.g., *Likkutei Amarim,* chaps. 32, 45), compassion can serve as a starting point for serving God, even when love is not possible. This is one way of interpreting the words "the house of Jacob that redeemed Abraham" (Isa. 29:22): Since Jacob embodies the attribute of compassion and Abraham the attribute of love, this verse can be read as saying, "Compassion redeems, awakens, and reveals love."

Sometimes a person may not feel love or even fear of God, yet he can still feel compassion for the divine spark within him. The attribute of love, on the other hand, demands a certain degree of closeness. The lover must have some sort of bond with the beloved; only then can love be cultivated. There is no love in a vacuum. It must be directed at a particular thing. If he has no knowledge of the thing, a person cannot feel love toward it.

This does not apply to the attribute of compassion. To have compassion for another person, one need not know or value him. The very fact that he is in need arouses compassion, almost like a reflex. If a person is walking down the street, and he slips and breaks his leg, people will run to help, even though they do not know him or have any connection to him. They do not need to love him to have compassion for him, and therefore a person can have compassion for someone who is extremely far from his own world, and even on something that is not human. A person can have compassion for an injured cat without loving it. He may even be repulsed by it, yet still have compassion for it.

---

4. See *Likkutei Torah,* Ex. 81c; *Zohar* 2:175b.

וְהִתְעוֹרְרוּת רַחֲמָנוּת זוֹ הִיא בָּאָה מֵהַתְּבוּנָה וְהַדַּעַת בִּגְדוּלַּת ה׳,

This awakening of compassion for the divine spark **stems from the understanding and knowledge of God's greatness,**

The author of the *Tanya* uses two different words for the knowledge that brings a person to sense the Divine, which is the precursor to cultivating compassion for it: *tevuna*, "understanding" and *da'at*, "knowledge." *Tevuna* is when a person contemplates a matter until he understands it well. When he internalizes this understanding until he manages to forge an emotional connection to it with all his soul, that is *da'at*. The contents of his contemplation are of "God's greatness," not of the divine essence itself, of which we have no apprehension, but rather of the illumination of that essence throughout the worlds.

אֵיךְ שֶׁאֲפִילּוּ הָעוֹלָמוֹת הָעֶלְיוֹנִים, לְמַעְלָה מַעְלָה עַד אֵין קֵץ, כְּלָא מַמָּשׁ חֲשִׁיבֵי קַמֵּיהּ,

how even the infinitely lofty higher worlds are literally considered nothingness before Him,

This contemplation is twofold. On the one hand, one should contemplate the greatness of God, and on the other hand, one should reflect on the darkness and nothingness of all the worlds, both higher and lower, those created and those emanated, which are all considered negligible compared to God.

Why should a person begin his contemplation with the greatness of God? Imagine trying to awaken one's compassion for a person who used to be wealthy but who now must collect charity. One must first understand how rich he was and the implications of this wealth before one can have true compassion for him in his changed circumstances.

Generally, others have compassion for children with developmental delays. But if you think about it, such a child probably does not even have compassion for himself. He does not feel that he is unfortunate, since he is not aware of the fact that he should be feeling unfortunate, that others should pity him. For him, this is his life.

Similarly, for a person to feel compassion for his divine spark, which suffered such a drastic descent, he must first contemplate the greatness of the Divine, which is the rightful abode of the infinite divine spark. Only then will he be truly impressed by the vast distance between the Divine and the limited created world in which the divine spark is captive. ☞

כִּי כָּל שִׁפְעָם וְחַיּוּתָם אֵינוֹ רַק מִזִּיו וְהֶאָרָה מֵאוֹת אֶחָד מִשְּׁמוֹ יִתְבָּרֵךְ,

because their entire sustenance and life force is nothing but glimmer and illumination drawn **from one letter of God's name,**

The wording here indicates three degrees of separation between the life force that sustains our world and God. First, the vitality of creation stems not from God Himself but from an illumination of the Divine. Second, this illumination radiates from His name, which, like a person's name, is only an external symbol through which others can relate to Him. Third, the illumination does not stem from His entire name but only from one letter of His name. The composition of several letters together conveys a certain meaning, while one letter expresses only one facet and no longer carries the entire meaning of the word of which it is a part.

COMPASSION FOR THE DIVINE SPARK

☞ The Talmud (*Yoma* 35b) relates how Rabbi Elazar ben Ḥarsum, one of the prominent and wealthy landowners in the Land of Israel, used to dress like a simple person and go from place to place to study Torah. One time, his servants saw a person wandering aimlessly and forced him to work for the great master (who was actually him). Rabbi Elazar begged them to leave him alone, but they refused.

A similar story is told of Rabbi Tarfon, whose servants caught him "stealing" from his own vineyards. Since they did not recognize him, they gave him a serious beating (see Jerusalem Talmud, *Shevi'it* 4:2).

This story happens, in a certain sense, within every person: God gives life to the world, as well as to every individual. He is the "owner of the vineyard," yet still a person does whatever he wants with his divine spark: subjugating it, beating it, and forcing it to participate and assist in that which is not only an insult to its honor but even antithetical to its will. If God would reveal Himself to man in all His infiniteness, in all His glory and greatness, no one could stand before Him. But God disguises Himself, as it were, within the workings of this world, making it hard for people to recognize His presence. The owner is here, in front of us, but we do not realize that He is the owner of the house, and so we treat Him in any way we wish.

כְּמַאֲמַר ״בְּיוּ״ד נִבְרָא עוֹלָם הַבָּא״ כו׳ (מנחות כט, ב).

as the Rabbis **stated,** "This world was created with the letter *heh;* **the World to Come was created with** the letter *yod*" (*Menaḥot* 29b).

The letter *yod,* the smallest of all the letters, represents the ultimate constriction, down to a single point. From this small letter were created the supernal spiritual worlds, which are all considered part of the rubric of the World to Come, the realm where souls exist beyond this physical world.

וְהִנֵּה בְּזִיו וְהֶאָרָה זוֹ, שֶׁהוּא הִתְפַּשְּׁטוּת הַחַיּוּת מִשְּׁמוֹ יִתְבָּרֵךְ לְהַחֲיוֹת עֶלְיוֹנִים וְתַחְתּוֹנִים, הוּא שֶׁיֵּשׁ הֶבְדֵּל וְהֶפְרֵשׁ בֵּין עֶלְיוֹנִים לְתַחְתּוֹנִים,

It is in this glimmer and illumination, which is an emanation of the life force from God's name to give life to the higher and lower worlds, **that there is a distinction and difference between higher and lower beings,**

It is only in the glimmer that emanates from the Divine, and not from the Creator Himself, that any distinction among the vast multiplicity of the created world is apparent. It is in the light of this emanation that the differences become recognizable between the highest of worlds and the lowest, between one time period and another, between supernal entities and lowly beings. All these differences, which for us are the whole world, are totally negligible and considered nothing at all in relation to Him. It is only from our perspective that there is any multiplicity in this world. It is analogous to the sun and its rays. The sun's rays can be felt to different degrees at different times and in varying locations, but these differences are recognizable only here on earth and not in the sun itself.

שֶׁעוֹלָם הַזֶּה נִבְרָא בְּה׳ וכו׳.

so that this world was created with the letter ***heh,*** whereas the World to Come was created with the letter *yod.*

It is only through the illumination that the worlds receive from the Divine, which constitutes the letters of His name and speech, that there are distinctions between the worlds. The distinction between this world and the next, between the higher worlds and the lower worlds, marks the most all-encompassing scope of differentiated reality. Moreover, the vitality and existence of these two worlds, of this world and the next, which encompass the entirety of reality, comes purely from the letters *yod* and *heh* of the name of *Havaya*. Just as two letters alone that a person may express are remote from the reality of his entire being, the relation between the worlds and God Himself is infinitely vast. ☞

THE WORLD TO COME VERSUS THIS WORLD

☞ As the author of the *Tanya* explained in the previous epistle, the essential difference between the higher worlds and lower worlds is related to the difference between these two letters, *heh* and *yod*. The life force of this world originates in the body of the letters, represented by the second *heh* of the name of *Havaya*, which corresponds to the sefira of *Malkhut* and the earth, while the vitality of the supernal worlds stems from the form and content that the letters symbolize, expressed by the letter *yod*, which corresponds to the *sefira* of *Hokhma*.

The difference between the higher worlds and the lower worlds is that the supernal realms are privy to direct and tangible perception of the Divine so that they are intrinsically incapable of straying beyond the bounds of their own realm. The lower worlds, on the other hand, are hardwired to prevent direct connection and perception of the Divine. As creatures of this world, we lack direct contact with the Divine. To reach a point of contact, we must create a framework that will allow us to bypass these limitations, such as in-depth study and faith.

There are phenomena even in our world that we know through direct contact. We need nothing else to know that they exist. This is how we know the physical world around us, and even certain spiritual realities and experiences: We palpably sense and experience them. By contrast, there are phenomena, even in the physical realm, that we do not experience directly but only learn about in a roundabout way. We do not see them, but we can train ourselves to relate to their reality as if we see them. We can only access them through other means that translate the coded messages of our surroundings and override our initial sensations and perceptions.

Not only people, but even holy *ḥayot* and the most supernal of angels, do not perceive the divine essence, as the verse states, "For man shall not see Me and live" (Ex. 33:20). Yet supernal beings in the higher worlds are able to perceive the divine illumination, the radiance of the divine vitality in all of creation, each according to its level. In the lower worlds, on the other hand, we see created entities but not the divine vitality within them; the container that conceals, yet not the light it contains. Our initial impression of reality is physical. To see beyond the physical, so that spirituality and, all the more so, the Divine, will

וְכֵן כָּל שִׁינּוּיֵי הַפְּרָטִים שֶׁבְּכָל עוֹלָם וְעוֹלָם הוּא לְפִי שִׁינּוּיֵי צֵירוּפֵי הָאוֹתִיּוֹת,

Likewise, the variations in the details of each and every world depend on the different combinations of the letters with which they were created,

As explained above, the vast, all-encompassing differences between the supernal worlds and the lower worlds are expressed in the distinction between the letters *heh* and *yod* of the divine name. The author of the *Tanya* now adds that the various differences within the minutiae within each and every world depend on the unique combinations of letters from which they stem.

The world of *Asiya* alone includes within it countless worlds. The physical world of *Asiya* encompasses the entire cosmos, and even a small and negligible part of it, such as planet Earth, is comprised of endless details. All these details, with all their distinctions in character and shape, stem from the differences in the combinations of the letters of divine speech that create them.

וְכֵן שִׁינּוּיֵי הַזְּמַנִּים בְּעָבָר הֹוֶה וְעָתִיד, וְשִׁינּוּיֵי כָּל הַקּוֹרוֹת בְּחִילּוּפֵי הַזְּמַנִּים,

and so too the variations in the dimensions of **time, of past, present, and future, and all the different events** that take place **through changing times,**

Creation is ever evolving and being renewed at every instant. The creation that existed in the past is not that of the present, and every single change is a result of new letter permutations. Moreover, just as there are combinations of letters that created every entity in the world, there are also permutations of letters that dictate the operation of the world: that which happened in the past, that which happens in the present, and that which will happen in the future. ☞

be a reality for us, we must work hard and train ourselves.

This is the significance of this world being created with the letter *heh*, and the next world being created with the letter *yod*. The entire creation is comprised of combinations of letters. In this world, reality is the body, the matter of the letters, while for beings that exist in the higher worlds, reality is the light and meaning behind the letters (see epistle 5 for a deeper explanation of the matter and content of letters).

הַכֹּל מִשִּׁינּוּיֵי צֵירוּפֵי הָאוֹתִיּוֹת שֶׁהֵן הֵן הַמְשָׁכַת הַחַיּוּת מִמִּדּוֹתָיו יִתְבָּרֵךְ שְׁמוֹ (כְּמוֹ שֶׁנִּתְבָּאֵר בְּלִקּוּטֵי אֲמָרִים חֵלֶק ב׳, פֶּרֶק י״א).

all stem from the various combinations of the letters of the ten utterances of divine speech, **which channel the life force from God's attributes (as explained in volume 2 of *Likkutei Amarim*,** *Sha'ar HaYiḥud VeHa'emuna,* **chap. 11).**

In *Sha'ar HaYiḥud VeHa'emuna,* the author of the *Tanya* explains that the revelation of the divine attributes and their activation in the lower realms during the six days of Creation is called an "utterance" or a "combination of letters." It follows that no manifestation of the attributes can happen without an accompanying combination of letters. Every letter has a certain creative force, a certain creative characteristic, and when letters combine, they create realities. Every combination creates a different essence in time and space. The reality

CHANGES IN TIME

☞ The author of the *Tanya* relates to time as a creation that has existence in and of itself and does not just exist relative to space or the awareness of man (see *Siddur Admor HaZaken, Sha'ar Keriat Shema*). Even if a person is not aware of a specific time, even if the world has not reached a certain time, it still exists.

Moreover, there are untold variations in the created entity called time. there are good times and bad times; there are years defined by abundance and kindness and years characterized by strict judgment. There are universal times that the whole world experiences, and there are individual times that relates only to a particular person. But not every person can sense the nature of a particular time, or the difference between various time periods, just as not every person can sense the differences between types of people or even between objects. Even to distinguish between stones, to discern which are valuable and which are worthless, one must be knowledgeable and aware. In the same way, it is impossible for every individual to be able to distinguish between moments of time.

This perspective of time has powerful implications for us: that every instant, every unit of time, is absolutely unique. Every moment constitutes a singular combination of divine letters that can never be repeated or revisited. If a person lost or destroyed a moment, even if he were to perform ten years' worth of good deeds in the attempt to rectify it, he could never bring it back. That moment will remain forever blemished. There will be other moments like it, but they will be different. In view of this, the colloquial expression "killing time" becomes actual. To kill a day, hour, or moment is like killing a person. True, there are millions of other people, but that individual unique person, like this unique present moment, will never return.

of every detail of every world and the definitions and distinctions between every single thing and between worlds are all due to changes in the illumination of the divine light that flows from the letters. The illumination does not flow and operate at every moment in the same way but rather shifts from one moment to the next and from one place to another.

אֲבָל לְגַבֵּי מַהוּתוֹ וְעַצְמוּתוֹ יִתְבָּרֵךְ כְּתִיב (מלאכי ג, ו): "אֲנִי ה' לֹא שָׁנִיתִי",

But in relation to God's essence and being, it is written, "For I the Lord did not change" (Mal. 3:6),

All the differences between worlds apply to the created universe, to revealed reality, but when it comes to the divine essence, there is no difference between the higher worlds and the lower worlds or between the time before the creation of the world and after it. The Creation, which included both the physical and spiritual realms at all levels and comprised endless, intricate systems, did not effect any change in God Himself.

בֵּין בִּבְחִינַת שִׁינּוּיֵי הַהִשְׁתַּלְשְׁלוּת, מֵרוּם הַמַּעֲלוֹת עַד לְמַטָּה מַטָּה, שֶׁכְּמוֹ שֶׁהוּא יִתְבָּרֵךְ מָצוּי בָּעֶלְיוֹנִים כָּךְ הוּא מַמָּשׁ בְּשָׁוֶה בַּתַּחְתּוֹנִים

neither in terms of the changes in the devolvement from the highest of levels to the lowest, for just as He is found in the higher worlds, so He is in precisely the same measure in the lower worlds

The highest of all supernal worlds, of which we have no comprehension, and the lowest of the physical worlds (even the lowliest realm of evil) differ only in the degree of light, in the magnitude of revelation, that is perceivable. Yet the essential, infinite Divine that exists in all of them is the same. In the highest worlds, the Divine is more accessible, more apparent, while in the lower worlds, particularly in our world, it is not recognizable or felt at all (at least not in one's initial impression of his surroundings), but God actually exists equally in all of them, in all realities and at all times, in the spiritual and the physical alike. This is the meaning of "I the Lord did not change." It is only the degree of divine revelation that changes from one point to the next, but God's infinite essence always remains the same.

(וּכְמוֹ שֶׁנִּתְבָּאֵר בְּלִקּוּטֵי אֲמָרִים חֵלֶק א׳ פֶּרֶק נ״א),

(as explained in volume 1 of *Likkutei Amarim*, chap. 51),

In *Likkutei Amarim*, the first section of the *Tanya*, the author distinguishes between the indwelling of the Divine Presence and the existence of the Divine Presence. The indwelling of the Divine Presence refers to the revelation of the Divine Presence, which differs based on time and place, so that it may be manifest to a greater or lesser degree. This does not apply to the existence of the Divine Presence. The Divine Presence itself does not exist more in one place than another.

וּבֵין בִּבְחִינַת שִׁינּוּיֵי הַזְּמַן, שֶׁכְּמוֹ שֶׁהָיָה הוּא לְבַדּוֹ הוּא יָחִיד וּמְיוּחָד לִפְנֵי שֵׁשֶׁת יְמֵי בְּרֵאשִׁית, כָּךְ הוּא עַתָּה אַחַר הַבְּרִיאָה.

nor in terms of changes in time, for just as He was alone, the one and only, before the six days of Creation, so He is now after Creation.

Just as there is no change in God from one world to the next, so too He does not change from one time to another. He is entirely the same now as He was before the creation of the world.

וְהַיְינוּ מִשּׁוּם שֶׁהַכֹּל כְּאַיִן וְאֶפֶס מַמָּשׁ לְגַבֵּי מַהוּתוֹ וְעַצְמוּתוֹ,

This is because everything is literally like absolute nothingness in relation to His essence and being,

How can it be that God is alone now just as He was before He created the world? The author of the *Tanya* explains that nothing, whether big or small, tall or short, takes up any room relative to Him. The endless multiplicity and distinctions between one thing and another bear significance within the paradigm of this world, but they are totally insignificant from God's vantage point.

וּכְמוֹ אוֹת אֶחָד מִדִּבּוּרוֹ שֶׁל אָדָם, אוֹ אֲפִילוּ מִמַּחֲשַׁבְתּוֹ, לְגַבֵּי כְּלָלוּת מַהוּת הַנֶּפֶשׁ הַשִּׂכְלִית וְעַצְמוּתָהּ.

just as one letter of a person's speech, or even one letter **of his thoughts,** is negligible **compared to the totality of the essence and being of the rational soul.**

The author of the *Tanya* adds here, "even [one letter] of his thoughts," because the letters of a person's thoughts are closer to his essence than his speech. Just as one letter that a person utters or thinks is but a tiny fraction of what he thinks and is capable of thinking, and even more so relative to all his potential thoughts, and even more so, relative to the essence of his soul, so too all the worlds are but a tiny fraction of the expression of God's being and essence.[5]

עַל דֶּרֶךְ מָשָׁל, לְשַׁבֵּךְ אֶת הָאֹזֶן, וּבֶאֱמֶת, "אֵין עֲרוֹךְ אֵלֶיךָ" כְּתִיב (תהלים מ, ו). וּכְמוֹ שֶׁנִּתְבָּאֵר בְּמָקוֹם אַחֵר (בְּלִקּוּטֵי אֲמָרִים חֵלֶק ב׳ פֶּרֶק ט׳) עַיֵּין שָׁם.

This comparison is only **by way of analogy, to attune the ear** by using terms it can appreciate. **In truth, it is written, "Nothing compares to You"** (Ps. 40:6), **as explained elsewhere (in volume 2 of *Likkutei Amarim*, *Sha'ar HaYiḥud VeHa'emuna*, chap. 9). See there.**

The analogy does not fully express the vast distance between God and His world. The human soul, with its capacity to think and speak to an endless extent, is still limited. Therefore, this metaphor is intrinsically defective; like all anthropomorphisms, it is inadequate. The purpose of the analogy is to "attune the ear," to provide imagery that will resonate and allow us to understand something of the relationship between God and the world, even though we are totally incapable of fully comprehending it.

The reality is that "nothing compares to You." "Comparison" implies relativity, large or small. That "nothing compares" means that essentially there is no comparison at all, not even between something very small to something unfathomably large. When there is a comparison, even one to a million, where the outer limits of these figures are incredibly far from each other, a comparison can still be drawn. But "nothing compares to You" means that any attempt at analogy is meaningless. This is not an issue of comparing that which is immense to something minute. The two sides cannot even be considered on the same plane of reality. In this sense, we do not nor cannot have any true example or metaphor that captures the essence of the Divine.

5. See also *Likkutei Amarim*, chaps. 20–21.

וְזֶהוּ שֶׁאוֹמְרִים "הַמֶּלֶךְ הַמְרוֹמָם לְבַדּוֹ מֵאָז". פֵּירוּשׁ, כְּמוֹ שֶׁמֵּאָז, קוֹדֶם הַבְּרִיאָה, הָיָה הוּא לְבַדּוֹ הוּא. כָּךְ עַתָּה, הוּא מְרוֹמָם כו', וּ"מִתְנַשֵּׂא מִימוֹת עוֹלָם". פֵּירוּשׁ, שֶׁהוּא רָם וְנִשָּׂא לְמַעְלָה מַעְלָה מִבְּחִינַת זְמַן הַנִּקְרָא בְּשֵׁם 'יְמוֹת עוֹלָם'.

This explains the words **that we say** in the *Yotzer Or* blessing, **"The King who alone is exalted from before," which means that just as "before," before the Creation, He was "alone," so too now "He is exalted... and He is elevated beyond the days of the world," meaning that He is exalted and elevated far beyond the dimension of time, which is called the "days of the world."**

In several places, the Sages say that that the term *me'az*, "from before," is not a point in time, but rather refers to time before the world existed, before the creation of time.[6] Just as before the creation of the world He was alone, now as well, after the creation of the world, with all its ever-evolving reality, He remains alone, separate from all the worlds. The emphasis here is on "He who is alone from before." The emphasis is that He is alone. The implication is far beyond the simple understanding of these words, that there are no other gods besides Him. It indicates that nothing at all exists besides Him.

The author of the *Tanya* extrapolates the rest of the blessing in the same vein: God is exalted beyond the world, not only in the spatial sense, but also beyond the "days of the world." A day is the most basic and tangible period of time. The "days of the world" refers not to a particular time but to time in general, since God's existence transcends the temporal construct. ☞

GOD AND TIME

☞ "Indeed, a thousand years in Your eyes are like yesterday gone by, like a watch of the night" (Ps. 90:4). This seems to imply that God does operate within time and that His time can be compared to our time, that one day for Him is a thousand years to us. Yet a closer look at the wording of the second half of the verse, "like yesterday gone by," tells us that yesterday is different from today. "Yesterday" no longer exists in time but is rather a memory of time, a thought of time. Similarly, "a

6. See, e.g., *Nedarim* 39b; *Sifrei*, Deut. 37.

וְהַיְינוּ לְפִי שֶׁחַיּוּת כָּל יְמוֹת עוֹלָם הוּא רַק מִבְּחִינַת "הַמֶּלֶךְ" כו', וּכְמוֹ שֶׁנִּתְבָּאֵר בְּמָקוֹם אַחֵר.

This is so because the life force of all the days of the world, of the dimension of time, **stems solely from the level of the king,** namely, from the *sefira* of *Malkhut,* **and so forth, as explained elsewhere** (*Sha'ar HaYiḥud VeHa'emuna,* chap. 7).

The author of the *Tanya* interprets the word *hamelekh,* "the king," from the verse he quoted as referring to the divine attribute of *Malkhut,* which is the lowest attribute. Therefore, all the created worlds stem from it, which are separate, as it were, from the divine essence. As established here, even time is a created entity, one facet of the entire created reality. Therefore, time as well stems from the *sefira* of *Malkhut.*

The attribute of *Malkhut,* then, is the only attribute that can be conjugated in time: He reigned, He reins, He will reign, past, present, and future.[7] This signifies that of all the *sefirot,* only *Malkhut* associates with the reality of time and the temporal details of the created world, which does not appertain to God's other, more supernal attributes.

וְאִי לְזֹאת, הָרַחֲמָנוּת גְּדוֹלָה מְאֹד מְאֹד עַל הַנִּיצוֹץ הַשּׁוֹכֵן בְּגוּף הֶחָשׁוּךְ וְהָאָפֵל,

Accordingly, upon contemplating all the above, one will feel **an exceedingly great amount of compassion for the** divine **spark that dwells in the dark and gloomy body,**

watch of the night" is not like a daytime watch but it too is like nothing. A person who stays awake all night may experience the nighttime watch as real time, but for a person who sleeps at night, it is nothing, as if no time elapsed. In this sense, for God a thousand years are therefore like "yesterday gone by," like a fleeting memory that passes in one flash. This is exactly what the author of the *Tanya* means in his explanation of the words of the verse "elevated beyond the days of the world." The "days of the world" all occur in another place, in another dimension, which is totally inapplicable to the context of the "exalted one."

7. In *Iggerot Kodesh,* vol. 20, letter 7, the Lubavitcher Rebbe, Rabbi Menaḥem Mendel Schneerson, notes that that this is most likely based on the words of the *Zohar* 1:34a. See also *Sefer HaBahir* 111, 127.

When a person contemplates all this, he prepares himself for divine service using his attribute of compassion. A person who lacks knowledge of the greatness of the Divine is incapable of cultivating compassion. Only when he ascertains, to whatever degree he is capable, the divine greatness, which is infinite, far transcending the uppermost reaches of this world, will he feel compassion for the divine spark, which is literally part of the divine essence.

Our bodies, with all its virtues and benefits, is mere flesh. The biological difference between it and a cow's body is very small. Our soul, which hails from the highest heights, resides in this piece of flesh. This must evoke compassion in us on the divine spark that is at the essence of the soul. ☞

'מַשְׁכָּא דְחִוְיָא' הֶעָלוּל לְקַבֵּל טוּמְאָה, וּלְהִתְגָּאֵל בְּכָל הַתַּאֲווֹת רַחֲמָנָא לִיצְּלַן,

the "snake's skin" that is prone to become impure and sullied by engaging in **all the desires** of this world, **God save us,**

Kabbalistic teachings call the body "the snake's skin."[8] The Torah states how God made for Adam and his wife tunics made out of hide and clothed them.[9] The *Zohar* comments that God stripped the snake of his

THE SPARK THAT RESIDES IN THE BODY

☞ In *Shivḥei HaBa'al Shem Tov* (Rubinstein ed., p. 313ff), the story is told about the son of the Maggid of Zelichov who was very sick and fainted. People thought he died, but three days later he started to sweat, and his soul returned to his body. When he recovered, he related what happened to him. The story is long and beyond the scope of this work, but at the end of it, he recounted that the heavenly court let him go and two people brought him back to earth. When he arrived, he saw a foul-smelling carcass that had been thrown in the garbage. They told him to enter the body, but he refused. They beat him, insisting that he enter the carcass against his will. When he went back in, he began to sweat, and his soul returned to him. This story illustrates how the soul sees the physical body after it disconnects from it even for a brief time.

8. See *Tikkunei Zohar* 10b, 92b.

9. Gen. 3:21.

skin and put it on man.[10] The human body is therefore likened to the skin of the primordial serpent. From a broader perspective, the snake skin is the *kelippa* that clothes the soul in this world.[11]

This term, "snake's skin," implies that the human body is not simply a physical entity. Rather, it is capable of becoming impure due to its physical desires. On one hand, it is a body like the body of an animal. But unlike an animal, the physical nature of man does not have any restraints, and it can descend even lower than its physical nature, into the realm of evil and sin. A person's body can become sullied even worse than an animal when he indulges in physical pleasures without inhibition. ☞

לוּלֵי שֶׁהַקָּדוֹשׁ בָּרוּךְ הוּא מָגֵן לוֹ וְנוֹתֵן לוֹ עוֹז וְתַעֲצוּמוֹת לִלְחוֹם עִם הַגּוּף וְתַאֲוֹתָיו וּלְנַצְּחָן.

if not for the fact that the Holy One, blessed be He, protects a person and gives him strength and might to wage war with the body and its desires and prevail over them.

THE SKIN OF THE SNAKE

☞ The expression "snake's skin" clearly draws a correlation with the sin of the tree of knowledge. The Talmud (*Shabbat* 146a) relates that the primordial sin consisted of the snake injecting Eve with venom, which lodged into all of humanity, until the Jewish people stood at Mount Sinai, whereupon their souls were rectified. When they sinned with the golden calf, however, it returned.

When it comes to sin, the human body is not like any other animalistic body, in that it draws a person to sin. Materiality in and of itself, like spirituality alone, is neutral and does not necessarily pose an impediment before the Divine. It is because of the body's association with the "snake's skin" and the sin of the tree of knowledge that it is no longer neutral but is relegated as an instrument destined for calamity.

In this sense, we cannot relate to our bodies like we do to the rest of physical reality, as neutral objects that do not have an inclination toward one side or another. Stones are neither good nor bad. They can be used to build a synagogue or other buildings. But our bodies, our "snake skins," have an inborn tendency toward impurity. This does not mean that they cannot lean toward holiness, but their primal inclination is toward impurity. If a person does not invest conscious effort, he will be led to the side of impurity, not to the side of holiness.

10. *Tikkunei Zohar* 10b; see also *Pirkei deRabbi Eliezer* 20; *Midrash Tehillim* 92.
11. See epistle 26; *Torah Or* 110d.

The divine spark descends so low that if God would not help it, it would not be able to emerge and ascend to its place, back to its origin in the Divine.[12]

But why do we need God's help? Why can't we do it on our own?

It is because the body is not neutral but rather draws a person to the realm of *kelippa* and evil. One cannot ignore his body. Even if he tries, his body will not allow it. If you put down an item somewhere, you can leave it there. You cannot do that with your body. You cannot just leave your body, even in a good place, to just sit quietly. Even after Yom Kippur, after a powerful repentance and total forgiveness of all of one's sins so that a person is like a newborn baby, one still cannot trust his body and assume that it will obey him and walk only on the good path. In a certain sense, what we can do with any animal, we cannot do with the body, and for this reason we need God's help. ☞

וְזֶהוּ שֶׁאוֹמְרִים, "אֲדוֹן עוּזֵּנוּ כו' מָגֵן יִשְׁעֵנוּ כו'".

This explains the verse that **is recited** in the continuation of the *Yotzer Or* blessing **"Master of our strength… Shield of our deliverance…."**

STRENGTH FROM GOD

☞ That God helps a person and protects him from this-worldly desires does not mean that an angel descends from Heaven and gets involved in a person's affairs. God's help is expressed mostly in the fact that He created light with an inherent benefit over darkness. This benefit is always there, but this assistance is perceptible only when a person succeeds in facing the struggle head-on. More than that, it is only when the forces of good and evil are more or less equal does God's promise to help come to the fore by imbuing a person with the strength to prevail over the body and its desires. After all, if the force of good were stronger, God's help would not be needed.

To get to this point, a person must invest immense, constant effort. Only after he succeeds in facing the good and evil elements within and weighing them against each other does God help him to feel the benefit of the light over the darkness so that ultimately, one way or another, he will get control over his body. Many people struggle to ever reach that point of balance, where the two sides are equal, and therefore are not privy to this divine assistance.

12. *Kiddushin* 30b; *Sukka* 52b; see *Likkutei Amarim*, chap. 13.

As mentioned above, this epistle is organized, to a certain degree, as a parallel to the blessing of *Yotzer Or.* First comes our praise of God, "who alone is exalted," through which one comes to an awakening of compassion and the supplication of "In your immense compassion, have compassion on us." The awakening of compassion in man's heart does not in and of itself save him but only serves as an awakening from below. To be truly saved, the awakening must come from above in the form of the help and protection from the forces of evil and the power and strength to prevail over them and triumph. It is in relation to this that we praise Him as the "Master of our strength... Shield of our deliverance" – the "strength" within us (the force that fills) and the "shield" around us (the force that encompasses). ☞

CONTEMPLATION THAT LEADS TO COMPASSION

☞ One must pay attention to the precise wording of the author of the *Tanya.* He speaks of the spark that resides "in the dark and gloomy body," which is "prone to become impure," but he does not refer explicitly to a person who is wicked and a sinner. These concepts, integral to the whole approach of the *Tanya,* the "Book of *Beinonim,*" are aimed at the general readership, and therefore one must begin from a universal human standpoint, not from a specific life circumstance. Clearly, a person who sinned, who dragged his soul down into spiritual filth and who forced God to sin with him, as it were, should feel shame and compassion for the divine spark within him that has been brought so low. Yet here he relates also to those who did not sin, so that those who have not fallen so low will also utilize this powerful tool of shame and compassion in his divine service. Therefore, he describes the condition of the divine soul within the physical body.

By way of analogy, imagine that a king is in exile, held captive, and he is placed under the control of a child who is not exceptionally smart or stupid and who is a little bit evil, and he is given permission to do whatever he wants with the king. He can let him go free for a day or ride on his back instead of on a horse, or he can give him candy. Compassion for the king does not arise only if the king is treated in an objectively humiliating way. The very fact that this insignificant person has been given the power to decide his fate is itself the indignity. That a person grants his coarse, lowly body the freedom and authority to do whatever it wants with his divine spark, whether it is engaging it in a degrading act or leaving it alone, constitutes the painfulness of captivity. For this, one should feel immense compassion.

The inner root of compassion comes from the highest place, from the level of the supernal *Keter.* This is also the root of God's primordial, all-encompassing compassion for reality (see *Likkutei Torah,* Deut. 13c). That God sustains the world at all and exists within reality is the ultimate show of compassion. Of course, there are many manifestations of His divine com-

20 Av

22 Av (leap year)

וְהִנֵּה מוּדַעַת זֹאת דְּיֵשׁ ב׳ מִינֵי דְּחִילוּ וּרְחִימוּ. הָרִאשׁוֹנוֹת הֵן הַנּוֹלָדוֹת מֵהַתְּבוּנָה וְהַדַּעַת בִּגְדוּלַּת ה׳ וּבִדְבָרִים הַמְּבִיאִין לִידֵי אַהֲבַת ה׳ וְיִרְאָתוֹ.

It is known that there are two kinds of fear and love of God. **The first** is fear and love that **are generated from the understanding and knowledge of God's greatness and** an awareness **of matters that lead to the love of God and the fear of Him.**

In a general sense, there are two levels of love and fear of God that a person can attain in his divine service. Whether a person feels love or fear of God depends on the manner and degree of one's contemplation of God's greatness. If he ponders God's exaltedness and the glory of His splendor, he will cultivate fear. If he reflects on God's kindness and compassion, he will awaken love within. The more a person develops his consciousness through the breadth and depth of his understanding, the loftier and more perfect the love and fear he evokes.

וְהָאַחֲרוֹנוֹת הֵן הַבָּאוֹת אַחַר כָּךְ מִלְמַעְלָה בִּבְחִינַת מַתָּנָה,

The latter is love and fear of God **that come afterward as a gift from above,**

Only after a person does everything in the power of his consciousness to attain intellectual love and fear of God does he merit an entirely different type of love and fear: love and fear that do not come directly from his contemplative work below but from above. This love and fear

passion. On the level of the world of *Yetzira*, God exists and enlivens the angels therein. There is also divine compassion in our world, where God gives life even to the wicked. At its essence, then, the attribute of compassion can extend from one extreme of reality to the other.

These concepts are related to that which will be explained below, that particularly through the attribute of compassion a person can go from one extreme to the other, from the lowest place to the highest. Even someone at rock bottom can grasp that he should have compassion. Even when contemplation of God's greatness evades him and he does not feel any love or fear of God, he is capable of understanding and awakening that primal spark of compassion. Once a person awakens the attribute of compassion, he can ascend higher and higher with it, since the attribute of compassion extends throughout all levels. Compassion is the foundation for all divine service. From a sense of compassion, a person is capable of transcending his limitations. This opening forges a channel of ascension through all the dimensions of his divine service, including love and fear.

are not a direct, automatic outcome of his prior level of love and fear, but they come from an other-worldly heavenly power, not as payment but as a gift. ☞

וּכְמוֹ שֶׁנִּתְבָּאֵר בְּמָקוֹם אַחֵר עַל פָּסוּק: "עֲבוֹדַת מַתָּנָה אֶתֵּן אֶת כְּהוּנַּתְכֶם" (במדבר יח, ז). שֶׁהִיא מִדַּת אַהֲבָה,

as explained elsewhere regarding the verse "As a service that is a gift I give your priesthood" (Num. 18:7). The priestly service **is the attribute of love,**

It is explained elsewhere that the priest represents the attribute of kindness, or love,[13] while the Levite service represents the attribute of restraint, or fear.[14] "Your priesthood" is therefore a general expression for any service that is performed out of love. The verse can thus be understood as saying that God gives the service of love to a person as a gift.

A GOD-GIVEN GIFT

☞ The concept of love and fear that one receives as a gift from above can be seen in the wording of our prayers. We ask, for instance, "Unite our hearts to love and fear Your name" (in the blessing of *Ahavat Olam*). This is puzzling: How can we ask God for love and fear? Isn't it an accepted truth that "everything is in the hands of Heaven except for fear of Heaven" (*Berakhot* 33b)? Furthermore, if it is truly a gift from above that is independent of a person's actions below, why isn't it distributed evenly between everyone?

The answer is in what is being discussed here, that there are two levels of love and fear. The first is acquired by a person through the work that he invests in his divine service. We do not pray for this kind of love and fear because God does not give it; it must be acquired by the person himself. When a person decides that he truly wants it, and he exerts effort to deepen his knowledge and contemplate the greatness of God, he attains love and fear. This is not easy. It is a long and difficult path of constant work. Moreover, it is a path that is not in the hands of Heaven but rather in the hands of man.

Then there is another type of love and fear that originates from above as a gift. It is not granted without any initiation or awakening on the receiver's part. There are extremely rare situations when this gift is given without any initial preparation on behalf of the receiver, but they are extremely uncommon and necessitate a fundamental reconfiguration of nature. One example of this is the revelation at Mount Sinai (see *Torah Or* 18a). Normally a person is privy to this type of love and fear when he is worthy, after he has done his part, doing everything he can to acquire the first type

13. See *Likkutei Amarim*, chap. 14; *Sha'ar HaYiḥud VeHa'emuna*, Introduction.
14. See *Torah Or* 62c, *Likkutei Torah*, Num. 54a, 55b.

וְכֵן הוּא גַּם כֵּן בְּיִרְאָה.

and likewise, there is **also** the gift of **fear.**

Like love, there is also a level of fear that a person merits as a gift from above. The principle at play here is that there are two starkly different categories of attributes, or emotions, that one feels toward God: those that stem from the power of human preparation and conscious work, and those that descend as a gift from above, from beyond one's reality.

וְהִנֵּה וַדַּאי אֵין עֲרוֹךְ כְּלָל בֵּין הָרִאשׁוֹנוֹת, שֶׁהֵן תּוֹלְדוֹת הַשֵּׂכֶל הַנִּבְרָא, לְגַבֵּי הָאַחֲרוֹנוֹת שֶׁהֵן מֵהַבּוֹרֵא יִתְבָּרֵךְ שְׁמוֹ.

There is certainly no comparison at all between the first level of love and fear, **which are products of the human intellect, and the latter** type of love and fear, **which are** a gift **from the Creator, blessed be He.**

The difference is that the first category of love and fear, where they are products of human cognitive processing, is limited by a person's intellectual capacity of consciousness, while the latter, granted by God, can be given without limitation. The crucial difference does not lie in

of love. Then, sometimes (though not always), God adds a major dose of the second type of love and fear that is not commensurate with the value of one's personal spiritual work.

That "everything is in the hands of Heaven except fear of Heaven" certainly does not mean that God is incapable of granting man fear of Heaven, but rather that He does not want to override man's free choice. In the broader picture, everything is truly in the hands of Heaven, including fear of Heaven. God did not include fear of Heaven as part of the framework of the created worlds; it is not part of the natural order, yet it is not totally separate from it. The reality is therefore complex: God sometimes gives a person a gift of love and fear, and other times the opposite is the case, and He takes a person's free choice away in the other direction, as in "I will harden Pharaoh's heart" (Ex. 7:3; see Rashi and Ramban there).

God does not veto a person's essential free will, but He may harden the heart of someone who already hardened his own heart, similar to the way that He gives love and fear to one who already possesses love and fear. As the verse states, "He grants wisdom to the wise" (Dan. 2:21), and "If it is to scoffers He will scoff" (Prov. 3:34). God does occasionally grant this gift to a person who has not done the preliminary spiritual work necessary as a type of credit that he will need to repay in the future (see *Likkutei Torah*, Lev. 1b). But at the end of the day, the ability to choose is always in the person's hands, only sometimes God grants him an augmentation of that which he already has as a gift from above.

the power of the emotion but in its origin, whether these emotions arise from within or they originate from above. Those that come from within are limited by the person's own cognitive abilities.

A person can only fathom things that are within a certain scope of his nature. The love and fear that a person cultivates with his conscious mind are necessarily confined to his level and spiritual makeup. By contrast, the love and fear that a person receives from above can transcend his capacity and, to a certain extent, exceed all comprehension because they come from the infinite Divine and not from a limited created being.

Yet the more significant difference, which this epistle addresses, touches on the degree to which the emotions ring true to their beholder. The love and fear cultivated from human consciousness are contingent on man's limitations, and the most significant limitation of one's life experience is the lack of certainty regarding the truth of what he is feeling. ☞

GENUINE VERSUS ILLUSORY EMOTIONS

☞ The Midrash (*Bereshit Rabba* 8:5) relates that when God wanted to create man, the angels gathered in groups and expressed their opinions, whether they were in favor of creating man or opposed. The attribute of truth said, "Let him not be created, for he is entirely lies." God, however, did not listen and "cast truth to the ground" (Dan. 8:12). Though God did not heed the angels and created man anyway, this does not mean that truth is not truth and that man is not filled with lies.

Lies come in many forms and degrees. There are simple lies, those that a person tells others. These can be verified and are easily exposed. Then there are more serious lies that are much harder for the person himself, as well as others, to deal with, those with which a person deludes himself. Here, since the person fills all the roles, that of witness, judge, and suspect, he lacks an objective frame of reference to assess the situation properly. The problem with this type of lie also plays a role in illusory experiences. In an experience that is full of falsehood, a person does not necessarily fake his emotions, pretending to love or fear or acting as if he is praying. The person himself may be convinced that he loves or fears God, that he is genuinely praying. That is when the problem is much more serious.

A certain tzaddik once said, half in bitter jest, "I believe that a person who lies and says that he fasts for three days is better than one who actually fasts for three days straight." The one who lies to others at least knows that he is lying, so the damage he does to his own spiritual well-being is reduced. But the person who actually fasts for three days may get stuck in a much more serious illusion. This is not about whether he ate or didn't eat, but a delusion about his own spiritual stature. Since there is no way to test this type of lie, there is also no way to escape from it. This risk of self-delusion poses a serious threat for every person who strives to serve God and tries to build a true awareness and understanding of the Divine.

In a certain sense, this is the biggest battle that confronts the devotee of God. It is not the difficulty of attaining love and fear in the first place but of staying authentic. Is what the person feeling and thinking real? In light of this, there is a significant difference between divine service that comes from his own efforts or service that comes as a gift from above. Whatever a person cultivates from his own energies comes with the risk of illusion and delusion. This problem is extremely subtle and deeply internal, and it exists on every level as a person grows, from one level to the next. This is not a simple case of pretending but a complex process of subtle deceit, one deception interwoven into the next. Due to the sheer subtlety of the self-illusion, a person can live an entire lifetime of deceit and have no idea that he is living a lie.

These issues primarily apply to one's service of God, since in our interpersonal relationships we generally do not need to delve into this degree of analysis regarding the authenticity of our modes of relating to each other. There is a certain point after which there is no longer a need to test the degree to which a relationship manifests from a place of inner truth. When a person loves his friend, he does not need to constantly ask himself questions like "Do I love him or do I just love myself? To what degree is this love a reflection of my own inner satisfaction? Am I fooling myself just to feel good? To what degree is this only a response to someone else's relating to me?"

When a relationship functions as it should, whether it is with family, a co-worker, or some other interpersonal interaction, that is proof of its integrity. Nothing else is necessary. This is not the case when it comes to service of God, where one is in relationship with a being who overtly is not in need of his love or is waiting to receive a response from him. When a person is not grounded in reality, when he is trying to play all the roles, that of suspect, verdict, and judge, the challenges in determining the truth are inestimably more severe.

The problem is that anything that the conscious self can formulate depends on a vast system of conditionality to which the self is restricted. Everything a person does, on almost every level, is conditional: If this, then that. When a person attempts to relate to a realm beyond that conditionality, the problem of authentication becomes virtually impossible, and at that moment, it becomes the most serious problem that a person has to grapple with.

Whether a person loves or fears, then, is less of an issue. The more serious task is to refine the emotions that he has, to distill them for authenticity. For a person to attain his personal "absolute truth" (see *Likkutei Amarim*, chap. 13) is virtually impossible. People strive to arrive at objective truth from subjective perspectives. While this is not a neat description of our efforts, it is very realistic. It could be that tomorrow, next week, or next year one will realize that the absolute truth that he previously attained is not actually true, not because what he attained previously was objectively false but because he was looking through the lens of that particular moment at the time, and it is only from that perspective that he reached what he thought was absolute truth.

וְלָכֵן הֵן הֵן הַנִּקְרָאוֹת בְּשֵׁם אֱמֶת, כִּי חוֹתָמוֹ שֶׁל הַקָּדוֹשׁ בָּרוּךְ הוּא אֱמֶת שֶׁהוּא אֱמֶת הָאֲמִיתִּי, וְכָל הָאֱמֶת שֶׁבַּנִּבְרָאִים כְּלָא חֲשִׁיבֵי קַמֵּיהּ.

Therefore, the second level of love and fear, which stem from God, **is the one called truth, because truth is the seal the Holy One, blessed be He, for He is the absolute truth, and any truth that is** found **among created beings is considered nothingness before Him.**

At the beginning of his work, Rambam states, "The meaning of the words of the prophet 'But my Lord God is truth' (Jer. 10:10) is that He alone is truth, and no other can claim that they have absolute truth. This relates to the Torah's statement 'There is no other besides Him' (Deut. 4:35), meaning that there is no extant truth besides Him or like Him" (*Mishneh Torah, Sefer HaMadda, Hilkhot Yesodei HaTorah* 1:2). This is the nature of truth: There is no half-truth, and there is no small truth or big truth. Either something is true through and through, or it is not true. In this sense, only God can represent absolute truth. All other definitions of truth are relative. Meaning, if they are true, it is only because they relate in some stipulative way to God's truth.

The truth that we establish, on all levels, is attained only through comparing one thing to another. One thing is true like something else that we know to be true. This is how we build our perspective of reality: by relating new concepts or experiences to true archetypes, which we compare to even truer truths, and so on. But within ourselves, when we as human beings are twisted and convoluted, fraught with distortion and falsehood, when our whole beings are upside down, inconsistent, and inauthentic, then we lack all objective tests of truth.

When we look inward and attempt to compare one thing to another, we come up with only relative truths. It is only about God that we say, "It is true and firm and correct, enduring, straight and faithful" (in the *Emet VeYatziv* prayer), like a tall building, at the top of which is (as the prayer concludes) "the Lord, your God who is truth." God's stamp is truth, and the truer something is, the closer it is to God. Since truth is the symbol emblazed on anything connected to God, on everything that comes from Him, we constantly search for truth. ☞

אַךְ אֵיזֶה הַדֶּרֶךְ שֶׁיִּזְכֶּה הָאָדָם לֶאֱמֶת ה'? הִנֵּה הוּא עַל יְדֵי שֶׁיְּעוֹרֵר רַחֲמִים רַבִּים לִפְנֵי ה' עַל הַנִּיצוֹץ שֶׁבְּנַפְשׁוֹ.

But what is the way for a person to merit God's truth? It is by awakening abundant compassion before God for the divine **spark that is in his soul.**

How does one merit this fabric of experience that is stamped with God's truth? How does one attain the love and fear of God, which are essentially a gift from above?

While the author of the *Tanya* previously stated that one must cultivate the first type of love and fear of his own volition before he can merit the second type, this alone is not enough. While this lays the necessary foundation, it does not guarantee that he will merit love and fear from above. From the first type of love and fear to the second is a gap that a person cannot cross by treading a certain number of steps, because the second type is not a consequence or payment for his effort and actions but a gift. A person cannot demand a gift – he must ask for it.

THE STAMP OF TRUTH

☞ The main difference between an attribute cultivated by a person and one that is God-given is not in size or intensity, nor in the degree that it impacts or moves its beholder. What characterizes the divine gift, if not intensity or degree of impact? The divine gift can be recognized in one way: in the stamp of God upon it, which is the stamp of truth.

Man-made metal instruments are comprised of a mixture of metals, mostly simple metals and, occasionally, silver and gold. Yet it is difficult to discern precisely which metals an item contains. Sometimes, what looks like a large and impressive piece is made almost entirely of tin and copper. Most people are not capable of deciphering whether precious metals are present. For this reason, the accepted practice is to put a special stamp on items that contain real gold and silver. The stamp not only states what it is, but more importantly, it testifies that it is real.

Similarly, the stamp of God testifies to the truth of a concept. An idea or emotion may not look any different, but the stamp indicates that it is intrinsically different from everything else. If a person merits one moment of this truth, then that moment becomes the ultimate point of reference for his whole reality, the measurement of whether other experiences are real or not. Everything else becomes relegated to the realm of speculation, to "what if" or "it resembles," while that experience, stamped with God's seal of truth, will forever remain one's definition of reality.

Some things are built on mutual reciprocity, on giving and taking. This is not how a gift works. A gift is a one-way expression. A poor person who asks for charity does not offer anything in return; he only arouses compassion. When asking for a free gift, one asks for compassion, not for what he deserves. So too, when we request a gift from God, we must arouse compassion. One's spiritual level does not matter. One must awaken compassion because the truth is that he cannot possibly buy it even if he were to give everything that he has.

The story is told about a certain tzaddik who in his old age used to say, "I have served God for seventy years, and I have not attained one word of truth. God should have compassion on an old man like me and give it a free gift."

This compassion is not directed toward our being, our self with whom we identify, but rather on the divine spark that is in exile within us.

Compassion **is the attribute of Jacob,** who is called **"the central bar** inside the boards **from end to end"** (Ex. 26:28), **implying** that this attribute passes **from the loftiest heights to the lowest depths,**

שֶׁהִיא מִדָּתוֹ שֶׁל יַעֲקֹב, "מַבְרִיחַ מֵהַקָּצֶה אֶל הַקָּצֶה" (שמות כו, כח), **דְּהַיְינוּ מֵרוּם הַמַּעֲלוֹת עַד לְמַטָּה מַטָּה,**

The forefathers, Abraham, Isaac, and Jacob, represent three paths in divine service though the attributes that they embodied: *Ḥesed*, Kindness; *Gevura*, Restraint; and *Tiferet*, which is synonymous with compassion.[15] These three paths are associated with the three sets of bars that secured the vertical beams of the Tabernacle: the upper bars, the lower bars, and a middle bar, which is described as extending "from end to end."

The upper and lower bars were fastened to the beams on the outside. Each bar had two sections, each of which extended halfway across the wall. The central bar, by contrast, passed through an opening inside the beams and extended the entire width of the wall, "from

15. See Gen. 31:42; Mic. 7:20: *Likkutei Torah*, Lev. 45b, Song 14a, 43b.

end to end."[16] This is why the central bar represents the attribute of compassion, the attribute of Jacob, which is a synthesis of *Ḥesed* and *Gevura*. Unlike the other attributes, the attribute of compassion penetrates every aspect of reality, reaching infinitely lofty heights and infinitely low depths.[17] It can penetrate the highest realms since relative to God even the most supernal beings need compassion, as well as the lowest depths, in the sense that even the lowest creature can still receive compassion.[18] ☞

FROM END TO END

☞ Just as Jacob's attribute of compassion extends from one end to the other, so does his attribute of truth (*Likkutei Amarim*, chap. 13). Every realm and every level in reality has its own core of truth. Like compassion, truth also descends all the way down to the depths, because something will be true even if others do not like it or agree with it. We may be opposed, we may not accept, we can choose not to look, yet that truth will stand.

Truth, like compassion, is the central bar that slices through everything and passes from one end to the other. This can be seen in other fields of thought as well, wherein particular concepts pass by each other, yet do not intersect or limit each other. In the same way, the line of truth passes through all of reality yet is not blemished or affected by it. If something is true, it is true; it cannot be falsified. It is stamped with God's seal of truth.

---

16. See *Shabbat* 98b, and *Tosafot* there, which states that the middle bar ran along the both the length and width of the Tabernacle so that it miraculously bent through the beams on three sides.

17. This concept is portrayed pictorially in the structure of the *sefirot* that is portrayed as three arrays. The right array is that of *Ḥesed*, Abraham's attribute; the left is that of *Gevura*, Isaac's attribute; and the middle array is that of *Tiferet*, Jacob's attribute. The middle array begins higher than the others, extending from *Keter*, which is higher than *Ḥokhma* and *Bina*, to the lowest point, to *Malkhut*, which lies below all the other *sefirot*.

18. Though the Sages state (see, e.g., *Berakhot* 33a; *Midrash Tanḥuma, Metzora* 1) that it is prohibited to have compassion on some people, such as evildoers or the person who has no *da'at*, discerning knowledge, this does not indicate a limitation of the attribute of compassion. On the contrary, it is specifically because compassion knows no bounds that one must be careful to not be compassionate toward some people. Love does not have to be limited in the same sense. If a person is repulsive, for example, no one loves him, but anyone can pity him.

לְהַמְשִׁיךְ אֱמֶת ה׳ לָעוֹלָם הַשָּׁפָל הַזֶּה הֶחָשׁוּךְ, וּכְמוֹ שֶׁכָּתוּב: ״כִּי אֵשֵׁב בַּחֹשֶׁךְ ה׳ אוֹר לִי״ (מיכה ז, ח). וְזֶהוּ ״כִּי גָבַר עָלֵינוּ חַסְדּוֹ כו׳״ (תהלים קיז, ב).

to draw down God's truth to this lowly, dark world, as it is written, "Though I sit in darkness, the Lord is a light for me" (Mic. 7:8). **This is** also **the meaning of** the verse **"For His kindness toward us is overwhelming…"** (Ps. 117:2).

Through prayerfully requesting an awakening of compassion, we can reach a point of true divine service. For one moment, we can reach that point of contact and experience true love and fear, as in the words of the siddur, "to serve You in truth."

This verse in Micah shows how divine truth shines through the attribute of compassion even in the darkness of this lowly world. The verse that the author of the *Tanya* quotes from Psalms implies that we attain that truth and compassion even though we may not deserve it. This is what we request when we ask for an awakening of compassion: that the attribute of truth, God's truth, reach even the level we are on, even if we do not deserve it. Compassion is therefore the vessel with which we may receive the gift of truth.

אַךְ הִתְעוֹרְרוּת רַחֲמִים רַבִּים לִפְנֵי ה׳ צְרִיכָה לִהְיוֹת גַּם כֵּן בֶּאֱמֶת.

However, the awakening of abundant compassion before God must also be truthful.

When a person comes to awaken the attribute of compassion to draw down God's eternal truth into his personal, lowly bubble of existence, the condition is that he must do so with a degree of truth. It is not enough for a person to mouth the words written in the siddur. He must be authentic. His words must truly reflect his own truth, his own true deficiency, his genuine desire. ☞

וְגַם כְּשֶׁהוּא בֶּאֱמֶת שֶׁלּוֹ, אֵיךְ יוּכַל עַל יְדֵי אֱמֶת שֶׁלּוֹ לְעוֹרֵר רַחֲמִים עֶלְיוֹנִים מֵאֱמֶת ה׳?

Yet even when it is true **according to one's own truth, how can one awaken supernal compassion from God's truth through his own** relative **truth?**

There is God's truth, and there is man's truth. A person can say something that is true from his standpoint, even from a universally human standpoint, yet it is not God's truth. We strive to inform our relative, limited sense of truth with a transcendent, absolute, infinite truth. We yearn for contact with the absolute yet from within a relative, limited, human paradigm. How can we attain divine truth through a human lens? ☞

THOSE WHO CALL OUT TO HIM IN TRUTH

☞ The verses in *Ashrei* (Ps. 145) are each comprised of two parts that complement each other, with one exception. In verse 18, the second clause does not add to the first but limits it. The verse begins, "The Lord is close to all who call Him," and then comes the limitation: "to all who call Him in truth." When we call out to God, asking him to turn to us, to have compassion upon us, to shower us with love, and inspire us with fear from above, the condition is that this request must be genuine, coming from the depths of the heart (see *Torah Or* 27a).

One may ask, is it possible that this prayerful request could be made without genuine intention? The answer is that there are many levels. The first, most common level is that the person is lying: He says one thing but thinks another. He is reading from the prayer book, but it is not affecting him at all. If he were to contemplate the content of the siddur, he would discover incredible things: powerful declarations, eternal obligations, and intimate expressions that he would never utter to another human being without serious intention, without really feeling them. When a person merely mouths the words in the siddur, he justifies it to himself by reasoning that he is obligated to pray three times a day and recite everything written in the siddur. When a person prays this way day after day, saying praises and putting forth requests insincerely, he resigns himself to this way of prayer.

TRUTH NEVER CHANGES

☞ Elsewhere, the author of the *Tanya* defines truth as that which is immutable. A feeling or experience that does not stand true at all times and on every level is not true. If a person can pray and immediately afterward think and do mundane or even sinful things, it is a sign that his prayer was not authentic. This does not apply only to someone who prays in a purely apathetic way, but even when he prays with fervor and has a spiritual experience, if afterward he can revert back to what he was before, as if he had not prayed, his experience was not really of God (see *Likkutei Amarim*, chaps. 12–13; *Torah Or* 28c–d). The moment a person reaches a crystal-clear truth, he is incapable of veering away from it. But as long as the experience stems from his subjective truth that comes to him at that moment in that situation, he remains stuck behind that unbridgeable gap between his truth and God's truth.

אַךְ הָעֵצָה לָזֶה הִיא מִדַּת הַצְּדָקָה, שֶׁהִיא מִדַּת הָרַחֲמִים עַל מַאן דְּלֵית לֵיהּ מִגַּרְמֵיהּ, "לְהַחֲיוֹת רוּחַ שְׁפָלִים כו'" (ישעיה נז, טו).

The solution for this is the attribute of charity, which is the attribute of compassion for one who has nothing of his own, "to revive the spirit of the humble" (Isa. 57:15).

The author of the *Tanya* returns now to the point with which he opened the letter: the meaning of the "sower of charity." This dilemma cannot be solved through personal, spiritual work, but rather the solution lies in the realm of action. A person's psychospiritual experience will always be relegated to the realm of the subjective, but an action performed in the world is objective, irrespective of what the person feels.

Charity is given to a person who does not have the means to repay the giver. The purpose of charity is to enliven and lift up the lowly. When one gives charity motivated by his attribute of compassion, he does not conduct a background check of the recipient. We do not ask the hungry man if he deserves the money. We do not pry and try to figure out whether it was his sins that caused him suffering. The mere fact that he is lowly, that he is lacking, deems him worthy of receiving charity.

The problem that the author of the *Tanya* strives to solve is how to engender objectivism when it comes to compassion. As long as a person has compassion for himself, as long as the extent of the expression of his attribute of compassion is an internal sensation of compassion, he is working only within the confines of his own inner world. But the moment he gives charity to someone in need, he has accomplished something that truly, objectively endures, irrespective of the giver's own personal experience. The giving of charity touches on God's absolute, objective truth and is no longer relegated to the person's own relative truth alone. His internal experience remains "his own truth," but the act of giving, objectively real from every frame of reference, is "God's eternal truth." ☞

CHARITY AS GOD'S TRUTH

☞ Essentially, all the action-based mitzvot take a person out of the confines of his own inner experience and affects the objective world, but the mitzva of charity is unique in the sense that it not only interfaces with the world but is entirely transferred to it. When a man lays *tefillin* or a woman lights the Sabbath candles, they

וּבְאִתְעֲרוּתָא דִלְתַתָּא אִתְעֲרוּתָא דִלְעֵילָּא, ה׳ מְעוֹרֵר יְשֵׁנִים וּמֵקִיץ נִרְדָּמִים, הֵם בְּחִינַת רַחֲמִים רַבִּים וַחֲסָדִים עֶלְיוֹנִים הַנֶּעֱלָמִים, לָצֵאת מֵהַהֶעְלֵם אֶל הַגִּילּוּי, וְהֶאָרָה רַבָּה לֵאוֹר בְּאוֹר הַחַיִּים אֱמֶת ה׳ לְעוֹלָם.

The awakening from below evokes an **awakening from above,** causing **God to rouse those who sleep and awaken those who slumber.** In other words, He awakens **the attributes of abundant compassion and supernal kindness, which are concealed,** causing them to **emerge from** their state of **concealment to** a state of **manifestation and great illumination,** so that a person is **enlightened with the light of life, the truth of God forever.**

The "abundant compassion" and "supernal kindness" are what is referred to as attributes in *Keter,* on a level beyond the levels of *Ḥokhma* and *Bina.*[19] These attributes are, in a certain sense, the attributes of God Himself, not those through which He actually runs the world, but rather His own hidden attributes. These concealed attributes, which constitute "the truth of God," are ancient, in the sense that they do not manifest down below in the ordinary workings of the world. It is only through an awakening from below they are roused from slumber and emerge from their state of concealment, shining the truth of God onto this world.

perform an objective act. But beyond the question of whether the *tefillin* are kosher and so on, the measure of these mitzvot is in the heavens.

From an objective standpoint, the donning of *tefillin* did not effect any change in our world. The impact and significance of this mitzva lie in the higher, spiritual worlds. While a person performs this physical action according to the *halakha,* what determines its degree of authenticity, its integrity, is the realm of his own personal truth. By contrast, the value of the mitzva of charity is determined, not by the spiritual level or intention of the doer, but rather by the recipient of the charity, who is, first and foremost, a person of flesh and blood in this world. Charity is not a mitzva that one can perform with supernal angels, where we have no frame of reference to estimate the impact we would have had. With charity, we know that so-and-so did not have any bread, and now he does. This action is therefore a true expression of compassion, which is no longer relegated to the realm of relative truth. At that moment, one can also awaken the compassion that is on the level of God's truth.

19. See *Torah Or* 63b, 70a; *Likkutei Torah,* Deut. 13c, 14a.

(וזה) [וְזֶהוּ] לְשׁוֹן זְרִיעָה הַנֶּאֱמַר בִּצְדָקָה, לְהַצְמִיחַ אֱמֶת הָעֶלְיוֹן, אֱמֶת ה'.

This is the meaning of the term "sowing" used with regard to charity, which causes **the supernal truth, God's truth, to sprout.**

This term, "sowing" is used with regard to charity in the verse that the author of the *Tanya* quoted at the beginning of the epistle: "The sower of charity has a true reward." When a person plants a seed in the ground, he ultimately reaps much more than he invested. Charity is similar: A person gives something physical and reaps supernal truth.

As explained above, supernal truth can be acquired only as a gift, because nothing man does or offers can possibly come close to being commensurate in value with God's truth. Yet there is something he can do that serves as an awakening from below to spark the revelation of God's truth. The revelation does not come as a direct outcome of the action, but rather the action creates a vessel capable of receiving the light of that supernal gift. We "sow" charity, and on the surface, the principal outcome of this action is that the money was acquired by another person, but we have done much more. This charity caused something inestimably huge to burgeon forth: We have engendered an awakening from below that caused an awakening from above and the revelation of God's truth.

וּבִפְרָט בִּצְדָקָה וְחֶסֶד שֶׁל אֱמֶת שֶׁעוֹשִׂים עִם אֶרֶץ הַקֹּדֶשׁ, תִּבָּנֶה וְתִכּוֹנֵן בִּמְהֵרָה בְיָמֵינוּ אָמֵן,

Particularly the charity and true kindness done for the Holy Land, may it be rebuilt and reestablished speedily in our days amen,

On the practical level, this epistle was intended to inspire the giving of charity to provide for the needs of the hasidic settlement in the Land of Israel. A group of hasidim who had moved to the Land of Israel not long before were in need of financial support, and Rabbi Menaḥem Mendel of Vitebsk, who stood at the helm of the group, appointed the author of the *Tanya* to collect funds for them.[20] This was not a simple matter, and in order to persuade and inspire the Jews living in the diaspora,

20. Rabbi Menaḥem Mendel took over the mantle of leadership from the Maggid of Mezeritch, and after the Maggid's death, the author of the *Tanya*, Rabbi Shneur Zalman of Liadi, accepted him as his Rebbe.

who lived in privation, to send monies to a faraway land and relieve the troubles of those living there, the author of the *Tanya* interwove mystical underpinnings into his call for donations.

לְקַיֵּים מַה שֶּׁכָּתוּב: "אֱמֶת מֵאֶרֶץ תִּצְמָח" (תהלים פה, יב), עַל יְדֵי זְרִיעַת הַצְּדָקָה בָּהּ.

in fulfillment of the verse "Truth will spring up from the land as charity looks down from heaven" (Ps. 85:12) **by sowing charity in it.**

To this end, the author of the *Tanya* addresses the spiritual side of the mitzva of charity. Charity is compared to sowing, which causes the divine attributes, which are rooted in truth, to spring forth. One sows in earth, and the Land of Israel is the paradigm of earth, the primary land. In light of this, the ultimate blossoming comes from seeds sown in the Land of Israel.

The earth is an embodiment of the *sefira* of *Malkhut*. There is a lower earth and a supernal earth, which corresponds to supernal *Malkhut*. The Land of Israel is perfectly oriented to the supernal earth[21] and is therefore the highest of all lands, serving as a conduit for all sustenance and vitality for all the other lands in the world. Sowing charity particularly in the Land of Israel causes truth to sprout forth in the most powerful, all-encompassing way.

וְחֶסֶד וְרַחֲמִים רַבִּים הַנֶּאֱסָפִים וְנִלְקָטִים לְתוֹכָהּ, הֵם מְעוֹרְרִים גַּם כֵּן חֲסָדִים עֶלְיוֹנִים הַצְּפוּנִים וְנֶעֱלָמִים (בְּנוּסַח אַחֵר: בָּהּ), כְּמוֹ שֶׁכָּתוּב: "אֲשֶׁר צָפַנְתָּ כוּ" (תהלים לא, כ), לְכוֹנְנָהּ וְלַהֲקִימָהּ,

The kindness and abundant compassion that are gathered and collected in it also awaken the supernal kindness that is hidden and concealed [alternatively: hidden and concealed within it], as it is written, "How great is the goodness **You have in store…"** (Ps. 31:20), so that the land **may be established and set up.**

The act of charity, which literally sows kindness and compassion in the earth, awakens the supernal, concealed kindnesses, which are then channeled to us in compassion in the form of a gift from above.

---

21. See *Etz Ḥayyim* 32:3; *Likkutei Torah*, Num. 36b, 89b.

"How great is the goodness You have in store for those who fear You," refers particularly to this hidden reward.[22] (The word *tzafanta*, "that You have in store," literally means, "that You have hidden away.") The blossoming inherently comes from the concealed dimension. When a person plants a seed, and the seed disappears in the earth, it is as if it ceases to exist. Yet a whole plant or an entire fruit-bearing tree grows from it that bears no resemblance whatsoever to the original seed. This is what it means to sow charity in the earth: A person gives a coin to a poor person, and even if it was not given in the most genuine, altruistic way, this act of charity causes true love and fear to blossom from above.

וְזֶהוּ שֶׁכָּתוּב: ״בִּצְדָקָה תִּכּוֹנָנִי״ (ישעיה נד, יד).

This is the meaning of the verse "With charity you will be established" (Isa. 54:14).

This verse, "With charity you will be established," is addressing the land itself. When a person sows the seeds of charity in the earth, he not only sustains the receiver and benefits himself, he nourishes the earth as well. In particular, charity given to the Land of Israel directly raises up the Divine Presence from the dust.

The Land of Israel, which is surrounded by other countries, parallels the Jewish people, who are surrounded by the nations. In another sense, it correlates to the Divine Presence itself. When a person physically builds the land by giving charity to those who live in it, he sustains the land, not just in the physical sense, but on a cosmic scope as well, sustaining the supernal land, the entire Jewish people, and the whole world on every level.

This epistle addressed two main points. The first is how to serve God with the attribute of compassion and what it means to have compassion for God. Then it explained that one must cultivate compassion for the divine spark within him, for the portion of God from on high that flickers within and has been brought to all kinds of lowly, degrading places. The Mishna depicts this with the words "When a person suffers,

22. See epistle 10 below; *Likkutei Torah*, Num. 29c.

what does the Divine Presence say? 'Woe to my head, woe to my arm'" (*Sanhedrin* 1:5). The Divine Presence suffers along with the Jewish people because every Jew is a limb of the Divine Presence. This is how a person should see himself: not as an independent entity, but rather, as part and parcel of the Divine Presence.

They say that the highest prayer that a person can pray for himself is when he makes a request "for the sake of God's name," when he feels compassion for the divine spark, for the Divine Presence within him, and makes his request on its behalf.[23] As the verse says, "I will be with him in times of trouble" (Ps. 91:15) and "In all their troubles, He was troubled" (Isa. 63:9). God joins us in our suffering, and we take part in His degradation, as it were. In this light, the suffering of the world, in all its forms, takes on a much deeper meaning in the sense that it is all God's suffering. Man's pain and lack is the pain and lack of the Divine Presence, and the compassion we request is ultimately for the Divine Presence. This is what it means to serve God with the attribute of compassion.

The second point that the letter discussed was with regard to the attribute of truth. More specifically, how can a person transcend his own subjective experience, even if true from his perspective, and access experiences of absolute truth, which are part of God's truth? The answer is that he must first of all ask for compassion, because he can only arrive at this ultimate truth through a gift from above. Furthermore, the request for compassion must be genuine, in line with the principle that an awakening from below causes the awakening from above that the person seeks to draw down.[24] The way to accomplish this is through the giving of charity, which makes a person a "sower of charity who receives the reward of truth."

This explanation is reminiscent of the axiom of our Sages, "Open for me one opening of repentance the size of a needlepoint... (*Shir HaShirim Rabba* 5:2). This image has double significance. The hole in the needlepoint is tiny, but it goes all the way through, from end to end. God says, "Open for me an opening, no matter how small, as long as it will be through and through, going from one end all the way through

---

23. See *Torah Or* 51a.
24. See *Torah Or* 24d.

to the other, and as a result, all the other openings will open for you." The question is, how can a person open an opening that will truly cut through from one end to the other? Aren't we locked in a maze with no exit? We work on ourselves inside ourselves, and everything that we perceive is essentially what is reflected back to us from our own being. How is it possible to reach a point of clarity that goes all the way through?

The answer is that we can achieve such clarity by performing an action in objective, physical reality. Then one accomplishes something that is truly through and through. Even if that action is small and negligible in relation to all the worlds, its doer will have touched on an objective point that slices through all the worlds and reaches the Divine. From that point, truly grandiose things can also permeate, such as supernal kindnesses and compassion. "How great is the goodness You have in store for those who fear You!"

Epistle 7

THIS EPISTLE IS ANOTHER LETTER MEANT TO FACILITATE and inspire the giving of charity to the hasidim living in the Land of Israel.[1] On a deeper level, it is a hasidic discourse in and of itself that addresses one particular topic: the unique connection between the commandments and the souls of the Jewish people. It explores the overarching, foundational bond between the two, as well as the way in which certain souls have a personal connection with particular mitzvot. These concepts are based on the interpretation of several verses that are explained here in a whole new light.

21 Av

23 Av (leap year)

״אַשְׁרֵינוּ מַה טּוֹב חֶלְקֵנוּ וּמַה נָּעִים גּוֹרָלֵנוּ״ כו׳ ״ה׳ מְנָת חֶלְקִי וְכוֹסִי וגו׳״ ״חֲבָלִים נָפְלוּ לִי וגו׳״ (תהלים טז, ה-ו).

In the morning prayers, we say, **“We are fortunate. How good is our portion and how pleasant our lot.…”** Similarly, it is written, **“The Lord is my lot and my portion.… The lots that have fallen to me** are pleasant.…” (Ps. 16:5–6).

The common thread between these verses are the terms “our portion” and “our lot.” This indicates that each of us have been allotted some sort of portion or inheritance, something unique to each individual that he received and no other, such as a special illumination or gift from God.

What is the significance of these two expressions, “our portion” and “our lot,” in this context and in general?

1. The epistle seems to have been written in 1798, as its conclusion, which does not appear in the *Iggeret HaKodesh* of the *Tanya*, attests. See *Iggerot Kodesh*, letter 55.

לְהָבִין לְשׁוֹן "חֶלְקֵנוּ" וְ"גוֹרָלֵנוּ" צָרִיךְ לְבָאֵר הֵיטֵב לְשׁוֹן הַשָּׁגוּר בְּמַאַמְרֵי רַבּוֹתֵינוּ זִכְרוֹנָם לִבְרָכָה: אֵין לוֹ חֵלֶק בֵּאלֹהֵי יִשְׂרָאֵל. כִּי הֲגַם דִּלְכְאוֹרָה, לֹא שַׁיָּיךְ לְשׁוֹן חֵלֶק כְּלָל בֶּאֱלֹקוּת יִתְבָּרֵךְ, שֶׁאֵינוֹ מִתְחַלֵּק לַחֲלָקִים חַס וְשָׁלוֹם.

To understand the terms "our portion" and "our lot," it is necessary to first **properly explain the common expression among the statements of our Rabbis** about one who commits certain sins, that **he has no portion in the God of Israel. It would seem that the term "portion" cannot be applied to God at all, for He cannot be divided into parts, God forbid.**

When a person commits a most grievous sin, the Sages say that "he has no portion in the God of Israel."[2] Just because this phrase is common, as the author of the *Tanya* points out, does not mean it is easily understood. The main challenge is understanding how we could apply the expression "portion" to God. One can speak about portions and inheritances of land, because land can be divided into parts, but how can one speak about a portion of the God of Israel? Is the Divine divisible, making it possible for a person to claim a stake in it? ☞

A COMMON EXPRESSION

☞ What is meant by this phrase "a common expression"? This question is characteristic of hasidic teachings and can even be viewed as one of its defining features. The essence of Hasidism is not in novel ideas, but rather in its ability to glean novelty out of old concepts. It takes something familiar to all, something that a person knows his whole life, and puts a totally new spin on it, asking, "What does this really mean and how is it relevant to me?" This is what the author of the *Tanya* is doing here. He asks: What does the common expression "He has no portion in the God of Israel" really mean? The answer to this question and the significance it holds for every person forms the basis of this letter.

2. See *Sanhedrin* 102b; *Otzar HaMidrashim*, p. 185. The Lubavitcher Rebbe, Rabbi Menaḥem Mendel Schneerson, comments: "Until now, I have found the source for this expression only in only one place: *Midrash Tanḥuma*, end of *Parashat Tazria*. Yet in many places, we find 'You have no [portion in the God of Israel]' (*Bereshit Rabba* 2:4) and 'They have no [portion in the God of Israel]' (*Berakhot* 63b). One can reconcile this by saying that the author of the *Tanya* did not want to use the second person or the plural."

אַךְ הָעִנְיָן כְּמוֹ שֶׁכָּתוּב בְּיַעֲקֹב: "וַיִּקְרָא לוֹ אֵל אֱלֹהֵי יִשְׂרָאֵל" (בראשית לג, כ).

The matter can be understood **based on a verse regarding Jacob:** "He established there an altar, **and he called it El Elohei Yisrael** [God of Israel]" (Gen. 33:20).

To explain this idea, another verse must be introduced, which all the commentaries have trouble explaining. After Jacob survived the encounter with his brother Esau, he built an altar to thank God. Then comes the ambiguous verse: "He established there an altar, and he called it El Elohei Yisrael," *El* being one of the names of God.

The question that the commentaries ask is, who called whom *El*? Rashi explains the verse literally, that Jacob named the altar *El* because of the miracle done for him there so that people who mentioned the name of the altar would automatically praise God. According to this, the meaning of the altar's name is "He who is God is God to me, whose name, my name, is Israel."[3] But as Rashi himself goes on to explain, the Sages interpret the verse differently: "The Holy One, blessed be He [the 'God of Israel] called Jacob *El*" (*Megilla* 18a). This explanation is shocking. How could a human being be called by God's name?

The author of the *Tanya* will explain this below and will even repeat this verse in order to give his interpretation. But first, before he can explain it, he introduces several points that touch on the foundations of faith.

פֵּירוּשׁ, כִּי הִנֵּה בֶּאֱמֶת הַקָּדוֹשׁ בָּרוּךְ הוּא כִּשְׁמוֹ כֵּן הוּא.

This means that in truth, the Holy One, blessed be He, is true to His name.

The name of God that the author of the *Tanya* mentions here, "the Holy One, blessed be He," a name used frequently by the Sages, is in and of itself a description that contains two seemingly contradictory concepts. He is "holy," meaning separate, since He exists on the other side of reality, disconnected from all physicality and every other aspect of existence.[4] Yet He is "blessed," meaning He is drawn down into

3. See Ramban, Gen. 33:20.
4. See *Likkutei Torah*, Lev. 4b, citing Maharal's introduction to *Gevurot Hashem*.

reality.[5] Logically speaking, if we posit one, we have to let go of the other. If He is drawn down into the worlds, then He is not truly holy and separate from them, and if He is holy and separate, then He should not actually exist within the worlds. Yet this is exactly the meaning of this name, that He is simultaneously holy and blessed.

כִּי אַף דְּאִיהוּ מְמַלֵּא כָּל עָלְמִין, עֶלְיוֹנִים וְתַחְתּוֹנִים, מֵרוּם הַמַּעֲלוֹת עַד מִתַּחַת לָאָרֶץ הַלֵּזוּ הַחוּמְרִית, כְּמוֹ שֶׁכָּתוּב: "הֲלֹא אֶת הַשָּׁמַיִם וְאֶת הָאָרֶץ אֲנִי מָלֵא" (ירמיה כג, כד), "אֲנִי" מַמָּשׁ, דְּהַיְינוּ מַהוּתוֹ וְעַצְמוּתוֹ כִּבְיָכוֹל וְלֹא כְּבוֹדוֹ לְבַד,

Although on the one hand He fills all the higher and lower worlds, from the highest spiritual heights to the bottom of this lowly corporeal earth, as it is written, "Do I not fill the heavens and the earth?" (Jer. 23:24) – **literally, "I," meaning** God's actual **essence and being, so to speak, and not just His glory** –

Elsewhere, we find two verses that echo this seeming contradiction:[6] the verse that is mentioned here, "Do I not fill the heavens and the earth?" and a verse from the book of Isaiah (6:3), "That which fills the entire world is His glory." At first glance, they seem to convey the same meaning, yet in actuality they relay two starkly different messages They both seem to be speaking about how God fills all the worlds, yet one uses the first person, "I," meaning God Himself, and the second speaks in the third person of "His glory." "Glory" implies an illumination, a connection with a more external aspect of God. This is echoed by the *Targum Yonatan*'s Aramaic translation of this phrase: "a ray of His honor," connoting a mere glimmer radiating from Him.

Another difference is that the first verse speaks of the heavens and the earth, of the higher and lower worlds, at the same time, while the second verse specifically refers to the earth, to this world. Hasidic teachings explain that the verse "That which fills the entire world is His glory" speaks of the light that fills all worlds, referring to the divine life force that fills and vitalizes every single aspect of reality, that permeates the very essence and inner workings of existence. This illumination is

---

5. See, e.g., *Likkutei Torah*, Deut. 16d, which explains that the term for blessing, *berakha*, connotes the drawing down from above to below in the form of a revelation.
6. See *Likkutei Torah*, Num. 53c; *Torah Or* 16a.

clearly not God's very essence but rather a force that emanates from Him to vivify the creation.

By contrast, the first verse conveys that "I" fill the heavens and the earth, literally My essence and being. God Himself, not just His glory, fills the heavens and the earth as one. This manner of God Himself relating to the world, to the heavens and the earth, is called the light that surrounds all worlds. It is an infinite illumination that represents God's very being in which the worlds, in all their multiplicity, are subsumed, negligible, and meaningless. In this light, heaven and earth are the same, as one.

He is nevertheless holy and separate from the higher and lower beings and is not contained within them at all, God forbid,

אַף עַל פִּי כֵן, הוּא קָדוֹשׁ, וּמוּבְדָּל מֵעֶלְיוֹנִים וְתַחְתּוֹנִים וְאֵינוֹ נִתְפָּס כְּלָל בְּתוֹכָם חַס וְשָׁלוֹם,

Though this essential light fills all of reality, it is also separate from it to the nth degree. "Holy" connotes intrinsically separate, totally other, evading any attempt at characterization. It is absolutely transcendent, with no medium between it and anything else whatsoever, but rather there exists an unbridgeable gap. The definition of "holy" here does not refer to the feeling of holiness at all but rather to its essential nature, which lies beyond all dimensions, beyond the highest and lowest worlds alike.

No matter how supernal the higher worlds may be, they are always embedded to some degree in the lower worlds. The lower worlds must always be able to register the higher worlds to some extent, to be a vessel for their light. Yet when it comes to God Himself, even though He fills everything, He Himself is not grasped by anything nor touches anything. ☞

NOT GRASPED AT ALL

☞ This concept is analogous (though only to a minimal degree) to certain phenomena that even in the physical realm cannot be felt. Radio waves are everywhere, filling every room. The proof is that if one turns on any radio, one will hear them. Yet we walk through these waves without hindrance. It does not make any difference what the radio waves are broadcasting, if at all. Radio waves exist close to us, encompass us, and are even within us, yet they are remote from us, inherently ungraspable (without the proper instrument), not observably touching us and totally separate from us.

כְּתְפִיסַת נִשְׁמַת הָאָדָם בְּגוּפוֹ, עַל דֶּרֶךְ מָשָׁל, כְּמוֹ שֶׁנִּתְבָּאֵר בְּמָקוֹם אַחֵר בַּאֲרִיכוּת.

as the human soul is contained within the body, for example, as explained elsewhere at length (*Likkutei Amarim*, chap. 42).

The parallel drawn between God in the world and the soul in the body is ancient and appears in the words of the Sages.[7] Yet still, despite the similarities, there is one fundamental difference: The soul does not just exist within the body and fill it; it also builds a two-way relationship with it. The soul vivifies the body and activates it. The body, on its part, activates the soul, or at the least has an effect on it. There is a mutual relationship between the body and the soul and even a certain degree of identification: The human sense of self is a composite of both the body and the soul. When the body is hungry, the soul cannot help but be affected. When someone is struck in the face, his soul hurts even more than his body. The soul, then, is considered to be contained within the body.

By contrast, although "I fill the heavens and the earth" although He exists in every molecule and iota of reality, He is not "grasped" within it. The relationship between God and the world is completely one way. His being fills reality, but reality does not encompass His being. It does not touch Him. Even when He is as close as can be, He is still unfathomably far.

Holiness, God's intrinsic separateness, is not just the type described in Ecclesiastes (5:1) – "God is in the heavens and you are on earth" – since God Himself is not in the heavens more than He is on land. God fills the heavens and the earth, yet He is separate and ungraspable on earth just as in the heavens. They sense His existence, since their whole existence comes from Him, yet they do not grasp Him at all, and they do not affect Him, negatively or positively. While He fills and enlivens everything, He remains forever the Holy One, distant and separate.

וְלָזֹאת לֹא הָיוּ יְכוֹלִים לְקַבֵּל חַיּוּתָם מִמַּהוּתוֹ וְעַצְמוּתוֹ לְבַדּוֹ כִּבְיָכוֹל.

Therefore, the worlds **could not receive their life force from His essence and being alone, so to speak.**

---

7. See *Berakhot* 10a; *Midrash Tehillim* 103.

The worlds cannot receive their particularized vitality directly from the divine essence. The divine essence is holy and transcendent; nothing else exists in its light. There can be no comparison between the world and God's essence; between them lies an unbridgeable gap. God's essence and being has no meaning in light of the minutiae and dimensions of the world. The farthest reaches of the imagination are incapable of measuring the reality of the world alongside the reality of God. They do not exist on the same plane at all. It is therefore impossible to speak of association between the two or the effect of one on the other.

Rather, the emanation of the life force into all the worlds **by which the Holy One, blessed be He, gives life to the higher and lower worlds is metaphorically analogous to an illumination shining forth from His name,**

רַק הִתְפַּשְּׁטוּת הַחַיּוּת אֲשֶׁר הַקָּדוֹשׁ בָּרוּךְ הוּא מְחַיֶּה עֶלְיוֹנִים וְתַחְתּוֹנִים, הוּא עַל דֶּרֶךְ מָשָׁל כְּמוֹ הֶאָרָה מְאִירָה מִשְּׁמוֹ יִתְבָּרֵךְ,

The life force that impacts and enlivens the world is just an illumination. To be precise, it is not even an illumination of the divine essence itself, but rather an illumination of God's name. God's name, like a person's name, is a type of illumination that radiates outward. The person does not need his name. Other people need it to refer to him, to relate to him. Yet, unlike other illuminations of that person's essence, such as character traits, the name points to the person himself. So too, though God's name is certainly not God Himself, one who calls Him by name addresses His very essence.

For He and His name are one.

שֶׁהוּא וּשְׁמוֹ אֶחָד.

The name of God is more than a title that we call Him. It is the initial illumination that emerges from His essence. The essence of God's name is one with the supernal divine essence, not because it is identical to it, but because it is not separate from it. As the Midrash states, "Until the world was created, there was only God and His great name" (*Pirkei deRabbi Eliezer* 3). Although His name is not His essence, but rather a revelation and an illumination of the Divine, it still far transcends all worlds and levels, and therefore this illumination from God's great name has the power to enliven all the worlds.

וּכְמוֹ שֶׁכָּתוּב: "כִּי נִשְׂגָּב שְׁמוֹ לְבַדּוֹ" (תהלים קמח, יג), רַק זִיווֹ, וְ"הוֹדוֹ עַל אֶרֶץ וְשָׁמַיִם וְגוֹ'".

Thus it is written, "For His name alone is exalted," while only the ray of "His glory" is "across earth and heaven..." (Ps. 148:13).

Not only is God's essence exalted, singular and totally separate from creation, but so is His name exalted and transcendent. Moreover, as the author of the *Tanya* explains here, the heavens and the earth receive only the glimmer and radiance that shines forth from his name, a "ray of His glory."

This concept is also found in the statement "Blessed is the name of His glorious kingdom forever and ever" (recited in the *Shema* prayer). We do not say "blessed is His name" or even "blessed is His glory" but rather "Blessed is the name of His glorious kingdom," expressing three degrees of separation that convey the vast distance between God and the worlds that He enlivens.

וְהֶאָרָה זוֹ מִתְלַבֶּשֶׁת מַמָּשׁ בָּעֶלְיוֹנִים וְתַחְתּוֹנִים לְהַחֲיוֹתָם,

This illumination actually becomes clothed within the higher and lower worlds to give them life,

This is the essential difference between God, who enlivens the world, and the soul, which enlivens the body. Unlike the soul, whose essence manifests in the body, God only manifests in the world as the glimmer of an illumination of Himself in the world, "a ray of His glory." It is this emanation of His being that constitutes the soul of the world. We are incapable of relating to the luminary, to the source of the divine light. Even though it exists and is the ultimate source of all life, it is not in our purview, and therefore it is as if it does not exist. All the vitality within us, our desires, awareness, sensations, and abilities, we receive from but a glimmer of a glimmer of an illumination.

וְנִתְפֶּסֶת בְּתוֹכָם עַל יְדֵי מְמוּצָּעִים רַבִּים וְצִמְצוּמִים רַבִּים וַעֲצוּמִים, בְּהִשְׁתַּלְשְׁלוּת הַמַּדְרֵגוֹת דֶּרֶךְ עִלָּה

and it is contained within them through many intermediary and numerous powerful constrictions

וְעָלוּל וכו׳. **through the unfolding succession of levels in a process of cause and effect, and so on.**

This divine illumination does not shine directly into the upper worlds and certainly not into our physical world. Rather it flows through various mediums, from world to world and level to level. Every level warrants further constriction relative to the level above it, and every constriction lends a unique filter that the light must pass through to manifest on that level and in that particular realm of creation. ☞

INTERMEDIARIES AND CONSTRICTIONS

☞ When a person lights a fire on a kerosene stove, he effectively ignites it with energy from the element of fire, but since the energy from the source itself is too immensely powerful to utilize directly, it must pass go through a particular pathway of intermediaries and constrictions, of illuminations and glimmers of illuminations, to the second and third degree and so forth, until it manifests, for example, in the fire produced from kerosene.

Every power plant is surrounded, at various distances, by transformers that constrict the electric voltage to a degree that we can use it. If we were to connect an electric cable from the power plant directly to our house, all our devices would immediately burn out. Similarly, we cannot look at the sun, but we can gaze at the moon, since the moon shines with but a glimmer of the sun's illumination; not with the illumination itself.

Similarly, the many constrictions of the divine light are meant to constrict the divine illumination so that it can enliven reality and not consume it. One of the explanations that the Rabbis give of how Sennacherib's soldiers died is that God opened their ears and they heard the song of the angels (see *Sanhedrin* 95b). This was not even a glimpse of God. It was merely the singing of the angels. But even that was enough to turn everyone who heard it into a corpse in an instant.

In several places in *Tanakh*, we read of people who are afraid to see even an angel. Mano'aḥ, Samson's father, was convinced that a person who sees an angel dies, and thus an angel must cover itself up so that a person might be able to look at it.

In the same sense, everything we see in this world is not the thing itself but a distant product of it. The original underwent the whole order of progression in a process of cause and effect until, after numerous constrictions and descents from one level to the next, the original illumination arrives at a level compatible with this world's distant level so that the lower world can safely utilize its energy.

The terms that the author of the *Tanya* employs to convey this idea, "intermediaries," "constrictions," the "unfolding succession," and "process of cause and effect," are each a whole concept in and of itself. The distinctions between them, qualitatively, characteristically, and categorically, create the system that the kabbalistic works call the "order of progression." Embedded in this sentence, then, is a con-

22 Av
24 Av (leap year)

וְהִנֵּה הֶאָרָה זוֹ, אַף שֶׁלְּמַעְלָה הִיא מְאִירָה וּמִתְפַּשֶּׁטֶת בִּבְחִינַת בְּלִי גְּבוּל וְתַכְלִית, לְהַחֲיוֹת עוֹלָמוֹת נֶעֱלָמִים לְאֵין קֵץ וְתַכְלִית, כְּמוֹ שֶׁכָּתוּב בָּ'אִדְרָא רַבָּא' (חלק ג קכז, ב),

This illumination, although above it shines and emanates boundlessly and infinitely, giving life to endless, infinite hidden worlds, as stated in *Idra Rabba* (3:127b),

Divine light itself is infinite. Its infinity expresses itself in that it gives life to an infinite number of worlds. Its macrocosmic scope manifests mostly in the upper worlds, which are by definition more all-encompassing realities. Every detail of each of these worlds is in and of itself a complete universe, an entire category of existence. By contrast, our world is one particular world, a specific occurrence, one possibility out of endless worlds. ☞

cise summary of this intricate and elaborate system. The author of the *Tanya* does not delve into its details, but we will provide a general explanation of them here.

The term "intermediary levels" refers to levels that lie in between the highest and lowest levels of the created world, connecting the highest and lowest realms. "Constrictions" refer to the significant shrinking of the divine light to the extent that one does not see from below the level above it. "Many" and "numerous" means a quantitatively vast number of constrictions, and "powerful" is the qualitative constriction that causes the light after the constriction to be not only weaker but also of a different type than before. "The unfolding succession of levels" and "process of cause and effect" express the descent of the light by way of causality, through a tightly precise path that goes from one level to the next, in which every higher level is the direct cause of the lower level below it and so can also be attained through it.

THE INFINITE SUPERNAL WORLDS VERSUS OUR WORLD

☞ Imagine numbers that are divided into groups, such as all the rational numbers or all the odd numbers. Some of these groups, or fields, overlap; some only meet others, and others intersect with each other. Every field is a whole world that may include infinite numbers that can be divided into an infinite number of groups. By contrast, any individual figure, one or three or eighteen thousand, is a particular number that relates to particular, defined frameworks.

Similarly, in contrast to our defined, particular world, there are abstract, all-encompassing worlds that are infinitely greater in number, size, and scope, and they receive their vitality from the divine illumination on a more supernal, all-encompassing degree.

אַף עַל פִּי כֵן, בִּרְדִתָּהּ לְמַטָּה, עַל יְדֵי צִמְצוּמִים רַבִּים לְהַחֲיוֹת הַנִּבְרָאִים וְהַיְּצוּרִים וְהַנַּעֲשִׂים,

nevertheless, when it descends below through many constrictions to give life to all the beings that have been created, formed, and made in the lower worlds of *Beria*, *Yetzira*, and *Asiya*,

The divine light descends below in the sense that it becomes funneled through constriction after constriction. When the divine illumination gets constricted into some parameter of reality, it enlivens and sustains that thing. Thus the constriction and descent of this illumination enlivens the worlds that progress from one to the next, which are, generally speaking, the worlds of *Beria, Yetzira*, and *Asiya*. ☞

הִיא נֶחְלֶקֶת דֶּרֶךְ כְּלָל לְמִסְפַּר תַּרְיָ"ג כְּנֶגֶד תַּרְיָ"ג מִצְוֹת הַתּוֹרָה.

it is generally divided into 613 rays, **corresponding to the 613 commandments of the Torah.**

The 613 divisions in which the divine illumination that enlivens the world is divided are like 613 colors, 613 pathways through which the

CONSTRICTION FROM INFINITE ILLUMINATION

☞ Although the source and essence of the illumination is infinite, it becomes contracted and divided into defined parts when it descends below. Yet the defined parts are still infinite in and of themselves. It is a transition from the undefined, unlimited infinite to a manifestation of the infinite that is in some sense constricted and defined. For example, the number of digits that are divisible by 777 is infinite, even though it is a defined, constricted group among all series of numbers. It is possible to formulate even more constricted parameters that will be only a part, a subcategory, of a wider and more complex system.

There are also things whose scope and nature are infinite but not qualitatively. People differ from each other. Their bodies take up a defined space, and two people cannot take up the same space at the same time. By contrast, angels, which do not fit into these physical parameters, differ from each other in a different way: in their essence and character. Therefore, one angel can be the size of the walking distance of five hundred years, and another, one-third the size of the world (see *Ḥagiga* 13a; *Bereshit Rabba* 68:12; *Likkutei Torah*, Lev. 41b; *Hemshekh Ayin Bet*, vol. 1, p. 339). In other words, an angel can be infinite in space, yet still be defined in terms of its essence in a restricted and particular way. These are parameters that, on the one hand, can be plotted and counted, yet, on the other, are actually infinite.

light is drawn down below. Each of the 613 commandments of the Torah characterizes one of these pathways and in a certain sense composes the fabric that the refraction that the illumination takes on in order to manifest itself in reality.

The 613 commandments can be defined as embodying the entirety of the contact between man and God, between the spiritual and the physical, between the Divine and the worlds. As such, the 613 commandments represent the roots and foundations of the worlds. Each one expresses a particular essence of reality, and the entire 613, albeit not obvious to all, express the entire reality of all the worlds. ☞

שֶׁהֵן הֵן תַּרְיָ"ג מִינֵי הַמְשָׁכוֹת הֶאָרָה זוֹ, מֵאוֹר אֵין סוֹף בָּרוּךְ הוּא,

These commandments **are 613 kinds of channels** that transmit **this illumination from the light of *Ein Sof*, blessed be He,**

The 613 lights in the divine illumination are 613 broad categories (which themselves are broken up into details and sub-details), which parallel the 613 mitzvot. Take, for example, physical light. When it refracts

EACH COMMANDMENT CORRESPONDS TO AN ASPECT OF THE WORLD

☞ Every commandment expresses a particular essence of the world. There are frequent mitzvot that a person performs every day, and then there are those that particular people perform at particular times and in particular places, and there are mitzvot that seem unrealistic and impractical almost all the time. There are prohibitions that a person applies regularly, such as "Do not kill," and "Do not commit adultery," and then there are prohibitions such as "The breast piece shall not be detached from upon the ephod" (Ex. 28:28) that cannot presently be applied at all. Yet every mitzva expresses a particular facet of reality. Some mitzvot manifest a familiar and obvious aspect of existence that every person encounters, and others, the rarely performed ones, manifest an aspect of reality that hardly anyone ever meets.

To illustrate, the degree to which the average person associates with helium gas is minuscule. He hardly ever encounters it. But in another entity, such as the sun, this gas plays an immensely crucial role. Only the fool would claim that he does not care if it exists, because if there were no helium, there would be no sun. Similarly, though an individual may rarely encounter something in his personal life, making it very foreign to him, it is crucial in another realm of life. The degree of importance that something holds in the greater scope of reality may be totally different from its significance in one's day-to-day life.

through a prism, it divides into a specific number of shades and primary colors that divide and recombine into infinite number of sub-colors.

לְהָאִיר לְנִשְׁמַת הָאָדָם הַכְּלוּלָה מֵרְמָ"ח אֵבָרִים וּשְׁסָ"ה גִּידִים,

to illuminate the human soul, which is comprised of 248 limbs and 365 sinews, which together totals 613,

Just as man, who is the ultimate purpose of the divine illumination to the worlds, is comprised of 613 limbs and sinews, so too the illumination that he contains is also divided into 613 lights. Not only is man's body composed of 248 limbs and 365 sinews, but parallel to his body, his soul is also composed of 613 fundamental elements.

אֲשֶׁר בַּעֲבוּרָהּ הוּא עִיקַּר תַּכְלִית יְרִידַת וְהַמְשָׁכַת הֶאָרָה זוֹ לְמַטָּה, לְכָל הַנִּבְרָאִים וְהַיְצוּרִים וְהַנַּעֲשִׂים, שֶׁתַּכְלִית כּוּלָּן הוּא הָאָדָם, כַּנּוֹדָע.

for whose sake is the primary purpose of the descent and flow of this illumination below to all the beings that have been created, formed, and made in the lower worlds of *Beria*, *Yetzira*, and *Asiya*, **because the purpose of them all is man, as is known.**

The main purpose of the divine light illuminating the worlds below – the worlds of *Beria*, *Yetzira*, and *Asiya*, which are all considered "below" in relation to the world of *Atzilut* – is for man to be able to exist in the lower world of *Asiya*. Therefore, the processes of illumination and progressive descent that are meant to sustain man and his world pass through all the upper worlds. ☞

THE WHOLE PURPOSE OF EXISTENCE

☞ There are 613 types of illumination, 613 commandments, and 613 components in a human being. The connection between them is not coincidental. The purpose of all the creations, those from the worlds of *Beria*, *Yetzira*, and *Asiya*, including all their worlds, chambers, and everything that happens within them, is man, who has 613 limbs and serves God through the 613 commandments of the Torah. Planet Earth, as huge as it is, is but a tiny speck in the vast created reality, beyond which lie heavens and heavens beyond the heavens, and all are nothing but mediums, platforms, that sustain man's reality. The verse "I made the earth and humanity upon it. (Isa. 45:12) does not speak of two different realities. It expresses how the earth is the canvas for the only being that holds any real significance, the

Even though man is not the largest creation in existence, neither in quantity nor in any other way, he is certainly the most important, since all of reality is tailored to him. Every illumination of vitality that flows to the worlds is fine-tuned to manifest man's reality with all its details, and man's reality parallels the supernal image from above of divine names and illuminations that flow from it. The 613 commandments are the practical human expression of all the hues of divine illumination and, in a certain sense, of the Divine itself.

23 Av
25 Av (leap year)

וְהִנֵּה מִסְפָּר זֶה הוּא בְּדֶרֶךְ כְּלָל, אֲבָל בְּדֶרֶךְ פְּרָט הִנֵּה כָּל מִצְוָה וּמִצְוָה מִתְחַלֶּקֶת לִפְרָטִים רַבִּים לְאֵין קֵץ וְתַכְלִית. וְהֵן הֵן גּוּפֵי הֲלָכוֹת פְּרָטִיּוֹת שֶׁבְּכָל מִצְוָה, שֶׁאֵין לָהֶם מִסְפָּר,

This number, 613, is a general division. **But specifically speaking, every single commandment is divided into numerous, endless, infinite details. These are the vast body of innumerable specific *halakhot* that pertain to every commandment,**

only one that fulfills the 613 commandments in his lifetime: man.

Consider, only for the sake of illustration, the immense investment of manpower, time, and money poured into the development of particle accelerators. Researchers build a huge, extremely expensive structure, sometimes miles long, all to measure the flicker of a single particle, whose entire life span is one-tenth to the twentieth power of a second. There seems to be no relationship between all the effort and finances involved in studying the particle, but that flicker is the whole point, and the entire, massive structure surrounding it was built only for that purpose.

The entire network of worlds is like God's large-scale experiment. He sustains this massive system whose whole purpose is to allow for the existence of a being called man, to enable the existence of a creature whose behavior is unpredictable and therefore testable. It is like when a person positions a subatomic particle in space using massive magnets with perfectly balanced forces, causing it to hover there as if there are no external forces acting upon it at all. The existence of the universes, with everything they encompass, all exist to do one thing: to allow for the reality of a being that stands exactly at the brink between holiness and impurity, between divine reality and mundanity. This being can attain awareness of God but is not forced to do so.

Man can reap the whole purpose of existence from exactly the life he has been given. If he succeeds, and the "experiment" is successful, he has elevated God's glory throughout all the worlds. When even a simple person thinks, *Maybe there is a God in the world!* he magnifies the glory of God more than one hundred thousand angels, whose sole purpose is to praise God. Since he is the only one who can deny God, when he declares, "There is a God," and acts on this thought, that is God's glory and pride.

There are many commandments that encompass an entire set of laws and instruction behind them. Even extremely specific commandments include a great number of details required for their proper fulfillment.

כְּמוֹ שֶׁכָּתוּב: "שִׁשִּׁים הֵמָּה מְלָכוֹת" (שיר השירים ו, ח), הֵן שִׁשִּׁים מַסֶּכְתּוֹת כו', "וַעֲלָמוֹת אֵין מִסְפָּר", הֵן הַהֲלָכוֹת כו' שֶׁהֵן הַמְשָׁכַת רָצוֹן הָעֶלְיוֹן כו'.

as it is written, "They are sixty queens" (Song 6:8), hinting at **the sixty tractates of the Mishna, and so on,** and, as the verse continues, **"And young women without number," which hints at the** ***halakhot*****, and so forth, which are drawn from the supernal will, and so on.**

The Sages extrapolate this correlation between the sixty queens mentioned in the Song of Songs and the sixty tractates of the Mishna.[8] The "young women without number" mentioned at the end of the verse refer to the endless halakhic details and directives that one constantly encounters with every new situation. Each and every halakhic decision is the expression of another aspect of the divine will that has never been revealed before. It is a revelation of what God wants from us within the corporeal confines of this world.

Like the light of the sun, the supernal will is one unified, all-encompassing light. This light is divided into a number of parts, each of which is its own all-encompassing realm. After that, they become further divided into specific details, until they amount to "young women without number," the multitude of *halakhot* that are divided down to the most minute detail, emblematic of the infinitude of the overarching divine light.

וְכֵן הוּא מַמָּשׁ בְּנִשְׁמַת הָאָדָם, כִּי הִנֵּה כָּל הַנְּשָׁמוֹת שֶׁבָּעוֹלָם הָיוּ כְּלוּלוֹת בְּאָדָם הָרִאשׁוֹן.

It is actually the same with regard to the human soul, for all the souls in the world were originally **encompassed in** the soul of **Adam.**

8. See *Shir HaShirim Rabba* 6:14; *Bemidbar Rabba* 18:21; *Zohar* 3:216a. Although the actual number of tractates adds up to sixty-three, the tractates of *Bava Kamma, Bava Metzia,* and *Bava Batra* are actually three sections of the larger tractate of *Nezikin,* and the tractate of *Makkot* is considered a continuation of *Sanhedrin.*

The human soul, which receives the divine light, the illumination that comprises the 613 commandments, is also an all-encompassing light that becomes divided into details and sub-details. This applies to the entirety of all souls in general and to each soul in particular.

Purely for the sake of example, a similar phenomenon is at work in the physical makeup of man. In every person's body reside the very cells that will function in all his future descendants. These cells were literally part of Adam's constitution and progressively increased and diverged into each of his progenitors. This is even more true in the spiritual realm regarding Adam's soul, which embodied the entire human race and included within it every component of every soul that would ever emerge from him.[9]

וְדֶרֶךְ כְּלָל הָיְתָה נִשְׁמָתוֹ נֶחְלֶקֶת לְמִסְפַּר תַּרְיַ"ג: רַמַ"ח אֵבָרִים וּשְׁסַ"ה גִּידִים.

Generally speaking, his soul, like his body, **was divided into 613** components, **248 limbs and 365 sinews,** corresponding to the 613 commandments.

Adam's soul was divided into 613 soul roots, so that every soul is rooted in one of the components of Adam's soul. Likewise, the soul of every one of Adam's descendants throughout the generations themselves are divided into 613 components.[10] ☞

THE 613 LIMBS THAT PARALLEL THE 613 COMMANDMENTS

☞ The limbs and commandments are not just the same in number. They are also fundamentally connected to each other: Each mitzva corresponds to a specific limb and on an even deeper level, each mitzva corresponds to a limb of one's spiritual body (see *Yalkut Shimoni, Tehillim* 723).

9. See *Shemot Rabba* 40b.

10. As the Midrash states, "When Adam was a lifeless mass, God showed him all the righteous men who would descend from him. Some were from his head, some from his hair, still others from his neck, some from his two eyes, some from his nose, some from his ears, and some from his arms..." (*Midrash Tanhuma, Ki Tisa* 12).

אַךְ דֶּרֶךְ פְּרָט, נֶחְלֶקֶת לְנִיצוֹצוֹת אֵין מִסְפָּר, שֶׁהֵן נִשְׁמוֹת כָּל יִשְׂרָאֵל מִימוֹת הָאָבוֹת וְהַשְּׁבָטִים עַד בִּיאַת הַמָּשִׁיחַ וְעַד בִּכְלָל,

But more **specifically,** Adam's soul **was divided into innumerable sparks, which are the** individual **souls of every Jew from the times of the forefathers and the tribes until the coming of the Messiah and beyond,**

Every individual soul is a spark of Adam's soul. Like the mitzvot, these sparks were divided into more detailed parts, each of which is a principal component in and of itself containing hundreds of thousands of myriad additional details, which make up all the souls that ever were and will ever be from the beginning of time until the end of history in messianic times.

שֶׁיְּקוּיַּם אָז מַה שֶּׁכָּתוּב: "וְהָיָה מִסְפַּר בְּנֵי יִשְׂרָאֵל כְּחוֹל הַיָּם אֲשֶׁר לֹא יִמַּד וְלֹא יִסָּפֵר" (הושע ב, א) מֵרוֹב.

when the following **verse will be fulfilled: "The number of the children of Israel will be like the sand of the sea, which cannot be measured and cannot be counted"** (Hos. 2:1) **due to their great number.**

Just as there will be numerous mitzvot to fulfill in messianic times, there will also be numerous souls that will fulfill them. In that future time, the Jewish people will be able to perform all 613 commandments since the Temple will be rebuilt and all Jews will be living in the Holy Land, so there will be no impediments to fulfilling the mitzvot. Moreover, that redemptive time will herald an age when all the work of the spiritual refinement of the world and the elevation of all the sparks by many souls will have come to completion.[11]

---

11. As a result of the shattering of the vessels, which occurred before the creation of the world, divine sparks have been trapped in the *kelippot*. By performing mitzvot, we release those sparks and elevate them so that they return to their origin, their source in the Divine.

וְהִנֵּה שׁוּפְרֵיהּ דְּיַעֲקֹב מֵעֵין שׁוּפְרֵיהּ דְּאָדָם הָרִאשׁוֹן (בבא מציעא פד, א), שֶׁתִּיקֵּן חֵטְא אָדָם הָרִאשׁוֹן,

The Rabbis taught, **"The beauty of Jacob is a semblance of the beauty of Adam"** (*Bava Metzia* 84a), **for** Jacob **rectified Adam's sin,**

Jacob resembled Adam in several respects. On a simple level, Jacob is the father of the Jewish people just as Adam is the father of humanity, and just as every person stems from Adam and only Adam, every Jewish soul comes from Jacob and only Jacob, who is the root from whom the entire Jewish people sprouted.

On a deeper level, Jacob's spiritual work brought him back to the level of Adam before the sin. Adam was the handiwork of God and therefore perfect. This is the deeper significance of the phrase "the beauty of Adam." Adam was beautiful in both body and soul, crafted in the most optimal of divine proportions.

The definition of beauty is harmony, in adhering to the optimal proportions, while sin, in this sense, is the distortion of them. Sin is like a deformity. It is not only like the loss of a limb, but it is also reminiscent of a limb that is not positioned correctly in relation to the others. A spiritual defect, like a physical one, is the loss of harmony, when a person is not living within the right proportions, and the components of his own being are not interacting with each other as they should. This is the meaning of "The beauty of Jacob resembled the beauty of Adam": Jacob rectified the original image, the "beauty of Adam," as it was before the sin. ☞

ASCENDING AND DESCENDING ANGELS

☞ The Midrash offers a very lofty understanding of the beauty of Jacob. In his dream about the angels ascending and descending the ladder that reached from the earth to the heavens, the angels were ascending to look at the image above (the likeness of man that was among the four likenesses that were around the throne of glory, as described in Ezekiel's vision), and then descending to look at the image of Jacob below (see *Ḥullin* 91b). The angels were ascending and descending the ladder to behold the incredible wonder: Jacob's face looked like the supernal image above.

וְהָיְתָה נִשְׁמָתוֹ גַּם כֵּן כְּלוּלָה מִכָּל הַנְּשָׁמוֹת שֶׁבְּיִשְׂרָאֵל מֵעוֹלָם וְעַד עוֹלָם.

and like Adam, **his soul was also comprised of all the souls of the Jewish people throughout time.**

Just as Adam's soul was the root of humankind, the soul of Jacob was the root of all the souls of Israel. He was the one to kickstart the new reality called the Jewish people. ☞

וְהָיָה מֶרְכָּבָה לַתּוֹרָה שֶׁלְּמַעְלָה, שֶׁנִּקְרֵאת בְּשֵׁם 'אָדָם',

He was a chariot for the spiritual root of the Torah above, which is called "Adam,"

When a person becomes a conduit and perfect expression for something, the Torah deems him a "chariot," a vehicle and medium through which that thing manifests. Jacob, as the expression of the perfection of the image of man, was a chariot for the image of supernal man, which is the Torah. As the Sages taught regarding the verse "This is the law [*haTorah*]: man" (Num. 19:14), the Torah is the depiction of the perfect image of man.[12] Since the Torah contains 613 commandments, which correspond to the components of man, both physical and spiritual, its spiritual root likewise corresponds to the supernal image of man. ☞

THE ESSENCE OF A JEW

☞ The essence of the Jewish people is, in a certain sense, the essence of primordial man channeled into Jacob, so that it will not become scattered throughout the distorted trends of society but rather will become concentrated in the rectified essence of the Jewish people. It is the mission of the Jewish people as a whole, and each Jew individually, to return to man the initial, rectified image of God. This is not an easy job. Like Jacob, every Jew in every generation must be careful to uphold the ideal proportions, the beauty and perfection of the image of man. This is the meaning of the talmudic statement "You are called man" (*Yevamot* 61a). You are the ones who are carrying the image of man from within the distortion of the world. You are the ones who must preserve the divine harmony of man's true essence.

"THE FOREFATHERS ARE THE VERY CHARIOT"

☞ This phrase appears in the Midrash (*Bereshit Rabba* 47:6, 82:6) and can be understood in light of the prophetic account that describes the divine chariot

12. *Zohar* 2:117b; see *Torah Or* 79c.

כְּמוֹ שֶׁכָּתוּב: "וְעַל דְּמוּת הַכִּסֵּא דְּמוּת כְּמַרְאֵה אָדָם וכו'" (יחזקאל א, כו),

as it is written, "Upon the likeness of the throne was a likeness, like the appearance of a person…" (Ezek. 1:26),

The author of the *Tanya* quotes this verse from the vision of the divine chariot in Ezekiel. The "likeness" that is manifest on the chariot is the image of God that is manifest in the world. It is the divine will, divine wisdom, divine kindness and so on, the attributes of God that that become clothed in the 613 commandments of the Torah, which are the "likeness, like the appearance of a person." The image of man is the prism through which the divine light shines. ☞

וּכְמוֹ שֶׁכָּתוּב: "וְזֹאת לְפָנִים בְּיִשְׂרָאֵל כו'" (רות ד, ז), אֵין "זֹאת" אֶלָּא תּוֹרָה כו' שֶׁהָיְתָה כְּלוּלָה וּמְלוּבֶּשֶׁת בְּנִשְׁמַת יִשְׂרָאֵל סָבָא הַכְּלוּלָה מִכָּל הַנְּשָׁמוֹת.

and it is written, "This was the tradition in Israel…" (Ruth 4:7). The Rabbis expounded, **"'This' is referring to nothing other than the Torah…"** (*Avoda Zara* 2b), **which was encompassed and clothed in the soul of Israel the patriarch,** who is Jacob, **which was comprised of all the souls.**

(Ezek. 1; Isa. 6; Zech. 1). The function of a chariot is to carry its rider from place to place, but it does not have an independent identity. It does not have a will of its own or any decision-making facilities. It is merely an instrument that the rider uses to get where he is going. It is in this sense that "the forefathers are the very chariot": that these men who reached their ultimate rectification became a chariot, a vehicle and instrument, for the Divine Presence.

THE TORAH AND THE LIKENESS OF MAN

☞ Since the Torah is built around the 613 commandments, and since the 613 commandments are aligned with the 613 components of the ideal image of man, the Torah constitutes the image of man at its essence. The image of man and the image of the Torah, though different in their external expression, are identical in every detail of their inner makeup.

For the sake of illustration, a telescope has a tiny focal point where one can hone in on the image of one lone star or an entire galaxy. All the light that comes from the star is focused into a miniature model of that star. This model is not a separate entity but is literally the image of that star. Similarly, there is an image above and an image below, and both have the appearance of man.

The soul of Jacob, of "Israel the patriarch" contains the entirety of the six hundred thousand souls of Israel in every incarnation. While all these souls were shrunk and folded into his soul, and all their facets are not outwardly revealed, still every aspect of every soul is encompassed in Jacob's soul.

The essence of the Jewish people, which is synonymous with the essence of Adam, as explained above, is also the way that the essence of the Torah, which is the divine light that shines into the world, is manifest. These are the paths through which the Divine is revealed in the world.

וְזֶהוּ "וַיִּקְרָא לוֹ אֵל אֱלוֹקֵי יִשְׂרָאֵל" (בראשית לג, כ).

This is the meaning of "And he called it El Elohei Yisrael [God of Israel]" (Gen. 33:20).

The author of the *Tanya* now explains the verse he quoted at the beginning of the letter. The Sages interpret this ambiguous verse as saying that God called Jacob "*El*." But how could this possibly be?

The answer is that the image that is called "a likeness, like the appearance of a person" in the prophetic vision of the divine chariot, which depicts the all-encompassing divine revelation within the worlds, is built on the pattern of "the appearance of a person." This appearance is what is meant when we refer to the "supernal man" or "man above." Corresponding to supernal man is what is called the paradigmatic likeness below, which is Jacob. Jacob is therefore the template that most closely reflects and embodies the supernal image and most clearly expresses the aspect of the Divine that manifests in the world. In other words, Jacob is the chariot for the God of Israel, and in this sense, he can be called "*El*," one of the names of God. ☞

THE SUPERNAL IMAGE OF MAN

☞ The verse states that Adam bore Seth "in his likeness, after his image" (Gen. 5:3). Before Seth was born, Adam and Eve bore other creatures, such as spirits and demons (*Eiruvin* 18b). In order for man to bear man, to produce his perfect image, he had to himself attain the ultimate likeness of man in his deepest depths. Then the illumination that emerged from him could also be in the appearance of man. But when a person sins, his inner appearance becomes distorted, and the creations he produces have

'אֵל' לְשׁוֹן הַמְשָׁכַת הַהֶאָרָה מֵאוֹר אֵין סוֹף בָּרוּךְ הוּא, מֵהַהֶעְלֵם אֶל הַגִּילּוּי, לְהָאִיר בִּבְחִינַת גִּילּוּי בְּנִשְׁמָתוֹ, וּכְמוֹ שֶׁכָּתוּב: "אֵל ה' וַיָּאֶר לָנוּ" (תהלים קיח, כז),

***El* connotes the flow and illumination from the light of *Ein Sof,* blessed be He,** when it emerges **from** a state of **concealment to** a state of **revelation to shine manifestly in the soul, as it is written, "The Lord is God; He has given us light"** (Ps. 118:27),

the appearances of monsters. He creates all kinds of spirits and demons, but not man.

In this light, of all the children that Adam had, not one returned to the initial perfect appearance that was in the likeness of God. It was only after a period of time, through a process of spiritual selection on the one hand and specific actions on the other that someone would emerge whose appearance was "as beautiful as Adam." Only then would the appearance of the ultimate Adam likeness, that of "the image of God," appear. This was Jacob, the paradigmatic image of essential man that is aligned with the Torah and the image of its Giver. The central axis of all the worlds are these two images: the image above and the likeness below and the bridge between the two is the internal heartbeat that pulsates throughout all the world.

When light passes through a small hole, it creates on the other side a miniature image of the source of the light. One might think that when the sun shines through a small hole partial shapes would appear, or the shape of the hole would be reproduced, but actually the sun's original circle shape is recreated over and over again. This can be proven by shining an incandescent bulb through a hole. One can see a reflection of the filament through the hole.

There are major differences between the light source and the reflection that shines through the hole, but both retain the same proportions and are therefore built on the same fundamental image. Similarly, God's image on the throne, "the likeness, like the appearance of a person," passes through the nexus of the worlds, through constriction after constriction, through numerous screens and tiny apertures, until finally an image of the appearance of a person is created.

However, since the divine image below is projected onto a flawed item, it creates an image that is not similar, not even close, to the original appearance. To illustrate, one can build anything through analytic geometry. One can build, for example, the shape of a snail. One creates the structure based on an equation made up of letters and numbers, and when it is projected onto a particular coordinate system, it creates the snail image. Obviously, the equation itself does not look like a snail, yet it is meant to produce a snail.

The Torah, made up of letters and words, is like that equation, but this one expresses the image of supernal man. When it is projected into the realm of the physical world, it creates the image of man below: "This is the Torah: man." The Torah is the image of a person, but the Torah image of man does not look to us like the familiar human image and not even like the human likeness that is on the throne. Still, each of these images expresses in its own unique language the form that from among all shapes and likenesses is the image of man.

Here the author of the *Tanya* explains why God called Jacob by this particular divine name. The name *El* is associated with the attribute of *Ḥesed,*[13] which is the *sefira* whose illumination emerges from a hidden state to a revealed state. It is the overarching force that moves from the inside out, as reflected in the verse quoted here that God is called *El* when His light shines forth and manifests within us, within the soul, when it issues forth from a state of concealment to a state of revelation.

Israel, which encompasses the entire Jewish people, as previously explained, is a chariot for the Divine Presence, and as such, its identity is absolutely subsumed within the Divine Presence itself. When God called Jacob *El,* He was attesting to the fact that Jacob had reached this level. He had become a perfect instrument for the revelation of the Divine in the world.

וְאַחֲרָיו כָּל יִשְׁרֵי לֵב הָעוֹסְקִים בַּתּוֹרָה וּבַמִּצְוֹת מֵאִיר אוֹר ה׳ אֵין סוֹף בָּרוּךְ הוּא בִּבְחִינַת גִּילּוּי בְּנִשְׁמָתָם.

and after Jacob, **the infinite divine light of *Ein Sof,* blessed be He, shines manifestly in the souls of all the upright of heart, who engage in Torah** study **and mitzvot.**

"The upright of heart" refers to each and every Jew.[14] What our forefather Jacob achieved with regard to the fundamental perfect likeness exists to a certain degree in every Jew. ☞

THE UPRIGHT OF HEART

☞ The usage of this term is significant since every Jew has the foundational template of our ancestor Israel (who is Jacob), who was the ultimate image of Adam, echoing the image of supernal man above. But this world and most people who inhabit it are filled with various corruptions, distortions, and blemishes of the body and, even

13. See *Torah Or* 10b.

14. Regarding this phrase, which appears in Ps. 94:15 and elsewhere. the Lubavitcher Rebbe, Rabbi Menaḥem Mendel Schneerson, comments: "The name Yisrael can be broken up into two words: *yashar el,*" which means "God made man straight." See *Likkutei Torah,* Num. 40c. "Straight" implies that he is the same below as he is above, that the upright among the Jewish people draw down the light of *Ein Sof* so that it is manifest below just as it is manifest above.

The upright of heart are those who study Torah and perform mitzvot. The Torah and mitzvot provide the tools that enable a person to take the straight path and receive the divine light. This means that this revelation can happen for every Jew at any time. Even if it is not necessarily to the ultimate degree, where the entire image of man is perfected, at certain auspicious moments any person can be a vessel for the divine light of supernal man. ☞

more so, of the soul. The author of the *Tanya* therefore speaks about "the upright of heart," about one who can preserve the image of man within in an upright fashion and not let it get distorted. Moreover, the term "heart" implies that most of the distortions can be traced to the heart. The intellect alone, when unaffected by the heart, registers things as they are. Those who can transmit that which they rationally know to be true to the heart, without any distortion, are called "the upright of heart."

THOSE WHO ENGAGE IN TORAH STUDY AND MITZVOT

☞ The author of the *Tanya* emphasizes that the illumination of one's soul with the light of *Ein Sof* comes about through Torah and mitzvot. There are people, extremely righteous, for whom God's light shines on whatever it is that they do, whether major or minor. Purely for the sake of example, there are people who have a certain grace. Whatever they do, they do well. These people do not have to try very hard to achieve that grace or learn how to achieve it. It is simply something they possess. Similarly, when certain people attain the likeness of supernal man and closely resemble the image from above, everything they do shines with divine light. These unique individuals, these tzaddikim who become chariots for the Divine Presence, do not just shine while they are performing mitzvot. Everything they do is automatically holy and shines with the light of divine wisdom. Every movement, word, and thought is aligned only with God.

Though the average Jew is not on this level of perfection, he too shines with the divine light when he aligns himself with the Torah and mitzvot. This illumination is revealed "in their souls," and does not usually surface as a conscious experience, not because the illumination is less but because of its immense power. The connection attained through Torah and mitzvot is truly greater than any other experience of oneness with God. When a person studies Torah or fulfills a mitzva, he is one with God in his actions, thoughts, and will.

Yet Torah and mitzvot are structures that operate within this world, and one must work within their constructs. For example, the Torah is an intellectual structure, and when a person studies Torah, his cognitive engagement may prevent him from feeling the revelation of the divine light concealed in the Torah. He cannot melt into that experience, because he must stay sharp to study properly, which is a necessary element to attaching oneself to God through the Torah. Similarly, when it comes to mitzvot, while one must evoke a deep, emotional experience through doing a mitzva, that authentic, heartfelt experience must be bridled within very specific parameters in order for him to perform the mitzva properly.

After the Torah gives the command-

וּזְמַן גִּילּוּי זֶה בְּיֶתֶר שְׂאֵת וְיֶתֶר עָז הַהֶאָרָה בְּמוֹחָם וְלִבָּם הוּא בִּשְׁעַת הַתְּפִלָּה, כְּמוֹ שֶׁנִּתְבָּאֵר בְּמָקוֹם אַחֵר.

The time of the greatest and most powerful manifestation of the illumination in their minds and hearts is during prayer, as explained elsewhere (see epistle 24).

While one studies Torah or performs mitzvot, this is not necessarily the time when the divine light manifests as a palpable spiritual experience. On the contrary, it can be an impediment. The fitting time for this, for the revelation of God's light in people's hearts and minds, is during prayer. The time of prayer, and particularly the prayer itself, removes one's masks and a living, palpable connection is forged between a person and God. This phenomenon is twofold: It is an opening of gates from above and, no less, an opening of gates from below, in the heart and soul of man.

Everyday life obscures the presence of God, but during prayer and other special moments, when the auspicious moment from above coincides with the service of prayer below, the divine light can manifest expressly in one's soul through the instruments of one's mind and heart. ☞

ment to light the candles of the *menora* in the Temple, it says, "And Aaron did so" (Num. 8:3). Rashi there explains that the Torah is praising Aaron because he did not change the commandment at all in his performance of it. Why is this praiseworthy? A certain tzaddik explains: If Rabbi Levi Yitzḥak of Berditchev was commanded to light the *menora*, in his immense excitement he would probably slip on the steps leading up to the *menora*, spill the oil, and tip over the *menora*. Aaron's excitement was certainly no less intense than Rabbi Levi Yitzḥak's, yet he was able to restrain himself and light the *menora* just as he was commanded.

This is how Rashi understands the Torah's praise of Aaron. This praise is meaningless for a person who does not feel the intensity of the divine light that is manifest upon the performance of a mitzva. But for a person like Aaron, who felt the enormity of the divine illumination brimming over when he fulfilled the mitzva, it was an extraordinary feat to be able to perform it with absolute precision.

This poses a fundamental problem. The awareness of the revelation of the divine light in the performance of mitzvot is bound to inhibit the optimal performance of it. In light of this, while a person studies Torah or performs a mitzva, which is when the divine light shines into his soul, he is not necessarily aware of it.

THE MOST POWERFUL REVELATION

☞ Unlike Torah study, prayer is a time for heartfelt emotion. If a person feels the light of God shining into him while he is praying, and he jumps out of sheer excitement,

Until this point, the author of the *Tanya* has been discussing the divine light, describing how it descends to our world and splits into 613 parts that correspond to the 613 commandments. This is the author of the *Tanya*'s explanation of the concept of a "portion in the God of Israel." This portion refers to a part of the divine revelation that manifests in its entirety through the Torah and mitzvot, which are themselves split up into many parts, every one of which is a "portion in the God of Israel." The author will now go on to explain the wording of the verses that he quoted at the very beginning of the epistle: the meaning of "our portion" and "our lot." What is the significance of "our portion" and how does a specific portion relate to a specific person?

24 Av / 26 Av (leap year)

וְהִנֵּה אַף שֶׁגִּילּוּי זֶה, עַל יְדֵי עֵסֶק הַתּוֹרָה וְהַמִּצְוֹת, הוּא שָׁוֶה לְכָל נֶפֶשׁ מִיִּשְׂרָאֵל בְּדֶרֶךְ כְּלָל, כִּי תּוֹרָה אַחַת וּמִשְׁפָּט אֶחָד לְכוּלָּנוּ,

Although this manifestation of divine light that occurs **through Torah study and mitzvot is generally the same for every Jew, for we all share one Torah and one law,**

The Torah and its laws are a revelation of the innermost supernal will, through which a connection between man and the Divine is forged. The performance of a mitzva is an expression of the essence of man, the essence of the Divine, and the essence of the world (which is another manifestation of the divine will). When a person studies Torah and performs a mitzva in this world, he reveals the divine will in the ultimate way, in all three aspects.

The author of the *Tanya* also points out here that one of the defining features of the Torah and all the mitzvot is that they are indivisible.

this does not impede his performance of the mitzva of prayer. On the contrary, it is the epitome of prayer. A person's prayerful words are merely external instruments for the emotions of his heart and its inspiration. Each word is a rung in the ladder on which he climbs higher and higher in his devotional service of love. There have been great people throughout the generations who did not stay planted in one place during prayers because they were overcome with such spiritual fervor that it was as if they were experiencing divine revelation (see *Berakhot* 31a; Rambam, *Mishneh Torah, Sefer HaMadda, Hilkhot Yesodei HaTorah* 7:2). Prayer is a time when a person is exposed to such intense illumination and emotions that he cannot remain in the place where he began. He must move and jump; he simply cannot stay where he was before.

The Torah is not meant for one type of person and not others. Every Jew has the obligation to live a Torah life, and no one is free to shirk this obligation.

אַף עַל פִּי כֵן, בְּדֶרֶךְ פְּרָט אֵין כָּל הַנְּפָשׁוֹת אוֹ הָרוּחוֹת וְהַנְּשָׁמוֹת שָׁווֹת בְּעִנְיָן זֶה לְפִי עֵת וּזְמַן גִּלְגּוּלָם וּבוֹאָם בָּעוֹלָם הַזֶּה,

nevertheless, specifically speaking, not every *nefesh, ruaḥ,* and *neshama* is equal in this regard. The manifestation **depends on the period and time of their incarnation and their coming to this world,**

That "this manifestation [of divine light that occurs] through Torah study and mitzvot is the same for every Jew" means that all Jews share the same collective lot. We are all human, and we all share the same history and Torah mission. But there are many individual differences between us, and in that sense, we are not all equal.

Beyond the basic categorization of people, there is also a deeper division that is connected to the levels of the soul: *nefesh, ruaḥ,* and *neshama.* A person's soul is not one basic unit. It is comprised of several levels, one higher than the next. These elements are, in a certain sense, separate. A person may damage or heal his *nefesh,* for instance, but not his *ruaḥ* and vice versa. It could be that on a *ruaḥ* level, he is one type of person, while on a *neshama* level, he is the opposite. Two people can be equal on one level, but different on another. It is like two musical instruments that share the same fundamental sounds, but in their higher tones they are completely different.

Another way that souls are distinct relates to the concept of reincarnation. Every time a soul returns to his world, it enters a new dimension of time and space. Depending on where and when he lives, a person has different types of experiences. A Jew who lived while the Temple was standing experienced a vastly different reality than a Jew who is living today. A Jew who lives today outside the Land of Israel has a different awareness of Torah and mitzvot than one who lives in the land. ☞

REINCARNATION

☞ A very rudimentary analogy for reincarnation is a child who stayed behind in school and repeated a certain grade in order to fulfill certain requirements that for some reason he failed to achieve the first time. If he fails the second time as well,

What each soul must accomplish depends on what level it is on when it comes into the world and what previous baggage it is carrying with it. Only a few souls, particularly in recent generations, are new souls, on their first round in this world. The vast majority of souls are old souls that have come back in a second, third, or higher incarnation. In light of this, even two seemingly similar people, born around the same time in the same place, experience life very differently. Each one carries with it the memories etched into him from previous lives, and each one has a special role and a unique mission that he came to the world to fulfill. One person must fix an entire lifetime, while another, who is nearing completion of the rectification of his soul, need only fix one particular facet.

Returning to this world time after time becomes demanding in and of itself, because every time a soul comes to the world, it may successfully fix one aspect but fail in another due to its new life circumstances. When an old soul gets a new body, it has all kinds of new issues to deal with: how to operate this particular body, how to function in his new home, how to navigate his new familial dynamics, how to succeed in an unfamiliar society and live in the strange new world to which he has been sent.

וּכְמַאֲמַר רַבּוֹתֵינוּ זִכְרוֹנָם לִבְרָכָה (שבת קיח, ב): אֲבוּךְ בְּמַאי הֲוֵי זָהִיר טְפֵי? אֲמַר לֵיהּ: בְּצִיצִית כו'.

As our Rabbis said, "Rav Yosef said to Rav Yosef, son of Rabba: **In what area was your father especially vigilant? He said to him:** It was **in** the mitzva of ***tzitzit*...**" (*Shabbat* 118b).

Rabba was surely meticulous in his performance of all the mitzvot. A person of his giant stature certainly performed every single mitzva as scrupulously as possible. Rather, as explained in hasidic works, the word for vigilant in this talmudic statement, *zahir,* shares the same letters as the Hebrew word *zohar,* shine. Rav Yosef was asking, "With which mitzva did your father shine? With which mitzva did your father's soul light up the most?"[15] ☞

then he will remain in the same grade a third and a fourth time. In the course of every life, whether it his second or third reincarnation, a person must perfect the image of Adam within his soul.

15. The Lubavitcher Rebbe, Rabbi Menaḥem Mendel Schneerson, comments:

וְכֵן אֵין כָּל הַדּוֹרוֹת שָׁוִין. Likewise, not all the generations are equal.

Beyond an individual's mission, which he fulfills in the context of his personal history, geographic location, and nature, there is also a particular role that he plays and obligations that he must fulfill in the larger scheme of his generation.[16] ☞

WHEN THE SOUL LIGHTS UP

☞ Every person feels this during prayers, when a certain word, sentence, or topic touches his soul, penetrates his essence, and shakes him to his core. Whenever he reaches that part of the prayers, his soul lights up. The same is true regarding mitzvot. A person may be very careful to perform all the mitzvot in the optimal way, yet there is always one particular mitzva that lights up his soul the most when he merits performing it.

Throughout a person's life, he comes to discover which mitzva that is. It is the mitzva that he often encounters, that he seeks out, that he must perform. These signs signify that this particular mitzva is the key to fixing that crucial element that requires rectification, the reason for which his soul descended in this incarnation and through which he will actualize his true potential and manifest his own unique facet of the image of Adam.

NOT ALL GENERATIONS ARE EQUAL

☞ Several sources compare the way in which the entire Jewish people are a complete structural analog in every generation to the way in which they form a complete structural analog throughout time. There is a division of devotional labor among the generations: One generation has one type of obligation to fulfill, while another has other types of obligations. Therefore, an individual who lives in a particular generation has specific obligations that he may not have had if he had lived in another generation.

"Every Jew is obligated to perform all 613 commandments, but each individual Jew has a particular mitzva through which all his Torah study and mitzva performance ascends" (see *Sefer HaSiḥot* [summer 5700], p. 22; *Iggerot Kodesh*, vol. 7, letter 2017). Elsewhere he states, "This [particular] mitzva serves as a gate through which all of one's Torah study and mitzva performance below ascend on high and through which all of one's vitality and blessings are drawn from above to below.… Of course, clarifying which particular devotional practice is relevant to a particular Jew almost always brings with it open divine providence by establishing for him how his chosen profession involves this mitzva or that practice, which proves that this is his particular gateway from below to above and above to below" (*Iggerot Kodesh*, vol. 10, letter 3011).

16. However, regarding these words of the author of the *Tanya*, "not all generations are equal," the Lubavitcher Rebbe, Rabbi Menaḥem Mendel Schneerson,

כִּי כְּמוֹ שֶׁאֵבְרֵי הָאָדָם, כׇּל אֵבֶר יֵשׁ לוֹ פְּעוּלָּה פְּרָטִית וּמְיוּחֶדֶת, הָעַיִן לִרְאוֹת וְהָאֹזֶן לִשְׁמוֹעַ, כָּךְ בְּכׇל מִצְוָה מֵאִיר אוֹר פְּרָטִי וּמְיוּחָד מֵאוֹר אֵין סוֹף בָּרוּךְ הוּא.

As with a person's limbs, where **each limb has a specific, distinct function,** such as **the** function of the **eye to see and the ear to hear, so too through every mitzva shines a specific, distinct light from the light of *Ein Sof,* blessed be He.**

The entirety of the 613 commandments are like the 613 limbs of the body. The body has a general life force that pulsates in the ear, the same as it does in the eye, the feet, and the brain, yet each limb also has a unique function all its own that is not interchangeable with any other. For instance, there is a single gene set in every cell of every limb that gives each one the same identifying DNA. Yet each limb has its own unique function as well. The eye is formed in a particular way and serves a purpose that no other limb in the body does. Similarly, each of the 613 commandments is an expression of the all-encompassing divine life force, yet each one is also a particular "limb," with a unique illumination all its own. ☞

This is also true regarding the larger analog of all the souls of Israel, which composes the template of a person. Some people are the manifest aspect of the eye, and the Torah calls them "the eyes of the congregation," and then there is the person whose role is to be the foot, and he must fulfill other corresponding missions in the world.

LIMBS AND MITZVOT

☞ The parallel between the mitzvot and the limbs of the body is not incidental. The mitzvot are intended to be fulfilled, and man was created to fulfill the mitzvot. It is said that this is how the Ba'al Shem Tov used to heal the sick. If a person suffered from an affliction in a particular limb, it meant that he had blemished its corresponding mitzva. The Ba'al Shem would tell his patient that he must speak to that limb and tell it to accept upon itself the corresponding mitzva. Only when it would do so would it be capable of healing.

---

comments, "It would seem that these words are encompassed in the aforementioned 'period and time' [discussed with regard to reincarnation], and one should research the handwritten manuscripts of *Iggeret HaKodesh* [for the correct phrasing]. Perhaps it is supposed to read 'mitzvot.'"

וְאַף שֶׁכׇּל נֶפֶשׁ מִיִּשְׂרָאֵל צְרִיכָה לָבוֹא בְּגִלְגּוּל לְקַיֵּים כׇּל תַּרְיַ"ג מִצְוֹת,

Although every Jewish soul must be reincarnated until it **fulfills all 613 commandments,**

One might think that if every soul is like a particular limb, the person must fulfill only one mitzva. But the bigger picture is more complex, since every soul, even in the context of the entire Jewish people and all the generations throughout time, embodies the entirety of the 613 commandments as well. In light of this, as explained in the writings of the Arizal, every soul must experience, in some way or another, every one of the 613 commandments. If he does not do so in one lifetime, he must come back in another incarnation until he completes them all.[17]

מִכׇּל מָקוֹם לֹא נִצְרְכָה אֶלָּא לְהַעְדָּפָה וְזְהִירוּת וּזְרִיזוּת יְתֵירָה, בְּיֶתֶר שְׂאֵת וְיֶתֶר עָז כְּפוּלָה וּמְכוּפֶּלֶת, לְמַעְלָה מַעְלָה מִזְּהִירוּת שְׁאָר הַמִּצְוֹת.

nevertheless, the emphasis on a specific mitzva **merely means an additional preference, vigilance, and alacrity** for that mitzva that is **of exceedingly greater magnitude and greater power above and beyond one's vigilance for the other commandments.**

This wording, "an additional preference, vigilance, and alacrity [for that mitzva that is] of exceedingly greater magnitude and greater power," describes how a person should conduct himself in relation to that one mitzva, "his" mitzva. The significance of this, that it is his mitzvah, is that he has a particular responsibility incumbent on him to do that which he and no one else can do.

On the other hand, this mitzva points to his essential weakness, since it is related to the particular mitzva that he blemished in a previous lifetime, and now it has become his particular challenge to overcome. Because the stakes are so high, he must be on alert for any impediments that will be thrown his way to prevent him from reaching his ultimate rectification. This is the reason that the author of the *Tanya* uses such

17. Elsewhere, this aspect of divine service is described as a garment that the soul must weave for its 613 limbs through the performance of the 613 mitzvot. This light-garment of the soul is what the soul will wear in the World to Come.

intense language when describing the immense effort a person must invest in the scrupulous performance of this particular mitzva.

וְזֶהוּ שֶׁאָמַר 'בְּמַאי הֲוֵי זָהִיר טְפֵי', 'טְפֵי' דַּיְיקָא.

This is why Rav Yosef **said, "In what area was** your father **especially vigilant?" specifically** using the word **"especially."**

Rav Yosef was not asking about which mitzva Rabba was most vigilant, since a person of his stature was certainly scrupulous in performing every mitzva. Rather, the question was regarding which mitzva he was particularly vigilant. Which mitzva lit up his soul in a special way, more than the other mitzvot.

As discussed above, this is the soul's special portion, the unique lot of this particular soul. It is in this area that the soul is particularly touched, that it receives extra fortitude to accomplish its mission in the world.

Up to this point, the author of the *Tanya* has explained the meaning of having a portion in the God of Israel. This does not mean that the Divine is divisible, but rather that there are various facets to divine revelation. It divides into infinite parts that are tailor-made for each individual. God apportions His divine bounty into 613 general categories, which correspond to our very beings. Every person has a particular portion of divine illumination that precisely relates to his soul. In this light, the concept that a person does not have "a portion in the God of Israel" means that that person is not fulfilling his unique part, that he is disconnected from his special allotment of the God of Israel. Since he disconnected himself to a certain degree from the image of supernal man, he lost his portion, the part that he was responsible for, in the building of the grand image of holiness in the world.

After clarifying the expression "our portion," posed as a question at the beginning of the epistle, the author of the *Tanya* concludes the letter by explaining the term "our lot." What is the meaning of the "lot" that relates to our "portion"?

וְהִנֵּה יִתְרוֹן הָאוֹר הַזֶּה הַפְּרָטִי לִנְשָׁמוֹת פְּרָטִיּוֹת אֵינוֹ בִּבְחִינַת טַעַם וָדַעַת מוּשָּׂג, אֶלָּא לְמַעְלָה מִבְּחִינַת הַדַּעַת,

The added measure of this individual light bestowed **on individual souls is not something rational that can be apprehended** intellectually. **Rather, it transcends reason,**

It is in the unique portion of each person, that area that he must work on the most, that his own personal power and abilities, his true essence, becomes the most manifest. This distinction, how one person needs to work on one specific mitzva in particular and another person is vigilant about a different mitzva, granting each an added measure of light and power in that area, is not something that lies within the grasp of their rational faculties. Rational considerations would posit that since a given person has certain abilities, his unique mitzva must be one that demands use of those skills. But the truth is much more complex, and we are incapable of understanding it entirely. The subtle and intricate considerations that assign certain missions to certain people are not based merely on their character strengths, but on the very roots of their soul and on the supernal divine will, which transcends not only our ability to understand it but every rational construct that exists.

שֶׁכָּךְ עָלָה בְּמַחֲשָׁבָה לְפָנָיו יִתְבָּרֵךְ. **for thus it arose in God's thoughts.**

The expression "arose in God's thoughts" characterizes the will that transcends reason.[18] It is pure will without a clear rationale. It is God's simple will that desires for a certain person to do a certain thing. This mysterious supernal will is that which determines one's personal destiny, the role that he must fulfill, his particular mitzva and portion in the world, all of which are inherently incomprehensible.

וְדוּגְמָתוֹ לְמַטָּה הוּא בְּחִינַת הַגּוֹרָל מַמָּשׁ. **The perfect analogy for this below is the concept of a lottery.**

In modern-day Hebrew, the words *goral*, lot, and *mazal*, luck, are synonymous. In the language of the Sages, *mazal* refers to the entire lifeline that encompasses all of a person,[19] his supernal root that descends and manifests as the very life and body of a person, while *goral* refers to fate.[20] In this context, *goral* refers to the seemingly arbitrary decision from above that does not have in and of itself any rational underpinnings. Therefore, when we speak of "our portion and our lot," we do

18. See *Menaḥot* 29b; *Torah Or* 87d, 92b.
19. See, e.g., *Shabbat* 156a; *Bereshit Rabba* 44:10.
20. See, e.g., Mishna *Yoma* 4:1.

not mean the portion that a person himself chooses or that he believes it is proper for him to take on, but rather that which he received, that which he was born with, like a note that says, "Such-and-such mitzva is your lot," a message that tells you which particular mitzva or portion in the Torah and life circumstance you will be handed. One's lot comes to signify his unique path on the journey of life. There is no rationale or explanation that determines this. Just as one cannot question why a person is the way he is, one cannot question why a person was dealt the portion and lot he was given.

An example that illustrates this idea is a raffle. A scrap of paper is picked at random, without any rational reason. The result does not depend on the skill of the person who extracts it or on the content of the note. This example is not just an analogy. It is a direct reference to the verses quoted at the beginning of the epistle: "How good is our portion and how pleasant our lot...." ☞ ☞

A DAY LIKE PURIM

☞ The motif of a lottery appears in two holidays: Purim and Yom Kippur. The lottery on Yom Kippur determined which goat was brought as an offering "to the Lord" and which was sent "to Azazel." A deeper look discloses the same motif in the Purim story, which centers around a lottery that produced two opposite outcomes (hence, the plural *purim*, lots): those who were saved and those who were put to death, those who went with God and those who went to Azazel. It is no wonder that the lottery that Haman cast fell out on a date with two-sided significance: Moses died on that day, but he was also born on that day. It is thus a day of death and also a day of life.

THE UNPUBLISHED CONCLUSION

As noted in the introduction to this epistle, the last section was not included in the published version of *Iggeret HaKodesh* of the *Tanya*. For those interested, here is the author's concluding passage:

"After presenting these matters and this truth, it is known in this land, in our country, the country of White Russia, Lithuania, and its environs, and to all those who have joined us, that 'the lots that have fallen to us are pleasant, and our estate is lovely' (see Ps. 16:6). I am referring to our ancestral portion, the Holy Land, may it be rebuilt and reestablished speedily in our days, amen. A great mitzva, which is to fortify its settlement on the basis of Torah and divine service, to sustain and nourish it, has fallen to our lot and our portion, in the light of the Lord, God of Israel, to toil in it with exceedingly great effort with all our souls and resources, with great vigilance and alacrity. This is the era of eras, mighty days, and blessed is the Lord who completes this for us and who has helped us to this point.

"We have made exceedingly great efforts to encourage those who are eager [to help] so that they may finish raising

This short epistle, which addresses the practical scope of the mitzva of charity, explained the deeper meaning of the "portion" and "lot" of every Jew. One's portion is his portion of the Divine, as it were, and his lot is his connection to his portion, an intrinsic connection that transcends reason. One's whole life revolves around these two elements, the perpetual search for one's personal mitzva, his portion and lot, as well as the knowledge that his portion and lot are determined on high, and he has no control over what his portion and lot will be. A person may stumble on his portion in the course of his life, and sometimes he may not even be aware that this is the focal point of his life, before and after which everything that happened was nothing but background and preparation. A person can never know with absolute certainty what that focal point is. It is one of those things a person must pray for, to be able to complete his portion and lot, to fulfill his life mission.

This personal discovery is the subject of the praise quoted at the beginning of the epistle: "How good is our portion and how pleasant

and collecting all the holy funds so that [the collection] will be completed before Passover in order that they may be brought up and arrive in the Holy Land by harvest time, when fruits and produce are cheap. Any sum that might be raised and collected after Passover would be outweighed by the great losses incurred on account of the expensive winter prices, so much so that it would cost almost double the amount.

"So far we have been unsuccessful, due to postponements and delays in collecting the monies from the Volhynia *kollel*, for which our agent was also sent, as you were commanded by the late holy Rebbe Rabbi [Menaḥem Mendel of Vitebsk], may the memory of the righteous be as a blessing for life in the World to Come. On this occasion, however, for various reasons it was agreed in the Holy Land that our agent would withdraw from [collecting] the funds of the Volhynia *kollel* and would not act for them as an agent for delivery. Rather, they would be sent through a member of the Polish community in the Holy Land, and our agent would not wait for him at all.

"To this end, I hereby redouble my efforts to strengthen those who are wavering [in contributing charity], the volunteers among the people, and to make firm the tottering knees of those who raise and collect funds in each and every city and prayer gathering. They should all be especially vigilant and alacritous to finish the entire campaign of raising and collecting the holy sum in advance and sending it on in orderly fashion specifically before Passover. They must not deviate from this mission, God forbid, so that the records in the account books will be completed before the upcoming festival of Shavuot. Then our agent will be able to set out on his travels and his holy journey immediately after the festival of Shavuot, with the help of God.

"I have been brief, in my great confidence, and I declare peace to the work of charity..."

our lot." This praise does not refer the commandments in general but rather to one's specific portion that he uniquely received. Some people search for their portion their whole lives. This is the main reason that people go to tzaddikim: It is to ask them this question, "What is my portion and lot?" Not "Where do I have to be vigilant?" but "Where do I have to be especially vigilant?" When a person feels that he has found his portion, he is so connected to it that he rejoices in the find of a lifetime and is overcome with gratitude at finding his place and role. He then offers praise and thanksgiving for being privy to his portion: "How good is our portion and how pleasant our lot!"

Epistle 8

THIS LETTER ALSO DISCUSSES THE MITZVA OF CHARITY IN general and charity for the Land of Israel in particular. But along with his words of inspiration regarding the giving of charity, the author of the *Tanya* also delves into the deepest and most profound aspects of divine service: prayer, love, reverence, and devotion. More specifically, this letter focuses on the relationship between giving charity before prayer and the divine revelation that an individual merits through that prayer. What is this divine revelation and illumination in prayer, and what is the connection between this gift and charity?

"זוֹרֵעַ צְדָקוֹת מַצְמִיחַ יְשׁוּעוֹת" (ברכת 'יוצר אור') הִנֵּה, מַה שֶּׁאוֹמֵר לְשׁוֹן זְרִיעָה בְּמִצְוַת הַצְּדָקָה וּכְמוֹ שֶׁכָּתוּב בַּפָּסוּק: "זִרְעוּ לָכֶם לִצְדָקָה כו'" (הושע י, יב),

25 Av

27 Av (leap year)

In the *Yotzer Or* blessing recited before the morning *Shema*, we say, **"He sows charity and brings forth salvation." The reason that the term "sowing" is used regarding the mitzva of charity, as it written, "Sow charity for yourselves..."** (Hos. 10:12),

The letter begins with a verse from the daily prayers, concerning which the author poses a question: Why is the term "sowing," which is related to planting, used in connection with the mitzva of charity? The same question can be posed regarding the verse from Hosea that he proceeds to quote.

יוּבַן עַל פִּי מַה שֶּׁאָמְרוּ רַבּוֹתֵינוּ זִכְרוֹנָם לִבְרָכָה (בבא בתרא י, א): רַבִּי אֶלְעָזָר יָהֵיב פְּרוּטָה לְעָנִי וַהֲדַר מְצַלֵּי דִּכְתִיב, "אֲנִי בְּצֶדֶק

can be understood based on the Rabbis' statement (*Bava Batra* 10a) **"Rabbi Elazar would** first **give a coin to a poor person and** only **then** would he **pray.** He said: **As it is**

אֶחֱזֶה פָנֶיךָ" (תהלים יז, טו).

written, 'I will behold Your face through charity' (Ps. 17:16)."

To support his practice of giving charity before prayer, Rabbi Elazar quoted the verse "I will behold Your face through charity," interpreting the verse as saying, "When I give charity, then I will behold Your face." Charity is a step, a precondition, by which one can achieve prayer, which is essentially "beholding Your face," the revelation and shining of the countenance of God, before whom one stands in prayer.

But this claim requires further elaboration. It would seem that the mitzvot of charity and prayer have no relevance to one another at all. Charity is the classic example of a mitzva performed between one person and another, whereas prayer is one of the clearest cases of an encounter between a person and God. Why, then, should it be necessary to perform the mitzva of charity before praying? What does prayer lack that is supplemented by charity?

פֵּירוּשׁ כִּי גִילּוּי אֱלָקוּתוֹ יִתְבָּרֵךְ הַמִּתְגַּלָּה בְּמַחֲשַׁבְתּוֹ שֶׁל אָדָם וְכַוָּנָתוֹ בִּתְפִלָּתוֹ,

The explanation for this is that the divine revelation of God that is manifest in a person's thoughts and intentions during prayer,

Prayer is a bond between us and God. We turn to Him so that He will turn to us, face-to-face, man to God. In this encounter, man anticipates a revelation from above. Prayer is not merely a declaration, nor is it only a request or a confession. Rather, prayer is a dialogue. It consists not only of what a person says to Heaven, but also what he receives from above in return. This response from Heaven does not always manifest clearly and explicitly (as in a prophecy or an open miracle), but there is some measure of illumination that is revealed to a person while he is praying.

כָּל חַד לְפוּם שִׁיעוּרָא דִילֵיהּ,

each according to his own capacity,

Although the words of the prayer book are the same for everyone, the intention behind the words and what is revealed to a person from within the words are not equal. No two people experience the exact same revelation. Everyone has his own aptitude for receiving the revelation. Prayer does not fall on people like rain, making everyone wet to the same degree. Rather, it is like a speech that is heard by many people, but each individual internalizes the contents in accordance with his own knowledge, understanding, and emotional disposition. ☞

הוּא בְּתוֹרַת צְדָקָה, "וְחֶסֶד ה' מֵעוֹלָם וְעַד עוֹלָם עַל יְרֵאָיו כו'" (תהלים קג, יז).

is granted by the charity of God, **"the kindness of the Lord** that **forever** comes **to those who fear Him…** (Ps. 103:17).

The illumination that a person receives from God during prayer, this revelation, ascension, and elevation of the heart that he feels while praying, even if it is only slight, is an act of charity and kindness from God. The person is not entitled to it by right or as part of the natural mechanism of prayer, a kind of automatic outcome of the bare fact that a person prays. It is a kindness and an unconditional gift.

כְּלוֹמַר, שֶׁאוֹר ה', אֵין סוֹף בָּרוּךְ הוּא, הַמֵּאִיר לְמַעְלָה בְּעוֹלָמוֹת עֶלְיוֹנִים בְּהֶאָרָה רַבָּה, בִּבְחִינַת גִּילּוּי רַב וְעָצוּם

In other words, the light of *Ein Sof*, blessed be He, that shines above in the higher worlds with a great illumination is such **a great and powerful manifestation that** the higher worlds

ACCORDING TO ONE'S CAPACITY

☞ A person's character, nature, and knowledge attained over the course of his lifetime all determine his capability to receive divine revelation. This applies both to the scale of the experience and its intensity. It is not enough for a person to be a God-fearing Jew. In order to attain a great revelation, he also needs to understand what he is receiving.

In the past, people proactively studied how to receive divine illumination. It is almost certain that the "disciples of the prophets" mentioned in *Tanakh* (see, e.g., II Kings 2:3) were those who trained their minds and developed their capacity for receiving prophecy. While study is not the exclusive method for achieving prophecy or even a revelation on a different level, it is necessary in order to understand it.

We can see this in the story of Samuel's first prophecy. Samuel heard a prophecy, but he did not know who was calling him or what was happening to him. He had to receive guidance from Eli, who explained to him what prophecy is and what he should do. Nevertheless, it should be kept in mind that a person's efforts to receive revelation does not guarantee that the revelation will come to him. After all, revelation is a divine gift, which does not hinge on a person's deeds but on the will of God (see Rambam, *Mishneh Torah, Sefer HaMadda, Hilkhot Yesodei HaTorah* 7:5).

Although God is everywhere equally, He does not reveal Himself everywhere to the same extent. This is the difference between the higher worlds and the lower worlds: In the lower worlds, there is a slight degree of revelation, whereas the upper worlds experience a greater and more powerful revelation of the Divine.

עַד שֶׁבֶּאֱמֶת הֵן בְּטֵלִין בִּמְצִיאוּת וּכְלָא מַמָּשׁ חֲשִׁיבֵי קַמֵּיהּ וְנִכְלָלִין בְּאוֹרוֹ יִתְבָּרֵךְ.

are completely subsumed and literally considered nothingness before Him and are encompassed in God's light.

Our world, in addition to its status as a material world, is a world of independent existence. It is a world whose material and spiritual existence views itself as an entity in and of itself and considers its existence as a separate reality. It does not sense the presence of the Divine, nor does it sense how dependent it is on God. In the higher worlds, by contrast, the divine revelation is so great that the reality of their existence is negated in the face of it. The higher worlds do not experience reality in opposition to God but as part of the divine light and not as its own entity at all. It can be said that the higher worlds are nothing more than combinations of lights, and therefore their reality appears ephemeral, mere shadows of a reality that actually does not exist, in contradistinction to our world, whose reality is so tangible to us.

וְהֵן הֵן הַהֵיכָלוֹת עִם הַמַּלְאָכִים וְהַנְּשָׁמוֹת שֶׁבָּהֶן הַמְבוֹאָרִים בַּזּוֹהַר הַקָּדוֹשׁ (חלק ב רס–רסא) בִּשְׁמוֹתָם לִמְקוֹמוֹתָם בְּסֵדֶר הַתְּפִלָּה שֶׁסִּדְּרוּ לָנוּ אַנְשֵׁי כְּנֶסֶת הַגְּדוֹלָה.

These higher worlds **are the chambers, together with the angels and souls within them, that are described in the holy *Zohar*** (2:260–61) **by their names and places,** as reflected **in the order of the prayers arranged for us by the members of the Great Assembly.**

The higher, spiritual worlds are called chambers in kabbalistic terms, and the beings and entities that live within them are angels and souls.

Kabbalistic terms are, at the end of the day, nothing more than metaphors and images. When we speak about a spiritual world, we are talking about a reality that is not like our material world, although it has certain parallels to it. We inevitably use words taken from our material existence, if only as illustrations that will enable us to have some grip on the concepts. In this sense, a chamber is a space that contains certain beings, both human and otherwise. In a spiritual world, these entities are also spiritual: angels and souls.

As the author of the *Tanya* points out, the *Zohar* enumerates the names of the chambers and their position in the order of the overall structure of the chambers. The formulation and sections of the prayers, in the order arranged by the members of the Great Assembly, correspond to these chambers and the various levels of the higher worlds. In kabbalistic literature, there are also highly detailed descriptions of the realm to which each part of prayer belongs, to which world and which chamber.[21] This reflects the purpose of prayer, which is to ascend from this world and climb to lofty levels, step by step, like a ladder set from the earth to Heaven.[22] The order of prayer thus parallels the order of the worlds, and the movements between the various sections of prayer reflects the transitions from one world to the threshold of another. ☞

It is from there that this **light, which is good, shines in this lowly world,**

הִנֵּה מִשָּׁם מֵאִיר הָאוֹר כִּי טוֹב לָעוֹלָם הַשָּׁפֵל הַזֶּה

When a person passes through a certain chamber, literally and spiritually, he receives a certain degree of illumination. Ascending to a higher level grants him a greater degree of revelation. At that

THE CHAMBERS AND THE PRAYERS

☞ When a person prays, and when his prayer truly brings about an ascension of his soul, it passes right through the chambers, from one chamber to another. One might say that he passes through the chamber, but one can equally say that the chamber passes through him. In essence, that is nothing more than a different way of saying the same thing, since in truth there is no actual place here or person within it; these are merely expressions we use for the purpose of illustration. In any case, the soul reaches a certain place and status through prayer that constitutes a specific chamber, a particular level of illumination.

21. See *Pri Etz Ḥayyim, Sha'ar HaTefilla,* chaps. 4, 6.
22. See *Zohar* 1:149b, 266b; *Torah Or* 2b; *Likkutei Torah,* Ex. 2b.

loftier level, he apprehends things at the higher level of revelation with the higher degree of illumination. This is one way of receiving divine revelation.

Then there is a level, which the author of the *Tanya* is referring to here, where the illumination descends from a higher world to a lower world. Although one did not ascend to the higher level, the revelation comes to him from above like a gift and has an effect on him even in the lower world where he is found.

עַל יְרֵאֵי ה׳ וְחוֹשְׁבֵי שְׁמוֹ הַחֲפֵצִים לְעָבְדוֹ בַּעֲבוֹדָה שֶׁבַּלֵּב זוֹ תְּפִלָּה,

on those who fear God and contemplate His name, who desire to serve Him with the service of the heart, which is prayer,

This is an important observation: The divine illumination is granted to those who desire it, to those who are open to it. As the author of the *Tanya* mentioned, each person experiences revelation in accordance with his capacity to receive it, with how he looks at the spiritual world, his capability, and above all what he wants to see. This can be compared to people who are walking through the king's palace. Each individual will absorb what he expects to see. Some will admire the decorations. Others will be impressed with the etiquette of the ministers. Yet others will hope to get a glimpse of the king so that they can show their fear and love for him.

וּכְמוֹ שֶׁכָּתוּב: "וַה׳ יַגִּיהַּ חָשְׁכִּי" (שמואל ב כב, כט).

as it is written, "And the Lord will illuminate my darkness" (II Sam. 22:29).

The illumination that comes during prayer is a light that comes from above and shines into the darkness of that individual. Any darkness of which a person is not aware will not be illuminated for him; only the gloom that troubles him, that he longs to brighten, will be lit up.

Another idea that can be learned from this verse – and this is its main message – is that this illumination does not shine of its own accord, merely because a person desires it. Rather, "the Lord will illuminate my darkness." It comes from God alone, through His will and kindness. ☞

וְהִנֵּה יְרִידַת הֶאָרָה זוֹ לְמַטָּה, לָעוֹלָם הַזֶּה, נִקְרֵאת בְּשֵׁם 'חֶסֶד ה'', הַמְכוּנֶּה בְּשֵׁם 'מַיִם', הַיּוֹרְדִים מִמָּקוֹם גָּבוֹהַּ לְמָקוֹם נָמוּךְ כוּ'.

The descent of this illumination below, to this world, is called God's kindness, referred to as water, which, like this illumination, **flows from a high place to a low place, and so on.**

The illumination from a higher world that is revealed in a lower world is an expression of kindness. The definition of kindness is bringing down a flow of blessing from a high place to a lower one, of giving from above to below, from the rich man to the poor man, from those who have to those who do not. Other attributes do not operate in this manner. When one performs justice or pays respect to someone, his action does not come from above to below. That is why the classic symbol of kindness is water, which always flows from a high place to a lower one.[23]

The divine illumination from a higher world to a lower one is always a type of breach, a breaking through, into a different reality. If we were to receive the illumination as it exists in the higher world, we would also be in that higher world. In order for the recipient to receive the supernal illumination even though he is on a lower level, he requires the kindness of God, which descends, like water, from a high place to a lower one, in order to allow the light to flow from the higher world to the lower world. ☞

THE WINDOWS OF PRAYER

☞ This gift breaks into the lower world through the windows that we open for it, which are typically the windows of prayer. Prayer creates points of contact between the worlds so that the supernal illumination can break through and reveal itself in the lower world. On a very cloudy day, when one cannot see the light of the sun at all, a gap might open up in the clouds if the wind suddenly blows, exposing a ray of sunlight. Likewise, in the spiritual worlds it can happen that the coverings, the layers and concealments of days, perhaps even years and generations, might suddenly be removed, and one will merit an illumination, a revelation that did not previously exist in his world.

ILLUSIONS FROM ABOVE

☞ The receiving of the illumination and revelation from another world into our own world raises serious concerns about the possibility of false experiences. What

23. *Tikkunei Zohar* 38a.

26 Av וְהִנֵּה מוּדַעַת זֹאת שֶׁיֵּשׁ לְמַעְלָה גַּם כֵּן מִדַּת הַגְּבוּרָה וְהַצִּמְצוּם לְצַמְצֵם וּלְהַסְתִּיר אוֹרוֹ יִתְבָּרֵךְ לְבַל יִתְגַּלֶּה לַתַּחְתּוֹנִים.

It is known that there is also an attribute of *Gevura* and constriction above, constricting and concealing God's light, preventing it from being manifest in the lower worlds.

Just as there is an attribute of *Ḥesed* above, the attribute of giving and the bestowal of blessings and illumination from above to below, from the abstract to the tangible, from the hidden to the visible, from those who have to those who do not, there is likewise an attribute of *Gevura* above. In a sense, *Gevura* is the opposite of *Ḥesed*. It is the attribute of convergence, a movement from the periphery to the center, which limits and hides the flow of the divine light.

The starting point of the attribute of *Gevura*, which is the attribute of judgment, is boundaries: Boundaries and restrictions exist between one world and another, and each of them are separate. When there are boundaries and limits, not only does the divine light not spill over outside the borders, but it confines itself to within itself. This state of convergence and seclusion is the main feature of the attribute of *Gevura*.

The situation described here is when a person praying enunciates the letters, utters the words, and thinks the correct thoughts, achieving

might seem genuine, an objectively higher reality, is actually nothing but an illusion. This is a concern because, as lowly beings, we do not have access to words and images that can identify the spiritual realm, and therefore we are compelled to continue using earthly metaphors and modes of thought. The way words are used, and even the inner experiences they convey, offer no real insight, since the images are basically the same: The ox that serves as a metaphor for spiritual essence looks exactly like a physical bull, while an angel can appear in human form. Thus the question of what a person really saw is not at all simple.

In the clear and tangible physical world, the discernment of falsehood is simpler and more obvious, and it is easier to distinguish between the truth and a lie. By contrast, when the experiences come from a loftier, spiritual plane, the higher the world the more elusive it is, and this requires greater caution, as well as a finer analysis of the essence and truth of each matter. This is why the parameters for serving God through prayer, especially according to the approach of Chabad Hasidism, are very strict. They define the experiences as much as possible to ensure that they will not be false. These include self-assessments and criteria that are designed to guarantee that one will not imagine that he is seeing and feeling what he does not see, that his experiences are authentic.

the status of one who is standing at the threshold of the higher worlds. The question is, what will the response of those worlds be? Will they treat him with kindness and offer their contents to him in a way that he can receive them (since they themselves are above and beyond man)? Will they allow him to peek and receive a glimpse of the light? Or will the threshold be characterized by *Gevura*: "What is your name? Who dares to approach?" The higher world can also see the distance that separates it from the person and perceive a person as someone who is unworthy and not entitled to receive anything.

There are, then, two attributes above: the attribute of *Ḥesed*, which gives generously and openly, and the attribute of *Gevura*, which closes off and conceals. The question is, what determines whether the attribute of *Ḥesed* or the attribute of *Gevura* will be revealed?

אַךְ הַכֹּל תָּלוּי בְּאִתְעָרוּתָא דִלְתַתָּא, שֶׁאִם הָאָדָם מִתְנַהֵג בַּחֲסִידוּת, לְהַשְׁפִּיעַ חַיִּים וָחֶסֶד כו׳ כָּךְ מְעוֹרֵר לְמַעְלָה,

But it all depends on the awakening from below. If a person behaves with kindness, bestowing life and kindness and so forth on others, **he likewise awakens** kindness **above.**

The awakening engendered by our actions below activates a corresponding awakening and giving from above. This is one of the most fundamental laws of creation and the divine operation of the world. It is how the world is built and how relationships between God and man operate. In other words, the manner in which the divine attributes are manifest in the world with regard to a specific individual, as well as to the world as a whole, depends to a very large extent on his own behavior. When we create the proper structure below, the need and the desire, the illumination from above enters it. In that case, when one "behaves with kindness" by "bestowing life and kindness" on other people, he awakens a similar attribute above, and kindness flows down into the reality of our world.

כְּמוֹ שֶׁאָמְרוּ רַבּוֹתֵינוּ זִכְרוֹנָם לִבְרָכָה: בַּמִּדָּה שֶׁאָדָם מוֹדֵד בָּהּ מוֹדְדִין לוֹ (סוטה פרק א משנה ז).

as the Sages stated, "With the measure that a person measures, he is measured with it" (Mishna *Sota* 1:7).

The attribute of *Ḥesed* from above is manifest below measure for measure. When one gives to the worthy and the unworthy alike, when he donates more than he is obligated to contribute to charity, he awakens the bestowal of *Ḥesed* from above to the same degree. On the other hand, one who is stingy with his possessions will be dealt with in a correspondingly strict manner.[24] If before praying, one gives charity to a pauper who is standing at his door, he will merit receiving from the higher world when he himself passes its threshold. When a person acts according to the letter of the law, and he gives only what is due to those who deserve it, without feeling obligated to give more, he will be treated in the same fashion.

אֶלָּא דִּלְכְאוֹרָה זוֹ אֵינָהּ מִן הַמִּדָּה כִּי אִם לְהַשְׁפִּיעַ לוֹ חַיֵּי הָעוֹלָם הַבָּא לְבַד כְּנֶגֶד מַה שֶּׁהוּא מַשְׁפִּיעַ חַיֵּי עוֹלָם הַזֶּה,

But it would seem that this kindness from above **is not of the** same **measure** as the kindness displayed by the person below, **but rather,** it would seem that the same measure would be **to bestow on him life in the World to Come alone, commensurate with his bestowing life** on others **in this world,**

We would expect that the concept of measure for measure should imply that the bestowal of kindness and flow from above would be of the same type that the person bestows. Since one gives life and kindness in this world, he should receive a similar reward in the World to Come, because generally the World to Come is the place where one is rewarded for one's service in this world. Although life in this world and life of the World to Come are not the same, they are both life. Granted, life in this world is physical whereas the life of the World to Come is spiritual, and its spiritual revelation is certainly greater than life in this world, it makes sense that if a person gives life to others below as much as he can, he should receive life above as much as it is possible to give him. A person gives a penny in this world, and he should receive the currency of the spiritual worlds in return. Since God's hand is larger and broader, His penny will be larger as well, but

24. See *Pesaḥim* 110a.

in the bigger picture a person should receive his reward in spiritual currency, which is eternal life.

אֲבָל לֹא לְהַשְׁפִּיעַ לוֹ חַיֵּי הֶאָרַת אוֹר ה׳ [נוּסָּח אַחֵר: אֵין סוֹף בָּרוּךְ הוּא] מַמָּשׁ, שֶׁיָּאִיר וְיַגִּיהַּ חָשְׁכּוֹ בַּעֲבוֹדָה שֶׁבַּלֵּב זוֹ תְּפִלָּה,

but not to bestow on him the life that stems from the illumination of the light of God [alternatively: of *Ein Sof*, blessed be He] itself for it to shine and illuminate his personal **darkness** when he engages **in the service of the heart, which is prayer.**

The illumination one receives through prayer is the actual light of God, the light of *Ein Sof*, which cannot be compared to the illumination of the restricted light that shines in the world, whether in this world or in the World to Come.

שֶׁהִיא בְּחִינַת וּמַדְרֵגַת ׳תְּשׁוּבָה עִילָּאָה׳ כַּנּוֹדָע,

This illumination **constitutes the higher** level of **repentance, as is known,**

It is explained elsewhere[25] that there are two levels of repentance: the lower level and the higher level. In contrast to the lower level of repentance, which is associated with a sin that one has committed and one's escape from its clutches, the higher level of repentance is not necessarily linked to any particular transgression. Rather, it involves a return to the primary source, the restoration of the soul, the divine spark within him, to the source and root of existence, to God Himself. This level of repentance transcends life in the World to Come. ☞

LOWER AND HIGHER REPENTANCE

☞ The lower level of repentance is fundamentally repentance that a person does because he has committed a transgression and now wishes to retract from his evil deeds. This repentance stems from regret, from an awareness of one's deficiencies and suffering, which awakens a thirst for a different life. By contrast, the higher level of repentance comes about when one is in a state of "an abundance of everything" (Deut. 28:47), and the yearning for it stems not from the concealed aspect of our real-

25. See *Iggeret HaTeshuva*, chap. 4; *Likkutei Torah*, Num. 73a, s.v. "*ma tovu*."

The illumination a person merits through prayer is the level of higher repentance. When one merits drawing the illumination from a higher world into his own world, he does not revert to being the same person he was before. As the verse states, "Taste and see that the Lord is good" (Ps. 34:9). Once one has tasted and seen "that the Lord is good," it is impossible for him to return to his previous state of existence. All he wants is to return to that state, to be once again in that place where he tasted and experienced the Divine. This is the higher level of repentance.

שֶׁהֲרֵי הִיא לְמַעְלָה מַעְלָה מִכָּל חַיֵּי עוֹלָם הַבָּא, כְּמוֹ שֶׁאָמְרוּ רַבּוֹתֵינוּ זִכְרוֹנָם לִבְרָכָה: יָפָה שָׁעָה אַחַת בִּתְשׁוּבָה וּמַעֲשִׂים טוֹבִים כו׳ וּכְמוֹ שֶׁנִּתְבָּאֵר בְּמָקוֹם אַחֵר בַּאֲרִיכוּת, דְּעוֹלָם הַבָּא אֵינוֹ אֶלָּא זִיו וְהֶאָרָה וכו׳.

which is above and beyond all the life of the world to Come, as the Rabbis stated, "One hour of repentance and good deeds in this world is more precious than an entire lifetime in the World to Come" (Mishna *Avot* 4:17), **and as explained elsewhere at length** (*Likkutei Amarim*, chap. 4), **the World to Come is only a ray and glimmer and so forth** of the Divine Presence.

ity, from a place of deficiency, but from the discovery of the other side, the revelation of the Divine. With the lower level of repentance, one feels compelled to act because he can no longer remain in the same place, and he must strive to climb upward, whereas the higher level of repentance comes from a calmer place, and from a certain perspective even a happy place. While it is true that there is a sense of deficiency here as well, it is of a different kind: The person is not like someone who is in pain and looking for a cure, but like someone who has tasted a good dish and now can no longer exist without it.

In both paths of repentance, there is a fundamental sense that "I cannot stay where I am," but the difference is that in one path it comes from the rejection of a negation, from the fight against darkness, whereas in the other it comes from affirmation, from a desire to remain in the light.

The higher level of repentance is considered the loftiest level of divine service. In essence, everyone wants to achieve such repentance, even the tzaddik, who wishes to merit greater illumination than he has attained. The problem of the righteous individual, in contrast to the penitent, is that he has attained a state of perfection, a sort of internal harmony, and therefore he does not have that same sense of lack that propels a person to take up the struggle and climb upward, to repent of his ways. The penitent, who feels his deficiency, burns with a passion to ascend higher and higher. The higher level of repentance is the level where the righteous person can also be a penitent. It is an unending repentance, through which every person, regardless of his rank, can rise ever higher.

A famous description of the World to Come is that "the righteous sit with their crowns upon their heads, enjoying the splendor of the Divine Presence" (*Berakhot* 17a). In the World to Come, there is only the splendor of the Divine Presence. Only the divine illumination that shines from the Divine Presence exists there, in contrast to the repentance and good deeds that are available in this world, where a person merits cleaving to the Divine Presence itself. One who cleaves to repentance and good deeds becomes attached to God Himself. Perhaps in this world one does not experience the same delight in God's light and splendor, but a person can achieve true attachment to the Divine, which goes above and beyond life in the World to Come. The question is, why does this person merit receiving such a reward, one that is not commensurate with the scope of what he gave?

אַךְ הָעִנְיָן הוּא עַל דֶּרֶךְ מָשָׁל: כְּמוֹ שֶׁזּוֹרְעִין זְרָעִים, אוֹ נוֹטְעִין גַּרְעִין, שֶׁהַשִּׁבּוֹלֶת הַצּוֹמַחַת מֵהַזֶּרַע וְהָאִילָן וּפֵירוֹתָיו מֵהַגַּרְעִין אֵינָן מַהוּתָן וְעַצְמוּתָן שֶׁל הַזֶּרַע וְהַגַּרְעִין כְּלָל,

27 Av **The matter can be explained by way of an analogy: It is like sowing seeds or planting a kernel. The stalk that sprouts from the seed and the tree with its fruits that sprout from the kernel are not of the essence and being of the seed or kernel at all,**

The author of the *Tanya* now returns to his starting point, which was his question regarding the meaning of the expression "sows charity" in our morning prayers and the juxtaposition of the terms "sowing" and "charity" in the verse from Hosea. The act of sowing follows an apparently simple pattern: One places a kernel of wheat in the ground and receives a whole stalk; one inserts an apple seed and an apple tree grows. But this is not a straightforward process, in which the seed itself grows and swells until it becomes a tree. Between the kernel and the tree there is murky phase in which the kernel completely disappears and the tree sprouts, as it were, from nothing.

כִּי מַהוּתָם וְעַצְמוּתָם כָּלֶה וְנִרְקָב בָּאָרֶץ, וְכֹחַ הַצּוֹמֵחַ שֶׁבָּאָרֶץ עַצְמָהּ [נוּסָּח אַחֵר: עַצְמוֹ] הוּא הַמּוֹצִיא

for their essence and being have been completely consumed and decayed within the soil of the

וְהַמְגַדֵּל הַשִּׁבּוֹלֶת וְהָאִילָן וּפֵירוֹתָיו.

earth. Rather, it is the vegetative power that is in the earth itself that brings forth and brings about the growth of the stalk and the tree with its fruits.

If one removes a seed from the soil before it germinates, not only does the seed itself not grow, it undergoes a process of decay until it completely wastes away, until there is practically nothing left of the seed that previously existed. If that is the case, what grows is not from the seed, which is already dead and rotting, but from the earth itself, from the combination of the materials found in the earth, as well as the sun, light, and air. A massive power is manifest from all these, and this is called the "vegetative power."[26]

רַק שֶׁאֵינוֹ מוֹצִיא וּמְגַלֶּה כֹּחוֹ לַחוּץ, מֵהַכֹּחַ אֶל הַפּוֹעַל, כִּי אִם עַל יְדֵי הַזֶּרַע וְהַגַּרְעִין שֶׁנִּרְקָבִין בָּאָרֶץ וְכָלֶה כָּל כֹּחָם בְּכֹחַ הַצּוֹמֵחַ שֶׁבָּאָרֶץ, וְנִתְאַחֲדוּ וְהָיוּ לַאֲחָדִים.

However, the earth **does not outwardly bring forth and manifest its vegetative power to actualize its potential except through the seed and kernel that decay in the earth and whose energy is consumed within the earth's vegetative power, uniting them as one.**

Although the materials that comprise a tree are always present, and the vegetative power exists in all plants, the earth does not sprout by itself but "through the seed and kernel." Although the kernel itself rots in the ground, it leaves something behind, not merely a genetic code but the power, desire, and interest to form and grow in a certain fashion, through which an entire fruit tree rises and comes into existence.

The stage of decay, of the wasting away of the kernel, is a necessary one. The growth process of the kernel incorporates within it the destruction of its own being. Without this destruction, the kernel

26. The term "vegetative power" is understood in hasidic teachings as a spiritual force nestled in the earth that bears the power of *Ein Sof* to spout and grow countless plants. This is a power that the lower worlds receives from *Ein Sof* to bring something into existence from nothingness, to create something physical from that which is spiritual. See also epistle 20 below.

would remain in its original state and would be unable to grow. The same is true of every living entity: The growth process requires the breaking down and negation of the previous state to a certain degree. An entity that remains in its current form is barren. It will neither grow nor reproduce. But decay alone does not create the growth, because there can be decay without growth. In order for the kernel to grow, it has to go through another process, along with the decay. This process is the return of the kernel, in its decayed form, to the earth in such a manner that it unites with the earth's vegetative power. This is how the kernel transfers to the vegetative power the code, the direction and form, that it bears.

וְעַל יְדֵי זֶה מוֹצִיא 'כֹּחַ הַצּוֹמֵחַ' אֶת כֹּחוֹ אֶל הַפּוֹעַל

In this way, the earth's **vegetative power actualizes its potential**

The process of sowing is the manner by which the vegetative power, which exists in the soil only in potential form, is actualized. This power of growth does not activate or grow anything of its own accord, because it is not a specific force. What all the seeds in the world do is awaken, define, and direct the raw vegetative power, causing it to bring forth one plant or another. This can be compared to a large reservoir of fresh water, where one must dig a hole and a channel so that the water will flow from it to the place where it is needed.

וּמַשְׁפִּיעַ חַיּוּת לְגַדֵּל שִׁבּוֹלֶת כְּעֵין הַזֶּרַע, אֲבָל בְּרִיבּוּי הַרְבֵּה מְאֹד בְּשִׁבּוֹלֶת אַחַת, וְכֵן פֵּירוֹת הַרְבֵּה עַל אִילָן אֶחָד.

and gives forth vitality to grow a stalk that is related to the seed from which it grows, **but with great abundance,** with many grains **in a single stalk, and likewise, many fruits** grow **on a single tree.**

When a person sows wheat, he does not receive another kernel in place of that seed but rather a whole grain that contains many kernels. Similarly, the seed of a fruit grows into a tree that yields many fruits. This abundant growth does not come from the power of the seed, which has rotted and no longer exists in and of itself, but from the vegetative power in the earth.

וְגַם מַהוּתָן וְעַצְמוּתָן שֶׁל הַפֵּירוֹת מְעוּלָּה בְּעִילּוּי רַב וְעָצוּם, לְמַעְלָה מַעְלָה מִמַּהוּתוֹ וְעַצְמוּתוֹ שֶׁל הַגַּרְעִין הַנָּטוּעַ, וְכֵן כְּהַאי גַּוְונָא בְּפֵירוֹת הָאָרֶץ הַגְּדֵלִים מִזֵּרְעוֹנִין כְּעֵין גַּרְעִינִין, כְּמוֹ קִשּׁוּאִים וּכְהַאי גַּוְונָא.

Also, the nature and essence of the fruit is of an immensely higher quality, above and beyond the nature and essence of the planted kernel from which it grew. **The same applies to the produce of the ground that grows from kernel-like seeds, such as cucumbers and the like.**

Besides the growth and multiplicity of the product, the essence of the fruit itself is of a higher quality than the kernel from which it sprouted. The kernel does not simply grow into many kernels, but rather it produces fruit. This fruit has a taste, odor, and color that the kernel does not possess, which means that the fruit possesses a different nature, one that is superior to that of the kernel. A single kernel grows into a whole plant that sprouts, not only similar kernels, but primarily fruits.

וְהַכֹּל הוּא מִפְּנֵי שֶׁעִיקַּר וְשֹׁרֶשׁ חַיּוּת הַפֵּירוֹת נִשְׁפָּע מִכֹּחַ הַצּוֹמֵחַ שֶׁבָּאָרֶץ הַכּוֹלֵל חַיּוּת כָּל הַפֵּירוֹת וְהַגַּרְעִינִין הַזְּרוּעִים בָּאָרֶץ אֵינָן אֶלָּא כְּעֵין 'אִתְעָרוּתָא דִלְתַתָּא',

All this is because the primary life force of the fruits issues forth from the earth's vegetative power, which encompasses the life force of all produce, and the kernels planted in the earth are like the awakening from below,

It is no surprise that the kernel can grow far beyond its own size and essence. That is because the growth stems from the general vegetative power, which can sprout and produce fruit without limit. The sowing of the ground is an awakening from below, which like any such process does not create by itself, but merely serves as an opening and catalyst for the manifestation of entities that are immeasurably greater and more numerous. ☞

הַנִּקְרֵאת בְּשֵׁם 'הַעֲלָאַת מַיִין נוּקְבִין' בְּכִתְבֵי הָאֲרִיזָ"ל.

which is called "the ascension of the feminine waters" in the writings of the Arizal.

This awakening from below, the process of a small action from below performed by man that releases far greater forces from above, is called "the ascension of the feminine waters" by the Arizal. The various terms are merely different ways of expressing the same concept: how a small action evokes a result that is not at all commensurate with the cause. A person invests a penny, and he receives eternity. There is no relation between the penny, or any number of pennies, and the nature of the ascent to the higher level of repentance, which is beyond all life in this world and the next and is the essence of contact with God.

To understand this idea, the author of the *Tanya* used the metaphor of sowing, which he explained at length. It is an example of not only a cause and its direct result, but a cause that awakens forces that are immeasurably greater than itself.

וְכָכָה מַמָּשׁ עַל דֶּרֶךְ מָשָׁל, כָּל מַעֲשֵׂה הַצְּדָקָה שֶׁעוֹשִׂין יִשְׂרָאֵל עוֹלֶה לְמַעְלָה בִּבְחִינַת הַעֲלָאַת מַיִין נוּקְבִין לְשׁוֹרֶשׁ נִשְׁמוֹתֵיהֶן לְמַעְלָה,

So too, exactly so, figuratively speaking, all the acts of charity that the Jewish people perform rise above like the ascent of the feminine waters to the root of their souls above, 28 Av

After a lengthy analysis, the letter returns to the lesson that is to be gleaned from the metaphor. When a person gives charity, he is

THE VEGETATIVE POWER IN NATURE

☞ The growth engendered by the vegetative power is unique among natural phenomena. In the physical realm, there is always a certain relationship between the force that drives and the entity that is driven, between the primary energy and the secondary energy. The source of the energy can change form, but every change and every process causes a reduction in energy, and there is certainly no addition to the energy that was initially introduced. The process of vegetative growth is entirely different, mainly because it is not an orderly causal progression, but rather there is one cause that triggers a number of processes that are on a different, infinitely larger scale. The large tree with its fruits is not restrained and concentrated within the kernel. Rather, the kernel is simply the switch that activates the growth. The act of sowing only releases energy that is in a different state. The mechanism that is activated is minuscule in terms of its potential and is in no way comparable to the growth that subsequently unfolds.

performing a spiritual deed that precisely parallels the physical act of sowing. He thereby causes the "feminine waters" to rise ever higher, all the way to the source of his soul, which is the source of the souls of all of Israel. This ascent is the sowing of the source of the souls of Israel in the supernal earth and supernal *Malkhut* above, which is the highest spiritual root of the earth and the level of *Malkhut* of below. ☞

הַנִּקְרָא בְּשֵׁם 'כְּנֶסֶת יִשְׂרָאֵל' וְ'אִימָּא תַּתָּאָה' בִּלְשׁוֹן הַזֹּהַר, וּ'שְׁכִינָה' בִּלְשׁוֹן הַגְּמָרָא,

which is called "congregation of Israel" and the "lower mother" in the *Zohar*'s terminology and the "Divine Presence" in the Talmud's terminology,

The root of the souls on high is called the "congregation of Israel." This is not just an umbrella term for all the Jews in the world. It is also the essence of the source and root of the souls of Israel. It is also called the "lower mother" because structurally it corresponds to the "higher mother," which is the *sefira* of *Bina*. It is "mother" because it receives the divine vitality from the *sefirot* above it and gives birth to the whole complex of created worlds. "Divine Presence" refers to the light of God that resides in all the worlds and is enclothed in them to sustain them, initially by being drawn down and enclothed within the souls of Israel.

All these appellations are connected, and they express a single essence that is called *Malkhut* in kabbalistic works. But since this is the essence that receives from everything above it while giving to all the

"EXACTLY SO, FIGURATIVELY SPEAKING"

☞ The author of the *Tanya* uses this expression on a regular basis. It signifies that even though the metaphor from the physical world is not like the spiritual realm in all regards and is only meant as a figurative way of speaking, it is nevertheless "exactly so." It is figurative because the lesson applies in our own world only to the extent that these concepts resonate with us. It is exact because the physical metaphor, even if it does not correspond to the spiritual reality in all respects, is still substantive for us, just as material substances in this world are perceived by our senses as reality. The nod toward reality is essential for the metaphor, since its whole purpose is not merely to explain a concept so that we can understand it intellectually, but to enable us to actually grasp it and feel it, just as we sense the physical reality in front of us.

created entities below it, it reflects a multitude of forms and likewise appears in a multitude of forms, appellations, and names. *Malkhut* is the great sea where all things converge and are stored before they are once again born from it.

הַכְּלוּלָה מִכָּל מִדּוֹתָיו שֶׁל הַקָּדוֹשׁ בָּרוּךְ הוּא, וּמְיוּחֶדֶת בָּהֶן בְּתַכְלִית,

which is comprised of all the attributes of the Holy One, blessed be He, and is utterly united with them,

Malkhut is the receptacle of all the attributes. It receives all of them and encompasses all of them within itself. This is not merely a superficial unity, like a box that contains everything placed within it, but unity at its essence, where the essence of *Malkhut* incorporates all the *sefirot* in a single unity. ☞

וְרֵאשִׁיתָן הִיא מִדַּת הַחֶסֶד.

the first of which is the attribute of *Ḥesed.*

The first of all the attributes that are incorporated within *Malkhut* is *Ḥesed*, the attribute of giving and kindness itself. It is the force that lies within all the attributes that come after it, enabling them to become manifest and give to others.

וְעַל יְדֵי הָעֲלָאָה זוֹ מִתְעוֹרֵר חֶסֶד ה׳ מַמָּשׁ, שֶׁהוּא גִּילּוּי אוֹרוֹ יִתְבָּרֵךְ, לֵירֵד וּלְהָאִיר לְמַטָּה לְנִשְׁמוֹת יִשְׂרָאֵל בִּבְחִינַת גִּילּוּי רַב וְעָצוּם

Through this ascent, the actual *Ḥesed* of God is awakened, which constitutes the revelation of His light descending below and shining into the souls of Israel with a great and powerful manifestation

MALKHUT IS GOVERNANCE

☞ In the human soul, the attribute of *Malkhut*, or Kingship, is what we call governance or control. On the one hand, governance is a power that controls and centralizes everything; on the other hand, "it has nothing of its own" (*Zohar* 1:191a, 2:142a). Governance by itself is a force without substance. Control by itself has no meaning. Its substance is in the essence that flows through it, whether in the form of kindness, justice, and so on. In this sense, the attribute of *Malkhut* is comprised of all the attributes, since they all express and actualize it. It is the background and the substance through which all the other attributes operate.

The ascent is our giving of charity, which is an awakening from below that ascends and causes an awakening from above. This is the feminine waters that rise and cause the masculine waters to give from above. In terms of the metaphor with which the letter began, charity is the sowing and investing of supernal earth, the earth that is the attribute of *Malkhut* and the root of the person's soul that is at the root of all the souls of Israel, from which "the actual *Ḥesed* of God is aroused."

As in the metaphor, when a person sows a seed, it grows something that is similar to itself. One does not sow peaches and get watermelons. Likewise, if a person sows charity and kindness, he will awaken a corresponding supernal kindness. The act of kindness performed below does no more than make space for the kindness of above, which is an immeasurably greater bounty than the kindness that man sows, like the seed that merely awakens the inestimable vegetative power in the earth to sprout a multitude of vegetation to which the seed that was sown cannot even be compared.

בִּשְׁעַת הַתְּפִלָּה עַל כָּל פָּנִים. **during the time of prayer at any rate.**

While the "time of prayer" refers to an auspicious time for prayer, a special time of openness and kindness, it refers mainly to the time when a person prays. The very act of saying the prayers with focus opens the doors from below. The time of prayer is thus the time when a person can receive the great light that was awakened through the act of charity that preceded his prayers. ☞

THE TIME OF PRAYER

☞ There is a difference between the awakening and emergence of kindness and its actual manifestation in the soul. Many things exist and operate within reality, and yet they are not noticeable from our perspective. Great events occur, compared to which what happens to us is meaningless, but they might not have a direct, tangible effect on what is occurring within us, either because they are not immediately perceived or because paying them any attention demands a lot of time. Similarly, with every act of kindness performed below, a flash of influence is awakened from above and made manifest. But this great light, God's kindness, is not necessarily revealed within the soul to its fullest extent. Its manifestation also depends on the preparedness of the soul. The time of prayer, when one stands in concentration, with all the faculties of his soul directed toward God, is when he can feel the light – if not all of it, then at least part of it – with his own senses.

כִּי אַף שֶׁלִּגְדוּלָּתוֹ אֵין חֵקֶר, עַד דְּכוּלָּא קַמֵּיהּ כְּלָא חֲשִׁיבֵי,

Although His greatness is unfathomable, to the extent that everything is considered nothingness before Him,

Since God's greatness and kindness are too lofty and immense for us to reach and relate to, what significance does all this have for us? Can a relationship even be formed between us and divine kindness?

הֲרֵי "בִּמְקוֹם שֶׁאַתָּה מוֹצֵא גְּדוּלָּתוֹ שָׁם אַתָּה מוֹצֵא עַנְוְתָנוּתוֹ" (מגילה לא, א), כְּמַיִם שֶׁיּוֹרְדִין כו'.

nevertheless, "wherever you find the greatness of the Holy One, blessed be He, you also **find His humility"** (*Megilla* 31a), **like water that flows** from a high place to a low place.

The esoteric interpretation of this talmudic saying is that God's greatness is His attribute of kindness, which is like water that flows from a high place to a lower one. The essence of kindness is giving and bestowing from inside oneself in an outward direction, from above downward. The greater the flow, the further down it goes. This quality is inherent to the nature of kindness: It is for those who are small, not great, for receivers rather than givers, and it reaches down as low as it can go. Accordingly, in the place where the kindness – or greatness – of the Holy One, blessed be He, is revealed, right there, in that very same attribute, you will find His humility, which is His descent "to revive the spirit of the humble and to revive the heart of the downtrodden" (Isa. 57:15).

In truth, all of God's attributes express His humility. Since He Himself transcends all attributes, and His attributes are merely the way in which He relates to the worlds, brings them into being, directs them, and reveals Himself in them, His revelation through them is an expression of humility. He lowers Himself through those attributes, which are separate from His essence, in order for us to be able to relate to Him so that we can exist at all. ☞

DIVINE PROVIDENCE AND DIVINE HUMILITY

☞ If one were to perceive divine conduct in the same terms as human leadership, by thinking of the Holy One, blessed be He, as a kind of large-scale manager of

וְזֶהוּ שֶׁכָּתוּב: "זָרַח בַּחֹשֶׁךְ אוֹר לַיְשָׁרִים חַנּוּן וְרַחוּם וְצַדִּיק" (תהלים קיב, ד), **דְּעַל יְדֵי שֶׁהָאָדָם חַנּוּן וְרַחוּם וְצַדִּיק צְדָקוֹת אֹהֵב, גּוֹרֵם לְאוֹר ה' שֶׁיִּזְרַח לְנִשְׁמָתוֹ הַמְלוּבֶּשֶׁת בְּגוּפוֹ הָעוֹמֵד בַּחֹשֶׁךְ שֶׁהוּא 'מַשְׁכָּא דְחִוְיָא'.**

This is the meaning of the verse "Light dawns in darkness for the upright, for he is gracious and compassionate and righteous" (Ps. 112:4). **By a person** being **gracious and compassionate, righteous and loving charity, he causes the light of God to shine into his soul, which is enclothed in his body that stands in darkness since it is the "skin of a serpent."**

By acting with compassion and performing charity and kindness in any manner that he can, a person "causes the light of God to shine into his soul." Just as he gives to those who do not have, he receives the light in a place where he does not have it, within the soul that resides in darkness, inside the body that hides the divine light.

The *Zohar* calls the concealing body the "skin of a serpent." After Adam's sin, God stripped the serpent of its skin and fashioned it into tunics for Adam and Eve.[27] Since then, the soul of man has been clothed in the skin of the serpent in terms of spiritual influence. The body was no longer a neutral material substance. Now it would operate and manifest as the garment of *kelippa*. It operates in such a manner that one sees and relates to the corporeal material, without direct awareness of the divine light and life force. ☞

the world, then of course He has no time to deal with the little things. He has to take care of the big matters within the billions of worlds in existence. From this perspective, when it comes to the details, He has to send the lower officials and junior clerks to take care of His affairs. This conception is the basis of all idolatry, which suggests that although God exists, He is so great that he does not relate directly to events in our limited, small world. By contrast, the outlook of Judaism is that God Himself is beyond our conception of big and small, and these have no relation to Him at all. What we perceive as big or small is meaningless in connection with God. For Him, not even the smallest detail differs from the largest generality. Everything deserves the same degree of consideration and attention.

27. See *Pirkei deRabbi Eliezer* 20; *Midrash Tehillim* 92.

Nevertheless, despite the veil of the dense body and the reality of a life of exile and stress that does not allow the divine light to penetrate the soul, "light dawns in darkness for the upright." When a person gives charity to the poor, he awakens the power of the Divine on high, illuminating the soul with the divine light.

וְזֶה נִקְרָא בְּשֵׁם "יְשׁוּעָה", כַּד אִתְהַפְּכָא חֲשׁוֹכָא לִנְהוֹרָא.

This revelation, **when darkness is transformed into light, is called salvation.**

Salvation does not merely imply that something good occurred but that one is rescued from a situation of siege and distress, so that the darkness turns into light. The revelation of the divine light in the human soul is thus rightly called salvation by the very fact that the light of God is revealed within the person who is situated in the darkness of the body. This is not necessarily an external salvation of the body itself, but it is always an internal salvation, that of the human soul groping in its own darkness before a light suddenly shines on it.

A GARMENT FOR *KELIPPA*

☞ Despite the differences in levels between various people, the extent and manner in which a person uses his body and how much he allows the amalgamation of body and soul to be swayed by the body alone, that the soul is within the body means that it is subject and enslaved to the body's grip. Since his attainments can be accomplished only through the body, he is effectively subjugated to the physical matters that relate to the body, through which he directs all areas of his life. Every person, even the greatest and most righteous, is confined within the darkness of his body and his senses. This is not merely an external constraint, in the sense the body and senses are limited, but an essential restriction that results from the fact that it is the body that directs one's desires and basic perception of reality.

Accordingly, even when the body itself does not tend toward evil, it still darkens and conceals the light of the soul and all its achievements and desires. In his famous introduction to *Perek Ḥelek* (the eleventh chapter of tractate *Sanhedrin*), Rambam describes this concept by means of the following metaphor: Just as a blind person is unable to apprehend what color is, what blue or red mean, so too a person stuck in a body, the "skin of a serpent," cannot grasp the meaning of an essence that is not physical. This is why it is difficult for him to develop a desire for divine service that is abstract and separate from the material world and the body's faculties.

וְזֶהוּ "מַצְמִיחַ יְשׁוּעוֹת", שֶׁיְּשׁוּעָה זוֹ צוֹמַחַת מִזְּרִיעַת הַצְּדָקָה, שֶׁזּוֹרְעִין בָּאָרֶץ הָעֶלְיוֹנָה,

This is the meaning of "He brings forth salvation," that this salvation sprouts from the sowing of charity, from the charity **sowed in the supernal land,**

The end of the letter returns to its opening inquiry regarding the relationship between sowing and charity. The phrase "He brings forth salvation" follows "He sows charity" in the citations from the morning *Shema* quoted above. When one sows the earth, comparable material entities grow. When a grain of wheat is sown, wheat stalks sprout. But when one sows a penny of charity in the "supernal land," one does not receive the same penny several times over, but rather an illumination from above. Although charity is given in the form of a physical penny, the essence of charity itself does not belong to the physical world, to the earth below. There is no earthly calculation that can compensate for the charity, but rather it is a spiritual, divine account, which is the "supernal land."

Moreover, the illumination that shines into the human soul and transforms the darkness into light is a form of salvation. Just as charity changes physicality into divine light, the salvation that sprouts from it is likewise a genuine divine light that penetrates one's being in this world. This illumination is called salvation because it is essentially a miracle that a person manages to see beyond the parameters of his mundane tools.

"אֶרֶץ חֵפֶץ" הִיא הַשְּׁכִינָה וּכְנֶסֶת יִשְׂרָאֵל, שֶׁנִּקְרֵאת כֵּן עַל שֵׁם שֶׁמִּתְלַבֶּשֶׁת בַּתַּחְתּוֹנִים לְהַחֲיוֹתָם,

which is called a **"desired land," which is the Divine Presence and the congregation of Israel, so called because it is clothed in the lower worlds to give them life,**

The supernal land is called a "desired land,"[28] the land that God desires, to which He turns. This is the essence of the Divine Presence, the power of the Divine that resides within all of reality as a whole and in its various details, sustaining it and giving it life. It is called the "supernal

28. See Mal. 3:12.

land" because it is the origin and purpose of all lands. Since God Himself desires it, as it were, when it is in its perfected and connected state, it is called the "desired land."

כְּמוֹ שֶׁכָּתוּב: "מַלְכוּתְךָ מַלְכוּת כָּל עוֹלָמִים" (תהלים קמה, יג).

as it is written, "Your kingship is an eternal kingship" (Ps. 145:13).

God's kingship, which is the Divine Presence, is "an eternal kingship," literally "the kingship of all worlds." In other words, it sustains all the worlds, from the hidden, supernal worlds all the way down to this physical world. This is the special divine illumination that brings into existence and vivifies the separate reality, so to speak, of the worlds.

וּבִפְרָט מִן הַפְּרָט כְּשֶׁזּוֹרְעִין בְּאֶרֶץ הַקּוֹדֶשׁ הַתַּחְתּוֹנָה הַמְכוּוֶּנֶת כְּנֶגְדָּהּ מַמָּשׁ,

This applies **most particularly when one sows** charity **in the Holy Land below, which is exactly aligned with** the supernal land.

Finally, the author of the *Tanya* turns his attention to the special nature of charity that is intended for those living in the Land of Israel.[29] In addition to everything that has been discussed, one earns a special advantage when giving charity to those living in the Land of Israel. Although the Land of Israel is a physical land, it is also the Holy Land. It is the land that is precisely aligned with the "supernal land," the "earth" in Heaven as it exists in the higher realm, within the divine will itself, beyond its enclothing in the lower reality.

שֶׁהַזְּרִיעָה נִקְלֶטֶת תֵּיכֶף וּמִיָּד בָּאָרֶץ הָעֶלְיוֹנָה, בְּלִי שׁוּם מְנִיעָה וְעִיכּוּב בָּעוֹלָם

The sowing of charity for the Holy Land **is absorbed immediately in the supernal land without any hindrance or delay in the world,**

Any charity that a person gives is sown in the supernal land, but this accomplishment is usually achieved in stages. Between the lands of the nations and the supernal land there is a fog, as well as obstacles and delays, so that the transition is not immediate, but rather is a process

29. See *Etz Ḥayyim* 43:2.

that takes time. By contrast, the Holy Land is exactly aligned with the supernal land, because one land parallels the other. This land is in a state of full resonance with the supernal land, with the Divine Presence above. An act of charity performed there is absorbed and its effect felt in the supernal land immediately, without delay.

מֵאַחַר שֶׁאֵין שׁוּם דָּבָר חוֹצֵץ וּמַפְסִיק כְּלָל בֵּין "אַרְצוֹת הַחַיִּים",

because nothing intervenes or separates at all between the lands of life, between the physical Holy Land and the supernal land,

The expression "lands of life"[30] is in the plural because it refers to two lands. There is the land of life in the perfect and pure sense, which the author of the *Tanya* refers to as the supernal land, the Divine Presence, and the congregation of Israel. It is called the land of life because life there is eternal. Corresponding to it is the land of life below, which is the physical Land of Israel. They are both termed the lands of life because they are interlinked, aligned with each other and open to one another in such a manner that nothing intervenes or separates between them.

כִּי "זֶה שַׁעַר הַשָּׁמָיִם" (בראשית כח, יז),

for the verse states regarding the Holy Land, **"This is the gate of the heavens"** (Gen. 28:17),

After receiving the vision in Beit El, Jacob declared, "This is nothing other than the house of God, and this is the gate of the heavens" (Gen. 28:17). The phrase "this is the gate of the heavens" is the definition of the essence of the Land of Israel, since it is the gate and entrance to Heaven. Since it is located directly opposite Heaven and is open to it, anything done there affects the supernal land without any delay.

מַה שֶּׁאֵין כֵּן בְּחוּץ לָאָרֶץ,

which is not the case outside the land.

Outside the land, there is a barrier so that there is no direct correspondence between the earth below and the supernal land. Consequently,

30. Based on Ps. 116:9; see also *Likkutei Torah*, Deut. 3d.

the charity performed there does not have an immediate effect on the supernal land, to awaken it to illuminate the one who gave charity at the time of prayer immediately with the divine light.

וְדַי לַמֵּבִין. This is **sufficient** explanation **for one who understands.**

There is no need to go into further detail, since this is not the place for that, and in general it is not the author of the *Tanya*'s style to delve into issues involving the *kelippot* and obstacles, whether outside the land or in the Land of Israel.

This letter dealt with the relationship between charity and prayer. The author of the *Tanya* illustrated this relationship with an analogy: Just as the seed a person sows generates, through the vegetative power inherent in the earth, numerous plants and trees that are immeasurably more valuable than the kernel that he sowed, the same is true regarding the mitzva of charity that precedes prayer. In general, one receives divine illumination that does not correspond to the value of his act of charity. The divine light shines into the darkness of his being in this world, an illumination that is the embodiment of salvation, which illuminates the soul in the darkness, in the confines of the body that conceals the Divine. This is the meaning of the verse "I will behold Your face through charity" (Ps. 17:16). When a person performs charity, he merits perceiving the divine countenance, the illumination of the divine light, at the time of prayer.

The Tzemaḥ Tzedek related the following story, which illustrates this idea: For a long time after the passing of his grandfather, Rabbi Shneur Zalman of Liadi, the author of the *Tanya,* to whom he was particularly close, he suffered great distress over the fact that he did not merit a vision from his grandfather, especially since he needed his advice and guidance. One morning, on his way to the synagogue, one of the local Jews approached him and asked him for an urgent loan. "The market is today, when the gentiles gather from the surrounding villages, and I do not have even a penny for trading." Since the Tzemaḥ Tzedek was on his way to pray, he did not want to be delayed and told the man that he would return to him after prayers.

The Tzemaḥ Tzedek entered the synagogue and prepared for prayer by donning his *tallit*. Then the thought came to him: "This Jew is in desperate need of this money, and here I am trying to pray devoutly?!" He immediately removed his *tallit*, raced back home, and took all the money he could find. He searched for the Jew who had appealed to him for help and gave him the money. Later, the Tzemaḥ Tzedek added, when he returned to the synagogue, for the first time in ages he was able to see the face of his grandfather.

Epistle 9

THIS LETTER ALSO DISCUSSES THE MITZVA OF CHARITY, but unlike the previous one, its main focus is not on the spiritual significance of charity and its relationship with prayer, but the manner of its fulfillment. More specifically, how much should one give of himself and his possessions? The answer this letter gives is, everything! But what does it mean to give everything – all of one's strength and time, everything that is precious to him? What kind of life is that, and who has the spiritual strength to go that far?

Yet if one follows this path, it will lead him beyond the mitzva of charity. It will impact all aspects of his life, and its effects will reach the very depths of his soul. The demand for a giving spirit of this kind is not easy, neither for the hasidim to accept nor for the Rebbe to ask it of them. The letter therefore also emphasizes the author of the *Tanya*'s love for the hasidim, whom he cherished like his own soul, because one can issue such a demand only out of great love.

29 Av / 28 Av (leap year)

אֲהוּבַיי אַחַיי וְרֵעַיי אֲשֶׁר כְּנַפְשִׁי

My beloved ones, my brethren and friends, who are like my own **soul,**

This is an especially affectionate address, partly because what the author of the *Tanya* will proceed to say will not be easy to hear.

בָּאתִי כְּמַזְכִּיר וּמְעוֹרֵר יְשֵׁנִים בְּתַרְדֵּמַת הַבְלֵי הֲבָלִים

I come as one who reminds and awakens those who sleep the slumber of futility of futilities

The phrase "futility of futilities," which is from Ecclesiastes (1:2), refers to all worldly affairs that have no real value, that are insignificant and of no substance in and of themselves, but in which people immerse themselves so that they remain in a kind of torpor, sleeping through life. ☞

וְלִפְקוֹחַ עֵינֵי הָעִוְרִים, **and to open the eyes of the blind.**

One whose life is guided by a vain purpose is compared to someone who is sleeping or to a blind person. The fact is that there is a purpose to everything, but sometimes one must first wake up from a dream in order to see it. The aim of the letter is to wake people up from this slumber and point to where they should invest their efforts, to show them what it truly means to live.

יַבִּיטוּ לִרְאוֹת לִהְיוֹת כָּל יִשְׁעָם וְחֶפְצָם וּמְגַמָּתָם לְכָל בָּהֶם חַיֵּי רוּחָם בִּמְקוֹר מַיִם חַיִּים חַיֵּי הַחַיִּים, **Let them look and see to it that their sole drive, desire, and aim, everything on which the life of their spirit depends, should be** invested **in the source of the living waters, the** infinite **source of life,**

One sign of purpose is that it is not fragmented at its root but rather is a comprehensive goal that necessarily occupies the whole of a person's being. As the author of the *Tanya* puts it, "their sole drive desire, and aim, everything on which the life of their spirit depends" – all their focus, their aspirations and goals in life – should be invested in the infinite source of life, God Himself.[1] In other words, all their desires and

THE SLUMBER OF "FUTILITY OF FUTILITIES"

☞ This does not mean that people live completely aimless lives. A person does not do anything without a reason. People work and invest their time in projects because they are driven by some goal. But this ambition is sometimes worthless. A man might to go work every day, but the reason he toils all year is to get two weeks' vacation or to receive a promotion. People travel to the other corner of the world, rationalizing that they will find a real life somewhere over there, but it often turns out that they were driven by fantasies and nothing more. The author of the *Tanya* calls all such ideas "futility of futilities."

1. See *Lilkkutei Amarim*, chap. 31.

longings, all the faculties of their soul on all levels, should be directed only to the source of life. He should be the exclusive focus of their yearning, and they should be subsumed and consumed in Him alone.

כָּל יְמֵי חַיֵּיהֶם מִנֶּפֶשׁ וְעַד בָּשָׂר, **all the days of their life.** This applies to everything, **from** matters of **the soul to** matters of **the flesh,**

When he says "all the days of their life," the author of the *Tanya* is defining the scope of this engagement: at all times and in all areas of life. Moreover, the extent of one's commitment should apply to everything "from [matters of] the soul to [matters of] the flesh," to all aspects of a person's spiritual life as well as his physical existence and all matters in which a person occupies himself. This does not only mean spiritual matters but also physical interests, one's health, one's livelihood – everything.

There are those who give God a percentage, like an income tax. They feel obligated to donate something, and they even understand that it is necessary, but the principle, remains with them. Yet when a person is prepared to give not only a certain sum or even a large contribution but everything, to be subsumed in the infinite source of life, this is a goal that has implications for everything else. When one does not merely pay lip service but actually keeps his word, this impacts all areas of life, "from [matters of] the soul to [matters of] the flesh."☞

דְּהַיְינוּ, כָּל מִילֵּי דְעָלְמָא וְעִסְקֵי פַּרְנָסָה. **meaning all material matters and the means by which one may earn a livelihood.**

The author of the *Tanya* proceeds to elaborate on the phrase "[matters of] the flesh." Even lowly, physical areas of life, which naturally have

"A JEW UP TO THE POCKET"

☞ There is a Yiddish saying that uses the phrase *ani betzedek*, "I, in righteousness" (Ps. 17:15), as an acronym for "*Ich nur Yid biz tzu di keshene*" – "I am a Jew only up to the pocket." Such an individual will pray, study Torah, and perform mitzvot, accepting that these areas of life belong to God, but when it comes to his wallet, he insists that it is his business alone. His Judaism reaches up to his pocket but goes no further.

a strong pull on one's attention and are very difficult to ignore, are included in this purpose and goal, in one's subsummation in the "infinite source of life."☞

It should be emphasized here that the author of the *Tanya* is not demanding from people that they ignore these primary, basic needs of existence. Jews must subsist in this world and live well. They must struggle unconditionally for their livelihoods. Nevertheless, they must also remember the true purpose of all these occupations.

לֹא יְהְיֶה כְּאִלּוּ דְּעָבְדִין לְגַרְמַיְיהוּ, וְלֹא יִהְיֶה בֵּית יִשְׂרָאֵל כְּכָל הַגּוֹיִם דְּזָנִין וּמְפַרְנְסִין וּמוֹקְרִין לִנְשַׁיְיהוּ וּבְנַיְיהוּ מֵאַהֲבָה,

One should not be like those who serve themselves, nor should the house of Israel be like the gentiles, who feed, sustain, and esteem their wives and children out of love,

THE LIVELIHOOD OF HASIDIM

☞ One should keep in mind that when these letters were written, Jews lived in a state of privation, pressured by the need to earn a basic income and suffering from harsh living conditions. When the author of the *Tanya* speaks of "the means by which one may earn a livelihood," he is not referring to luxuries but a minimal subsistence. With a few exceptions, most Jews lived by peddling or performing menial labor. One does not grow wealthy from such occupations, and they had to work hard, far more than eight hours a day, to earn the bare minimum. With all that, none of the effort they expended guaranteed anyone the continuance of this humble existence.

The jokes they would tell reflected this reality. For example: If the local rabbi did not fast every Monday and Thursday, he would die of hunger. One can also see this in the contracts that communities made with the rabbis they hired, in which they promised him "half a goat" (that is, the right to receive half the milk of a particular goat). This was not because the community did not want to give more. They would have adorned their rabbi with gold if they could have afforded it. It was because they were unable to offer more than that. Likewise, yeshivot did not have enough money to feed their students. These pupils were called "daily eaters" because every evening they were sent to a different family for supper. The head of the family who hosted them was often desperately poor himself and had several other mouths to feed apart from his guest, so the yeshiva student went hungry more often than not.

Accordingly, while the phrase "all material matters" includes all worldly affairs, the author of the *Tanya* specifies one's livelihood because this was the matter that took up most people's attention, that which preoccupied them and disturbed their peace of mind.

This means out of love for one's wife and children, an emotion that is intrinsic to a man's physical nature. Although a Jew does not have less problems or troubles than a gentile, and sometimes he has even more, the Jew may not live the same kind of life as his non-Jewish counterpart. Even animals maintain a (sometimes temporary) relationship with their offspring, but a Jew must ensure that there is another element to his relationships, that there is a higher purpose to everything he does.

The difference between a Jew and a gentile does not boil down to merely a certain type of behavior, such as the fact that one performs a mitzva and the other does not, and there is no distinction between them in all other areas of life. Rather, the difference is intrinsic and internal, and it should be reflected in everything the Jew does or feels. The dissimilarity that the author of the *Tanya* is noting out here lies within a person. It applies not only to deeds but also, and primarily, to the feelings that accompanies those deeds. Even when a gentile acts for others, it is because he loves them. This love, as explained in the first chapter of the *Tanya*, is at its core self-love. He loves others and acts on their behalf as an extension of his own existence. His being has expanded and now includes others – his wife and children, his relatives and the residents of his town – but they are merely an extension of his own being that he is caring for, raising, and nurturing.

כִּי "מִי כְּעַמְּךָ יִשְׂרָאֵל גּוֹי אֶחָד בָּאָרֶץ" כְּתִיב (דברי הימים א יז, כא). דְּהַיְינוּ שֶׁגַּם בְּעִנְיְנֵי אֶרֶץ לֹא יַפְרִידוּ [נוּסָח אַחֵר: יִפָּרְדוּ] מֵאֶחָד הָאֱמֶת חַס וְשָׁלוֹם

for it is written, "Who is like Your people Israel, one nation on the earth?" (I Chron. 17:21), **meaning that even earthly matters they do not separate [alternatively: even in earthly matters they are not separate] from the one true** God, **God forbid,**

A Jew must be "one on earth" so that even when he is involved in material concerns, which might seem remote and separate from God, he must remain "one," united with God, the one true reality. The author of the *Tanya* is saying that such unity is not only possible in Heaven, where the divine unity is manifest, but also on earth, where that unity is concealed and seemingly separate.

לְהָעִיד עֵדוּת שֶׁקֶר חַס וְשָׁלוֹם בִּקְרִיאַת שְׁמַע עֶרֶב וָבוֹקֶר בְּעֵינַיִם סְגוּרוֹת "ה' אֶחָד" בְּאַרְבַּע רוּחוֹת וּבַשָּׁמַיִם מִמַּעַל וּבָאָרֶץ מִתַּחַת,

bearing false witness, God forbid, by reciting the *Shema* in the evening and morning with eyes closed, proclaiming that **"God is one,"** omnipresent **in the four directions and in the heavens above and the earth below,**

When we recite the *Shema* in the evening and morning, we close our eyes at the words "God is one" and have in mind that He is one "in the four directions and in the heavens above and the earth below." As explained in several places,[2] this is alluded to in the word for "one," *eḥad,* spelled *alef-ḥet-dalet.* The letter *alef* represents the *Aluf,* or Captain, of the world, who is one in the seven firmaments and on earth, which together make eight, the numerical value of *ḥet,* and in the four directions, four being the numerical value of *dalet.* ☞

וּבִפְקוֹחַ עֵינֵי הָעִוְרִים, "הֲתָעִיף עֵינֶיךָ בּוֹ וְאֵינֶנּוּ" (משלי כג, ה) חַס וְשָׁלוֹם.

and **when the eyes of the blind are opened,** when after the recitation of the *Shema* one opens his eyes, **by "casting your eyes on** the world **and** behaving as though God **is gone"** (Prov. 23:5), **God forbid.**

BEARING WITNESS

☞ The declaration that we make in the *Shema,* "The Lord is our God, the Lord is one," is a sort of testimony. We, the souls who descended into a body on this earth, testify to the entire world and to this earth that God is also one here on earth. This is not immediately evident down here, so that it is necessary for someone to attest that this is the actual state of affairs. We therefore come and testify that it is indeed the truth: God is one here as well, from the highest to the lowest places (the seven firmaments and the earth) and in all four directions, which appear to be separate from each other. He is the only one and everything is incorporated and united in Him in an absolute union.

2. See, e.g., *Sefer Mitzvot Katan* 104, cited in *Beit Yosef* and *Shulḥan Arukh, Oraḥ Ḥayyim* 61:6; see also *Torah Or* 55b.

After reciting the *Shema*, one opens his eyes. The idea here is that when a person emerges from those moments that he is concentrating on his prayers, from his connection with that which is holy, and he returns his focus on the world, he immediately "casts his eyes on the world and behaves as though God is gone," God forbid. Now he no longer sees the one God but the world and its distractions, which appear to be a separate reality from the Divine. In that moment, when one has opened his eyes after prayer, when he no longer sees the divine unity and is dealing with the world and its concerns, it is as though he is bearing false witness. That he fails to retain his focus on spiritual matters once he has finished reciting the prayers attests that what he said was not the truth.[3]

אַךְ בְּזֹאת יֵאוֹת לָנוּ לִהְיוֹת [נוּסָּח אַחֵר: בִּהְיוֹת] כָּל עֲסָקֵינוּ בְּמִילֵּי דְעָלְמָא לָא לְגַרְמַיְיהוּ

Rather, it is befitting for us that our entire involvement in material matters should not be for our own sake

Even when we are engaged in worldly matters, we do not cease to be "one nation on earth." We remain connected to the one God, so that we have no desire for those things for their own sake.[4]

The key difference is that gentiles generally occupy themselves with their faith only at a specific time and place, and then they lock up the building and venture outside, with no connection between what happened inside and what goes on outside. By contrast, a Jew's faith does not belong to the synagogue alone. If someone speaks in a certain manner in the synagogue and behaves differently when he leaves, then he was not holy in the synagogue either. If matters of sanctity are confined to specific situations, everything a person says and thinks about holy matters is worthless.

It is like a child's game, where one child pretends to be a king and the other is a soldier. As soon as the game is over, they instantly drop their roles. One's prayers and even his Judaism in general can likewise

3. See *Likkutei Amarim*, chap. 13.

4. The other side of the coin is described in *Likkutei Amarim*, chap. 1: "This is not the case with regard to the souls of the [gentile] nations of the world, which are derived from the other, impure *kelippot*, which contain no good whatsoever, as it is written in *Etz Ḥayyim* 49:3. [As the *Zohar* states,] any good [deed] performed by the nations is performed for their own [selfish purposes]."

become a kind of game. The real test begins when we leave the synagogue: Can we be one nation not only in Heaven but also, and most importantly, on earth? ☞

כִּי אִם לְהַחֲיוֹת נַפְשׁוֹת חֶלְקֵי אֱלֹקוּת **but for the sake of giving life to the souls** of others in need, **portions of God,**

In practice, how should a person conduct himself if he is not acting for his own sake? The answer is, he should act "for sake of giving life to the souls of others in need, portions of God." This refers both to Jewish souls, which are a "portion of God on high" (Job 31:2), and to the sparks of holiness that constitute the divine component of every entity in existence. Everything one does should be to sustain and promote life, to give of his strength and his life to those divine portions. The abstract conception of directing one's attention to the Divine, which is beyond the reality of this world, finds practical expression in one's focus on the portions of the Divine that are located within the world. In simple terms, when a person provides for himself and his family members, he should have in mind that he is supporting, not himself and his loved ones, but those portions of God that are within them. In this way, his love for God finds expression.

וּלְמַלְּאוֹת מַחְסוֹרֵיהֶם בְּחֶסֶד חִנָּם. **and to provide** them with **whatever they lack out of unconditional kindness.**

"FOR OUR OWN SAKE"

☞ This term *legarmayhu* literally means "for itself," but the hasidic teachings explain that it is a concept that encompasses the natural order of the mineral, vegetable, animal, and human realms (see *Likkutei Amarim*, chap. 1). By this natural order, each entity acts for its own sake. The inanimate simply exists, the vegetable realm grows in a place of water and light, while animals and humans do what is beneficial and pleasurable for them. Each acts "for itself." This is not evil, but simply natural and even necessary, yet it is not what is required of a Jew. This is not why a holy soul was brought down to the world. If a Jew conducts himself in that manner, he is acting improperly. Granted, he must take care of himself, his wife and children, but that should only be a means, not an end in itself. A Jew's roots go beyond the world and its nature, and he should live his life accordingly. The purpose of his life lies outside the system. He should live, not for himself, but for the sake of the transcendent, with his focus on the Divine, which is beyond all affairs of this world.

A Jew should not do anything out of a sense of obligation, whether for himself or for his family, but as an act of kindness. Not only should he perform charitable acts, but they should be done out of "unconditional kindness," without any calculations, without expectations of reward, neither in this world nor in the next. It is only when a person performs kindness, real kindness, unconditional kindness, that he escapes from the closed circle of *legarmayhu*, "for his own sake," of doing things for his own benefit, and is able to focus his gaze on the portions of God around him.

שֶׁבָּזֶה אָנוּ מְדַמִּין הַצּוּרָה לְיוֹצְרָהּ - ה' אֶחָד אֲשֶׁר "חֶסֶד אֵל כָּל הַיּוֹם" (תהלים נב, ג), **'חֶסֶד שֶׁל אֱמֶת', לְהַחֲיוֹת הָעוֹלָם וּמְלוֹאוֹ בְּכָל רֶגַע וָרֶגַע.**

In this way, we make our **form,** which is in God's image, **resemble the one who formed him, the one God, for "the kindness of the Almighty is all day long"** (Ps. 52:1). His is **true kindness, giving life to the world and everything in it at every moment.**

Since a person is created in the image of God, he can actually resemble God if he conducts himself like Him by performing acts of kindness unconditionally, without expecting anything in return.[5] God's kindness is considered true kindness because He sustains the world at every moment and does not need anything in exchange. A person must strive to emulate the attributes of God: Just as He feeds and nourishes all creations and does not need anything from them, so too one must toil for his livelihood and perform acts of kindness for others, not in order to receive anything for himself but for the sake of giving life to other souls, which are a portion of God on high. ☞

UNCONDITIONAL KINDNESS

☞ God's kindness is a gift that comes without an accompanying account. It is not only that God does not require anything in return, but neither does He make any calculations. When a person makes the calculated decision to give charity solely to those who deserve it, only to beautiful, good, and decent people, this is not un-

5. See *Bereshit Rabba* 96:5, which states that true kindness is the act of kindness one performs for the dead since one cannot expect the dead to return the favor. See also *Likkutei Torah*, Num. 30d, 93c.

The author of the *Tanya* singles out one's livelihood and the performance of kindness as paths through which one can emulate God, because one does not have to be a scholar or learned, or even a particularly God-fearing person, to execute such tasks. One simply has to perform acts of kindness. But when one remains on the plane of action alone, even if he does good deeds, he is not necessarily emulating God. Perhaps he is emulating the gentiles, who also provide for their family. He might be imitating the wild beasts: After they tear apart their prey and eat it, they leave some for others if they are unable to finish it all. He therefore stated, "The house of Israel should not be like the gentiles," that their deeds should not be for their own sake at all, but "for sake of giving life to the souls [of others in need]."

רַק שֶׁאִשְׁתּוֹ וּבָנָיו שֶׁל אָדָם קוֹדְמִין לַכֹּל עַל פִּי הַתּוֹרָה,

It is only that a person's wife and children take precedence over everyone else according to Torah law,

There are orders of precedence when it comes to charity.[6] These are not dictated by rights but rather they are formal orders of precedence. There is the sphere of a person's family: Whoever is closest to a person

conditional kindness. Unconditional kindness is when one gives even to drunkards and frauds, because they too need compassion. We thereby resemble God.

The Talmud (*Berakhot* 17b) quotes the verse "Hear Me, hard-hearted, who are far from charity" (Isa. 46:12) and asks, "Who are hard-hearted who are far from charity?" The answer is that these are righteous people who do not need God's kindness, since they truly deserve what they receive. But such individuals are few and far between, the likes of Rabbi Ḥanina ben Dosa, whereas everyone else does require charity, God's unconditional kindness, in order to survive. Not because they deserve it, not because they have anything to give back, but simply because they need it, like simple beggars, without questions or preconditions.

Yet people do not always feel that they are dependent on God's unconditional kindness. When one is healthy and has a regular source of income, he does not sense that he receives everything through unconditional kindness. Yet when his world is shaken, and he feels needy, he begins to realize how much he needs compassion and kindness for his each and every breath.

6. See *Shulḥan Arukh, Yoreh De'a* 251:3.

is the first to receive charity from him. His immediate family takes priority, his father and mother, his wife and children, followed by his extended family, then the people of his city, the residents of the country, and so on. A man's duty to provide for his wife and children does not negate his obligations toward others, but merely establishes his order of priorities.[7]

חוּץ מִצַּדִּיקִים שֶׁבַּדּוֹר שֶׁהֵן קוֹדְמִין לְבָנָיו, וְצַדִּיקִים שֶׁבְּאֶרֶץ יִשְׂרָאֵל קוֹדְמִין לַצַּדִּיקִים שֶׁבְּחוּץ לָאָרֶץ, לְבַד מִזֹּאת שֶׁלֹּא הִנִּיחוּ כְּמוֹתָן בְּחוּץ לָאָרֶץ, וְדַי לַמֵּבִין.

except for the tzaddikim of the generation, who take precedence over one's children, and the tzaddikim in the Land of Israel take precedence over the tzaddikim outside the land, aside from the fact that the tzaddikim who traveled to the land **did not leave anyone of their stature** behind **outside the land.** This is **sufficient** explanation **for one who understands.**

This particular passage does not appear in the standard printed editions, but is found in *Luaḥ HaTikkun*.[8] These letters that deal with charity were written for the most part with regard to the charity of the Land of Israel, and therefore this addition concerning the order of precedence in giving charity in relation to the righteous is logical.

עַל כֵּן אֲהוּבַיי אַחַיי שִׂימוּ נָא לְבַבְכֶם לָאֵלֶּה הַדְּבָרִים הַנֶּאֱמָרִים בִּקְצָרָה מְאֹד (וְאִם יִרְצֶה הַשֵּׁם פֶּה אֶל פֶּה אֲדַבֵּר בָּם בַּאֲרוּכָּה).

Therefore, my beloved ones, my brethren, pay attention to these words, which are stated here **very briefly (and God willing, I will speak about them at length** when we meet **in person).** 30 Av / 29 Av (leap year)

7. There are other criteria as well. For example, if a particular item is a luxury for one person but a necessity for another, the order of preference will change accordingly. See epistle 16 below.

8. This is a list of emendations that were made to the printed text of the *Tanya* and was subsequently inserted in the back matter of recent editions.

The brevity of the letter does not mean that its content is not important and does not require the reader's full attention. Yet for various reasons the author of the *Tanya* did not wish to write about these concepts here at length.

As explained in the introduction to the *Tanya,* certain matters cannot be clarified in writing. In general, it is difficult to address serious concerns that touch on highly sensitive and personal issues through the medium of the written word. One should attempt to broach such topics only in person, face-to-face, by speaking directly to the listener. It is for this reason that the author of the *Tanya* was brief, and in a departure from his usual manner of writing, he added a request that the reader pay particular attention to his words. Though they are not easy to hear, they come from a place of love.

אֵיךְ הֱיוֹת כָּל עִיקַּר עֲבוֹדַת ה' בְּעִתִּים הַלָּלוּ, בְּ'עִקְּבוֹת מְשִׁיחָא' הִיא עֲבוֹדַת הַצְּדָקָה, כְּמוֹ שֶׁאָמְרוּ רַבּוֹתֵינוּ זִכְרוֹנָם לִבְרָכָה: אֵין יִשְׂרָאֵל נִגְאָלִין אֶלָּא בִּצְדָקָה.

Remember **that the primary** means of **divine service at these times,** which are described as **the heels of the Messiah, is the service of charity, as the Sages stated, "The Jewish people will be redeemed only through charity"** (see Rambam, *Mishneh Torah, Sefer Zera'im, Hilkhot Mattenot Aniyim* 10:1).

Jewish history is not a random sequence of events but a meaningful pattern of the service that the Jewish nation is required to perform over the course of the generations. This pattern can be discerned as taking on the form of man, which in a certain sense is the figure of the Messiah, with different eras representing different parts of that form. The era of the *tanna'im,* for example, which followed the destruction of the Temple, was the embodiment of the cognitive attributes that represent the head: *Ḥokhma, Bina,* and *Da'at.* In that era, the souls were rectified through these attributes. The times in which we live, by contrast, are described as the "heels of the Messiah," when the exile will come to an end and the redemption is imminent. In this era, the principal service is the mitzva of charity, an action-based mitzva, which will bring rectification to this world of *Asiya,* the world of Action. When the service of the Jewish people in all generations has been accomplished, the image of the Messiah will also be complete and he will arrive, at which point history will also come to an end.[9]

וְלֹא אָמְרוּ רַבּוֹתֵינוּ זִכְרוֹנָם לִבְרָכָה תַּלְמוּד תּוֹרָה שָׁקוּל כְּנֶגֶד גְּמִילוּת חֲסָדִים, אֶלָּא בִּימֵיהֶם, שֶׁתַּלְמוּד תּוֹרָה הָיָה עִיקַּר הָעֲבוֹדָה אֶצְלָם, וְעַל כֵּן הָיוּ חֲכָמִים גְּדוֹלִים, תַּנָּאִים וְאָמוֹרָאִים.

The Sages' statement that Torah study is equivalent to kind deeds applied only to their days, when Torah study was their primary occupation, which is why they were great scholars, *tanna'im* and *amora'im*.

This statement, "Torah study is equivalent to all of them," which includes kind deeds, appears in the Mishna.[10] Although each person in every generation is obligated to perform the same mitzvot, there are different emphases for various people, places, and generations. The era of the Sages was a period of Torah study, when Torah study was their main occupation, and therefore there were individuals in those generations for whom that was their primary task and who were qualified for such work.

מַה שֶּׁאֵין כֵּן בְּ'עִקְּבוֹת מְשִׁיחָא', שֶׁנָּפְלָה 'סוּכַּת דָּוִד' עַד בְּחִינַת רַגְלַיִם וַעֲקֵבַיִם, שֶׁהִיא בְּחִינַת 'עֲשִׂיָּה',

By contrast, in these times described as **the heels of the Messiah, when the booth of David has fallen** all the way **to the level of feet and heels, which is the level of *Asiya*,**

The *sukka*, or booth, of David is reference to David's monarchy[11] and so is an appellation for *Malkhut* of *Atzilut*, which descends to the worlds of *Beria*, *Yetzira*, and, finally, *Asiya*.[12] The divine attribute of *Malkhut* descends in order to bring life to these worlds. The world of *Beria* represents the head – the intellect and awareness. *Yetzira* corresponds to the torso, to the heart and the attributes or emotions. The feet and the heels are the embodiment of *Asiya* and action.

9. See *Likkutei Torah*, Numbers 63d; *Or HaTorah*, *Ḥukkat*, p. 874.
10. *Pe'a* 1:1.
11. Based on Amos 9:11; see also epistle 21.
12. See *Sha'ar HaKavanot*, *Derushei Keriat Shema* 6.

אֵין דֶּרֶךְ לְדָבְקָה בָּהּ בֶּאֱמֶת, וּלְהַפְּכָא חֲשׁוֹכָא לִנְהוֹרָא דִּילָהּ [נוּסָח אַחֵר: דִּילֵיהּ] כִּי אִם בִּבְחִינַת עֲשִׂיָּה גַּם כֵּן, שֶׁהִיא מַעֲשֵׂה הַצְּדָקָה.

there is no way to truly cleave to it and transform darkness into its light without also engaging in **action, namely, the act of charity.**

When the "booth of David," or *Malkhut,* is on the lowly level of *Asiya,* our primary service is also through *asiya,* or action.[13] We must operate primarily through action, which entails the act of charity. ☞

כַּיָּדוּעַ לַמַּשְׂכִּילִים, שֶׁבְּחִינַת עֲשִׂיָּה בֶּאֱלֹקוּת הִיא בְּחִינַת הַשְׁפָּעַת וְהַמְשָׁכַת הַחַיּוּת לְמַטָּה מַטָּה, לְמַאן דְּלֵית לֵיהּ מִגַּרְמֵיהּ כְּלוּם.

As known to the scholars of Kabbala, **action in** relation to **the Divine is when the life force is bestowed and drawn down below to one who has nothing of his own.**

The world of *Asiya* is the level of divine activity. It is the lowest and most distant level from the origin of the divine light. It is a place that has no inner relationship with the Divine. In view of this, God gives to this world as an act of unconditional kindness, to one who has nothing and no ability to repay the kindness. In human terms, when you give to someone who owns property, you expect to receive something in return, in one form or another, but when you bestow a gift on someone who has nothing, you don't expect anything in return. Such giving is related to the attribute of *Malkhut,* which according to the teachings

---

13. See the *Iggerot Kodesh* of the Lubavitcher Rebbe, Rabbi Menaḥem Mendel Schneerson, vol. 19, letter 7094, in response to Rabbi Shlomo Yosef Zevin's suggestion that this text should be read as "to truly cleave to God." He states there: "Regarding his comment that in *Iggeret HaKodesh,* end of section 9, 'and to cleave to it' should read 'to God,' it would seem that this does not fit in well with the continuation, *dila,* 'its [light]' (which refers to the booth of David), and also, the text above refers to cleaving to the service of God, or the booth of David, not cleaving to God. The early editions of *Iggeret HaKodesh* are like ours, only the alternative versions do not appear there. It would seem that 'to it' refers to the booth of David, or *Malkhut,* which is the Divine Presence, as our Rabbis state in several places...."

of Kabbala has nothing of its own. Everything it possesses it receives from the levels above it, which it then projects to the worlds below.

The same is true of us, in this world and at this time called the heels of the Messiah, which is the level of *Asiya* in time and place: The service required of us is also at the level of action, which entails giving charity, donating specifically to those who have nothing of their own.

וְכָל הַזּוֹבֵחַ אֶת יִצְרוֹ בָּזֶה וּפוֹתֵחַ יָדוֹ וּלְבָבוֹ - אִתְכַּפְיָא סִטְרָא אַחֲרָא

One who slaughters his inclination in this regard, by opening his hand and heart to give charity, **subdues the** ***sitra aḥara***

One has to "slaughter his inclination" through the mitzva of charity, like the slaughter of an offering, which is a gift to Heaven without any designs on making a profit here on earth in return, and "open his hand and heart" to give wholeheartedly, without the expectation of receiving a reward. The mitzva of charity, then, involves opening not only one's hand but also one's heart: One should smile, show empathy, take an interest in the other person's problems, and so on.[14]

When a person gives charity in this manner, he "subdues the *sitra aḥara*," which is the evil inclination, the *kelippa*. Two aspects of this statement are particularly noteworthy. First, that subduing the evil inclination does not mean that evil is transformed into good. It is not

CHARITY IS ACTION

☞ While other mitzvot entail action as well, they also include a certain element of intent and understanding to the extent that it is said that a mitzva without intent is like a body without a soul (see *Likkutei Amarim*, chap. 38). By contrast, there is no need to have intent when giving charity. Charity also takes effect without intent. In the case of other mitzvot, we perform an action below that primarily resonates above. For example, when one shakes a *lulav* below, that act has no significance down here. Without its attendant, lofty meaning, the act has no import. It is nothing more than the mere shaking of branches. But when one gives charity and thereby enables someone to survive, the act of giving has significance in this world as well, since it brings about rectification and change in the world whether or not the giver had that intention in mind.

14. See Rambam, *Mishneh Torah, Sefer Zera'im, Hilkhot Mattenot Aniyim* 10:4.

persuaded that giving charity is for its benefit. Rather, it is subdued against its will. This is the essence of charity, this unconditional act of kindness: giving even when he fails to understand the reason for it.

Second, when it comes to subduing evil, even the slightest crack that one manages to inflict on it will contribute to shattering the *sitra aḥara*, the other side, completely. The existence of evil is like a disease that metastasizes everywhere and in every person. When one overcomes it, when he cuts off part of the evil, he also strikes at its root, its essence. ☞

וּמְהַפֵּךְ חֲשׁוֹכָא לִנְהוֹרָא וְאוֹר הַשֵּׁם יִתְבָּרֵךְ, הַשּׁוֹכֵן עָלֵינוּ בִּבְחִינַת עֲשִׂיָּה בְּ׳עִקְבוֹת מְשִׁיחָא׳,

and transforms darkness into the light of God, blessed be he, who in these times described as **the heels of the Messiah, dwells upon us in a state of action,**

During this period called the heels of the Messiah, the light of God is the light of action. Through the light of our actions, through our giving of charity, we transform the darkness of his era, the heels of the Messiah, into light and divine revelation at this lowly level of action. ☞

SUBDUING THE *SITRA AḤARA* THROUGH CHARITY

☞ There are several types of evil inclinations. There is, for example, the inclination for illicit sexual relations and the inclination for pride. But the most fundamental evil inclination, which in a sense encompasses all of them, is the evil inclination for selfishness. This is the inclination to act for my own sake and for those close to me, but not for the benefit of others to whom I have no obligation. The inner struggle entailed in the service of charity is first and foremost a battle against this evil inclination. One gives charity even though he does not have enough for himself, even though he is taking something of his own that he will lack. For this reason, it is specifically through the mitzva of charity, when one "slaughters his inclination," that he strikes at the root of the *sitra aḥara*.

TRANSFORMING DARKNESS INTO LIGHT

☞ In the realm of nature, we find that the sun and moon are constantly changing location and appearance. There is a morning sun and an evening sun, a summer sun and a winter sun, each occupying different places in the sky. Likewise, there is a moon of the beginning of the month and a moon of the middle of the month, and they are not identical. The same applies to the spiritual world. The light is not always situated

וְיִזְכֶּה לִרְאוֹת עַיִן בְּעַיִן בְּשׁוּב ה' צִיּוֹן כו'.

and will merit seeing with actual eyes the return of God to Zion and so forth.

In the merit of giving charity, we will be able to see below that which can be seen above. The world of action and materiality will no longer conceal and obscure spirituality. The Divine will be revealed in all its glory.[15]

This short letter was written for a specific audience: the hasidim of the author of the *Tanya*. He is telling this group that a Jew cannot allow himself to be a regular person. When we recite, "Who has not made us like the nations of the lands, nor placed us like the families of the earth..." (from the *Aleinu* prayer), this is not simply a description of the distinction between whom we bow down to and whom we do not bow to. Rather, it reflects the essence of life, its purpose. While on an external level there may not be a difference between Jew and gentile, internally there is an immeasurable chasm between them, in their intention regarding the things they do and see. A Jew is not merely a creation in the world. He is a messenger of the Creator of the universe. He is not an entity in and of himself, nor does he do anything for himself. He is like the hand, head, and mouth of God, and he has been bestowed with the divine mission to "give life to the souls, portions of God."

The mitzva of charity applies to every Jew. "Even a poor person who is sustained from charity is obligated to give charity" (Rambam,

in the same spot. The divine light shifts its position on each occasion, in every generation, shining through a different window. In our times the windows are in the world of *Asiya*, the world of Action, and therefore one's struggle is also in the realm of action, in the mitzvot of charity and kind deeds in particular. When we emerge victorious in these battles, we transform darkness into light. It is true that a person can also overcome his inclination in other areas, and it is certainly the case that he "slaughters his inclination" through such actions as well. But that is comparable to someone who opens a window on a side of the house where the sun is not shining: Some light will enter, but it is not the same as opening a window that faces the sun, where the darkness itself is transformed into light.

15. See *Likkutei Torah*, Rosh HaShana 55a.

Mishneh Torah, Sefer Zera'im, Hilkhot Mattenot Aniyim 7:5, based on *Gittin* 7b). In addition, charity is not performed merely with money. People need all kinds of assistance: to find a match, to seek guidance, or simply to receive a smile and a little attention. A bus driver can add a "good morning" while he is selling tickets and giving change and brighten a passenger's day. It's not about the money or the sum involved, but that he gives of himself, which makes all the difference between a person who lives for himself, for his own sake, and one who lives for another purpose, to "give life to the souls, portions of God."

The general principle of charity is to seek to emulate God as much as possible. God sustains all creatures with unconditional kindness, from the smallest gnat to the largest whale, and one should likewise give with unconditional kindness to all, whether close relatives or strangers, great or small. He should give, not because they deserve it, and not because he thereby reaps reward, whether material or spiritual, but because he is currently in a position to help those who are beneath him at that point in time. Since he has the power of sight, he must show those who are unable to see; since he has knowledge, he is required to teach those who lack it.

It is the nature of man to feel close to those who are near him and far from those who are distant from him. It might seem that one cannot really be like God and bestow true unconditional kindness, without any personal interests. But that is only the nature of man when he lives his life like the nations, in "the slumber of futility of futilities," immersed in the affairs and entanglements of this world. When one lives as a Jew, as a member of the "one nation on the earth," so that even when involved in earthly affairs he is not separated from God, then he is not performing kind deeds for people as they are on earth, because of their mundane relationships with him. Rather, he does so because they are souls that are a portion of God. In this manner, his kindness is also unconditional, and the created being resembles his Creator, the one God.

Epistle 10

THIS LETTER, LIKE MANY OF THE LETTERS, DISCUSSES the mitzva of charity. According to the *halakha*, one is obligated to give a specific share of his income to charity. But this letter explains that at certain times, and for certain individuals, it is permitted and even required to give more.

The author of the *Tanya* characterizes the charity that a person gives as reflecting the nature and scale of the charity and kindness that he receives from God. When a person requires more kindness than his worth and attributes warrant, the charity he gives must likewise be greater than his relative value.

The letter analyzes these two levels of divine kindness, one that is given in accordance with a person's worth and the other that is bestowed without such considerations, as well as the corresponding two levels of human charity.

1 Elul

30 Av (leap year)

אַחַר דְּרִישַׁת שָׁלוֹם וְחַיִּים, פֵּתַח דְּבָרַי יָעִיר אֹזֶן שׁוֹמַעַת תּוֹכַחַת חַיִּים

After greetings of peace and life, may my opening words awaken the ear to listen to reproof of life

Like the majority of the letters, this one begins with words of blessing and peace originating in biblical sources.[1]

אֲשֶׁר הוֹכִיחַ ה׳ חַיִּים עַל יְדֵי נְבִיאוֹ וְאָמַר: "חַסְדֵי ה׳ כִּי לֹא תָמְנוּ וגו׳" (איכה ג, כב) וַהֲוָה לֵיהּ לְמֵימַר 'כִּי לֹא תַמּוּ' כְּמוֹ שֶׁכָּתוּב

with which the living God rebuked through His prophet, saying, "It is the Lord's kindnesses that we have not ceased..." (Lam. 3:22). **It seems**

1. See Ps. 119:130; Isa.50:4; Prov. 15:31.

"כִּי לֹא תַמּוּ חֲסָדֶיךָ וגו'".

that it should have said *"ki lo tamu,"* that the kindnesses have not ceased, **as it is written** elsewhere (in the *Amida* prayer), **"For Your kindnesses have not ceased** [*lo tamu*] **...."**

The life-giving rebuke that the author of the *Tanya* refers to is the reproof that God gave "through His prophet."[2] The author then raises a question regarding the precise phraseology of this verse, citing a counterexample from the *Amida* prayer: If the verse refers to the kindnesses, that they have not ceased, it should have said *lo tamu* rather than *lo tamnu*, which implies that "we have not ceased."

וְיוּבַן עַל פִּי מַה שֶּׁכָּתוּב בַּזּוֹהַר הַקָּדוֹשׁ (חלק ג קלג, ב): אִית חֶסֶד וְאִית חֶסֶד, אִית 'חֶסֶד עוֹלָם' כו', וְאִית חֶסֶד עִילָּאָה דְּהוּא 'רַב חֶסֶד' כו'.

This can be understood based on the what is written in the holy *Zohar* (3:113b): **"There is *Ḥesed*, and there is** another type of ***Ḥesed*: There is world-centered *Ḥesed*... and there is supernal *Ḥesed*, which is** called **abundant *Ḥesed*...."**

In order to grasp the reason behind the unusual wording of the verse and its status as "reproof of life," it is necessary to understand the *Zohar*'s statement that there are two types of *Ḥesed*: world-centered *Ḥesed*, which is a lower level of *Ḥesed*, and supernal *Ḥesed*, which is also called abundant *Ḥesed*.[3] These are both forms of divine kindness, but the difference is that world-centered *Ḥesed* is God's kindness in relation to the world, the divine kindness that is manifest and active within the world, whereas abundant *Ḥesed* is on a higher plane. It is not defined by its association with the world, but rather from the perspective of God Himself. It is therefore called the kindness of God and supernal kindness, since it transcends the limitations of the world.

2. Although the verse that the author of the *Tanya* quotes here is from Writings, the author states that it was delivered "through His prophet" because according to rabbinic tradition the book of Lamentations was composed by the prophet Jeremiah.

3. A phrase derived from Ex. 34:6.

It is known that the Torah is called *oz,* might, **which is an expression of** *Gevura,* **as our Sages stated, "Six hundred thirteen commandments were said to Moses at Sinai from the mouth of the Almighty** [*Gevura*]" (*Makkot* 23b),

כִּי הִנֵּה מוּדַעַת זֹאת הַתּוֹרָה נִקְרֵאת 'עֹז' שֶׁהוּא לְשׁוֹן גְּבוּרָה, וּכְמוֹ שֶׁאָמְרוּ חֲכָמֵינוּ זִכְרוֹנָם לִבְרָכָה: תַּרְיַ"ג מִצְוֹת נֶאֶמְרוּ לְמֹשֶׁה מִסִּינַי מִפִּי הַגְּבוּרָה (מכות כג, ב),

To grasp this point, we must first clarify several ideas regarding the relationship between God's holy attributes and the world in general. The Torah is called *oz,* or might, which the Sages derived from the verse "The Lord gives strength [*oz*] to His people" (Ps. 29:11).[4] This is an expression of the attribute of *Gevura.* There are many appellations for God: great, powerful, awesome, among others. But in the context of the giving of the Torah, He is called *Gevura,* "Almighty," indicating that the giving of the Torah was an expression of divine strength.

and it is also written, "From His right, a fiery law for them" (Deut. 33:2), **meaning that the source and root of the Torah is nothing but kindnesses of God, which are called** the **right** side.

וּכְדִכְתִיב "מִימִינוֹ אֵשׁ דָּת לָמוֹ" (דברים לג, ב), פֵּירוּשׁ, שֶׁהַתּוֹרָה מְקוֹרָהּ וְשָׁרְשָׁהּ הוּא רַק חַסְדֵי ה' הַמְכוּנִּים בְּשֵׁם 'יָמִין',

This verse is part of the description of the giving of the Torah, where fire represents God's attribute of *Gevura,*[5] while the right side represents *Ḥesed* (as opposed to the left, which is *Gevura*).[6] In that case, there seems to be a contradiction in the expression "from His right, a fiery law." If it was given from "His right," through the attribute *Ḥesed,* then that which was given should be through the attribute of *Ḥesed,* not fire, or *Gevura.*

The author of the *Tanya* proceeds to explain that *Ḥesed* represents the array of giving and flow, of movement from the inside outward, from the source to the environs. Its path is one of spreading out and

4. *Zevaḥim* 116b; *Zohar* 1:94a; see also *Torah Or* 67a.

5. See *Pardes Rimmonim* 23:1, s.v. "*esh*"; see also *Torah Or* 25b, 45c, 86c; *Sha'ar HaYiḥud VeHa'emuna,* chap. 5.

6. *Tikkunei Zohar* 17a.

expansion. This is in contrast to *Gevura*, which represents constriction and limits and entails a focus on specific points and particular definitions, as will be explained below. Moreover, *Ḥesed* and revelation is part of the essence of the Torah.

דְּהַיְינוּ הַמְשָׁכַת בְּחִינַת אֱלֹהוּתוֹ יִתְבָּרֵךְ וְהֶאָרָה מֵאוֹר אֵין סוֹף בָּרוּךְ הוּא אֶל הָעוֹלָמוֹת עֶלְיוֹנִים וְתַחְתּוֹנִים

That is, the drawing down of Godliness and illumination from the light of *Ein Sof*, blessed be He, to the higher and lower worlds

Divine revelation is the essence of the Torah. Beyond its manifest content, the Torah is the expression of the light of *Ein Sof* and divine revelation in the world. The Torah is the hand sent forth to the world, the finger of God that crosses all partitions, bridging the chasm between the Divine and man and reaching all the way down to the depths. ☞

עַל יְדֵי הָאָדָם הַמַּמְשִׁיךְ הָאוֹר עַל עַצְמוֹ, בְּקִיּוּם רַמַ״ח מִצְוֹת עֲשֵׂה,

comes about **through** the actions of **man, who draws the light upon himself by performing the 248 positive commandments,**

This bond that is established between God and man through the Torah is not unilateral. It is not forged only through the revelation of God's desire to form a connection with man. It is also attained "through [the actions of] man, who draws the light upon himself by performing the 248 positive commandments." After the giving of the Torah, the relationship between God and man developed into one of mutual cooperation: on the one hand, through divine illumination, which pierces the infinite empty chasm that exists between the Divine and creation and is revealed in the Torah, and on the other hand, through the agency man, who binds himself to the Torah and God through the mitzvot, which constitute the divine will. This is, after all, the whole purpose of a mitzva: to forge a relationship between man and God. ☞

שֶׁהֵן רַמַ״ח אֵבָרִים דְּמַלְכָּא.

which are the 248 limbs of the king.

The purpose of the Torah and mitzvot is to draw down the revelation and presence of the Divine in the world. They provide a framework, a system of vessels, to receive divine revelation in this world. This framework is likened to the human body,[7] which contains 248 limbs. In terms of the revelation, they are called "limbs of the king,"[8] since the divine revelation generally unfolds through the divine attribute of *Malkhut*, Kingship, and thus the particulars of the revelation are like the limbs of the king. Furthermore, the 248 limbs of the king are the 248 positive commandments, the mitzvot of the King who commands us. In view of this, when we perform the mitzvot, it is as though we are constructing the image of the King within the reality of this world.

THE TORAH IS NOT A BOOK OF REMEDIES

☞ The main value of the Torah is not that it teaches one how to be healthy and happy, nor even how to be a better, more productive person. God did not shake up all the worlds in order to give man a book of remedies for the improvement of body and mind (see Mishna *Sanhedrin* 10:1). Rather, the significance of the Torah is that it constitutes divine revelation within the world, and the giving of the Torah was itself a revelation of God's desire to establish a connection between Himself and man.

MITZVOT AND RELATIONSHIP WITH THE DIVINE

☞ While a mitzva is fulfilled, brought into existence, by the person who carries it out, it was not created by him. Man merely forges a connection with the mitzva through his action. By fulfilling a mitzva, he activates an existing mechanism, revealing a light that already exists but cannot operate without his participation. This can be compared to activating an electric current. A house might be full of electrical appliances that are connected to wires that are in turn linked to power sources, but if there is no one there to press the switch, nothing will work. The person who comes and flips the switch does not create the light. He simply connects the systems that cause the light to illuminate through this slight action.

Many physical actions that we do achieve a similar objective. With the simplest activities, such as eating, we only do our part. Everything that happens next, digestion, absorption, the transformation of food from one form to another, are part of an existing mechanism that does not need the assistance of conscious human action at all in order to function. When we eat, we do not create the enzymatic system that enables digestion, which allows the human body to absorb substances that it ingested. These systems already existed; they are simply being activated. Similarly, our role in the performance of mitzvot is to execute certain actions that will activate this entire complex and wondrous mechanism.

---

7. See Ezek. 1:26.
8. See *Tikkunei Zohar* 74a–b; *Likkutei Amarim*, chaps. 23–24.

פֵּירוּשׁ, רְמַ"ח כֵּלִים וּלְבוּשִׁים לַהֶאָרָה [נִרְאֶה דְּצָרִיךְ לוֹמַר "לְהַהֶאָרָה"] מֵאוֹר אֵין סוֹף בָּרוּךְ הוּא הַמְלוּבָּשׁ בָּהֶן

This means that the positive commandments constitute **248 vessels and garments for the illumination of the light of *Ein Sof*, blessed be He, that is clothed in them**

Identifying the 248 positive commandments as the 248 limbs of the king adds another layer of meaning to these mitzvot. They are not isolated units but parts of an organic whole. Moreover, just as the limbs of the body are external tools that reveal the life-giving faculties of the soul within, so too the mitzvot are tools of expression and receptacles for the divine illumination that is enclothed in them. For the divine light to be revealed in the world, it requires a vessel, certain modes of expression, which are called garments. These garments are not merely random expressions of divine revelation, but are parts of a unifying system that fashions, in its entirety, the revelation of God within the world.

(וּמֵאוֹר זֶה יוּמְשַׁךְ לוֹ דְּחִילוּ וּרְחִימוּ בְּכָל מִצְוָה כַּנּוֹדָע).

(and from this light, fear and love of God **are** also **drawn down on him through every mitzva** he performs, **as is known).**

When a person performs a mitzva, he receives his own personal light, which illuminates his soul, from the light of *Ein Sof* that is drawn to the world. For that person, the illumination is substantial and real. It is not merely a subjective experience but a true emotional and cognitive connection, an actual encounter with the Divine. Yet the experience, awareness, and exhilaration are only byproducts of the mitzva, which at most indicate that a connection was formed but does not prove anything about the essential nature or strength of this bond.

We see that the giving of the Torah in general is an act of kindness from God, in the sense that it constitutes the divine revelation in the world, the manner in which God reveals Himself on earth. The Torah is a gift from above to below, the expansion and revelation of the Divine through all the firmaments all the way down to our world. It is God's greatest act of kindness, since He gives the world this unparalleled gift: the ability to connect to Him.

The Talmud states that the word *anokhi*, the first word of the Ten

Commandments, is an acronym for *ana nafshi ketivat yehavit*, "I myself wrote [and] gave." (*Shabbat* 105a). The plain meaning of this statement is that God declared, "I Myself wrote and gave the Torah." In kabbalistic writings this is interpreted on a deeper level, as "I wrote Myself and gave."[9] This is the essence of the giving of the Torah: that God gives Himself, so to speak.

Until this point, the author of the *Tanya* focused on God's kindness in giving us the Torah "from His right arm," which enables us to illuminate all the worlds when we perform a mitzva. The author now turns his attention to the aspect of *Gevura* in the giving of the Torah, the fire referred to in the verse.

רַק שֶׁהַמְשָׁכָה זוֹ נִתְלַבְּשָׁה תְּחִלָּה בְּמִדַּת גְּבוּרָתוֹ שֶׁל הַקָּדוֹשׁ בָּרוּךְ הוּא, הַמְכוּנָּה בְּשֵׁם "אֵשׁ", שֶׁהִיא בְּחִינַת צִמְצוּם הָאוֹר וְהַחַיּוּת הַנִּמְשָׁכוֹת מֵאוֹר אֵין סוֹף בָּרוּךְ הוּא, כְּדֵי שֶׁתּוּכַל לְהִתְלַבֵּשׁ בְּמַעֲשֵׂה הַמִּצְוֹת, שֶׁרוּבָּן כְּכוּלָּן הֵם בִּדְבָרִים חוּמְרִיִּים,

But this flow of divine light **is first clothed in the attribute of *Gevura* of the Holy One, blessed be He, which is called "fire"** and **which constitutes the constriction of the light and life force that are drawn down from the light of *Ein Sof*, blessed be He, so that it can become enclothed in the performance of the mitzvot, which are almost entirely** performed **with material objects,**

In order for the Torah, which contains the divine revelation, to be revealed in this material world, within mitzvot that are limited and circumscribed in certain specific ways, it has to go through a process of inestimable constriction. This constriction and limitation of the great kindness and revelation constitutes the attribute of *Gevura*, through which the Torah could be given to a material world. ☞

GEVURA AS CONSTRICTION

☞ While *Gevura* means power and strength here, the term is an expression of constriction and convergence. In truth, the two ideas are connected, since *Ge-*

9. See the Arizal's *Likkutei Torah, Parashat Yitro*; *Me'orei Or* 1; *Likkutei Torah*, Num. 48d; *Degel Maḥaneh Efrayim, Parashat Yitro* and *Parashat Ki Tisa*, s.v. "*pesol*."

כְּצִיצִית וּתְפִילִּין וְקָרְבָּנוֹת וּצְדָקָה.

such as *tzitzit* and *tefillin*, sacrifices and charity.

Tzitzit are made from wool, while *tefillin* must be fashioned from parchment and ink and sacrifices consist of animals. The mitzva of charity, in particular, which is universal in nature, in that it rectifies the entire material world in general, as explained elsewhere,[10] is defined by material parameters.

וְאַף מִצְוֹת שֶׁהֵן בְּרוּחָנִיּוּת הָאָדָם כְּמוֹ יִרְאָה וְאַהֲבָה, אַף עַל פִּי כֵן הֵן בִּבְחִינַת גְּבוּל וּמִדָּה וְלֹא בִּבְחִינַת אֵין סוֹף כְּלָל.

Even mitzvot involving a person's spirit, such as the commandments to **fear and love** God, **are nevertheless of a limited, measured nature and are by no means infinite,**

Our world is distinct not only because it is a material world, but because it is limited. The spiritual aspects of man and the world are also not boundless; they too are circumscribed. Although their spiritual dimensions and designations are not restricted in terms of length and weight and such, they are most certainly constrained and limited. Thus, even those mitzvot that might appear to be entirely spiritual and not physical at all, such as the fear and love of God, have defined limits.[11] Even though these are not fulfilled through physical actions

vura as an expression of power does not exist as a manifestation of pure strength, but mainly in the form the strength takes on and how it functions in reality. The activation of any force, in any field, is based on its ability to constrict itself in order to operate at a specific point.

It is said that when a certain tzaddik passed by a train locomotive, he said to his disciples, "Do you know why this locomotive is so powerful? Because it can hold the steam inside it!" The strength of the locomotive does not come from the existence of the steam, but from the fact that the steam is constricted and limited. This is what creates the power. Undefined and undirected strength will not create power. Rather, it dissipates without leaving any impression. The essential quality of *Gevura* is therefore not the strength itself, but its ability to limit and constrict it. This contrasts with *Ḥesed*, which is expansive and unlimited.

10. See *Likkutei Amarim*, chap. 37.
11. See Rambam, *Mishneh Torah, Sefer HaMadda, Hilkhot Yesodei HaTorah* 2:1.

but through the soul's faculties, by developing feelings of love and awe toward God, they are still confined by certain parameters.

כִּי אַהֲבָה רַבָּה לַה׳, בְּלִי קֵץ וּגְבוּל וּמִדָּה, אֵין הָאָדָם יָכוֹל לְסוֹבְלָהּ בְּלִבּוֹ וְלִהְיוֹת קַיָּים בְּגוּפוֹ אֲפִילוּ רֶגַע.

for it is impossible for a person to bear a great love for God that is without end, limit, or measure in his heart and maintain his bodily existence even for a second.

It might seem that love and awe in themselves have no boundaries, but in practice our love is minimal and limited, the kind that we can bear. Even if the soul itself can tolerate a greater and more powerful love, a person in this world, as a soul within a body, is unable to abide such emotion. The amalgamation of soul and body greatly reduces each of their capabilities.

וּכְמַאֲמַר רַבּוֹתֵינוּ זִכְרוֹנָם לִבְרָכָה שֶׁבִּשְׁעַת מַתַּן תּוֹרָה, שֶׁהָיְתָה הִתְגַּלּוּת אֱלֹהוּתוֹ יִתְבָּרֵךְ וְאוֹר אֵין סוֹף בָּרוּךְ הוּא בִּבְחִינַת דִּיבּוּר וְהִתְגַּלּוּת - פָּרְחָה נִשְׁמָתָן כו׳.

As our Rabbis stated, when the Torah was given, when God's divinity and the light of *Ein Sof*, blessed be He, were manifest as speech, their souls departed from their bodies.

At the giving of the Torah there was a revelation of the Divine in the world to the extent that the Jewish people achieved an unlimited degree of love of God, and immediately "their souls departed [from their bodies]."[12] As mortals they could not bear it. Their souls could not contain such feelings and still remain in their bodies. ☞

IMPOSSIBLE TO BEAR

☞ This implies that not only one's physical life, but also the life of his soul – his love, awe, faith, and so on – are limited and constricted. God only makes certain demands from us, even in the spiritual realm. His expectations of us are commensurate with our capacities and our attributes, and these are so specific and defined that any small de-

12. *Shabbat* 88b; *Shemot Rabba* 29:4; *Shir HaShirim Rabba* 63; see also *Likkutei*

2 Elul
1 Elul (leap year)

וְהִנֵּה לְפִי שֶׁהַמִּצְוֹת נִיתְּנוּ לָנוּ עַל יְדֵי הִתְלַבְּשׁוּת בְּמִדַּת גְּבוּרָה וְצִמְצוּם הַהֶאָרָה כו׳,

Because the commandments were given to us by being enclothed in the attribute of *Gevura* and through the **constriction of the illumination** of the divine light,

The mitzvot were not given as abstract concepts or in general terms, but rather "from the mouth of the *Gevura*, the Almighty," in a constricted

viation can undermine our entire existence. This is true in all areas of life. We cannot bear either an excess of punishment or an excess of good (see *Ta'anit* 23a), neither too much heat nor too much cold. Our material and spiritual spheres are concentrated within very limited and delineated spaces. From this point to that one, a person can act, but beyond that he will die; he will disintegrate. As a result, everything that is given to us, both physically and spiritually, is extremely limited and constricted.

The same applies to the greatest gift of all, the giving of the Torah. For us to be able to connect to the Torah and live with it, to prevent it becoming a fatal revelation that we could not bear, it is not enough for God to reveal Himself. This revelation must also be commensurate with our capacity to handle it: constricted, one degree after another, until we reach the level where we can build a relationship with Him. The same is true of the physical world: Water is a blessing, a kindness and a source of all life in the world, but beyond a certain limit it becomes a flood that can wipe out all of existence from upon the face of the earth.

This leads us to one of the reasons most of the mitzvot are physical rather than spiritual. It is because spirituality is less easily constricted and narrowed down since we do not have defined standards for spiritual matters. When God instructs us to fashion *tzitzit* from wool, which can be measured by the centimeter, a person can be relied on to make such-and-such centimeters of woolen thread, at which point the bond that has been created is complete. This is not the case when the demands are spiritual. How can one measure love? Accordingly, it is when the Torah addresses the physical aspects of reality, and the mitzvot involve the material world, that the relationship can be built.

This can be compared to an adult who wants to talk to a small child. If he speaks in his own language and at his level, this will be beyond the child's comprehension, as wonderful as the person's ideas may be. No connection will be made, and no information will be passed along. To build a relationship with someone so much younger than him, he must constrict himself, in his thoughts, concepts, and language, so that his listener can form a connection with him. This is what is called *Gevura* in *Ḥesed*. The constriction serves as a means of giving, which is essential in order to transfer and deliver the message.

Amarim, chap. 36.

manner and with certain material limitations. Although a mitzva itself is an illumination of *Ein Sof*, the mitzvot do not reach us as an unconstrained expression of *Ein Sof*. Rather, they come within our confines, within the boundaries of the world.

לָכֵן רוֹב הַמִּצְוֹת יֵשׁ לָהֶן שִׁיעוּר מְצוּמְצָם.

therefore most of the commandments have a limited measure to their performance.

An essential part of every mitzva is the measurement that applies to it. We are required to do a specific act at a specific time in a specific way. Any more or less than this measure, and it is no longer a mitzva. Sometimes the act is no longer desirable and might even be harmful.

כְּמוֹ אוֹרֶךְ הַצִּיצִית י"ב גּוּדָלִין, וְהַתְּפִילִּין אֶצְבָּעַיִם עַל אֶצְבָּעַיִם, וּמְרוּבָּעוֹת דַּוְקָא, וְהַלּוּלָב ד' טְפָחִים, וְהַסּוּכָּה ז' טְפָחִים וְהַשּׁוֹפָר טֶפַח, וְהַמִּקְוֶה מ' סְאָה. וְכֵן בַּקָּרְבָּנוֹת, יֵשׁ לָהֶן שִׁיעוּר מְצוּמְצָם לִזְמַן, כְּמוֹ כְּבָשִׂים בְּנֵי שָׁנָה, וְאֵילִים בְּנֵי שְׁתַּיִם, וּפָרִים כו'.

For example, the length of *tzitzit* must be at least **twelve thumbbreadths, and *tefillin*** must be at least **two fingerbreadths by two fingerbreadths, and they must be square. A *lulav*** must be at least **four handbreadths** long, **while a *sukka*** must be at least **seven handbreadths** tall, **and a *shofar*** must be at least one **handbreadth** long. **A *mikveh*** must contain at least **forty *se'a*** of water. **The same is true of the sacrifices; they have a limited measure in terms of timing. For example, lambs** must be **in their first year, rams** must be **in their second year, as well as bulls, and so on.**

Each mitzva is limited in its own area. In other words, all the mitzvot were given from the mouth of the *Gevura* – that is, through *Gevura*, with constriction and restraint.

וְכֵן בְּמַעֲשֵׂה הַצְּדָקָה וּגְמִילוּת חֲסָדִים בְּמָמוֹנוֹ, אַף שֶׁהִיא מֵהָעַמּוּדִים שֶׁהָעוֹלָם עוֹמֵד עֲלֵיהֶם, וּכְדִכְתִיב: "עוֹלָם חֶסֶד יִבָּנֶה" (תהלים פט, ג), אֲפִילוּ הָכִי יֵשׁ לָהּ שִׁיעוּר קָצוּב: חוֹמֶשׁ - לְמִצְוָה מִן הַמּוּבְחָר, וּמַעֲשֵׂר - לְמִדָּה בֵּינוֹנִית, כו'.

So too with regard to the act of charity and to kind deeds that one performs **with his money: Although** charity **is one of the pillars on which the world stands, as it is written, "The world is built with kindness"** (Ps. 89:3), **it nevertheless has a set limit,** namely, **one-fifth** of one's income to fulfill **the mitzva in the most desirable manner and one-tenth for an average measure, and so on.**

Ḥesed, which is the quality of giving and unrestrained bounty, is one of the foundations on which the world is sustained. Yet even the mitzvot of charity and kind deeds that are required of us have a set limit: One may give no more than one-fifth of his property or income to charity, and this is the amount for a person who fulfills the mitzva in the most desirable fashion.[13] This is the upper limit, in accordance with the dictum that "one who dispenses [his money to charity] should not dispense more than one-fifth" (*Ketubot* 50a).

וְזֶה נִקְרָא 'חֶסֶד עוֹלָם' פֵּירוּשׁ "חֶסֶד אֵל כָּל הַיּוֹם" (תהלים נב, ג),

This divine *Ḥesed* clothed in the commandments **is called world-centered kindness, meaning "the kindness of the Almighty** that **is all day long"** (Ps. 52:3).

The divine *Ḥesed* enclothed in the mitzvot that have a set limit is the world-centered kindness mentioned at the beginning of the letter, the *Ḥesed* that is confined within the boundaries of the world in which it operates. World-centered kindness can be defined with the verse "The kindness of the Almighty is all day long." "Day" represents the world, as in the six days of Creation and the six supernal attributes with which the world was created. The kindness that is drawn into the "day," or world, is enclothed within the attributes of the world,

13. *Shulḥan Arukh, Yoreh De'a* 249:1.

functioning through them. For this reason, it is called world-centered kindness.

הַמִּתְלַבֵּשׁ בְּעוֹלָמוֹת עֶלְיוֹנִים וְתַחְתּוֹנִים עַל יְדֵי אִתְעָרוּתָא דִלְתַתָּא,

This is the kindness **that is clothed in the higher and lower worlds through an awakening from below,**

In order for the infinite *Ḥesed* to descend and be enclothed in world-centered kindness, within the limitations of the world, there must be something below that will awaken it for this purpose. In a certain sense, this *Ḥesed* depends on the world itself, on its level of preparation and readiness to receive it. In the terminology of the *Zohar*, this is achieved through an awakening from below.

הִיא מִצְוַת הַצְּדָקָה וְחֶסֶד שֶׁעוֹשִׂים בְּנֵי אָדָם זֶה עִם זֶה.

namely, through **the mitzva of charity and the kindness that people do for one another.**

One might think that in order to awaken divine kindness, we would have to perform kindness toward God. Why, then, does the author of the *Tanya* say that it is drawn through the kindness that people perform with each other?

The principle of measure for measure, of receiving reward in kind, applies to divine kindness, yet in this instance, measure for measure does not refer to what we do for God. Such a gesture is meaningless to God: "If you are righteous, what have you given Him … ?" (Job 35:7). Likewise, one who prays is not doing God a favor. If someone dons *tefillin*, God is not thereby in his debt. He does not need man's benevolence or his mitzvot, no matter how grand their scale. Consequently, God bestows kindness in response to the acts of kindness that people perform for each other, the haves for the benefit of the have-nots. ☞

A MITZVA FOR ITS OWN SAKE

☞ One should perform the mitzvot in the name of God, but not for the sake of God. There is a huge difference. Doing something in His name means one wishes to bring glory to God's name in the world, to bring about divine revelation in this lower realm. Through this revelation, one adds to the vitality and sustenance that the world receives from God.

וּלְפִי שֶׁהָעוֹלָם הוּא בִּבְחִינַת גְּבוּל וּמִדָּה מֵהָאָרֶץ עַד לָרָקִיעַ ת"ק שָׁנָה, וְכֵן מֵרָקִיעַ לְרָקִיעַ כו' (חגיגה יג, א), וְשִׁית אַלְפֵי שְׁנֵי הָוֵי עָלְמָא כו',

Since the world is finite and limited, as the Talmud states, **"From the earth to the firmament** is a walking distance of **five hundred years, and a similar** distance exists **between each and every one of the firmaments..."** (*Ḥagiga* 13a), **and "The world will exist for six thousand years... "** (*Rosh HaShana* 31a),

The world was created with boundaries. Everything it contains is circumscribed and limited, such as the distance from the earth to the firmament. Although a walking distance of five hundred years is immense, it is still limited. With respect to the dimension of time as well, the world is constrained and delineated. The world, then, is not immeasurable, but rather it is entirely composed of dimensions and proportions.

לָכֵן נִיתַּן שִׁיעוּר וּמִדָּה גַּם כֵּן לְמִצְוַת הַצְּדָקָה וְהַחֶסֶד שֶׁבַּתּוֹרָה, כְּמוֹ לִשְׁאָר מִצְוֹת הַתּוֹרָה.

therefore the mitzva of charity and kindness in the Torah was also given a set measure, just like the rest of the Torah's commandments.

Since the world consists of measures and limits, and man is circumscribed and restricted in his physical form, the mitzvot of charity and kind deeds were also given with limits. Although limitless at its essence, the mitzva of charity entered the framework of a boundary when it entered this limited world. Within this framework, charity awakens God's kindness so that He bestows vitality and blessings on the world in accordance with its limitations. This is world-centered kindness.

3 Elul אַךְ הַיְינוּ דַּוְקָא לְשׁוֹמֵר הַתּוֹרָה וְלֹא סָר מִמֶּנָּה יָמִין וּשְׂמֹאל, אֲפִילּוּ כִּמְלֹא נִימָא.

Yet this set limit given to charity **applies only to one who keeps the Torah, without veering from it right or left even by a hairbreadth.**

The limits imposed on the mitzva of charity – one-tenth for an average measure and one-fifth as the most desirable ratio – were provided with respect to one who follows the letter of the law in other areas of life. If a person eats, sleeps, and conducts himself in all matters according to the requirements of the law, he can do the same when it comes to charity as well. ☞

ONE WHO KEEPS THE TORAH

☞ Commenting on the verse "Hear Me, hard-hearted, who are far from charity" (Isa. 46:12), the Talmud states that it is referring to the righteous: "The entire world is sustained by [God's] charity, while [the righteous who are far from God's charity] are sustained by force" (*Berakhot* 17b). There are people who are "far from charity" in the sense that they do not need God's charity because they can demand it by right. Such individuals, who do not require gifts beyond that which they deserve, do not have to awaken the supernal attribute of *Ḥesed*, what the author of the *Tanya* calls "abundant *Ḥesed*," since world-centered kindness is enough for them.

In life, there are normal and abnormal situations. A normal situation is when the entire system progresses in harmonious perfection, without any deviations from the standard operation of the mechanism. This is true in many areas. When any apparatus works perfectly, without disruptions or aberrations, it requires a minimum of investment. This applies to the amount of oil that one must put in a car, the tuning of a piano, or even the human body. A healthy person can make do with limited and even sometimes very small amounts of vitamins and minerals, provided that he does not have to compensate for deficiencies caused by unusual circumstances.

The same is the case for one's spiritual life. When the system is operating normally, when a person lives according to the laws of the Torah, there is no need to shake him up. It is enough to alert him to a mistake in order for him to change the direction of his behavior. But when the system breaks down and stops working properly, this leads to a deficiency and distortion that must be corrected, and for this purpose the minimum amount is no longer sufficient. In order to restore a machine that has broken down to its equilibrium, one must make a special effort that goes far beyond the energy invested in its normal operation. In order to restore a sick human body to normal functioning, it must be supplemented with medicines and extra food, in much larger quantities than those that suffice for normal existence.

This is the approach some have taken to explain why the study of the esoteric teachings of the Torah have become more popular in recent generations, not only for great and wise individuals, but for the average individual. Furthermore, there is a difference with regard to the content of this study itself: Whereas in earlier times they were satisfied with allusions and general statements, in our days the ideas are spelled out explicitly. The claim is that in former generations, which were healthy and strong, one would hear a hint of an idea, and that was enough to fill his soul with everything it required. But as people became weaker, they needed more

אֲבָל מִי שֶׁהֶעֱבִיר עָלָיו הַדֶּרֶךְ, חַס וְשָׁלוֹם, מֵאַחַר שֶׁהֶעֱוָה דַּרְכּוֹ, לָתֵת מִגְרָעוֹת בְּקֹדֶשׁ הָעֶלְיוֹן,

But regarding one who has strayed from the path of the Torah, **God forbid, because he has corrupted his path, thus diminishing the** flow of **supernal holiness,**

When a person strays from the path of the Torah, he "diminishes the flow of supernal holiness," since he has damaged the entire framework of holiness. ☞

שֶׁגָּרַע עֶרְכּוֹ, בִּבְחִינַת הַמְשָׁכָתוֹ מַה שֶּׁהָיָה יָכוֹל לְהַמְשִׁיךְ מִבְּחִינַת אֱלֹהוּתוֹ וְהֶאָרַת הָאוֹר מֵאוֹר אֵין סוֹף בָּרוּךְ הוּא, אִילּוּ הָיָה שׁוֹמֵר הַתּוֹרָה וּמְקַיְּימָהּ כְּהִלְכָתָהּ,

since he has diminished its value in terms of its flow into the world, by not drawing down **what he could have drawn down from God's divinity and** from **the illumination of the light from the light of *Ein Sof,* blessed be He, had he kept the Torah and fulfilled it properly,**

teachings of a special quality to create the same impact.

The same is true in other areas of life. In a balanced framework, one can learn from the slightest hint; one can construct grand edifices from tiny particles. By contrast, if the structure is not balanced, a much greater investment is required, with far more attention and consideration. This also applies to the emotional realm: A child who grows up in a harmonious, happy home does not need to be shown excessive affection. One smile from his parents can fulfill all his soul's requirements for decades afterward. This is not the case if his family structure is unstable. Then it is necessary to show excessive and frequent affection, through caresses and kisses, to prevent the child from feeling deprived. Once the balance is undermined, the standard investment is no longer enough, and an exceptional effort is required to put one back on his feet.

THE ONE WHO HAS STRAYED FROM THE PATH

☞ It must be stressed once again that when the author of the *Tanya* is discussing one who is on a low level, who "strayed from the path of the Torah," the person he is referring to is on a much higher level than our concept of someone who is lowly. When he talks about corruption or one who strayed from the right path, he does not mean someone who committed serious transgressions, who committed adultery or murdered someone. Such deeds are not considered part of a Jew's life at all.

The author of the *Tanya* proceeds to clarify what it means to "diminish the flow of supernal holiness." It means that one has "diminished its value" because he had the potential, based on his soul's source and capabilities, to attain certain achievements, to achieve loftier levels, and he should have acted accordingly, but he failed to do so. ☞

הֲרֵי מְעֻוָּת זֶה לֹא יוּכַל לִתְקֹן **such corruption cannot be fixed**

This corruption cannot be fixed by means of a normal drawing down of the divine light. In other words, when a person is required to perform a mitzva, he has to invest a certain amount of time and energy. But if he has neglected to fulfill the mitzva altogether, and he wants to make up for his shortcoming, he can no longer make do with the same degree of investment that was required for the performance of that mitzva at the outset.

From his perspective, one who has strayed and corrupted his path has not even actually sinned, but is merely guilty of "diminishing the flow of supernal holiness."

DIMINISHED VALUE

☞ Every person faces various forms of accountability. There is the law, as imposed in a criminal court: Did the accused rob or murder or did he not? Is he guilty or innocent? But there is also another type of accounting, which is subtler and more demanding: One is asked not only, "What did you do?" or "Are you guilty or not?" but also, "What is the connection between what you could have done and what you actually did?" It is always possible to find some way out of the first judgment. There are many good excuses, not only in an earthly court, but in the heavenly court as well: The temptations were too strong. I was confronted with difficult circumstances. I was facing huge social pressure. I was not feeling well, and so on and so forth. But none of these justifications are acceptable when we are dealing with the integrity of the system.

The question then is not which rationale was given and will it be accepted, but simply: What was done or what was not done? Was it effective or not? This is the case when one must execute a highly complex task, such as operating a spaceship or performing a mitzva. Granted, there might have been good reasons for the failure. The person was tired or a small screw became loose, leading to a tiny deviation. But at the end of the day, the spaceship will not reach its destination. Here no one is guilty in the legal sense, because in terms of criminal law it can be proven that he acted reasonably: He was compelled by external forces, while internally he had good reasons for behaving the way he did. Yet when it comes to the integrity of the system, whether that of the soul or of holiness itself, the flow of supernal holiness has been diminished.

כִּי אִם בְּהַמְשָׁכַת הָאוֹר הָעֶלְיוֹן, שֶׁלְּמַעְלָה מֵהָעוֹלָמוֹת וְאֵינוֹ מִתְלַבֵּשׁ בָּהֶן, הַנִּקְרָא 'חֶסֶד עִילָּאָה' וְ'רַב חֶסֶד'. לְפִי שֶׁמֵּאִיר וּמִתְפַּשֵּׁט בִּבְחִינַת אֵין סוֹף, בְּלִי גְּבוּל וּמִדָּה, מֵאַחַר שֶׁאֵינֶנּוּ מְצוּמְצָם תּוֹךְ הָעוֹלָמוֹת אֶלָּא בִּבְחִינַת מַקִּיף עֲלֵיהֶן מִלְמַעְלָה,

except by drawing down the supernal light, which transcends the worlds and is not enclothed in them. This light **is called "supernal *Ḥesed*" and "abundant *Ḥesed*,"** for this light **illuminates and shines infinitely, without limit or measure, since it is not constricted within the worlds but encompasses them from above,**

The corruption cannot be fixed from within the world. It is impossible to change the laws of reality from the inside, and yesterday's deficiency cannot be mended within the world's framework. The rectification and completion of what was not drawn forth and not performed in its proper time and place can be attained only through the power of kindness that comes from without, from beyond that reality, which does not enter it but surrounds it and its laws. The encompassing light, which does not apply specifically to any point in time and place, can be drawn forth in some manner to any person at any time and place. The author of the *Tanya* will go on to clarify how a person can awaken and draw the encompassing light into his life. ☞

ENCOMPASSING FROM ABOVE

☞ World-centered kindness is the light that flows into the normal state of the world and its vessels, what can also be called the inner light. This light and its vessels hinge on one another: If the light is much greater than the size of the vessel, the vessel will break. If the light falls short of the vessel's capacity, the vessel will smother it. Within each world, as within each person, there is a certain amount of light that fits the vessel of its existence. This balance is part of the essence and existence of the world. By contrast, supernal *Ḥesed*, which is also called abundant *Ḥesed*, is the *Ḥesed* that comes from the level of *Ein Sof*. For this reason, it cannot be a kindness within the world, a world-centered kindness, because the world cannot contain *Ein Sof*. The world and *Ein Sof* cannot relate to each other on the same scale. By its very definition, *Ein Sof* cannot be constricted. We cannot fit it into any unit of measure or vessel. Rather, this light encompasses it from above.

As has been explained elsewhere (*Likkutei Amarim*, chap. 48–49), when we discuss the relationship between the inner light and the encompassing light, we are not talking about a connection that is dependent on a place or on any other material dimension. Even with regard to the spiritual realm, we use the concepts of lights and vessels, lights in vessels, and lights that encompass the vessels, where the light is the content and the vessel is the spiritual structure that contains it. To use the example of speech, certain content, such as an idea, has words that express it. Between the words and the idea there is a certain connection, which is the relationship between the idea (the light) and the words (the vessel). In order for the words to be meaningful, and for the content to be manifest, there must be a close, compatible relationship between the content and the words. To put it another way, when the words encompass and enclothe the content, they can express it. But when the words are unable to encompass the light, we say that the light is not within the vessels, but rather it surrounds them. At that stage, there is no internal connection, and the content remains beyond the limits of experience and verbal communication.

This does not mean that when the light is encompassing the vessels, it has no influence on the world at all. Rather, it means that the influence is not internal – familiar and comprehensible – but it is an encompassing influence in the form of an obscure experience, of an unfathomable recognition. Admittedly, there are also degrees of encompassment (see *Likkutei Torah*, Num. 52:4; *Derekh Mitzvotekha* 15:1). Some supernal encompassments are not found in any consciousness and have almost no personal meaning for anyone. There are also more intimate encompassments, which we cannot absorb and attain internally, yet they influence us in other ways.

If you speak to a person in a way that he cannot hear the words at all, the message will not get across at all. But if you address someone in a language he does not understand, but he can at least hear the words, he may be able to absorb the ideas from an encompassing perspective. Even though he does not comprehend a single word, he can still grasp something from the tone and rhythm; he can distinguish between a negative statement and consent. Although his internal comprehension is insignificant, the encompassment can have a great effect.

Not all influences have to be received internally. Aside from the direct message, there is an atmosphere, emotions and moods, as well as the ever-present influence of society and the environment. None of these factors affect a person in a conscious, intentional fashion, but are unquestionably influential. Sometimes the influence of the encompassing factor is even stronger and more significant than the internal absorption of the message. Whether a person hears a joke when he is alone, for example, or he hears it when he is part of a large crowd makes a big difference. If you are a member of an audience, there is much less need to understand the joke in order to laugh, since the surrounding audience has its effect. The influence of the encompassing factor can be such that it penetrates the mind even when the internal effect is minimal and one does not comprehend what is being said.

These two forms of influence differ in their modes of operation. One can be clarified and analyzed, while the other works in such a way that we do not know how to define what happened and how. A great personality could say a few words, and they could have an enormous impact. Yet later, when one tries to analyze what happened, one will not be able to identify anything special. The words he said were ordinary, his statements were simple, and it is difficult to ascertain what exactly caused such a strong impact. This is because it was not

מֵרֵישׁ כָּל דַּרְגִּין עַד סוֹף וכו'.

from the top of all spiritual **levels to the end** of all spiritual levels.

The encompassing effect always operates on the entire system, since to the influence of the Divine affects every level in the system, whether low or high. It encompasses and incorporates all of them together.

וּכְשֶׁהָאָדָם מַמְשִׁיכוֹ לְמַטָּה, בְּמַעֲשָׂיו וְ'אִתְעָרוּתָא דִּלְתַתָּא',

When a person draws the supernal *Hesed* **down below through his actions and an awakening from below,**

The drawing down of the encompassing light is not the same as the inner light. We do not actually draw down the encompassing light but merely awaken it from below. An interest is awakened, as it were, and the vessels are prepared, and then in its own time and manner it issues forth and flows down. The rule is that the awakening from above depends on the awakening from below. The actions and intentions of man below effect the awakening and flow of the light of *Ein Sof* from above. ☞

the inner content that created the effect, but the encompassing factors.

It is known that many people who visited the Lubavitcher Rebbe could not understand him, and even if they could, they were often unable to hear him, and yet there is no question that he had a great effect on them. In the hasidic world in general, the absorption of the hasid who visits the tzaddik is usually in the form of encompassment. People go to the tzaddik and perhaps catch a few syllables of what he says, and what they do hear they do not comprehend, yet and even so they receive a great gift, which gives them strength and fortitude for years to come.

HOW TO DRAW DOWN THE LIGHT OF *EIN SOF*

☞ There appears to be a contradiction here: How can a mere mortal affect the infinite Divine? How can an act of man break through the boundaries of his limited existence and somehow make contact with the light of *Ein Sof*?

As stated elsewhere, even if a person cannot reach the Divine, he can nevertheless breach the limits of the finite. Even if he cannot relate directly and fully to the Divine, he can relate to the limitless part of himself. As soon as he succeeds in breaking through his own limits, he has established some sort of relationship with the absolutely infinite Divine as well.

אֲזַי אוֹר עֶלְיוֹן זֶה מֵאִיר וּמִתְפַּשֵּׁט תּוֹךְ הָעוֹלָמוֹת, וּמְתַקֵּן כׇּל מְעֻוָּת וְכׇל מִגְרָעוֹת שֶׁנִּיתְּנוּ בַּ׳קֹּדֶשׁ הָעֶלְיוֹן׳, וּמְחַדֵּשׁ אוֹרָן וְטוּבָן בְּיֶתֶר שְׂאֵת וְיֶתֶר עָז, בִּבְחִינַת אוֹר חָדָשׁ מַמָּשׁ.

then this supernal light illuminates and spreads within the worlds, rectifying all corruption and every deficiency that had been caused to the supernal holiness, renewing their light and goodness with greater magnitude and greater power, literally infusing them **with a new light.**

The rectification of the deficiencies within the world can be achieved only by drawing down the encompassing light – not the measured light of world-centered *Ḥesed* but the light of abundant *Ḥesed* that comes directly from *Ein Sof*. Since it is from *Ein Sof*, it fills in all the deficiencies and fashions things afresh. This light, which comes from outside the system, is called a "new light," in contrast to the old light, which is the life force of the worlds in their current state. The old light is the one that is formed and placed within the boundaries and laws of the world, which are the laws of nature and of the soul, and to a certain extent even the laws of the Torah and the mitzvot. When there is a deficiency and corruption in reality, it cannot be repaired by its own power, but only by means of a light that is renewed, the light from which the whole world was initially created, so that the whole world can be created afresh. ☞

REPAIRING ALL CORRUPTION

☞ When a system that should be perfect is damaged, this constitutes a fundamental failure, which one might think cannot be fully repaired. It is true that the Sages provide a list of items to which they apply the maxim "That which is warped cannot be mended" (Eccles. 1:15; see *Berakhot* 26a; *Ḥagiga* 9b), from which it can be inferred that everything else can be mended. Yet that sort of repair refers to measures we can take so that the system is not impaired too severely. On a profound level, every flaw is a corruption that cannot be fixed, and there is no real way to repair it completely. When we view life as a random collection of events, it is always possible to add and replace what is missing and defective. But when the events of life are treated as points in the systems of time and place, there is no real way to repair an imperfection. A transgression committed at a certain time and place, a good deed that was not performed – these cannot be taken back. Just as it is impossible to restore a moment that has passed, so too it is impossible to rectify a defect that one has caused, and one cannot make up a deficiency that he has created.

The author of the *Tanya* therefore reiterates here that in order to rectify that which is corrupt and cannot be mended, one has to rely on *Ein Sof*, to rely on

לָכֵן אָמְרוּ: "בִּמְקוֹם שֶׁבַּעֲלֵי תְשׁוּבָה עוֹמְדִין" וכו' (ברכות לד, ב).

Therefore the Sages **said, "In the place where penitents stand,** even the full-fledged righteous do not stand" (*Berakhot* 34b).

Through *teshuva*, repentance, which is essentially the act of rectifying and perfecting defects, one can draw down the divine light from the level of *Ein Sof* itself. This is beyond the level that a righteous person, who has always preserved his level and boundaries, can reach. The tzaddik has attained his optimal state of being. He has used his faculties, abilities, and circumstances to the maximum. But the penitent, who touches the infinite, can go beyond even these limits.[14] ☞

4 Elul
2 Elul (leap year)

וְהִנֵּה עִיקַּר הַתְּשׁוּבָה הוּא בַּלֵּב כִּי עַל יְדֵי הַחֲרָטָה מֵעוּמְקָא דְלִבָּא

The essence of repentance is in the heart, because through the regret that one feels **from the depths of the heart,**

Repentance is achieved, not primarily through a particular action, such as fasting or bringing a sacrifice, but through what unfolds within a person's heart. The regret he feels in the depths of his heart, after he has worked on himself as much as he can, is the point at which he manages to do more. The expression "from the depths of the heart" serves to emphasize that this is not the kind of regret that caters to others, to improve one's relationships. It is a fundamental change, where a person

abundant *Ḥesed* rather than world-centered *Ḥesed*. For *Ein Sof*, all limits, that of time and place, that of man and deed, are equalized. True perfection is possible only by touching infinity, where the laws and limits of the world no longer apply.

THE PLACE WHERE PENITENTS STAND

☞ Repentance not only rectifies defects and restores the situation to its original state. In order for this to occur, a new illumination must be drawn forth, one that goes beyond the bounds of reality, since this alone accounts for the illogical nature of *teshuva*. The new illumination creates a world that is more complete than the previous one, since now a new divine light shines on it, a light that is greater than that which was initially revealed in the worlds. That is why the new place created by the penitent is greater and higher than the world of the tzaddik. The tzaddik knows

14. See *Likkutei Amarim*, chap. 7; *Iggeret HaTeshuva*, chap. 8.

breaches his own limits, beyond what he could have done on his own. This is the prerequisite for true rectification and perfection of the self.

מְעוֹרֵר עוֹמֶק אוֹר הָעֶלְיוֹן הַזֶּה. **one awakens the depth of this supernal light.**

By truly reaching the depths of one's heart, one thereby "awakens the depth of this supernal light." This phrase recalls a similar phrase in *Sefer Yetzira*, "the highest depths" (1:5), a paradoxical expression that conveys exactly this point of breaking forth to make contact with the Divine. A person discovers within the recesses of his soul the essence of infinity, and from there he can reach the "highest depths," the depths of reality, what lies beyond visible existence. This is the reason that throughout the days of repentance, Psalm 130, which begins, "Out of the depths I call to You, Lord," is recited. From the depths of the human soul one can reach the heights of supernal illumination. From the regret that lies deep within the heart, at that point where one is truly touched, when he feels that his whole life depends on his repentance and rectification,[15] it is from there that he draws forth the divine light in truth.[16] ☞

how to relate to a defined world, to a world of rules he can abide by, but he cannot stand in the world of *teshuva*, which defies any definition or limits.

FROM THE DEPTHS

☞ The words "Out of the depths I call to You" express the entreaties of a person from that inner point within, where he makes no calculations, where he is ready to give even what he does not wish to relinquish. As long as a person gives up only what he does not need anyway, such gestures are of little value, merely external acts. They might appear impressive from the outside, but they lack true worth. What may seem like a great sacrifice to one person is not necessarily so for someone else. For some people, going without food entails genuine mental suffering, whereas others do not care so much if they get to eat or not.

The Talmud states that "a single regret in one's heart is preferable to many lashes" (*Berakhot* 7a). A person's internal suffering can hurt much more than physical pain. At the end of the day, external pain that is physical has limits, and people can usually bear it, whereas internal pain has no limits. When it comes to physical distress, the body might hurt, but not the soul. Although the pain does touch the soul on the surface, it remains intact at its essence. This is not the case when it comes to the

15. See epistle 4 above.
16. See *Likkutei Torah*, Rosh HaShana 62b; *Sefer HaMa'amarim Melukat* vol. 2, p. 115.

אַךְ כְּדֵי לְהַמְשִׁיכוֹ לְהָאִיר בְּעוֹלָמוֹת עֶלְיוֹנִים וְתַחְתּוֹנִים צָרִיךְ אִתְעָרוּתָא דִלְתַתָּא מַמָּשׁ, בִּבְחִינַת מַעֲשֶׂה,

But in order to draw down this light **so that it may shine in the higher and lower worlds, there must be an actual awakening from below in the form of an action,**

Granted, repentance is first and foremost an internal transformation that takes place within the heart, but for this change to have a real impact on reality, he must give it expression in the world of action. In order for the light of *Ein Sof* to reach down to the worlds and maintain a proper hold within them, it is not enough for a person to have internal feelings. He must perform some action that expresses those feelings and carve out an impression in reality outside himself.

דְּהַיְינוּ מַעֲשֵׂה הַצְּדָקָה וְחֶסֶד בְּלִי גְּבוּל וּמִדָּה.

namely, an act charity and kindness without limit or measure.

Of course, a person's actions cannot really be without limit or measure, because for man the very concept of that which is boundless is itself limited. Yet a person can be unlimited in relation to his limited essence. If there are restrictions, he can go beyond them. Accordingly, if he breaks through the existing framework of constraints, he can perform an act that is reminiscent of infinity: He can bestow "abundant kindness," giving more than he is obligated to give.

דִּכְמוֹ שֶׁהָאָדָם מַשְׁפִּיעַ רֹב חֶסֶד, פֵּירוּשׁ ח"ס דָּלֶ"ת, דְּהַיְינוּ לְדַל וְאֶבְיוֹן, דְּלֵית לֵיהּ מִגַּרְמֵיהּ כְּלוּם וְאֵינוֹ נוֹתֵן גְּבוּל וּמִדָּה לִנְתִינָתוֹ וְהַשְׁפָּעָתוֹ,

For just as a person bestows abundant kindness [*ḥesed*] **on another, meaning** ***ḥas dalet,*** "have pity on one who lacks," **referring to a destitute pauper who has nothing of his own, setting no limit or measure to his giving and bestowing,**

"depths of the heart." Therefore, the test of "out of the depths," whether the repentance is truly internal, is if one is willing to give even what he is unable relinquish. He reaches his breaking point where he feels that he cannot hold on any longer, and yet prevails over this feeling and reaches a place from which he can declare, "Out of the depths I call to You."

The word for kindness, *ḥesed*, is a composite of *ḥas dalet*, the *dalet* implying the Aramaic word for "one who lacks."[17] Since the pauper has nothing to give in return, the giver sets "no limit or measure to his giving and bestowing." True *ḥesed*, then, constitutes giving to a pauper who has nothing of his own, who is owed nothing and cannot give anything in return for the donation. Under these conditions, the giving does not depend at all on the recipient's merits, or what the giver may receive from him, but on absolute, unconditional kindness without any restrictions on the part of the giver. ☞

כָּךְ הַקָּדוֹשׁ בָּרוּךְ הוּא מַשְׁפִּיעַ אוֹרוֹ וְטוּבוֹ בִּבְחִינַת חֶסֶד עִילָּאָה הַנִּקְרָא 'רַב חֶסֶד', הַמֵּאִיר בִּבְחִינַת אֵין סוֹף, בְּלִי גְּבוּל וּמִדָּה, תּוֹךְ הָעוֹלָמוֹת

so too the Holy One, blessed be He, bestows His light and goodness from the level of supernal *Ḥesed*, called "abundant *Ḥesed*," which illuminates infinitely, without

GIVING WITHOUT LIMIT

☞ It has been said, with regard to the request in the Grace after Meals that states, "Do not make us dependent on the gifts of mortals, nor on their loans," that "their loans" is not an addition to "the gifts of mortals," but rather, it clarifies the meaning of a gift from a mortal.

A gift of this type is generally granted in the form of a loan, like an investment in a business, a sort of deposit in a bank, whether an actual bank or a "spiritual bank." Accordingly, the author of the *Tanya* emphasizes here that the perfect act of kindness is when one gives to the poor, which is an unconditional gift for which nothing is expected in return, neither in the material realm nor the spiritual plane. Such kindness is called "abundant kindness," which is bestowed even on those paupers who have no merit.

In the story of Abraham and the angels (Gen. 18:1–10), the Torah stresses that Abraham's test did not involve a poor person who was a scholar, a pleasant and grateful person, or even a regular pauper, but someone whom there was every reason not to tolerate. A similar story is related about the father of the Ba'al Shem Tov. In order to test him, the prophet Elijah appeared in the form of a poor man on the Sabbath, arriving in such a manner that it was clear that he had desecrated the Sabbath. Yet the Ba'al Shem Tov's father welcomed him into his home, fed him, and gave him a drink without saying a word to him about the Sabbath desecration. It is said that in reward for this mitzva, he merited being the father of the Ba'al Shem Tov.

---

17. See also II Kings 25:12 and *Shabbat* 104a, which states that the Hebrew letter *dalet* itself means "one who is impoverished."

עֶלְיוֹנִים וְתַחְתּוֹנִים.

limit or measure, within the higher and lower worlds.

The awakening from below leads to an awakening from above; the action below creates the action above. When one gives to a pauper without the restrictions, beyond the limits of his ability, God responds in kind. He too gives to all the worlds in the manner of "abundant kindness," without limit or measure.

שֶׁכּוּלָּם הֵם בִּבְחִינַת דְּלֵי"ת אֶצְלוֹ יִתְבָּרֵךְ, דְּלֵית לְהוֹן מִגַּרְמֵיהוֹן כְּלוּם, וְכוּלָּא קַמֵּיהּ כְּלָא חֲשִׁיבֵי.

All the worlds **are considered lacking before God, in that they have nothing of their own. Everything before Him is considered nothingness.**

All the worlds are like paupers in relation to God. They are considered as nothing in relation to the Creator, who brings them to life from nothingness and an absolute void.

וְעַל יְדֵי זֶה נִתְקְנוּ כָּל הַפְּגָמִים שֶׁפָּגַם הָאָדָם בַּעֲוֹנוֹתָיו לְמַעְלָה, בְּעוֹלָמוֹת עֶלְיוֹנִים וְתַחְתּוֹנִים.

Through this act of charity, **all the blemishes that a person caused above in the higher and lower worlds through his sins are rectified.**

If a person gives without limits, God does likewise. God's unlimited gift, which is given in response to man's immeasurable effort, can rectify and amend all the flaws man has caused, both the defects of an individual person in particular and all the flaws of humankind in general. This applies both above, in the supernal reality, the root of everything, and also below, in this low, material world where we are meant to build a dwelling place for God.

וְזֶהוּ שֶׁכָּתוּב: "עֲשֹׂה צְדָקָה וּמִשְׁפָּט נִבְחָר לַה' מִזָּבַח" (משלי כא, ג), לְפִי שֶׁהַקָּרְבָּנוֹת הֵן בִּבְחִינַת שִׁיעוּר וּמִדָּה וּגְבוּל. מַה שֶּׁאֵין כֵּן בִּצְדָקָה, שֶׁיּוּכַל לְפַזֵּר בְּלִי גְּבוּל לְתַקֵּן עֲוֹנוֹתָיו.

This is the meaning of the verse "Acting with charity and justice is preferential to the Lord than sacrifice" (Prov. 21:3), **for the sacrifices have a set measure, limit, and parameter, unlike charity, which one may dispense without** any **limit** at all, **in order to rectify his sins.**

Performing acts of charity and justice below toward others is even better and more desirable than offering a sacrifice to God above. The sacrifices have defined parameters: what kind of animal must be brought, how old it must be, when it should be offered, when it is eaten, and so on. If a person deviates from these parameters, whether he does more or less, the sacrifice is not valid.

A sacrifice, like charity, serves to atone for one's transgressions, but it atones only in proportion and measure, if performed in the particular manner prescribed by Torah law. By contrast, the atonement of charity comes from a loftier place, even higher in a sense than the will that is contained in the mitzvot. It derives from the root of the will itself, so that it can compensate for the particulars of the will that the person lacked when he fulfilled the mitzvot. This is the very essence of charity, that it is not bound by any measure or parameters. One does not contribute charity according to what is due but as an unconditional gift. Since it is not limited, it draws from the God's kindness, which is immeasurable and which can rectify all defects.

וּמַה שֶּׁאָמְרוּ "הַמְבַזְבֵּז אַל יְבַזְבֵּז יוֹתֵר מֵחוֹמֶשׁ" (כתובות נ, א) הַיְינוּ דַּוְקָא בְּמִי שֶׁלֹּא חָטָא אוֹ שֶׁתִּיקֵּן חֲטָאָיו בְּסִיגּוּפִים וְתַעֲנִיּוֹת כָּרָאוּי לְתַקֵּן כָּל הַפְּגָמִים לְמַעְלָה.

As for the statement of our Sages that **"one who dispenses** his money to charity **should not dispense more than one-fifth"** (*Ketubot* 50a), **this refers only to one who has not sinned or who has rectified his sins through the appropriate self-afflictions and fasts** necessary **to rectify all the blemishes above.**

This directive of the Sages not only limits one's obligation, but establishes that it is prohibited to give more.[18] This does not contradict the claim made here, that charity is boundless, because the Sages' statement refers to someone who has not sinned. Such an individual is not required to bestow an unconditional gift on the needy in order to bring about a rectification of his soul. Consequently, the sum he gives does not serve the purpose of rectifying and healing

18. See Rambam, *Mishneh Torah, Sefer Hafla'a, Hilkhot Arakhim* 8:14; *Shulḥan Arukh, Yoreh De'a* 349:1; see also epistle 13; *Iggeret HaTeshuva*, chap. 3.

the soul, but is ordinary charity and falls within the scope of the mitzva according to the *halakha*. Alternatively, the person in question might have already rectified his sins by other means. When a person has corrected his flaws through self-afflictions and fasting, he has achieved atonement in some measure, and in a certain sense he has attained rectification in accordance with the law, like someone who has brought a sacrifice.[19] Therefore, he too does not need the divine *Ḥesed* that has no measure.

אֲבָל מִי שֶׁצָּרִיךְ לְתַקֵּן נַפְשׁוֹ עֲדַיִין, פְּשִׁיטָא דְּלָא גָּרְעָה רְפוּאַת הַנֶּפֶשׁ מֵרְפוּאַת הַגּוּף, שֶׁ״אֵין כֶּסֶף נֶחְשָׁב״ (דברי הימים ב ט, כ), ״וְכֹל אֲשֶׁר לָאִישׁ יִתֵּן בְּעַד נַפְשׁוֹ״ כְּתִיב (איוב ב, ד).

But as for one who must still rectify his soul, it is obvious that the healing of the soul is no less important **than the healing of the body,** that in that case, **"silver is not considered anything"** (II Chron. 9:20) **and "everything that a man has he will give for his life"** (Job 2:4).

Someone who is seeking to achieve the rectification of his soul does not give charity like someone who is fulfilling the mitzva, but as someone who seeking a remedy for a physical illness. Every individual makes a budget for himself: how much he will set aside for each of his own needs and how much he will provide for others. But when a person is fighting for his life, for his very existence, all such calculations lose their meaning, and he will give everything he has, and even more, to save himself.

5 Elul / 3 Elul (leap year)

וְהִנֵּה מִדַּת חֶסֶד זוֹ, בְּלִי גְּבוּל וּמִדָּה, נִקְרֵאת עַל שְׁמוֹ שֶׁל הַקָּדוֹשׁ בָּרוּךְ הוּא – ׳חַסְדֵי ה׳״. כִּדְכְתִיב: ״וְחֶסֶד ה׳ מֵעוֹלָם וְעַד עוֹלָם כו׳״ (תהלים קג, יז).

This degree of kindness, without limit or measure, is called by the name of the Holy One, blessed be He, as in **"the kindnesses of the Lord," as it is written, "The kindness of the Lord is forever..."** (Ps. 103:17).

19. See *Iggeret HaTeshuva*, chaps. 3–4.

This description of God's kindnesses does not refer to the one who performs them, but to the essence of the acts of kindness themselves: This is kindness without limit or measure. Since God is infinite, His kindnesses are likewise infinite, boundless, and immeasurable.

כִּי הֲגַם שֶׁכָּל יִשְׂרָאֵל הֵם רַחֲמָנִים וְגוֹמְלֵי חֲסָדִים, בְּרַם יֵשׁ גְּבוּל וּמִדָּה לְרַחֲמֵי הָאָדָם, אֲבָל הַקָּדוֹשׁ בָּרוּךְ הוּא נִקְרָא 'אֵין סוֹף בָּרוּךְ הוּא' וּלְמִדּוֹתָיו אֵין סוֹף, כְּדִכְתִיב: "כִּי לֹא כָלוּ רַחֲמָיו וכו'" (איכה ג, כב).

Although all of Israel are compassionate and kind, there is still a limit and measure to human compassion. But the Holy One, blessed be He, is called *Ein Sof*, blessed be He, the Infinite One, **and His attributes are** likewise **infinite, as it is written, "For His mercies have not ended..."** (Lam. 3:22).

Even if someone is merciful and kind by nature, his compassion is inevitably limited. By contrast, God's mercy has no limit in any respect whatsoever.

וְזֶה שֶׁאָמַר הַנָּבִיא אַחַר הַחוּרְבָּן וְהַגָּלוּת "חַסְדֵי ה' כִּי לֹא תָמְנוּ וגו'",

This is the meaning of the prophet's statement after the destruction of the Temple **and the** onset of **exile: "It is the Lord's kindnesses that we have not ceased** [*lo tamnu*]... " (Lam. 3:22).

The author of the *Tanya* now returns to the question with which he began the letter: What is the meaning of the phrase "It is the Lord's kindnesses that we have not ceased [*ki lo tamnu*]," which was formulated after the destruction of the Temple, when the world in general, and souls in particular, were now in an incomplete state.

פֵּירוּשׁ: לְפִי שֶׁ"לֹּא תָמְנוּ" - שֶׁאֵין אָנוּ תְּמִימִים וּשְׁלֵמִים בְּלִי שׁוּם חֵטְא וּפְגָם בַּנֶּפֶשׁ וּבְעוֹלָמוֹת עֶלְיוֹנִים,

This implies that since *lo tamnu*, that we are not perfect and complete, without any sin or blemish in the soul or in the higher worlds,

The word *tam* has two virtually opposite meanings: In one sense it connotes something that is finished or ceased, and it also connotes perfection. Here the author of the *Tanya* applies the second meaning, so that one can read the verse as saying, "It is the Lord's kindnesses, because we are not perfect." We ask for God's kindness because we are not perfect, because we are incomplete. Furthermore, every flaw that a person creates through his sins is effectively a double defect: It brings about a blemish both in his own soul and in the higher worlds. The flaw exists in all the worlds, but in the lower worlds it is not currently apparent. At present, it is manifest only at its spiritual root, which is in the higher worlds.

עַל כֵּן צְרִיכִין אָנוּ לְהִתְנַהֵג בְּ'חַסְדֵי ה'', שֶׁהֵם בְּלִי גְּבוּל וְתַכְלִית,

we must therefore behave in accordance with "the Lord's kindnesses," which are without limit or end

Since we are not perfect, and there are deficiencies and flaws in our being that must be amended and perfected specifically through the unlimited kindness of God, we must therefore practice the mitzva of charity in the manner of God's kindnesses, by giving without limitation ourselves.

כְּדֵי לְעוֹרֵר עָלֵינוּ רַחֲמִים וְ'חֶסֶד עִילָּאָה' שֶׁהוּא 'רַב חֶסֶד' וְרַחֲמִים בְּלִי גְּבוּל וְתַכְלִית. כְּמוֹ שֶׁכָּתוּב: "כִּי לֹא כָלוּ רַחֲמָיו וגו'".

in order to awaken compassion and supernal kindness, which constitutes abundant kindness and compassion without limit or end, upon ourselves, as it is written at the conclusion of the verse, **"For His mercies have not ended…."**

The supernal kindnesses and mercies of God, which stem from His essence, so to speak, are unlimited. It is only through God's kindness that we can perfect the deficiencies and flaws in our souls and in the world. The only way to awaken these kindnesses is by performing unlimited kindness ourselves, at the very least acts of kindness that defy our limits, the restraints of our character, and our financial resources.

וְזֶהוּ שֶׁאָמְרוּ רַבּוֹתֵינוּ זִכְרוֹנָם לִבְרָכָה: אֵין יִשְׂרָאֵל נִגְאָלִין אֶלָּא בִּצְדָקָה, שֶׁיַּעֲשׂוּ גַּם אִם יִהְיוּ פְּטוּרִים מִדִּינָא כִּי "אֵין בֶּן דָּוִד בָּא" כו' (סנהדרין צז, א).

This is the meaning of our Rabbis' statement that the Jewish people will be redeemed only through charity that they will perform even when they are legally exempt, for "the son of David, the Messiah, **will not come** until the *peruta* will cease from the purse" (*Sanhedrin* 97a).

In order to bring about the redemption, to emerge from the state where "we are not perfect," we must give charity even when we are legally exempt from giving charity.

The author of the *Tanya* proceeds to cite a statement of the Sages regarding the time of the Messiah's arrival.[20] He interprets it to mean that the Messiah will come, not due to our poverty and destitution, but when we give without limit, "until the *peruta* will cease from the purse" – from the giver's purse, since he is not legally required to donate so much. ☞

"THE SON OF DAVID WILL NOT COME"

☞ In the book of Proverbs it is written, "A wise man judged with a foolish man may be wrathful or amused, but there is no satisfaction" (Prov. 29:9). The Midrash (*Eikha Rabba, Petiḥta* 14). explains that this is a parable for the relationship between God and Israel: When He afflicts them, they do not understand or respond, and when He smiles on them, they do not respond either. After all approaches have failed to bring about the desired end, neither an excess of punishment nor an excess of good, it seems that the redemption will arrive only when we break through the boundaries, particularly in our generation, after we have faced a worse oppressor than Haman, as well as great salvations. The only way to perfect what is left undone is through the kindnesses of God, His unlimited, abundant *Ḥesed*.

20. The author of the *Tanya* does not quote the teaching in full. Regarding his omission of its concluding phrase, "until the *peruta* will cease from the purse," the Lubavitcher Rebbe suggests that "perhaps the author of the *Tanya* did not want to cite these words explicitly, since this saying of the Sages also applies on the spiritual plane, when Jews think of themselves only as paupers and lacking in everything."

This letter, like others in the book, dealt with the spiritual aspect of the mitzva of charity, its effect on the soul of the giver and its impact on the higher worlds. Yet this letter focused in particular on how we can touch the infinite through this mitzva, how the act of charity can awaken, not only the vitalizing divine life force that is bestowed on the worlds, but also the infinite power of God that transcends the worlds: infinite kindness itself. The letter explains that we require this kindness precisely because we are flawed and imperfect, that our world is so deficient that we do not have the ability rectify and perfect it ourselves. We need supernal kindness, the kindness of God Himself, to pour its influence into our world once again and bring us completion.

This power of the mitzva of charity is manifest only when it is performed in such a way that one ventures beyond his limits, beyond the boundaries and restrictions of his soul, body, and resources and proceeds to give what is truly precious and important to him – not only what he can and should donate according to the *halakha,* but even more than that. This "more than that" is what evokes the kindness of God from above, the infinite divine kindness itself, which can perfect and heal us, even if "we are not perfect."

The author of the *Tanya* concludes the letter by stressing that just as an individual achieves perfection through the mitzva of charity, so too, both the collective redemption of the Jewish people from among the nations and the redemption of the Divine Presence from its exile also depend on the fulfillment of the mitzva of charity in this abundant manner.

Epistle 11

THIS LETTER IS ONE OF THE MOST DIFFICULT ONES IN the book,[1] not because it is hard to understand the words, but because the message is difficult to accept and live by. It demands absolute devotion to God and the renunciation of any desire for worldly affairs, including the most basic aspects of a person's life: his own life and that of his family.

The author of the *Tanya* did not write these words in the manner of a person directing them to himself, but rather he was addressing a particular hasid or group of hasidim. It would appear from the letter that he believed that its teachings were relevant to all his hasidim and that they were capable of fulfilling them.

In explaining his demands, what he means and how it affects each and every individual, he touches on the fundamental issues of life: the meaning of evil and suffering and belief in divine providence over every person and at all times, along with the belief that everything is for good and no evil comes from Heaven. While clarifying these matters, the author of the *Tanya* teaches his followers how to strengthen and internalize their faith to the extent that it will change their view of reality and will even transform reality itself.

לְהַשְׂכִּילְךָ בִּינָה, כִּי לֹא זוֹ הַדֶּרֶךְ יִשְׁכּוֹן אוֹר ה', לִהְיוֹת חָפֵץ בְּחַיֵּי בְשָׂרִים וּבְנֵי וּמְזוֹנֵי

This letter comes **to enlighten you with understanding, that this is not the way in which the light of God dwells** within a person, **by desiring the life of the flesh, children, and sustenance,** 6 Elul / 4 Elul (leap year)

1. According to *Iggerot Kodesh* of the Lubavitcher Rebbe, Rabbi Menaḥem Mendel Schneerson, this epistle was apparently written before 1790 to a hasid from Smalyany, a village in Belarus.

The letter opens with an unequivocal statement:[2] The light of God does not reveal itself in a person whose innermost desire is directed toward worldly matters,[3] including children, life, and sustenance. Children are a person's offspring, life refers to life and good health, and sustenance relates to livelihood. It is around these three elements that life generally revolves. These are things that bring a person joy, and when they are absent, he suffers. People dream about them and struggle to attain them, each in his own way.[4] ☞

NOT IN THIS WAY

☞ The indwelling of the divine light within a person involves a revelation of God in the person's mind, emotions, and senses. But when those conduits are filled with this-worldly affairs, when those are always more urgent and concrete, the divine light cannot be revealed through them. The divine light of God is abstract, and it is seemingly neither here nor urgent. In order to feel it and to become connected to it, a person needs a clear expanse, both of time and in his soul. If a person's soul and desires are constantly connected to the concrete matters of the world, he will never come to even think about the divine light in a serious manner, and certainly not to sense it.

Moreover, when it comes to the divine light, there is no room for compromise. There cannot be the "light of God" and also "life of the flesh, children, and sustenance." The light of God is a revelation of the light of *Ein Sof*, which cannot be manifest with anything else in the world. Otherwise it would not be a revelation of *Ein Sof* – the Infinite One.

The fundamental question that a person has to ask himself is, *What is the purpose of life? What do I truly desire?* As long as a person's desires lies in the realm of "life of the flesh," even if it is in the most refined manner, his ideology and theology are insignificant. What he says and what he thinks make no difference. They are merely intellectual and emotional games, merely lip service. This is why the first question one must ask himself is, *What is the focus of my life? What truly matters to me? Where is the innermost point of my heart?*

---

2. The letter's opening statement is essentially a string of biblical and rabbinic sources. See Dan. 9:22; II Kings 6:19; Job 38:19; Ps. 34:13; Prov. 14:30; *Mo'ed Katan* 22a.

3. Note that the author of the *Tanya* uses the word *ḥefetz* to refer to a person's inner desire. For the difference between *ḥefetz* and *ratzon*, will, see *Likkutei* Torah, Song 28d, and *Likkutei Amarim*, chap. 41.

4. It would seem that since the author of the *Tanya* says that desiring physical life, children, and sustenance is "not the way" to draw down the divine light, one could say that such a way exists and he comes to reject it. How is that possible? The Lubavitcher Rebbe, Rabbi Menaḥem Mendel Schneerson, explains this by quoting a statement of the Sages: "One should not say, 'I have no desire to eat

כִּי עַל זֶה אָמְרוּ רַבּוֹתֵינוּ זִכְרוֹנָם לִבְרָכָה: "בַּטֵּל רְצוֹנְךָ כו'" (אבות פרק ב משנה ד), דְּהַיְינוּ שֶׁיִּהְיֶה רְצוֹנוֹ בָּטֵל בִּמְצִיאוּת, וְלֹא יִהְיֶה לוֹ שׁוּם רָצוֹן כְּלָל בְּעִנְיְנֵי עוֹלָם הַזֶּה כּוּלָּם, הַנִּכְלָלִים בִּ'בְנֵי חַיֵּי וּמְזוֹנֵי',

for concerning this desire for children, life, and sustenance, **our Rabbis said, "Set aside your will** in the face of His will" (Mishna *Avot* 2:4). **That is, one's will should literally be subsumed in** the divine **reality, and one should not have any desire of his own at all for any of the matters of this world, which are comprised of "children, life, and sustenance,"**

The author of the *Tanya* emphasizes the first part of the rabbinic dictum "Set aside your will in the face of His will," as if it were a statement that stands on its own. Setting aside your will means setting aside the very essence of your will, not just a particular desire when God desires something else. It means that your will is completely subsumed in the divine will. It is not that man has a will that he nullifies at certain points, but rather that he has no will of his own whatsoever.

וּכְמַאֲמַר רַבּוֹתֵינוּ זִכְרוֹנָם לִבְרָכָה: "שֶׁעַל כָּרְחֲךָ אַתָּה חַי" (אבות פרק ד משנה כב).

in accordance with our Rabbis' statement "It is **against your will** that **you live**" (Mishna *Avot* 4:22).

When a person has no desire for life in this world, any involvement he may have in "children, life, and sustenance" is in the manner of "it is against your will that you live." He lives, takes care of his health, and

The author of the *Tanya* is not preaching asceticism, but demanding that every person examine where he is, what is the true focus of his life. A person can restrict himself to bread and salt and sleep on the ground, but still be immersed in "life of the flesh," and he can eat meat and fish and drink fine wine, but still not be a glutton. The question is not what he does and does not do, but rather what he feels his life revolves around.

---

pork, but rather one should say, 'I wish to do so, but what can I do? My Father in Heaven forbade me to do so'" (*Yalkut Shimoni, Kedoshim* 626). There is indeed such a mode of service, but the author of the *Tanya* comes to say that this is not the way by which the light of God will dwell within a person. See *Likkutei Torah,* Deut. 9d.

raises children, not because this is what he desires and yearns for, but because it is something he must do, because this is the will of God. This does not mean that one should hate the need to be involved in these things, but neither does it mean that he should immerse himself in these matters and eagerly attend to them. ☞

These opening words of the epistle serve as a prelude to the loftier ideas that follow: that there is a sublime, spiritual goal to attain a close attachment to God and cause the light of God to dwell in the soul. The way to achieve this, by setting aside one's essential will, seems unattainable. But the rest of the letter will tie everything together. The author of the *Tanya* goes on to explain how this can be achieved with the tools at our disposal, those of deep contemplation and faith.

וּבֵיאוּר הָעִנְיָן הוּא רַק אֱמוּנָה אֲמִיתִּית בְּיוֹצֵר בְּרֵאשִׁית,

The explanation of this concept, how to attain this abrogation of one's will, **is** that this is **only** possible **with true faith in the Creator of the universe,**

What enables such an attitude toward life, that "it is against your will that you live," so that one may remove his desire for all worldly affairs? The author of the *Tanya* tells us this is only possible with true faith in

LIVING AGAINST YOUR WILL

☞ Every person has obligations simply because he has a body and he is subject to the physiological needs of that body. He must eat and drink, sleep and get dressed, and no one can live without taking these matters into consideration. Many people deal with these things, at least partially, only because they must, whether or not they want to. Many people go to work every day with that feeling of "against one's will." They do not hate it, and somehow they manage, but they do their work without passion and out of necessity, as part of the demands of life.

This does not mean that a person should not accomplish things in his life or that he should not enjoy what this world has to offer. The question is, what is important to him? This needs to be clearly defined from the very outset. Everything that follows, in this epistle in particular and regarding these matters in general, hinges on this point. The ability to resist evil, the capacity to justify God's justice, assumes a definition, a conviction of what is important and what is not. This is true at every level, not only in the upper realms. To be able to relate, even at the simplest levels, to the reality of reward and punishment, there must be a basic recognition that a sin is a sin. One who does not acknowledge this will feel that any punishment is excessive.

the Creator of the universe. This is faith that not only penetrates deeply into one's soul but is infused in every aspect of life.

דְּהַיְינוּ שֶׁהַבְּרִיאָה יֵשׁ מֵאַיִן, הַנִּקְרֵאת 'רֵאשִׁית חָכְמָה' וְהִיא חָכְמָתוֹ שֶׁאֵינָהּ מוּשֶּׂגֶת לְשׁוּם נִבְרָא.

that the creation came into existence from nothingness, which is called the "beginning of wisdom," and this is God's **wisdom, which is not apprehended by any created being.**

When the author of the *Tanya* refers to true faith in the Creator of the universe, he is referring to the very beginning of Creation. It means that one believes that the world came into existence from nothingness, and this nothingness that preceded existence is called the "beginning," which is the level of the wisdom. The nothingness is a concept that belongs to the realm of cognition. It is not absolute nonexistence, the absence of existence, but rather that which is not subject to cognition, that which cannot be comprehended. This point of nothingness is the starting point of cognition, the first flash of wisdom, from which the realm of the intellect and the emotive attributes develop. When this process is completed, not within the soul, but in the creation of the worlds, it constitutes a transition from nothingness to the reality of the created worlds. This is what the Jerusalem Targum means when it translates the words "*bereshit bara*" from the first verse in Genesis as "with wisdom He created." The reality of the world begins with divine wisdom and was created through that wisdom.

הַבְּרִיאָה הַזֹּאת הִיא בְּכָל עֵת וָרֶגַע, שֶׁמִּתְהַוִּים כָּל הַבְּרוּאִים יֵשׁ מֵאַיִן מֵחָכְמָתוֹ יִתְבָּרֵךְ הַמְחַיָּה אֶת הַכֹּל.

This creation from nothingness occurs **at every moment and second, so that all created beings come into existence from nothingness, through God's wisdom, which gives life to all.**

True belief in the Creator does not entail only belief that the world was created from nothingness at the beginning, but also that this creation from nothingness takes place at every moment and second. This is the meaning of the term "Creator of the universe," the word *yotzer*, Creator, being in the present tense. It conveys that even now, at every moment, all created beings come into existence from nothingness.

The notion that the Creation was not a onetime event is one of the principles of Hasidism. It is true that God began the Creation at a certain point in time, but since then He continues to activate it without pause. God "renews every day, continually, the work of creation." At every moment and second, the existence of the world is renewed, from nothingness to existence, from incomprehensible divine wisdom to modes of reality that are known and familiar to us. ☞ ☞

וּכְשֶׁיִּתְבּוֹנֵן הָאָדָם בְּעוֹמֶק הֲבָנָתוֹ, וִיצַיֵּיר בְּדַעְתּוֹ הֲוָויָיתוֹ מֵאַיִן בְּכָל רֶגַע וָרֶגַע מַמָּשׁ,

When a person contemplates this creation **with the depths of his understanding and imagines in his mind how he comes into existence from nothingness literally every single moment,**

CREATION AT EVERY MOMENT AND SECOND

☞ The notion of creation at every moment and second rules out other conceptions of the creation of the world. Not only does it run counter to the opinion of those who compare it to the building of a house, which no longer needs the builder once it is built, but it even negates the view of those who compare creation to the production of a clock, which runs on its own once the clockmaker has finished his work, and only from time to time must it be adjusted or repaired. Some see the creation of the world in the same way: From time to time, God gives the world a glance, checks what is happening, and makes some minor adjustments, but all in all the world runs by itself. By contrast, the perception presented here maintains that the creation of the world is a constant process. It does not entail occasional involvement, but renewal of the creation from nothingness at every moment and second.

GOD'S WISDOM

When it comes to man, there is a difference between wisdom and the other faculties of the soul, which are a reflection of the divine attributes. The other faculties exist within the soul and undergo a process within: moving from intellect to emotive attribute and from emotive attribute to thought, speech, and action. It is not the essence of the thing that develops into something new, but its form, the way it finds expression. Wisdom, on the other hand, starts from nothingness and comes into existence. It constitutes true renewal, from the nothingness that was not yet in reality to the existence that comes into being anew at every moment.

As the author of the *Tanya* explained in *Sha'ar HaYiḥud VeHa'emuna* (chaps. 1–2), the significance of creation through speech ("And God said..."; "For He spoke and it was done"), as opposed to creation through action, is that with speech a one-time utterance is not enough, but rather the speech must continue and perpetuate. When the speech ceases, there is silence. God creates the world by speaking the world into existence, and when He speaks again, the world is created anew.

In order to attain true faith, a person must contemplate this process of creation from nothingness at every moment. How must he contemplate it? "With the depths of his understanding" – in an intellectual manner, to the best of his ability. Then he must also "imagine it in his mind." He must provide his intellectual understanding with an image he can relate to, an image that will also have emotional meaning. This is all to be understood "literally," and not as a metaphor. This matter, that one's existence is created from nothingness every single moment is literally so. ☞

הָאֵיךְ יַעֲלֶה עַל דַּעְתּוֹ כִּי רַע לוֹ, אוֹ שׁוּם יִסּוּרִים מִ'בְּנֵי חַיֵּי וּמְזוֹנֵי', אוֹ שְׁאָרֵי יִסּוּרִין בָּעוֹלָם?

how can it even occur to him that his situation **is bad for him or** that he is experiencing **any suffering with regard to children, life, or sustenance, or any other kind of suffering in the world?**

After contemplating this, how the entire world, including himself, receives its life force and existence from God at every moment, and not through any specific mechanism or another, but rather through the decision of God Himself at this very moment concerning any particular being, it should not even occur to a person that his life circumstances are bad for him or entail any suffering.

If God Himself is the direct cause of this reality, it cannot truly contain evil. There is no denial here of the reality of suffering, but along with sensitivity toward suffering, loftier sensitivities can develop in the

LITERALLY AT EVERY SINGLE MOMENT

☞ A story is related about a yeshiva student who fled the house of his father-in-law, who was an opponent of Hasidism, and stayed for a while with his Rebbe. When he returned, his annoyed father-in-law asked him, "Why did you go there? What have you learned?"

The hasid said to him, "I learned that there is a God who created the world."

His father-in-law laughed. He summoned the maid and asked her, "Tell me, who created the world?" and she answered, "God, of course."

His father-in-law turned to his son-in-law in anger and said to him, "For this you went to your Rebbe? To learn what every maid knows?"

The son-in-law answered, "She said. But I know!"

This is what the author of the *Tanya* means when he says "literally at every single moment."

soul, so that a person will not even consider that his situation is bad and that he is experiencing anguish. ☞

הֲרֵי הָ'אַיִן', שֶׁהִיא חָכְמָתוֹ יִתְבָּרֵךְ, הוּא מְקוֹר הַחַיִּים וְהַטּוֹב וְהָעוֹנֶג,

After all, the state of **nothingness, which is God's wisdom,** from which everything is created, **is the source of life, goodness, and pleasure,**

Divine wisdom is not only an intellectual concept, nor is it just the beginning of existence. In a certain sense, it reflects the innermost aspects of the divine essence. Wisdom, the source of existence and the source of life, is also the source of goodness and the source of pleasure. ☞

וְהוּא הָ'עֵדֶן' שֶׁלְּמַעְלָה מֵעוֹלָם הַבָּא.

and it is the level of **Eden, which transcends the World to Come.**

The World to Come is the future world for the soul after life in this world. It is also called the Garden of Eden, literally, the "garden of delight," since it is the place where the soul delights. It is the place where

THE AWARENESS OF SUFFERING

☞ The author of the *Tanya* does not say this because he is a stranger to suffering. Without going into detail about his personal history, people of distinction are generally extremely sensitive, and this does not preclude suffering.

Suffering is the product of complex life events and mental constructs, of an awareness and association with certain emotions and faculties. To feel even simple pain requires a certain degree of sensitivity. Even in the biological realm, the simpler a creature, the greater its inability to sense pain. This sensitivity becomes more acute in direct correlation with the refinement of a person's being and not the other way around. When the author of the *Tanya* speaks about suffering, he is speaking from personal experience, and he feels it even more than others. But there are additional sensitivities, another level of reality in which one can live, a level that is open not only to the elite, where suffering and pain are placed in a totally different perspective.

LIFE, GOODNESS, AND PLEASURE

☞ These three elements, life, goodness, and pleasure, parallel concepts from the field of ethics and morality, where that which is useful, desirable, and pleasing define the criteria for what is considered good. These qualities are found together only at the point of nothingness, which is wisdom, where what is right existentially is also right morally and experientially.

the divine light is visible and where the soul apprehends, experiences, and basks in it. The source of the Garden of Eden is Eden: "And a river emerged from Eden to water the garden" (Gen. 2:10). The plain meaning of this verse is that Eden is the source and spring from which the river flowed. According to kabbalistic teachings, Eden is the point of *Ḥokhma,* Wisdom, while the river is *Bina,* Understanding, and the garden is *Malkhut,* Kingship.[5] From this perspective, the Garden of Eden is the place where the divine rationale can be comprehended, which is not the case with Eden itself. While it is the source of all the apprehension and delight that can be found in the Garden of Eden, it cannot be apprehended or understood in itself.

רַק מִפְּנֵי שֶׁאֵינוֹ מוּשָּׂג, לָכֵן נִדְמֶה לוֹ רַע אוֹ יִסּוּרִים.

It is only because this lofty level of Eden **is not apprehended** by the human intellect **that it therefore appears to him that his situation is bad or** that he is **suffering.**

The Eden that is beyond the garden cannot be grasped.[6] We have no comprehension or sense of this point of the wisdom that brings all of reality into existence at every moment. Since we do not see the source of things and events, we experience certain situations as evil or as suffering. It is only because our perception of reality is rife with holes, with parts we do not understand, that we relate to them in this way.

אֲבָל בֶּאֱמֶת אֵין רַע יוֹרֵד מִלְמַעְלָה וְהַכֹּל טוֹב,

But in truth, no evil descends from Heaven, and everything is good,

In the divine reality that is above the world, in the nothingness that cannot be comprehended, there is no evil.[7] There is only good. When the flow of divine light and vitality descends and is revealed in the world, it is not evil, but may seem to be so because we cannot comprehend

5. See *Torah Or* 9b, 27b; *Likkutei Torah,* Lev. 45a.

6. See *Berakhot* 34b.

7. See *Bereshit Rabba* 79:1; *Yalkut Shimoni, Tehillim* 11; *Tikkunei Zohar* 41a; *Avodat HaKodesh,* vol. 1, chap. 12; see also *Torah Or* 92b; *Likkutei Torah,* Num. 62b, Deut. 35b.

it. Evil exists in the apparent absence, in the negation, of divine reality. But if one believes that it is God who brings all of reality into existence and sustains it, and there is no other besides Him, it is impossible for evil to come down from above.

רַק שֶׁאֵינוֹ מוּשָּׂג לְגוֹדְלוֹ וְרַב טוּבוֹ.

only the goodness **is not apprehended due to its greatness and abundant goodness.**

The difference between good and bad events from our perspective lies in how much we are able to sense the good. There is no objective definition, since it depends on our subjective senses. What seems to us as darkness, anguish, and pain is not inherently evil. It is only that our perception is incapable of perceiving the good in it. The less we perceive the source of things, and the more disconnected we are from the things we experience, the more suffering and anguish we feel. At the least, there is a sense of triviality and even boredom, but then they may escalate and become unpleasant, painful, and even excruciating.

On high there is only good, and sometimes the perception of the good is even within our purview. But our entire human experience, both physical and spiritual, is restricted to a fairly small range. The spectrum of temperatures within which we feel good is very narrow. A few degrees more or less, and we feel uncomfortable, too cold or too hot. So too in all areas of life. Everything we receive, even when we ask for it, is good within a very limited parameter, and beyond that it is meaningless, and even unpleasant and painful. ☞

EVERYTHING IS GOOD ON HIGH

☞ This is not to say that everything that we view as bad is good and all pain is a delight. If a person is plagued with afflictions, if he feels pain, he is truly hurting. It is not just in his imagination. Evil does not descend from above, but there can certainly be pain. Even when we perceive God's governance of the world, there are many things that are painful and unpleasant, but they are not evil. The difference is in the attitude, how we relate to things. The question is not whether or not a person is hurting, but whether or not it is bad for him. Suffering exists in the world, and not only as a result of our lack of understanding. By contrast, our attitude toward suffering and

וְזֶהוּ עִיקַּר הָאֱמוּנָה שֶׁבִּשְׁבִילָהּ נִבְרָא הָאָדָם, לְהַאֲמִין דְּלֵית אֲתַר פָּנוּי מִינֵּיהּ,

This is the essence of the faith for which man was created: believing that there is no space void of Him,

A person lives in a world in which there is darkness and pain, because the Divine is concealed and hidden. When in spite of this one believes that God exists, that there is no place void of Him, he fulfills the purpose for which he and the world were created. The belief that "there is no space void of Him" is not just an abstract idea. It has emotional and practical consequences as well. This belief cannot cause pain to not be painful or evil to not be evil, but it can affect a person's attitude toward these matters, and as a result, his afflictions will not cause such anguish.

וּ"בְאוֹר פְּנֵי מֶלֶךְ חַיִּים" (משלי טז, טו).

and that **"life is in the light of the King's countenance"** (Prov. 16:15).

evil is to some extent subject to training and education.

In every person's life there is the realization that certain things may be unpleasant, but they are not necessarily bad. Everyone learns that a painful injection is a good thing and sometimes even lifesaving. Over time, one may acquire new tastes, some of which may not be pleasant at first, but after a period time in which one gets used to them, they come to be even more pleasant than simpler tastes of the past. The same is true in other areas, in music, in poetry, in other branches of literature. There is always a stage of learning that requires time and involves a certain amount of pain and discomfort. The more abstract the subject, the longer it takes to acquire. There are, of course, things concerning which some people never go through such a phase, and as a result they will never learn to find enjoyment in those things. A small number of people can get excited about a mathematical formula, whereas most, even those who understand math, will never appreciate it.

One aspect of our experience of suffering and pain is our inability to see the larger picture, to know the full range of causes and effects. We see things as fragmented, only a partial picture. Sometimes, over time, this picture is filled in to a certain extent, and then a person can rethink and reexperience past events. But for the most part, suffering has nothing to do with the individual's inability to understand the big picture but rather with the very fact that he was created a human being. Even if God sometimes bestows His gifts in a more restricted and limited manner so that we can better understand and adapt to them, fundamentally these things are beyond our comprehension, and for this reason, life in this world constitutes a constant framework for pain and anguish.

Not only is there no space void of God, but His existence in our lives constitutes life. Our life comes from Him, from the "light of His countenance," from His desire for us and for our good. The author of the *Tanya* here points to the light that comes from "the King's countenance," an illumination that shines from the face, so to speak. In this form, the flow of life and goodness is manifest and evident.

7 Elul

וְעַל כֵּן, "עֹז וְחֶדְוָה בִּמְקוֹמוֹ" (דברי הימים א טז, כז) הוֹאִיל וְהוּא רַק טוֹב כָּל הַיּוֹם.

Accordingly, "might and joy are in His place" (I Chron. 16:27), **because He is only good all the time.**

Wherever one discovers God, that is "His place," and there one will find "might and joy." This is not the case in a place of concealment, where one might also find what appears to be evil. Yet just as God's presence in the vitality that He bestows on the world is everywhere at all times, so too should we rejoice in His presence everywhere and at all times.

וְעַל כֵּן, רֵאשִׁית הַכֹּל שֶׁיִּשְׂמַח הָאָדָם וְיָגֵל בְּכָל עֵת וְשָׁעָה, וְיִחְיֶה מַמָּשׁ בֶּאֱמוּנָתוֹ בַּה׳, הַמְחַיֶּה וּמֵטִיב עִמּוֹ בְּכָל רֶגַע.

Therefore, a person must first of all be happy and rejoice at every moment and hour and truly live by his faith in God, who sustains him **and bestows goodness on him at every second.**

The gist of the matter is that "the righteous will live by his faith" (Hab. 2:4). The life of the believer, of one who walks in the path of the righteous, is intertwined with his faith in God. This is true not only in the simple sense, that he lives in accordance with the contents of his faith, but also in the sense that his vitality, desires, and yearnings are encompassed by his faith. Faith is the focus of his life, and it is where his innermost feelings are found. The righteous lives, not only in the sense that he is not dead, but in the sense that he takes pleasure and joy in life. His faith in God who sustains him and bestows goodness on him at every moment infuses him with life and constitutes his pleasure, excitement, aspirations, and satisfaction.

וּמִי שֶׁמִּתְעַצֵּב וּמִתְאוֹנֵן, מַרְאֶה בְּעַצְמוֹ שֶׁיֵּשׁ לוֹ מְעַט רַע וְיִסּוּרִין וְחָסֵר לוֹ אֵיזֶה טוֹבָה, וַהֲרֵי זֶה כְּכוֹפֵר חַס וְשָׁלוֹם.

But one who becomes sad and complains demonstrates about himself that he is experiencing some trouble and suffering and lacks some good, and he is thus **like a heretic, God forbid.**

When a person is sad, he is essentially declaring that things are not going well for him, that something is missing in his life. Thus, he is like a heretic, God forbid. Anyone who declares that things are not good for him in a particular situation is in effect declaring that God is not there. He pushes God away, as it were, from that time and place, for it states, "Might and joy are in His place." God's presence is in itself might and joy, it is the very definition of the good. When a person argues that reality is not positive, he ostensibly proclaims that God is not present and does not belong in that point of reality, and thus he is like a heretic, God forbid.

וְעַל כֵּן הִרְחִיקוּ מִדַּת הָעַצְבוּת בִּמְאֹד חַכְמֵי הָאֱמֶת.

Therefore, the scholars of the truth, the kabbalists, **vehemently rejected the attribute of sadness.**

The sages of the esoteric teachings, the kabbalists and the great hasidic leaders, totally negated the attribute of sadness, calling it an evil attribute from which one must absolutely distance himself to the extreme. Sadness results in a lack of progress and growth, in an inability to cope, of sinking to the depths in every sense. It is, unequivocally, an evil attribute, no matter its source and what lies behind it.

This includes sadness stemming from sin or a person's defective spiritual state, and it is considered even worse than the sin itself. A transgression can lead a person to repentance, whereas sadness will always bring him down, so that he cannot find his way out. Moreover, sadness is not a static emotion, one that comes and goes, but it expands and proliferates and brings a person to sink into it more and more. ☞

SADNESS AND LACK OF FAITH

☞ The attribute of sadness referred to here is usually the emotional expression of the notion that "I deserve more." When a person feels that he has received what

אֲבָל הַמַּאֲמִין לֹא יָחוּשׁ מִשּׁוּם יִסּוּרִין בָּעוֹלָם,

By contrast, one who believes in God **is not perturbed by any suffering in the world,**

A true believer is not troubled by suffering because he believes in God and trusts in Him, and he knows that whatever comes from above is good. Faith does not change the fact that things hurt, but it changes the way one relates to them. This may be compared to a young child who cries in the dark because he feels alone and fears the unknown, but when he knows that his father is there, he is no longer afraid. The same is true of life in this world: We are in the dark and do not see the divine light, and that is why we feel anguish and pain. The essence of faith is when a person hears, as it were, the voice of God telling him, "I am here." He knows and believes that "there is no space void of Him," that He is right here. While outwardly the darkness remains darkness and the pain remains pain, when a person believes that God is there with him, he is no longer afraid. There is greater meaning and providence that envelops and embraces everything.

וּבְכָל עִנְיְנֵי הָעוֹלָם הֵן וָלָאו שָׁוִין אֶצְלוֹ בְּהַשְׁוָאָה אֲמִיתִית,

and with regard to all worldly matters, yes and no are the same to him, truly equal,

For a person who truly believes in God, yes and no should be the same to him. The absence or presence of any particular thing should not make any difference, and failures or successes should not change his attitude. God's presence is so real and significant to him that he

he deserves, that he is rightly being punished for his transgressions, he will feel the pain, but it does not cause him sadness. A person is sad when he feels that he has been wronged. People resent human evil and evil in general, not because it exists, but because they cannot accept it or relate to it. When one begins with questions about evil, that is where faith enters and that is when it leaves. This is not about the questions raised by an individual about his particular situation, about what he deserves and does not deserve. A person may or may not be able to justify the judgment issued against him. But those questions are localized, applying only to a particular situation and individual. Here the author of the *Tanya* conducts a grand reckoning of good and evil, saying that the general conception that there is evil in the world fundamentally stems from a lack of faith.

relates to the rest of reality with complete equanimity. It is not that he denies the existence of things and events, but he experiences them without an undue emotional response. He views the events of life without engaging with them or attributing significance to them that they do not deserve. It is as if he is merely seeing the facts of the events from afar, some of which he understands and some of which he does not. ☞

וּמִי שֶׁאֵין שָׁוִין לוֹ, מַרְאֶה בְּעַצְמוֹ שֶׁהוּא מֵ'עֵרֶב רַב' דִּלְגַרְמַיְיהוּ עָבְדִין,

and one to whom yes and no **are not the same demonstrates that he is** a member **of the mixed multitude, who act** only **for themselves,**

When the Jewish people left Egypt, members of other nations who joined the people of Israel went out with them. They were called "the

TRUE EQUALITY

☞ These words apparently refer to the Ba'al Shem Tov's comment concerning the verse "I set [*shiviti*] the Lord before me always" (Ps. 16:8). If God's presence is always before me, then the reaction is one of *shiviti*, in the sense of *hishtavut*, equality. Whatever happens to a person, it is all the same to him, whether people praise him or humiliate him. The same is true of other things, for example, whether he eats delicacies or more simple foods – it is all equal in his eyes. Since his sole intention in life is to act for the sake of Heaven, intrinsically it makes no difference. The Ba'al Shem Tov concludes, "This is a very high level."

Let us analyze the matter in more concrete terms: When tragedy strikes, a person's attitude toward it consists of two parts. On the one hand, he relates to what happened in an objective manner. On the other hand, there are his personal and subjective attitude and feelings. When one reads in the newspaper about the death of a certain person whom he does not know personally, he usually does not even bother to say, "Blessed is the true Judge." He knows that people die, and it is a reality of life. But the closer he is to the deceased, the more his feelings change. Death as a phenomenon is death, whether the deceased is one of a billion Chinese people or one's closest and dearest friend. The difference between the two lies in his relationship with the deceased. A person does not weep over the fact that there is death and evil in the world, but he resents that it causes him pain. He does not cry for the world; he cries for himself. When the author of the *Tanya* says that "yes and no are the same to him," he means that a person can relate to everything that happens in the world solely from an objective perspective, whereas his personal feelings are reserved for God alone. There lies his awareness, excitement, and caring, while in all other matters, yes and no are the same to him.

mixed multitude."[8] These mixed multitude worshipped God, but not because that was their essence, like it is for Israel, but for their own interests.[9] They served God because at the present time it served them. By contrast, the inner truth of a Jew is to be God's servant, and if that is not the case, it is because now he is not acting like a Jew. ☞

וְאוֹהֵב אֶת עַצְמוֹ **and** that **he loves himself**

These words are primarily a description of a person's emotional conclusions. The question is where his focal point lies, by what standards his values are measured. When a person loves himself, the focal point, the concrete standard for everything, is "I." What is good for me defines what is good, and what is inconvenient or unpleasant for me defines what is evil. ☞

The expectation here is very lofty, even from those who have thoroughly prepared themselves for such a level, in both the command-

THE MIXED MULTITUDE

☞ The mixed multitude, who joined the Jewish people when they went out of Egypt, some of whom have certainly remained with us to this very day, appear again and again in the Midrash and other Jewish literature (see, e.g., *Beitza* 32b; Rashi, Ex. 32:4 and Num. 11:4; *Zohar* 1:25a), as those whose Jewish identity is incomplete. They behave like Jews and do what a Jew should do, yet their inner connection to Judaism is not essential. They are bound by habit or because it is now convenient and appropriate for them to be Jews. But whenever it is inconvenient to be a Jew, they do not act like Jews.

The mixed multitude is not necessarily determined by lineage. A person may be a member of the Jewish people by his lineage, yet in terms of the essence of his soul, he belongs to the mixed multitude that became intermingled with Israel.

WHEN A PERSON SERVES HIMSELF

☞ The essential question in the service of God is whether a person serves God because he loves God or because he loves himself. There is a manner of divine service that is a type of long-term investment. Some people invest in stocks that will bear fruit in thirty years, while others invest in "stocks" that will bear fruit in the World to Come. A person will constantly check what is currently accounted to him as reward and what remains as the principal. When he feels he is not getting

8. Ex. 12:3, and Rashi ad loc.
9. See *Likkutei Amarim*, chap. 1.

ments governing the relationship between man and his fellow and the commandments governing the relationship between man and God. In order for a person to truly achieve this level, where he is struck by tragedy yet does not experience it as tragedy, his point of service must be completely selfless. As long as there is a trace of self-interest, he is still in a state of loving himself.

לָצֵאת מִתַּחַת יַד ה׳ וְלִחְיוֹת בְּחַיֵּי הַגּוֹיִם בִּשְׁבִיל אַהֲבָתוֹ אֶת עַצְמוֹ.

to the extent that he **removes himself from under God's authority and lives the life of the nations out of his self-love.**

When one's starting point is self-love, when his focus is on what is comfortable and good for him, he removes himself from under God's authority. Self-love is a form of idolatry, since it establishes another central point, another absolute value in relation to reality, instead of the true center of reality: God Himself. Idolatry, even in its subtlest form, is no less idolatrous than a graven image before which a person prostrates. On the contrary, the same person who can mock fools who

what he expected, he can decide, as every investor does, that his investment is not good, and that he should transfer his resources to a different investment fund. The question is, what is the ultimate goal? If the purpose is to serve God, then it is all worthwhile. But if the purpose is to live better, there are many ways to do that, everyone according to his own imaginings, among which there is also the path of divine service, where a person serves God only because he thinks that it is a more promising path than others.

In other religions, such a perception is a legal one. A kind of contract of giving and receiving exists between man and the gods. One undertakes to give certain things, and in exchange he is entitled to receive other things. He may also lodge a claim against his god if the latter fails to fulfill his obligation to his satisfaction. The prophet Isaiah describes this phenomenon: "And it shall be, when he is hungry, he will become angry and curse his king and his gods..." (Isa. 8:21). Though this is a system that is not natural in the physical sense, it operates according to the same principles: One invests in order to receive, and one receives in accordance with what one has invested. Today there are entire worlds of mysticism based on this same principle. The reason a person does what he does is to receive pleasure. The difference lies only in the type of pleasure he wishes to receive. Some engage in certain activities in order to attain physical pleasures. Others engage in other activities in order to attain spiritual pleasures. This is a difference solely of preference, not a difference of substance.

bow down to images of wood and stone is unable to acknowledge when he is in a similar situation, when he bows down to himself.

וְעַל כֵּן הוּא חָפֵץ בְּחַיֵּי בְּשָׂרִים וּ'בָנֵי' וּ'מְזוֹנֵי', כִּי זֶה טוֹב לוֹ.

That is why he desires the life of the flesh, children, and sustenance: because that is what benefits him.

These three things, children, life, and sustenance, even when sought after with honesty and integrity, maintain and serve a person's existence in this world and so express self-love. One who desires and craves them may also be considered a religious person, someone who fulfills the mitzvot and prays. He goes to synagogue because it is convenient, and perhaps even enjoyable, for him to do so, much like another person goes to a lecture or a concert. The problem here is not that the person has violated any sort of prohibition, but that the essence and center of his life, what he considers good, is his own life.

וְנוֹחַ לוֹ שֶׁלֹּא נִבְרָא, כִּי עִיקַּר בְּרִיאַת הָאָדָם בָּעוֹלָם הַזֶּה הוּא בִּשְׁבִיל לְנַסּוֹתוֹ בְּנִסְיוֹנוֹת אֵלּוּ וְלָדַעַת אֶת אֲשֶׁר בִּלְבָבוֹ,

It would have been better for him had he not been created because the main purpose of man's creation in this world is to test him with such tests and to ascertain what is in his heart,

Man's great challenge is not just to live in reality but to stand up to it. He was not created to be a part of reality. The soul did not descend into the body to be like the body. It came down to the body and to this world to prove something that would be impossible to know from the world itself, like a test, which if it succeeds, proves something very important, and if it fails, disproves it. But if a person does not put himself at all to the test, and does not even try to transcend the boundaries of this world, it is better for him had he not been created.[10] But when a person stands up to the test for which he was created, it becomes clear that there is something deep in his heart, something larger and more important than the outside world.

---

10. See *Berakhot* 17a; *Eiruvin* 13b.

אִם יִפְנֶה לְבָבוֹ אַחֲרֵי אֱלֹהִים אֲחֵרִים שֶׁהֵם תַּאֲוֹות הַגּוּף הַמִּשְׁתַּלְשְׁלִים מִסִּטְרָא אָחֳרָא וּבָהֶם הוּא חָפֵץ,

whether his heart will turn to other gods, which are the desires of the body that evolve from the *sitra aḥara*, and desire them,

These "other gods" include, not only other religious rites or meditations in foreign temples, but also a wide range of human activities. Just as the names of the idols change from time to time – once they were called Baal and Ashtoret, and today they are called by other names – so too their forms and modes of service change. Put simply, other gods are the desires of the body that evolve from the *sitra aḥara*, the forces of the other side. There are idols of power, wealth, lust, and materiality, none of which require any special rite to worship them. This is what such a person desires. Here lies his innermost will, and it is in these desires that he truly delights. If a person's heart turns toward these other gods, he does not stand the test. He makes himself part of the material world and shows that there is nothing beyond that.

אוֹ אִם חֶפְצוֹ וּרְצוֹנוֹ לִחְיוֹת חַיִּים אֲמִיתִּים הַמִּשְׁתַּלְשְׁלִים מֵאֱלוֹקִים חַיִּים,

or whether his desire and will is to live a life of truth, which evolves from the living God,

The desired goal is that a person withstand the test and prove that there is something beyond the appearances of this world, that he wishes to live only a life of truth, a life that evolves from the Divine.[11] When a person binds himself to all sorts of falsities and substitutes for life, he lives a life that is not true. On the other hand, when one attaches himself to the primary and only source of life, to the Divine, then one is living a life of truth.

The test of life in this world lies in the fact that it does not reveal, and even conceals, the divine vitality in it. In order to withstand the test, a person must, in a certain sense, live in opposition to the world and what it says. This world has standards for assessing success in life, how much money a person has, whether he is healthy or sick, whether he is

11. See *Likkutei Torah*, Deut. 11b.

admired and respected by others. The question is, can a person assess himself using other standards, such as his connection to God? ☞

אַף שֶׁאֵינוֹ יָכוֹל.

even if he is unable to actually live this kind of true life.

These words are particularly pertinent to us. Note the preciseness of the author of the *Tanya*'s wording: He is not saying that a person withstands the test only if he is able to actually live a life of truth. What he is saying is only that it should be one's desire and will to do so. Not everyone can truly live in this manner, of living by one's faith alone, but everyone can wish and desire that he be able to do so.

From this it may be understood that this letter was written neither for people who actually feel and live in this manner, since for them it is unnecessary, nor for those who cannot at all relate to this point, because for them it is meaningless. Rather, it was intended for those who, though they are unable to live this way, wish and desire it. It is precisely in that place where the struggle happens. Sometimes one overcomes the struggles and sometimes one fails, but as long as they exist, there is something to talk about.

(צָרִיךְ עִיּוּן, וּבְאֵיזֶה כִּתְבֵי יָד לֵיתָא תֵּיבוֹת אֵלּוּ [אַף שֶׁאֵינוֹ יָכוֹל]. וּבְנוּסְחָא אַחֶרֶת מָצָאנוּ כָּךְ: "אוֹ אִם חֶפְצוֹ וּרְצוֹנוֹ אַף שֶׁאֵינוֹ יָכוֹל לִחְיוֹת חַיֵּי אֲמִיתִּיִּים כו'". וּלְפִי נוּסְחָא זוֹ נִרְאֶה

[Printer's note:] (**The matter requires further study. In some manuscripts these words, "even if he is unable," do not appear, while in another version we find as follows: "or whether his desire and will, even if he is unable, is to live a life of truth…." According**

THE TEST OF FAITH

☞ The test of faith is the greatest challenge presented to us by the world. The important thing is not whether or not we believe in the existence of God. The true question is what place a person's faith occupies in his life. Does it stand at the center of a person's life, at the center of his being and experience? When a person lives by his faith, everything he does and everything he feels stems from the fact that he lives by that faith in God. Then all the affairs of this world, though they are happening around him and he must respond to them as necessary, are equal in terms of his attitude toward them.

שֶׁתֵּיבוֹת [אַף שֶׁאֵינוֹ יָכוֹל] הוּא מַאֲמָר מוּסְגָּר).

to this version, the words [“even if he is unable”] seem to be a parenthetical remark.)

וְיַאֲמִין שֶׁבֶּאֱמֶת הוּא חַי בָּהֶם, וְכָל צְרָכָיו וְכָל עִנְיָנָיו מִשְׁתַּלְשְׁלִים בֶּאֱמֶת, בִּפְרָטֵי פְּרָטִיּוֹתֵיהֶם, שֶׁלֹּא מִ'סִּיטְרָא אַחֲרָא'

One should believe that he truly lives a life of truth **and that all his needs and all his** personal **affairs truly evolve, down to their every detail, not from the** ***sitra aḥara,*** but from the Divine,

Even when a person does not feel that he lives a true life bound to God, he must believe that this is the case. He must feel that the life he lives, not only in general but down to the smallest detail, is a life that stems from God and from God alone. He believes that all his needs and everything else in his life come from God and from the side of holiness and not from the other side, that which the world calls chance, fate, luck, the economy, society, or whatever other name people give it.

כִּי "מֵה' מִצְעֲדֵי גֶבֶר כּוֹנָנוּ" (תהלים לז, כג) וְ"אֵין מִלָּה כו'" (תהלים קלט, ד), וְאִם כֵּן הַכֹּל טוֹב בְּתַכְלִית, רַק שֶׁאֵינוֹ מוּשָּׂג.

for “the Lord sets the footsteps of man” (Ps. 37:23), **and** “even **when** there is yet **no word on my tongue,** truly, Lord, You know it all” (Ps. 139:4), **and if so, everything** a person experiences **is ultimately good. It is just that it is not apprehended** as such by the human mind.

Everything that happens to a person stems from God and comes about through His providence. As the Sages said, “A person injures his finger below only if they declare about him on high [that he should be injured], as it states, ‘The Lord sets the footsteps of man’” (*Ḥullin* 7b).[12]

---

12. The Lubavitcher Rebbe, Rabbi Menaḥem Mendel Schneerson, comments, “Ostensibly, it is difficult to understand why it is specifically this verse that is quoted here when many other verses that appear earlier in *Tanakh* speak of divine providence. This can be understood in light of the fact that it was specifically in connection to this verse that the Sages said, ‘A person injures….’ Here too we see the magnitude of the precision of the author of the *Tanya*.”

It is not only a person's actions that come from God, but even the words that a person utters, his thoughts, and even his desire to think. Moreover, not only do we believe that God "sets every footstep," but that everything He does, He does for good. If a person does not see things this way, it is because he does not understand how it is so. A person may not apprehend a particular event or course of events in reality because it is too complicated for him to understand, and therefore it appears to him as evil, as an injustice done to him. But true faith entails believing that even that which appears dark and negative is a divine revelation, and even through this God reveals His existence and His goodness.

What appears to us as the difference between good and evil is only the difference between two types of good, between good at a level that we can perceive and good at a perhaps higher level that we are unable to perceive. The Talmud says something similar about "afflictions of love."[13] Sometimes afflictions come, not as a punishment for sin, but as a manifestation of great love. ☞

וּבֶאֱמוּנָה זוֹ בֶּאֱמֶת, נַעֲשֶׂה הַכֹּל טוֹב גַּם בְּגָלוּי שֶׁבֶּאֱמוּנָה זוֹ, שֶׁמַּאֲמִין שֶׁהָרַע הַנִּדְמֶה בְּגָלוּי, כָּל חַיּוּתוֹ הוּא מִטּוּב הָעֶלְיוֹן, שֶׁהִיא חָכְמָתוֹ יִתְבָּרֵךְ שֶׁאֵינָהּ מוּשֶּׂגֶת,

When one truly believes this, that everything he experiences is good, **everything becomes good even in a revealed sense, because with this faith, where one believes that** even **what appears to be openly evil** really **derives its entire life force from the supernal goodness, which is God's wisdom that cannot be apprehended** by man

THE CHALLENGE OF "SETTING GOD ALWAYS BEFORE ME"

☞ The challenge of setting God in one's center is found both in a life of anguish and in a life of well-being. The tests of wealth, honor, and well-being may be even more challenging than the test of humiliation, privation, and poverty. The gifts that a person receives through God's excessive goodness can turn into a disadvantage and cause corruption when a person does not know how to receive them. The dan-

13. *Berakhot* 5a.

When a person truly believes that this is the case, that everything he experiences is utterly good, the good is manifest and experienced as good even openly. When a person reaches this level and recognizes what appears to be evil, and he truly believes (or at least he wants to truly believe) that it is not actually evil but rather concealed good, there is already a change. He knows that there are answers, even if he does not see it.

To illustrate, consider a young child who encounters a bizarre and threatening mask. The moment he realizes that behind the mask is his father's face, he is no longer afraid. A person fears what he perceives as threatening, as alien, as that which is an arbitrary independent force. But the moment he internalizes the knowledge that what he sees is nothing but a veil, that it is not arbitrary at all, but rather his Father, God, behind the mask, that which had been threatening is no longer threatening and that which had been strange is no longer strange.

וְהִיא הָ'עֵדֶן' שֶׁלְּמַעְלָה מֵעוֹלָם הַבָּא,

and which is the supernal level of **Eden that transcends the Word to Come,**

Just as Eden is the hidden source that "no eye has seen" for all the delight attained in the World to Come (the "Garden of Eden"), so too that which is not apprehended in this world, that which appears to be evil and painful, is loftier than all that seems good and pleasant in this world.

הֲרֵי בֶּאֱמוּנָה זוֹ נִכְלָל וּמִתְעַלֶּה בֶּאֱמֶת הָרַע הַמְּדוּמֶּה בַּטּוֹב הָעֶלְיוֹן הַגָּנוּז.

with this faith, the apparent evil truly becomes incorporated in the concealed supernal goodness.

ger is not only that a person will develop overbearing pride, but it may impair that person's very ability to act. When a person is not subject to any criticism, whether from himself or from an external source, he ceases to grow or have any value.

The challenge of "setting God always before me" means that one need not ask God for a loan, to bestow goodness on him against one's merits, nor does one have to ask God to take back from him what he has received. Whether from a place of well-being or a place of privation, one need only believe that "the Lord sets the footsteps of man," that everything comes from Heaven and everything is perfectly good, even though he does not always understand how.

Here is an additional facet: The ability to see the Divine everywhere in the world, in the manner of "setting the Lord always before me," is also the key to seeing the good within the evil. In view of this, not only is the evil no longer evil, but it itself becomes the revealed good. ☞

SUFFERING AS A LIFELINE

☞ There is another point in relation to this belief. When we assume that what is happening to us is void of cause and purpose, our reaction will generally be the wrong one. If we cannot attribute what is happening in reality to the Divine, to a future purpose, we also cannot respond appropriately. We become resentful where there is no need to be resentful, or we fall prey to paralyzing sadness where we need to act. A person is drowning, and he can feel that something has been thrown on his head. He feels depressed and humiliated: Not only is he struggling for his life, but he is still being hit on the head! But were he less resentful – about the world being full of evil and inflexibility and about why he is on the way to death – he would see that the blow he received to his head is actually a lifeline that was thrown to him, and he would respond differently.

Moreover, when a person feels that his problem has no solution, he becomes paralyzed, and instead of searching for a way out, he sinks even lower. The very knowledge that the problem has a solution creates a fundamental change in his attitude. Even if the problem is not completely resolved, some part of it will surely work out. The great secret of the atomic bomb was revealed when the first bomb exploded. From then onward, with and without espionage, it was only a matter of time before others were able to develop the technology.

The same is true with life: As long as we see the course of events in the world as evil that befall us arbitrarily, as causeless and purposeless, there is really no answer to what is happening in the world. Answers to specific questions may be found, but no attempt will be made to find the fundamental solutions, since the basic premise is that the problems by their very nature have no solution. But when a person believes in the "Creator of the universe" and that "no evil descends from Heaven," he assumes that there is an answer, that what appears to be evil is a difficult problem, but not a problem that has no solution. The solution may not be at hand right now, but the very knowledge that the solution exists is itself a kind of solution.

The answer to all the questions, even the broadest in scope, those related to death and evil (which will only be revealed at the end of days), is based primarily, not on changing this world's reality, but on changing our perspective of them. You can place a person in the Garden of Eden, but that does not mean he will have the Garden of Eden. Not only does the person have to enter the Garden of Eden, but the Garden of Eden must also enter him. Otherwise, he will not know that he is in the Garden of Eden.

If a horse were brought to a Rembrandt exhibition, it will not enjoy the art, not because of a flaw in the paintings, but because of a deficiency in the horse's comprehension. It takes a certain degree of awareness for a person to know where he is, for him to understand the meaning of the things he is going through.

This short letter dealt with a big question: What is the way to bring the light of God to dwell in man? The condition set by the author of the *Tanya* from the very outset seems impossible, that a person must have no inner desire for the affairs of this world, no yearning or emotional connection to them. His desires must be directed solely to God. When the author of the *Tanya* tries to explain this to his followers, he talks of faith. It is only true faith at all times in the Creator of the universe that can help a person transfer his innermost relationship from the affairs of the world to God, who brings everything into existence. Only true faith can distract a person from challenges and suffering so that he does not sink into depression and so that he can see only the good and delight that descends from above, even if he cannot apprehend how it is all good.

This too seems difficult. Not every person can live this way; not every person can refrain from relating to the suffering and anguish afflicting him and those close to him. Yet by the power of faith, he can change the way he relates to them. Man's suffering is twofold: He suffers to a certain extent from the evil itself, but above all, he suffers from the feeling that it has no purpose, that he does not deserve it, that it is a labyrinth that has no solution and no meaning. Without a doubt, faith can change this aspect of the torment, which is also the most difficult part of it. True faith maintains that even evil and suffering are fundamentally good. The whole distinction between what seems to us to be good or bad is actually a distinction between two different languages. The language of good is one that we understand (at least in part), whereas the more complex language of what we perceive as evil, we are unable to understand. We must relate to it through faith, complete faith in God, that no evil descends from Heaven.

The stronger the faith that this is the truth, the more things change in concrete reality. It is impossible to explain this, it is not something we can define, but over the course of time, the believer comes to know that this is really the case.

In several places in the *Tanya*, the author speaks of goals that a person can set for himself. Even if he does not achieve them today, and may perhaps attain them tomorrow, perhaps some time in the future, or perhaps never, he is already proceeding along the path and his name is already inscribed on it.

Epistle 12

THIS LETTER DEALS ENTIRELY WITH A SINGLE VERSE from the book of Isaiah that speaks of two levels of giving charity. As discussed in the other letters that focus on this mitzva, the mitzva of charity relates to the inner emotional makeup of the person who is giving the charity. The two levels that will be discussed here are two levels in the service of the soul and in the soul itself: one where a person performs service that is in line with his nature, and a second, deeper level, which reveals itself when the person performs service that goes beyond his nature and even contrary to it.

The fundamental example of these two levels is found in the two ways the mitzva of charity can be fulfilled. Yet the letter goes on to discuss prayer and the feelings of devotion that follow in its wake, as well as the enlightenment a person receives from above in accordance with the level at which he fulfilled the commandment below.

8 Elul

5 Elul (leap year)

"וְהָיָה מַעֲשֵׂה הַצְּדָקָה שָׁלוֹם וַעֲבוֹדַת הַצְּדָקָה הַשְׁקֵט וָבֶטַח עַד עוֹלָם" (ישעיה לב, יז). לְהָבִין הַהֶפְרֵשׁ שֶׁבֵּין "מַעֲשֶׂה" לַ"עֲבוֹדָה" וּבֵין "שָׁלוֹם" לְ"הַשְׁקֵט וָבֶטַח כו'"

It is written, **"The act of charity will be peace, and the service of charity will be quiet and security forever"** (Isa. 32:17). **One may understand the difference between an "act" and "service" and between "peace" and "quiet and security," and so on,**

The author of the *Tanya* points out that the verse is composed of two parts, and they are not identical. The first part speaks of an "act of charity," of giving charity in the form of an action, the reward for which is "peace." The second part refers to giving charity in the manner of a service, the reward for which is "quiet and security forever." What is the difference between an "act" and "service," and what is the difference between "peace" and "quiet and security"?

עַל פִּי מַה שֶּׁאָמְרוּ רַבּוֹתֵינוּ זִכְרוֹנָם לִבְרָכָה עַל פָּסוּק: "עוֹשֶׂה שָׁלוֹם בִּמְרוֹמָיו" (איוב כה, ב).

in light of our Rabbis' statement regarding the verse "He makes peace in His heights" (Job 25:2).

It is clear that peace must be made below in this world, where there is envy, competition, and war. But what does it mean to make peace "in His heights"? What quarrel or fighting is there between the angels or between the supernal attributes that requires that peace be made above?

כִּי מִיכָאֵל שַׂר שֶׁל מַיִם וְגַבְרִיאֵל שַׂר שֶׁל אֵשׁ וְאֵין מְכַבִּין זֶה אֶת זֶה (דברים רבה פרשה ה, יב).

The Rabbis stated **that Michael is the minister of water, and Gabriel is the minister of fire, and** yet **they do not extinguish one another** (*Devarim Rabba* 5:12).

The angels do not quarrel, but there are differences between them. The supernal reality is neither unequivocal nor uniform; there are differences there too, even contrasts. Michael and Gabriel are both holy angels.[14] The angel Michael is the "minister of Israel,"[15] and in a certain sense the same is true of the angel Gabriel. Both are at the head of the "camps of the Divine Presence" that stand on the same side, the side of Israel.[16] Yet they are so different that peace must be made between them. The image used to describe the difference between them is that one is the angel of water while the other is the angel of fire. Water and fire, even as spiritual essences, are two opposites that seemingly cancel each other out. In order for Michael and Gabriel to

14. These are the only two angels that are mentioned by name in *Tanakh*. See, e.g., Dan. 9:21, 10:13.

15. *Midrash Shoḥer Tov* 23:20.

16. As it says in the evening recitation of the *Shema*, the Divine Presence is accompanied by four groups of angels, and at the head of two of them is Michael and Gabriel. See also *Zohar* 1:26b, 3:118b.

coexist in the same place and perform their service without interfering with each other and without contradicting each other, God must make peace between them.

כְּלוֹמַר, שֶׁמִּיכָאֵל שַׂר שֶׁל חֶסֶד, הַנִּקְרָא בְּשֵׁם מַיִם הַיּוֹרְדִים מִמָּקוֹם גָּבוֹהַּ לְמָקוֹם נָמוּךְ,

That is, Michael is **the minister of *Ḥesed*, which is called water,** because water **descends from a higher place to a lower place,**

It goes without saying that in Heaven there is no actual water or fire. There are only spiritual essences: the essence of *Ḥesed,* of Kindness, and the essence of *Gevura,* of Restraint. *Ḥesed* is described as water, because it is the nature of water, like *Ḥesed,* to flow downward from a high point to a low point, from a place where there is water to a place where there is not.

וְהוּא בְּחִינַת הַהַשְׁפָּעָה וְהִתְפַּשְּׁטוּת הַחַיּוּת מֵעוֹלָמוֹת עֶלְיוֹנִים לְתַחְתּוֹנִים

and *Ḥesed* **is the flow and emanation of the life force from the higher worlds to the lower worlds.**

This is the essence of kindness, material or spiritual: that it descends from above to below, that one who has gives to another who does not have. It is the flow from the center to the periphery, from the inner essence to the outer essence.

וּבְחִינַת אֵשׁ, שֶׁטִּבְעָהּ לַעֲלוֹת לְמַעְלָה, הִיא בְּחִינַת הַגְּבוּרָה וְהִסְתַּלְּקוּת הַשְׁפָּעַת הַחַיִּים מִמַּטָּה לְמַעְלָה,

By contrast, **the element of fire, whose nature is to rise above, represents the attribute of *Gevura* and the withdrawal of the flow of life force from below to above,**

By contrast, the attribute of *Gevura* operates in the opposite direction. It starts at the periphery and is pulled to the center and its influence flows from below upward. Of course, up and down should be understood here, not in the geographical sense, but in the spiritual one. Up and down are meaningful only when one assumes that "up" is the more important and fuller place, and "down" is the empty and deficient place, toward which there can be expansion.

In terms borrowed from another realm, it may be argued that "up" is high energy and "down" is low energy. In this sense, *Ḥesed* is the flow from a high level to the low level, and *Gevura* is the opposite: It involves emptying out, as things on the periphery converge inward to their center point.

so that it flows only in an immensely constricted manner. שֶׁלֹּא לְהַשְׁפִּיעַ רַק בְּצִמְצוּם עָצוּם וָרָב.

As opposed to the attribute of *Ḥesed,* which bestows and flows outward, the attribute of *Gevura* constricts its influence toward the center. This constriction is not out of malice, but out of justice, to give only to those who are deserving. *Gevura* is the power to constrict and to concentrate on the manifestly most important and most significant point. To do so, one must cut off and exclude everything that is on the periphery, that is not at the center point. ☞

These attributes of *Ḥesed* and *Gevura* **contradict and oppose one another,** וְהֵן מִדּוֹת נֶגְדִּיּוֹת וְהָפְכִּיּוֹת זוֹ לְזוֹ,

The attribute of *Ḥesed* operates on the assumption that in a place of lack, there must be giving, whereas the attribute of *Gevura* operates on the assumption that in a place of lack, there need not be giving. One who is lacking is apparently unworthy and undeserving, and therefore matters should be left as they are, constricted to the center. The attribute of *Ḥesed* relates to the experience of "I lack," while the attribute of *Gevura* relates to the experience of "I deserve." These are two extremely different and opposing points of view. ☞

GEVURA AND JUSTICE ARE NOT *KELIPPA*

☞ The attribute of justice does not entail a total abstinence from giving. Total abstention from giving is an attribute of malice, of *kelippa*, whereas the attribute of justice is one of holiness. One of the definitions of *kelippa* is that which only takes but gives nothing. Therefore, a place that is void of giving is not a place of holiness.

ḤESED AND *GEVURA* AMONG PEOPLE

☞ This distinction between the two attributes is also a distinction that occurs between different people. One person acts in all situations in a spirit of expansion and

וְהַיְינוּ כְּשֶׁהֵן בִּבְחִינַת מִדּוֹת לְבַדָּן.

when they are in their pure **state** as emotive **attributes.**

When do these two attributes contradict each other? When these attributes are not exposed to the enlightenment of the intellect that gives rise to them, when they are restricted to a completely emotional reality, then they are uncompromising opposites. Intellects can understand other intellects. They can communicate and, in a certain sense, accept each other's existence. But between one disparate emotion and another, emotions such as love and fear, there can be no compromise. There can be no connection between them where they are able to act as a single unit.

אַךְ הַקָּדוֹשׁ בָּרוּךְ הוּא עוֹשֶׂה שָׁלוֹם בֵּינֵיהֶם, דְּהַיְינוּ עַל יְדֵי גִילּוּי שֶׁמִּתְגַּלֶּה בָּהֶן הֶאָרָה רַבָּה וְהַשְׁפָּעָה עֲצוּמָה מְאֹד מֵאוֹר אֵין סוֹף בָּרוּךְ הוּא.

But the Holy One, blessed by He, makes peace between them by means of a revelation, where a great illumination and an extremely immense flow from the light of *Ein Sof,* blessed be He, is manifest in them. 6 Elul (leap year)

The peace established by God does not entail only the prevention of conflict. In order for water and fire not to extinguish each other, it would suffice to give each one its own space and limit each to its own realm and role. This is often done in politics, as well as in other areas: The parties are separated to the point that they cannot come in contact with each other and do each other harm. Yet the peace that God brings about is almost the opposite: Instead of separating them, He joins the opposites together, in peace and in a single wholeness. ☞

giving, while another does everything in a spirit of constriction and precision. One person is extravagant, giving beyond the usual bounds, while another is frugal, giving only as necessary.

PEACE THROUGH REVELATION

☞ An ordinary joining of opposites is achieved by eliminating and neutralizing the contrasts between them. Each of the different sides refrains from expressing itself in its uniqueness and exclusivity, and thus there is "peace" between them. Such

אֲשֶׁר כִּשְׁמוֹ כֵּן הוּא, שֶׁאֵינוֹ בִּבְחִינַת מִדָּה, חַס וְשָׁלוֹם.

True to His name, the light of *Ein Sof* **is without measure, God forbid.**

The author comments here on the term "the light of *Ein Sof*," which is associated with that name, the Infinite One, because it is infinite, unlimited, indefinite, and cannot be measured at all. Thus one cannot speak of it in terms of justice or kindness, *Gevura* or *Ḥesed*.

The author of the *Tanya*'s addition of the phrase "God forbid" comes to emphasize the severity of even raising the possibility of speaking about *Ein Sof* in terms of any designation or unit of measure. There are certain things that may not make sense when you think about them, but one can resonate with them at a certain level. There are other things, like attributing limits to *Ein Sof*, where the very utterance, even as a possibility that is rejected, is shocking. ☞

peace, which is built on breaking apart the parties who had been quarreling with each other, is also found in a cemetery. After all, those who lie in the ground are no longer fighting with each other. But here we are dealing with peace in life, and such peace is built not on breaking apart the opposing parties, but on harmony. It takes into account the tension that exists between the opposites, yet a stronger essence imposes itself on the opposites so that the opposing attributes become equal. This essence before which everything becomes equal is the essence of *Ein Sof*. Before *Ein Sof* there is no big or small, no right or left. In its shadow, all are at peace.

WITHOUT MEASURE

☞ When we talk about a particular thing, describing it and giving it a name, we also say that it is not the opposite. Every statement, no matter how positive and exaggerated, also includes within it a certain limitation. In light of this, nothing can be said about God. In the Talmud, it is related that a particular individual descended before the ark as prayer leader in the presence of Rabbi Ḥanina and praised God with the words "God, the great, mighty, awesome, powerful, mighty, awe-inspiring, strong, fearless, steadfast, and honored." Rabbi Ḥanina waited for him to complete his prayer and then rebuked him: "Have you concluded all the praises of your Master? Even concerning the three praises that we recite, 'the great, mighty, and awesome,' had Moses our teacher not said them in the Torah and had the members of the Great Assembly not come and incorporated them into the *Amida* prayer, we would not be permitted to recite them" (*Berakhot* 33b).

When we say that God is "great, mighty, and awesome," it is not because that is all there is to say about God, but because that is what we are permitted to say about God. In truth, even that He is "great, might, and awesome" is impossible to say.

If we had to turn to God properly, then "for You, silence is praise" (Ps. 65:2). But

אֶלָּא לְמַעְלָה מַעְלָה עַד אֵין קֵץ, אֲפִילּוּ מִבְּחִינַת חָכְמָה בִּינָה וָדַעַת, מְקוֹר הַמִּדּוֹת.

Rather, the light of *Ein Sof* **is infinitely above and beyond** the realm of divine attributes, **even the attributes of *Ḥokhma, Bina,* and *Da'at,* the source of the** emotive **attributes.**

The light of *Ein Sof* is a supernal illumination, above and beyond the confines of reality that are characterized through the emotive attributes, and even above the source of those attributes.

These attributes, the primary ones being *Ḥesed* and *Gevura,* are the attributes through which God relates to the world, and therefore they are the attributes and dimensions through which our world operates. *Ḥokhma, Bina,* and *Da'at* are the source of the attributes and the hidden source of our reality. Yet even *Ḥokhma, Bina,* and Da'at, while they are the source of the attributes, have limitations. The author of the *Tanya,* then, adds that the light of *Ein Sof* is above even *Ḥokhma, Bina,* and *Da'at* to emphasize that in no sense whatsoever does it have a limit or measure.

וַאֲזַי הַמִּדּוֹת נֶגְדִּיּוֹת שֶׁל מִיכָאֵל וְגַבְרִיאֵל נִכְלָלוֹת בִּמְקוֹרָן וְשָׁרְשָׁן וְהָיוּ לַאֲחָדִים מַמָּשׁ, וּבְטֵלִים בְּאוֹרוֹ יִתְבָּרֵךְ הַמֵּאִיר לָהֶם בִּבְחִינַת גִּילּוּי,

Then, when the light of *Ein Sof* is manifest in them, **these contradictory attributes of Michael and Gabriel are encompassed in their source and root and become truly unified and subsumed in God's light, which illuminates them in a revealed manner,**

When the illumination that is above even the source and essence of the attributes becomes manifest, all the attributes are subsumed and

because we want to pray, and because we have been granted permission to do so, we say what we have been permitted to say. It is like a young child who does not yet talk and cannot even say "Father" or "Daddy." Even when he makes some unidentifiable sounds, his father is pleased, because he loves him. The same is true with us. Though essentially we have no appropriate words with which to praise God, we pray and say what we have been taught to say: "the great, mighty, and awesome."

they become one essence, as they were originally in the divine unity, before they were manifest and activated in the world.

Making peace, then, entails increasing the illumination that will bring things, and even push them, to their point of origin. This is also a description of the end of days, when "nation will not lift sword against nation" (Isa. 2:4). This will happen, not because people will be smarter or more cowardly, but because of the increase in illumination, when "all flesh will see together that the mouth of the Lord has spoken" (Isa. 40:5), when all essences will be brought together to the point that the differences and contrasts between them will no longer establish the essence of the relationship between them. ☞

THE ESSENCE OF THE ATTRIBUTES AND THEIR SOURCE

☞ This can be compared to a king who has many ministers who, both because of their nature and because of their office, are constantly quarreling. This is not necessarily a personal rivalry but rather a controversy over the way the kingdom should be run. The minister in charge of war has a different point of view from that of the minister in charge of education. The minister in charge of the treasury sees things differently from the minister in charge of taxes. All this is true when they are alone in their offices. Then they are in a constant debate that seemingly has no solution. Yet when the king enters, they all kneel down and prostrate themselves before him. They forget their disagreements and suddenly discover that there is no opposition among them, that the way to run the kingdom consists of all the approaches and wishes that they promote.

When the king enters, they are brought back to their source and root, as it were. They return to the root and essence of their role, which is to do the king's will. They realize that their job is not to promote their own character and interests, but to serve the king and fulfill his wishes.

The same is true of each of the attributes. When it reveals its source and root, the attribute reveals the inner experience, the inner desire within it. Even though each attribute has a different manner of manifesting itself, the differences between the attributes and their various manifestations become meaningless with the revelation of each one's inner essence.

All created entities in the world, whether spiritual or material, have undergone a certain process of evolution from a simple nucleus. As the relationship between the inside and the outside becomes more distant, a greater multiplicity of forms and subforms comes into being. As things return to their original source, they become simpler, gradually losing the differences between them, and refocusing on the inner point. The basic components are the same, and as one ascends to higher degrees of abstraction, one finds that the fundamental components are more and more uniform, until one reaches the one fundamental component in which the differences become insignificant.

A similar phenomenon is found in the

וְאָז מִתְמַזְּגִים וּמִתְמַתְּקִים הַגְּבוּרוֹת בַּחֲסָדִים

and then the aspects of *Gevura*, the restraining forces, **are tempered and sweetened by the aspects of *Ḥesed*,** the quality of kindness,

When things return to the source in a way that there is no more conflict between them, they may stop functioning entirely. The angel Michael and the angel Gabriel no longer act like one or the other; they are silent. The problem here is not how to silence things absolutely, but how to bring them to operate in a way that they do not act against each other but with each other. To do this, there must be a fusion between the attributes, *Ḥesed* and *Gevura*, in such a way that the restraining forces are sweetened by the forces of kindness. *Gevura* is harsh. It cuts things in a sharp, hard, and not always pleasant manner. The fusion with *Ḥesed* sweetens the *Gevura*, causing it to lean toward the side of *Ḥesed* in such a way that it is clear that the cutting and limiting are deliberate and for good. The moment a person understands that the challenge he is undergoing is for his own good, the harsh experience and the suffering are mitigated. ☞

material world: The finite forms of things are the same at their source. There is a big difference between a piece of wood and refined gasoline, but fundamentally they are both composed of carbon. The way by which different materials become joined is similar to what was said here: One should strive to find the fundamental components of each of the materials, and thus try to connect them with each other, to see their common denominators. Only there is it possible to combine them and create a new essence that will encompass and express the two contrasting essences.

In one of the central chapters of *Likkutei Amarim*, which deals with the love of a fellow Jew (chap. 32), the same idea is found with regard to souls. People may hate each other as long as they are far from the source, but the closer they come to the source, and the more meaningful the soul and the source of the soul are to them, the more hate and separation are impossible, and the love becomes more real and intense.

TEMPERED AND SWEETENED

☞ Why does the fusion involve sweetening *Gevura* with *Ḥesed*? One explanation is connected to the essence of the attribute of compassion, which fuses the two, but "leans toward *Ḥesed*," as will be explained below. Yet there is also a more comprehensive explanation, which is part of a broader issue, of defining the world of rectification as op-

עַל יְדֵי בְּחִינָה מְמוּצַּעַת, קַו הַמַּכְרִיעַ וּמַטֶּה כְּלַפֵּי חֶסֶד, הִיא מִדַּת הָרַחֲמִים,

through an intermediating force, the determining factor between the attributes that leans toward *Ḥesed*. This intermediating force **is the attribute of compassion,**

When these two attributes, *Ḥesed* and *Gevura*, touch each other, not in rivalry but in harmony, they reveal a new, intermediating attribute, the attribute of compassion. This attribute is essentially a synthesis of *Ḥesed* and *Gevura*, but as emphasized here, it is the determining factor, which does not stand precisely in the middle but rather leans toward *Ḥesed*. ☞ ☞

הַנִּקְרֵאת בְּשֵׁם 'תִּפְאֶרֶת', בְּדִבְרֵי חַכְמֵי הָאֱמֶת,

which is called *Tiferet* in the words of the scholars of truth, the scholars of Kabbala,

posed to the world of chaos. The world of chaos is the world that preceded our world, the world that was and no longer exists, after its infrastructure collapsed. The essence of the world of chaos, also called the world of *nekudim*, or points, is that the attributes were manifest as isolated, point-like vessels, without interaction. It emerged from the realm of unity that could hold things together, the world of *akudim*, or binding, but did not attain a new state of unity. This situation, in which opposites are unable to reach a state of completion or fusion, cannot endure, and it collapses. Attributes that do not limit each other, that exist in their ultimate perfection and purity without any compromises, cannot exist in a world that is inherently limited. Unlimited giving, just like unbounded restraint, can be dangerous, and even fatal. This was the world of chaos, and so it collapsed.

Something similar can be seen in young children. In children, the attributes have not yet been tempered by each other. The fundamental impulses are unadulterated and unambiguous. This is why people avoid giving young children small animals to play with. Because of their excessive love for them, they are liable to harm them.

The world of rectification is, fundamentally, our world, the world that is constantly rectifying its reality. In the world of rectification, every force has attributes that limit it. Every instance of justice has a limitation beyond which it must not be stretched. Every expression of love has a restriction to ensure that the beloved does not suffocate. In the world of rectification, there are no pure attributes, but rather each attribute is some fusion of all the attributes within it. There is *Ḥesed* in *Gevura*, and *Gevura* in *Ḥesed*, and so on. By contrast, the world of chaos is a world of justice, in which the forces contained therein are totally separated from each other, where the boundary between them cannot be crossed, and each of them is stretched without limit. In the world of rectification, where there is a fusion of the attributes, *Gevura* is tempered and sweetened by *Ḥesed*.

THE INTERMEDIATING ATTRIBUTE

☞ The three attributes of *Ḥesed*, *Gevura*, and *Tiferet* are arranged as a triangle of thesis, antithesis, and synthesis. As stated in *Pataḥ Eliyahu* (the introduction to *Tikkunei Zohar* 17a), "One is long, one is short, and one is medium." The third attribute does not only stand in the middle in the sense that it is not as extreme as the first or the second, simply because it is unable to reach one of the sides. Between giving too much and not giving anything, one can give a little, but this little, as a middle ground, can be flawed in both directions. One who needs a lot may receive too little, and one who needs nothing may receive too much.

The Kotzker Rebbe was once asked about such a middle ground: Why was he so extreme? The Rebbe took the questioner to a window that overlooked the street and said, "See, people walk on the right side and on the left side of the street. Only horses walk down the middle!" Such a middle ground is for people who cannot decide which side to walk on.

The attribute of compassion is not just a midline. It is an additional attribute that contains within it the two attributes of *Ḥesed* and *Gevura* in a kind of synthesis that reveals a reality that is beyond the two and therefore encompasses them both together.

LEANING TOWARD *ḤESED*

☞ The attribute of *Ḥesed* entails giving to all, while *Gevura* entails giving only to those who are deserving. The attribute of compassion, on the other hand, entails giving to those in need. The one who gives out of kindness gives, not because the recipient needs it, but because the benefactor wishes to give. A person who welcomes guests welcomes anyone, rich or poor, respectable or disreputable, and he gives them all to eat and drink (see, e.g., Rashi, Gen. 18:1, regarding Abraham; *Bereshit Rabba* 54:6; *Likkutei Siḥot*, vol. 23, p. 770).

Giving based on the attribute of restraint is limited to those to whom the benefactor is obligated to give. He gives to his wife and children, because he is obligated to provide for them. But to one to whom he has no obligation, he does not give. Not that he gives nothing at all, but even charity he gives only as he is required, only as much the recipient deserves, and nothing more.

The attribute of compassion entails giving to those who need it. This means giving even to those who are undeserving, and even beyond the limit and obligation, when that is necessary. On the contrary, since the attribute of compassion relates to what the other person needs, it is unlimited giving in an even deeper sense. Any limitation that exists is on the part of the recipient, but on the part of the giver there is no limitation whatsoever. For this reason, because there is in the attribute of compassion aspects of giving and expansion that is not found even in the attribute of *Ḥesed* itself, the author of the *Tanya* tells us that this attribute "leans toward *Ḥesed*."

Though the kabbalists identify the attribute of compassion with that of *Tiferet*,[17] the latter is not a synonym for the attribute of compassion but rather has implications of his own. The connection between *Tiferet* and compassion is a deep connection that denotes additional meanings and facets, as will be explained below.

לְפִי שֶׁהִיא כְּלוּלָה מִ־ב׳ גְּוָונִין, לוֹבֶן וְאוֹדֶם, הַמְרַמְּזִים לְחֶסֶד וּגְבוּרָה.

for it is comprised of two colors, white and red, which allude to *Ḥesed* and *Gevura*.

The name *Tiferet* adds to the attribute of compassion the facet of beauty and harmony.[18] Harmony is never comprised of only one variety, one type, or one essence. It is always the product of a harmonious combination of opposite, or at least different, elements, whether sounds, colors, shapes, or mental processes. When in harmonious combination, the opposites do not contradict each other, nor do they cancel each other out, but rather they strengthen and beautify one another and act in complementary fashion as one essence toward one goal.

וְלָכֵן סְתָם שֵׁם הֲוָיָ״ה בָּרוּךְ הוּא שֶׁבְּכָל הַתּוֹרָה מוֹרֶה עַל מִדַּת הַתִּפְאֶרֶת, כְּמוֹ שֶׁכָּתוּב בַּזּוֹהַר הַקָּדוֹשׁ (חלק ג יא, א),

Therefore, generally, the blessed name of *Havaya* as it appears **throughout the Torah represents the attribute of *Tiferet*, as stated in the holy *Zohar*** (3:11a),

As is explained in several places,[19] the names of God relate to the *sefirot*: the name *El* to the attribute of *Ḥesed*, the name *Elokim* to the attribute of *Gevura*, the name of *Havaya* to the attribute of *Tiferet*, and so on.[20] Elsewhere,[21] it is noted that the name of *Havaya* is unique among the divine names in that apart from its association with the *sefira* of

---

17. *Pardes Rimmonim, Sha'ar Arkhei HaKinuyim*, chap. 20; *Me'orei Or*, s.v. "*raḥamim*."
18. See *Pardes Rimmonim, Sha'ar HaGevanim*, chap. 4.
19. See *Torah Or* 10b; *Likkutei Torah*, Lev. 23c.
20. These refer to the seven names of God that may not be erased. See *Shevuot* 35b; Rambam, *Mishneh Torah, Sefer HaMadda, Hilkhot Yesodei HaTorah* 6:2, *Shulḥan Arukh, Yoreh De'a* 276:9.
21. *Torah Or* 60a; *Likkutei Torah*, additions to Lev. 51c; *Derekh Mitzvotekha, Shoresh Mitzvat HaTefilla*; see also *Bati LeGani* (5721).

Tiferet, it is also the essence of all the divine names. It is the name that expresses the essence itself, as opposed to the attributes through which the Divine is expressed.[22] In other words, it expresses the light that is enclothed in the vessels of the *sefirot*, while the other names represent the attributes or vessels that contain that light.[23] Therefore, the name of *Havaya* is found in combination with other divine names, such as *Havaya Elokim* and *Havaya Tzevakot*, which together give expression to the combination of light and vessel. But when the name of *Havaya* appears alone, without another divine name, it represents the light and its own unique vessel, the *sefira* of *Tiferet*.

לְפִי שֶׁכָּאן הוּא בְּחִינַת גִּילּוּי אוֹר אֵין סוֹף בָּרוּךְ הוּא, הֶאָרָה רַבָּה בְּיֶתֶר שְׂאֵת מִשְּׁאָר מִדּוֹתָיו הַקְּדוֹשׁוֹת יִתְבָּרַךְ.

because here, within the attribute of *Tiferet,* **the light of *Ein Sof,* blessed be He, is manifest with a great illumination in a greater magnitude than the rest of God's holy attributes.**

What is unique about the *sefira* of *Tiferet* is that it reveals within it a light that is greater and deeper than that of the other attributes. As explained above, in order for something to truly mediate between different sides, it must be greater and more inclusive than either one of them. It must stem from the root that preceded the contrasts, from the place where they are still one. In a certain sense, the light must not only be greater, but also without limitations, so that its illumination negates all boundaries.

וְהִנֵּה אִתְעָרוּתָא דִּלְעֵילָּא לְעוֹרֵר גִּילּוּי הֶאָרָה רַבָּה וְהַשְׁפָּעָה עֲצוּמָה, הַנִּזְכָּר לְעֵיל, מֵאוֹר אֵין סוֹף בָּרוּךְ הוּא, לַעֲשׂוֹת שָׁלוֹם הַנִּזְכָּר לְעֵיל הִיא בְּאִתְעָרוּתָא דִּלְתַתָּא,

9 Elul
7 Elul (leap year)

The awakening from above, which evokes the aforementioned great illumination and immense flow from the light of *Ein Sof* to make the aforementioned peace between the attributes of *Ḥesed* and *Gevura,* is caused **by the awakening from below,**

22. See *Pardes Rimmonim, Sha'ar Shem Ben Dalet*, chap. 1.
23. See *Bati LeGani* (5721), chaps. 4–5.

To make peace between the heavenly attributes, there must be an awakening of the light of *Ein Sof* from above, which will effect that peace. The awakening from above, in turn, depends on an awakening from below. The awakening from above comes from far above, from the Creator Himself, the primary source, while the awakening from below comes from man who inhabits in this world and performs his service down here below. This is not service performed through heavenly forces, but with his own limited human power. Why is this the case? It is because this is what the supernal will desires, that the lowly agent below should awaken the great light, the true Agent above. Small as he may be, making almost no difference in his own space, man has great impact, provided that his actions emulate the divine attributes that flow from above.

בְּמַעֲשֵׂה הַצְּדָקָה וְהַשְׁפָּעַת חַיִּים חֵן וָחֶסֶד וְרַחֲמִים, לְמַאן דְּלֵית לֵיהּ מִגַּרְמֵיהּ כְּלוּם וּלְהַחֲיוֹת רוּחַ שְׁפָלִים כו'.

through the act of charity and the bestowal of life, graciousness, kindness, and compassion to one who has nothing of his own, reviving the spirit of the lowly and the heart of the downtrodden.

The awakening from below that brings about peace above comes about through charity and through "the bestowal of life, graciousness, kindness, and compassion."[24] The act of charity involves not only giving money, but also entails kindness and compassion, both with respect to the manner in which the money is given and also as an expression of those feelings in themselves, because sometimes a person needs kindness and compassion no less than he needs the money.

As stated above, the vessel that makes peace is the attribute of compassion, and in order to awaken compassion from above, one must express the attribute of compassion below. One must give to the person who has nothing, because he is lowly and downtrodden. This is the essence of compassion. When a person shows compassion below,

24. The Lubavitcher Rebbe, Rabbi Menaḥem Mendel Schneerson, points out that this phrase originates from the *Sim Shalom* blessing in the *Amida* prayer because the essence of the awakening below is to establish peace. See also epistle 30 below.

he is shown compassion above. This is what the Sages say regarding the verse "And He will give you mercy and be merciful to you" (Deut. 13:18): that God gives you the attribute of mercy, and when you use it, He will have compassion on you.[25]

וּמוּדַעַת זֹאת מַה שֶּׁאָמְרוּ רַבּוֹתֵינוּ זִכְרוֹנָם לִבְרָכָה, עַל הָעוֹסֵק בַּתּוֹרָה לִשְׁמָהּ: מֵשִׂים שָׁלוֹם בְּפָמַלְיָא שֶׁל מַעְלָה וּבְפָמַלְיָא שֶׁל מַטָּה (סנהדרין צט, ב).

It is well known that our Sages state concerning one who studies Torah for its own sake, "He introduces peace into the heavenly **entourage above and into the** earthly **entourage below"** (*Sanhedrin* 99b).

Another way of bringing down this supernal attribute of compassion and *Tiferet* is through Torah study, which also expresses the attribute of *Tiferet*.[26] According to our Rabbis, studying Torah for its own sake draws illumination from the light of *Ein Sof*, making peace among the heavenly entourage and among the earthly entourage.[27] This entourage is a system of forces that contains opposites, such as left and right. For the system to operate properly, there must be peace between its constituent elements. There is such a system at the root of things that is hidden above, and there is such a system below. ☞

THE HEAVENLY ENTOURAGE ABOVE AND THE EARTHLY ENTOURAGE BELOW

☞ Within man as well, there are two such systems. One example of the relationship between the two systems is the relationship between body and soul: The entourage above is the soul, and the entourage below is the body. This is the way the Ba'al Shem Tov explained how he healed the sick where other doctors failed. He healed "the entourage above," the system of the divine soul and its connection to God, and in that way the entourage below, the mental and physical system, also healed.

25. See *Shabbat* 151b; *Sifrei*, Deut. 96.
26. See *Berakhot* 58a.
27. See also *Likkutei Torah*, Num. 83a, 86d.

'פְּמַלְיָא שֶׁל מַעְלָה' - הֵם הַשָּׂרִים וְהַמִּדּוֹת הַנִּזְכָּרִים לְעֵיל, שֶׁהֵן הַהֵיכָלוֹת עֶלְיוֹנִים בְּעוֹלַם הַבְּרִיאָה שֶׁבַּזֹּהַר הַקָּדוֹשׁ, 'וּפַמַלְיָא שֶׁל מַטָּה' - הֵן הַהֵיכָלוֹת הַתַּחְתּוֹנִים,

The "entourage above" comprises the aforementioned heavenly **and** divine **attributes, which are the supernal chambers in the world of *Beria* that are** mentioned **in the holy *Zohar*. The "entourage below" comprises the lower chambers** found in the lower worlds,

The entourage above refers to the heavenly ministers, Michael and Gabriel, who are mentioned in the talmudic passage cited above along with their attributes. In the *Zohar*, it is further explained that they are the heavenly chambers in the world of *Beria*.

The entourage below are the lower chambers found in the lower worlds of *Yetzira* and *Asiya*. It consists not only of our material world, but also of various spiritual worlds that relate to it. The entourage below, of the lower chambers, is defined by the fact that they are derivative chambers that stand below the supernal chambers and are in the position of recipients in relation to the supernal chambers above them.

וּבִפְרָט עוֹלָם הַזֶּה הַשָּׁפָל, הַמְעוֹרָב טוֹב וָרַע מֵחֵטְא אָדָם הָרִאשׁוֹן

particularly this lowly physical **world, which, since Adam's sin, is** comprised of both **good and evil intermingled** together,

The essential definition of this world is not its being a material world or connected to a material world, nor is it at all dependent on the dimensions of space and time, but on a unique phenomenon that exists in this world and does not exist in any other world: the intermingling of good and evil.[28]

This intermingling of good and evil exists since the time of Adam's sin. Adam's sin did not create evil, but rather it created the mixture of good and evil in this world so that they are no longer distinct from each other. ☞

---

28. See *Torah Or* 5c.

וְהָרַע שׁוֹלֵט עַל הַטּוֹב, with the evil dominating the good,

In this world, the mixture of good and evil is not even, but rather the evil dominates and prevails over the good. From the time that good and evil became intermingled, evil has had a certain advantage in its ability to triumph over good. When a righteous and a wicked man, meet, it is the nature of this world that the evil man has the advantage.

In the book of Ecclesiastes, there is a parable about "a small city, but few men in it, and a great king came against it and surrounded it, and built great siege works against it. A poor and wise man was found in it, and he saved the city in his wisdom" (Eccles. 9:14–15). The "great king" is the evil inclination, and the "poor and wise man" is the good inclination.[29] This is the relationship between them when they meet in

THE INTERMINGLING OF GOOD AND EVIL

☞ It can be said that God created a world of possibilities, and at a certain stage, when he sinned, Adam (and mankind in general) chose this form of the world to live in. From that moment, there is no good in this world that does not contain some trace of evil, and there is no evil without some aspect of good. Good and evil overlap and are interwoven with each other, to the point that at times it is impossible to determine which of the two is greater. What this means for us relates primarily to the matter of choice. Before the sin, the main difficulty was choosing between good and evil. Now the difficulty lies in recognizing what is good and what is evil. Good and evil are not situated in their own corners, and there are no signs to guide us as to what defines good and what entails evil. They are intermingled, and even resemble each other.

Were good and evil separate and distinct, good would have all the virtues and evil all the flaws, but instead what is good is not necessarily beautiful and what tastes good may be harmful. The same is true of people. There is almost no one who is totally good, just as there is almost no one who is totally evil. The mixture is so deep that not only do others not know where is the good and where is the evil, but one cannot even be sure what is good and what is evil within himself.

Regarding this, the last prophet, Malachi, said after the exile to Babylonia, "You will return and see the difference between the righteous and the wicked, between one who serves God and one who does not serve Him" (Mal. 3:18). In other words, one must look again and again (implied by the words "return and see") to be able to discern who is righteous and who is wicked, what is good and what is evil.

29. See *Nedarim* 32b.

the "small city," in this world: the "poor man" as opposed to the "great king," with the advantage that a king has over a poor man.

Elsewhere, the Talmud says that were God not there to help him, man would not be able to overcome the evil inclination.[30] Were the matter to depend only on the balance of natural forces, the evil inclination would prevail. ☞

כְּמוֹ שֶׁכָּתוּב: "אֲשֶׁר שָׁלַט הָאָדָם בְּאָדָם כו'" (קהלת ח, ט), "וּלְאוֹם מִלְאוֹם יֶאֱמָץ" (בראשית כה, כג).

as it is written, "Whenever man controlled man, it was to his detriment" (Eccles. 8:9), **and "One nation will prevail over the other nation"** (Gen. 25:23).

When the "man of *kelippa*" controls the "man of holiness," it is ultimately "to his detriment" – to the detriment of the man who is on the side of *kelippa*. Nevertheless, this situation of *kelippa* prevailing over holiness is the reality of our lower world, in which evil is intermingled with good and can prevail over it.[31]

The verse from Genesis, "One nation will prevail over the other nation," refers to the struggle between Jacob and Esau. As explained

THE IMPURE INTO THE HANDS OF THE PURE

☞ In the *Al HaNissim* prayer that is recited on Hanukkah, we say, "You delivered the mighty into the hands of the weak, the many into the hands of the few, the impure into the hands of the pure, the wicked into the hands of the righteous, and the wanton sinners into the hands of those who occupy themselves with your Torah." "The mighty into the hands of the weak" is indeed a miracle; but what is the miracle inherent in God delivering "the wicked into the hands of the righteous" and "the impure into the hands of the pure"? The answer is that the wicked have many advantages. They are prepared to use any means to achieve their ends. They have no inhibitions and do what the righteous cannot and are unwilling to do. For this reason, in the material struggle between them, where there is no distinction between good and evil, the wicked man has a fundamental advantage. If nonetheless the good and the righteous emerge on top, it is a miracle.

---

30. *Kiddushin* 30b.

31. See epistle 25 below, which states that this is the mystical understanding of the exile of the Divine Presence. See also *Torah Or* 6a.

in *Likkutei Amarim*,[32] this verse also speaks of an internal battle within a person, between his divine soul and his animal soul, between good and evil.

וְכַנִּרְאֶה בְּחוּשׁ בָּאָדָם הַתַּחְתּוֹן הַנִּקְרָא בְּשֵׁם 'עוֹלָם קָטָן', שֶׁלִּפְעָמִים הַטּוֹב גּוֹבֵר וְלִפְעָמִים לְהֵיפֶךְ, חַס וְשָׁלוֹם,

We see this empirically in mortal man, who is called a miniature world, where sometimes the good within him **prevails and sometimes the opposite, God forbid.**

Man is a microcosm, encompassing within him the entire world.[33] In order to know and understand what is happening in the world at large, both in the material world and even more so in the spiritual worlds, a person can look inside himself and see there what is contained in the worlds: which forces are at work, how they relate to each other, what is their purpose and significance. The advantage that the small world has over the larger world is that we know the small world from within ourselves, by way of our senses, directly and not through intermediaries.

וְאֵין שָׁלוֹם בָּעוֹלָם עַד עֵת קֵץ,

Therefore, **there is no peace in the world until the end of time,**

Both in man and in the world, the duality of good and evil is part and parcel of the basic structure of reality. Therefore, true and essential reconciliation is impossible within reality as it is. Only at the end of days, after time and the reality of this world will be over, when the entire structure of reality will change, will peace also come to the world.

שֶׁיִּתְבָּרֵר הַטּוֹב מֵהָרַע לִידָּבֵק בְּשָׁרְשׁוֹ וּמְקוֹרוֹ מְקוֹר הַחַיִּים בָּרוּךְ הוּא. וַאֲזַי יִתְפָּרְדוּ כָּל פּוֹעֲלֵי אָוֶן וְרוּחַ הַטּוּמְאָה יַעֲבוֹר מִן הָאָרֶץ, כְּשֶׁיִּתְבָּרֵר מִתּוֹכוֹ

when the good will be extracted from the evil to become attached to its root and source, the source of life, blessed be He. Then all evildoers will be scattered, and

32. Chap. 12.

33. *Midrash Tanḥuma, Pekudei* 3; *Tikkunei Zohar* 100a.

בְּחִינַת הַטּוֹב הַמְחַיֵּיהוּ.

the spirit of impurity will be removed from the earth, when the element of good that gives life to the spirit of impurity **will be extracted from it.**

The problem of this world is the intermingling of good and evil, and therefore the world's rectification will involve the extraction and separation of good from evil. What will happen after the extraction? The good will rise and become attached to its root and source, God, the source of life. As for evil, all the evildoers will be scattered, and the spirit of impurity will be removed from the earth,[34] because the element of truth that sustains that spirit of impurity will be extracted from it. Evil, the spirit of impurity, sucks all its life and existence from the good that is intermingled with it. But at the end of days, when all good will be extracted from it, and the good will be absolutely extracted from the evil, the very existence of evil will be obliterated from the earth.

In order for transgression to exist, for a person to commit sin, it must have an aspect of good. If non-kosher food were not tasty, no one would eat it, and the same is true of other offenses. To the good side belong all the good things: beauty, grace, pleasantness, and purpose. To the bad side belong all the other things. But in our reality, they are intermingled. This intermingling, which began with the tree of the knowledge of good and evil, is the life force of all evil in the world, and when the work of extraction and separation between them is complete, the existence of evil in the world will also come to an end. ☞

WHEN EVIL WILL BE REMOVED FROM THE EARTH

☞ As was stated above, the essence of evil in itself is one of absence, defect, and negation. If so, how does it exist? The answer is that it exists because it is always intermingled with good. Evil sucks on the good, taking crumbs from it and using them by distorting them until the life force in them goes to the evil instead of the good so that it may grow and become stronger. Were it possible to isolate the evil and extract the good from it, there would be no further need to wage war against it, since it would die out by itself.

Consider a parasite, which has no capacity for an independent existence. A virus has no existence of its own but ex-

34. Based on Ps. 92:10 and Zech. 13:2.

8 Elul (leap year)

וּבֵירוּר זֶה יִהְיֶה גַּם כֵּן עַל יְדֵי גִּילּוּי אֱלֹקוּתוֹ לְמַטָּה בְּהֶאָרָה רַבָּה וְהַשְׁפָּעָה עֲצוּמָה. כְּמוֹ שֶׁכָּתוּב: "כִּי מָלְאָה הָאָרֶץ דֵּעָה אֶת ה'" (ישעיה יא, ט), "וְנִגְלָה כְּבוֹד ה' כו'" (שם מ, ה).

This extraction of good from evil at the end time **will likewise be caused by the manifestation of the Divine below with a great illumination and an immense flow** of divine light, **as it is written, "For the earth will be filled with knowledge of the Lord"** (Isa. 11:9), **and "The glory of the Lord will be revealed** and all flesh will see together that the mouth of the Lord has spoken" (Isa. 40:5).

The complete and absolute extraction of good from evil can occur only through a great and immense revelation of the Divine beyond all that is usually revealed in the world. When the great light shines, it draws into it all the smaller lights, as depicted by the well-known parable of the candle flame that is extinguished by the flame of a great fire. When "the glory of the Lord will be revealed," all the sparks and bits of holiness will be drawn out from where they can be found in the husks of impurity and concealment, in the materiality and vitality of the mundane, and they will ascend and cling to Him. At that moment, evil will be completely abolished and will no longer be able to exist.

This revelation, which clarifies the good from the evil, will create peace in the world, when all the divisions and chasms in the world will merge and complete each other. This is why this illumination is called a

ists only within the living cell to which it has attached itself. There it lives, grows, and reproduces, and from the moment it is removed from the living cell it no longer exists.

Another example from an altogether different field: Let us imagine a situation in which no one is prepared to buy stolen goods from a thief. In that case, thieves could not exist. The thief lives by virtue of the fact that there is someone who is willing to buy from him, and someone else is prepared to buy from the person who bought from the thief, and so on. Were it possible to cut the underworld's chain of existence from the legitimate economy, the underworld and everything connected to it would cease to exist and there would be no need to wage war against it (see *Gittin* 45a).

Evil is like a lie. An absolute lie, which contains nothing of the truth, cannot exist in reality. The lie itself is a negation of reality, and in order for it to exist, it must contain elements of truth. A falsehood that endures merely changes the relationship between the given elements and distorts the connections between them, but it does not create a new reality that is entirely false.

"tabernacle of peace."[35] Like a *sukka*, or tabernacle, this revelation will cover and surround the world to the point that all aspects of reality will become subsumed in it, and all the divisions and contrasts between them will be eliminated.

וְזֶהוּ בִּכְלָלוּת הָעוֹלָם לֶעָתִיד, **This applies to world in general** and its state **in the future,**

With respect to the world as a whole, this process of extraction will reach completion only in the future, at the end of time, when the service of all generations will come to its conclusion.

אַךְ בָּאָדָם הַתַּחְתּוֹן בְּכָל עֵת מְצוֹא, זוֹ תְּפִלָּה, **but with regard to mortal man, at every auspicious time, which is** during the time of **prayer,**

Every person is a microcosm, which contains not only the geography and zoology of the larger world but also its history. Every person contains within him the events of the past, such as the exile in Egypt and the exodus, as well as the future events of the great revelation, when "the earth will be filled with knowledge of the Lord." These historical events do not manifest in their full force and full scope, as the exodus from Egypt was in its time and as the redemption will be in the future, but only partially, and within the human aspect that relates to it, and even then, only at certain times.

The author of the *Tanya* pinpoints such a time: Every person can merit experiencing the extraction of good from evil at an auspicious time, which refers to any time that man finds God, which is during times of prayer.[36] The time of prayer is a time of divine revelation and illumination that is reminiscent of the great revelation that will occur at the end of time. It is a time when the glory of God is revealed to a person, similar to the way it will be revealed in the future. The time of prayer, both on account of the time, which is a time fit for praying, and

35. In the *Hashkivenu* blessing of the *Arvit* prayer. See *Sefer HaMa'amarim Melukat*, vol. 1, p. 177, where this is explained.
36. See Ibn Ezra, Ps. 32:6; Jerusalem Talmud, *Berakhot* 4:1; *Bereshit Rabba* 92:2.

the act of prayer, is a time of clarity, when good is refined from evil and opposites will be reconciled with each other. ☞

אוֹ שְׁאָר עִתִּים מְזוּמָּנִים לְהִתְבּוֹדֵד עִם קוֹנוֹ,

or other times designated for secluding oneself with one's Maker,

A person can achieve such clarity, not only through prayer, but also in other ways. There is the path of seclusion, where a person turns away from everything and isolates himself with God. Such seclusion is not connected to any particular place, time, or action that the person performs, but only to the fact that he is occupied with nothing else, that he is found in his thoughts exclusively with God and he is not engaging in anything else that will interfere with the light of truth revealing itself in him.

כָּל אֶחָד לְפִי מַעֲשָׂיו זוֹכֶה לְמֵעֵין בֵּירוּר זֶה עַל יְדֵי עֵסֶק הַתּוֹרָה לִשְׁמָהּ,

every individual merits a semblance of this extraction of good from evil **in accordance with his deeds, through** the revelation that comes about through **Torah study for its own sake.**

AN AUSPICIOUS TIME

☞ The time of prayer is the time when a person unites with his Maker, when the concealments, hindrances, and internal battles disappear for a while from his consciousness. At such a time, the evil leaves a person for a moment, nothing bad fills his heart and mind, and he is capable of feeling a clarity that is, in fact, a taste of the future world within his present world.

The tzaddik Rabbi Chaim of Sanz had a crippled foot, apparently the result of a childhood wound that did not heal properly, and it caused him great torment. Once, when he was with the tzaddik Rabbi Naftali of Ropshitz, he prayed with great devotion, divesting himself of his materiality in his usual manner, and he broke into a dance. Rabbi Naftali's wife, who could not bear to see a tzaddik suffering, went to her righteous husband and said to him, "Why do you allow him to stomp on his ailing foot. Tell him at least to dance on his healthy foot."

"I would tell him," the tzaddik answered, "if he knew while he was praying on which foot he was stomping!"

When Rabbi Chaim prayed, everything disappeared. All suffering vanished and never even entered his thoughts.

Another way to experience the clarity resulting from the extraction of the good from the evil is through Torah study for its own sake. The essence of studying Torah for its own sake is that a person engages in something that is pure and clean, that illuminates all of reality with the clarity that is found within it. But if he studies Torah for other purposes, for his own interests, if he defiles the Torah itself, it will not bring him such clarity.

וְכֵן עַל יְדֵי הַצְּדָקָה, כְּמוֹ שֶׁאָמְרוּ (בבא בתרא י, א) רַבִּי אֶלְעָזָר יָהֵיב פְּרוּטָה לְעָנִי וַהֲדַר מְצַלֵּי, דִּכְתִיב: "אֲנִי בְּצֶדֶק אֶחֱזֶה פָנֶיךָ" (תהלים יז, טו).

Likewise, one may achieve such clarity **through charity, as** the Rabbis **stated** (*Bava Batra* 10a), **"Rabbi Elazar would** first **give a *peruta* to a poor person and** only **then** would he **pray.** He said: **As it is written, 'I will behold Your face through charity'** (Ps. 17:15)."

Yet another way to attain the clarity that can be arrived at through prayer is through the giving of charity.[37] Charity itself does not evoke a revelation of divine light, but it serves as a starting point from which one can go out to pray and reveal that light. This is a common Jewish practice, to give charity before prayer, as preparation and training for the revelation and transcendence of prayer.

This applies to any deed that does not require preparation, such as showing respect to the elderly, that it can serve as that initial spark, but it applies particularly to the act of giving charity. It is the nature of charity to open boundaries, whether between one person and another, or between one person's property and that of another, and when boundaries are opened below on earth, even just a little, they open above as well, to illuminate for him the lights of his portion of the World to Come already in this world. ☞

BREACHING BOUNDARIES THROUGH CHARITY

☞ The giving of charily must involve a substantial gift, something that is important to the person, something that he needs yet gives away as charity. Rabbi Elazar, the

37. See also Rambam, *Mishneh Torah, Sefer Zera'im, Hilkhot Mattenot Aniyim* 10:15; *Shulḥan Arukh, Yoreh De'a* 246:14, *Oraḥ Ḥayyim* 92:14.

הִיא בְּחִינַת גִּילּוּי הֶאָרָה וְהַשְׁפָּעַת הַדַּעַת וְהַתְּבוּנָה, לְהִתְבּוֹנֵן בִּגְדוּלַּת ה׳ וּלְהוֹלִיד מִזֶּה דְּחִילוּ וּרְחִימוּ שִׂכְלִיִּים כַּנּוֹדָע.

This revelation that a person experiences during prayer **is a manifest illumination and a flow of knowledge and understanding, so that one may contemplate God's greatness and generate from it an intellectual fear and love** of God, **as is known.**

The illumination that is revealed to a person while he is engaged in prayer is first and foremost an illumination of knowledge and understanding, of contemplating the greatness of God as it becomes manifest through contemplation of the worlds. As explained in many hasidic texts, this contemplation may give rise to an intellectual love and fear of God, to emotions that are connected to the contemplation of God's greatness and other subjects of contemplation and knowledge that develop from them.

וְעַל יְדֵי זֶה נִבְרָר הַטּוֹב לַה׳ וְנִפְרָד הָרַע,

Through this, the good is thereby extracted for God, while the evil is separated,

These feelings of love and fear serve to extract the good from the evil. The intellect alone cannot achieve this extraction by itself. It lacks the mental involvement in reality, the ability to operate within it. Neither can emotion alone achieve this extraction, since it cannot distinguish between good and evil, nor does it discern where the reality that one experiences in such a concrete manner is headed, what the next step will be, what direction it will take, what will lead to good and what will

Sage mentioned in the talmudic statement quoted above, was wretchedly poor, and therefore for him a gift of a *peruta* was a substantial gift. It is related about Rabbi Yaakov Yitzḥak of Peshisḥa that when his son fell ill and the situation was beyond despair, he asked his wife to give all that he owned to charity: his money, his house, his clothing, all his property. This is the essence of charity, that precisely when a person breaks boundaries, without any consideration for himself and his needs, the same is done for him from above.

lead to evil. Only through the intellectual fear and love of God can the good be extracted and separated from the evil. ☞

כְּמוֹ שֶׁכָּתוּב: "מַצְרֵף לַכֶּסֶף וְכוּר לַזָּהָב וְאִישׁ לְפִי מַהֲלָלוֹ" (משלי כז, כא), פֵּירוּשׁ לְפִי הִילּוּלוֹ אֶת ה', בְּעוֹמֶק הַדַּעַת לְהוֹלִיד דְּחִילוּ וּרְחִימוּ, כָּכָה נִבְרָר הַטּוֹב וְנִפְרָד הָרַע, כְּבֵירוּר וּפֵירוּד הַסִּיגִים מִכֶּסֶף וְזָהָב בְּמַצְרֵף וְכוּר.

as it is written, "The refining pot is for silver and the crucible for gold, and a man is according to his praise" (Prov. 27:21), **meaning, according to his praise of God** during prayer, by contemplating God's greatness **with the depths of the mind to generate fear and love** of God, **the good is thus extracted and the evil is separated, like the extraction and separation of dross from silver and gold through the refining pot and crucible.**

Gold has a crucible to extract it from the dross, silver has a refining pot, and man has prayer. Just as gold is extracted from the dross through the fire of the crucible, so the good in a person is extracted when he praises God in his prayers. Prayer is man's service through contemplation in the depths of his mind, which gives rise to the love and fear of God. It is known that silver symbolizes love, and fear represents gold. In other words, they are the aspects of silver and gold in the human soul,[38] the

INTELLECTUAL FEAR AND LOVE OF GOD

☞ When religious life is based solely on blind faith, when the emotions are not illuminated by the intellect, the clarification that results in the world is also partial and random. This is not the case when love and fear are drawn from the intellect, from a cognitive awareness, and are illuminated by it. Then there is no place in reality for a mixture of good and evil. When one has a sense of clarity, when one sees the way by which one may descend to the abyss on the one hand and the way by which one ascends from it on the other, there is no struggle between the two paths. The good ascends to the place where it belongs, and the evil ceases on its own to exist. The struggle exists only in the dark, in a place where one cannot see and does not know. But where there is illumination, the greater the light, the clearer things become.

38. See *Torah Or*, Gen. 26d.

essence of his goodness, and they are clarified during prayer and set the person on the side of holiness. ☞

10 Elul

9 Elul (leap year)

וְהִנֵּה מוּדַעַת זֹאת שֶׁיִּשְׂרָאֵל בְּטִבְעָם הֵם רַחֲמָנִים וְגוֹמְלֵי חֲסָדִים, מִפְּנֵי הֱיוֹת נַפְשׁוֹתֵיהֶם נִמְשָׁכוֹת מִמִּדּוֹתָיו יִתְבָּרֵךְ, אֲשֶׁר הַחֶסֶד גּוֹבֵר בָּהֶן עַל מִדַּת הַדִּין וְהַגְּבוּרָה וְהַצִּמְצוּם. וּכְמוֹ שֶׁכָּתוּב: "גָּבַר חַסְדּוֹ עַל יְרֵאָיו" (תהלים קג, יא).

It is known that the Jewish people by nature are compassionate and kind since their souls are drawn from God's attributes, wherein the attribute of ***Ḥesed*** **prevails over the attribute of judgment,** ***Gevura,*** **and constriction, as it is written, "His kindness prevails over those who fear Him"** (Ps. 103:11)**.**

The Jewish people by nature are compassionate and kind, because their souls are derived from God's attributes, wherein the attribute of *Ḥesed* prevails over the attribute of *Gevura.*[39] Regarding the supernal attributes of *Atzilut,* as well as all the attributes on the side of holiness (and in the soul of man), the midline between the right array of attributes, those that align with *Ḥesed,* and those of the left array, which align with *Gevura,* is not exactly in the middle. Rather, it leans to the right. There is more right than left, more *Ḥesed* than *Gevura.* In a certain sense, the

THE REFINING POT

☞ Prayer is measured by its ability to serve as a "refining pot for silver," for love. Whether or not that love was engendered is not determined by the person's personal experience of the love. Rather the question is, did a change take place in the person's soul or not? Did the prayer operate like a refining pot or a crucible, so that something become clarified through it? If the prayer was offered in the proper manner, the person after the prayer is not the same person as he was before the prayer. Something within him became clear, and another part of his essence now belongs to the side of holiness, to the love and fear of God.

39. See *Yevamot* 79a; *Likkutei Amarim,* end of chap. 1; see also *Iggerot Kodesh* of the Lubavitcher Rebbe, Rabbi Menaḥem Mendel Schneerson, vol. 2, letter 326.

side of holiness belongs entirely to the right side, whereas the left side is subject to the right and serves it.☞

שֶׁלָּכֵן נִקְרֵאת הַנְּשָׁמָה "בַּת כֹּהֵן", כְּמוֹ שֶׁכָּתוּב בַּזּוֹהַר הַקָּדוֹשׁ (חלק ב צה, א).

This is why the soul is called the "daughter of a priest," as stated in the holy *Zohar* (2:95a).

Regarding the verse "And if the daughter of a priest is married to a non-priest" (Lev. 22:12), the *Zohar* states that "daughter of the priest" is the soul, and being "married to a non-priest" refers to its descent into the world to be clothed in a body and an animal soul, the natural soul that animates the body. The entire portion there can be explained along these lines. For our purposes, the "priest" in all contexts is the side of *Ḥesed* (as opposed to the Levite, who represents *Gevura*), and therefore the "daughter of the priest" is the supreme divine soul, which belongs to the side of *Ḥesed*, just like the holy, supreme attributes, which lean in general to the side of *Ḥesed.*[40]

וְהִנֵּה הַצְּדָקָה הַנִּמְשֶׁכֶת מִבְּחִינָה זוֹ נִקְרֵאת בְּשֵׁם "מַעֲשֵׂה הַצְּדָקָה", כִּי

The charity that issues from this element of kindness ingrained in

THE DOMINANCE OF THE ATTRIBUTE OF *ḤESED*

☞ The dominance of *Ḥesed* finds expression in that same statement of the Rabbis that says the Jewish people are distinguished by three characteristics: They are merciful, bashful, and kind. These three traits correspond to three heavenly attributes. Kindness corresponds to the attribute of *Ḥesed*, bashfulness corresponds to the attribute of *Gevura*, and mercy corresponds to the attribute of compassion. It turns out that the attribute of *Gevura* reveals itself in the souls of Israel in their bashfulness. Bashfulness, indeed, belongs to the attribute of *Gevura*, to restraint and constriction, but this is *Gevura* that belongs to the side of *Ḥesed* and serves it. Even compassion, which is in the center, is essentially an attribute characterized by a flow of *Ḥesed* and giving.

40. See *Likkutei Torah*, Lev. 86d, which states, "The essence of peace in the entourage below is to include the left in the right. What this means is that the attributes in the divine soul are called the aspect of right, with *Ḥesed* dominating, and therefore the soul is called 'a priest's daughter.' But the attributes of the animal soul are the aspect of left, for the root and source of the animal soul is the ox on the left."

שֵׁם ׳מַעֲשֶׂה׳ נוֹפֵל עַל דָּבָר שֶׁכְּבָר נַעֲשָׂה, אוֹ שֶׁנַּעֲשֶׂה תָּמִיד מִמֵּילָא, וְהִיא דָּבָר הַהֹוֶה וְרָגִיל תָּמִיד.

a Jew's nature **is referred to as the act of charity, because the term "act" applies to something that has already been done or that is always done by default, which is something that happens regularly and constantly.**

When a person gives charity because it is his nature to be compassionate and kind, and in a certain sense he cannot do otherwise, then his giving of charity is called an "act of charity." As will be explained below, the distinction being made here is between an act and service. An act is a mechanism that is implanted in the soul, a fixed process that may affected by different variables but at its essence remains the same. It was done in the past and is done again in the present.

וְאַף כָּאן, הֲרֵי מִדַּת הַחֶסֶד וְהָרַחֲמָנוּת הוּטְבְּעָה בְּנַפְשׁוֹת כָּל בֵּית יִשְׂרָאֵל מִכְּבָר, מֵעֵת בְּרִיאוּתָן וְהִשְׁתַּלְשְׁלוּתָן מִמִּדּוֹתָיו יִתְבָּרֵךְ, כְּמוֹ שֶׁכָּתוּב: "וַיִּפַּח בְּאַפָּיו כו׳" (בראשית ב, ז), "וְאַתָּה נְפַחְתָּ בִּי"; "וּמַאן דְּנָפַח כו׳".

Here too, the attribute of kindness and compassion are already ingrained in the souls of the entire Jewish people, from the time they were created through their evolvement from God's attributes, as it is written, "And He breathed into his nostrils the soul of life" (Gen. 2:7), **and** as we say in the morning blessings, **"You blew it into me," and "one who blows,** within himself he blows."

The author of the *Tanya* explains elsewhere[41] that in contrast to the entire world, which was created through speech, the divine soul was

41. *Likkutei Amarim*, chap. 2. There the author of the *Tanya* also quotes these sources and states that the latter comes from the *Zohar*. Yet regarding this quotation, the Lubavitcher Rebbe, Rabbi Menaḥem Mendel Schneerson, comments, "It appears not to be found in the *Zohar* or in the *Tikkunei Zohar* that we possess, but it is found in the name of the early sages, among them our Rabbis."

given to man through breath. A person's speech does not constitute his actual spirit, but merely represents assorted forms that he creates with what emerges from his mouth, whereas his exhalation of air is the very spirit of life that he breathes from within him. In this sense, the human soul that God blew into his nostrils is literally a portion of God from above, whereas the entire world is merely speech, an external expression of the divine essence. For this reason, the very traits that are found in the supernal attributes, where the attribute of *Ḥesed* prevails over the attribute of *Gevura*, are implanted within the souls of Israel.

וְגַם בְּכָל יוֹם וָיוֹם בְּטוּבוֹ מְחַדֵּשׁ מַעֲשֵׂה בְרֵאשִׁית, וַ"חֲדָשִׁים לַבְּקָרִים כו'" (איכה ג, כג).

Likewise, every single day God **in His goodness** constantly **renews the act of Creation, and** also the breath of the soul is **"renewed every morning…"** (Lam. 3:23).

Like all of creation, this blowing of the soul into the nostrils of man is renewed every day and at every moment, and together with it is the implanting of the supernal attributes and the empowerment of the soul where the attributes of compassion and *Ḥesed* prevail.

Just as the whole of creation is not an independent, fixed reality but rather a reality that is made anew every day, so too the attributes imbued in the soul, like the attribute of *Ḥesed*, do not exist and operate on their own. A person must practice them each time anew. It is not enough that the attribute of *Ḥesed* is part of his nature, but rather he must go forth and give charity, to perform an act of kindness. This is not self-evident, and it can also be difficult, when the act runs counter to the other attributes, such as the attribute of justice and *Gevura*, which are also holy attributes. Yet the capacity to do so, the ability to prevail even in the face of obstacles, is implanted in the human soul, and a person need not do anything against his nature or beyond his nature. This is similar to God renewing the act of creation. Every day the world is created anew. Every day there is a new world, even though the world of today is no different by its nature than the world of yesterday.

אַךְ לְשׁוֹן עֲבוֹדָה אֵינוֹ נוֹפֵל אֶלָּא עַל דָּבָר שֶׁהָאָדָם עוֹשֶׂה בִּיגִיעָה עֲצוּמָה נֶגֶד טֶבַע נַפְשׁוֹ, רַק שֶׁמְּבַטֵּל טִבְעוֹ וּרְצוֹנוֹ מִפְּנֵי רָצוֹן הָעֶלְיוֹן בָּרוּךְ הוּא, כְּגוֹן לְיַיגֵּעַ עַצְמוֹ בְּתוֹרָה וּבִתְפִלָּה עַד מִיצּוּי הַנֶּפֶשׁ כו'.

But the term "service" applies only to something a person does with immense effort, that goes against his soul's nature, yet he sets aside his nature and will in the face of God's supernal will, for example, exerting himself in Torah study **and prayer, to the extent that he squeezes out the soul, and so on.**

When a person engages in service, he acts against his nature and habits, so that he must change and correct his nature, which requires great effort. An example of such service is studying Torah by exerting great effort. It is certainly possible that a person may naturally want to study Torah and even enjoy it. But when a person learns in this manner, he is occupied in the act of study and not in its service. When a person feels that he has no desire to study, that he is no longer able to do so, yet he continues to study because that is what God wants of him, that is service. When a person prays because he cannot help it, that is not the service of prayer. But when he nullifies his will and being and envelops them in the will and being of God, that is service. ☞

וְאַף כָּאן בְּמִצְוַת הַצְּדָקָה, לִיתֵּן הַרְבֵּה יוֹתֵר מִטֶּבַע רַחֲמָנוּתוֹ וּרְצוֹנוֹ, וּכְמוֹ שֶׁאָמְרוּ רַבּוֹתֵינוּ זִכְרוֹנָם לִבְרָכָה עַל פָּסוּק: "נָתוֹן תִּתֵּן" (דברים טו, י) – אֲפִילוּ מֵאָה פְּעָמִים וכו' (ספרי שם).

Here too with regard to the mitzva of charity, the service of charity means **giving much more that one's natural compassion and will** dictate, **as our Rabbis stated regarding the verse "You shall give him"** (Deut. 15:10), that one should give **"even one hundred times..."** (*Sifrei* ad loc.).

NULLIFYING ONE'S NATURE

☞ Why would a person change his essence? What brings a person to act against his nature and will? The only thing that can cause a person to do this is God's supreme will. Any other reason is ultimately connected to some calculation, great or small, of whether it is worthwhile, centered, at the end of the day, around the self.

When a man has compassion for an impoverished person and his heart aches for the needy, and he has the means and is able to give him, he gives the amount that his compassion obligates him to give. But if he gives beyond his means, even though he does not want to, this is the service of charity.

Here lies the difficulty: When a person comes asking for charity, one is inclined to show him compassion and give him willingly. When he returns the next day and asks again, and then again and again, the compassion diminishes and the patience slowly runs out. When the Torah says, "You shall give [*naton titen*] him," which the Rabbis understood as implying that one must give him "even a hundred times," this means that one must give his fellow Jew as much as he needs, even though there is no longer any compassion or desire to give.

11 Elul

10 Elul (leap year)

וְזֶהוּ שֶׁכָּתוּב: "וְהָיָה מַעֲשֵׂה הַצְּדָקָה", שֶׁגַּם הַצְּדָקָה הַנִּקְרֵאת בְּשֵׁם 'מַעֲשֶׂה' וְלֹא בְּשֵׁם 'עֲבוֹדָה', אַף עַל פִּי כֵן, בְּאִתְעָרוּתָא דִלְתַתָּא אִתְעָרוּתָא דִלְעֵילָּא מְעוֹרֵר גִּילּוּי אוֹר אֵין סוֹף בָּרוּךְ הוּא בְּהֶאָרָה רַבָּה וְהַשְׁפָּעָה עֲצוּמָה, וְנַעֲשָׂה שָׁלוֹם בִּמְרוֹמָיו, וְגַם בַּפָּמַלְיָא שֶׁל מַטָּה.

This is the meaning of the verse cited at the beginning of the letter, "**The act of charity** will be peace," **that even the** kind of **charity that is called an act and not service still** serves as **an awakening from below that causes an awakening above, evoking the revelation of the light of *Ein Sof,* blessed be He, with a great illumination and an immense flow** of divine light. **Thus peace is made in His heights,** in the entourage above, **as well as the entourage below,** in this world.

Even the kind of charity that is called an act and not service is considered charity. Whenever a person performs an act of charity below, when he gives and benefits others, not in accordance with what they deserve but as an act of kindness, he awakens in turn a revelation of the divine light over and beyond the illumination of the worlds through justice. Through such illumination peace is achieved above and also below.

רַק שֶׁבָּעוֹלָם הַזֶּה, הַשָּׁפֵל, לֹא יִתְגַּלֶּה הַשָּׁלוֹם וְהַבֵּירוּר וּפֵירוּד הָרָע מֵהַטּוֹב עַד עֵת קֵץ, וְלֹא בִּזְמַן הַגָּלוּת כַּנִּזְכָּר לְעֵיל,

However, in this lowly physical **world, the peace** resulting from **the extraction** of good from evil **and the separation of the evil from the good will not be revealed until the end of time and not in the era of the exile, as mentioned above,**

Our world is not only the world most distant from the divine light, but also a world in which there is a distortion of the supernal light, created by man and his sins. As long as the impression left by human sins is evident in the world, which is essentially during the entire period of exile, that illumination will not be revealed in the world.

רַק בְּ'עוֹלָם קָטָן' הוּא הָאָדָם בְּכָל עֵת מְצוֹא זוֹ תְּפִלָּה, כְּמוֹ שֶׁכָּתוּב: "בְּצֶדֶק אֶחֱזֶה פָנֶיךָ" (תהלים יז, טו), כַּנִּזְכָּר לְעֵיל.

but only in the miniature world, meaning a person at every auspicious time, which is the time of **prayer, as it is written, "I will behold Your face through charity"** (Ps. 17:15)**, as mentioned above.**

Even if the illumination is not revealed in its entirety in the reality of the larger world, it is partially revealed within man, who is a miniature world. Even then, it is not revealed at all times and not in the entire being of man, but only at auspicious times, such as the time of prayer. Through an act of charity below, a great light is awakened above, only this great light does not penetrate all the way down to be revealed in this lower world and in the daily reality in which we live. There are, however, certain areas within reality where the screen is not so opaque, and it opens partially from time to time. One such area is prayer, and in a certain sense also the Sabbath.[42] Prayer is like a semblance of the Sabbath every day, and the Sabbath itself is a semblance of the World to Come. For this reason, through prayer, and even more so through the Sabbath prayer, there may be the clarifications of peace, not only "in His heights," but also "upon us."

This is the meaning of the verse "I will behold Your face through

42. See *Torah Or* 86d.

charity" (Ps. 17:15): that the illumination above, which is awakened by an act of charity performed below, becomes revealed through prayer.

אַךְ אַחַר הַתְּפִלָּה יוּכַל לִהְיוֹת הָרַע חוֹזֵר וְנֵיעוֹר בְּקַל וּלְהִתְעָרֵב בַּטּוֹב, כַּאֲשֶׁר יִתְהַלֵּךְ בְּחֶשְׁכַת עוֹלָם הַזֶּה.

But after prayer, it is possible that the evil will easily reawaken and become intermingled with the good once more, **as a person walks in the darkness of this world.**

The time of prayer is a clear window, when it is obvious to the person what is good and what is evil, what should be done and what should not. But after concluding his prayer, he once again reverts to a reality that does not allow for such clarity. This world returns to him, with all its affairs and troubles. Once again, things begin to intermingle and blur, and very quickly a person finds himself in the same place he was before. In other words, when charity is performed as an act of charity, which a person performs without deviating from his nature, the illumination it awakens will also not deviate from the nature of the world, nor will it change it in a concrete manner.

אַךְ הַצְּדָקָה בִּבְחִינַת 'עֲבוֹדָה', הִנֵּה מֵאֲשֶׁר יָקְרָה וְגָדְלָה מַעֲלָתָהּ בִּמְאֹד מְאֹד,

Yet the kind of **charity that is a service, inasmuch as its quality is exceedingly precious and great**

When charity is given in the form of service, with an extraordinary effort to break and change one's nature, this service is exceedingly precious and great within the soul of the giver.

בִּהְיוֹתוֹ מְבַטֵּל טִבְעוֹ וּרְצוֹנוֹ הַגּוּפָנִי מִפְּנֵי רְצוֹן הָעֶלְיוֹן בָּרוּךְ הוּא וְאִתְכַּפְיָא סִטְרָא אָחֳרָא

in that one sets aside his nature and bodily will in the face of God's supernal will, thereby **subduing the *sitra aḥara***

It is the nature of every person, even a man of virtue, to serve his own interests. His own body is more important to him than those of others. In everyone's life, there are crossroads, when a person must decide: Does he take more for himself or give to others? When he decides to set aside his nature and will in deference to God's will, and he gives to another, this is the service of charity.

By virtue of the fact that a person sets aside his own will, he subdues the *sitra aḥara*, the other side. If a person does not break his nature and engage in service, there is, in turn, no subjugation. Within the nature of every member of Israel, there is a certain side of good and compassion. An act of doing good, of giving to another, does not necessarily involve a mental struggle or crisis, because that is his nature. For example, there are animals that at certain times are pleasant and delightful, and at other times they scratch. These two states do not constitute a deviation from the creature's nature but are part of its nature and essence. Similarly, in every person are implanted certain characteristics and desires that are part of his nature and heredity, and as long as he acts within that framework, he does not coerce his nature and does not break anything within himself. But when he engages in service, he comes into conflict and confrontation with the other sides of his nature, and since he cannot persuade them to yield, he must coerce them. This is what it means to subdue the *sitra aḥara*. ☞

וַאֲזַי אִסְתַּלֵּק יְקָרָא דְקוּדְשָׁא בְּרִיךְ הוּא כו',

and causing **the glory of the Holy One, blessed be He, to then be exalted** throughout all the worlds,

The Sages taught that when God sought to create man, the ministering angels protested, "What is man, that You are mindful of him?"[43] Why create such a creature, who is weak, dangerous, and prone to calamity? Yet God created man nevertheless. Ever since then, man's creation has

SUBDUING THE *SITRA AḤARA*

☞ When a person acts in a way that he is able to subdue the *sitra aḥara*, his action has an effect that goes beyond the *kelippa* within himself. It is not just a temporary, localized coercion but a general coercion of the evil within all of reality.

When a person acts in accordance with his nature, he acts within the framework of his own will and for his own benefit, which is the focus of his reality. Even when he gives, he does so because he wants to do so, and because in the end it is he who receives. When he subdues the *sitra aḥara* within him, and his own nature in general, his action has an effect on the essence of evil in the whole of reality.

43. *Sanhedrin* 38b; *Pirkei deRabbi Eliezer* 12; *Zohar* 1:3a.

been constantly subject to a test. God, as it were, gambled on man, believing and investing in him. Every time a person reaches a point of confrontation and emerges victorious, subduing the *sitra aḥara*, he elevates the glory of God even higher.

וְ״כִּיתְרוֹן הָאוֹר מִן הַחֹשֶׁךְ״ (קהלת ב, יג) דַּוְקָא כַּנּוֹדָע.

like the "advantage of light over darkness" (Eccles. 2:13), **specifically** where the light emerges from the darkness, **as is known,**

The light that emerges from the confrontation with the *sitra aḥara* and the victory over it is light that emerges from the darkness. This light not only repelled the darkness, but in a sense emerged from it, and therefore this light has a great advantage over the ordinary light found in the world. Such light reveals within it an essence that is higher and more transcendent than anything found within the world. ☞

אִי לָזֹאת, אֵין הָרַע יָכוֹל לִהְיוֹת עוֹד חוֹזֵר וְנֵיעוֹר בְּקַלּוּת כָּל כָּךְ מֵאֵלָיו

in that case the evil is no longer able to reawaken so easily on its own

When one performs a mitzva (or gives charity or prays) in accordance with his nature, when he finds his prayer sweet and beautiful, when he offers it without struggle, then after he has finished praying, he returns to his routine life, to the same place he was before. The spiritual

THE ADVANTAGE OF LIGHT OVER DARKNESS

☞ The teachings of Hasidism explain this concept in several ways. There is the cognitive advantage, that light is more noticeable and effective when it appears in contrast to darkness, whether after the darkness or alongside it. It is like joy that emerges from sadness, health from sickness, wisdom from folly. But there is also a deeper advantage, in that light that emerges from darkness illuminates the darkness itself. The idea is that the greater light is not that which is revealed but that which is hidden from us. Due to the limits of our understanding, it is clear that what we do not take in is loftier than what we do take in, that what we see is only an immeasurably small part of what we do not see. Thus, light that emerges from the darkness constitutes an illumination that was previously in the realm of darkness and concealment, an illumination that stems from the divine essence about which it states, "He engulfed His secret place in darkness" (Ps. 18:12).

elevation he attained during prayer did not effect a permanent change but was only for a limited time.

This is not the case when the charity or prayer falls into the category of service. Even if the illumination that he had acquired will not continue to illuminate for him in the same way, a certain change took place in his essence, which remains even after prayer. The person after prayer is not the same person he was before. He has changed to the point that he no longer identifies with the evil forces that dominated him before he prayed.

רַק אִם הָאָדָם יְעוֹרְרֶנּוּ וְיַמְשִׁיכֶנּוּ עַל עַצְמוֹ חַס וְשָׁלוֹם.

but only if the person awakens it and draws it down on himself, God forbid.

The person is now in a different atmosphere. He is no longer subject to the same forces as he was before. Yet he still retains his free choice. He may not be aware of it, but he can always decide, for one reason or another, that he is going to sin. A person may be able to get out of a swamp and take a straight, dry path, where the slime no longer adheres to him, but nothing prevents him from jumping back into the muck. In this sense, even the greatest act of charity does not provide a person with permanent immunity. On the other hand, a change took place. A new equilibrium was created within his life, which is neither canceled nor easily washed away by the stream of life.

וְזֶהוּ שֶׁכָּתוּב: "הַשְׁקֵט וָבֶטַח עַד עוֹלָם". "הַשְׁקֵט" הוּא מִלְּשׁוֹן "שׁוֹקֵט עַל שְׁמָרָיו", דְּהַיְינוּ שֶׁהַשְּׁמָרִים נִפְרָדִים לְגַמְרֵי מִן הַיַּיִן וְנוֹפְלִין לְמַטָּה לְגַמְרֵי, וְהַיַּיִן לְמַעְלָה זַךְ וְצָלוּל בְּתַכְלִית.

This is the meaning of the second part of the **verse,** "And the service of charity will be **quiet and security forever.**" The word for quiet, ***hashket,* is related to** the word *shoket* in the phrase **"it is settled** [*shoket*] **on its sediments." That is, the sediment is completely separated from the wine and falls all the way down,** leaving **the wine above perfectly pure and clear.**

In the early stages of wine preparation, the yeast is intermingled with the wine, and even after the fermentation process ceases, the yeast continues to float on top of the wine for a certain amount of time.

At this stage, the wine is cloudy and does not taste good. Only after the wine has sat quietly for a while, without fermentation or other processes taking place, does it become "settled on its sediments," where the yeast and other solid material settles to the bottom of the container and the wine becomes perfectly pure and clear at the top. Thus the use of the word *al*, "on," in the phrase "it is settled on its sediments." The wine is not mixed with the sediments, but rather it rests on top of them.

וְעַל דֶּרֶךְ זֶה הוּא בַּעֲבוֹדַת הַצְּדָקָה: הַשְּׁמָרִים הֵן בְּחִינַת תַּעֲרוֹבֶת רַע שֶׁבְּנַפְשׁוֹ נִבְרָר וְנִפְרָד מְעַט מְעַט, עַד שֶׁנּוֹפֵל לְמַטָּה לִמְקוֹרוֹ וְשָׁרְשׁוֹ,

So it is with the service of charity: The sediment represents the evil intermingled in a person's soul, which is **extracted and separated little by little, until it falls below to its source and root,**

The yeast in the soul, which elsewhere is called the "yeast in the dough" (*Berakhot* 17a), is the evil inclination that agitates a person, changing and distorting his essence. Through the service of charity, it becomes extracted and separated little by little, until it falls below to its source and root. Separating the yeast from the wine is a metaphor for the separation of the evil from the good. The yeast is the waste and evil that falls down, while the wine is the holiness that rises up.[44]

Man's problem is not the reality of evil, but rather the mixture of good and evil, that evil is found within life, within everything that man does and thinks. For this reason, rectification lies in the separation of the good from the evil. The good becomes better, clearer, and holier, while the evil, if it remains, becomes coarser and more repulsive. The person merits "quiet and security," an inner quiet in which good and evil are no longer intermingled. Yet it is always possible to stir the wine in which the sediments have settled to the bottom and raise them back into the wine. But from now on, this will depend on the voluntary act of the person, where he chooses to bring the evil, but the evil will no longer leap at him and come to him against his will.

---

44. See *Torah Or* 97b; *Likkutei Torah*, Num. 42b.

וּכְמוֹ שֶׁכָּתוּב: "וְתַשְׁלִיךְ בִּמְצוּלוֹת יָם כָּל חַטֹּאתָם" (מיכה ז, יט).

as it is written, "And You will cast all their sins into the depths of the sea" (Mic. 7:19).

When the sins are cast to the depths of the sea, the water becomes clear. The emphasis here is on "the depths of the sea," from which it is impossible to ascend. This is what a person merits for his service of charity. The illumination and clarity that he achieves is not temporary but permanent. The clear water cannot easily become sullied once the evil has been cast into the depths of the sea, into a place from which it cannot readily rise again.

This epistle discussed the mitzva of charity and its effect on man's soul and his service of God through Torah study and the performance of the commandments, and particularly through prayer. Giving charity in general, which involves giving that is not based on justice, even to one who does not deserve it and cannot pay for it, awakens a flow of light and life force from above that is also given without measure, beyond, as it were, what the person deserves according to the standards of justice. This great illumination is the illumination that makes "peace," where all contrasts are eliminated.

It was further stated that just as there are two levels to the performance of the mitzva of charity, either as an act or service, there are two levels to the illumination from above that arises from it. The first one creates peace in His heights as well as in this world, only it is not revealed in this world through a manifest change in its nature, but only in a way that a person can reveal it temporarily, at special times and with special effort, such as during the time of prayer. The second level, like the service of charity, which abolishes the basic nature of a person and reveals his hidden point, penetrates and reveals that which is concealed in the world and even establishes a new order, below as above, in the form of "quiet and security forever."

Epistle 13

THIS LETTER, APPARENTLY WRITTEN IN 1792, IS THE first part of an epistle that was intended to encourage the hasidim to donate to a special charity fund through a particular emissary who had been sent for that purpose. The main part of the letter, which is presented here, addresses a person who is being asked to give beyond his means and do more than he can, and that is because he has within him the ability to do so, even if this is not evident and even if the person himself is unaware of it. To evoke this ability, the person needs to know of its existence. Does it exist in every person? Where is it hidden? How is it awakened, from below and from above?

This epistle comes to answer these questions.

"מָה רַב טוּבְךָ אֲשֶׁר צָפַנְתָּ לִּירֵאֶיךָ וגו'" (תהלים לא, כ).

12 Elul / 11 Elul (leap year)

It is written, **"How great is the goodness You have in store for those who fear You,** which You have created for those taking refuge in You…" (Ps. 31:20).

The letter opens with an explanation of a verse from Psalms that talks about the reward God gives to those who serve Him, for the good deeds they do, and He rewards them in accordance with the manner and intention with which they do those deeds. Yet what the author of the *Tanya* focuses on is not the reward but the service of the soul that is revealed by the reward, and he will clarify this through his explanation of the verse.

The author points to the two parts of the verse, the first one revolving around "those who fear You," and the second speaking of "those taking refuge in You." As will be explained below, "those who fear you" and "those taking refuge in You," are two types of people. The author of the *Tanya* goes on to explain the nature of each one and how they differ from one another.

הִנֵּה בִּכְלַל עוֹבְדֵי ה׳ יֵשׁ ב׳ בְּחִינוֹת וּמַדְרֵגוֹת חֲלוּקוֹת,

Generally speaking, among those who serve God there are two different categories and levels,

In the *Tanya* there is much discussion about the distinction between the tzaddik and the *beinoni*, (one who is neither righteous nor wicked), between one who serves God and one who does not. These distinctions are distinctions of rank, differences in the intensity of the person's service and its level, differences in the degree of individual revelation. The tzaddik and the *beinoni* are not on the same plane; one is above the other. It is not that they deal with the same problems in different ways, but rather they deal with different problems. Here, on the other hand, we are talking about a different type of distinction: a distinction between people who are on the same level, but differ in character, personality, and the way in which they approach life.

If one person could perfectly fill the place of another person, God would not have created him. Each person has a certain facet, a particular point, that does not exist in anyone else. On the one hand, it can be argued that just as the roots of the souls of Israel number six hundred thousand, so do different types of people. Yet there are divisions that are more inclusive. There is the division into twelve tribes, with each Jew belonging to one of them at the root of his soul.[45] There is the division into seventy (meaning the seventy people who first went down to Egypt),[46] which is also the division into the seven attributes.[47] But the most inclusive division is the division into two, into two different categories and levels. ☞

מִצַּד שׁוֹרֶשׁ נִשְׁמָתָם לְמַעְלָה מִבְּחִינַת יָמִין וּשְׂמֹאל.

depending on the root of their souls above, whether they stem **from the right** side **or the left.**

45. See *Torah Or* 49d, 55a.

46. Deut. 10:22.

47. See *Torah Or* 32b.

The distinction between the two types of service is not only an external expression of character or mode of behavior, but a distinction that stems from the root of the soul. The division here is on the horizontal plane, of right and left, as opposed to a division of above and below. This refers to right and left, not in the physical sense, but as spiritual directions, ways of conceptual and emotional progression in one direction or another.

דְּהַיְינוּ שֶׁבְּחִינַת שְׂמֹאל הִיא מִדַּת הַצִּמְצוּם וְהַהֶסְתֵּר בַּעֲבוֹדַת ה',

That is, the left side **is the attribute of constriction and concealment in the service of God,**

In general, the left side is the side of restraint, fear, and justice. These are not expressions of evil as opposed to good. They are expressions of convergence, of constriction from the periphery to the center, of restraint and concealment, and therefore they are liable to be seen as harsh expressions of resistance to giving and even of evil. In the service of God, the left side is always the side that refers primarily to what occurs internally – inside the house, inside the walls, within boundaries and limitations.

כְּמוֹ שֶׁכָּתוּב: "וְהַצְנֵעַ לֶכֶת כוּ'" (מיכה ו, ח),

as it is written, "And to walk humbly with your God" (Mic. 6:8),

TWO WAYS TO DIVINE SERVICE

☞ Why should we engage in such questions of classification in the first place? Why is it important to categorize other types of people who are not like us? Apart from the general idea, that there are two levels in divine service, which is good for a person to know, there is also another reason, which was expressed by one of the hasidic masters. In his interpretation of the verse "You shall not hate your brother in your heart" (Lev. 19:17), he said, "You shall not hate your brother because his heart is not like your heart." A person may have a certain tendency or a relationship with a certain thing. When he sees that other people do not have that same relationship, it may disturb him that they are not like him, and he is liable to think that there is something wrong with them. In order to understand that people can be different, even very different, from each other, and yet they can all be servants of God, in order to understand that the service of God does not always follow the same pattern or share the same characteristics, one must know that there are other types of people and other ways of serving God.

There is a mode of divine service that involves "walking humbly with your God," serving Him in a discreet manner, on the inside. This is mainly a matter of character, the mark of a person who does not make his thoughts and actions known because that would bother him and he does not need it. There is also something virtuous about "walking humbly" in the realm of holiness. ☞

"בְּמִסְתָּרִים תִּבְכֶּה כו'" (ירמיה יג, יז), "כָּל הָעוֹסֵק בַּתּוֹרָה בַּסֵּתֶר כו'".

and it is written, "My soul **will weep in concealed places...**" (Jer. 13:17). Similarly, our Sages speak of **one who studies Torah in secret, and so on.**

Even regarding God Himself there are aspects of revelation, of "might and joy in His place" (I Chron. 16:27), and there are aspects of concealment, where "My soul will weep in concealed places." The verse expresses the personality trait of a person who does not reveal his affairs in public. When he is in a concealed place, a place fit for crying, he cries. But he does not cry in public, nor does he reveal his feelings and experiences, but rather he keeps them to himself.

The same is true of Torah study: There are those who study Torah in secret.[48] They study Torah in secret, not because they are embarrassed to reveal what they are doing, but because they are that way, and that is the nature of their Torah study, which is no one else's business.

The three expressions that the author of the *Tanya* uses here encom-

WALKING HUMBLY WITH GOD

☞ In contrast to people who invest effort to advertise their piety, there are those who invest even greater effort to hide it. Chabad hasidim talk about standing out as a negative quality. It is frowned upon not only in reference to offensive attributes, but even with regard to good attributes. When a person has a good quality, and he and others know that he has it, it is not a virtue. Kotzker hasidim were even known to perform certain ruses to appear light-headed and reckless (and this too required great care, so that the deception itself did not involve a trace of standing out). The assumption is that what a person does with God is private, and other people need not know about it. The long-standing tradition of the hidden tzaddik is built on this approach, and there are people who deliberately live this way, where they do not want other people to know who they are and what they know and are able to do.

48. See *Mo'ed Katan* 16b.

pass all areas of divine service: Torah, prayer, and mitzvot. "Walking humbly" is related to the performance of mitzvot. "My soul will weep in concealed places" refers to the service of prayer performed with weeping and supplications. "Anyone who studies Torah in secret" describes the service of Torah study. This highlights how the two categories of divine service being discussed here is not a distinction between a higher level of service and a lower one, but between the different ways that people do the same thing, and this distinction applies to every area: Torah study, prayer, and the performance of mitzvot.

וְהִנֵּה מִמִּדָּה זוֹ נִמְשְׁכָה גַּם כֵּן בְּחִינַת הַצִּמְצוּם וְהַגְּבוּל בַּעֲבוֹדַת ה׳,

From this trait of the left side **is also derived the aspect of constriction and limitation in the service of God,**

The trait of humility and concealment is also a trait of restriction, of setting limits in the service of God. All forms of refraining from something – from doing, from revealing, from thinking or from speaking – stems from the left, from the force of limitation, justice, and restraint. Even *Gevura* finds expression, not in a burst of strength, but rather in refraining from any outburst. The same is true of the attribute of justice and of "walking humbly" with God. ☞

כְּמוֹ בִּצְדָקָה, לִהְיוֹת נִידּוֹן בְּהֶשֵּׂג יָד וְהַמְבַזְבֵּז אַל יְבַזְבֵּז יוֹתֵר מֵחוֹמֶשׁ,

such as charity being determined and limited **according to** one's **means and** abiding by the dictum that **one who dispenses his money to charity should not dispense more than one-fifth.**

RESTRICTION AND LIMITATION IN THE SERVICE OF GOD

☞ A person who does not give what he must or do what has to be done may not necessarily be a miser. He may act in that manner because his character and service of God are built on law and order, on internal and external discipline, on the idea that things must be done within certain boundaries and not beyond them. Such a person attaches great importance to fences and limits, and it is the preservation of boundaries and limitations that guides him in his service. This finds expression not only in the way he distances himself from evil, but also in the manner that he does good: within boundaries and limitations.

The mitzva of charity has certain halakhic parameters. A person may give only in accordance with his means and no more than that.[49] A person must calculate how much he has and how much he can afford to give, and that is what he will give. Moreover, a person who dispenses charity should not dispense more than one-fifth of his assets,[50] so that he does not end up in a situation where he himself is in need of charity.

וּכְהַאי גַּוְונָא בְּתַלְמוּד תּוֹרָה וּשְׁאָרֵי מִצְוֹת, דַּי לוֹ שֶׁיּוֹצֵא יְדֵי חוֹבָתוֹ מֵחִיּוּב מְפוֹרָשׁ שֶׁחִיְּיבַתּוּ הַתּוֹרָה בְּפֵירוּשׁ, לִקְבּוֹעַ עִתִּים כו׳.

Similarly, regarding Torah study and the other commandments, it is enough for him to discharge his obligation by fulfilling **the duty that the Torah explicitly obligates him** to do, **to set times** for Torah study by day and by night.

It suffices for such a person to fulfill his obligations regarding the commandments as dictated by the *halakha*. When it comes to Torah study, for example, a person is commanded to set fixed times to study Torah by day and by night, as the verse states, "You shall ponder it day and night" (Josh. 1:8).[51] Such a person sets frameworks for his study: He has fixed times and fixed classes, and he sticks to his schedule and he will not give up one of his fixed classes under any circumstances. He will invest his energy and strength in meeting the times and classes he set for himself.

אַךְ בְּחִינַת יָמִין הִיא מִדַּת הַחֶסֶד וְהַהִתְפַּשְּׁטוּת בַּעֲבוֹדַת ה׳, בְּהִתְרַחֲבוּת בְּלִי צִמְצוּם וְהֶסְתֵּר כְּלָל, כְּמוֹ שֶׁכָּתוּב: "וְאֶתְהַלְּכָה בָרְחָבָה כו׳" (תהלים קיט, מה).

But the right side **is the attribute of kindness and expansiveness in the service of God,** serving Him **openhandedly without any constriction or concealment at all, as it is written, "Let me walk in a wide, expansive place..."** (Ps. 119:45).

49. See *Tur* and *Shulḥan Arukh, Yoreh De'a* 247:1, 249:1, based on Rambam, *Mishneh Torah, Sefer Zera'im, Hilkhot Mattenot Aniyim* 7:5.

50. *Ketubot* 50a; see also Rambam, *Mishneh Torah, Sefer Hafla'a, Hilkhot Arakhim* 8:13.

51. See *Shulḥan Arukh, Yoreh De' a* 246:1.

In contrast to the constriction, convergence, and withdrawal on the left side, the right side is characterized by openness, expansion, and going beyond boundaries.[52] When such a person performs a mitzva, studies Torah, or prays, he does not adhere to fixed boundaries but rather expands and proceeds wherever possible. Such service, which does not stop at the borders, does not remain in the realm of "humbly walking with God." It is visible to the world. ☞

Also derived from this attribute is the trait described **by our Rabbis' statement "Cast fear upon** your **students..."** (*Ketubot* 103b). [Editor's note: The appearance of this last sentence here **requires scrutiny; apparently, it ought to appear before** the words **"But the right side...."**]

וּמִמֶּנָּה נִמְשָׁךְ גַּם כֵּן מַה שֶּׁאָמְרוּ רַבּוֹתֵינוּ זִכְרוֹנָם לִבְרָכָה: זְרוֹק מָרָה בְּתַלְמִידִים כו' (כתובות קג, ב). [הערת העורך: צָרִיךְ עִיּוּן, וְנִרְאֶה שֶׁצָּרִיךְ לִהְיוֹת קוֹדֶם "אַךְ בְּחִינַת יָמִין כו'"].

The talmudic Sage Rabbi Yehuda HaNasi made this statement when his eldest son, Rabban Gamliel, was appointed *nasi*, the head of the Sanhedrin, and he transmitted to him the procedures of the position. He said to him, "Conduct your term as *nasi* with assertiveness, and cast

EXPANSIVENESS IN THE SERVICE OF GOD

☞ Ostensibly, it should be that with regard to everything related to sin and affairs of this world, a person should make use of the attributes of restraint and constriction, but when it comes to the performance of mitzvot, he should make use of the attributes of kindness and expansion. But in reality people are built differently. A person is made with a certain character that dictates how he will conduct himself in everything he does, whether in holy matters or in his mundane affairs. A person cannot be miserly by nature in all matters, but not when it comes to the mitzvot, nor can he be generous only with regard to mitzvot. A person with a closed and withdrawn disposition is closed and withdrawn in all areas of his life. Admittedly, there are people who can overcome their essential nature at certain points (for example, the Midrash in *Esther Rabba* 2:3 describes a person who was exceedingly frugal when it came to his household's needs but was generous with his charity), but this is extremely difficult.

52. See *Likkutei Torah*, Lev. 49e.

fear upon your students."[53] These words express restraint, adherence to boundaries, and a refusal to compromise, all characteristics of the attribute of *Gevura*.

In light of this, it would appear, as the parenthetical note points out, that this sentence was printed in the wrong place, since its content suggests that it relates to what was stated above regarding the left side.

וְגַם בְּלִי צִמְצוּם וּגְבוּל כְּלָל, וְאֵין מַעֲצוֹר לְרוּחַ נִדְבָתוֹ, בֵּין בִּצְדָקָה וּבֵין בְּתַלְמוּד תּוֹרָה וּשְׁאָרֵי מִצְוֹת, וְלֹא דַי לוֹ לָצֵאת יְדֵי חוֹבָתוֹ בִּלְבַד, אֶלָּא עַד בְּלִי דַי כו'.

The right side **also** means serving God **without any constriction or limit at all and with no constraint to one's generous spirit, whether with regard to charity, Torah study, or any of the other mitzvot.** Such a person **does not suffice with fulfilling his obligation alone, but rather** exerts himself **endlessly, and so on.**

Such a person does everything in an expansive manner, above and beyond what is required of him. He knows that there are limits, but they are of no consequence to him, and therefore he breaches them, whether in the realm of charity, giving more than required and more than he can afford, or in the realm of Torah study, or with regard to the rest of the mitzvot. He does not act this way to fulfill an obligation, because he does not live with the sense of obligation but with the sense that he is acting willingly, with the sense of giving and benefaction that is never enough. He never feels that what he has done suffices, so he breaks out and continues doing more without limit.

וְהִנֵּה כָּל אִישׁ יִשְׂרָאֵל צָרִיךְ לִהְיוֹת כָּלוּל מִ־ב' בְּחִינוֹת אֵלּוּ,

Every Jew must comprise both these traits,

In reality, this distinction between right and left is not so clear-cut. Almost no one epitomizes one side alone. For the most part, people are merely inclined to one side or the other, sometimes in a more extreme manner and sometimes less so. What is more, we are required to work on the nature of our soul in order to combine these traits and not express only

53. See also Rambam, *Mishneh Torah, Sefer HaMadda, Hilkhot Talmud Torah* 4:5, and *Shulḥan Arukh, Yoreh De'a* 246:11.

one side. Part of our mission in this world is to try to live within ourselves also with the other attributes that are not natural to us.

וְאֵין לְךָ דָבָר שֶׁאֵין לוֹ מָקוֹם (אבות פרק ד משנה ג).

and "there is no thing that does not have its place" (Mishna *Avot* 4:3).

This division is not between good and bad attributes, but between different attributes, each of which has a time, place, and proportion that are appropriate for it. Everything in the world has a place, and the same is true of the different sides of a person's soul. It is only a question of finding the appropriate time, place, and manner for each side to find expression. Admittedly, an individual has more room for the particular attributes that are more active in his soul, but the other traits also have their time and place. A person who is incapable of uncovering a certain attribute inside himself is not fulfilling his mission completely. A person who has perfected himself can find all the sides and attributes within himself, and not in a way that they contradict each other but in a way that each one has its place, that he knows when and where to employ each attribute. ☞

וְלָכֵן מָצִינוּ כַּמָּה דְבָרִים מִקּוּלֵּי בֵית שַׁמַּאי וּמֵחוּמְרֵי בֵית הִלֵּל,

Therefore, we find several matters where the Sages of **Beit Shammai ruled leniently and** the Sages of **Beit Hillel ruled stringently.**

NO THING THAT DOES NOT HAVE ITS PLACE

☞ Some people talk extensively about a wide variety of topics with expansive explanations, while others speak with restraint, uttering every sentence with deliberation, saying what must be said and nothing more. The truth is that both are ways of influencing others, but one needs to know when and where to use each of them. There were certain sages who spoke expansively and offered lengthy explanations in their oral discourse, but when they committed their words to writing did so in an abridged manner. For instance, it is related about the Rogatchover Gaon, Rabbi Yosef Rosen, who was famous for his exceedingly concise writing, that in face-to-face communications he conducted himself differently, explaining matters at great length. Likewise, to a small child or to a person of limited intellectual capacity, it is necessary to explain matters in great detail. But using the same approach with a person who understands matters on his own, offering repeated explanations of things he already knows, is out of place, ineffective, and even harmful.

Though Beit Shammai usually rules stringently, and Beit Hillel rules in a more lenient manner, there are matters regarding which Beit Shammai is lenient and Beit Hillel is stringent.[54]

לְלַמְּדֵנוּ שֶׁאַף בֵּית שַׁמַּאי, שֶׁשֹּׁרֶשׁ נִשְׁמָתָם מִבְּחִינַת שְׂמֹאל הָעֶלְיוֹן,

This **teaches us that even** the Sages of **Beit Shammai, whose souls were rooted in the supernal left** side,

Every soul below has a root and source above in the supernal attributes from which it receives its character traits. When the soul is rooted in one of the attributes belonging to the left side, this will also find expression in the person below: in his character, in his deliberations, in the way he sees things. This also explains why there are groups of people who think and feel in a similar manner (even if they are seemingly unrelated), in contrast to other groups, such as the Sages who belonged to the school of Shammai as opposed to the Sages who belonged to the school of Hillel.

וְלָכֵן הָיוּ דָנִין לְהַחְמִיר תָּמִיד בְּכָל אִיסּוּרֵי הַתּוֹרָה. וּבֵית הִלֵּל שֶׁהָיוּ מִבְּחִינַת יָמִין הָעֶלְיוֹן, הָיוּ מְלַמְּדִין זְכוּת לְהָקֵל וּלְהַתִּיר אִיסּוּרֵי בֵּית שַׁמַּאי,

and therefore they would always rule stringently regarding all the prohibitions of the Torah, while the Sages of **Beit Hillel, who** stemmed **from the supernal right** side, **would find arguments to be lenient and to permit that which Beit Shammai prohibited,**

Since the left side is the side of boundaries and limitations, the side of caution and concern, the Sages of Beit Shammai, whose souls were rooted in the supernal left side, was inclined to be stringent, to set limits and erect fences. The Sages of Beit Hillel, on the other hand, stemmed from the supernal right side and so tended to rule leniently and "permit that which Beit Shammai prohibited."

When one performs a mitzva with a certain object or person (and not only a mitzva, but anything a Jew is occupied with in this world, such as eating), the goal is to elevate the object and everything related

54. See Mishna *Eduyot*, chaps. 4–5; *Shabbat* 77b; *Eruvin* 6b; *Rosh HaShana* 14b.

to it from the neutral realm to the realm of holiness. When something is ruled as prohibited, this means that it is bound to the material reality and to *kelippa* and cannot be released and elevated, and therefore a Jew must not engage with it. In light of this, the author of the *Tanya* explains elsewhere that the word for a prohibition, *issur,* is derived from the word *assur,* tied and bound.[55] When something is ruled as *mutar,* permitted or "unbound," this means that it can be elevated. If a person makes an effort, if he directs his mind in the proper manner, it is possible to elevate the light and holiness within this permitted thing so that it is lifted out of this world and join them to the Divine. Therefore, Beit Hillel "would find arguments to be lenient." They recognized the difficulties and the problems, and they understood why Beit Shammai declared it prohibited, but nevertheless they sought a way to permit that which is prohibited, to loosen its ties to the *kelippot* and attach it to holiness. ☞

PERMITTING THAT WHICH IS PERMITTED

☞ A famous story is related about Shammai and Hillel concerning a gentile who wanted to become a proselyte on condition that he be appointed a High Priest (*Shabbat* 31a). Shammai immediately rejected him, as he rightly deserved. Hillel, on the other hand, converted him, but told him that before he became a High Priest, he should learn what that entailed. After a short course of study, the proselyte understood on his own that he could not be a High Priest.

The story expresses the complex relationship between the two sides. Ostensibly, Shammai was right and Hillel was wrong. According to all halakhic parameters, the gentile should not have been accepted as a proselyte. If a person wishes to attach a condition to his conversion, and all the more so a condition such as this, it is inappropriate to convert him. Yet Hillel tried to push the limits, to find an allowance, to expand what is permitted to the extent possible. This is the nature of the attribute of *Ḥesed,* to try to be lenient, to be flexible, to breach the limits. There is, however, a limit beyond which flexibility loses its substance and turns into anarchy. Therefore, it is by no means a simple matter to draw an overall conclusion from the story, neither that one should be soft like Hillel and not harsh like Shammai, nor the other way around.

A similar question arises as to who is a good doctor. Is it the doctor who permits everything, for the patient to eat, drink, and behave as he wishes? Or is it the doctor who forbids? Is the bighearted engineer, who turns a blind eye to the fact that the building does not meet all the required standards, a good person? Surely this good

55. *Likkutei Amarim,* chap. 7.

שֶׁיִּהְיוּ מוּתָּרִים מֵאִיסּוּרָם וְיוּכְלוּ לַעֲלוֹת לְמַעְלָה,

so that they would be released from their prohibited state and be able to ascend above,

The definition of *Ḥesed* as leniency and *Gevura* as stringency relates not to the person, but to reality. When we say that something is prohibited, the emphasis is not on the fact that it is prohibited to a certain person, but that is prohibited in itself. When we permit it, it is like the release of a prisoner. That which is prohibited is released from its shackles. It goes free, and it is able to ascend to holiness. ☞

Generally the Sages of Beit Shammai were more stringent, because they stem from the left side, from the attribute of justice. According to this approach, not everyone can ascend to holiness. Only those who actually meet the qualifications can do so. The Sages of Beit Hillel, on the other hand, were more lenient. Their basic approach is to accept that which extends even beyond the limitations and boundaries.

אַף עַל פִּי כֵן, בְּכַמָּה דְּבָרִים הָיוּ בֵּית שַׁמַּאי מְקִילִין, מִפְּנֵי הִתְכַּלְּלוּת שֹׁרֶשׁ נִשְׁמָתָם, שֶׁהוּא כָּלוּל גַּם מִיָּמִין, וְכֵן שׁוֹרֶשׁ נִשְׁמַת בֵּית הִלֵּל כָּלוּל גַּם מִשְּׂמֹאל.

in certain matters Beit Shammai were nevertheless lenient. This is **due to the integration** between the different attributes **in the root of their soul, which also comprised of the right** side. **Likewise, the root of Beit Hillel's soul comprised** attributes **from the left** side **as well.**

man is also responsible for everything that might happen if the building collapses.

Some people are expansive in all areas; it is easy for them to conduct themselves in an unreserved manner. Others find it easy to act with severity, to insist that boundaries be respected. This is an indication of a person's approach to the world around him. But in terms of the issues themselves, this does not indicate what is right and what is good.

REINCARNATION IN PROHIBITED AND PERMITTED ANIMALS

☞ Many stories are told about reincarnated souls trapped in the bodies of slaughtered animals (see, e.g., *Kol Sippurei HaBa'al Shem Tov*, vol. 3, pp. 17, 35). In one such story, a goose was declared non-kosher when a question was raised about the validity of the slaughter. The matter was brought before a tzaddik, who cried out, "Is it possible? A soul transmigrated into this goose and has been waiting many

The soul of Beit Shammai belongs to the left side, and at the end of the unfolding succession, once a soul descends to this world from on high, where things are said and done, the left seems separate from the right. But at the soul's root, from which the attributes of the left and the right sides emerge, these attributes are integrated with one another, essentially a single essence that splits apart once they have descended to the worlds.

Since there is an integration of the different attributes at the root of the soul, even down below nothing is entirely one-sided. This finds expression in the realm of *halakha,* since there are matters about which Beit Shammai are lenient and matters about which Beit Hillel are stringent, even more so than Beit Shammai. ☞

כַּיָּדוּעַ דֶּרֶךְ וּמִדּוֹת קֹדֶשׁ הָעֶלְיוֹן, דְּלֵית תַּמָּן קִיצּוּץ וּפֵירוּד חַס וְשָׁלוֹם,

As is known, it is the way of the supernal holy attributes that there is no division or separation there, God forbid,

The tzaddik reviewed and deliberated over the matter, trying as hard as possible to permit the animal so that the reincarnated soul could be released.

years for this moment, and you disqualify the slaughter and send the soul back for another lifetime in a goose, or perhaps even worse?"

ONE SINGLE TRUTH

☞ When we say that certain authorities are stringent, while others are lenient, we are not talking about an erroneous ruling or a distortion of the law, because reality is not such that every question has only one correct answer. Sometimes the same question has several correct answers, and one has to choose between them. There are those whose nature it is to see the negative side, what is liable to happen. They are afraid that it might come to pass, and therefore they rule stringently. There are others who see the chances of success, and they generally rule leniently.

To give a concrete example of this phenomenon, it is possible to reach agreement that the color blue is blue and red is red, and so on. But when people are asked to choose a certain color, everyone chooses a different color. Every answer is correct, since everyone chooses what resonates with him and the root of his soul. In a similar fashion, one person studies a page of Talmud and understands with the same approach as Rashi, while another studies the same page and raises objections in the manner of *Tosafot*. This does not mean that one has more intelligence and the other less. It is merely the way each of them sees and perceives things.

As the holy attributes are found above, before they become intermingled and clothed in the lower worlds, so they are found below to the point that this is one of the most distinctive signs of holiness: Any attribute stemming from the side of holiness cannot be severed and detached from its origin or from other attributes. Conversely, wherever things are severed, when they cannot relate to each other and take each other into consideration, that is a sign that they are not from the side of holiness. Wherever you find extremism, where a thing cannot be incorporated into something else, it means that it is not from the side of holiness, that it stems from impurity. ☞

The Talmud says that "Beit Shammai did not refrain from marrying women from Beit Hillel, nor did Beit Hillel refrain from marrying women from Beit Shammai. This serves to teach you that they practiced affection and camaraderie between them" (*Yevamot* 14b). Despite their halakhic disputes, there was no division or hatred between them. This

DIVISION AND SEPARATION

☞ When someone cannot tolerate another person or a different trait, this is an expression of a deficiency in his soul. Sometimes it stems from *kelippa* itself, and sometimes it is merely a root of evil, the state of evil before it is fully manifest. This is also evident in the realm of Torah and the service of God. When a person sees only one side of the Torah, and neither understands nor relates to any other side, his Torah is divided and separated. If he belongs to the side of holiness, even if he primarily and essentially relates to one thing, he can also digest and understand other things. But if he has only one thing in his head to the exclusion of all else, even if it is entirely holy, this is an evil root. As explained in kabbalistic works, the process of shattering the vessels, of creating the possibility of evil, was at this very point: when the supernal attributes were separated and could no longer relate to the existence of other attributes.

Just as in the laws of the Sabbath a distinction is made between a private domain and a public domain, a similar distinction is made in kabbalistic texts regarding spirituality, between a private domain, the domain and place of God, and a public domain, the place of the worlds (see the introduction to *Tikkunei Zohar* 11b, 20a; *Likkutei Torah*, Deut. 30a, 86d; *Likkutei Amarim*, chap. 33). Everything related to holiness and the Divine is connected to unity, and there can be no division or separation there. This is intimated by the concept of the *reshut hayaḥid*, private domain, which can also mean "the domain of the One." Only in the world below, where the existence of the one God is hidden, does it seem that there is multiplicity and separation. This is conveyed by the concept of the *reshut harabim*, public domain, which can also be translated as "the domain of the many."

is a sign of holiness: when people who are not of the same nature, who disagree with each other, can live together and be integrated with one another.

וְכָל הַמִּדּוֹת כְּלוּלוֹת זוֹ מִזוֹ, וְלָכֵן הֵם מְיוּחָדוֹת זוֹ בָּזוֹ, כַּיָּדוּעַ לְיוֹדְעֵי חֵ"ן,

and all the attributes are incorporated into one another. Therefore, they are united with one another, as is known to those initiated in the esoteric wisdom of Kabbala,

When the attributes cannot unite and integrate with each other, when each attribute is a separate entity in itself, this is the world of chaos and broken vessels.[56] It is a world and reality that cannot endure, that can exist only as fragments of what could not exist. This is in contrast to the world of rectification, where the attributes are integrated with each other, where the attribute of *Ḥesed* has a trace of the attribute of *Gevura* and the attribute of *Gevura* has a trace of the attribute of *Ḥesed*. If the attributes were completely separate, with the attribute of *Ḥesed* being all *Ḥesed*, and the attribute of *Gevura* being exclusively *Gevura*, there would be no possibility of contact and connection between *Ḥesed* and *Gevura*. In holiness, even though every attribute has one fundamental hue, the hue is complex, and therefore it also connects with other sides and other colors, until all of them together complete one picture of unity. ☞

THE INTEGRATION OF THE ATTRIBUTES

☞ This is also the difference between man and beast (and the other creatures in the world). The leopard is always "bold as a leopard." It preys on other animals and tears them apart and cannot act with kindness and mercy. The sheep is meek and deferential and will never attack another animal. Man, on the other hand, can be both one way and the other. This ability characterizes the uniqueness and the magnificence of man. When a person lives in accordance with a particular attribute, that is his heart's desire, and when he can change his attribute as necessary, that is his glory. If a person puts his hand in the mouth of a leopard, it will undoubtedly bite him. A man of holiness, by contrast, even if he is known to be zealous and strict, can also be loving and merciful.

56. See *Me'orei Or*, s.v. "*reshut*."

וּכְדִכְתִיב בְּאַבְרָהָם, שֶׁהוּא מִדַּת הַחֶסֶד וְהָאַהֲבָה, "עַתָּה יָדַעְתִּי כִּי יְרֵא אֱלֹהִים אַתָּה" (בראשית כב, יב),

as it is written regarding Abraham, who represents the attribute of kindness and love, "Now I know that you are God fearing, and you did not withhold your son, your only one, from Me" (Gen. 22:12).

After passing the test of the binding of Isaac, Abraham, who was the perfect human expression of the attribute of kindness and love, was told by God, "Now I know that you are God fearing...." The emphasis is on his fear of God and not on his love for Him. Abraham's test related, not to the attribute of kindness, but rather to the opposite attribute. When the angels appeared to him in human form on the third day, when Abraham was sick and in pain, this was not a test for Abraham. On the contrary, it may have been more difficult for him on the previous two days, when no guests arrived.

This was true of all his trials. In all of them, he was asked to do something against his character, to break his nature and habits: from his leaving Ur Kasdim, his abandoning and severing of all his ties, until the binding of Isaac, where the man of kindness proved that he was God fearing.

עַל יְדֵי שֶׁלָּבַשׁ מִדַּת הַגְּבוּרָה "וַיַּעֲקֹד אֶת יִצְחָק בְּנוֹ... וַיִּקַּח אֶת הַמַּאֲכֶלֶת כוּ'" (שם פסוקים ט–י).

Abraham demonstrated his fear of God **by adopting the attribute of *Gevura*** at the binding of Isaac, as it is written, **"And he bound Isaac his son...and took the knife** to slaughter his son" (Gen. 22:9–10).

At the binding of Isaac, Abraham conducted himself in a manner that was the opposite of Abraham. Abraham embodied *Ḥesed* with every fiber of his being, whereas the binding of Isaac, which involved overcoming and prevailing over his nature, his impulses, his feelings, and his opinions to the furthest extreme, was all *Gevura*. It is precisely for this reason that this test emphasizes Abraham's perfection. That Abraham was "Abraham who loved Me" had long been known, but now it became clear that he was also "God fearing," and this revelation immeasurably changed and elevated everything that had come before.

The same is true on the other side: When a person conducts himself in accordance with the attribute of *Gevura*, we do not know whether this is merely a character trait, that he is closed and restricted within himself, maintaining limits and boundaries, or whether this flows from the side of holiness and the integration of the attributes. But when he also exposes another side, of love and broad-mindedness, he reveals that everything that came before was not just melancholy but *Gevura* in holiness. ☞

וּמַה שֶּׁאָמַר הַכָּתוּב: "אַבְרָהָם אוֹהֲבִי" (ישעיה מא, ח) וּ"פַחַד יִצְחָק" (בראשית לא, מב), הִנֵּה הַהֶפְרֵשׁ וְהַהֶבְדֵּל הַזֶּה הוּא בִּבְחִינַת גִּילּוּי וְהֶעְלֵם, שֶׁבְּמִדַּת יִצְחָק הַפַּחַד הוּא בִּבְחִינַת גִּילּוּי וְהָאַהֲבָה מְסוּתֶּרֶת, בִּבְחִינַת הֶעְלֵם וְהֶסְתֵּר, וְהַהֵיפֶךְ בְּמִדַּת אַבְרָהָם אָבִינוּ עָלָיו הַשָּׁלוֹם.

As for the expressions in the verses "Abraham who loved me" (Isa. 41:8) **and "the fear of Isaac"** (Gen. 31:42), **this difference and distinction pertains to** which attribute is in **a state of revelation and** which is in state of **hiddenness. In the trait of Isaac, the fear is manifest and the love is concealed, in a state of hiddenness and concealment. The opposite is true of the trait of Abraham, our father, may he rest in peace.**

If the holy attributes are incorporated into one another, why do the verses assign a particular attribute to each of the forefathers: to Abraham the attribute of love and kindness and to Isaac the attribute of justice and fear?

But defining Abraham as a man of kindness does not deprive him of the attribute of fear, just as attributing to Isaac the attribute of fear does not deprive him of the attribute of love. Abraham is not only

WHEN ONE'S ATTRIBUTES ARE NOT INTEGRATED

☞ The Rebbe of Peshisḥa expressed this idea in exceedingly harsh terms: "One who is only kindness is an adulterer. One who is only God fearing is a monk. One who is only restraint is a murderer." Of course, he does not mean that this is the case in actuality, but when a person exclusively embodies one single attribute, everything he does with that attribute is a revelation of his ego, of his desires and impulses. That is why the emphasis on Abraham's fearing God is so important: because it is precisely in this that his superiority over other lovers, angels, and souls was revealed.

Ḥesed, and Isaac is not exclusively *Gevura*. The difference between them relates to which attribute is manifest and which is concealed, which is the revealed attribute and which is the hidden one in their respective souls.

In Abraham, kindness is the manifest attribute, while fear is the attribute that is concealed, but the opposite is the case with regard to Isaac. When we characterize a person with a certain attribute, we mean that this attribute is the manifest one, the dominant attribute in his personality and in his life. But in that person's inner essence, all the attributes may be found.

וְזֶהוּ שֶׁאָמַר דָּוִד הַמֶּלֶךְ עָלָיו הַשָּׁלוֹם: "מָה רַב טוּבְךָ וגו'" (תהלים לא, כ). כְּלוֹמַר: שֶׁמִּדַּת הַטּוֹב וְהַחֶסֶד, אֲשֶׁר הִיא בִּבְחִינַת הֶעְלֵם וְהֶסְתֵּר אֵצֶל כָּל מִי שֶׁשּׁוֹרֶשׁ נִשְׁמָתוֹ מִבְּחִינַת שְׂמֹאל, הַנִּקְרָאת בְּשֵׁם "יְרֵאֶיךָ", כְּמִדַּת בֵּית שַׁמַּאי, הִנֵּה אַף שֶׁהוּא טוֹב הַגָּנוּז וְצָפוּן, אַף עַל פִּי כֵן הוּא רַב וְגָדוֹל מְאֹד, כְּמוֹ מִדַּת הַגְּדוּלָּה וְהַחֶסֶד מַמָּשׁ שֶׁמִּבְּחִינַת יָמִין.

This the meaning of the following statement of King David, may he rest in peace: "How great is the goodness You have in store for those who fear You" (Ps. 31:20). **In other words, the attribute of goodness and kindness, which is in a hidden and concealed state in anyone whose soul is rooted in the left side,** in those who are **called "those who fear You," like the attribute of Beit Shammai, it is nevertheless very abundant and great, like the actual attribute of greatness and kindness that stems from the right side, even though the goodness is concealed and hidden.**

The author of the *Tanya* returns here to the verse with which he opened this epistle. The emphasis is on the abundant goodness, that the good that is hidden, though it does not appear so in a manifest manner, is in a certain sense even more abundant than the revealed attribute of kindness.

וּשְׁתֵּיהֶן הֵן מִבְּחִינַת גִּילּוּי, בְּלִי גְּבוּל וּמִדָּה וְשִׁיעוּר.

Both of these degrees of kindness, that which is in a revealed state and that which is concealed, **are manifest without limit, measure, or estimation.**

This is the characteristic of *Ḥesed*: manifestation and expansion without limit. Even the hidden kindness of those who fall into the category of "those who fear You," is also kindness in the same manner. It is only a question of the appropriate place and need for it to be revealed in a way that is "without limit, measure, or estimation."

וְזֶהוּ שֶׁכָּתוּב "מָה רַב טוּבְךָ", כְּלוֹמַר בְּלִי גְּבוּל וּמִדָּה. בֵּין הַטּוֹב "אֲשֶׁר צָפַנְתָּ לִּירֵאֶיךָ", וּבֵין "אֲשֶׁר פָּעַלְתָּ לַחוֹסִים בָּךְ", שֶׁהֵם בַּעֲלֵי הַבִּטָּחוֹן שֶׁמִּבְּחִינַת יָמִין.

This is the meaning of the verse "How great is Your goodness": without limit or measure. This applies to **both the** concealed **good that "You have in store for those who fear You,"** and the revealed good that **"You have created for those taking refuge in You," those who embody trust** in God, **which comes from the right** side.

The one who takes refuge in God trusts in Him and confidently follows Him without calculations. On the other hand, everything that one who is fearful does is calculated and restrained. He will only choose a proven path that is guaranteed in advance after it has all the proper justifications. ☞

וַחֲסָדִם וְטוּבָם הוּא גַּם כֵּן בִּבְחִינַת גִּילּוּי וְהִתְפַּשְּׁטוּת "נֶגֶד בְּנֵי אָדָם", וְלֹא בִּבְחִינַת צִמְצוּם וְהֶסְתֵּר כְּלָל.

The kindness and goodness of "those who fear you" **are also in a state of manifestation and expansion "to be bestowed openly to the sons of man" and not in a constricted or concealed manner at all.**

ONE WHO TRUSTS IN GOD

☞ One who fears God also trusts Him, but he first counts the money and only then does he believe that he has received the amount in full. By contrast, one who trusts in God is one for whom life is open: All will be good. Everything will work out. Since he has a foundation of trust, of devotion and of confidence, he can give and share – his charity, his qualities, his time, himself – without calculations.

The attribute of *Ḥesed* is found equally in those who fear You and in those who embody trust in You. There is a difference between them as to the degree of the attribute's accessibility and clarity to other people, but there is no difference regarding its existence and its ability to appear in a revealed and expansive state.

(וּמַה שֶּׁכָּתוּב "לִירֵאֶיךָ" וְלֹא "בִּירֵאֶיךָ", הַיְינוּ מִשּׁוּם שֶׁכָּל מַה שֶּׁהוּא בִּבְחִינַת הֶעְלֵם בְּכָל נְשָׁמָה, הִנֵּה בְּחִינָה זוֹ אֵינָהּ מְלוּבֶּשֶׁת תּוֹךְ הַגּוּף בְּמוֹחוֹ וְלִבּוֹ, אֶלָּא הוּא בִּבְחִינַת מַקִּיף, מִלְמַעְלָה,

(As for the verse using the phrase **"to those who fear you" rather than "in those who fear you," this is because any** attribute **that is in a concealed state within any soul is not manifest within the body, in his mind and heart, but rather it encompasses from above,**

The author of the *Tanya* here adds a parenthetical note derived from a precise reading of the verse that illuminates all that has been said with more profound meaning. He points out that it has been explained that abundant goodness is stored within "those who fear You." If so, the verse should read "in those who fear You" and not "to those who fear You."

He answers that in every person's soul there are parts that are manifest and there are parts that are concealed, that are not usually evident in the actions and expressions of the soul. The visible parts of a person's soul are those that are manifest within him, in his body and in his soul's faculties, his cognitive and emotive attributes – "his mind and heart" – and find expression in them. The person thinks and feels these parts of his soul in an active and conscious way. By contrast, the concealed parts of his soul, those parts that are not manifest in him, are found in him in an encompassing way. They affect him, because if they did not affect him at all, it would be impossible to say that they belong to him in any sense, but this influence is not direct and visible, but rather encompasses from above. These parts are concealed not only from other people, but in a deeper sense, are not directly and explicitly revealed even to the person himself. Those parts of his soul are manifest only in the way he sees things, in the atmosphere that envelops him, or they do not reveal themselves at all. In any event, they exist for him and have an impact, as will be explained below. ☞

וּמִשָּׁם הִיא מְאִירָה לְמוֹחוֹ וְלִבּוֹ לְעִתִּים הַצְּרִיכִים לְהִתְעוֹרְרוּת בְּחִינָה זוֹ, שֶׁתִּתְעוֹרֵר וְתָאִיר לְמוֹחוֹ וְלִבּוֹ כְּדֵי לָבֹא לִידֵי מַעֲשֶׂה בְּפוֹעַל מַמָּשׁ.)

and from there it radiates to his mind and heart at those times when it is necessary for this attribute to be awakened, so that it will be awakened and radiate to his mind and heart in order to result in an actual deed.)

As has been stated, a sign of holiness is that the hidden, encompassing part of the soul does not always remain in that state. Even an attribute that is the complete opposite of the manifest attributes in a person's soul, an attribute that is found only in the hidden and encompassing aspect of his personality, is sometimes revealed in practice in his consciousness and emotions, and of course in his thoughts and actions. Even in a person who embodies *Gevura*, for example, in whom the side

ENCOMPASSING FROM ABOVE

☞ "Encompassing" and "inner" should not be understood as spatial terms, not with regard to the forces operating in the world and certainly not with regard to the faculties of the soul (see *Likkutei Amarim*, chap. 48). Using modern terms, it may be suggested that the terms "inner" and "encompassing" reflect the distinction between the manifest part of the soul found in the conscious realm and its hidden part in the subconscious realm. In this respect, it can be argued that most of us live the majority of our lives in only a small part of our psyche, and the majority of our psyche is outside of us. Sometimes people live with only a memory of the existence of the soul, with only the vitality that is found also in animals, and the rest is found only in potential outside their being. The greater and holier a person is, the more he is aware of the other parts of his soul and the more he uses them.

This has far-reaching consequences in several areas. It establishes an internal perception of equality between people. In *halakha*, this perception finds expression in the statement "What did you think, that your blood is redder? Perhaps that man's blood is redder" (*Pesaḥim* 25b; *Yoma* 82b). That is to say, in what way are you better than another person? If a certain person is considered a great and righteous scholar, and another person is deemed a boor, a fool, and a sinner, and one must decide which of the two shall die, the Torah scholar holds no advantage. This equality of their souls is in relation to the souls in themselves, even though the manifestation of the souls exhibits great differences.

of *Ḥesed* is completely hidden, the attribute of kindness and love, of openness and going beyond the limits, becomes manifest from time to time, where it is necessary. ☞

וְאָמַר עַל כֵּן, אֲשֶׁר "רַב טוּב" לְבֵית יִשְׂרָאֵל הַצָּפוּן וְהַגָּלוּי הוּא בִּבְחִינַת בְּלִי גְּבוּל וּמִדָּה לְפִי עֶרֶךְ נַפְשׁוֹתָם הַמְלוּבֶּשֶׁת בַּגּוּף,

Thus King David **said that inasmuch as the abundant goodness in the house of Israel,** both **the hidden** goodness **and the revealed** goodness, **is unlimited and immeasurable compared to** the component of **their soul that is enclothed in the body,**

The attribute of goodness and kindness, the readiness to give without limit and measure, is found in every member of Israel.[57] This attribute is greater than the component of the soul that manifests itself in the physical life of this world. The soul is revealed in vessels, and when these vessels are limited material vessels, the element of the soul that is manifest in them is also small and limited in comparison to the hidden part of the soul that is not revealed in these vessels at this time. ☞

THE HIDDEN FACULTIES IN THE SOUL

☞ The reality of hidden faculties in the soul, in ways and degrees of which the person is unaware, is the basis of the author of the *Tanya*'s educational approach. When one studies the *Tanya*, the question arises: How is it possible to make such extreme demands, which sometimes seem as if they have nothing to do with that person's situation?

The answer is that every person has a holy soul containing all the virtues and faculties. When a person comes to educate himself for great things, he does not need to build a new essence for his soul. All that is required of him is to reveal the faculties that are already a part of him in an encompassing state. In a certain sense, the entire *Tanya* is about building the relationship between the manifest part of the soul and its hidden part so that the person will be able to reveal the faculties stored in him, not only in extraordinary stressful situations, but even in his everyday life.

WITHOUT LIMIT AND MEASURE

☞ Within man's being, there is nothing that is unlimited and immeasurable. Man, after all, is a created being and therefore limited at his essence. Thus the author

57. See Isa. 63:7.

לָכֵן, גַּם אַתָּה ה׳ תִּתְנַהֵג עִמָּהֶם בְּמִדַּת חַסְדְּךָ הַגָּדוֹל בְּלִי גְּבוּל וְתַכְלִית, הַנִּקְרֵאת ״רַב חֶסֶד״.

therefore, you too, God, act toward them with Your great, unlimited, and unending kindness, which is called "abundant kindness."

Just as the Jewish people reveal within themselves, or can potentially reveal within themselves when necessary, kindness that is beyond limit and measure, so too we ask God to behave toward them with the same attribute of infinite kindness, which is called "abundant kindness."

דְּאִית חֶסֶד וְאִית חֶסֶד (זהר חלק ג קלג, ב). אִית ׳חֶסֶד עוֹלָם׳, שֶׁיֵּשׁ כְּנֶגְדּוֹ וּלְעוּמָּתוֹ מִדַּת הַדִּין, חַס וְשָׁלוֹם, לְמַעֵט וּלְצַמְצֵם חַסְדּוֹ וְטוּבוֹ,

For "there is kindness, and there is kindness" (*Zohar* 3:113b). **There is world-centered kindness, which has opposed and counter to it the attribute of judgment, God forbid, to minimize and constrict His kindness and goodness,**

The *Zohar* explains there are two general levels of *Ḥesed*: The first is *Ḥesed* that relates to the boundaries of the world and is limited by them, called "world-centered kindness." This level of *Ḥesed* has a counterpart in the attribute of judgment, which can minimize and constrict God's kindness and goodness.[58] This world-centered kindness is part of the reality of the world, in which are also found the attributes of judgment and constriction. The pattern of the world is essentially a limited

of the *Tanya* adds that the goodness that is contained in any member of the Jewish people is unlimited only "compared to [the component of] their soul that is enclothed in the body." The idea appears in many places in his writings: How can a limited, finite person awaken the unlimited, infinite light of *Ein Sof* above? After all, every awakening from below must resemble the awakening from above. His answer is that it is by breaching the boundaries, where a person manages to reach beyond his own limits, even with regard to something small. In this way, an awakening from below brings about an awakening above, which in turn illuminate and affect the reality of the person below.

58. See also *Torah Or* 82a–b, which speaks of the kindness of Abraham as being the natural attribute of love found in the hearts of all of Israel, only that it is hidden and must be awakened, this being awakening from below. With awakening from

pattern: Nothing contained within it expands without limit. Every force is limited by other forces, and every reality is limited by other realities. With regard to the attribute of kindness, for example, even that of a person who is kind and a great lover of mankind, there are necessarily limits set by the attribute of judgment that restrict his kindness. He loves people, but there are some who are difficult even for him to love. He gives to everyone, but there are amounts that even he will not give, and there are some people that even he will concede do not deserve to receive. This is the attribute of world-centered kindness, of kindness that is limited within the dimensions of reality.

אֲבָל ׳חֶסֶד עֶלְיוֹן׳, הַנִּקְרָא ״רַב חֶסֶד״, אֵין כְּנֶגְדּוֹ מִדַּת הַדִּין לְמַעֵט וּלְצַמְצֵם רוֹב חַסְדּוֹ מִלְּהִתְפַּשֵּׁט בְּלִי גְּבוּל וְתַכְלִית. כִּי הוּא נִמְשָׁךְ מִבְּחִינַת ׳סוֹבֵב כָּל עָלְמִין׳, וּ׳טְמִירָא דְּכָל טְמִירִין׳ הַנִּקְרָא ׳כֶּתֶר עֶלְיוֹן׳.

but in the case of **supernal kindness, which is** called **"abundant kindness," there is no attribute of judgment opposing it to minimize and constrict His abundant kindness from expanding without limit or end, for it is derived from the level of encompassing all worlds, and that which is hidden even from all that is hidden, which is called the "supernal crown."**

Supernal kindness exists above and beyond the world's infrastructure. It derives from the level of "encompassing all worlds," which transcends the reality of the world, and from that which is hidden even from all that is hidden, also called the "supernal crown." Like a crown that is above the head and surrounds it, so too the level of encompassing all worlds is completely above all the worlds, encompassing and distinct from all of existence. The *Ḥesed* that comes from the supernal crown is therefore unlimited. It is the *Ḥesed* of *Ein Sof*. Nothing counters it, and nothing can limit it.

World-centered kindness is the attribute of *Ḥesed* of the inner attributes, which relate to each other and limit one another. By contrast, supernal kindness flows from the inner will, the simple will that is at

---

below there is awakening from above, called "abundant kindness," and this is the aspect of Aaron, the High Priest.

the root of all the soul's faculties, with nothing opposing it and no force limiting it.

This is how one should understand the verse "How great is the goodness You have in store for those who fear You." In the soul of every Jew, both those in whom goodness is manifest as well as those in whom it is hidden within the attribute of *Gevura* that is manifest in them, there is the attribute of abundant goodness. This is the abundant goodness that is beyond the revealed attribute of goodness. It is the goodness that is found beyond the limits of the soul, yet operates within it. With this attribute of abundant goodness, one awakens the attribute of supernal kindness so that the abundant kindness may flow without limit.

וְזֶהוּ שֶׁכָּתוּב: "תַּסְתִּירֵם בְּסֵתֶר פָּנֶיךָ וגו' תִּצְפְּנֵם בְּסוּכָּה וגו'" (תהלים לא, כא).

This is the meaning of the next **verse, "Conceal them in the secret place of Your presence; shelter them…in Your pavilion…"** (Ps. 31:21).

These words are expressions of supernal *Ḥesed*, of "abundant kindness," which is stored away and hidden in the supernal crown that hangs over and encompasses reality. This is the implication of the word *sukka* in the verse, which has the same root as the word *sokheh*, which connotes a covering or that which envelops. This level of *Ḥesed* can reveal itself even in Jews whose souls are rooted in the left side, where the attribute of judgment conceals the attribute of *Ḥesed* in them. There is no judgment that cancels or limits supernal *Ḥesed*. ☞

ADDITION OF THE LUBAVITCHER REBBE

☞ In this epistle, the entire section dealing with the application of the ideas herein was omitted. The Lubavitcher Rebbe, Rabbi Menaḥem Mendel Schneerson, addresses this issue in his comments and adds a short passage that summarizes the rest of the epistle:

"What emerges from the aforementioned holy epistle, which was delivered by an emissary…for the collection of charity is that even those who serve God with their souls rooted in the left side, and even if they are like Beit Shammai, they are absolutely righteous people (who are not required to give charity, in accordance with what is explained in epistle 10). 'For they have not ceased' – the kindness within them is 'very great and abundant' and 'when necessary, results in action in actual practice,' as explained at the end of the epistle, which was not printed by the rabbis, may they live [long lives], the sons

This letter is in a certain sense a short essay in praise of Israel. The Jewish people comprise different types of Jews. There are those whose souls are rooted in the right side, in whom we see the good qualities of kindness, love, and giving, and there are those whose souls are rooted in the left side, in whom we see constriction, judgment, and strictness. The author of the *Tanya* explains that with respect to a Jew's holy essence, there is actually no difference between one person and another. There may be a difference in the way the individual's attributes are manifest, but at their essence they are integrated with one another so that every individual possesses both sides, both that of *Gevura* and that of *Ḥesed*, which can become manifest in any one of them as giving without measure or limit.

of the *gaon*, the author, of blessed memory. The conclusion of the epistle states as follows:

"'After these words, it is my request from the depths of my soul to awaken the abundant goodness hidden in the heart of every member of our community, to bring it from a state of concealment to a state of manifestation, so that it may result in deed by filling their hands for God, with a full and open hand, through the trusted bearer of this letter. What is written in the letter is sufficient for one who understands. I am not writing it explicitly because it is unnecessary, and this is sufficient for one who understands.

"'These are the words of one who loves you with all his soul, who seeks your welfare with the longing of the heart and soul,

"'Shneur Zalman, son of my master, my father, our teacher, the master Rabbi Baruch.'"

The full version of the letter's conclusion has been printed in *Iggerot Kodesh* of the Lubavitcher Rebbe (letter 28).

Epistle 14

THE PARTICULAR FOCUS OF THIS LETTER, WHICH WAS probably composed in 1776[1] and which also deals with the mitzva of charity, is the charity of the Land of Israel and the Land of Israel in general. In 1777, a large group of hasidim and their families led by Rabbi Menaḥem Mendel of Vitebsk emigrated to the Land of Israel. It was the first large-scale, organized aliya after a lengthy period during which only a few moved to the land.[2] To meet their material needs and to maintain the unique character of the small hasidic community, they required substantial assistance. The author of the *Tanya* had a special interest in this cause, both because of his affection for the land and its inhabitants and because he considered the leader of the group his own Rebbe to a certain extent and the successor of the Maggid of Mezeritch.

Collecting the funds and sending them to the Land of Israel was a demanding and complicated endeavor. As a rule, the hasidic communities were poor. They did not have abundant financial support even from the beginning, and persecution at home and abroad only worsened the situation. Moreover, the Land of Israel was then governed by the Ottoman Empire, which was in continuous conflict with the Russians. As a consequence, sending funds from Eastern Europe to the land was a complex and dangerous task.[3] All these factors together made the collection of funds

---

1. According to the Lubavitcher Rebbe, Rabbi Menaḥem Mendel Schneerson, *Iggerot Kodesh*, letter 48.
2. These include the Ba'al Shem Tov's brother-in-law, Rabbi Gershon of Kitov.
3. One of the accusations leveled against the author of the *Tanya* while he was

for the community in the land a formidable challenge, both for the Rebbe and for the hasidim in general, and this letter attests to the great efforts they invested in this regard.

As is typical of these letters from the Rebbe to the hasidim, the practical topic at hand serves as a framework for the hasidic ideas that it explores. This letter clarifies the special virtue of charity in the Land of Israel, which leads to the topic of the Land of Israel itself: What is the nature of the divine influence over the land, and what is the special day when this influence is renewed every year? Also explored is the meaning of time, particularly Rosh HaShana as its annual starting point.[4]

15 Elul / 12 Elul (leap year)

לְעוֹרֵר אֶת הָאַהֲבָה הַיְשָׁנָה וְחִבַּת אֶרֶץ הַקֹּדֶשׁ

This letter was written **to awaken the old love and affection for the Holy Land,**

The letter begins by expressing the need to awaken our erstwhile love for the Holy Land, which has perhaps grown old and is currently lying dormant.

לִהְיוֹת בּוֹעֶרֶת כְּרִשְׁפֵּי אֵשׁ מִקֶּרֶב אִישׁ וְלֵב עָמוֹק, כְּאִלּוּ הַיּוֹם מַמָּשׁ נָתַן ה׳ רוּחוֹ עָלֵינוּ, רוּחַ נְדִיבָה בְּהִתְנַדֵּב עָם, לְמַלֹּאוֹת יָדָם לַה׳ בְּיָד מְלֵאָה וּרְחָבָה,

so that it burns like sparks of fire from within man and the depths of the heart, as though God literally placed His spirit upon us on this very day, a generous spirit, so that the people volunteer to dedicate themselves to God with great generosity

When the hasidim decided to help their brothers in the Land of Israel, there was initially great enthusiasm. In the subsequent year and the one after that, their fervor waned, and it became harder to collect the same amounts. The purpose of this letter is to inspire the hasidim, not only to give, but also to feel the same enthusiasm they felt the first time and to an even greater extent.

---

imprisoned in St. Petersburg was that he was conspiring with the enemy, a claim based on the large sums he had transferred to Israel. See epistle 2 above.

4. See *Likkutei Torah*, Deut. 53c.

בְּרִיבּוּי אַחַר רִיבּוּי מִדֵּי שָׁנָה בְּשָׁנָה,

with one **increase after another, from year to year,**

Every year should see an increase of charity over the previous one. The author of the *Tanya* is asking that they not only refrain from reducing what they had promised to give in advance or what they are accustomed to giving, but rather they should increase the sum. In order to preserve the novelty, one must fashion an experience that somewhat resembles the first time one encountered it by consistently adding something to the previous instance.

הוֹלֵךְ וְעוֹלֶה לְמַעְלָה רֹאשׁ, כְּמִדַּת קֹדֶשׁ הָעֶלְיוֹן,

consistently ascending and rising like the measure of supernal holiness,

There is a rabbinical concept that we rise in level in matters of sanctity.[5] The mark of holiness is that one is constantly on the increase. When one is not growing in sanctity, when there is no advancement or ascent, the result is deterioration, which is the opposite of holiness.

הַמֵּאִיר לְאֶרֶץ הַקֹּדֶשׁ, הַמִּתְחַדֵּשׁ וּמִתְרַבֶּה תָּמִיד,

that shines on the Holy Land, which is constantly renewing and increasing,

One essential aspect of the attribute of holiness, which is a quality of the Holy Land, of the Land of Israel, is the quality of renewal, constantly increasing and ascending in level. In the case of man, this is expressed through a persistent increase in one's spiritual aspirations, awareness, and devotion. Practically speaking, this can be expressed in constantly augmenting the amount of charity one gives to the inhabitants of the land. ☞

SUPERNAL HOLINESS

☞ In kabbalistic terminology, this expressions alludes to the *sefira* of *Ḥokhma*, or Wisdom, which is considered the first or highest level of the *sefirot*, while that which is merely called "holy" or the "Holy Land" refers to the *sefira* of *Malkhut*, the

5. See, e.g., Mishna *Shekalim* 6:4; *Berakhot* 28a; *Shabbat* 21a.

כִּדְכְתִיב: "תָּמִיד עֵינֵי ה' אֱלֹהֶיךָ בָּהּ, מֵרֵשִׁית הַשָּׁנָה וְעַד אַחֲרִית שָׁנָה" (דברים יא, יב).

as it is written, "A land that the Lord your God seeks; **always the eyes of the Lord your God are upon it, from the beginning of the year until the end of the year"** (Deut. 11:12).

The illumination of the supernal holiness is expressed in this verse, which the author of the *Tanya* will elucidate below. The verse mentions the special status of the Land of Israel: It is not like other lands, but rather it is "a land that the Lord your God seeks" and "always the eyes of the Lord your God are upon it." It is blessed with a special level of divine providence.

דְּהַאי "וְעַד אַחֲרִית כו'" אֵינוֹ מוּבָן לִכְאוֹרָה, שֶׁהֲרֵי בְּאַחֲרִית שָׁנָה זוֹ מַתְחֶלֶת שָׁנָה שְׁנִיָּה, וְאִם כֵּן הֲוָה לֵיהּ לְמֵימַר 'לְעוֹלָם וָעֶד'!

It would seem that the meaning of **this** phrase **"until the end** of the year" **is not clear, since at the end of the year another year begins, and in that case, it should have said "forever."**

If the eyes of God are "always" on the land, the verse should have said that God's eyes are on it "forever." What is the verse implying with this unusual phrase, "from the beginning of the year until the end of the year"? What is the significance of this break between one year and another, this division of time into distinct units? ☞

lowest of the *sefirot*. The verse tells us that "the Lord founded the earth with wisdom [*ḥokhma*]" (Prov. 3:19), intimating that the *sefira* of *Ḥokhma* illuminates the earth, which is the *sefira* of *Malkhut*.

THE NATURE OF TIME

☞ A year is not simply a period of time but a meaningful unit. It should not be viewed as merely the sum of a regular cycle of insignificant units that one could divide into sections: two days, seven days, three hundred and sixty-five days. Rather, time is an organic entity, with a head and a foot, a beginning and an end, that can maintain its essential nature only if it remains whole. If one chops it up, each part will have a different character and nature. A 100-meter thread can be cut into two threads each 50 meters long, but if one were to cut a living thing in half, one would be left with a head on one side and legs on the other, and neither of them will remain alive. It is

אַךְ הָעִנְיָן יוּבַן עַל פִּי מַה שֶּׁכָּתוּב: "ה' בְּחָכְמָה יָסַד אָרֶץ" (משלי ג, יט), שֶׁיְּסוֹד הָאָרֶץ הָעֶלְיוֹנָה הִיא בְּחִינַת 'מְמַלֵּא כָּל עָלְמִין',

Rather, the idea can be understood on the basis of the verse "The Lord founded the earth with wisdom" (Prov. 3:19), **that the foundation of the supernal land is an expression of** the divine light and life force **filling all worlds,**

According to the teachings of Kabbala, wisdom refers to the *sefira* of *Ḥokhma,* while the earth refers to the *sefira* of *Malkhut.* The supernal land is the spiritual essence of our material world and thus is also an expression of the divine *sefira* of *Malkhut.* It is the *sefira* of *Malkhut* that descends from the divine essence of the *sefirot* into the worlds. The whole of existence and the impact of the *sefirot* on the worlds, down to the physical earth below, is channeled through the *sefira* of *Malkhut.* This *sefira* does not merely draw down the divine light and life force from above. It actually descends into the worlds to sustain and guide them from within. This is why *Malkhut* is called "the supernal land" that "fills all worlds." It is the immanent divine life force within all of reality, the earth, bringing it into existence and sustaining it.

וְהַתַּחְתּוֹנָה הִיא 'אֶרֶץ חֵפֶץ' הַמְכוּוֶּנֶת כְּנֶגְדָּהּ מַמָּשׁ,

and the lower land, the Land of Israel, which **is called a "desired land," is literally** situated **opposite** the supernal land,

The Land of Israel is called "a desired land"[6] and is situated "opposite the supernal land." Of course, this does not refer to a geographic location. The supernal land is not located in a physical place. Rather, the idea is that they resonate with each other: The physical Land of

a difference not merely in dimensions, but of essence. In view of this, "from the beginning of the year until the end of the year" is not simply a period of time, consisting of a defined number of days, but the specific unit called year, which has both a beginning and an end.

6. See Mal. 3:12.

Israel is counterpart to the supernal entity called "land." In light of this, the terms "Divine Presence," "*Malkhut*," "congregation of Israel" and "Land of Israel" are often used synonymously. ☞

וְנִקְרֵאת עַל שְׁמָהּ 'אֶרֶץ הַחַיִּים',

and it is named after the supernal land, **the land of the living.**

The lower land, the Land of Israel, is named after the supernal land, which is the divine attribute of *Malkhut*. It is called the land of the living – the land that receives and gives life.[7] There are thus two lands of the living, one above and the other below. Just as the supernal land receives and gives supernal life, as will be explained below, so too the lower land, the Land of Israel, receives and gives life to all the worlds in a direct and real sense.

הִנֵּה הוּא נִמְשָׁךְ מֵהַמְשָׁכַת וְהֶאָרַת "חָכְמָה עִילָּאָה", מְקוֹר הַחַיִּים הָעֶלְיוֹנִים, כְּדִכְתִיב: "הַחָכְמָה תְּחַיֶּה בְעָלֶיהָ וכו'" (קהלת ז, יב).

The life force **issues forth from the flow and illumination of supernal *Ḥokhma*, the source of supernal life, as it is written, "Wisdom preserves the life of its possessors…"** (Eccles. 7:12).

A DESIRED LAND

☞ The "desired land" is the land that God desires. According to hasidic teachings, this desire refers to the inner will, and the desired land is the land that God wants with His inner will as opposed to the other lands, which are considered like the mere framework in relation to Israel. The lands receive their life force only through the life force and providence bestowed on the Holy Land. The desired land thus expresses the essence of the land, the purpose of all the other lands' existence, where God directs His attention and through which all the other lands receive their measure of providence.

---

7. See Ps. 116:9. It is explained elsewhere that this refers to two lands, the land below and the land above, which are positioned opposite one another and operate in tandem and in conjunction with one another. See *Torah Or* 26c.

The *sefira* of *Ḥokhma* is the first *sefira*, the loftiest of the ten *sefirot*. It is the first to receive the divine light and life force from *Ein Sof*, which encompasses all worlds, and infuses it with the light that fills all worlds, which is an aspect of the supernal land, as the author of the *Tanya* stated above. Consequently, *Ḥokhma* is the source of all of existence and life for the worlds. ☞

וְהֶאָרָה וְהַמְשָׁכָה זוֹ הִיא מִתְחַדֶּשֶׁת בְּאוֹר חָדָשׁ מַמָּשׁ בְּכָל שָׁנָה וְשָׁנָה,

This illumination and flow from supernal *Ḥokhma* is renewed each and every year with an actual new light,

While this illumination of light from *Ḥokhma* to the worlds is constant, because otherwise the worlds would cease to exist, it is not fixed and monotonous. The illumination renews itself regularly, with its most prominent revitalization occurring "each and every year." Every year presents a fresh link between the higher and lower realms, and a new entity is created that did not previously exist. Naturally, the new year also replicates some of the features of the previous year, since there are aspects that are similar between them along with the differences, but in essence each unit of time is its own entity.

Consider family relationships. All the children of one set of parents share a bond and resemble each other; the second child is similar in some ways to the first. But they are not the continuation of a single entity. There is always a distinct division between one individual

WISDOM VERSUS INTELLECT

☞ When discussing the attribute of wisdom, one should avoid identifying these concepts (as one instinctively tends to do) with the intellect. This does not mean that there is no connection between them, but "intellect" is an inadequate term to ascribe to wisdom. The intellect is a manifestation of the mind, but it is not its essence. The same can be said about the brain: It cannot be defined as the intellect. The brain is the seat of thought, of the intellect, but it is far more than its intellectual capacity. It is the center of life, the functioning hub of a living creature. In this sense, the brain of a spider and that of a human being serve the same function: It is the core of life, of everything that happens to the creature as a living being. Furthermore, and to an even greater extent, when we refer to *Ḥokhma*, we are not speaking merely of knowledge. Rather, the term is far more expansive, intimating that it is the primary source of life.

and the next. Similarly, there is a break between the years. They bear a resemblance to each other, but in fact each year is "an actual new light." ☞

כִּי הוּא יִתְבָּרֵךְ וְחָכְמָתוֹ אֶחָד בְּתַכְלִית הַיִּחוּד, **for God and His wisdom are one, in absolute unity,**

In the words of Rambam, "He is the knower, He is the known, and He is the knowledge itself..." (*Sefer HaMadda, Hilkhot Yesodei HaTorah* 2:10). Since His knowledge constitutes knowledge of Himself, all three aspects of His knowledge – the object of His knowledge, the knowledge He possesses, and He, the knower – are one and the same. Notwithstanding the limitations of this explanation, it conveys the

EVERY YEAR A NEW LIGHT

☞ No time is precisely like another, just as no person is exactly the same as any other, and no place is identical to another place. It might appear to us that there is no difference, that time is a uniform period that can be divided into fixed, homogeneous units, just as the clock divides the day into finite, equal units. This view stems from a perfunctory conception of time. The dimension of place can also be perceived in this superficial manner. If one analyzes places only in terms of their external dimensions, one might say that there are such-and-such miles from one end of Israel to the other, and each mile is the same as the next. But the truth is that some areas are hilly whereas others consist of valleys, and various kinds of vegetation grow in each spot, and so each area is a distinct place. It is impossible to equate the arid south of Israel to the region near the Sea of Galilee.

In the same vein, there are countless stars, all of which look identical to us, and yet God "sets a number for the stars and calls them all by name" (Ps. 147:4). Each of them has its own name; they are all unique entities. In the case of people as well, one can present them in numerical terms – two people, a hundred, a million – and this captures them to a certain extent. But when it comes to what these numbers represent, each person is a unique individual.

This is how units of time are understood here. Each unit is an entity unto itself, a living entity, one that has a beginning and an end, that is born and dies, the like of which never existed before and will never recur again.

This idea has far-reaching ramifications for everything a person does, especially in his service of God. What is important is not only what a person does in life, but also the time when he performs those actions. If a person does not execute a deed at a particular hour, he cannot reassure himself by saying, "I will do it tomorrow" or "I will get back to that next week," because the next day will not be identical to the present one. This day, this very moment, will never return. Anything a person does on some other day will belong to that time and will become part of the essential nature of that very different day.

idea that divine wisdom and the divine essence are united in a single essence.[8] ☞

וְנִקְרָא בְּשֵׁם 'אוֹר אֵין סוֹף בָּרוּךְ הוּא', שֶׁאֵין סוֹף וְאֵין קֵץ לְמַעֲלַת וּגְדוּלַּת הָאוֹר וְהַחַיּוּת הַנִּמְשָׁךְ מִמֶּנּוּ יִתְבָּרֵךְ וּמֵחָכְמָתוֹ, בְּעִילּוּי אַחַר עִילּוּי עַד אֵין קֵץ וְתַכְלִית, לְרוּם הַמַּעֲלוֹת לְמַעְלָה מַעְלָה.

and the light that issues forth from *Ḥokhma* **is called the light of *Ein Sof*, blessed be He, since there is no end and no limit to the quality and greatness of the light and life force that issues forth from God and from His wisdom, through one elevation after another, endlessly without limit, at the pinnacle of** all **heights, above and beyond.**

The vessel of *Ḥokhma* is, in a certain sense, the vessel of *Ein Sof*. Supernal *Ḥokhma* is not a distinct entity in any respect, but rather is a receptacle for the light and life force of *Ein Sof*. This is the divine light that comes from high above, an encompassing light that reaches all the way down to the lowest levels of the lowest world of *Asiya*. It is the illumination that everywhere and in all manners embodies *Ein*

"GOD AND HIS WISDOM ARE ONE"

☞ Why is this unity attributed specifically to wisdom? The Hebrew letters of the word for wisdom, *ḥokhma*, can be rearranged to spell *ko'aḥ mah*, the "potential of what" (see, e.g., *Likkutei Amarim*, chap. 18), referring to the most primal force of life that cannot yet be distinguished, that does not yet recognize itself as a separate entity. Accordingly, even though the level of *Ḥokhma* is not identical to the essence of the soul, and, of course, the divine attribute of *Ḥokhma*, God's wisdom, must not be identified with His essence, it is still unified with it, since it has no separate identity, no distinct sense of self.

Moreover, the author of the *Tanya* explains elsewhere that this unity of wisdom, or knowledge, in Rambam's terminology, exists in all the *sefirot*, not only in *Ḥokhma*. The manifestation and effect of each *sefira* is of itself and within itself. There is nothing apart from it in that plane of the *sefirot*. One of the reasons the author of the *Tanya* refers specifically to *Ḥokhma* is because this *sefira* corresponds to *Atzilut*, the highest of all the worlds, and it is the highest of all the *sefirot* in every world.

8. See *Likkutei Amarim*, chap. 2.

Sof, endlessly giving in quantity and quality, with infinite patience and boundless exaltation.

A question then arises concerning the relationship between *Ḥokhma* and the earth, of which the verse states, "The Lord founded the earth with wisdom [*ḥokhma*]." There are two possibilities: Either there is no direct connection between this attribute and the world, because *Ḥokhma* is indeed entirely inconceivable and does not exist in relation to reality, or there is a connection, in which case reality would be subsumed in the divine light.

Though this attribute is indeed lofty, its connection to the earth, to the worlds below, is nevertheless preserved through the mode of "running and returning." The divine light and life force do not descend to the world in a direct, uniform manner, but in the form of pulses, like the life that flows through our veins, in our heartbeats and our breathing, and as is the case for many facets of our existence. The divine beneficence to the worlds pulsates in a similar fashion: Like pulses that come and go, rising up and dying out, from day to day and from year to year.

13 Elul (leap year)

וּבְכָל שָׁנָה וְשָׁנָה יוֹרֵד וּמֵאִיר מֵחָכְמָה עִילָּאָה אוֹר חָדָשׁ וּמְחוּדָּשׁ, שֶׁלֹּא הָיָה מֵאִיר עֲדַיִין מֵעוֹלָם לָאָרֶץ הָעֶלְיוֹנָה.

Each and every year a new, renewed light descends and radiates from supernal *Ḥokhma*, one that has never yet shone, to the supernal land,

On Rosh HaShana every year a new light arrives, one that never existed before and will never return. This is the pulse of the divine beneficence, which comes in fixed, disparate portions, each of which is a new entity with respect to the others. These pulses have diverse rhythms. Some consist of immense rhythms of a thousand years, while others are tiny, lasting mere moments. But the most significant rhythm, around which our lives are structured, is that of the year. Each year is like a heartbeat, and the body lives from one pulse to the next, which passes only to be replaced by another. ☞

The phrase "from the beginning of the year until the end of the year" thus expresses the essence of a year that has a beginning and an end, of the pulse of a life that starts and finishes. The new year is not merely a date written in the calendar, but a revelation, an actual change in reality that is no longer the same as it was. The former existence is no longer, and what will be in the new year is an entity that was not there before.

כִּי אוֹר כָּל שָׁנָה וְשָׁנָה מִסְתַּלֵּק לְשָׁרְשׁוֹ בְּכָל עֶרֶב רֹאשׁ הַשָּׁנָה, כְּשֶׁהַחֹדֶשׁ מִתְכַּסֶּה בּוֹ.

for the light of each and every year withdraws to its source on every Rosh HaShana eve, when the new moon is covered and hidden.

Rosh HaShana is the only festival that falls on Rosh Ḥodesh, the day of the new moon, when the new moon is hidden from sight.[9] This is not coincidental but conveys the essence of this day. Rosh HaShana, the beginning of the new year, is a time when all is hidden. The previous year has vanished and expired, like a person who has run out of oxygen. Without new blood or a fresh source of life, his life will come to an end. This metaphor represents the eve of Rosh HaShana, when the previous year has faded away, returning to the primal source, and no longer has a relationship with our reality.

וְאַחַר כָּךְ, עַל יְדֵי תְּקִיעַת שׁוֹפָר וְהַתְּפִלּוֹת, נִמְשָׁךְ אוֹר חָדָשׁ עֶלְיוֹן

Subsequently, on Rosh HaShana itself, **through the *shofar* blasts and the prayers, a new supernal light issues forth**

THE YEAR AS A UNIT OF TIME

☞ A year is a unit in its own right, a living entity, a reality that has several ramifications. On the broad scale, this is true for any segment of time; they are all singular and unique. The expression "killing time" conveys precisely this point: When one kills time, one actually does destroy it. It is not as one might think, that this moment is simply replaced by another, that one "gets rid" of a year and another year is there in its stead. The next year is different, a completely new entity, unrelated to the previous year, and one cannot be exchanged for the other. This is precisely like the way two people differ from each other. Although it is possible for one person to do the same kind of work as another, no one can entirely fill the shoes of another, because he is not the same person. One who has killed someone can seek to atone for his sin, but he cannot bring back the person he killed.

9. See *Rosh HaShana* 8a–b.

The prayers of Rosh HaShana and the sounding of the *shofar* accompany the birth of a new time period, heralding, awakening, and even directing it. ☞

מִבְּחִינָה עֶלְיוֹנָה יוֹתֵר, שֶׁבְּמַדְרֵגַת חָכְמָה עִילָּאָה, **from a higher aspect in the level of supernal *Ḥokhma***

Before Rosh HaShana, the new year is in a potential state, at the highest level of *Ḥokhma,* offering loftier and greater possibilities than the previous years. This is because time increasingly progresses and accumulates, so that each new year has greater potential than the previous ones. ☞

לְהָאִיר לְ'אָרֶץ עֶלְיוֹנָה' וְלַדָּרִים עָלֶיהָ, הֵם כָּל הָעוֹלָמוֹת הָעֶלְיוֹנִים וְהַתַּחְתּוֹנִים הַמְקַבְּלִים חַיּוּתָם מִמֶּנָּה, **to illuminate the supernal land and those who dwell in it, which are all the higher and lower worlds that receive their vitality from it,**

THE SOUNDING OF THE *SHOFAR*

☞ The *shofar* emits several sounds. One is "the blast of the King" (Num. 23:21), pronouncing a new reign, the arrival of a fresh time, the germination of a new world. For this reason, at the conclusion of the Rosh HaShana evening service we recite the verse "Lift up your heads, gates; be raised up, infinite portals, so the King of glory may enter" (Ps. 24:7). The sound of the shofar, with its staccato and broken blasts, also represents the cries of a mother in labor: The one hundred shofar blasts that are sounded on Rosh HaShana (see *Shulḥan Arukh HaRav, Oraḥ Ḥayyim* 596:1) correspond to one hundred wails of a woman giving birth (*Vayikra Rabba* 27:7; *Tanḥuma, Tazria* 4). A woman in labor emits a cry, a sound of pain. She does not make gentle sounds that are pleasing to listeners. The same is true of the shofar: It is the sound of a world torn apart, screaming, weeping, wailing. Like the sounds of a child-bearing woman, it projects a mixture of emotions: of joy and fear, of pain, apprehension, and hope.

A GREATER RISK

☞ The loftier status of the new year does not necessarily come to fruition in practice. It is possible that the opposite will occur, because as time progresses the danger that the new year will be a more difficult one also increases. When a person is sitting on the ground, he has nowhere to fall and hurt himself, but when he climbs to a higher spot, he is in a more precarious position. Each new year thus presents more opportunities, but also greater risk.

The supernal land is a reservoir of life that encompasses all the worlds. Just as we receive our physical life, directly or indirectly, from the earth, the material, lower realm, so too, in a more complex and wider scope, all the worlds sprout from the essence of divine *Malkhut*, which is the supernal land.

דְּהַיְינוּ, מִן הָאוֹר אֵין סוֹף בָּרוּךְ הוּא וְחָכְמָתוֹ הַמְלוּבָּשׁ בָּהּ, כְּדִכְתִיב: "כִּי עִמְּךָ מְקוֹר חַיִּים בְּאוֹרְךָ נִרְאֶה אוֹר" (תהלים לו, י), דְּהַיְינוּ אוֹר הַמֵּאִיר מֵחָכְמָה עִילָּאָה מְקוֹר הַחַיִּים

that is, from the light of *Ein Sof*, blessed be He, and His wisdom, which is enclothed in it, as it is written, "For the source of life is with You; through Your light we see light" (Ps. 36:10). **This refers to the light that shines forth from supernal *Ḥokhma*, the source of life**

The supernal land, or *Malkhut*, does not bestow the life force from itself but from the light of *Ein Sof* that is enclothed in it, whose origin is high above, in the source of all life.[10] Accordingly, the light that is renewed on Rosh HaShana is not a continuation and development of the previous year, of a light that already descended into the world and is enclothed within it (whether in potential or actuality). Rather, it is an entirely new light that emerges from the primal source, the source of life.

(וְכַנּוֹדָע לְיוֹדְעֵי חֵ"ן, שֶׁבְּכָל רֹאשׁ הַשָּׁנָה הִיא הַ'נְּסִירָה' וּמְקַבֶּלֶת מוֹחִין חֲדָשִׁים עֶלְיוֹנִים יוֹתֵר כוּ').

(and as is known to those initiated in the esoteric wisdom of Kabbala, **on every Rosh HaShana the *nesira*,** a cutting or separation, takes place, **and it receives newer, loftier *moḥin*, and so on).**

According to the teachings of Kabbala,[11] the *nesira* is one of the main themes of Rosh HaShana. On the most basic level, *nesira* is a description of the creation of the woman. Man and woman were

10. See *Likkutei Torah*, Lev. 52a.

11. See *Pri Etz Ḥayyim, Sha'ar Rosh HaShana*, chaps. 1, 5; see also *Likkutei Torah*, Deut. 42b, 47e.

originally created as one being, back-to-back, and the creation of woman was in actuality a separation of the woman from the man so that she became a distinct entity. In broader terms, it refers to the separation of *Malkhut* from the divine essence, as it were, so that it becomes a distinct essence with its own *moḥin,* its own consciousness, as it were. This separation is the beginning and foundation of the creation and existence of all worlds, which arise and receive their life from *Malkhut.* ☞ ☞

THE *NESIRA*

☞ It should be noted that Rosh HaShana is not the anniversary of the creation of the world, but rather marks the sixth day, when man was created. When we call it a commemoration of the first day, this refers to the first day to which memory or consciousness is applicable. It is the beginning of time that has meaning, that can be experiences, a time that begins with man.

One of the most significant events of this day was the *nesira*, the separation of Adam and Eve. This separation has far-reaching symbolic meaning that goes beyond the creation of woman. The relationship between Adam and Eve, between the first man and the first woman, is the prototype of a bond that repeats itself on all levels of reality, all the way to the loftiest heights. Before the *nesira*, the woman was part of man's form, which also incorporated the woman. In this archetypal figure, the woman was not a distinct being unto herself, just as the man was not a separate entity in his own right. It is the *nesira* that fashioned her into a new determinate being.

The creation of woman and her transformation into a separate creature symbolizes the creation of *Malkhut*, the "land." This is a process by which the configuration of the *sefirot* was transformed from a closed system that was complete and whole in and of itself into one that bore a new infrastructure that could grow and develop outward. The *nesira* constructed the *sefira* of *Malkhut*, step by step, as its own entity. Consequently, instead of being just a meaningless mirror image (as Eve was to Adam when they were back-to-back), it would now receive substance and meaning of its own, becoming "the mother of all living" (Gen. 3:20).

The *nesira*, the building of *Malkhut*, is described as a process through which this *sefira* received new *moḥin*, not by means of *Zeir Anpin* (the array of six *sefirot* that correspond to the emotive attributes: *Ḥesed, Gevura, Tiferet, Netzaḥ, Hod*, and *Yesod*), but from the cognitive *sefira* of *Bina* itself (*Likkutei Torah*, Deut. 42b). When *Malkhut* (woman) is joined with the *sefira* above it (man), it receives *moḥin* through it and from it. It is like the way a person's foot has no consciousness or viewpoint of its own. Any sentience it has is part of the person's general awareness, of the head and the body that are above it, and it moves accordingly. In the process of *nesira*, which is the formation of *Malkhut* as a separate entity, it receives *moḥin*, or a consciousness, so to speak, of its own.

The *moḥin* that *Malkhut* receives on

וּבִפְרָטֵי פְּרָטִיּוֹת כֵּן הוּא בְּכָל יוֹם וָיוֹם. **On a more specific level, the same is the case each and every day.**

Just as the year manifests in large units of time, so too it unfolds in small units: "In His goodness, He continually renews the work of creation every day" (*Yotzer Or* blessing). Every day sees a total renewal of existence from the source of life. Each day is a new time and a fresh world that did not exist before, with all that this implies. Like the judgment that

Rosh HaShana is the fresh vitality from the supernal *Ḥokhma* that reinvigorates the world, like a newly created being. This entity is the new world that is born on Rosh HaShana, the new pulse that will pump life into the existing world from the beginning of the upcoming year until its conclusion.

ROSH HASHANA AS THE DAY OF JUDGMENT

☞ This interpretation of Rosh HaShana as the pulse of new life, stemming from the source of all existence, also explains why this festival is considered the day of judgment, as expressed in the verses "Blow the shofar at the showing of the New Moon, at the appointed time of our holiday, for it is a statute for Israel, a law of the God of Jacob" (Ps. 81:4–5). Rosh HaShana starts at the conclusion of the previous year. The flow of life from the previous year is over, and now a new life must start. This is a stage of judgment: Will the gift of life be given or not? Is it deserved or undeserved? If we desire life, we must justify our collective and personal existence. On this day, and to a certain extent on all the Days of Awe, the world receives a kind of conditional present. We are duty-bound to explain: Why do we deserve another year? What justifies our continued existence?

This judgment goes beyond the basic question of whether or not a person has sinned. It is based on a more fundamental inquiry: Does the past justify the future? Does what transpired last year provide a reason for us to carry on or not? This is a far more intimidating judgment, since it puts our very existence into question. When we must provide an account of all the good and bad deeds we have done, we might have to pay a price. But if we fall short of the account taken on Rosh HaShana, there might not be another year at all.

This can be compared to the practice of a farmer. At the beginning of each season, he inspects his harvest and makes a calculation for each planting: Did the fruits the tree grew the previous year justify his investment in water, land, and labor? Is success more likely in the forthcoming year? He will accordingly decide whether or not to give that crop another try.

This whole line of thought comes from our understanding of the year, and of time in general, as an entity that must be created afresh on each occasion. For that renewal to be justified, it has to be better and of finer quality than what existed before.

the whole world faces on Rosh HaShana, so too it stands in judgment every day, to determine whether a new day is justified.[12] ☞

נִמְשָׁכִין מוֹחִין עֶלְיוֹנִים יוֹתֵר בְּכָל תְּפִלַּת הַשַּׁחַר, **Loftier *moḥin* are drawn down during each morning prayer service,**

The drawing down of the *moḥin* refers to the fresh vitality of the new day, which is superior and more developed than the previous one, as explained above. If a person does not corrupt his ways, he will merit a new revelation every day, as he ascends from one level to the next, day by day.

These *moḥin* of the nascent day are drawn down to the world

FEELING THE CONSTANT RENEWAL OF CREATION

☞ Although each day is a new creation, a new world, we generally do not feel it. There are several reasons for this. First, we are usually busy with our affairs, and when someone is preoccupied, he does not feel time passing. He does not pay attention to the changes that are transpiring around him. A second reason is that in order to feel time, its existence and uniqueness, one requires a special sensitivity. The third reason is that we are not typically aware of anything that does not change in big leaps. One who is living with a child will not notice him growing, whereas those who have not seen him for a long time will immediately observe how much he has grown. Likewise, although there are changes from day to day, and no day is the same as the one before, the course of change is usually continuous, without sharp jumps, and therefore we cannot feel it. Indeed, sometimes a big change occurs, and then one truly does wake up in the morning with the feeling that today the world is entirely different.

Nevertheless, there are undoubtedly people who have the ability to discern these changes in time, just as in every realm of life certain individuals are blessed with a special insight and comprehension. Such people will immediately notice changes that others do not see. Experts in diamonds will instantly detect the small differences, those singular qualities that other people are not aware of at all. The same applies to time: There are people who can grasp the essence of time, just as others instinctively understand the mechanics of a machine or a computer program, and yet others can intuit the nature of a certain person. These individuals can grasp the unique essence of a certain time as a complete entity, from beginning to end, and therefore they can in a sense also ascertain what will happen over the course of time. It is related about the Ḥozeh of Lublin, Rabbi Yaakov Yitzḥak HaLevi Horowitz, that he could see from the beginning of the year what kind of year it would be.

---

12. *Likkutei Torah, Derushim LeRosh HaShana* 53d; see also *Rosh HaShana* 16a.

and to one's soul during the morning service, through both the special qualities of the time and by virtue of the prayer he offers at that hour.

וְאֵינָן מוֹחִין הָרִאשׁוֹנִים שֶׁנִּסְתַּלְּקוּ אַחַר הַתְּפִלָּה, רַק גְּבוֹהִין יוֹתֵר.

and they are not the original *moḥin* that were withdrawn after the prayer of the day before, **but loftier ones.**

As a rule, the world should grow and become progressively better day by day. Every day it should receive a loftier and greater illumination. What it does with this illumination is the world's own affair, because it can also ruin it. Yet the day itself is always loftier than the previous one. ☞

וְדֶרֶךְ כְּלָל, בִּכְלָלוּת הָעוֹלָם, בְּשֵׁית אַלְפֵי שְׁנִין, כֵּן הוּא בְּכָל רֹאשׁ הַשָּׁנָה וְרֹאשׁ הַשָּׁנָה.

In general, with regard to the world as a whole, over the course of the six thousand years of its existence, **this is the case on each and every Rosh HaShana.**

The broadest cycle of the world's existence will endure for six thousand years. In keeping with the cycle of the seven days of the week and the seven years of the sabbatical year cycle, the largest cycle is that of six thousand years and the seventh millennium.[13] During the course of those six thousand years, every Rosh HaShana is also a time of renewal.

LOFTIER THAN THE DAY BEFORE

☞ This principle derives from the same idea that every day is a new unit, an incipient entity in time. Time is not a featureless plane on which events occur. It is a novel creation in a real sense, a divine creation where there is no evil or failure at all but rather the loftiest of elevations. This means that each fledgling unit of time and burgeoning world is a fresh cycle, an additional and more elaborate effort built on the previous day, from which it developed. It forms the link on the next rung in a ladder that ascends to the Divine.

13. *Rosh HaShana* 31a; *Avoda Zara* 9a.

16 Elul

וְזֶהוּ שֶׁכָּתוּב: "תָּמִיד עֵינֵי ה' אֱלֹהֶיךָ בָּהּ" (דברים יא, יב), שֶׁהָעֵינַיִם הֵם כִּינּוּיִם לְהַמְשָׁכַת וְהֶאָרַת אוֹר הַחָכְמָה, שֶׁלָּכֵן נִקְרָאוּ חֲכָמִים "עֵינֵי הָעֵדָה",

This is the meaning of the verse cited above, **"Always the eyes of the Lord your God are upon it"** (Deut. 11:12), **that the eyes represent the drawing down and illumination of the light of *Ḥokhma*, since it is for this reason that sages are called the "eyes of the congregation,"**

In Hebrew, expressions involving sight invariably refer to intellectually grasping a matter, to thought and awareness. (Similarly, in English one regularly says "I see what you mean" to convey understanding.) Specifically, the eyes and the sense of sight represent *Ḥokhma*.

Just as the eyes are the body's means of sight, so too the wisdom of a sage "sees" on behalf of the congregation, and they are therefore called the "eyes of the congregation."[14] It is sages who must perceive and understand matters, and they draw down the light of *Ḥokhma* to our level of reality. ☞

וַאֲוִירָא דְּאֶרֶץ יִשְׂרָאֵל מַחְכִּים.

and this is also the meaning of the teaching that **the air of the Land of Israel makes one wise.**

ḤOKHMA AND *BINA*, SEEING AND HEARING

☞ *Ḥokhma* is related to the eye and the sense of sight, whereas *Bina* involves the sense of hearing. One of the differences between hearing and seeing is that when a person looks at something, he sees a complete picture in one glance, but when he hears a description from others, he receives disparate and distinct segments, which must be joined together to complete the portrait.

The advantage of *Ḥokhma* over *Bina* lies in the ability to grasp a matter as a whole, as a single image. One who cannot see the complete picture might be talented and intelligent and able to solve any problem he encounters, but he is not wise.

There are examples of this in various fields. Some chess players can see the whole board in one glance, while others will see only one piece, one or two moves ahead, but they cannot take into account what will happen beyond that. In many areas a person can make a successful move without noticing that there is another part of the board, other factors and influences in the great tapestry of life that he fails to grasp. This is why sages are called the "eyes of the congregation": They see the overall state of affairs, and so it is they who can direct and coordinate all the talented but "sightless" people in order to complete the big picture.

---

14. Num. 15:24; see *Ta'anit* 24a; *Likkutei Amarim*, chap. 24; see also *Torah Or* 40a; *Likkutei Torah*, Deut. 3c.

Since "the eyes of the Lord your God are upon it" refers to the illumination of divine wisdom that shines on the Land of Israel, the land itself takes on the essence of *Ḥokhma* that provides wisdom to its inhabitants, and from there to the entire world.[15] This is in line with the talmudic teaching that "the Land of Israel was created first, and the rest of the entire world was created afterward.... The Land of Israel is watered by the Holy One, blessed be He, Himself, while the rest of the entire world is watered through an intermediary..." (*Ta'anit* 10a). The key point here is that the Land of Israel contains the illumination of divine wisdom itself. Just as all the other *sefirot* and forces receive light and vitality from *Ḥokhma*, the other lands receive from the Land of Israel.

וְהֶאָרָה וְהַמְשָׁכָה זוֹ אַף שֶׁהִיא תְּמִידִית, אַף עַל פִּי כֵן אֵינָהּ בִּבְחִינָה וּמַדְרֵגָה אַחַת לְבַדָּהּ מִימֵי עוֹלָם, אֶלָּא שֶׁבְּכָל שָׁנָה וְשָׁנָה הוּא אוֹר חָדָשׁ עֶלְיוֹן,

This illumination and flow of divine light and life force, **although it is constant, is nevertheless not only on one single level since time immemorial. Rather, each and every year there is a new supernal light,**

"Always the eyes of the Lord your God are upon it," but the gaze is different each time. Each year there is a fresh look that takes a different form and that should be better and finer than the previous one. ☞

A NEW SUPERNAL LIGHT

☞ Every innovation, each addition, contains an element of ascent, since each novel item is built on what came before. That is why it is said about Torah scholars that as they get older, their minds become more composed (Mishna *Kinnim* 3:6). It is not inevitable that a person stops developing. Physical growth indeed has is limits, and it must come to a halt. Spiritual growth, by contrast, has no boundaries. The reason that spiritual growth ceases is because it does not happen automatically. In order to know more, one has to study; to comprehend more, one must reflect on matters. If one does not do so, he will not grow.

Each year, then, constitutes an embryonic, higher light that is unlike the previous one. One who renews himself is aligned with the time, growing and advancing. The converse is also true: One who does not refresh himself will decline as time progresses. This is why one can-

15. The idea that "the air of the Land of Israel makes one wise" is from *Bava Batra* 158b. See also *Bava Metzia* 85a; *Kiddushin* 49b.

כִּי הָאוֹר שֶׁנִּתְחַדֵּשׁ וְהֵאִיר בְּרֹאשׁ הַשָּׁנָה זֶה הוּא מִסְתַּלֵּק בְּעֶרֶב רֹאשׁ הַשָּׁנָה הַבָּאָה לְשָׁרְשׁוֹ. וְזֶהוּ שֶׁכָּתוּב: "מֵרֵשִׁית הַשָּׁנָה וְעַד אַחֲרִית שָׁנָה" - לְבַדָּהּ.

because the light that was renewed and illuminated this Rosh HaShana withdraws to its source on the eve of the next Rosh HaShana. This is the meaning of the verse cited above: "Always the eyes of the Lord your God are upon it, **from the beginning of the year until the end of the year" alone.**

The end of the year is the conclusion of a unit of time, of a unit of life and the unique vitality of that year. It is as though the year is dead, since it no longer has any vitalizing influence in the world. The vigor of the previous year departs from the world, returning to its source and root above. Its specific flow and illumination were meant for that year alone and do not carry over to the ensuing year. No year passes along anything to the next. Each year starts over from scratch, with no former assets available for use. ☞

וְלָכֵן כְּתִיב "מֵרֵשִׁית" חָסֵר א', רוֹמֵז עַל הִסְתַּלְּקוּת הָאוֹר שֶׁמִּסְתַּלֵּק בְּלֵיל רֹאשׁ הַשָּׁנָה עַד אַחַר הַתְּקִיעוֹת,

Therefore, the word ***mereshit*** in the verse **is written without an *alef*, alluding to the withdrawal of the light that withdraws on the night of Rosh HaShana until after the** shofar **blasts,**

not remain in the same place he was in the previous year and why anyone who does not ascend will inevitably decline. In a certain sense, the same applies to everything in our world. It is impossible for anything to remain on an even keel: It will either go up or fall down.

ONE ATOM OF TIME

☞ The Mishna states, "On Rosh HaShana, all who enter the world pass before Him like sheep, as it states (Ps. 33:15), 'He who fashions all their hearts, who understands all their deeds'" (*Rosh HaShana* 1:2; see *Torah Or* 57c; *Likkutei Torah*, Lev. 45b). On Rosh HaShana the entire year converges to a single point. At this gathering point, God scans the entire world with a single glance, and there is, so to speak, only one atom of time. Subsequently, time spreads and expands and is then reviewed with a second glance, one that focuses on the results of things, what we see as actual reality. "From the beginning of the year until the end of the year" is the entirety of the year, which is first reviewed with a single glance, before it is split into its myriad details that evolved from one moment to the next.

Without the letter *alef,* the word *mereshit* alludes to the word *rash,* which means pauper. The beginning of the year is thus the poverty of the year.[16] On the night of Rosh HaShana, from the start of the festival until the sounding of the *shofar,* the world is in a state of hibernation, without vitality, or in kabbalistic terminology, in a deep sleep.[17] It preserves only the external husk of vitality but does not receive an inner life force until the new time is born, which occurs after the *shofar* has been sounded.[18] "Until after the blasts" means until the following morning. The *shofar* blasts are blasts heralding the new king, the arrival of the new time.

שֶׁיּוֹרֵד אוֹר חָדָשׁ, עֶלְיוֹן יוֹתֵר, שֶׁלֹּא הָיָה מֵאִיר עֲדַיִין מִימֵי עוֹלָם אוֹר עֶלְיוֹן כָּזֶה.

when a new, loftier light descends, a lofty light that has never yet illuminated the world **from time immemorial.**

The new light that now descends is not merely a change. It must be a loftier light, which, although new, aligns with the natural order and direction of life. This direction is one of constant ascension and elevation, even if this is not always evident.

וְהוּא מִתְלַבֵּשׁ וּמִסְתַּתֵּר בְּ'אֶרֶץ הַחַיִּים' שֶׁלְּמַעְלָה, וְשֶׁלְּמַטָּה לְהַחֲיוֹת אֶת כָּל הָעוֹלָמוֹת כָּל מֶשֶׁךְ שָׁנָה זוֹ.

This light **enclothes and conceals itself in the land of the living above and below to sustain all the worlds throughout the duration of this year.**

The new vitality, which comes from *Ein Sof* by means of the gaze of *Ḥokhma,* passes through the land of the living as through a conductor, within a mediating essence. We do not receive the light directly into our consciousness and senses, but only after it has been hidden and

16. See also *Rosh HaShana* 16b.

17. This is reminiscent of Adam's slumber during the *nesira,* when the woman was separated from him to become a distinct being. See Gen. 2:21, and *Pri Etz Ḥayyim* there.

18. This is the basis for the custom not to sleep on Rosh HaShana. It is said in the name of the Arizal that one should be careful not to sleep until after the *shofar* blasts have been sounded. See *Sha'ar HaKavanot, Derushei Rosh HaShana,* s.v. "*inyan hasheina.*"

enclothed in the "land of the living above," which is *Malkhut* of *Atzilut*, "and below," in the Land of Israel. Each and every year the world suckles all life and blessing by way of the supernal land directly to the lower land, which is the Land of Israel, and from there they spread throughout the entire world.

אַךְ גִּילּוּיוֹ מֵהֶסְתֵּר הַזֶּה תָּלוּי בְּמַעֲשֵׂה הַתַּחְתּוֹנִים

But its manifestation from this concealment depends on the deeds of the lower creations

This new illumination, the likes of which have never been seen before, a light that is loftier than anything that previously existed, is still concealed on Rosh HaShana, secured as if in a safe. All the instructions have been issued from above. Everything is ready for a new and superior year, one that has never transpired before. In order for it to be extracted from the safe and to have a real effect on the lower realm, action from below is required. The renewal and change from above can be absorbed only if there is a similar renewal and change below. ☞

וּזְכוּתָם וּתְשׁוּבָתָם בַּעֲשֶׂרֶת יְמֵי תְשׁוּבָה,

and their merits and repentance during the Ten Days of Repentance,

THE DEEDS OF LOWER CREATIONS

☞ The new life force that descends upon the advent of the new year is hidden in the existing, former elements of the world. It does not paint the roses a different color. Although this light is new, it still passes through the mechanisms of the existing reality, and its originality and uniqueness are hidden within that system.

We can only ever see something new in light of the old. We perceive objects by relating one thing to another. Something that is completely novel, which we cannot relate to anything already in existence, cannot be perceived at all. Incidentally, this is why the language of the Kabbala, and in a sense any language that attempts to deal with matters that have no counterpart in this world, no terminology in our world, is a language that is neither eloquent nor clear. To describe something that is entirely original, we can say, at best, that it is unlike anything else, and even then we are still using the same modes of thought. Consequently, as long as we do not change anything about ourselves down here below, we cannot perceive or receive anything new from above, neither innovative ideas, nor even a new time or year.

These merits and repentance prepare one's soul and the world to receive the illumination of the new year. This is the essential work of the Ten Days of Repentance, the period from Rosh HaShana to Yom Kippur. This repentance and purification toward change and renewal on the part of man below renders him fit to participate in the process of overall renewal that comes from above during this time of the year.

There is a structure and order to reality, with its natural, physical, and spiritual processes that proceed methodically, step by step. These include the mechanisms through which one who has performed a mitzva receives a reward and one who has committed a sin is punished. All those transgressions enclothe and conceal the new light, but repentance stands in counterpart to them. Repentance is the attempt to breach the spiritual infrastructure that declares, "The soul that sins, it will die" (Ezek. 18:4). That "repentance preceded the world"[19] implies that repentance is not part of the structure and order of the world. Instead, it was implanted within the world to provide the possibility of breaking those rules. The laws do not cease to exist; they continue to maintain the world's operation, the existence of reality. But the repentance that illuminates through them and beyond them reveals a new light the likes of which have never been present before, as well as the new world that is now created through its power.

וְדַי לַמֵּבִין. **and** this is **sufficient** explanation **for one who understands.**

The letter concludes with the terse comment "And [this is] sufficient [explanation] for one who understands." Despite the relatively lengthy discussion of this matter, its purpose was not to discuss Rosh HaShana. The ideas are clarified briefly and in a manner that those who are familiar with the background and the necessary preliminaries will comprehend them.

The main aim of this letter was to awaken the readers' affection for the land, to cherish its inhabitants, and to urge the hasidim to share the burden of its residents and help them as best they can. At the same time,

19. See *Pesaḥim* 54a; *Bereshit Rabba* 1:5.

as is the case for all the letters of the author of the *Tanya* and his timeless inner vision, his observations go far beyond their time and place.

The fundamental theme of the letter, at any rate the main section printed here in *Iggeret HaKodesh*, is renewal: The revitalization of the beginning of the year, and the corresponding rebirth and reinvigoration that man himself must generate. The author of the *Tanya* demands that the hasidim give charity with that same sense of renewal, again and again each year, every time in a novel fashion, rising above the efforts of the previous occasion. After all, this is a time of rejuvenation, when the year is renewed and the world is revived. If we too renew ourselves, we will discover the renewal and elevation that God brings to all of reality at this time. The author of the *Tanya* thus refers to the land, to the "land of the living," which is the source of this renewal.

The connection between the renewal of the new year and the personal regeneration of each individual is the main theme of this letter. If one does not renew himself, his year will not only be the same as the previous year, but worse than the previous year. As the author of the *Tanya* explained, the light increasingly grows year by year, and each time it is loftier and of a finer quality. When the light shines brighter, the demands are also greater, and the possibility of failure is amplified. The potential increases the corresponding risk.

This can be seen in all areas of life, from technology to the realms of thought and emotion. The more one's options proliferate, and the more promising the situation, the more compelling becomes the question of what one has achieved. In the past, someone who wanted to influence humanity had to exert a great deal of effort for his message to spread. Now, through the current-day media and the possibility of global communication, one can reach masses of people with incalculable speed and ease. The modern world offers extremely fluctuations: It is more open and willing to accept ideas, but the possibilities of failure are correspondingly great. The progression of time is one of elevation, of increasing holiness, and one who does not want this progression to push him down should seek to connect to it by increasing sanctity in the world himself, particularly in the Holy Land, which is the counterpart to the "land of the living."

The giving of charity to the inhabitants of the Holy Land, especially when they are worthy of these contributions, creates a partnership with the land, which is the source of life. By virtue of this partnership, the giver also receives the new light. One who wishes to receive from the land of the living must open up a channel between himself and the land. The way to open this conduit is by donating to those who are living there. When the channel is open, it flows in both directions. Since at the beginning of each year the reservoir and passageway to the light and life force that belonged to the previous year has run out, that passage must be reopened each year. We must create a new, superior passageway every time by augmenting what came before, in order to elevate and renew ourselves together with the new year.

Epistle 15

APPARENTLY THIS EPISTLE WAS ORIGINALLY WRITTEN as a hasidic discourse on one of the central topics in Kabbala: the ten *sefirot*. The significance of this discourse is twofold: It addresses a topic that constitutes the foundation of all the teachings of Kabbala, and it offers a methodological discussion of this topic from a hasidic perspective, providing a basic explanation of each *sefira*. As a result, this epistle is quoted extensively in hasidic literature.

The author of the *Tanya* prefaces the discourse with Hasidism's approach to understanding the divine *sefirot*, along with other essential kabbalistic concepts. This approach is unique in that it explains these concepts not only in the realm of Kabbala, describing the relationships among the *sefirot*, but it strives to make these teachings accessible to any person, to the way in which an individual experiences life in this world. This approach is based on the connection and parallel between the human soul and the Divine, taking into account the necessary limitations of such a comparison.

11 Elul

14 Elul (leap year)

"לְהָבִין מָשָׁל וּמְלִיצָה דִּבְרֵי חֲכָמִים וְחִידוֹתָם" (משלי א, ו) בְּעִנְיַן הַסְּפִירוֹת.

"To understand proverbs and aphorisms, the words of the wise and their riddles" (Prov. 1:6), **with regard to the *sefirot*:**

The author of the *Tanya* associates this verse from Proverbs with the study of Kabbala, particularly the topic of the *sefirot*. This verse indicates that these kabbalistic teachings, whether transmitted orally or in writing, are expressed through allegory and metaphor. They are not meant to be understood in their simple sense but as an allegory from which the intended meaning may be understood. Even "the words of the wise," those statements made by the kabbalistic masters in their explanations of these teachings, are riddles that only one who is wise and who understands on his own can know. ☞ ☞

THE MYSTICAL TEACHINGS OF THE TORAH

☞ These teachings are often referred to as "mystical" or as "secrets," not because the kabbalists wished to conceal these concepts, but because they deal with spiritual states that do not exist in our familiar physical and linguistic domain. In a certain sense, this is the definition of a secret: Only a person who is wise and understands without the need to have it explained to him, only a person who knows of such matters in some manner because he has personally experienced them, can understand the deeper meaning behind them. For someone else, they remain metaphors and allegories, riddles and secrets that he cannot discern. At most, he can study the connections between the ideas, how they relate to each other and how they are discussed in one text as opposed to another.

HASIDISM AND THE TEACHINGS OF KABBALA

☞ From its inception, Hasidism aspired to remove the barrier before these mystical teachings and, more broadly, to reveal the deeper meaning of everything that a person does: in the performance of mitzvot, in prayer, and in Torah study. Many of the descriptions of how the Ba'al Shem Tov revealed himself and his teachings tell how he transmitted these mystical ideas to others so that they tangibly experienced them. For the Ba'al Shem Tov, these revelations were essentially experiential: true and impactful, but dependent on the teacher's personality and ability to transmit his life experience. Yet the author of the *Tanya* presents these teachings as a systematic, intellectual revelation so that they will become accessible to an even broader scope of people. This letter is an example of his approach, and the introduction to the epistle establishes the foundations of how to contemplate this topic, as well as the possibilities and limitations inherent in that contemplation.

When the Ba'al Shem Tov first met the Maggid of Mezeritch, the Ba'al Shem Tov asked the Maggid if he knew Kabbala, to which the Maggid replied in the affirmative. The Ba'al Shem Tov showed him a passage in the teachings of the Arizal, in the work titled *Etz Ḥayyim*, and asked him to explain it. When the Maggid did so after taking the time to study it at length, the Ba'al Shem Tov told him, "You do not know anything."

"My explanation was correct," the Maggid replied. "If you have another explanation, please say it, and I will hear who is correct."

The Ba'al Shem Tov told the Maggid to stand up, and the Ba'al Shem Tov recited the passage, which contained several names of angels. The house was immediately filled with light and flames, and they saw the angels. The Ba'al Shem Tov concluded, "The explanation you gave was correct, but your analysis lacked a soul" (*Keter Shem Tov* 424).

מוּדַעַת זֹאת בָּאָרֶץ מִפִּי קְדוֹשֵׁי עֶלְיוֹן נִשְׁמָתָם עֵדֶן, **It is widely known from the mouths of the holy masters, whose souls** are in the Garden of **Eden,**

Knowledge of these lofty matters may be "widely known" (literally, "known upon the earth"), clothed in human thought and concepts. Such explanations come directly from "the holy masters," the teachers of the author of the *Tanya,* who were the first hasidic masters.[1] Though he does not quote from his teachers directly in this epistle, their teachings are the source of the words that follow.

לְקָרֵב קְצָת אֶל הַשֵּׂכֶל that they sought **to make somewhat more intelligible**

The innovation of the author of the *Tanya* was to make these matters accessible not only to the heart but also to the intellect. As explained in *Likkutei Amarim* and elsewhere, the approach to the service of God in Chabad Hasidism is by means of the intellect, through the faculties of wisdom, understanding, and knowledge, the cognitive attributes through which the emotive attributes are affected. This approach truly brings a person closer to God, and it can influence many people, because when these mystical concepts are clothed in an intellectual form, they become more accessible even to a person who lacks mystical experience of the spiritual worlds.

מַאי דִּכְתִיב "וּמִבְּשָׂרִי אֶחֱזֶה אֱלוֹהַּ" (איוב יט, כו). **the verse "And from my flesh I will view God"** (Job 19:26).

This verse expresses the general idea that all of our knowledge of divinity, and of reality in general, comes from our knowledge of ourselves. The simple explanation for this is that this is how human awareness functions. Our conceptions and language emerge from within ourselves, and we project them onto everything else. On a deeper level,

1. The author of the *Tanya* was a prize student of the Maggid of Mezeritch. He also received his approach to Torah study and modes of conduct from the Ba'al Shem Tov, whom he called his spiritual grandfather. In addition, he studied under the tutelage Rabbi Avraham HaMalakh, the son of the Maggid, Rabbi Menaḥem Mendel of Vitebsk, and his own colleagues, the great students of the Maggid.

this is how things actually are: A human being is a microcosm, made in the divine pattern that generates and guides existence, as the verse states, "God created man in His own image; in the image of God He created him" (Gen. 1:27).

This concept is the foundation of the hasidic way of understanding man and his relationship to the Divine: that by knowing himself, one can know divinity as well, and conversely, by knowing divinity, he can know himself. However, this idea is not easy to internalize, so one must be very careful in studying it.[2]

שֶׁהַכַּוָּונָה הִיא לְהָבִין קְצָת אֱלֹהוּתוֹ יִתְבָּרֵךְ מִנֶּפֶשׁ הַמְלוּבֶּשֶׁת בִּבְשַׂר הָאָדָם,

They taught **that this refers to understanding a little of God's divinity from the soul, which is enclothed in the flesh of man,**

The author of the *Tanya* makes it clear that man's similarity to God is inherent not in the structure of his physical body but in the structure of the soul contained in the body.[3]

וְעַל פִּי מַאֲמַר רַבּוֹתֵינוּ ז"ל (ברכות י, א) עַל פָּסוּק "בָּרְכִי נַפְשִׁי וגו'" (תהלים קג, א) – מָה הַקָּדוֹשׁ בָּרוּךְ הוּא כו' אַף הַנְּשָׁמָה כו', וְעַל פִּי מַאֲמַר הַזֹּהַר עַל פָּסוּק "וַיִּפַּח בְּאַפָּיו נִשְׁמַת חַיִּים" (בראשית ב, ז) – מַאן דְּנָפַח מִתּוֹכֵיהּ נָפַח.

in accordance with our Rabbis' statement (*Berakhot* 10a) **regarding the verse "Bless** the Lord, **my soul…"** (Ps. 103:1): **Just as the Holy One, blessed be He,** fills the world, **so does the soul** fill the body. It is also **in accordance with the statement of the holy *Zohar* regarding the verse "And He blew into his nostrils the breath of life"** (Gen. 2:7), that **one who blows, from within himself he blows.**

2. See also *Likkutei Torah*, Lev. 31b, Deut. 4a, which state that this refers to divinity as it "fills all worlds." See also *Likkutei Dibburim*, by the sixth Lubavitcher Rebbe, Rabbi Yosef Yitzḥak Schneerson, vol. 2, p. 334; *Sefer HaMa'amarim Melukat* (5720), vol. 3, s.v. "*lekha amar libi.*"

3. It is common in kabbalistic literature to find concepts that utilize the imagery of the body, for example, that "*Ḥesed* is the right arm; *Gevura* is the left arm…" (*Pataḥ Eliyahu*, introduction to *Tikkunei Zohar* 17a). It is important to emphasize that this does not refer to the actual body itself.

This statement establishes a comparison between the Divine, which is clothed in the world and gives it life, and a person's soul, which is clothed in the body and gives it life.[4]

Furthermore, when a person speaks, he transmits a thought or an idea, as well as some of the breath that he exhales from within. But when he blows air from within himself, he brings forth the essence of his inner being from within himself. The author of the *Tanya* compares this to the process by which God blew from His essence to create the soul of man, in contrast to His creation of the rest of existence.[5]

The rest of creation was created by God's speech. Speech is external to the speaker in that the speaker transmits knowledge and meaning through the words he utters, yet these words do not represent the speaker himself, only his insights, ideas, and feelings. But when it came to the creation of the soul, God "blew into his nostrils the breath of life." When God created man, He blew of His essence into man, as it were. In view of this, the human soul draws from the actual life-giving soul of God, literally "a portion of God on high."

At its root, the human soul is an ultimately profound entity: loftier than all the worlds, loftier than all revelations in the worlds. Yet it is also a created entity clothed in a physical body and manifest in the worlds. As a result, one can contemplate the soul with the human intellect, a contemplation that is like contemplating the Divine itself. It is regarding this that the verse states of this, "And from my flesh I will view God."

וַאֲפִילוּ נֶפֶשׁ דַּעֲשִׂיָּה **Even the *nefesh* of** the world of ***Asiya***

The soul is a portion of the Divine that God breathed from within Himself. That is not only the case regarding the loftiest of souls, those that belong to the loftiest of worlds, the world of *Atzilut*, which is united and one with the Divine, but even to lowlier souls, even to

4. See *Likkutei Torah*, Lev. 31b.

5. This statement from the *Zohar* also appears in *Likkutei Amarim*, chap. 2, and in *Iggeret HaTeshuva*, chap. 4. The Lubavitcher Rebbe, Rabbi Menaḥem Mendel Schneerson, comments, "It appears to me that this [statement] is not found in the *Zohar* nor in the *Tikkunei Zohar* that we possess but that it does appear in the books of the early sages." See also *Likkutei Siḥot*, vol. 9, p. 437, and the note there.

souls that belong to the lowly world of *Asiya*, which is, as it were, completely separate from the Divine. It is precisely the fact that the essence of divinity can be clothed in the soul that is found in *Asiya* that reveals the profound connection between the human soul and the Divine, a profundity that transcends all revelations in the worlds. In the face of this profundity, all distinctions between souls are meaningless. ☞

הִיא בָּאָה מִזִּיווּג זְעֵיר וְנוּקְבָא דַּעֲשִׂיָּה, **is derived from a union of *Zeir*** *Anpin* of *Asiya* **and *Nukva* of *Asiya***

Zeir Anpin consists of the six *sefirot* that are called the emotive attributes: *Ḥesed, Gevura, Tiferet, Netzaḥ, Hod,* and *Yesod*. *Nukva* is the *sefira* of *Malkhut*. In each of the four worlds, the *nefesh* is manifest and clothed through the union of the *sefirot* in that respective world. The union of the divine *sefirot* engenders the *nefesh* so that the *nefesh* is derived from the essence of the *sefirot* united in divinity. This is comparable to a physical union. A child, born of a union between his father and mother, is not only an extension of his parents, like a person's thoughts or speech. Rather, he is literally of their essence.

וְהַמּוֹחִין שֶׁלָּהֶם, **and** of the union of **their *moḥin*,**

THE *NEFESH* OF *ASIYA*

☞ The soul can actually be divided into five levels: *nefesh, ruaḥ, neshama, ḥaya,* and *yeḥida*, of which *nefesh* is the lowest. (The term *nefesh*, then, can either refer to the soul in general or to the lowest level of the five levels of the soul.) Likewise, *Asiya* is the lowest of the four worlds: *Atzilut, Beria, Yetzira,* and *Asiya*. The level of *nefesh* is associated with the world of *Asiya*, the level of *ruaḥ* to *Yetzira*, and so on. Yet even though the world of *Asiya* is the place of the *nefesh*, and the *nefesh* is rooted in *Asiya*, the level of *ruaḥ* and higher levels of the soul may also be revealed in the world of *Asiya*.

For instance, the *nefesh* of *Asiya* is revealed in a person when he performs the practical mitzvot (the word *asiya* connoting "action") solely because God commanded us to do them. He does not act out of feelings of love and fear, nor out of a comprehension of the value of these actions. When a person performs a mitzva out of love and fear, on the other hand, the level of *ruaḥ* is manifest within him and within the world of *Asiya*. If he performs a mitzva because he understands intellectually the reasons behind it, the level of *neshama* is now revealed within him and within the world of *Asiya*.

The *moḥin,* literally, "brains," are the cognitive *sefirot*: *Ḥokhma* and *Bina,* Wisdom and Understanding. Every world has its own ten *sefirot,* which means there are *moḥin* of *Atzilut, moḥin* of *Beria, moḥin* of *Yetzira,* and *moḥin* of *Asiya.* The *moḥin* are a vessel that draws forth and reveals the flow of divine light and life force that comes to them from above. The *moḥin* of *Asiya* receive from the *moḥin* of *Yetzira, Beria, Atzilut,* and beyond to the most elevated plane at the level of the light of *Ein Sof.*[6]

שֶׁהֵם בְּחִינַת חַיָּה וּנְשָׁמָה דִּזְעֵיר וְנוּקְבָא.

those being the *ḥaya* and *neshama* of *Zeir Anpin* and *Nukva.*

There is a parallel between the *sefirot* and the levels of the soul. *Ḥaya* and *neshama* correspond to the *moḥin,* the *sefirot* of *Ḥokhma* and *Bina, ruaḥ* corresponds to *Zeir Anpin,* and *nefesh* corresponds to *Nukva.* If so, the *ḥaya* and *neshama* of *Zeir Anpin* and *Nukva* in *Asiya* are the *moḥin,* the cognitive *sefirot,* of *Asiya.*

More specifically, these are the *moḥin* of the *partzufim* of *Zeir Anpin* and *Nukva. Partzufim,* literally, "countenances," are structures or composites that encompass within them all ten *sefirot,* only the *sefirot* to which they correspond are more dominant within the structure (for example, in *Nukva,* the *sefira* of *Malkhut* is dominant). This means that besides the general *moḥin* of the world of *Asiya,* the *partzufim* of *Zeir Anpin* and *Nukva* of the world of *Asiya* have their own *moḥin,* which parallel and receive from the *moḥin* of the world of *Asiya.* ☞

ḤAYA AND NESHAMA OF ZEIR ANPIN AND NUKVA

☞ Kabbalistic terminology has various constellations of terms. In general, each relates to a different realm of existence. The terms *Atzilut, Beria, Yetzira,* and *Asiya* relate to the realm of worlds. The terms *Ḥesed, Gevura,* and so forth (and the *partzufim* of *Zeir Anpin* and *Nukva*) relate to the realm of the *sefirot.* The terms *nefesh, ruaḥ, neshama,* and so forth relate to the realm of the soul. Yet the works of Kabbala and Hasidism mingle these terms and connect them to each other so that they are not exclusive to one realm. Rather, each set of terminology can apply to any realm. This imparts more extensive, profound, and complex layers of meaning to all these terminologies. Perhaps this intermingling of concepts is intended to indicate the bond between the human soul and the divine *sefirot,* that at their essence, the *sefirot* and the soul are connected, since

6. See *Likkutei Amarim,* chap. 18.

שֶׁהֵן הֵן אֲחוֹרַיִים דְּכֵלִים דִּזְעֵיר אַנְפִּין וְנוּקְבָא דַּאֲצִילוּת,

These *moḥin* are the "back side" of the vessels of *Zeir Anpin* and *Nukva* of *Atzilut*,

The *moḥin* of *Asiya* only constitute the back side of the *sefirot* of *Atzilut*. Through these *moḥin*, the light and life force that emanate from the divine *sefirot* of *Atzilut* are channeled into all the worlds. ☞

שֶׁהֵם אֱלֹהוּת מַמָּשׁ,

which are actual divinity,

This refers to the vessels in *Atzilut*. This is a unique aspect of the world of *Atzilut*: It is not separate from the Divine, *Atzilut* connoting *etzel*, "near." It is so close to the Divine that it does not appear separate from it. Viewed from the perspective of the three worlds below it, *Atzilut* is not a world at all but divinity: divine *Ḥokhma*, divine *Ḥesed*, and so on. To illustrate, a person's deeds and even his speech and thoughts, may be viewed as separate from him. Yet it is impossible to consider his soul's faculties, his intellect and emotive attributes,

they are constructed from the same code, as it were. That makes it possible for us to learn about one from the other, as in "From my flesh I will view God," and "one who blows, from within himself he blows."

THE BACK SIDE AND THE VESSELS

☞ In the language of Kabbala, the "back side" indicates exteriority. In terms of descent from level to level, the level that pours onto what is below it is relatively exterior to the inner aspect of the level that does not descend. This exterior level is called the "back side" of the level above it. This is comparable to the body (exterior) and essence (inner aspect) of a thing.

In the language of Kabbala, this is also referred to as vessels and lights. In this sense, the vessels are the "back side" to the lights. The worlds in general, including *Atzilut*, are a reality of lights within vessels, the vessels being the *sefirot*. The light is revealed only when it is in a vessel, and the vessel only has significance and vitality when it contains light. That being the case, with regard to the back side, in the sense of channeling outward and downward, the flow comes down by means of the vessels into which it is channeled. To illustrate, letters and words are vessels in relation to the meaning behind them. When a teacher needs to explain something to his student, he speaks words that can transmit meaning, but he cannot transmit the pure meaning inherent in them. Similarly, the divine lights of the worlds are channeled and transmitted through the *sefirot* within each world.

as separate from him. From the standpoint of an onlooker, they are the person himself.[7]

שֶׁבְּתוֹכָם מֵאִיר אוֹר אֵין סוֹף בָּרוּךְ הוּא, הַמְלוּבָּשׁ וְגָנוּז בְּחָכְמָה דַּאֲצִילוּת,

in which the light of *Ein Sof*, blessed be He, which is **enclothed and hidden in the *Ḥokhma* of *Atzilut*, shines,**

The light that shines in the vessels of *Atzilut* is the light of *Ein Sof* Himself. It is not the limited light of the created worlds, but the infinite, divine light. Therefore, the entire world of *Atzilut* is permeated with the divine light, without any limitation, so that it is entirely one with the Divine.

Though the light of *Ein Sof* shines and is clothed in the world of *Atzilut*, it must first be clothed in *Ḥokhma* of *Atzilut*. The reason for this was explained in *Likkutei Amarim*:[8] The light of *Ein Sof* is singular and unique, so that only the level of *Ḥokhma* can absorb it to some extent. *Ḥokhma* itself is not an independent entity, but a flash of the essential absorption of a thing. It absorbs the thing itself but does not give it definition (unlike all created entities). It does not place a thing within any parameters, because it does not have its own parameters. In that sense, although *Ḥokhma* only receives a flash of the light of *Ein Sof*, it is unified with that light with a simple, indivisible unity. Thus, *Ḥokhma* has the ability to enclothe the light of *Ein Sof*. ☞

ḤOKHMA OF ATZILUT

☞ Kabbalistic literature explains that *Atzilut* in comparison to the other worlds is analogous to *Ḥokhma* in comparison to the other *sefirot*. (Similarly, the *sefirot* are divided into four groups, or *partzufim*, which parallel the four worlds and the four letters of the name of *Havaya*. *Ḥokhma*, or the *partzuf* of *Abba* is in *Atzilut* and corresponds to the letter *yod*. *Bina*, or the *partzuf* of *Ima*, is in *Beria* and corresponds to the first *heh*. The *partzuf* of *Zeir Anpin* is in *Yetzira* and corresponds to the letter *vav*, and *Malkhut* is in *Asiya* and corresponds to the second *heh*.) *Atzilut* is

7. As explained in *Likkutei Amarim*, chaps. 3–4, the *sefirot* of *Atzilut* are like the soul's faculties (its intellect and emotive attributes), in contrast to the worlds of *Beria*, *Yetzira* and *Asiya*, which are like the three garments of the soul – thought, speech, and deed.

8. See the gloss in chap. 35.

דְּאִיהוּ וְגַרְמוֹהִי חַד בַּאֲצִילוּת.

for in *Atzilut* God **and His vessels are one.**

The world of *Atzilut* is united with God Himself.[9] It is not only the light in *Atzilut*, which is the light of *Ein Sof*, that is one with God, but even the vessels in *Atzilut*, the *sefirot* in *Atzilut*, which clothe and conceal the light, are a revelation of the Divine. The kabbalistic literature explains that since the vessels in *Atzilut* are literally a part of the Divine, even their concealment of the light and placing it within defined parameters are a revelation of the Divine, a revelation of the power of the concealment of the Divine and placing it within parameters.[10] At any rate, the vessels in *Atzilut* are united with the Divine itself.

וְעַל כֵּן גַּם בְּנִשְׁמַת הָאָדָם מֵאִיר אוֹר אֵין סוֹף בָּרוּךְ הוּא, מְלוּבָּשׁ וְגָנוּז בְּאוֹר הַחָכְמָה שֶׁבָּהּ לְהַחֲיוֹת אֶת הָאָדָם.

Therefore, the light of *Ein Sof*, blessed be He, shines also in the soul of man, enclothed and hidden in the light of *Ḥokhma* within the soul **to sustain the person.**

The light of *Ein Sof* is the source of the life force that sustains everything, overall and in particular. It issues forth and is revealed through the *sefira* of *Ḥokhma* in *Atzilut*,[11] and from there through the *sefira* of *Ḥokhma* in every world, down to the corresponding faculty of wisdom in the soul. This life force, then, is clothed within the faculty of wisdom in the soul. The life force itself is transcendent, the nothingness that is the beginning of existence, which receives from beyond it to sustain existence. This means that the life force within the soul, even in the world of *Asiya*, is the light of *Ein Sof*, the divine light itself, that is clothed in *Ḥokhma*.

subsumed completely in the Divine that is revealed in it. But viewed from above, *Atzilut* is a world, the source and root of all the created worlds. Therefore, even in the world of *Atzilut* there is a point that is *Atzilut* of *Atzilut*, *Ḥokhma* of *Ḥokhma*, in which the light of *Ein Sof* is clothed and concealed.

9. See introduction to *Tikkunei Zohar* 2b; see also epistle 20 at length.

10. See *Hemshekh Ayin Bet* 9 and onward, which states that in a certain senses the vessels are even loftier than the light and revelation itself.

11. See also *Likkutei Amarim*, chaps. 18, 53.

וּמִמֶּנָּה יוּכַל הָאָדָם לְהָבִין קְצָת בַּסְּפִירוֹת הָעֶלְיוֹנוֹת, שֶׁכּוּלָּן מְאִירוֹת בְּנִשְׁמָתוֹ הַכְּלוּלָה מֵהֶן.

From his soul, **a person can understand a little of the supernal** ***sefirot,*** **since they all shine in his soul, which comprises them.**

Having shown how a person's soul is connected to the Divine on high, and in particular to the divinity revealed in the ten supernal *sefirot,* the author of the *Tanya* returns to exposit the approach of Hasidism in understanding the *sefirot,* which says that a person can understand the divine *sefirot* through his soul. ☞ ☞

COMPRISED OF THE *SEFIROT*

☞ The author of the *Tanya* makes two points here: that all the *sefirot* shine within a person's soul, and that his soul comprises them. All the *sefirot* shine in a person's soul because his soul possesses faculties that parallel the *sefirot*. These faculties reflect the corresponding *sefirot*. Moreover, the soul is composed of the *sefirot*. It not only has a structure similar to that of the *sefirot,* but it is an actual part of their essence and thus it is a part of the divine essence that is clothed in the *sefirot*. All of its external manifestations and forms are constantly bound with this inner essence.

This concept that the soul comprises the divine *sefirot* and is therefore bound to the Divine is relevant in the realm of holiness. In the side of holiness, things work together and can be incorporated within one another, while the other side is characterized by disconnection (see *Torah Or* 24d). The soul's external manifestations and faculties constitute the vessel that reveals the inner light that transcends those manifestations. In light of this, when a person engages in contemplation, which is a faculty of his soul, he can achieve a true understanding of the divine *sefirot,* even though the soul is constricted within the vessel of the *nefesh* and the human intellect.

LEARNING FROM DISSIMILARITY

☞ There is a basic axiom that we learn about the Divine from the human soul. Yet as part of that truth, we must know that whatever we can understand is constricted and immeasurably far from the essential character of the Divine. Although the soul is divine, a part of the Divine, that is not at all mean that the Divine is like the soul. It is important to point this out, because it is a part of the truth. Just as it is true that there is an aspect of the Divine that is connected to us, it also true that the Divine is separate from us, that it is not similar or connected to us, that it is loftier and holier than us. Emphasizing the connection and similarity provides tools to understand the divine attributes and the faculties of the soul so that as a result we will know how to conduct ourselves properly. On the other hand, an appreciation of the difference is just as essential, the recognition that the distance between the soul and God is infinite, immeasurably beyond our comprehension, so that we will be humble and fear God and so that our understanding will be true and not illusory.

18 Elul
15 Elul (leap year)

אַךְ צָרִיךְ לְהַקְדִּים מַה שֶּׁשָּׁמַעְתִּי מִמּוֹרִי עָלָיו הַשָּׁלוֹם, עַל פָּסוּק: "וְאָנֹכִי עָפָר וָאֵפֶר" (בראשית יח, כז), שֶׁאָמַר אַבְרָהָם אָבִינוּ עָלָיו הַשָּׁלוֹם עַל הֶאָרַת נִשְׁמָתוֹ הַמְּאִירָה בְּגוּפוֹ מֵאוֹר חֶסֶד עֶלְיוֹן.

However, it is necessary to first explain what I heard from my teacher, the Maggid of Mezeritch, **may he rest in peace, regarding the verse "And I am dust and ashes"** (Gen. 18:27), **that our forefather Abraham, may he rest in peace, said** this **in reference to the illumination of his soul shining in his body from the light of supernal *Ḥesed*.**

After the author of the *Tanya* has explained that there is a parallel in structure, and even an essential connection, between the human soul and the Divine, he goes on to qualify his statement with a discussion of Abraham and the divine attribute of *Ḥesed*.

Abraham's soul was in the heights of *Atzilut*, as high as it is possible for a human soul to reach. Yet he chose to emphasize his distance from the Divine, which is manifest in the *sefirot*, comparing himself and his trait of kindness to "dust and ashes," in contrast to the trait of the supernal *Ḥesed* of God.

וְהִיא מִדָּתוֹ מִדַּת 'אַהֲבָה רַבָּה' (נוסח אַחֵר: שֶׁבָּהּ הָיָה) שֶׁהָיָה אוֹהֵב אֶת הַקָּדוֹשׁ בָּרוּךְ הוּא אַהֲבָה גְּדוֹלָה וְעֶלְיוֹנָה כָּל כָּךְ עַד שֶׁנַּעֲשָׂה מֶרְכָּבָה לְהַקָּדוֹשׁ בָּרוּךְ הוּא.

This is Abraham's **attribute: the attribute of great love, for he** [**alternatively: with which he**] **loved the Holy One, blessed be He, with a such a great, lofty love that he became a vehicle for the Holy One, blessed be He.**

The illumination of Abraham's soul was a total expression of divine *Ḥesed*. This was Abraham's unique trait, a love so great that he became a vehicle for God. Elsewhere, it states that great love, unlike "small love," is love in which a person no longer relates to himself, thinking of how this love benefits him. Rather, it is about the subject of the love, and a love for the other's actions or impact but a love for his very self, his essence, even if that essence cannot be defined or comprehended.[12]

12. See *Torah Or* 47b; *Likkutei Torah*, Lev. 2b, Deut. 30b.

Abraham loved God with such love, with a great and supernal love that involved an absolute nullification of himself. His love was identified with an absolute unification with God's own love. It was the love of a person who wants nothing for himself, who wants only what God wants, who loves what God loves. This is what the author of the *Tanya* means when it says that Abraham became a vehicle for God: His love was a pure vessel for God's supernal love. ☞

וְסָלְקָא דַעְתָּךְ אֲמִינָא שֶׁבְּחִינַת חֶסֶד וְאַהֲבָה שֶׁלְּמַעְלָה, בַּסְּפִירוֹת הָעֶלְיוֹנוֹת, הִיא מֵעֵין וְסוּג מַהוּת מִדַּת אַהֲבָה רַבָּה שֶׁל אַבְרָהָם אָבִינוּ עָלָיו הַשָּׁלוֹם.

It might enter your mind to say that the level of *Ḥesed* and love that exists **above in the supernal *sefirot* is of the same nature and type as the attribute of the great love of our forefather Abraham, may he rest in peace.**

A SOUL FROM *ATZILUT*

☞ The supernal *sefirot* shine in every person's soul. Yet with regard to the forefathers, we are told that they were vehicles for the Divine (*Bereshit Rabba* 47:6; see *Likkutei Amarim*, chaps. 18, 23, 34 et al.). Every person has a divine spark (clothed in *Ḥokhma*), and that spark is usually an obscured, potential point in his soul, without form, image, definition, or ability to relate to the manifestations of the soul. Therefore, this spark may not have any explicit effect on who the person is and on his life.

This is not the case with a person who is a vehicle for the Divine. Being a vehicle is a lofty level that the forefathers attained (and in a sense so do all tzaddikim in every generation), where not only the concealed spark but the entire soul, all its levels and all its faculties, actively exist in unity with the Divine, absolutely nullified to the Divine. Moreover, even the soul's garments, the person's thoughts, speech, and deeds, become an unalloyed vessel for the expression and revelation of the Divine in the world. In contrast to the low level discussed above, that of the *nefesh* of *Asiya*, the forefathers were on the level of the *neshama* of *Atzilut* – the loftiest soul level in the loftiest world. The *neshama* as it exists in *Atzilut*, as a vehicle for the supernal attributes of *Atzilut*, was revealed in actuality in their bodies in this world.

For each of the forefathers, this nullification occurred in a particular attribute and facet related to his nature and life. For Abraham it was in the attribute of *Ḥesed*, for Isaac in *Gevura*, and for Jacob in *Tiferet*. In light of this, the author of the *Tanya* here refers to the illumination of Abraham's soul "shining in his body from the light of supernal *Ḥesed*."

It is clear to us that God's supernal love is not the same as the average person's emotive attribute of kindness and love. A person's love is connected to his body and to his reality as an independent, separate being. Therefore, that love is limited by what he wants and thinks that he wants for himself. It is necessarily distinct and separate from supernal love, both in its objects and in its scope. But the love of Abraham was not bound by these limitations and was not affected by any of that. We might therefore think this great love is of the same sort of love as the divine love of the *sefira* of *Ḥesed*.

רַק שֶׁהִיא גְּדוֹלָה וְנִפְלָאָה מִמֶּנָּה, לְמַעְלָה מַעְלָה עַד אֵין קֵץ וְתַכְלִית.

But supernal love **is greater and more wondrous than** Abraham's love, **transcending it to an infinite and endless degree.**

One might have thought that the supernal traits are in the same category and type as Abraham's traits, and the only difference between them is in their scope and size.

כַּנּוֹדָע מִמִּדּוֹת הָעֶלְיוֹנוֹת שֶׁאֵין לָהֶם [נוּסָח אַחֵר: קֵץ] סוֹף וְתַכְלִית מִצַּד עַצְמָן,

As is known, the supernal attributes have no end and limit of their own,

The infinitude of the supernal attributes is intrinsic to them. Although even the supernal attributes are attributes, and the Hebrew word for "attribute," *midda*, connotes something measured and meted out, something finite, they are finite only in the sense that they limit each other. For instance, *Ḥesed* is limited by *Gevura* in the sense that it is not *Gevura*. But *Ḥesed* in itself, *Gevura* in itself, are both infinite. *Ḥesed* gives and bestows without measure, without any limitation on the power of giving and on the character of that which is given. *Gevura*'s power of restraint and constriction, which is intrinsically infinite, is expressed in *Gevura*'s ability to limit the infinite *Ḥesed*.

כִּי אוֹר אֵין סוֹף בָּרוּךְ הוּא מֵאִיר וּמְלוּבָּשׁ בְּתוֹכָם מַמָּשׁ, וְאִיהוּ וְגַרְמוֹהִי חַד.

because the light of *Ein Sof*, blessed be He, actually illuminates and is enclothed within them, and He and His vessels are one.

What is unique about the supernal attributes in *Atzilut* is that the light clothed in them is literally the divine light of *Ein Sof*, united with them and revealed in them in its infinitude. Although in general the vessels reveal the light, they also conceal and limit it. But the vessels in the world of *Atzilut* are different, because they do not conceal. They only reveal the light, and since the light is infinite, the vessels too, the attributes, in *Atzilut* are infinite. Just as the light is always united with its source and has no existence independent of its source, so too a vessel in the world of *Atzilut*, which has no separate existence that conceals divinity, reveals the infinite divine essence.[13]

מַה שֶּׁאֵין כֵּן בְּנִשְׁמַת הָאָדָם הַמְלוּבֶּשֶׁת בַּחוֹמֶר, שֶׁיֵּשׁ לְמִדּוֹתֶיהָ קֵץ וּגְבוּל.

This is not the case with regard to the human soul, which is enclothed in the physical body, whose attributes are finite and limited.

A person's soul is clothed in the vessel of his physical body, confined and limited by the limits of physicality. Therefore, these limitations are attributed on some level to its spiritual attributes as well. In that sense, they are not infinite in the way that God's supernal attributes are infinite.

אֲבָל מִכָּל מָקוֹם, סָלְקָא דַּעְתָּךְ אֲמִינָא שֶׁמִּדּוֹתֶיהָ הֵן מֵעֵין וְסוּג מִדּוֹת הָעֶלְיוֹנוֹת.

But nevertheless, it might enter your mind to say that the soul's **attributes are of the same type as the supernal attributes.**

One might still think that even if the soul's attributes are not of the same scope as the attributes of *Atzilut*, they still possess the same quality as the supernal attributes.

There are two polarities here. On the one hand, "From my flesh I will view God" and "One who blows, from within himself he blows." This implies that there is a connection between the human soul and its faculties and divinity as it is revealed in the ten *sefirot*. On the other hand, there is an infinite gap between the light of *Ein Sof* clothed in *Atzilut* and the human soul clothed in a corporeal body. To understand

13. Introduction to *Tikkunei Zohar* 3b.

this relationship, which is the basis for almost every kabbalistic discussion about the *sefirot*, and to negate what a person might have thought, the author of the *Tanya* quotes what he heard from his teacher, the Maggid of Mezeritch.

וְלָזֶה אָמַר "וְאָנֹכִי עָפָר וָאֵפֶר". דִּכְמוֹ שֶׁהָאֵפֶר הוּא מַהוּתוֹ וְעַצְמוּתוֹ שֶׁל הָעֵץ הַנִּשְׂרָף, שֶׁהָיָה מוּרְכָּב מִ־ד׳ יְסוֹדוֹת: אֵשׁ, רוּחַ, מַיִם, עָפָר. וְ־ג׳ יְסוֹדוֹת - אֵשׁ, מַיִם, רוּחַ - חָלְפוּ וְהָלְכוּ לָהֶם וְכָלוּ בֶּעָשָׁן הַמִּתְהַוֶּה מֵהַרְכָּבָתָן, כַּנּוֹדָע. וִיסוֹד הַ־ד׳ שֶׁהָיָה בָּעֵץ, שֶׁהוּא הֶעָפָר שֶׁבּוֹ, הַיּוֹרֵד לְמַטָּה, וְאֵין הָאֵשׁ שׁוֹלֶטֶת בּוֹ, הוּא הַנִּשְׁאָר קַיָּם, וְהוּא הָאֵפֶר.

It is with regard to this that Abraham **said, "And I am dust and ashes."** He was **like ashes, which are the essence and substance of burned wood, which had been comprised of four elements – fire, wind, water,** and **earth** – of which **three elements, fire, water,** and **wind, vanished and were consumed in the smoke that came into being from their compound, as is known. The fourth element that was in the wood, which is the** element of **earth within it, which descends and over which fire does not rule, remains in existence, and that is the ashes.**

Fire, wind, water, and earth are the elements from which everything material is composed.[14] The smoke that rises from burning wood is composed of fire, water, and wind. Only the fourth element in the wood, the earth, remains below, because it is heavier and more material than the other elements.

וְהִנֵּה כָּל מַהוּת הָעֵץ וּמַמָּשׁוֹ וְחוּמְרוֹ וְצוּרָתוֹ, בְּאוֹרֶךְ וְרוֹחַב וְעוֹבִי, שֶׁהָיָה נִרְאֶה לָעַיִן קוֹדֶם שֶׁנִּשְׂרַף, עִיקָּרוֹ הָיָה מִיְּסוֹד הֶעָפָר שֶׁבּוֹ, רַק שֶׁאֵשׁ מַיִם רוּחַ כְּלוּלִים בּוֹ.

The whole essence of the wood and its substance, materiality, and form in terms of **length, width, and depth, which were visible before it was burned, was primarily from the element of earth within it, except that fire, water,** and **wind were** also **incorporated in it.**

14. This principle was accepted and widespread in the ancient world. See Rambam, *Mishneh Torah, Sefer HaMadda, Hilkhot Yesodei HaTorah*, chap. 4; see also *Likkutei Amarim*, chap. 1.

Furthermore, these components are not only four distinct elements, but they are intrinsically different from each other. Even before the wood burned, the element of earth was its central component, a sort of basic material, whereas the other elements only gave it its form: the size, color, smell, and taste unique to wood.

כִּי הֶעָפָר הוּא חוּמְרִי יוֹתֵר מִכּוּלָּן, וְיֵשׁ לוֹ אוֹרֶךְ וְרוֹחַב וְעוֹבִי, מַה שֶּׁאֵין כֵּן בְּאֵשׁ וְרוּחַ, וְגַם הַמַּיִם הֵם מְעַט מִזְּעֵיר בָּעֵץ. וְכָל אָרְכּוֹ וְרָחְבּוֹ וְעוֹבְיוֹ - הַכֹּל הָיָה מִן הֶעָפָר וְהַכֹּל שָׁב אֶל הֶעָפָר, שֶׁהוּא הָאֵפֶר הַנִּשְׁאָר אַחֲרֵי שֶׁנִּפְרְדוּ מִמֶּנּוּ אֵשׁ מַיִם רוּחַ.

That is **because earth is more material than all the other** elements, **having length, width, and depth, which is not the case for fire and wind. Even water is a minuscule component of wood. The wood's length, width, and depth all came from the** element of **earth and all returns to the earth, which is the ashes that remain after the fire,** **water,** and **wind separated from it.**

Earth is a tangible, material component, with dimensions such as length, width. and thickness, all material dimensions, whereas fire and wind lack those dimensions. The dimensions of water are changeable, and in any case very little of it is present in wood.

וְהִנֵּה, כְּמוֹ שֶׁהָאֵפֶר אֵין לוֹ דִּמְיוֹן וְעֵרֶךְ אֶל מַהוּת הָעֵץ הַגָּדוֹל בְּאוֹרֶךְ וְרוֹחַב וְעוֹבִי קוֹדֶם שֶׁנִּשְׂרַף, לֹא בְּכַמּוּתוֹ וְלֹא בְּאֵיכוּתוֹ, אַף שֶׁהוּא [הוּא] מַהוּתוֹ וְעַצְמוּתוֹ וּמִמֶּנּוּ נִתְהַוָּה,

Just as there is no parallel or comparison between the ashes and the essence of the large tree in length, width, and thickness before it was burned, neither in its quantity nor in its quality, even though the ash **constitutes** the tree's **nature and essence, and** the ashes **came into being from** the wood,

The burned tree is not a miniature version of the tree. It is only ash. Although the source of the ash is the wood, it is not similar to wood. True, the material that comprises the ashes is essentially the same material that once was wood, and the quantity may even be the same quantity, if we look at the large fruit-bearing tree and at the heap of ash, there is apparently no connection and similarity between them. To illustrate with an example closer to home: If we grind a watch into powder, nothing of the watch has been lost. The metal, the glass, the fluorescence all remain. Yet it is impossible to construct any relationship between the powder and the watch.

כָּךְ עַל דֶּרֶךְ מָשָׁל אָמַר אַבְרָהָם אָבִינוּ עָלָיו הַשָּׁלוֹם עַל מִדָּתוֹ, מִדַּת הַחֶסֶד וְהָאַהֲבָה הַמְּאִירָה בּוֹ וּמְלוּבֶּשֶׁת בְּגוּפוֹ. דְּאַף שֶׁהִיא [הִיא] מִדַּת הָאַהֲבָה וְחֶסֶד הָעֶלְיוֹן שֶׁבַּאֲצִילוּת הַמֵּאִיר בְּנִשְׁמָתוֹ, שֶׁהָיְתָה מֶרְכָּבָה עֶלְיוֹנָה, אַף עַל פִּי כֵן בְּרִדְתָּהּ לְמַטָּה, לְהִתְלַבֵּשׁ בְּגוּפוֹ עַל יְדֵי הִשְׁתַּלְשְׁלוּת הָעוֹלָמוֹת מִמַּדְרֵגָה לְמַדְרֵגָה עַל יְדֵי צִמְצוּמִים רַבִּים,

so too, figuratively speaking, our forefather Abraham, may he rest in peace, spoke of his attribute, the attribute of kindness and love that shone in him and was enclothed in his body. Although it was the attribute of supernal *Ḥesed* and love in *Atzilut* that shone in his soul, which was a supernal vehicle for the Divine, **even so, as it descended to be enclothed in his body, by means of the transmutations of the worlds from one level to another, through numerous constrictions,**

Abraham's soul was a supernal vehicle transmitting the divine attributes to this world without anything else intermingled with it. Yet when the attribute of *Ḥesed* in *Atzilut* descended to be clothed in Abraham's corporeal body, in the physical world of *Asiya,* it did not clothe itself in it purely as it exists in the world of *Atzilut,* but it necessarily descended via the transmutations of the worlds, through numerous constrictions.

אֵין דִּמְיוֹן וְעֵרֶךְ מַהוּת אוֹר הָאַהֲבָה הַמֵּאִיר בּוֹ, אֶל מַהוּת אוֹר אַהֲבָה וְחֶסֶד עֶלְיוֹן שֶׁבַּאֲצִילוּת, אֶלָּא כְּעֵרֶךְ וְדִמְיוֹן מַהוּת הֶעָפָר שֶׁנַּעֲשָׂה אֵפֶר אֶל מַהוּתוֹ וְאֵיכוּתוֹ כְּשֶׁהָיָה

there is no parallel or comparison between the essence of the light of the love that shone within him to the essence of the light of the supernal love and *Ḥesed* that is in *Atzilut*. Rather, it is like the comparison and parallel between the essence of

עֵץ נֶחְמָד לְמַרְאֶה וְטוֹב לְמַאֲכָל.

the element of **earth that became ashes and its essence and quality when it was in the tree that is pleasant to the sight and good for food.**

As the divine attribute of *Ḥesed* descends from *Atzilut* to our world, it necessarily undergoes what the divine light that vitalizes the worlds undergoes: the entire scope of devolution, concealment, and constriction, level after level, until it turns into the materiality and physicality of this world. Moreover, just as there is no similarity between this world and the world of *Atzilut*, so too there is no similarity between the love that was manifest in Abraham in the physical world and the light of supernal love and *Ḥesed* in *Atzilut*. Compared to supernal *Ḥesed*, the attribute of Abraham was like the ashes that remain from a tree that was burnt compared to the living tree. There is no comparison between them, neither in appearance, taste, scent, nor function.

עַל דֶּרֶךְ מָשָׁל, וְיוֹתֵר מִזֶּה לְהַבְדִּיל בְּאַלְפִּים הַבְדָּלוֹת,

This is only **figuratively speaking, and one should differentiate** between the two cases **even more so, thousands of times over.**

The difference between the wood and the ashes is minuscule in relation to the difference between divine *Ḥesed* and Abraham's attribute of kindness. The difference is so great that the two are separated from each other not by one transmutation or even a few degrees, but by thousands of transmutations, level upon level, each one of which is so much higher than the one beneath it that it is absolutely impossible for one to perceive the other.

רַק שֶׁדִּבְּרָה תּוֹרָה כִּלְשׁוֹן בְּנֵי אָדָם בְּמָשָׁל וּמְלִיצָה.

But the Torah spoke in the language of human beings, through allegory and metaphor.

Abraham's statement, "And I am dust and ashes," is only a metaphor employing concepts that people can discuss and think about. In truth, the distance is much greater and entirely different from any concept we can possibly fathom. ☞

But why is it that if the supernal attributes are so different from human attributes, the Torah offers metaphors from the language of human beings?

It is because, despite all these differences, a human being and his soul are a unique reality within the totality of creation, possessing a special status and connection to the Creator. Were that not the case, the statement "From my flesh I will view God" would be meaningless. A person is able to contemplate and apprehend the divine *sefirot* by contemplating the nature of the soul clothed in his body. Although it is vitally important not to conflate the two realms, to acknowledge the vast distance between the metaphor and its referent, the human soul – and not only that of Abraham – can serve as a model through which one may understand the divine *sefirot*. ☞

19 Elul
16 Elul (leap year)

וְהִנֵּה כְּלָלוּת הָעֶשֶׂר סְפִירוֹת שֶׁבְּנִשְׁמַת הָאָדָם, נוֹדַע לַכֹּל [בְּדֶרֶךְ כְּלָל - בִּכְתַב יָד לֵיתָא] שֶׁהַמִּדּוֹת נֶחֱלָקוֹת בְּדֶרֶךְ כְּלָל לְ־ז׳ מִדּוֹת, וְכָל פְּרָטֵי הַמִּדּוֹת שֶׁבָּאָדָם בָּאוֹת מֵאַחַת מִ־ז׳ מִדּוֹת אֵלּוּ, שֶׁהֵן שׁוֹרֶשׁ כָּל הַמִּדּוֹת וּכְלָלוּתָן.

Regarding the totality of the ten *sefirot* within the soul of man, it is known to all [in general terms (this does not appear in the original manuscript)] that the emotive **attributes are typically divided into seven attributes, and each of the specific attributes in man comes from one of these seven attributes, which are the root and totality of all the attributes.**

METAPHOR AND ABSTRACT THOUGHT

☞ When we compare one entity to another, we necessarily relate to matters that we apprehend, to concepts that are familiar to us whether within us or within the world outside. When we wish to relate to an unfamiliar concept and experience, we can only relate to it by invoking the extremity of our comprehension, but no more.

Here too we contrast a living tree, which is the peak of complexity and perfection in the material world, with dust and ashes, which is the lowest and most primitive state of materiality. Within the material realm, there is no greater difference. When Abraham speaks of the difference between the attribute of kindness within him and the *Ḥesed* in *Atzilut*, he uses this analogy. But undoubtedly, it is meant only as a metaphor.

Following the above introduction, which dealt with the way in which we think about and study hasidic teachings, the author of the *Tanya* now proceeds to the main topic of the epistle: an explanation of the ten *sefirot*.

The ten *sefirot* are divided into two groups: the cognitive attributes and the emotive attributes.[15] The three cognitive *sefirot*, *Ḥokhma*, *Bina*, and *Da'at*, are the faculties of awareness with which we become aware of the reality and find our place in it. The emotive attributes constitute a person's senses and his relationships with things through his emotions and deeds. This epistle mainly discusses the emotive attributes, and so the author of the *Tanya* lists them first. The cognitive *sefirot* are mentioned afterward and then principally in terms of their role as the source and root of the emotive attributes.[16]

In the most general sense, this epistle explains the *sefirot* from three

THE ANALOGY OF THE HUMAN SOUL

☞ We can learn about the divine *sefirot* through contemplation of the soul, and not only because the source and root of the faculties in the soul are the supernal *sefirot*. In a sense, the entire world, including inanimate matter and vegetation, is rooted and sourced in the spiritual, supernal worlds, but unlike everything else in creation, the human soul is a complete structure. It is an entity that encompasses (although distantly) the totality of the components of the world of *Atzilut*: the *sefirot*, which include *Ḥesed* as well as *Gevura*, the cognitive *sefirot* as well as the emotive attributes. Therefore, even when the specific components of *Atzilut* are not at all similar to those that comprise man, something of a relationship exists between them. Our left hand is not similar to that which is the left on high and our right hand is not like the right in spiritual terms, but the relationship between left and right in Heaven in some way parallels that relationship in a human being, despite all the differences.

An additional point is that the divine soul in man is not only loftier than anything else in existence, but the soul maintains something of its uniqueness on all the levels through which it descends and in which it is clothed. Even when it is in a corporeal body, it is divine, supernal, and unique within the reality around it. Granted, there are differences between people, depending on the quality of their soul, their deeds, and their lifestyle. The higher the level of a person's soul and the more pristine his conduct, the more his soul retains its structure, its state of refinement, as it exists above in the worlds of *Yetzira*, *Beria*, and even *Atzilut*.

---

15. See *Likkutei Amarim*, chap. 3.

16. Perhaps this is because the intellect recognizes things as they are at their

perspectives. The first explanation deals solely with the emotive attributes as they exist in the external aspect of man's animal-rational soul, how they manifest in his reactions and deeds. The second explanation deals with the inner aspect of the emotive attributes, the inner causes of those reactions and deeds and the way they manifest as emotions within (such as the feeling of fear that leads to restraint, or *Gevura*, or of love that fuels an act of kindness, or *Ḥesed*). It also touches on the intellect, primarily on *Da'at*, the awareness that generates the expression and manifestation of all the emotive attributes, as will be explained. The third explanation, the principal one and the most detailed, deals with all ten *sefirot* as they are manifest in the divine soul and in *Atzilut*, as well as we can apprehend them.

The author of the *Tanya* will first delineate and explain the seven emotive attributes in descending order: *Ḥesed* (or love), *Gevura* (or fear), *Tiferet* (or compassion), *Netzaḥ*, *Hod*, *Yesod*, and *Malkhut*. These are general classifications that represent the emotions. In actuality, people can have endless gradations of feelings. No two people have exactly the same feelings, and even the feelings of a single individual are always shifting. The reason for this is that feelings are complex. For instance, love for someone is never only love. It is also comprised of worry and jealousy related to fear (which is associated with *Gevura*), compassion and beauty (associated with *Tiferet*), subjugation (associated with *Netzaḥ*), dominion or acceptance (associated with *Malkhut*), and so on. This combination of attributes constantly forms different shades, which we experience as feelings. But they all have their roots in the seven emotive attributes. ☞

This epistle will go on to discuss how the emotive attributes are manifest in action. For instance, if a person has the attribute of kindness, how does he conduct himself? What do we see when looking at him from the outside? After that, the epistle will discuss the inner aspect

---

essence without any sense of personal connection to them, whereas his emotive attributes express his relationship with other matters. Just as a person's emotive attributes express his relationship to things outside him, so do they define the person and express who he is, what he feels, what he wants, and so forth. Thus, a person's emotive attributes are related to his sense of self, how he experiences himself. Since this epistle deals with understanding the *sefirot* in light of a person's experience of himself, it principally discusses the emotive attributes.

of a person's emotive attributes: What does this person who employs the attribute of kindness feel? What is the inner trait that impels him to conduct himself and act as he does? The distinction between the outer expression of the attribute and its inner aspect is reflected in an attribute having one designation for its outer expression and another for its inner manifestation. For instance, the outer expression of *Ḥesed* is called kindness, while its inner manifestation is called love.

שֶׁהֵן מִדַּת הַחֶסֶד לְהַשְׁפִּיעַ בְּלִי גְּבוּל,

They are the attribute of *Ḥesed*, which constitutes **giving without limit,**

The attribute of *Ḥesed* is the trait of expansion, movement from the center outward through giving, bestowing, expanding. The description here of "giving without limit" does not apply specifically to the *Ḥesed* of God, who is infinite and whose attributes are infinite, but to the attribute of *Ḥesed* in itself, which constitutes giving without limitation at its essence. The attribute of *Ḥesed* in itself is that of pouring forth without parameters, while the parameters, such as how much to give and where to give, are limitations that come from the influence of other emotive attributes, as well as the limitations of the reality into which the *Ḥesed* flows.

וּמִדַּת הַגְּבוּרָה לְצַמְצֵם מִלְּהַשְׁפִּיעַ כָּל כָּךְ, אוֹ שֶׁלֹּא לְהַשְׁפִּיעַ [נוּסָח אַחֵר: כָּל עִיקָּר] כְּלָל,

the attribute of *Gevura*, which constitutes **refraining from giving too much or from giving at all [alternatively: altogether],**

The attribute of *Gevura* is the opposite of the attribute of *Ḥesed*. But the attributes always interact with each other and function together, exhibiting a dynamic relationship. Separate, discrete emotive attributes

THE EMOTIVE ATTRIBUTES IN MAN

☞ To illustrate, there are numerous colors and hues. No two leaves have exactly the same color, and the color of the sky today is not the same as it was yesterday. The human eye can see approximately a million colors. Yet there are only three primary colors (red, blue, and yellow), whose mixture in various ratios creates all of the colors in existence.

do not exist. When we discuss the attributes of *Ḥesed* and *Gevura*, we always relate them to each other. *Ḥesed* is shaped by *Gevura* and *Gevura* by *Ḥesed*. In this case, the attribute of *Gevura* expresses itself in its constriction of the pouring forth of *Ḥesed*, whether partially or totally.

A more intrinsic definition of *Gevura* is constriction and convergence toward the center: movement from the outside inward, from outside the limits into parameters and boundaries. By contrast, the attribute of *Ḥesed* is expansiveness, spreading out from within and breaking through boundaries.

וּמִדַּת הָרַחֲמִים לְרַחֵם עַל מִי שֶׁשַּׁיָּיךְ לְשׁוֹן רַחֲמָנוּת עָלָיו,

and the attribute of *Tiferet*, which manifests as **compassion, as having compassion on one to whom the term "compassion" pertains,**

Raḥamim, or compassion, is another term for *Tiferet*, which represents a balance between *Ḥesed* and *Gevura*. Like *Ḥesed*, the attribute of kindness, compassion entails giving. But unlike *Ḥesed*, the trait of compassion is meted out in accordance with the recipient. *Raḥamim* does not give everything to everyone, but rather gives that which is lacking to one who is in need – to one who deserves compassion. Whereas *Ḥesed*'s giving comes from an inner impulse to give, to pour forth from within outward, almost without relating to the recipient, the attribute of compassion focuses on the recipient, and the giving is therefore limited. Compassion is felt for the recipient who is lacking and needs to receive, and it is meted out in keeping with the recipient's lack and ability to receive. ☞

THE UNLIMITED ATTRIBUTE OF COMPASSION

☞ From another perspective, the limitation of compassion comes from the recipient, whose lack and needs evoke this attribute. But from the perspective of the giver, there is an aspect of this trait that makes it almost unlimited. *Ḥesed*'s giving requires to a certain extent a personal relationship with the recipient and, on a deeper level, a feeling of love. The attribute of *Ḥesed* is not limited by the recipient, by whether he deserves or needs a gift, because it is solely an expression of an inner compulsion to give. But there is an inner boundary, which is whether the giver feels love, and it is not

וְהִיא מִדָּה מְמוּצַּעַת בֵּין גְּבוּרָה לְחֶסֶד. **which is the intermediate attribute between *Gevura* and *Ḥesed*.**

The ten *sefirot* relate to each other, giving and receiving from each other, limiting and defining each other. In this context, an "intermediate attribute" is not a compromise between two attributes that are opposites. It does not represent the common denominator shared by the two opposites, which is generally weighted toward the lower of the two extremes, nor is it only a silhouette, a reflection, of the two sides. Rather, it is an entity in itself. Not only is this third entity not lower than the other two attributes, but it is even loftier than them and can encompass and integrate them. ☞

always possible to feel love, nor is it possible to feel love for everyone.

This is not the case with the trait of compassion, which is dependent on a different factor: on lack in the recipient. If someone is lacking, it makes sense to have compassion on him and give to him. From that perspective, there is no limitation to compassion. A person can only love someone who is like him, someone whose qualities he shares, someone with a similar degree of intelligence, a similar soul root, or the same goals. But a person can have compassion on anything, even a wet cat or a broken tree. Furthermore, with compassion the recipient's lack and the distance between the recipient and the giver does not get in the way of the giving. In fact, they are the very reason one gives. When someone is lacking, people have compassion on him and give to him, and the more he lacks, the more they give.

THREE ARRAYS

☞ These relationships exist in every part of the infrastructure of *sefirot*. They are described, verbally and graphically, by the wording that appears in *Tikkunei Zohar* (*Pataḥ Eliyahu*): "One long and one short and one intermediary." In accordance with this, all of the *sefirot* are divided graphically into three vertical lines, or arrays: a right array, a left array, and an intermediate array (see *Tikkunei Zohar* 17a, where the *sefirot* are described in terms of the image of the human body, so that *Ḥesed* is the right arm, *Gevura* is the left arm, *Tiferet* is the torso, and so on). Generally speaking, the right array, consisting of *Ḥokhma*, *Ḥesed*, and *Netzaḥ*, is characterized by pouring forth and spreading out, by initiative and activism. The left array, consisting of *Bina*, *Gevura*, and *Hod*, is characterized by strength, constraint, and converging inward, by receiving and passivity. The middle array, consisting of *Da'at*, *Tiferet*, and *Yesod*, is the intermediate array.

שֶׁהִיא לְהַשְׁפִּיעַ לַכֹּל, גַּם לְמִי שֶׁלֹּא שַׁיָּיךְ לְשׁוֹן רַחֲמָנוּת עָלָיו כְּלָל, מִפְּנֵי שֶׁאֵינוֹ חָסֵר כְּלוּם וְאֵינוֹ שָׁרוּי בְּצַעַר כְּלָל.

Ḥesed constitutes **giving to everyone, even to one to whom the term "compassion" does not apply at all because he lacks nothing and is not besieged by any troubles at all.**

The unlimited flow that pours forth from *Ḥesed,* a pouring forth out of love, is not in response to a recipient who requires what is being given, but because the giver wants to actualize his love. The giver does not consider whether the recipient needs, wants, or is deserving of the gift. This is in contrast to the trait of compassion, which incorporates the attribute of *Gevura,* limiting and restricting the giving, constraining the giving to one who is lacking and needs to receive.

וּלְפִי שֶׁהִיא מִדָּה מְמוּצַּעַת - נִקְרֵאת תִּפְאֶרֶת. כְּמוֹ בִּגְדֵי תִפְאֶרֶת עַל דֶּרֶךְ מָשָׁל, שֶׁהוּא בֶּגֶד צָבוּעַ בִּגְוָונִים הַרְבֵּה מְעוֹרָבִים [בּוֹ - בִּכְתַב יָד לֵיתָא] בְּדֶרֶךְ שֶׁהוּא תִּפְאֶרֶת וְנוֹי. מַה שֶּׁאֵין כֵּן בֶּגֶד הַצָּבוּעַ בְּגָוֶן אֶחָד, לֹא שַׁיָּיךְ בּוֹ לְשׁוֹן תִּפְאֶרֶת.

Since compassion **is an intermediate attribute, it is called *Tiferet*,** Beauty, **like, for example, beautiful garments that are dyed with many colors blended [in it (this does not appear in the manuscript)] in a manner that makes them beautiful and ornamental. This is not the case regarding a garment dyed in a single color, to which the term *tiferet* does not apply.**

Tiferet indicates beauty, and beauty is revealed through harmony, in proper relationships between entities.[17] There are various types of harmony: a harmony of colors, shapes, or tones, harmony among people, harmony among the faculties of the soul. Just as a single line or a single note cannot be harmonious, so too a single feeling, a single faculty, cannot be beautiful. The attribute of *Tiferet* always involves a combination of opposites as they relate to each other, combine and

17. Similar language appears in the mishnaic statement "Rabbi [Yehuda HaNasi] would say: What is a straight path that a person should choose for himself? Whatever is harmonious [*tiferet*] for the one who does it and harmonious for mankind" (*Pirkei Avot* 2:1).

separate, emphasize and deemphasize, always in a complementary relationship. It is true that some combinations are not beautiful but ugly and grating. But perhaps that is merely the other side of the same coin, since beauty can emerge specifically from a place that could also have been ugly.

Ḥesed, Gevura, and *Tiferet* are the fundamental *sefirot,* summing up the entire infrastructure of an entity with a right, left, and middle: There is a relationship between them from below to above, from above to below, and the harmonious movement back and forth. In other terms, they are the basic triangle of thesis, antithesis, and synthesis.

The next three *sefirot, Netzaḥ, Hod,* and *Yesod,* are secondary attributes. They do not determine an emotional relationship but only the way to relate to the relationship, how to elicit and actualize that which has been established through the fundamental *sefirot.* Nevertheless, on their level, they too are fundamental in the sense that they exist in every feeling and flow that pours through the soul.

וְאַחַר כָּךְ, בְּבוֹא הַהַשְׁפָּעָה לִידֵי מַעֲשֶׂה,

Subsequently, when the flow of love and kindness **is actualized** –

The order of the *sefirot,* what comes first and what comes later, is not relevant to the intrinsic being of the *sefirot* but to the flow that pours through them. The beginning of the flow is received from above. Afterward, that which was poured forth is developed within us through intellectual understanding and feeling. After that, it is actualized in speech and action that are directed outward, an actualization that passes through the *sefirot* of *Netzaḥ* and *Hod.*

דְּהַיְינוּ בִּשְׁעַת הַהַשְׁפָּעָה מַמָּשׁ, צָרִיךְ לְהִתְיַיעֵץ אֵיךְ לְהַשְׁפִּיעַ בְּדֶרֶךְ שֶׁיּוּכַל הַמְקַבֵּל לְקַבֵּל הַהַשְׁפָּעָה.

that is, at the time of the actual pouring forth – it is necessary to deliberate regarding **how to give** it **in a manner that the recipient will be able to receive the flow.**

Between the impulse to act and pour forth within the *sefirot* of *Ḥesed, Gevura,* and *Tiferet,* and the actual giving and receiving through the *sefirot* of *Yesod* and *Malkhut,* there must be a preparatory stage. This exists in the *sefirot* of *Netzaḥ* and *Hod.* They are the passageway from the what to the how: How is it possible to give to someone, and how is it possible for him to receive?

Parents certainly love their child and want to feed him, and the baby is certainly deserving and needs to be fed, but they cannot give him their own food. There must be a how: how to feed him. There must be a stage in which the food is prepared and measured so that the baby will be able to receive it.

כְּגוֹן שֶׁרוֹצֶה לְהַשְׁפִּיעַ דְּבַר חָכְמָה לְלַמְּדָהּ לִבְנוֹ, אִם יֹאמְרֶנָּה לוֹ כּוּלָּהּ כְּמוֹ שֶׁהִיא בְּשִׂכְלוֹ, לֹא יוּכַל הַבֵּן לְהָבִין וּלְקַבֵּל, רַק שֶׁצָּרִיךְ לְסַדֵּר לוֹ בְּסֵדֶר וְעִנְיָן אַחֵר, דָּבָר דָּבוּר עַל אוֹפַנָּיו, מְעַט מְעַט.

For example, when one wishes to convey and teach some matter of wisdom to his child, if he tells it all to him as it is in his mind, the child will be unable to understand and receive it. **Instead,** the father **must organize it for** his child **in a different order and context, with the proper phrasing, little by little.**

This example expresses the burning desire to give, because the father certainly wants to give everything good to his child, but along with that comes the challenge in transmitting that goodness, because there is a vast gap between the father's intellect and the child's intellect. For the child to be able to receive, it is not enough for the father to pour onto him what he knows. He must rearrange the information and hand it out little by little, not in accordance with his own understanding, but in keeping with what the child is able to absorb. The process must begin from the child – what he knows, what he wants, and how he thinks. ☞

וּבְחִינַת עֵצָה זוֹ נִקְרֵאת נֵצַח וְהוֹד, שֶׁהֵן כְּלָיוֹת יוֹעֲצוֹת,

This deliberation is called *Netzaḥ*, Dominance, **and *Hod*,** Splendor, **which are "the kidneys that advise."**

The *sefirot* and the corresponding faculties of the soul have many parallels to the human body.[18] *Netzaḥ* and *Hod* are described as two legs, parallel to the two arms, which are *Ḥesed* and *Gevura*. Here, with regard to the flow that pours forth and the advice on how it should

18. See *Tikkunei Zohar* 85a.

pour forth, the author of the *Tanya* uses the talmudic imagery of "the kidneys that advise."

The Talmud explains that the kidneys advise the heart with the good inclination or with the evil inclination. In other words, the kidneys advise the heart on how to relate to its feelings and how to act on them, what to feel and what not to feel in actuality, and subsequently, whether to act or not to act in accordance with those feelings.

וְגַם [נוסח אַחֵר: וְהֵן] תְּרֵין בֵּיעִין הַמְבַשְּׁלִים הַזֶּרַע, שֶׁהִיא הַטִּפָּה הַנִּמְשֶׁכֶת מֵהַמּוֹחַ.

Also, [**alternatively: and they are**] **the two testicles that prepare the semen, which** begins as **the drop that is issued from the brain.**

Another metaphor (or, according to the variant reading, a continuation of the previous metaphor) for the *sefirot* of *Netzaḥ* and *Hod* is the two testicles, which prepare the semen that begins as a drop that issues from the brain. That drop of semen is the innermost, most essential part of oneself that a man can give forth. Its source is actually in the brain, in a substance that is extremely fine that is on the borderline between the physical and the spiritual. It descends through the body until it

THE FATHER'S INTELLECT AND THE CHILD'S INTELLECT

☞ The difference between the father's intellect and the child's intellect, between a greater intellect and a smaller intellect, is the difference between an intellect in which the elements of a topic are organized into a complex picture, and an intellect that absorbs ideas in a rudimentary manner. The picture in the father's intellect is composed of many pieces of detailed knowledge that he has acquired and organized over time. Ideas that seem simple and self-understood to him are not at all comprehensible to his child. When the father must communicate information to his child, he must dismantle that picture, reveal its details anew, and rebuild them in a different order and context that align with the child's ability to absorb them.

Furthermore, there are some things whose deeper meaning the child is entirely incapable of understanding. If the father would state them as they are without explanation, the child will not assimilate them. In such a case, the father must provide other explanations that are not the actual, deeper explanation. This raises the question of which explanation to provide. One might offer an explanation that is not entirely correct, but that might do more harm than good. This way of thinking about how to verbalize and explain matters, with one explanation or another, is done using the attributes of *Netzaḥ* and *Hod*, which are called "the kidneys that advise" (*Berakhot* 61a), as the author of the *Tanya* goes on to state.

becomes a physical drop of semen, and the place in the body in which this essence, this spiritual-physical distillation of the mind and feelings, is transformed into an actual drop of seed is in the two testicles.

דְּהַיְינוּ דְּבַר חָכְמָה וְשֵׂכֶל הַנִּמְשָׁךְ מִשֵּׂכֶל הָאָב, שֶׁלֹּא יוּמְשַׁךְ כְּמוֹ שֶׁהוּא שֵׂכֶל דַּק מְאֹד בְּמוֹחוֹ וְשִׂכְלוֹ, רַק יִשְׁתַּנֶּה קְצָת מִדַּקּוּת שִׂכְלוֹ וְיִתְהַוֶּה שֵׂכֶל שֶׁאֵינוֹ דַּק כָּל כָּךְ, כְּדֵי שֶׁיּוּכַל הַבֵּן לְקַבֵּל בְּמוֹחוֹ וַהֲבָנָתוֹ.

That is to say, from a more spiritual perspective, **a concept of wisdom and intellect that issues forth from the father's mind is not drawn forth as the very subtle** matter of **intelligence that is in his mind and intellect. Rather, it changes somewhat from the subtle** concept in **his intellect and becomes a concept that is not so subtle so that the child can absorb** it **with his mind and understanding.**

Now the author of the *Tanya* offers a more spiritual metaphor. A refined intellect is an abstract intellect, whose ideas, in word and thought, do not resonate directly with a material existence but with higher and more spiritual frameworks. Intellect on that level cannot be apprehended by a mind whose mental concepts are based principally on the physical plane of existence. For a person to transmit a subtle, abstract idea to a mind that is not so rarefied, he must coarsen the concepts by lowering the level of abstraction and using concrete analogies and examples. ☞

NETZAḤ AND *HOD* IN EMOTIONS

☞ Just as a father can transmit an idea to his child, who possesses a simpler understanding, so can he transmit the emotive attributes of love and fear. If the love within a person is infinitely fine and sensitive, and he needs to communicate it to someone else, to the reality that is outside him, he might need to break it down in order to relate it to a defined reality. When one loves a specific person, it is impossible to give him everything, to express everything beloved by the one who loves that person. Rather, we must take into account what the recipient wants and is able to receive. That is the stage of *Netzaḥ* and *Hod*, that of the necessity to differentiate, constrict, and align.

וְהוּא מַמָּשׁ עַל דֶּרֶךְ מָשָׁל כְּטִפָּה הַיּוֹרֶדֶת מֵהַמּוֹחַ, שֶׁהִיא דַּקָּה מְאֹד [מְאֹד], וְנַעֲשֵׂית גַּסָּה וְחוֹמְרִית מַמָּשׁ בַּכְּלָיוֹת וּתְרֵין בֵּיעִין.

This is, figuratively speaking, actually analogous to a drop of semen **that descends from the brain, which is very, [very] fine and literally becomes coarse and corporeal in the kidneys and the two testicles.**

Like the intellect, the drop of seed exists in the brain in a subtle form, like the spiritual source of the physical drop. But while it is in the brain, it cannot father children. For that drop to pass onward, to be absorbed into material existence and truly father a physical child, it must be coarsened and receive a physical form.

וְגַם נֶצַח וְהוֹד נִקְרָאִים 'שְׁחָקִים' וְ'רֵחַיִים', שֶׁשּׁוֹחֲקִים מָן לַצַּדִּיקִים.

***Netzaḥ* and *Hod* are also called grinders and millstones, because they grind manna for the righteous.**

The imagery that the author of the *Tanya* offers here emphasizes that *Netzaḥ* and *Hod* work together as a pair. This is epitomized by the use of the Hebrew words for grinder and millstone, *reḥayim* and *shoḥakim*, which are in the plural. There cannot be a mill made of one stone. In order to grind and mill, two grinders or millstones are needed, two forces that work one against the other.[19] So too in spirituality, when a person wants to break down a broad and abstract idea in order to communicate it to someone else, he needs opposing, balancing ideas, opposite counsels. Only then can he communicate concrete formulations and concepts.

כְּמוֹ הַטּוֹחֵן [חִטִּים] בְּרֵחַיִים, עַל דֶּרֶךְ מָשָׁל, שֶׁמְּפָרֵר הַחִטִּים לַחֲלָקִים דַּקִּים מְאֹד, כָּךְ צָרִיךְ הָאָב לְהַקְטִין הַשֵּׂכֶל וּדְבַר חָכְמָה שֶׁרוֹצֶה לְהַשְׁפִּיעַ לִבְנוֹ, וּלְחַלְּקָם לַחֲלָקִים רַבִּים, וְלוֹמַר לוֹ מְעַט

They are, **figuratively speaking, like one who grinds [wheat] in a mill, crumbling the wheat into very fine pieces. Likewise, the father must reduce the concept and matter of wisdom that he wants to transmit to his child, divide it into many**

19. See *Ḥagiga* 12b; *Zohar* 3:26a; *Me'orei Or*, s.v. *shoḥakim*; *Pardes Rimmonim, Sha'ar HaShemot*, chap. 12; *Sha'ar HaKavanot, Derushei Ḥag HaSukkot*.

מְעַט בְּמוֹעֵצוֹת וָדַעַת.

parts, and communicate them **to** his child **little by little, with counsel and knowledge.**

That is what every educator does: He takes a general idea and breaks it down into small parts that he can transmit. He does all this "with counsel and knowledge." The division and arrangement of the material should be with "counsel," as a result of taking advice on how to do this. It should also be done with "knowledge," by connecting to the recipient through his faculty of knowledge.[20]

וְגַם בִּכְלָל, בְּחִינַת נֵצַח הוּא לְנַצֵּחַ וְלַעֲמוֹד נֶגֶד כָּל מוֹנֵעַ הַהַשְׁפָּעָה

In general, ***Netzaḥ*** **expresses** the ability **to triumph and stand firm against anything that prevents the transmission** of wisdom

Until now, the author of the *Tanya* has discussed *Netzaḥ* and *Hod* in terms of internal obstacles that impede the pouring forth of goodness. Whether it comes to transmitting wisdom, which needs to be broken down so that the receiver can absorb the ideas, or whether emotions must be redefined in order to be aligned with the receiving vessel and have any influence on the physical reality. The author of the *Tanya* will go on to discuss external obstacles that involve impediments placed by existence, and in particular, physical existence, to any change or growth.

All movement in our world requires effort. It requires overcoming layers and constructs that are unprepared to move and change. The seed must push through layers of earth and rocks in order to reach the light outside and sprout into a plant. So too a new idea must push through layers of previous knowledge, habits, and preconceptions in order to pass from being a flash of wisdom to understanding and, beyond that, to actualization that can influence others.

The author of the *Tanya* has been discussing *Netzaḥ* and *Hod* as a unit. Now he focuses on *Netzaḥ* alone. *Netzaḥ* is related to vanquishing.

---

20. The Hebrew word for knowledge, *da'at*, connotes a bond, as in the verse "And the man had been intimate with Eve" (Gen. 4:1). The word for intimacy in the verse is *yada*, which literally means that the man "knew" Eve.

The power to vanquish is an independent faculty of the soul in itself, unlike kindness, love, and compassion, which are faculties of the soul that relate to another in a certain sense. *Netzaḥ* is the essence of the desire to vanquish. A person engages in competition, in struggle, without consideration for the nature of what he is battling against. He simply wants to overcome and vanquish. This drive to vanquish is very strong, sometimes stronger than any desire that stems from recognition or feeling, yearning or fear.

This power is employed in sports competitions. To extract more from a person, he is made to face people against whom he will compete. At peak moments of effort, the drive for victory is decisive. It can push a person beyond what he thought he was capable of achieving.

There are obstacles to actualizing a deed, a word, or even a thought, even when the thing one wants to accomplish is desirable and proper. In order to overcome these obstacles, one needs a special fortitude, not additional encouragement, whether intellectual or emotional, but a rawer power so that one can prevail and overcome the difficulties and obstacles to do what needs to be done.

וְהַלִּימּוּד מִבְּנוֹ. מִבַּיִת וּמִחוּץ. מִבַּיִת, הַיְינוּ לְהִתְחַזֵּק נֶגֶד מִדַּת הַגְּבוּרָה וְהַצִּמְצוּם שֶׁבָּאָב עַצְמוֹ, שֶׁהִיא מְעוֹרֶרֶת דִּינִים בִּרְצוֹנוֹ עַל בְּנוֹ, לוֹמַר שֶׁאֵינוֹ רָאוּי לְכָךְ עֲדַיִין.

and prevents **the teaching** from reaching **his child, whether from within or from without. "From within" means the father strengthening himself against the attribute of *Gevura* and constriction within, which evokes in his will contentions against his child, saying that** his child **is not yet ready** to receive **this** teaching.

Even when it comes to something that a person wants and desires, such as when a father desires to transmit his wisdom to his child, there are obstacles that a person must vanquish. The obstacles come from two directions. There are external obstacles that come from without, such as distance, time constraints, or the hostile actions of people and governments. As for obstacles that come from within, it may happen that a person wants to do something and is intellectually prepared to do it, but certain considerations and feelings keep him from acting. In order to follow through, he must overcome his inner hesitation, his ambivalent thoughts and feelings, and despite them realize his wish and desire in actuality.

A person does so by employing the attribute of *Netzaḥ,* which is a branch of *Ḥesed,* the attribute of giving and action. When doing so, he can overcome the considerations that have prevented him from acting. Although the author of the *Tanya* does not speak of it here, the preventive force is the attribute of *Hod*. *Hod,* which is a branch of *Gevura,* opposes the voices that urge a person to act. It prevents him from doing so even though he has reason and the desire to do so. ☞

(בִּכְתַב יָד נִרְשַׁם: חָסֵר) (A note **in the manuscript indicates: omission.**)

Parts of the text are apparently missing. This may consist of a few lines about the obstacles that come from without, since only the inner obstacles are discussed in the extant text. Moreover, the text does not discuss the attribute of *Hod* in detail, but only the composite of *Netzaḥ* and *Hod*.

Hod, like *Netzaḥ,* is the faculty of overcoming an obstacle, of defying existence, but on the left side. When employing this faculty, a person stands firm. He does not surrender, does not retreat, does not break down, even when there is no hope, even at the cost of destruction and death, so that he will not lose the essential point for which he is fighting. ☞

וּבְחִינַת יְסוֹד הִיא, עַל דֶּרֶךְ מָשָׁל, הַהִתְקַשְּׁרוּת **The attribute of *Yesod* is, figuratively speaking, the bond**

THE ROOT OF *NETZAḤ*

☞ *Netzaḥ* has the power to prevail over the mind and even feelings that express something different from the will. That testifies to the power of *Netzaḥ,* which comes from the essence of the soul, higher than the mind and feelings. In a sense, it is even higher than the soul's faculty for pleasure. Although *Netzaḥ* is a branch of *Ḥesed,* which expresses itself in love and giving, *Netzaḥ* is the faculty of dominance and victory. *Netzaḥ* comes into play when the struggle to prevail over opposition creates a buildup of forces that sweep the person along with them and give him the ability to act despite opposing voices.

Yesod is the attribute that follows *Netzaḥ* and *Hod,* parallel to *Tiferet,* which is the attribute that follows *Ḥesed* and *Gevura.* This triad, of *Netzaḥ, Hod,* and *Yesod,* brings the flow of light and life force into existence. *Netzaḥ* and *Hod* prepare the flow. They dismantle the mechanisms of this flow, overcome difficulties and obstacles, coming as close as possible to the recipient itself, but not quite reaching it.

Yesod is the connection between the two. It is not yet the ultimate recipient – that role belongs to *Malkhut* – but *Yesod* offers a tangible, intrinsic connection, the passageway or channel between *Netzaḥ* and *Hod* and *Malkhut* to allow the life force and divine light bestowed by the higher *sefirot* to be manifest in the world. This connection is a faculty of the soul, and the nature of this bond or connection, whether from

NETZAḤ AND *HOD* ARE ALWAYS TOGETHER

☞ A detailed and separate explanation for *Netzaḥ* and *Hod* is not as necessary and meaningful as it is for *Ḥesed* and *Gevura,* because *Netzaḥ* and *Hod* are primarily treated as a unit. They work together as a team to actualize that which has been incipient, despite obstacles from within and from without, from the person himself and from outside reality. There is no difference in their goals nor even in the way that they operate. They are essentially two aspects of the same mechanism. Unlike *Ḥesed* and *Gevura,* whose essential characteristics are very different, *Netzaḥ* and *Hod* only differ externally. They do not deal with inner content, with awareness and emotions. Their function is purely operative: how to transmit content, actualize it, and overcome any impediments to that actualization. Therefore, the disparities between them are neither deep nor detailed because they diverge only in how they operate, whereas their inner content is identical.

The *sefirot* of *Netzaḥ* and *Hod,* and in a sense, *Yesod* as well, are secondary attributes in relation to *Ḥesed* and *Gevura,* and lower in the order of the *sefirot.* Yet, in actuality, they are sometimes more important. By analogy, a person may have an expansive awareness and be overcome with love and fear, and he even wants to express that love and display a great amount of kindness. But if he lacks *Netzaḥ* and *Hod,* nothing will happen. None of his wisdom, love, or kindness will be actualized, neither in deed, nor in speech, and to some degree not even in thought. Such a person will remain stuck, and nothing of his abilities and desires will develop, grow, or change.

There is another advantage to these attributes. The attributes of *Ḥesed* and *Gevura* are compared to the right hand and the left hand, respectively, while *Netzaḥ* and *Hod* are compared to the feet. The hands are higher: They perform refined work, they write, they reveal the depth and subtlety of the soul. By contrast, the feet are coarse and crude. Yet a person stands on his feet and not on his hands (see epistle 1 above). In this sense, the feet have a greater and more basic power that holds up all the higher structures that follow them.

the perspective of the giver or from the perspective of the recipient, has a decisive impact on the giving.

The emotion associated with *Yesod* is principally a sense of pleasure in the connection itself, a sense of pleasure in which the essence of the giver is revealed and connects with the essence of the recipient. The nature of this connection, then, is the degree of pleasure felt on either side of the equation. The more the giver enjoys giving and the more the recipient feels good about receiving, the more the giver will bestow on the recipient, and the stronger their bond will be.

שֶׁמְּקַשֵּׁר הָאָב שִׂכְלוֹ בְּשֵׂכֶל בְּנוֹ בְּשָׁעַת לִמּוּדוֹ עִמּוֹ בְּאַהֲבָה וְרָצוֹן, שֶׁרוֹצֶה שֶׁיָּבִין בְּנוֹ.

with which the father, for example, **binds his intellect to his child's intellect when he is teaching him, lovingly and willingly, since he wants his child to understand.**

This analogy shows that the associations and feelings related to the connection between giver and recipient – the love, the desire, the pleasure – plays a meaningful role with regard to the actual pouring forth. This does not refer to the father's love and desire to give of his wisdom to his child, but the love and desire revealed in the connection itself at the moment that the giver and receiver bond.

וּבִלְעֲדֵי זֶה, גַּם אִם הָיָה הַבֵּן שׁוֹמֵעַ דִּבּוּרִים אֵלּוּ עַצְמָם מִפִּי אָבִיו [שֶׁמְּדַבֵּר בַּעֲדוֹ וְלוֹמֵד לְעַצְמוֹ, בִּכְתַב יַד קֹדֶשׁ אַדְמוֹ״ר בַּעַל ׳צֶמַח צֶדֶק׳ נִשְׁמָתוֹ עֵדֶן (בִּדְרוּשׁ ״כִּי יְדַעְתִּיו״ סְעִיף י״ג שֶׁהוּעְתַּק שָׁם לָשׁוֹן זֶה) לֵיתָא תֵּיבוֹת אֵלּוּ] לֹא הָיָה מֵבִין כָּל כָּךְ כְּמוֹ עַכְשָׁיו, שֶׁאָבִיו מְקַשֵּׁר שִׂכְלוֹ אֵלָיו וּמְדַבֵּר עִמּוֹ פָּנִים אֶל פָּנִים, בְּאַהֲבָה וְחֵשֶׁק, שֶׁחוֹשֵׁק מְאֹד שֶׁיָּבִין בְּנוֹ, וְכָל מַה שֶּׁהַחֵשֶׁק

Without this connection, **even if the son would hear the words themselves from his father's mouth (when** the father **was speaking to himself and learning on his own – in the holy manuscript of the author of *Tzemah Tzedek*, may his soul rest in peace, these words do not appear [**in his **sermon "For I Have Known Him," section 13, where this phrase was transcribed]), he would not have understood as well as** he does **now, when his father binds his intellect to him and speaks to him face-to-face,**

וְהַתַּעֲנוּג גָּדוֹל - כָּךְ הַהַשְׁפָּעָה וְהַלִּימּוּד גָּדוֹל. שֶׁהַבֵּן יוּכַל לְקַבֵּל יוֹתֵר וְהָאָב מַשְׁפִּיעַ יוֹתֵר, כִּי עַל יְדֵי הַחֵשֶׁק וְהַתַּעֲנוּג מִתְרַבֶּה וּמִתְגַּדֵּל שִׂכְלוֹ בְּהַרְחָבַת הַדַּעַת לְהַשְׁפִּיעַ וּלְלַמֵּד לִבְנוֹ.

with love and desire, since the father **very much desires that his son will understand. The greater the** father's **desire and pleasure, the greater the pouring forth and learning. The son can absorb more, and the father** can **transmit more, because as a result of the** father's **desire and pleasure, his intellect is increased and magnified with a broadening of the mind, so that he may transmit** his wisdom **and teach his son.**

The essence of the connection, though one is usually not conscious of it, is a powerful force that enhances and changes what is happening, what is being transmitted, including the core of what is being transmitted.

The pleasure in this connection is not intellectual. It does not express the intellect in the giving, nor even the love that the giving expresses. Like *Netzaḥ* and *Hod,* which do not deal with the content being given but only with its transference, the attribute of *Yesod* is not connected to the essence and content of the giving but to the connection itself. In the example brought here of a father who is giving of his wisdom to his child, the father connects to his child, not because the child is smart, nor because the father loves him, but because the child is his child, a product of his essence. Ultimately, whatever the father's feelings and thoughts, he loves his child and gives to him for the sake of it. The content of the giving, whatever it may be, whether wisdom, love, even rebuke, is carried on the intrinsic connection, on those essential sparks passing and connecting to each other.

The connection between father and child is merely an example to illustrate the connection that is *Yesod.* Just as the relationship between father and child is a function of *Yesod,* so are the connections between husband and wife, teacher and student, rich person and pauper a manifestation of *Yesod.* When such a connection, the connection rooted in *Yesod,* occurs and is felt, that which is connected and transmitted is transferred from the very essence of the giver to the very essence of the receiver.

(וּכְמוֹ עַל דֶּרֶךְ מָשָׁל בְּגַשְׁמִיּוּת מַמָּשׁ, רִבּוּי הַזֶּרַע הוּא מֵרוֹב הַחֵשֶׁק וְהַתַּעֲנוּג, וְעַל יְדֵי זֶה מַמְשִׁיךְ הַרְבֵּה מֵהַמּוֹחַ, וְלָכֵן הִמְשִׁילוּ חַכְמֵי הָאֱמֶת לְזִיוּוּג גַּשְׁמִי כְּמוֹ שֶׁיִּתְבָּאֵר.)

(This is like, figuratively speaking, in the realm of actual physicality, an increase of semen as a result of an intense desire and pleasure, through which a great deal issues from the brain. This is why the scholars of the truth, of Kabbala, **compared** teaching **to physical relations, as will be explained.)**

In the imagery of the human body, *Yesod* corresponds to the organ via which a man and woman bond. The Kabbala compares any spiritual flow, any bond, unification, and fusion to physical relations. The physical analogy expresses the importance and power of *Yesod* more than spiritual descriptions can. *Yesod* is the intrinsic connection between giver and receiver. Within this bond, aside from the nature of what is being transmitted, there is a great deal of yearning and pleasure.[21] This pleasure is the spiritual-emotional expression of the connection itself, and it indicates the intensity of the connection. The extent of the pleasure is not an inconsequential side effect but is, like the connection itself, extremely significant with regard to the quality and quantity of that which is being transmitted, both from the aspect of *Yesod* that pours forth from above to below and from the aspect of *Yesod* that receives. As the author of the *Tanya* has shown using spiritual-intellectual imagery, that which occurs at the locus of connection affects the roots of the giving on the highest levels. It can lead to drawing down the flow from even loftier and more hidden levels than before, because the bond itself touches on the essence of the soul, and this affects all its faculties. ☞

Until this point, the epistle has discussed the *sefirot* on a relatively external level, only referring to the six middle *sefirot*, to the exclusion of the cognitive *sefirot* that precede them and the *sefira* of *Malkhut* that follows.[22] The epistle will now discuss the *sefirot* on a deeper level.

---

21. See *Ba'al Shem Tov al HaTorah, Parashat Noaḥ, Amud HaTefillah* 16.

22. The Lubavitcher Rebbe, Rabbi Menaḥem Mendel Schneerson, explains that the reason the epistle does not discuss the *sefira* of *Malkhut* here is that at this

17 Elul (leap year)

וְהִנֵּה מִדּוֹת אֵלּוּ הֵן בְּחִינוֹת חִיצוֹנִיּוֹת שֶׁבַּנֶּפֶשׁ, וּבְתוֹכָן מְלוּבָּשׁוֹת מִדּוֹת פְּנִימִיּוֹת,

These emotive **attributes are the external aspects of the soul, and within them are enclothed the internal attributes,**

"External" describes an action and mode of behavior that is directed outward, whereas "internal" describes the inner causes of that action, to the viewpoint of the one doing the action or displaying that mode of behavior. On a deeper level, it relates to the intrinsic characteristics of the person who acts. ☞

שֶׁהֵן בְּחִינוֹת אַהֲבָה וְיִרְאָה כו'.

which are love, fear, and so on.

WHY *YESOD*?

☞ The connection that constitutes *Yesod* is the coming together of all the attributes and faculties in a person's soul. In light of this, the connection is also the foundation – the *yesod* – on which all these attributes and faculties are built from the outset. Moreover, *Yesod* is not only a general coming together. Rather, the connection in *Yesod* reveals the essence of the soul: the foundation of all its faculties and self-expression in the *sefirot*.

THE INTERNAL AND EXTERNAL ASPECTS OF THE EMOTIVE ATTRIBUTES

☞ These are not just two facets of the same thing. It is true that the internal attributes are the inner aspect of the external attributes, but they are also attributes in and of themselves. They stand on their own and not just as internal attributes in relation to the external attributes. The external attributes likewise stand on their own, with their own source of sustenance that does not come through the internal attributes.

Something of this model exists among the *sefirot* on different levels, such as the relationship between the cognitive *sefirot* and the emotive *sefirot*. The intellect is the internal aspect of the emotive attributes in the sense that it engenders and directs them. But it also has an external expression of its own that is not channeled through the emotive attributes. Likewise, the emotive attributes have a source in a loftier plane than the intellect that does not pass through the intellect. Within the emotive attributes themselves, there is a similar relationship between the archetypal triad (*Ḥesed*, *Gevura*, and *Tiferet*) and the secondary triad (*Netzaḥ*, *Hod*, and *Yesod*).

---

point the author is discussing the pouring forth as it exists within the entity that is giving forth, which is not relevant to *Malkhut*, the ultimate receiver.

Love is the internal aspect of *Ḥesed*, and fear is the internal aspect of *Gevura*. Such a division also exists with regard to the other emotive attributes: Compassion is the internal aspect of *Tiferet*, and while the remaining attributes – *Netzaḥ*, *Hod*, and *Yesod* – do not have separate names for their internal dimension, they do have an internal dimension as well as an external dimension.

דְּהַיְינוּ, עַל דֶּרֶךְ מָשָׁל בְּאָב הַמַּשְׁפִּיעַ לִבְנוֹ מֵחֲמַת אַהֲבָתוֹ, וּמוֹנֵעַ הַשְׁפָּעָתוֹ מִפַּחְדּוֹ וְיִרְאָתוֹ שֶׁלֹּא יָבֹא לִידֵי מִכְשׁוֹל חַס וְשָׁלוֹם.

This is analogous to a father who gives to his child out of his love for him, **and he withholds his giving due to his dread and fear that** his child **might come to transgress, God forbid.**

Love is a positive inclination of the lover toward the beloved. It is empathy, the desire to be with the other, a wish that the beloved should fare well. All this leads to an intimacy between the lover and beloved, to the lover giving to the beloved both physically and spiritually. As a consequence, the love attains full expression.

Conversely, the expression of fear manifests as anxiety and concern that the other may harm or be harmed. As a result, one withholds his giving to the other and refrains from intimacy so that the object of the fear will not cause harm and one can maintain the status quo.

The analogy that the epistle describes here does not speak of two objects, one an object of love and another an object of fear. Rather, there is one object: the child whose benefit the father desires. The variable is in the father's feelings toward him. To this one object, the father directs two feelings: love and kindness on the one hand, and fear and caution on the other.

The advantage of this analogy is that it highlights the internal traits, love and fear, without intermingling other factors. Furthermore, and principally, this teaching and metaphor is directly analogous to the divine *sefirot*. That is to say, it is a human metaphor for divine love and fear. Although God certainly does not fear others, as a person does, He may, so to speak, fear that harm may come to a person, so this particular analogy is quite apt.

וּמְקוֹר וְשֹׁרֶשׁ מִדּוֹת אֵלּוּ, הַפְּנִימִיּוֹת וְהַחִיצוֹנִיּוֹת, הוּא מֵחָכְמָה בִּינָה דַּעַת שֶׁבְּנַפְשׁוֹ,

The source and root of these emotive **attributes, internal and external, stems from the *Ḥokhma, Bina,*** and ***Da'at* in** a person's **soul,**

Ḥokhma, Bina, and *Da'at* are the cognitive *sefirot,* which comprise a person's intellectual awareness. This awareness is the source and locus in the soul where a person's feelings and traits develop. Furthermore, they are the traits through which he acts and affects the world around him. ☞

כִּי לְפִי שֵׂכֶל הָאָדָם כָּךְ הֵן מִדּוֹתָיו.

for a person's emotive **attributes are commensurate with his intellect.**

The connections that exist between the intellect and the emotive attributes may be different from one person to the next, but as a general rule a certain understanding leads to a certain feeling. A broader, deeper understanding leads to broader and deeper feelings. Reuven, for example, loves Shimon. If Reuven gives it thought and finds additional good traits in Shimon, his feeling of love will grow. Moreover, if a person's intellect grows aware of factors that it had not previously been aware of, through this greater clarity and verisimilitude, he will develop a

THE SOURCE AND ROOT OF THE EMOTIVE ATTRIBUTES

☞ That intellectual awareness is the source and root of the emotive attributes is a complex concept. Intellectual awareness does not create the emotive attributes, the emotions. Rather, it formulates the objects toward which the emotive attributes relate. The emotive attributes exist in the soul, and their root is very deep, deeper than the reality of the intellect. But in order for an emotive attribute to coalesce in some form, it needs a kernel of awareness, an idea, something that it favors or disfavors, something in relation to which it can make a goal and actualize it. That idea need not be something deep, such as that which a person contemplates before praying. Any sort of idea around which the emotive attributes may array themselves, that they may relate to and as a result develop into love and fear, will suffice.

Since the emotive attributes are not literally created by the intellect but are only manifest and develop via the intellect, they do not depend only on intellect. A person might have a small intellect yet his feelings will be intense, deeply felt, and genuine, while another may have a broad intellect yet it is possible for him to be disassociated from his emotions.

feeling of love or fear toward them. This insight opens a wider path in the service of God: By contemplating God's greatness as reflected in His creations and His world, by attaining a more tangible awareness of God, one may increase his love and fear of Him.

כַּנִּרְאֶה בְּחוּשׁ, שֶׁהַקָּטָן, שֶׁהַחָכְמָה בִּינָה דַּעַת שֶׁלּוֹ הֵן בִּבְחִינַת קַטְנוּת, כָּךְ כָּל מִדּוֹתָיו הֵן בִּדְבָרִים קְטַנֵּי הָעֵרֶךְ. וְגַם בִּגְדוֹלִים, "לְפִי שִׂכְלוֹ יְהוּלַּל אִישׁ" (משלי יב, ח).

As seen in actuality, that in the case of a minor, whose *Ḥokhma*, *Bina*, and *Da'at* are in a state of smallness, all his emotive **attributes are likewise focused on things of insignificant value. With regard to adults as well, "according to his sense, a man will be praised"** (Prov. 12:8).

This concept applies not only to contemplation of spiritual subtleties, to matters that only the person himself apprehends, but also to the reality around him. A child takes an interest in relatively insignificant things – toys, candy – because his attributes, his intellect and emotions, resonate with them. This does not mean that his yearnings or fears are insignificant. On the contrary, he may have a fierce yearning for something small, or a terrible anger and fear regarding something foolish.

Likewise, there are adults whose intellect is directed toward trivial matters and who also direct their emotions toward such things. Conversely, when a person's intellect engages in great things, his feelings will grow to match them. ☞

A MAN AND HIS INTELLECT

☞ Hasidic teachings (see *Likkutei Torah*, Song 25a; *Sefer HaMa'amarim* [5700], p. 96; *Torat Menaḥem*, vol. 3, pp. 118–19) explain that there are four Hebrew synonyms for man: *adam*, *ish*, *gever*, and *enosh*. These words allude to four levels within an individual. *Ish* corresponds to a person's emotive attributes, as opposed to *adam*, which corresponds to the intellect. In light of this, the verse that the author of the *Tanya* quotes, which employes the term *ish*, implies that a person's attributes are commensurate with his intellect. A great person who thinks about great things will have correspondingly great feelings.

כִּי לְפִי רוֹב חָכְמָתוֹ כָּךְ הוּא רוֹב אַהֲבָתוֹ וְחַסְדּוֹ, וְכֵן שְׁאָר כָּל מִדּוֹתָיו, פְּנִימִיּוֹת וְחִיצוֹנִיּוֹת, מְקוֹרָן הוּא מֵחָכְמָה בִּינָה דַּעַת שֶׁבּוֹ.

The amount of love and kindness a person possesses **is commensurate with the amount of wisdom** he possesses, **and the same applies to all the rest of his attributes, internal and external: Their source stems from the** faculties of **wisdom, understanding,** and **knowledge within him.**

In the most basic sense, a person's awareness determines which reality his emotive attributes will relate to, toward what he will develop a feeling of love and what he will affect, whether physically or spiritually. His sense of what is real and tangible within his perspective of the world is the basis for everything that comes afterward: what he will feel, what he will decide to say and do, and what he will accomplish. ☞

CONSTRICTED AND EXPANDED CONSCIOUSNESS

☞ This epistle has been discussing *moḥin*, the intellect or consciousness, in terms of engaging in insignificant, simple thinking as opposed to contemplating important, abstract concepts. But the issue is deeper and more complex than that. Expansiveness in reference to the *moḥin* does not only mean that one thinks of particularly great and abstract matters. Expansiveness primarily means that the relationship between the intellect and the emotive attributes changes. For a child, his emotive attributes are the main thing: He lives by them and thinks and acts in accordance with them, so much so that his intellect, although it is the source of his feelings, is directed primarily by his feelings. It is not that his intellect has no influence on his feelings, but it does not direct them. Instead, his feelings occur spontaneously. This characterizes a constricted consciousness or small-mindedness.

For an adult, on the other hand, the intellect has its own province, and it is not engendered by the emotions, nor directed by them, but rather it is directed by the faculties of the intellect itself. This is what characterizes the expanded consciousness, of a mature mind. In fact, this is the true definition of an adult, of a mature person. In this sense, an adult is the opposite of a child: Rather than being led by the emotions, the emotions are determined and directed by his intellect. That does not mean that his emotions do not influence his intellect, but it is not an influence that engenders something new but rather merely reveals what already exists. It fortifies and expands, bringing to the fore the intellect's intent and goals.

וְהָעִיקָּר הוּא הַדַּעַת שֶׁבּוֹ, הַנִּמְשָׁךְ מִבְּחִינוֹת הַחָכְמָה וּבִינָה שֶׁבּוֹ.

The primary faculty **is the knowledge within him, which is drawn from the wisdom and understanding within him.**

When discussing the connection between the cognitive attributes and the emotive attributes, the most important faculty is *da'at*, knowledge. This does not refer merely to information that one knows. It is an attribute in itself, a unique spiritual faculty among the three cognitive attributes. In terms of the *sefirot*, *Da'at* occupies the middle array, below *Ḥokhma* and *Bina*, and it is the attribute that binds the other two together and draws them down to the emotive attributes and, in essence, to a connection with the soul. Therefore, when we speak of the intellect as the source and root of the emotive attributes, we are principally referring to *Da'at*.

Ḥokhma, Wisdom, is the first flash of awareness that stems from nothingness. *Bina*, Understanding, then develops and magnifies that flash to form a picture of a particular reality. *Ḥokhma* and *Bina* may be compared to a father and mother. The father provides the initial drop, like a mere point that has no apparent form and definition. The mother absorbs the drop and develops and grows it within herself until it a baby is born. All this constitutes the first stage of awareness, of the creation of an object, an idea or concept. The second stage is that of categorization: Where do we place the object? How do we label it? How do we relate to it? Is it good or bad? Do we like it or hate it, and how strongly? Making such determinations, taking a personal stance toward the object (though still in the intellectual and not the emotional realm), is in the purview of *Da'at*.

Determining one's stance toward the object of thought and how it relates to reality is not yet directly related to the emotions, to love or fear. Rather, it constitutes the power and drive of those emotive attributes. It occurs within the intellect in a state of concealment, in "pregnancy," but in a way in which the distinction between love and fear is already recognizable. This distinction is the source of the feelings that exist in *Da'at* itself. This is the meaning of the author of the *Tanya*'s statement that the principal root of the emotive attributes is *Da'at*, because if the intellect lacks *Da'at*, then even if a person has a deep intellectual understanding of a topic, it will not arouse any feelings in him at all and he may have no connection to those feelings in accordance with which he acts.

This epistle will go on to discuss this attribute and faculty as one of connection. A person's intellect alone is cold and disconnected from him. A person can understand something, and even understand it well, but it might not touch him. He may understand that it is proper that people act in a certain way, yet that does not say anything about his own conduct. This factor, the connection between a person's intellect and himself, the way in which his intellect communicates with him, is the province of *Da'at*.

כַּנִּרְאֶה בְּחוּשׁ, כִּי לְפִי שִׁינּוּי דֵּעוֹת בְּנֵי אָדָם זֶה מִזֶּה כָּךְ הוּא שִׁינּוּי מִדּוֹתֵיהֶם.

It is seen in actuality that knowledge is the primary faculty in that **the emotive attributes differ in accordance with people's various perspectives.**

Different people will see the same object and respond to it differently. This is because their faculty of knowledge, their *da'at*, their personal connection with the thing that they understand intellectually, determines what their feelings and decisions will be toward it.

Up to this point, the epistle has discussed two aspects in the manifestation of the emotive attributes. The first refers to their external expression, the way they are manifest in the animal soul and how they function within the world. The other is their internal aspect, such as the love within a person that leads him to express kindness. There is a third aspect, which the author of the *Tanya* will go on to discuss, involving the attributes of a person's divine soul. These attributes do not relate to matters of this world, but rather they relate directly to the Divine.

וְהִנֵּה כָּל זֶה הוּא רַק עַל דֶּרֶךְ מָשָׁל לְבַד. כִּי כָּל זֶה הוּא בְּנֶפֶשׁ הַשִּׂכְלִית הַתַּחְתּוֹנָה שֶׁבָּאָדָם הַבָּאָה מִקְּלִיפַּת נוֹגַהּ.

All this is meant only figuratively, because all this applies to the lower, rational soul of man, which stems from the *kelippa* of *noga*. 20 Elul
18 Elul (leap year)

Up to this point, the epistle has focused on the lower, rational soul.[23] As the author of the *Tanya* has discussed until now, the faculties of the soul within man, his cognitive and emotive attributes, are parallel to the supernal *sefirot*. Now the epistle will discuss the divine soul, which God "blew from within Himself," and is literally a portion of the Divine on high. This is more than a mere analogy for the supernal *sefirot*, as in the case of the faculties of the rational soul. What is said of the divine soul applies equally to the supernal *sefirot*.

The rational soul (as well as the animal soul) stems from the *kelippa* of *noga*, the "luminescent husk" that is composed of both good and evil, as opposed to the impure *kelippa*, which consists solely of evil. The *kelippa* of *noga* is set apart from that which is divine, as it were, since it relates solely to matters of this world. In that case, the attributes of the rational and animal soul are only an analogy for the supernal *sefirot*, parallel to them but not of them. For instance, the attribute of love in the animal soul will not necessarily manifest as a love of God, but may also be expressed as love for another person or even an object. ☞

THE RATIONAL SOUL

☞ The concept of the rational soul as distinct from the animal soul is not explained in the *Tanya*, but is mentioned only in passing in a few places (such as *Likkutei Amarim*, chap. 42, and *Ḥinukh Katan*). The author of the *Tanya* does, however, explain it in other texts (see *Likkutei Torah*, Lev. 4c–d). He states there that it is possible to speak of three souls in a human being: the animal soul, the divine soul, and the rational soul, which connects the animal soul to the divine soul. The rational soul, like the animal soul, belongs to the reality of this world and of *kelippat noga*, in contrast to the divine soul, which essentially belongs to the Divine. The *Tanya* itself speaks only of two souls, because in a general sense the three souls are two: the divine soul and the lower soul, which stems from *kelippa* of *noga* and can be subdivided into an animal soul and a rational soul.

As its name indicates, the animal soul is the life force of the animalistic side of a person: his body, his senses, and his emotions. Conversely, the rational soul relates to a person's intellectual faculties, the human intellect that can apprehend abstraction and spirituality. It can also apprehend divine existence in the world, and so it can understand and connect with the divine soul. When the author of the *Tanya* explains how it is possible to discern the entire infrastructure of the ten *sefirot* – the cognitive *sefirot* and the emotive attributes – within the faculties of the soul and how one can see that the cognitive *sefirot* are the source of the emotive attributes, he is referring specifically to the rational soul.

23. See *Likkutei Amarim*, chaps. 1–2.

אַךְ בֶּאֱמֶת לַאֲמִיתּוֹ, בְּנֶפֶשׁ הָעֶלְיוֹנָה הָאֱלֹהִית, שֶׁהִיא חֵלֶק אֱלוֹהַּ מִמַּעַל כָּל הַמִּדּוֹת, פְּנִימִיּוֹת וְחִיצוֹנִיּוֹת, הֵן לַה' לְבַדּוֹ.

Yet in the absolute truest sense, all the internal and external attributes in the higher divine soul, which is a portion of God on high, are directed to God alone.

The divine soul is literally a portion of God from above.[24] In light of this, its faculties are actually a precise parallel to the divine *sefirot*. All of the faculties of the divine soul, whether cognitive or emotive, whether the inner feelings or their external expression, are directed solely to God. The attributes in the divine soul are true because they reveal themselves only in their relationship to God. Conversely, the faculties in the animal soul are only an analogy for the supernal *sefirot,* because they relate to the world and are revealed in various forms that represent only an imitation and image of the divine reality. ☞

THE ABSOLUTE TRUTH

☞ Not only are the divine soul and its attributes rooted in truth, but they are "absolute truth." They are not only truth in contrast to the attributes of the animal soul, with the animal soul serving merely as an analogy for the divine soul, but they are, in a sense, unequivocally true. The basis for the teaching that "from my flesh I will view God," that a person can learn about the Divine from his divine soul, is that there is a structural similarity between the human body, and even more the soul, and higher states of existence. Moreover, the human soul is a portion of God on high. This means that the divine soul is not only similar to the divine *sefirot*, but is the actual essence of the divine *sefirot*, which issue forth from the Divine and exist in a person's divine soul.

Since the divine soul is literally a portion of the Divine, all its faculties are expressed, not in relation to the world, but only in relation to God. This is why the author of the *Tanya* states here that all of the faculties are "directed to God alone." The author of the *Tanya* clarifies in *Likkutei Amarim* that this occurs through the garments of Torah study and mitzvot. The Torah is literally the revelation of the divine will and wisdom, though greatly constricted within the conceptions that relate to the material world. Although the human intellect cannot always comprehend this connection, when the divine soul, which is clothed in the body and in the world, fulfills the commandments, it reveals the Divine that it contains within to the world.

24. See *Likkutei Amarim,* chap. 2.

כִּי מֵחֲמַת אַהֲבַת ה׳, וּמֵרוֹב חֶפְצוֹ לְדָבְקָה בוֹ, הוּא חָפֵץ חֶסֶד כְּדֵי לִידָּבֵק בְּמִדּוֹתָיו, כְּמַאֲמַר רַבּוֹתֵינוּ ז״ל עַל פָּסוּק ״וּלְדָבְקָה בוֹ״ (דברים יא, כב) – הִדָּבֵק בְּמִדּוֹתָיו (ספרי דברים פיסקא מט).

This is **because on account of** a person's **love of God, and out of his great desire to cleave to Him, one desires** to perform **kindness in order to cleave to** God's **attributes, as our Rabbis stated regarding the verse "And to cleave to Him"** (Deut. 11:22): **"Cleave to His attributes"** (*Sifrei, Devarim* 49).

A person's love for God is the internal aspect of the divine soul's faculty of kindness. This attribute as expressed by the divine soul differs from that of the rational soul. In the rational soul, which relates to this world, kindness means loving another person and giving him what he needs. Through the divine soul, which relates to God alone, it is impossible to give to Him, since He lacks nothing. If someone whom we love is incomparably greater than we are and we cannot give him anything, we transform our attribute of kindness: Instead of giving to him, we connect ourselves to his attribute of kindness, by giving to others unconditionally, just as he gives. In light of this, the attributes of the divine soul are employed in this fashion, in clinging to God's supernal traits by emulating Him.

וְכֵן בְּמִדַּת הַגְּבוּרָה לְהִפָּרַע מִן הָרְשָׁעִים וּלְעָנְשָׁם בְּעוֹנְשֵׁי הַתּוֹרָה.

The same applies to the attribute of *Gevura*, to exacting retribution from the wicked and to punishing them with the punishments dictated by **the Torah,**

The attribute of restraint within the divine soul, which is the external aspect of fear, identifies with the supernal attribute of *Gevura*, the attribute with which God punishes the wicked. The wicked transgress God's will, and the supernal attribute of *Gevura*, as revealed in the laws of the Torah, dictate that a person who commits a particular deed should receive a particular punishment. One who cleaves to God's attributes fulfills the laws of the Torah given into the hands of man by punishing the wicked accordingly.

וְכֵן לְהִתְגַּבֵּר עַל יִצְרוֹ וּלְקַדֵּשׁ אֶת עַצְמוֹ בַּמּוּתָּר לוֹ,

and likewise to making it possible for a person **to overcome his** evil **inclination and sanctify himself by** refraining from **that which is permitted to him,**

Overcoming the evil inclination and sanctifying oneself by refraining from what is permitted[25] is another expression of this attribute within the divine soul. There is no need to look for wicked people in order to cleave to supernal *Gevura*. Every person has a wicked person within himself: his evil inclination. Of course, the epistle is not speaking here literally of a wicked person who must be subjected to the Torah's punishments. As a rule, the author of the *Tanya* does not discuss wicked people but *beinonim*, those who have not committed any transgressions, yet the potential is there in the guise of the evil inclination within them (as opposed to the righteous, who have vanquished their evil inclination). He is not referring to someone who transgresses the Torah's prohibitions, but whose struggle is to sanctify themselves by refraining from indulging in that which is permitted to them, though certainly this also applies to a person who must struggle to overcome his evil inclination so as not to commit a sin. ☞

REFRAINING FROM THAT WHICH IS PERMITTED

☞ The nature of the struggle described here is specifically with regard to gaining control over matters that are permitted. Overcoming one's evil inclination in matters that are prohibited means prevailing over the coarse, impure *kelippa*. A person who lives life from a Torah perspective, who views the world through the lens of the Torah and who associates with others who fulfill the Torah, generally will not face this struggle. Instead, such a person's struggle is in the realm of what is permitted to him: how he acts when eating kosher food, in his relationship with his wife, his friends, his mitzvot, and his Torah study.

Furthermore, a person sanctifies himself specifically in that which is permitted to him. The concept of holiness connotes "separate." A person attains holiness only when he separates himself from his previous, relatively unenlightened dealings with matters that are permitted to him. This means not only that they are permitted to him by the *Shulḥan Arukh*, the strict code of *halakha*, but they are what he has permitted himself, in keeping with his sense

25. See *Yevamot* 20a.

וְלַעֲשׂוֹת גָּדֵר וּסְיָיג לַתּוֹרָה, מִפְּנֵי פַּחַד ה׳ וְיִרְאָתוֹ פֶּן יָבֹא לִידֵי חֵטְא חַס וְשָׁלוֹם.

as well as erecting a fence and a safeguard for the Torah, on account of one's awe of God and one's fear that one may come to sin, God forbid.

The internal aspect of *Gevura* is fear. In this context, it is the fear of sin. The external expression of *Gevura*, on the other hand, consists of making fences and barriers even with regard to that which is permitted in order to ensure that one will not even approach that which is prohibited.

וְכֵן לְפָאֵר אֶת ה׳

Likewise, it is manifest **by glorifying God**

Glorifying God is an expression of the attribute of *Tiferet* in the divine soul. In the rational soul it manifests in appreciating the glory and beauty of the world, the appreciation of its harmony. But in the divine soul, this attribute relates to the divine life force that vitalizes existence, which is wondrous and harmonious. Moreover, it glorifies God Himself, because the divine soul has an appreciation of divinity beyond the parameters of the world, and with that appreciation, it glorifies Him and praises Him.

וְתוֹרָתוֹ בְּכָל מִינֵי פְּאֵר, וּלְדָבְקָה בִּשְׁבָחָיו בְּכָל בְּחִינוֹת נַפְשׁוֹ, דְּהַיְינוּ בְּהִתְבּוֹנְנוּת שִׂכְלוֹ וּמַחֲשַׁבְתּוֹ, גַּם בְּדִיבּוּרוֹ.

and His Torah by all means of glory and cleaving to His praises with all the faculties of one's soul through contemplation with one's intellect and thoughts and **also through one's speech.**

Since the revelation of God's essence comes about specifically via the Torah, the principal way in which a person can think and speak in order to praise Him is through His Torah. We cannot comprehend God's praiseworthiness. In truth, "for You, God of Zion, silence is praise" (Ps. 65:2). Therefore, the only way that we can praise God is with the terms

and view of his level and circumstances. When he sanctifies himself with what is permitted to him, he goes beyond his previous parameters and so becomes holy in relation to himself and his situation.

that God Himself has disclosed and applied to Himself in His Torah through His prophets and sages.[26]

We "cleave to God's praises" that are mentioned in His Torah principally in prayer, when a person is fervent with love for God while contemplating His greatness with his intellect and the garments of his intellect, which are thought and speech. ☞

וְכֵן לַעֲמוֹד בְּנִצָּחוֹן נֶגֶד כָּל מוֹנֵעַ מֵעֲבוֹדַת ה׳ וּמִלְּדָבְקָה בּוֹ,

Similarly, with the attribute of *Netzaḥ* within the divine soul, a person **prevails over any impediment to serving God and to cleaving to Him**

The attribute of *Netzaḥ* manifests in the divine soul when it triumphs over every obstacle to serving God and cleaving to Him. That triumph is comparable to victory in war and competition. In the human soul, there is a constant war between good and evil, between the divine soul and the animal soul. The desire of the divine soul is to serve God and cling to Him, but the world in general and the animal soul in particular do not accept that and attempt to prevent it from happening. Prevailing over the forces that prevent a person from serving God is the expression of the faculty of *Netzaḥ* in his divine soul. ☞

THE TORAH IN *TIFERET*

☞ In the order of the *sefirot*, the Torah is associated with the attribute of *Tiferet*. *Ḥesed* involves love and giving without limit, while *Gevura* characterizes judgment, constriction, and strength. *Tiferet* is related to the Torah. Thus a verse that describes the giving of the Torah states, "On His right, a fiery law for them" (Deut. 33:2). "On His right" corresponds to *Ḥesed*, which is on the right side, pouring forth the light of *Ein Sof*. "Fiery" corresponds to *Gevura*, which constricts that light within the Torah and its mitzvot so that it may be revealed in this world. The Torah itself is the center rod that passes from the highest polarity to the lowest, from above to below, bringing the divine light from the highest plane to the lowest. It is literally the drawing down of the divine essence to this world in a way that the world can endure it: within the Torah and mitzvot.

BATTLING WITH THE ATTRIBUTES OF *NETZAḤ* AND *HOD*

☞ In the higher triad of the emotive attributes – *Ḥesed*, *Gevura*, and *Tiferet* – what occurs is principally internal. The forces of holiness are formed, and other forces are

26. See *Berakhot* 33b.

This concept of war exists in the divine *sefirot* as well. Though it is impossible to speak of opposition and victory with regard to God, that applies only at the essence and root of the attributes where only the will of the Divine exists. There, at the essence and root, the sefirot are unified, subsumed in the divine light. But when the divine light is revealed through the *sefirot* within the physical world, their unique characteristics are uncovered. At that stage, even the holy attributes have their own considerations. A decision to act in one necessarily has an opposing counterpart (consider the *sefirot* of *Ḥesed* and *Gevura,* the outpouring of kindness versus restraint and constriction), and that leads to a war. ☞

וְנֶגֶד כָּל מוֹנֵעַ מִלִּהְיוֹת כְּבוֹד ה׳ מָלֵא אֶת כָּל הָאָרֶץ, כְּמִלְחֲמוֹת ה׳ אֲשֶׁר נִלְחַם דָּוִד הַמֶּלֶךְ עָלָיו הַשָּׁלוֹם.

and over anything that prevents the glory of God from filling the entire earth, such as in the wars of God fought by King David, may he rest in peace.

prevented from coming into formation. Through *Netzaḥ*, as well as *Hod*, the struggle is channeled outward to actualization. At this point, there is an actual battle between the supernal *sefirot* and the *kelippot*. As in an earthly war, it occurs only after lines have been drawn, after determining who is the enemy and what the battle is about, after there is no more chance to negotiate and for the enemy to change into an ally. At this point, when one must choose sides, one is confronted with a battle. As long as it was confined to feelings and thoughts, it was possible to reason one way or the other and to be swayed in different directions. But when it all comes to the fore, when one is faced with a call to action, one must make a decision. If the enemy prevents a person from doing the right thing, if he attacks, one must wage war to overcome him.

THE ATTRIBUTE OF *HOD*

☞ The *sefira* of *Hod* is also one of triumph and victory, no less than *Netzaḥ*. The difference between them is that when employing the attribute of *Netzaḥ*, one takes action, whereas *Hod* entails standing firm so that one will not end up taking a different action or so as not to refrain from any ongoing action. It is like a physical war in this world. In battle, an army can take the offensive, where it takes action and conquers the enemy, where it moves forward and vanquishes. This is *Netzaḥ*. An army can also be on the defensive, where it fights to the death so as not to be forced to retreat from its borders. That is *Hod*.

In the time of King David, when the character of a king of Israel was shaped and formed,[27] the external wars of the Jewish nation were the wars of God,

War can take place within the soul, in the form of internal struggles, or in the world outside, between people and between countries. One is an analogy for the other. Sometimes that which is described in terms of the soul also relates to happenings in the world, and sometimes a struggle described in terms of the world, like a war between one nation and another, apply as well to the soul.

וְכֵן לְהִשְׁתַּחֲווֹת וּלְהוֹדוֹת לַה׳, **Likewise,** a person employs the attribute of *Hod* in the divine soul **when bowing and giving thanks to God,**

The word *hod* is related to *hoda'a,* giving thanks. Bowing and giving thanks are very often linked, such as in the prayer of *Aleinu,* where we recite, "We bow and prostrate ourselves and give thanks…," and in the *Amida,* in which a person bows as he recites the thanksgiving prayer of *Modim.* The deeper import of bowing and giving thanks is self-nullification. When a person bows, that symbolizes his self-abnegation. This is particularly true when the bowing takes the form of prostrating oneself with one's hands and feet outstretched. When a person prostrates himself and stretches himself out as much as possible, he expresses the nullification of his existence and being as an independent entity. Similarly, giving thanks is a spiritual self-nullification. It is not a self-abnegation in the intellectual sense nor even in an emotional sense, but the total nullification of one's existence within the essence of the Divine. ☞

TWO LEVELS OF SELF-NULLIFICATION

☞ Some texts delineate two acts of bowing: the bending of the knees and bowing at the waist, corresponding to the two levels of giving thanks and reciting blessings, which in turn parallel two levels of self-nullification. Giving thanks is like bending the knees: Both correspond to *bitul hayesh,* the nullification of the self, subjugating oneself to the divine will. Bowing conveys the type of self-nullification epitomized by

27. See I Sam. 18:17, 25:28.

אֲשֶׁר מְחַיֶּה וּמְהַוֶּה אֶת הַכֹּל, וְהַכֹּל בָּטֵל בִּמְצִיאוּת אֶצְלוֹ, וְכוּלָּא קַמֵּיהּ כְּלָא חֲשִׁיב וּכְאַיִן וְאֶפֶס מַמָּשׁ.

who gives life to everything **and brings everything into existence. Everything is subsumed in** the divine **reality before Him, and everything before Him is literally considered as absolute nothingness.**

The more a person internalizes the concept that God is essentially everything – life, existence, and also the person himself – the more he bows, thanks, and nullifies himself to God.

וְאַף שֶׁאֵין אָנוּ מַשִּׂיגִים אֵיךְ הוּא הַכֹּל אֶפֶס מַמָּשׁ קַמֵּיהּ,

Although we cannot apprehend how everything is literally nothingness before Him,

A created entity is intrinsically unable to comprehend a state in which it does not exist. The human intellect, including the most fundamental thoughts and concepts, is based on the existence of the self. The nullification of the self is inconceivable to the intellect and to the feelings engendered by the intellect. There is, of course, the intellectual comprehension that one must nullify oneself, that such a concept can exist, but the intellect cannot grasp with true awareness the actual experience of self-nullification.

אַף עַל פִּי כֵן מוֹדִים אֲנַחְנוּ בְּהוֹדָאָה אֲמִיתִּית שֶׁכֵּן הוּא בֶּאֱמֶת לַאֲמִיתּוֹ.

we nevertheless concede with genuine acknowledgment that it is the absolute truth.

Although it is impossible to apprehend the concept of self-nullification, it is possible to acknowledge it. *Hod* is therefore the unique faculty in the soul that can acknowledge and concede to this even if a person cannot comprehend it intellectually. ☞

the blessings of the *Amida*. This refers to *bitul bimetziut*, the nullification of one's existence within reality, where one abnegates oneself to the point that one is no longer aware of oneself as an independent being (see *Likkutei Torah*, Deut. 1a–b).

וּבִכְלָל זֶה גַם כֵּן לְהוֹדוֹת לַה׳ עַל כָּל הַטּוֹבוֹת אֲשֶׁר גְּמָלָנוּ, וְלֹא לִהְיוֹת כְּפוּי טוֹבָה חַס וְשָׁלוֹם.

This attribute of *Hod* **also includes giving thanks to God for all the favors that He has bestowed on us and not being ungrateful, God forbid.**

Hod also entails thanking God for all that He has done for us and not being ungrateful. We teach even small children to say thank you and not be ungrateful. The nature of the divine soul to thank God is part of an overall perspective of the all-encompassing divine providence over all of existence down to every detail, one that appreciates that nothing is natural and self-evident. Everything – daylight, the air we breathe at every moment, the food we eat – is a gift from God, a favor that He bestows on us. If we do not give thanks, whether with a blessing, in prayer, or by cleaving to Him, we are being ungrateful.

THANKING, ACKNOWLEDGING, AND CONCEDING

☞ The root of the word *hod* connotes three meanings: thanking, acknowledging, and conceding or admitting (see *Likkutei Torah*, Num. 89a; *Siddur Admor HaZaken*, *Sha'ar Lag BaOmer*). Thus, for instance, we find that "the Sages conceded to Rabbi Meir" (see, e.g., Mishna *Menaḥot* 2:5). The Sages conceded not because they understood and agreed with Rabbi Meir's view. If they had, they would have adapted his view as their own. Rather, "concede" means that they did not understand it, did not feel any identification with it, yet they conceded that he was right.

Similarly, between ourselves and God there is, as it were, a dispute. We view the world as existence and God as nothingness, whereas from His perspective, He is existence and the world is nothing. That is because we comprehend existence with *da'at taḥton*, lower knowledge, the apprehension of the Divine in relation to the existence of the world below. This world is the tangible reality, and the existence of God is impossible to comprehend. But there is also *da'at elyon*, higher knowledge, the perspective of the Divine from above, perceiving the world through a divine lens. There, God is the tangible reality, while the created world lacks substance.

In view of this, "We give thanks to You" means "We do not understand. We are unable to view reality, as You do, with higher knowledge. But we nullify our view, our sense of independent existence and the existence of the world, and we concede to You that You are right."

This is *Hod*: the faculty of self-nullification, nullification of conceptualizing, nullification of knowing, nullification of feeling, and nullification of our very existence as an independent entity.

וּבִכְלָל זֶה לְהוֹדוֹת עַל כָּל שְׁבָחָיו וּמִדּוֹתָיו וּפְעוּלּוֹתָיו בַּאֲצִילוּת וּבְרִיאוּת עֶלְיוֹנִים וְתַחְתּוֹנִים שֶׁהֵם מְשׁוּבָּחִים עַד אֵין תַּכְלִית [נוּסָח אַחֵר: חֵקֶר], וְנָאִים וּרְאוּיִם אֵלָיו יִתְבָּרֵךְ וְיִתְעַלֶּה.

This also includes giving thanks for all of God's **praiseworthy** actions, **attributes, and deeds in the emanation and creation of the higher and lower worlds, which are praiseworthy to no end [alternatively: beyond comprehension] and which are fitting and becoming to Him, may He be blessed and exalted.**

The attribute of *Hod* also possesses a higher property. It does not just entail thanking God for the good He has bestowed on us, but thanking and acknowledging Him in the sense of praise. This praise is related not only to His relationship with us and with His creations in general, but also to Him intrinsically, that He is great, mighty, and so forth, and to His actions with which He created all the infinitely great and wondrous worlds. This is connected to what was stated earlier regarding *Hod* as the force that guards the existence of holiness. This praise does not create or reveal things that did not previously exist, but only relates to things that exist. It acclaims and praises them, and in so doing, it keeps them within a person's consciousness and reality.

וְהוּא מִלְּשׁוֹן הוֹד וְהָדָר.

The word *hod* **is thus used in the same sense as in** the phrase ***hod vehadar,*** splendor and glory.

Hod has a broader connotation than thanks. It is the praise and splendor of the Creator Himself. ☞

THE ACTUALIZATION OF HOLINESS IN THE WORLDS

☞ More than any of the other *sefirot*, the name of this *sefira*, *Hod*, is elusive. One meaning of *Hod*, which it shares with *Netzaḥ*, is that of preparing for actualization despite the opposition that constantly exists at this stage. *Netzaḥ* is the attribute of actualizing and revealing the Divine in the world, even if it is beyond one's ability to understand. *Hod* is the other side of the same coin. It entails strengthening and acknowledging this divine revelation, so that it will be manifest in reality, guarding it so that it will endure. As the Divine is actualized in the worlds in speech and

וְכֵן בְּמִדַּת צַדִּיק יְסוֹד עוֹלָם, לִהְיוֹת נַפְשׁוֹ קְשׁוּרָה בַּה׳ חַיֵּי הַחַיִּים וּלְדָבְקָה בוֹ

Likewise, through the attribute of the tzaddik, who is the foundation of the world, the attribute of *Yesod*, a person's **soul is bound to God, the infinite** source of **life, and cleaves to Him**

The *sefira* of *Yesod* expresses the persona of the tzaddik and his actions in the world. The tzaddik's uniqueness is not that he teaches the Torah's wisdom or that he pours physical and spiritual goodness into the world, but that he connects people to God. He is the connection between above and below, between the world and God.

The same is true for every person. Whereas *Yesod* in the rational soul involves forming connections between people, between husband and wife, between parent and child, in the divine soul this attribute is manifest through connection to God. ☞

in deed, *Hod* guards it so that it will be able to endure in this world, so that it will not be damaged.

Hod fights to preserve the boundaries of holiness through self-nullification, because the sense of independent existence, of the individual and of the world, unravels the parameters of holiness. The sense of independent human existence necessarily nullifies a sense of divine existence, and in order to preserve the sense of the Divine, the human self must bow and thank, praise and acknowledge the Divine.

This is the meaning of *hoda'a*. The person who thanks and praises is not thinking about his own existence and what he lacks, but rather about what He whom he is thanking and praising is giving him. The person is not an independent self, but rather one who supports and maintains divine existence here below.

THE TZADDIK AND *YESOD*

☞ There is another connection between the tzaddik and the attribute of *Yesod*. The tzaddik stands between God and other people (and the world overall), like *Yesod*, which stands between the emotive attributes (*Ze'ir Anpin*) and *Malkhut*, between the giver and the recipient.

Everything that *Malkhut* receives passes through *Yesod*, but there is a difference between *Yesod* and *Malkhut*. In *Yesod*, the divine sustenance and life force that is channeled down through the *sefirot* is not yet defined as it is in *Malkhut*. It is not like something that has already been received but like something just before the receiving. Therefore, the tzaddik, associated with *Yesod*, can change, broaden, deepen, rectify, and sweeten reality before it reaches its final destination in *Malkhut*. This is why God may issue a decree, and the righteous can nullify it, and similarly, the righteous man decrees and God fulfills that decree (see *Mo'ed Katan* 16b; *Tanna deVei Eliyahu Rabba* 2).

בִּדְבִיקָה וַחֲשִׁיקָה בְּחֵשֶׁק וְתַעֲנוּג נִפְלָא. **with devotion and longing, out of wondrous desire and pleasure.**

The emotion associated with *Yesod* is pleasure. In *Ḥesed,* the emotion associated with it is that of love, the desire to give and the desire for closeness. In *Gevura,* the emotion is that of fear and distance. In *Yesod,* the emotion is pleasure itself. This is because *Yesod* essentially constitutes connection. It is neither an attribute of transmission nor of receiving, giving, or relating, but rather that of cleaving to God, which engenders a feeling of pleasure. This is also the trait of the tzaddik: He experiences a wondrous, intrinsic pleasure in the cleaving itself, in being with God and not in what he receives from God. ☞

PLEASURE AND CONNECTION

☞ The essence of the connection that constitutes *Yesod* is also an essential connection: essence connecting to essence. Therefore, it is delight and pleasure, the innermost and most essential expression of the soul that is evoked through the sense of connection. The other faculties of the soul, the faculties that precede *Yesod*, entail illumination, insights, and feelings, but each one is still an isolated faculty. *Malkhut*, on the other hand, is the outcome. *Yesod* is the sole point of connection within the entire system between *Ze'ir Anpin* and *Malkhut*. It is precisely at this connecting point that the essence is felt, the essence that transcends all boundaries and conceptions. This locus encompasses everything and binds everything together, and the emotion experienced at this point of connection is pleasure and delight.

Every connection, bond, coupling, is pleasure. When people who were separated meet, that is delight. When letters bind together into words, and words bind together into sentences to express a certain meaning, that is delight (see *Keter Shem Tov* 387; *Ba'al Shem Tov al HaTorah, Parashat Noaḥ*). When we feel the bond and unification between God and the Divine Presence through the performance of a mitzvah, Torah study, prayer, or thought, that evokes pleasure and wondrous delight. Where essence is revealed, that is delight. When there is a revelation of the divine essence, and when there is the revelation of one essence bonding to another essence, and an essence that is higher than both of them, encompassing both of them, is revealed, that is an even greater delight. In this sense, the attribute of *Yesod* in the divine soul, which is the soul's connection with God, manifests itself as delight and pleasure on the highest and most profound level.

Regarding each of the attributes in the divine soul, it is said that the attribute in the soul identifies with the corresponding supernal, divine attribute. This is especially marked in the case of *Yesod*. In that connection itself, in the actual unification and fusion, there is (almost) no difference between above and below, between giver and receiver. The more complete the bond, the

וּבְמִדַּת מַלְכוּת לְקַבֵּל עָלָיו עוֹל מַלְכוּתוֹ וַעֲבוֹדָתוֹ, **As for the attribute of *Malkhut*,** it entails **accepting upon oneself the yoke of His kingship and service,**

The unique power of *Malkhut* in the divine soul is the power to receive and accept divine sovereignty. In our Sages' words, "A person should accept upon himself the yoke of the kingdom of Heaven" (Mishna *Berakhot* 2:2). ☞

כַּעֲבוֹדַת כָּל עֶבֶד לַאֲדוֹנוֹ, **like the service of any servant to his master,**

The servant does his master's will even if he does not understand why. His personal opinion makes no difference at all, nor whether he has any opinion at all. He acts because he is a servant who performs his master's will.

more the delight and connection experienced below are the same as the delight and connection that exists above in the realm of the Divine.

THE ESSENCE OF RULERSHIP

☞ The divine attribute of *Malkhut* is characterized by sovereignty. From God's viewpoint, being king necessitates the creation of a kingdom over which to be king. This is what is meant by the saying that "there is no king without a nation": Sovereignty has no significance unless it is exercised over subjects (see *Sha'ar HaYiḥud VeHa'emuna*, chap. 7). Moreover, the Hebrew word for "nation," *am*, is related to the Hebrew word for "dim" (*Pesaḥim* 27a). The connection between the nation and its source is dimmed, hidden, so that the nation possesses an existence apart from the king, as it were. Since a king needs a nation to rule, one may say that by virtue of the fact that God is King, the nation is automatically created, and that nation is, in the broadest scope, all of creation.

Malkhut alone has no substance. It is not a particular power that is active in the world. It is not necessarily a pouring forth of *Ḥesed* or *Ḥokhma*. It is not necessarily a framework of laws, neither those of love nor of fear. *Malkhut* is everything, and so it is nothing in particular. It is in a sense like an enveloping influence by virtue of whose existence the entire world exists. Nevertheless, there is one power, whose parallel also exists in the soul, that can be defined as the power of *Malkhut*, and that is rulership. Rulership expresses relationship, the relationship between ruler and subject, but without any particular trait. The nature of rulership is not necessarily to punish, to give, or to forgive. Rather, it is expressed through all these characteristics, and not through only one of them in particular.

So too accepting the yoke of the kingship of Heaven occurs when a person acts, not because he understands nor because he agrees that the matter is important, but because he is a servant who obeys God and accepts His authority. ☞

בְּאֵימָה וּבְיִרְאָה. with awe and fear.

Although *Malkhut* and the faculty of accepting the yoke of the kingship of Heaven is a discrete attribute and faculty in the soul, *Malkhut* is associated with the attribute of judgment and fear.[28] *Malkhut*, kingship, is exercised specifically over an entity that is separate and distinct. A person is not considered king over his limbs nor over his children, yet he may be king over a nation. Maintaining a distance between the king and his nation is essential to the existence of sovereignty: "There is no king without a nation."[29] The concept of a king cannot exist without differentiation and distance between him and his subjects. This attribute of limitation and maintaining boundaries is associated with the left array in the structure of the *sefirot*, the attribute of fear and awe in particular. Such awe, which is essentially directed toward that which is beyond bounds, toward the unknown, toward that which is separate and exalted (in terms of God), evokes a feeling of dread and fear in the heart.

MALKHUT FIRST AND LAST

☞ Divine *Malkhut* is called "first and last" (see Isa. 44:6; *Likkutei Torah*, Song 2c; *Torat Menaḥem*, vol. 8, p. 53). It is *Malkhut* at the bottom of one realm, and it is *Keter*, the highest *sefira*, at the top of the next, lower realm. It is both will (*Keter*), that which initiates any process, and outcome (*Malkhut*), the recipient and result. So too in a person's divine soul, the attribute of *Malkhut* is the initial will that a person imposes on himself, on his soul and body, to perform the divine will prior to all explanations, desires, and fears. It is also the end result, the essence of the actual deed, the speech employed in the study of Torah, the deed in the performance of a mitzva.

---

28. As in the statement "The law of the kingdom is the law" (*Nedarim* 28a). See *Pardes Rimmonim, Sha'ar Arkhei HaKinuyim* 4.

29. See Rabbeinu Baḥya, Gen. 38:30; *Kad HaKemaḥ, Rosh HaShana* 2; *Pirkei deRabbi Eliezer* 3.

Until now the epistle has focused on the emotive attributes. From this point onward, it will discuss the cognitive *sefirot*: *Ḥokhma, Bina,* and *Da'at.*

וּמְקוֹר וְשׁוֹרֶשׁ כָּל הַמִּדּוֹת הֵן מֵחָכְמָה בִּינָה דַּעַת.

The source and root of all the emotive attributes are *Ḥokhma, Bina,* and *Da'at.* 21 Elul

That which applies to the rational soul and to the animal soul applies to the divine soul in relationship to the Divine. The awareness of existence is the source and root of the entire array of emotive attributes, to the emotions, associations, conclusions, and deeds. ☞

Similarly, the supernal emotive attributes constitute the structure of the world: *Ḥesed* is the divine attribute of giving and pouring forth. *Gevura* is the constriction and restraint of that giving, and so on until *Malkhut,* which is the actualized speech of the Creator, that which operates and sustains the universe. The epistle explains here that the source and root of all of this pouring forth and sustenance are the cognitive *sefirot*: *Ḥokhma, Bina,* and *Da'at.* They are like God's seeing, understanding, and knowing of the worlds that He wants to create:

BEGINNING WITH THE EMOTIVE ATTRIBUTES AND CONCLUDING WITH THE COGNITIVE ATTRIBUTES

☞ Why does this epistle begin with the emotive attributes and conclude with the *moḥin*, the cognitive attributes, in contrast to the discussion of this topic in *Likkutei Amarim* (chap. 3), where the author of the *Tanya* begins with the cognitive attributes and continues with the emotive attributes?

Perhaps, in consonance with a comment made by the Lubavitcher Rebbe, Rabbi Menaḥem Mendel Schneerson, toward the end of the epistle, here the author of the *Tanya* is dealing principally with the emotive attributes. He discusses the cognitive attributes solely as the source of the emotive attributes. Perhaps this is because the teachings of this epistle are derived from the verse "From my flesh I will view God." "My flesh" is associated with the emotive attributes, which is like the "flesh" in the soul, as opposed to the "bones," which are the cognitive attributes (see *Likkutei Torah*, Lev. 78a). It is thus primarily from the emotive attributes that we learn the meaning of "From my flesh I will view God." By contrast, in *Likkutei Amarim*, the primary focus is the connection between the cognitive attributes and the emotive attributes, how the brain rules over the heart, and the way to serve God using the cognitive attributes, which affect and influence the emotive attributes.

an awareness that leads to His relationship with them, which in turn leads to actualized creation.

דְּהַיְינוּ הַחָכְמָה, הִיא מְקוֹר הַשֵּׂכֶל הַמַּשִּׂיג אֶת ה׳ **That is, *Ḥokhma* is the source of the intellect that apprehends God**

Ḥokhma itself is not the intellect but the source of the intellect, which is manifest in *Bina* and *Da'at*. It is impossible to apprehend God, *Ein Sof* Himself, with the intellect. Therefore, *Ḥokhma*, which is not the intellect, because it is not yet anything specific, is the doorway and key to the intellect with which to apprehend God.

וְחָכְמָתוֹ וּגְדוּלָּתוֹ וּמִדּוֹתָיו הַקְּדוֹשׁוֹת, שֶׁמַּנְהִיג וּמְחַיֶּה בָּהֶן כָּל הָעוֹלָמוֹת עֶלְיוֹנִים וְתַחְתּוֹנִים. **and His wisdom, greatness, and holy attributes with which He guides and sustains all the higher and lower worlds.**

No thought can grasp God. Nevertheless, there can be a certain conception and awareness of His essence as it is clothed in the *sefirot*. Like the soul's faculties, in which the essence of the soul is clothed and revealed, so the Divine is clothed and manifest through the *sefirot*.[30] The human intellect cannot apprehend the supernal *sefirot* themselves but only how they guide and sustain the worlds. The human intellect primarily apprehends the lower worlds, from which it extrapolates to the higher worlds. From those upper worlds it extrapolates even higher to the supernal *sefirot* themselves. *Ḥokhma* is the source of this intellect as opposed to the intellect itself. By analogy, it is like the image a person sees before he absorbs and thinks about what he is seeing.

וּבִינָה הִיא הַהִתְבּוֹנְנוּת בְּהַשָּׂגָה זוֹ ***Bina* is the contemplation of this apprehension** of God's greatness

Bina has breadth. *Ḥokhma* is like a flash of light that illuminates an entire world, but so quickly that there is no time to look and contemplate what one sees. That is the nature of *Ḥokhma*: It takes in the object itself, and the flash is necessarily merely a flash, because it is followed

30. See *Likkutei Amarim*, chaps. 3–4; *Torah Or* 13c.

by another flash different from the first. By way of analogy, a picture is an image of something that was. In essence, it is impossible to receive a picture of what is, of what is alive now. That which is alive can only be branded by the flash of *Ḥokhma*. *Bina* then forms a picture of that which was, of that flash, that instant. As soon as *Bina* enters the picture, the flash no longer shines in *Ḥokhma*. But precisely because of that, *Bina* has the time and breadth to contemplate, think, and analyze the impression of *Ḥokhma*'s flash and to build an image that attempts to describe *Ḥokhma's* illuminations and relate to them. ☞

בְּאוֹרֶךְ וְרוֹחַב וְעוֹמֶק בִּינָתוֹ, **in the length, breadth, and depth of one's understanding,**

Though *Ḥokhma* encompasses everything in an instant, in a flash, from the aspect of the awareness and recognition of the thinker, it is like a dot. All he knows about the dot is that it exists. But he does not know anything about it, neither the who nor the how.[31] The dot itself is only itself, without dimensions. It is only when *Bina* enters the picture, when contemplation ensues, that the initial flash of awareness takes on the dimensions of length, breadth, and depth. Therefore, *Ḥokhma* is represented by the letter *yod,* which appears as a dot alone without dimensions, while *Bina* is represented by the letter *heh,* which has the dimensions of length and breadth.[32]

The length of *Bina* entails spreading out from above to below. It is the ability to bring something into increasingly constricted limitations, to bring a concept down and explain it on the simplest levels to a person

ḤOKHMA AND *BINA*, FATHER AND MOTHER

☞ The relationship between *Ḥokhma* and *Bina* is like that between a father and mother. The father confers a drop of seed, a kernel that does no more than provide the stimulus and appropriate directive. From that point onward, everything tangible occurs in the mother: the fetus's growth, its development, and the formation of its limbs. This process requires a space and time, and the kernel of *Ḥokhma* receives that in *Bina*.

---

31. Thus *Ḥokhma* is associated with the question "What?" This is the primary question that relates to something only in terms of its essential existence. *Bina*, on the other hand, is associated with "Who?"

32. See *Iggeret HaTeshuva*, chap. 4.

who is not on the same plane as that of abstract concepts and feelings. *Bina*'s breadth is the ability to spread out to all sides, the ability to understand broadly, with great inclusiveness and with many details, and the ability to explain something in various aspects and ways.[33] The depth of *Bina*, which is also called the internal aspect of *Bina*, is the ability to grasp the essence and root of an idea. It is the ability to understand the essence of a concept, beyond analogies and explanations that are employed to make something loosely comprehensible. It is an understanding that follows extended contemplation and study, that grasps the substance and essence of the subject.[34]

לְהָבִין דָּבָר מִתּוֹךְ דָּבָר, **so that one comprehends one matter from another,**

Ḥokhma is the initial grasp of wisdom. Beyond that, it adds nothing, and therefore, it in itself is passive. By contrast, the essence of *Bina* is to add, build, and form. It can comprehend something additional that had not been revealed by the light of *Ḥokhma*, something additional from the matter that was.[35] ☞

Hasidic teachings explain that "understanding one matter from another" refers to apprehending He who surrounds all worlds as a result

SERVICE BY WAY OF CONTEMPLATION

☞ The author of the *Tanya*'s explanation of the animal soul speaks about awareness that is the foundation on which the emotive attributes are built and grow. His explanation does not speak about active contemplation that engenders the emotive attributes. Conversely, in his explanation relating to the faculties of the divine soul, he has a more detailed explanation of *Ḥokhma* and *Bina* in connection to the contemplation that engenders the emotive attributes. That is because with regard to the spiritual realm, and principally that which is related to the Divine, awareness of the Divine, as well as love and fear, do not automatically and intrinsically awaken. It is specifically regarding the divine soul that there is a need for the service of contemplation, in order to bring something additional — the transcendent Divine — into awareness and afterward to bring it into a relationship with the emotive attributes of love and fear.

33. See *Iggeret Teshuva*, chap. 4; *Torah Or* 54c.
34. See *Torat Ḥayyim*, Gen. 46d, Ex. 292b.
35. See *Ḥagiga* 14b; Rashi, Deut. 1:13.

of contemplating He who fills all worlds.[36] "He who fills all worlds" refers to the divine life force that is clothed in the world, that brings it into existence and sustains it on all levels and in all its details. This is what a wise person sees within things. "He who surrounds all worlds" refers to the transcendent divine essence, which is not revealed within things and which *Ḥokhma* does not actually see. But *Bina* understands, by way of understanding one matter from another, that there is a divine existence beyond that which is revealed. This understanding engenders an infinite love for God, as well as awe and absolute self-nullification.

The author of the *Tanya* now returns to discussing the emotive attributes in a person's divine soul as they are engendered by contemplation and the connection between the emotive attributes and the intellect.

וּלְהוֹלִיד מֵהַשָּׂגָה זוֹ תּוֹלְדוֹתֶיהָ, **and from this comprehension are engendered its offspring,**

A person's intellectual awareness consists of *Ḥokhma* and *Bina*, which are like a father and mother, while his emotive attributes are their offspring. Just as *Ḥokhma* and *Bina* engender God's greatness (another designation for His *Ḥesed*) and His other supernal attributes, a person's intellectual awareness engender love for God, fear of God, and so forth. Therefore, there is a simple principle: When a person contemplates love, that contemplation engenders love. When he contemplates *Gevura*, or fear, that contemplation engenders fear, and so on.

שֶׁהֵן מִדּוֹת אַהֲבָה וְיִרְאָה, **which are the attributes of love and fear,**

In a person's divine soul, the offspring of intellectual awareness are the emotive attributes of love and fear. Love and fear are the progenitors of all the remaining emotive attributes, which are permutations and variations of these two fundamental attributes.

As explained above, love and fear are the internal dimensions of *Ḥesed* and *Gevura*. Here the epistle speaks of how the emotive attributes are engendered by intellectual awareness, which always begins from within, from the essence of the emotive attribute and the

36. See *Torah Or* 1a, 113a.

feeling, before it is manifest and expressed. Only then do the first two emotive attributes develop and gain their exterior aspects, which are *Ḥesed* and *Gevura.*

וּשְׁאָרֵי מִדּוֹת הַנּוֹלָדוֹת בַּנֶּפֶשׁ הָאֱלֹהִית,

and the rest of the attributes, *Tiferet, Netzaḥ, Hod, Yesod,* and *Malkhut,* **that are born in the divine soul,**

The emotive attributes of the divine soul are generated by the intellect. Without employing intellect, without active contemplation, the emotive attributes will not be generated. In the animal soul, the emotive attributes may be engendered without the intellect and without contemplation, but these attributes are not holy. They are born from the very fact that a person exists in this world, and they are associated with the senses and stimuli that he experiences in this world, through his physical body and from the people around him. Whether intentionally or unwittingly, he encounters things with his senses and awareness, and that awareness engenders a connection with them.

This is not the case regarding the emotive attributes engendered in the divine soul. Generally a person does not happen upon God's greatness. He has to make an effort to meditate and contemplate deeply to understand one matter from another until an awareness develops that is distinctly separate from physical existence so that it acquires its own tangible and experiential dimensions: its own form, its own head and body, its own left and right. This in turn evokes in a person love, fear, and the other emotive attributes to be channeled toward the Divine.

הַמַּשְׂכֶּלֶת וּמִתְבּוֹנֶנֶת בִּגְדוּלַּת ה׳,

which comprehends and contemplates the greatness of God,

The word for greatness, *gedula,* is also an expression for the attribute of *Ḥesed* when it was activated and manifest during the creation of the world.[37] Contemplating God's greatness, then, is not about contemplating God's essence and being, but rather His power and life force bring the world into existence and sustain it. ☞

---

37. See *Likkutei Torah,* Num. 12d; see also *Zohar* 3:5a, 2:235a, which describes other ways that God's greatness is manifest.

כִּי לִגְדוּלָּתוֹ אֵין חֵקֶר. **how His greatness is unfathomable.**

God's greatness is infinite. Although a person can apprehend that it exists, a person cannot truly fathom it. He cannot relate to it as he relates to a physical created entity but must relate to it as he does the Divine, the holy, the exalted, the One, as something remote and unattainable.

The emotional ramifications of contemplating God's greatness will have varied results. The emotion engendered in a person as a result of his contemplation of a particular topic depends on the perspective and context of his contemplation. So too contemplating God's greatness can have a variety of emotional outcomes. Generally there are two outcomes, love and fear, which can be broken down into four: the lower level of fear, the higher level of fear, great love, and a lesser love.

וְיֵשׁ בְּחִינַת גְּדוּלַּת ה׳ שֶׁעַל יְדֵי הִתְבּוֹנְנוּת הַנֶּפֶשׁ הָאֱלֹהִית בָּהּ תִּפּוֹל עָלֶיהָ אֵימָתָה וָפַחַד, שֶׁהִיא ׳יִרְאָה תַּתָּאָה׳ שֶׁהִיא בְּחִינַת מַלְכוּת,

One aspect of God's greatness is that when the divine soul contemplates it, it is overcome by fear and trepidation. This is the lower level of **fear, which is an aspect of *Malkhut*,**

A person's contemplation of God's greatness, of His lovingkindness, may evoke fear. This initial feeling of fear stems from the revelation of divine greatness to the individual in his present world and reality. This contemplation, which essentially focuses on the sovereignty of the Divine, strengthens a person's relationship to God as a subject to a king, and a person's relationship with God as King is initiated with this lower level of fear.

CONTEMPLATING THE GREATNESS OF GOD

☞ Greatness is the attribute of divine *Ḥesed* (see *Sha'ar HaYiḥud VeHa'emuna*, chap. 4), the first of the emotive attributes that in a sense includes them all. Contemplating God's greatness, then, means contemplating all the emotive attributes. Furthermore, among the emotive attributes, *Ḥesed* is the attribute of giving and revelation, in contrast to *Gevura*, which is the attribute of concealment and constriction. Therefore, the essence of what we contemplate with the divine soul is always greatness and revelation, which the other emotive attributes then constrict, define, and direct.

Essentially, the lower level of fear is the sense that something transcendent is here in this world. It is not clear what and how, but it is sufficiently clear to a person that it is true and real, and this sense of a Divine Presence evokes in a person a feeling of fear. As Rabban Yoḥanan ben Zakkai told his students, "May it be His will that the fear of Heaven shall be upon you like the fear of flesh and blood" (*Berakhot* 28b).[38] It is not necessary for a person to be aware of the entirety of God's greatness, which is unfathomable, in order to evoke fear of Him. The main thing is the tangibility of one's awareness, just as a person is aware of the presence of another human being, though that awareness is not truly analogous because it relates to earthly dimensions and concepts.

In any case, a person's sense of this presence, the sense that he is not alone, has the power to guard him from sin even more than higher levels of love and fear are able to do. For this reason, this lower level of fear is also called the fear of sin and the fear of punishment. As Rabban Yoḥanan concludes, "Know that when one commits a transgression, he says to himself, 'I hope that no man will see me.'"

The lower level of fear is also lower in the sense that it is not a person's fear of God Himself, but fear for himself, for what will happen to him. This applies whether he fears punishment or whether, more subtly, he is concerned for his spiritual fate because he knows that by sinning he is rebelling against God and is separated from Him. ☞

THE LOWER LEVEL OF FEAR AND *MALKHUT*

☞ *Malkhut* constitutes sovereignty on the one hand and the kingdom's obedience on the other. The lower level of fear does not involve understanding the reasons for the king's commandments, nor even enjoying them, but adhering to them: not to transgress that which is prohibited and doing that which one is commanded to do. Furthermore, as explained in hasidic teachings, *Malkhut* in relation to God Himself is like a name, like an illumination. It is not God Himself but only His mode of operation and illumination. Similarly, the lower level of fear is so called because it does not relate to fear of God Himself, of His glory and greatness, but to His revelation as it affects us, of what might occur if we disobey Him.

38. See *Likkutei Amarim*, chap. 41.

וְיֵשׁ בְּחִינַת גְּדוּלַּת ה׳ שֶׁמִּמֶּנָּה בָּאָה ׳יִרְאָה עִילָּאָה׳, יִרְאָה בּוֹשֶׁת.

and there is an aspect of contemplating **God's greatness that leads to the higher** level of **fear,** which is **fear involving shame.**

There is another, much higher level of contemplation, which evokes the higher level of fear. Whereas the lower level of fear is that initial feeling of awe, which is associated with the reality of this lower world and is the initial way of relating to God, the higher level of fear is a loftier way of relating to Him. It is the ultimate level that a person can attain with regard to his feelings toward God.

The ultimate apprehension of God's greatness is the awareness that He is incomparably greater than anything we can imagine. It is the realization that all conceivable existence constitutes the word of God: His speech, His utterance, His thought. It is the understanding that no thoughts or feelings of a human being can grasp Him beyond a great and awesome fear that overcomes him from above.

This lofty fear is called fear involving shame because it is alloyed with shame. All shame with regard to God is the inner response to such fear, in which a person does not fear what God will do to him, nor even what God will think of him, but rather he has a sense of shame at being in God's presence. He cannot stand before God having done something improper, or even without having done anything wrong, because "Who am I to stand before Him?" This is comparable to feeling overcome with shame when standing before a great and righteous person. It is the feeling of shame that overwhelms a person because of who the righteous person is, because of his intrinsic greatness, and not because of anything one might perceive of him on the outside.

וְיֵשׁ בְּחִינָה שֶׁמִּמֶּנָּה בָּאָה ׳אַהֲבָה רַבָּה׳,

There is also **an aspect** of the contemplation of God's greatness **that leads to great love,**

Generally speaking, fear of God derives from a person's awareness that God is great, exalted, and singular. It is like a person's fear of a king who sits on an exalted, elevated throne. On the other hand, a person's love for God stems from his sense of closeness to Him, from his awareness that God's greatness is the source of all of vitality and existence, that everything that exists and happens comes from Him, that all goodness, light, and pleasure are provided by Him. This love is the person's ever-growing, ever-deeper desire and yearning for God, to become ever closer to Him and attach oneself to Him.

Great love is parallel to the higher level of fear, which relates to God Himself. Beyond His presence, which is clothed in the world, in whatever form and within whatever parameters, and beyond all the goodness and delight that He bestows on a person, is love of God's essence, which is infinite, just as God himself is infinite. ☞

וְיֵשׁ בְּחִינָה שֶׁמִּמֶּנָּה בָּאָה 'אַהֲבָה זוּטָא'. **and there is an aspect that leads to a lesser love.**

The contemplation of God's greatness from which the lesser love develops is a contemplation of that which a person's intellect can grasp, of what he can feel, of what exists in this world. In contrast to the contemplation that leads to great love, the higher level of love, whose purpose is to arrive at a point where he sees that which is unfathomable, the contemplation that brings a person to the lesser love entails understanding the object of the contemplation. Here one develops this comprehension as much as possible, with all the details involved, until the picture is so tangible and so close that the person's emotional relationship to the object is inevitable.

This love is "lesser" because it is limited by its vessels, whether it

THE GIFT OF GREAT LOVE

☞ Although the author of the *Tanya* is speaking here about a person's contemplation of God's greatness leading to this higher level of love, other sources explain that this love is not a love that a person can engender. A person can evoke and generate love that resonates with him and with the world, that is associated with that which he can apprehend. But a person has no comprehension of God's being and essence, so he cannot generate a genuine feeling of love toward Him. This great love, then, is a gift, a love that comes from above, from God, because it is God's love, on His scale of greatness (see *Ḥinukh Katan*, the introduction to *Sha'ar HaYiḥud VeHa'emuna*). A human being has at most a vessel with which to receive this great love. Even then, it is only received in the essence of the soul, which transcends the aspect that is clothed in the intellect and emotive attributes. A person's contemplation can only prepare this vessel, broaden it, and cleanse it in order to receive the great love, if and when it comes.

is the vessel of the person who loves or whether it is the vessels and parameters of the object of the love. This is a love that is engendered by a person's contemplation and imagination. Therefore, it relates only to the divine illumination that is clothed in the worlds, to that which the intellect can apprehend. This is in contrast to great love, where the essence of the soul, which transcends all the soul's faculties, relates to the divine essence that transcends the worlds.[39]

וְכֵן בַּמִּדּוֹת הַחִיצוֹנִיּוֹת שֶׁהֵן חֶסֶד כו׳, **The same applies to the external attributes, to *Ḥesed*, and so on.**

Like the emotive attributes of the animal soul, the emotive attributes of the divine soul have external aspects and internal aspects. Just as contemplation of God's greatness leads to the internal dimensions of the first two emotive attributes of the divine soul, to levels of love and fear, it also leads to their external expression, to *Ḥesed, Gevura,* and the rest of the *sefirot.*

It may seem that the external aspects of the emotive attributes stem from their internal aspects, that because a person loves God, for instance, he desires God's lovingkindness. But as explained regarding the emotive attributes of the animal soul, so too in the divine soul the external emotive attributes are not just an external outcome and expression of the internal aspects of the emotive attributes. They have their own root of existence independent of the internal attributes. One may say that they also have an independent root as a result of contemplation. Just as contemplation of God's greatness leads to love of God, there is contemplation that leads to *Ḥesed.* Often, when we do not succeed via contemplation in evoking the internal feeling of love, one can attain the external expression that feeling, the outcome of that emotive attribute: to desire *Ḥesed* and, subsequently, to engage in acts of *Ḥesed.*[40]

---

39. Hasidic teachings state that these four levels of fear and love are four levels in serving God. First comes the lower level of fear, then the lesser love, then great love, and finally the higher level of fear. See *Zohar* 2:123a; *Tikkunei Zohar* 21b; *Likkutei Torah*, Num. 73a.

40. See *Likkutei Amarim*, chaps. 16–17.

וּבְכוּלָּן צָרִיךְ לִהְיוֹת מְלוּבָּשׁ בָּהֶן בְּחִינַת הַדַּעַת, **All these** manners of contemplation **must be clothed in *Da'at*,** the third of the cognitive *sefirot,*

Ḥokhma and *Bina* are like a father and mother that engender the emotive attributes. What, then, is the role of the third cognitive *sefira*, *Da'at*? Does *Da'at* also have a place in the entire process of engendering the emotive attributes?

The author of the *Tanya* goes on to explain that not only does *Da'at* have a central function in this process, but without *Da'at*, the birth of the emotive attributes would not be possible.[41]

שֶׁהוּא בְּחִינַת הִתְקַשְּׁרוּת הַנֶּפֶשׁ **which represents the soul's bond** to the emotive attributes

Da'at is the faculty of connection in the intellect, which binds the emotive attributes to the essence of the soul, which transcends the intellect. ☞

Da'at's relationship to *Ḥokhma* and *Bina* is similar to that of *Tiferet*'s relationship to *Ḥesed* and *Gevura*. *Da'at* is not an additional, third attribute on the same plane as *Ḥokhma* and *Bina*, but an attribute that is expressed in the connection between the two. *Da'at* is an intellectual

DA'AT IS CONNECTION

☞ The connotation of *Da'at* as connection and even union is found in several places in *Tanakh*, such as in the verse "And the man had been intimate [*yada*] with Eve his wife" (Gen. 4:1), and "Only you have I known from all the families of the earth" (Amos 3:2). At any rate, *Da'at* universally expresses a sort of deeper awareness. It is not only an understanding of a matter, but a recognition and knowledge that permeates all the faculties of the soul. Therefore, it connotes empathy, caring, an awareness that resonates deeply so that it has an effect on one's senses and emotions. Even in modern Hebrew, where *da'at* denotes information, it connotes a stage beyond understanding, that of remembering, of organizing ideas and pieces of information in one's thoughts and the manner in which the soul associates with these ideas and pieces of information. Without such a connection, without forming an association with the knowledge, one will not retain it and arrive at the proper awareness that these ideas engender.

41. See also *Likkutei Amarim*, chap. 3.

capability, lofty and concealed in itself, that is revealed only in the connection and bond that forms between *Ḥokhma* and *Bina*,[42] between the intellect and the emotive attributes,[43] and between the intellect and the faculties of thought, speech, and action. In a certain sense, *Da'at* is the connecting faculty that transmits messages and conclusions, warnings and intuition from the emotions, from one part of the soul to the other, and from one faculty of the soul to another.

הַקְּשׁוּרָה וּתְקוּעָה בְּהַשָּׂגָה זוֹ שֶׁמַּשֶּׂגֶת אֵיזֶה עִנְיָן מִגְּדוּלַּת ה', שֶׁמִּמֶּנָּה נוֹלְדָה בָּהּ אֵיזֶה מִדָּה מֵהַמִּדּוֹת.

with which the soul **is connected and attached to this apprehension, wherein** the soul **apprehends some facet of God's greatness, from which one of** these **attributes is engendered in** the soul.

How do we create and reveal *Da'at*? We do so exactly as it functions in the psyche: by not allowing an insight to simply pass by. Rather, we tie it down and grasp it. We embed the soul in it for a period of time. In this way one connects the point of *Ḥokhma*, the initial flash of awareness, to *Bina*, and likewise one connects *Bina* to the emotive attributes.

Having a passive awareness of God's greatness is insufficient to engender love or fear. Rather, a person must ponder that awareness, focusing his mind and heart on it. As mentioned regarding the attributes of the animal soul, the nature of the emotive attributes is that they are engendered from awareness. The awareness flows and the emotive attributes are engendered from it and relate to it. But clearly, not everything that passes through a person's awareness, just as not everything that the eye sees, generates a deep emotional relationship. Here *Da'at* comes into play: Where there is *Da'at*, where something matters, where awareness is focused, the emotive attributes are born.

כִּי בְּהֶיסַּח הַדַּעַת כְּרֶגַע מֵהַשָּׂגָה זוֹ מִסְתַּלֶּקֶת גַּם כֵּן הַמִּדָּה הַנּוֹלָדָה מִמֶּנָּה,

When *Da'at* is momentarily diverted from this apprehension, the attribute that was engendered from this insight **is also withdrawn**

42. *Torah Or* 75d.
43. *Likkutei Amarim*, chap. 3.

The moment a person's *Da'at* shifts away from a certain matter, the moment he no longer ponders it, the emotive attribute that the awareness generated, the love or fear born of that awareness, withdraws. For an attribute to remain and be active, it needs a constant connection to the person's awareness. Love for God needs an awareness of His greatness; fear of God needs a different type of awareness of His greatness, and so on. This applies particularly with regard to the emotive attributes of the divine soul, in which the attributes relate to abstract insight, which is not a natural and initial part of life in this world. In order for a person's insight to engender an emotive attribute, it must be well developed with *Ḥokhma*, *Bina*, and *Da'at*. The image must be clear and tangible, and it must be bound to the soul, in the same way that the soul is bound to daily physical reality. Then, in order to hold on to the insight, a person must invest constant effort into focusing his *Da'at* on it so that his *Da'at* will not be withdrawn from it.

מֵהַגִּילּוּי בַּנֶּפֶשׁ אֶל הַהֶעְלֵם לִהְיוֹת בָּהּ בְּכֹחַ וְלֹא בְּפוֹעַל.

from its state of **manifestation in the soul to** that of **concealment, so that it is within** the soul **only in potential and not in actuality.**

The attribute engendered in a person's divine soul is real and tangible to the degree that his apprehension of God's greatness is actual and to the degree that his divine soul is real and exists. Then, even if a person's *Da'at* is temporarily diverted, the emotive attribute does not dissipate like a passing illusion, but is only hidden in the soul, in a potential and unactualized state. This means that even if a person does not sense it in a moment of distraction, it will return and emerge from its potential state once he refocuses his mind on it. It reverts to the same state it had been previously and does not need to be reborn and grow entirely anew.

וְלָכֵן נִקְרָא הַזִּיווּג בִּלְשׁוֹן דַּעַת, מִפְּנֵי שֶׁהוּא לְשׁוֹן הִתְקַשְּׁרוּת.

Therefore, physical relations are called *Da'at*, **because** *Da'at* **connotes connection.**

Physical relations are connection. The male connects with the female, the giver with the recipient. As explained above regarding the attribute of *Yesod*, this connection is not a pouring forth, but rather it constitutes the connection of the giver itself with the recipient. Giving alone is merely illumination, a matter of the spirit, like the teacher transmitting information to the student. But in order for there to be actual giving, a transference from the giver to the recipient, in order for there to be a child, there must be a union, a bond between the giver and the recipient.

The same applies to *Da'at*. Intellectual understanding alone, deep and extensive as it may be, cannot engender the emotive attributes. An emotive attribute, like a child, is not only an illumination of the intellect but an entity in itself. In order for a person's love for God to be born, there must be *Da'at*. There must be a coupling. In this sense, *Da'at* is a descent of the intellect itself into the emotive attributes and its connection to them, and it ceases to exist as a disconnected intellect and becomes meaningful and personal, binding to a person's personality and becoming a part of it. Only then, when a person cares about something, when his soul is incapable of disassociating from it, are his emotive attributes engendered: the lesser and great love, the lower level of fear and the higher level of fear. From that point onward, his entire soul conducts itself differently.

וְזֶהוּ בְּחִינַת 'דַּעַת תַּחְתּוֹן' [נוּסָח אַחֵר: הַדַּעַת הַתַּחְתּוֹן] הַמִּתְפַּשֵּׁט בַּמִּדּוֹת וּמִתְלַבֵּשׁ בָּהֶן לְהַחֲיוֹתָן וּלְקַיְּימָן.

This is the level of lower knowledge [alternatively: the lower knowledge], which spreads through the attributes and is enclothed in them in order **to give them life and sustain them.**

Elsewhere, the author of the *Tanya* explains that there are two levels of *Da'at*: lower knowledge and higher knowledge.[44] In the supernal *sefirot*, these are two levels, two models for God's knowledge. One is knowledge as it is clothed in the worlds, which constitutes His divine providence as it is contained in this-worldly concepts. This is what the author of the *Tanya* calls lower knowledge. The other is higher knowledge, which is His inherent knowledge that both transcends and encompasses the world.

---

44. See *Torah Or* 14d and the note there.

A parallel of these two levels exists in the faculty of knowledge within the divine soul. There lower knowledge is a person's knowledge of God's greatness as it is revealed in the world. This knowledge spreads through the emotive attributes, vitalizing and sustaining them.

The author of the *Tanya* now goes on to explain the nature of higher knowledge in the soul.

וְיֵשׁ בְּחִינַת 'דַּעַת הָעֶלְיוֹן', שֶׁהוּא בְּחִינַת הִתְקַשְּׁרוּת וְחִיבּוּר מְקוֹר הַשֵּׂכֶל הַמַּשִּׂיג עוֹמֶק הַמּוּשָּׂג, שֶׁהוּא כִּנְקוּדָּה וּכְבָרָק הַמַּבְרִיק עַל שִׂכְלוֹ שֶׁיִּתְפַּשֵּׁט לְמַטָּה וְיָבֹא עוֹמֶק הַמּוּשָּׂג לִידֵי הֲבָנָה בְּהַרְחָבַת הַבֵּיאוּר בְּאוֹרֶךְ וְרוֹחַב, שֶׁהִיא בְּחִינַת בִּינָה הַנִּקְרֵאת 'רְחוֹבוֹת הַנָּהָר',

There is also the level of higher knowledge, through which the source of the intellect that comprehends the depth of a concept creates a connection and bond to the concept. This is like a point and lightning flash that flashes through a person's **intellect, so that** the point of wisdom **will spread downward and the depth of the concept will come to be understood extensively, in length and breadth. This is the attribute of *Bina*, which is called the "expanses of the river,"**

Ḥokhma is like a wellspring, the source from which the water, or the illumination or insight, flows. *Bina*, on the other hand, is like a river that has breadth and length.[45] Higher knowledge therefore binds *Ḥokhma* and *Bina*. It binds the point of wisdom, the initial flash of awareness, to the analysis and development of that awareness through an understanding that has length and breadth. ☞

This bond does not come about by itself. In order for it to occur, in order for *Ḥokhma* to descend and be constricted in *Bina*, in order for *Bina* to not only receive from *Ḥokhma* but to receive *Ḥokhma* itself, there must be an outpouring and revelation that transcends them both, in which both of them will be nullified and bound together as one. This revelation is that of higher knowledge. As explained above regarding

45. See *Zohar* 3:142a.

Tiferet, although *Da'at* is between and below *Ḥokhma* and *Bina* in the structure of the *sefirot*, its ability to bind them together attests that its root is higher than both of them. *Da'at* is actually connected to the *sefira* of *Keter*,[46] in which *Ḥokhma* and *Bina* are nullified as separate entities and in which they are bound together as one.

With regard to the divine soul, it is possible to say that higher knowledge is the illumination of the will within the soul, in the sense that a person desires and is interested in something. Within this will, although it does not yet have a form and comprehensible logic, *Ḥokhma* and *Bina* are as one. Each of the subsequent *sefirot* will reveal that will differently. But at the initial stage within the will itself, *Ḥokhma* and *Bina* are still united, with no difference between them. They both want the same thing.

כְּמוֹ שֶׁיִּתְבָּאֵר בִּמְקוֹמוֹ. as will be explained in its place.

It is not clear to which place the author of the *Tanya* is referring. Perhaps he means passages in the *Tanya* or perhaps teachings that were published in *Likkutei Torah*.

THE REQUISITE BOND BETWEEN *ḤOKHMA* AND *BINA*

☞ The bond between *Ḥokhma* and *Bina* is even more requisite than the bond between the intellect and the emotive attributes, so much so that, practically speaking, there is no existence and meaning to *Ḥokhma* without *Bina* and vice versa. It is possible to see this in certain people who are essentially wise and others who are essentially insightful. A wise person has flashes, epiphanies, but without the insightful person to take the flashes of wisdom and make something of them, they will go to waste. On the other hand, if a person who knows how to build and develop ideas does not receive the idea from without, he will be unable to move forward and develop anything meaningful. Therefore, the bond between *Ḥokhma* and *Bina* is the source of all phenomena and vitality in the soul, like the bond between a wellspring and a river.

---

46. The kabbalistic literature teaches that when *Da'at* is counted among the *sefirot*, *Keter* is not counted, and vice versa. Like *Keter*, *Da'at* also connotes will. See *Torah Or* 88a.

This epistle explained each of the ten supernal *sefirot,* as well as how the *sefirot* are manifest in the divine soul and in the animal soul. But one may venture to say that this epistle not only dealt with the ten *sefirot* themselves, but also discussed the way in which we understand them. It presented the parallel between the faculties of the soul and the supernal *sefirot* themselves.

The epistle began with a long introduction that presented the analogy – the human soul, its uniqueness and its limitations – and the object of the analogy, the divine *sefirot.* It went on to describe the unique parallels between the analogy and the object of the analogy, between various frameworks in which the ten *sefirot* may be understood, from the most sensory stage of the animal soul to the most abstract stages of the divine soul, in which the analogy (the soul) and its object (the divine *sefirot*) touch and are almost completely identified with each other.

First, the epistle explained the emotive attributes as they are manifest in the animal soul. Then it described how they are expressed in the world: as the attributes of *Ḥesed, Gevura,* and so on, which impact and define the lifegiving sustenance that is bestowed on the world. After that, the epistle explained the internal dimensions of these *sefirot* and their parallels, the faculties of the soul, not as they are manifest and are activated, but their intrinsic essence: the attributes of love and fear, and so on. The epistle then went on to discuss the cognitive *sefirot* – *Ḥokhma, Bina,* and *Da'at* – which are the source and root of the emotive attributes of love and fear.

The epistle proceeded to a more internal framework of the *sefirot* as it exists in the faculties of the divine soul. All the emotive attributes were explained again, one by one: first the emotive attributes and then the cognitive *sefirot.* It was also explained how a person can engender and develop the divine attributes in his divine soul with which to love and fear God by contemplating and meditating on God's greatness

In the midst of all the allegories and metaphors, the supernal *sefirot* are revealed. From the crudest analogy of the animal soul, in which the concealment of the Divine is great but the analogy is tangible, to the *sefirot* as they are manifest in the divine soul, which is literally a portion of the Divine, the *sefirot* of God Himself as they exist in the world of *Atzilut* are manifest. In contrast to the animal soul, the analogy in the divine soul is so subtle that it is almost like the object of the analogy itself. Who, besides God Himself, can understand the difference between the divine soul's love for God and God's love for the soul? And who, besides God Himself, can understand the difference between the soul's wisdom and understanding as it contemplates God's greatness, His creation of the world, and His providence over it and His wisdom, understanding, and all His holy traits, which create, fashion, and exercise providence over all His creations and deeds?

It is true that the divine soul is not always revealed in this world in all its purity and its full identification with the supernal *sefirot*. Generally its faculties are revealed only partially and with a certain distortion. This is because of the body, because of the animal soul, and in general because of the exile of the Divine Presence. But as explained in the epistle's introduction, even a person like Abraham, who was a vehicle for the revelation of the Divine, whose manifestations of the supernal attributes in his divine soul were perfect, who made no movement, physical or spiritual, that was not an absolute expression of the supernal traits, said of himself, "I am dust and ashes."

God teaches that "My thoughts are not your thoughts" (Isa. 55:8). There is an essential difference between a person's thoughts and God's thoughts (aside from the topics one thinks about and their scope). One difference is that unlike a person's thoughts, God's thoughts create the reality that it thinks about. One may say that the same applies to the divine attributes, the *sefirot*. God's attributes are the root of all of existence. Regarding the verse "In six days the Lord made the heavens and the earth" (Ex. 20:11), hasidic teachings explain that the world was created with the six emotive attributes, one for each day. Conversely, a person's emotive attributes at the most change his inner sensibilities, his relationship to reality.

This difference is expressed in Abraham's statement, "I am dust and ashes." Even if Abraham's attribute of *Ḥesed* was identified absolutely with divine *Ḥesed*, even if he poured forth only divine love and *Ḥesed*, the nature of his love was only a shadow of supernal love, the endpoint and conclusion of a process whose entire depth, greatness, and meaning cannot be imagined. It was like ashes that remain of a large tree in relation to the tree itself.

Nevertheless, this epistle discussed these matters in order "to understand proverbs and aphorisms" – in order that they may be understood simply, in human terms. This is possible only when a person feels the emotive attributes in his soul as his own. Only by way of analogy (the soul) can a person understand the object of the analogy (the divine *sefirot*). The conceptualization of the supernal attributes, after all the explanations, is a concept that may be described, in the language of the *Zohar*, as "touching and not touching." When a person comprehends, he comprehends only allegory and metaphor, which are essentially no more than dust and ashes. A person's attempt to truly understand will result in his not understanding anything.[47]

47. As the *Zohar* states, "No thought grasps Him at all." No thought, no matter how high it may be, grasps Him. However, although no thought grasps Him, "the desire of the heart," the inner recesses of the heart, does grasp Him.

Epistle 16

THIS LETTER WAS APPARENTLY WRITTEN AROUND THE year 1794[1] regarding a charity collection on behalf of residents of the Land of Israel. What is unique about this letter is that it is addressed to a particular community, and although the author of the *Tanya* was aware that the community members were experiencing unusual financial difficulties that year, he nonetheless asked that they continue giving charity to their brethren in the Land of Israel.

In this context, the letter touches on the question of how far one must go in giving charity, even when one does not have superfluous funds and must give money that he would otherwise use for his own basic necessities. This discussion focuses both on the letter of the law and on what can be expected or encouraged beyond the letter of the law, based on both halakhic and kabbalistic sources and in circumstances when it is difficult, or even very difficult, to contribute.

לְאַנְשֵׁי קְהִלַּת וכו' **To the members of the community of…**

22 Elul
19 Elul (leap year)

This letter is one of the most specific, addressed to a particular community in light of particular events. But the identifying details have been omitted in the printed edition of the *Tanya*, including the name of the community to which this letter was addressed and the specific events that served as the backdrop for its writing.

1. See *Iggerot Kodesh* (2012), letter 41.

אֲהוּבַיי אַחַיי וְרֵעַיי אֲשֶׁר כְּנַפְשִׁי

My beloved ones, my brethren and friends, who are like my own **soul,**

These words are not mere hyperbole. They give true expression to the relationship between the author of the *Tanya*, Rabbi Shneur Zalman of Liadi, and his hasidim, and to the essence of the relationship in general between a Rebbe and his hasidim. ☞

Before the author of the *Tanya* proceeds to the content of his letter, which includes some words of criticism that may be difficult for the recipients to hear, he states that his care and devotion for them is like that which he has for himself. His critique, then, is almost like words of criticism a person might direct at himself, which are easier to hear.

הִנֵּה לֹא נֶעְלַם מִמֶּנִּי צוּק הָעִתִּים אֲשֶׁר נִתְדַּלְדְּלָה הַפַּרְנָסָה, וּבִפְרָט הַיְּדוּעִים לִי, מִמַּחֲנֵיכֶם, אֲשֶׁר מָטָה יָדָם בְּלִי שׁוּם מַשְׁעֵן וּמַשְׁעֵנָה, וּמַמָּשׁ לוֹוִים וְאוֹכְלִים, ה׳ יְרַחֵם עֲלֵיהֶם וְיַרְחִיב לָהֶם בַּצָּר בְּקָרוֹב.

the desperateness of the current **times, in which livelihoods have dwindled, have not escaped my notice. I am particularly aware of those** members **of your community who have become destitute without any support. They literally borrow in order to eat. May God have mercy on them and soon grant them respite from their distress.**

The author of the *Tanya* notes the financial distress of the members of the community he is addressing, some of whom are lacking basic

"MY BELOVED ONES, MY BRETHREN AND FRIENDS"

☞ These two different forms of address accurately reflect the deep and substantive relationship between a Rebbe and his hasidim. The love the Rebbe feels for his followers is that of both a brother and a friend, two distinct types of love (see *Likkutei Torah*, Lev. 40a). The love one has for a brother, to whom one is related by birth, is constant and unchangeable, even if at times it is less overt. By contrast, one is not inherently and automatically connected to a friend, but precisely for that reason, when one does establish a close friendship, the feelings of love and affinity can be deeper than the feelings one has for a brother. When the author of the *Tanya* refers to his hasidim as his brethren and friends, he means that his relationship with them encompasses both types of love: It is constant and unchangeable and also deep and intense.

staples. They take small loans simply in order to buy food for the day with no way to ensure their most basic needs for the following day. He first blesses them that God may grant them respite from this distress. The particular form of the blessing, that God should have mercy on them, foreshadows the rest of the letter, where he states that when they have mercy on those even more destitute than they are, God will have mercy on them.

וְעִם כָּל זֶה, לֹא טוֹב הֵם עוֹשִׂים לְנַפְשָׁם,

Nevertheless, they are not acting beneficially toward themselves

Despite their financial distress, the behavior of the members of this community is damaging to themselves both materially and spiritually. This is consistent with what the author of the *Tanya* wrote in previous letters, that when one gives charity, one benefits himself even more than he benefits the recipient of his charity. Furthermore, the author of the *Tanya* explains that refraining from giving causes spiritual damage to one's soul.

לְפִי הַנִּשְׁמָע אֲשֶׁר קָפְצוּ יָדָם הַפְּתוּחָה מֵעוֹדָם עַד הַיּוֹם הַזֶּה, לִיתֵּן בְּיַד מְלֵאָה וְעַיִן יָפָה לְכָל הִצְטָרְכוּת הַהֶכְרֵחִיִּים לְדֵי מַחְסוֹרֵי הָאֶבְיוֹנִים נְקִיִּים, אֲשֶׁר עֵינֵיהֶם נְשׂוּאוֹת אֵלֵינוּ, וְאִם אָנוּ לֹא נְרַחֵם עֲלֵיהֶם חַס וְשָׁלוֹם, מִי יְרַחֵם עֲלֵיהֶם? "וְחֵי אָחִיךָ עִמָּךְ" (ויקרא כה, לו) כְּתִיב.

according to reports that they have closed their hands, which had been open their whole lives until this day, from giving fully and generously all the necessities that the destitute, whose eyes are raised to us, lack. If we do not have mercy on them, God forbid, who will have mercy on them? As it is written, "And your brother shall live with you" (Lev. 25:36).

The reference here is to the hasidim who immigrated to the Land of Israel in 1777. These individuals suffered from even greater poverty and persecution than other communities there. This letter concerns a collection undertaken for their benefit.

וְלֹא אָמְרוּ ׳חַיֶּיךָ קוֹדְמִין׳ (בבא מציעא סב, א), אֶלָּא כְּשֶׁבְּיַד אֶחָד קִיתוֹן שֶׁל מַיִם וכו׳ שֶׁהוּא דָּבָר הַשָּׁוֶה לִשְׁנֵיהֶם בְּשָׁוֶה לִשְׁתּוֹת לְהָשִׁיב נַפְשָׁם בַּצָּמָא,

Regarding this verse, the Sages **said, "Your life takes precedence"** (*Bava Metzia* 62a) **only** in a case **where one has a pitcher of water** to share between himself and another, **and so on, which is something that is equally essential to both of them so that they may drink to relieve themselves of thirst.**

The Talmud cites a case where two people are traveling in the wilderness and only one of them has a pitcher of water. If both drink, neither will survive since there will not be enough water between them, whereas if only one person drinks, he will make it back to civilization. Rabbi Akiva derives from the verse "And your brother shall live with you" that "your life takes precedence over the life of your brother." Yet the author of the *Tanya* points out that this principle applies only when the two individuals are in equal need of what they lack and when only one may survive while the other will die.

אֲבָל אִם הֶעָנִי צָרִיךְ לֶחֶם לְפִי הַטַּף וְעֵצִים וּכְסוּת בַּקָּרָה וּכְהַאי גַּוְונָא - כָּל דְּבָרִים אֵלּוּ קוֹדְמִין לְכָל מַלְבּוּשֵׁי כָּבוֹד וְזֶבַח מִשְׁפָּחָה, בָּשָׂר וְדָגִים וְכָל מַטְעַמִּים שֶׁל הָאָדָם וְכָל בְּנֵי בֵיתוֹ.

But if the pauper requires bread to feed his **children, and wood and clothing in the cold and the like, all such things take precedence over any fine garments or a family feast of meat, fish, and all** other **delicacies for a person and all the members of his household.**

If one person lacks the most basic necessities without which he cannot survive, his needs take precedence over another person's legitimate needs that are nevertheless not essential for his survival.

וְלֹא שַׁיָּיךְ בָּזֶה ׳חַיֶּיךָ קוֹדְמִין׳ מֵאַחַר שֶׁאֵינָן חַיֵּי נֶפֶשׁ מַמָּשׁ כְּמוֹ שֶׁל הֶעָנִי שָׁוֶה בְּשָׁוֶה מַמָּשׁ, כִּדְאִיתָא בִּנְדָרִים דַּף פ׳ (עמוד ב).

The principle of **"Your life takes precedence" does not apply here, since these are not actually vital essentials that are equivalent to those of the pauper, as stated in *Nedarim* 80b.**

The Talmud states that if a city does not have sufficient water for all its inhabitants, the needs of the residents of the city take precedence over the needs of nonresidents. This principle extends to the need of water for livestock and for washing as well. But this applies when the needs are equal, where both groups need drinking water or need water for their animals or to wash their clothes. In such a case, the residents do not need to give up their own needs in order to satisfy the needs of others. But if the needs are not equal, if the nonresidents lack drinking water and the residents merely need the water to wash their clothes, the principle that "your life takes precedence" does not apply.

23 Elul
20 Elul (leap year)

וְהִנֵּה זֶהוּ עַל פִּי שׁוּרַת הַדִּין גָּמוּר. אֲבָל בֶּאֱמֶת גַּם אִם הוּא עִנְיָן דְּלָא שַׁיָּיךְ כָּל כָּךְ הַאי טַעְמָא, רָאוּי לְכָל אָדָם שֶׁלֹּא לְדַקְדֵּק לְהַעֲמִיד עַל הַדִּין, רַק לִדְחוֹק חַיָּיו וְלִיכָּנֵס לִפְנַי וְלִפְנִים מִשּׁוּרַת הַדִּין,

This is in accordance with the strict letter of the law. But in truth, even if it is a case where this reason does not really apply, it behooves every person not to be scrupulous about fulfilling only the letter of **the law. Rather, he should live a life of hardship and go far beyond the letter of the law.**

According to the letter of the law, one must give up on one's own needs where they are not absolutely essential in order to provide for another's most basic necessities. But the reality was that the hasidim of Russia were not necessarily less impoverished than of the community in the Land of Israel. Even so, the author of the *Tanya* urges his followers not to merely follow the letter of the law. Though their needs are the same as those of the hasidim in the Land of Israel, they should go beyond the letter of the law and contribute nonetheless.

וְלִדְאוֹג לְעַצְמוֹ מִמַּאֲמַר רַבּוֹתֵינוּ ז״ל שֶׁכָּל הַמְדַקְדֵּק בְּכָךְ סוֹף בָּא לִידֵי כָּךְ חַס וְשָׁלוֹם.

He would thereby **be taking care of himself,** as derived **from our Rabbis' statement that whoever is excessively fastidious in this regard will ultimately come to that state** himself, **God forbid.**

The letter of the law appears to be logical and just. Why, then, did the Sages state that "whoever is [excessively] fastidious in this regard will ultimately come to that state [himself]"?[2] The nature of the world is that people's fortunes rise and fall. If one only fulfills the letter of the law with regard to others, people are likely to treat him the same way when he is in need. On a deeper level, the way a person treats others affects his relationship with God. When one does no more than required for others, he will do the same with God.

וְגַם כִּי כּוּלָּנוּ צְרִיכִים לְרַחֲמֵי שָׁמַיִם בְּכָל עֵת, **Also, because we are all in need of the compassion of Heaven at all times,**

Even someone who is not currently struggling with financial or medical hardships is constantly in need of divine mercy. At the end of the day, only God can provide one's needs, and in relation to God, a person is always in a state of need. One who does not recognize this is either foolish or heretical.

בְּאִתְעֲרוּתָא דִלְתַתָּא דַּוְקָא, which are evoked **specifically through an awakening from below,**

Divine mercy is elicited through our own actions, what is called "an awakening from below." More generally, the way God relates to us is influenced by the way we act here below. The divine awakening is stirred on high in parallel to the action done below. Moreover, this action from below prepares us to receive the heavenly compassion that has been aroused.

בְּכָל עֵת וּבְכָל שָׁעָה, לְעוֹרֵר רַחֲמֵינוּ עַל הַצְּרִיכִים לְרַחֲמִים. **at all times and at all hours, by evoking our compassion for those who require compassion.**

Fundamentally, an awakening from below does not mean simply praying for what we need but rather initiating the relevant action

---

2. The Talmud in *Bava Metzia* 33a states that attending to one's own lost item takes precedence over returning another person's lost item, but that one who is punctilious in that regard and does not act beyond the requirements of the law will ultimately experience that state himself. Rashi explains that although by law one may give precedence to his own needs, he thereby ceases to be involved in charity and acts of kindness even when the financial loss is not significant. Eventually he himself will need help from others. See also *Shulḥan Arukh, Ḥoshen Mishpat* 264:1.

ourselves. This concept characterizes the fundamental hasidic concept of prayer: We are not just asking for something but creating it ourselves by verbalizing it in prayer. This is not merely inwardly directed either. We are praying and creating new realities not only for ourselves, but for the world in general and, in a more abstract way, for the sake of the Divine Presence. This is the case with all awakenings from below that serve to awaken divine compassion for the individual with regard to a specific concrete need. We are not arousing compassion for ourselves, but rather for our fellow Jews, who are in need of divine mercy, and for the Divine Presence, which itself is in need of abundant mercy.[3]

וְכָל הַמְאַמֵּץ לְבָבוֹ וְכוֹבֵשׁ רַחֲמָיו, יִהְיֶה מֵאֵיזֶה טַעַם שֶׁיִּהְיֶה, גּוֹרֵם כָּךְ לְמַעְלָה לִכְבּוֹשׁ וכו׳, חַס וְשָׁלוֹם.

Anyone who hardens his heart and suppresses his compassion, for whatever reason, causes compassion **to be suppressed above, and so forth, God forbid,**

Just as acting with compassion toward those in need awakens divine compassion toward us, the opposite is also true: Withholding our compassion from others can cause a withholding of divine compassion from us, God forbid. When we evoke compassion within ourselves for those in need of compassion, we thereby awaken divine compassion for ourselves. Conversely, if we stifle our compassion toward others, this engenders a corresponding restriction of compassion from above, God forbid.

This is one reason for giving charity even beyond the letter of the law: to arouse divine compassion beyond the letter of the law. This will result in a qualitatively different reality – a reality infused with compassion and giving beyond what is deserved. This applies to everyone, but there is an additional reason that the author of the *Tanya* will present below, one that is relevant to a person who is lacking and needs atonement, a medical cure, a livelihood, and so on. In that case,

3. On the contrary, if one prays only for the fulfillment of his own needs, the result is likely to be divine judgment rather than divine mercy. See *Torah Or* 51a, where it is explained that praying for oneself causes divine judgment as to whether one is worthy to stand before God in prayer and serve Him. Rather, one should pray for mercy for the Divine Presence, which is in exile. See also *Likkutei Siḥot*, vol. 19, Rosh HaShana (6 Tishrei).

charity is portrayed as a kind of remedy that the supplicant urgently needs and for which he is willing to give everything he has.[4]

וּמַה גַּם "כִּי אָדָם אֵין צַדִּיק בָּאָרֶץ אֲשֶׁר יַעֲשֶׂה טּוֹב" - תָּמִיד - "וְלֹא יֶחֱטָא" (קהלת ז, כ), וְהַצְּדָקָה מְכַפֶּרֶת וּמְגִינָּה מִן הַפּוּרְעָנוּת וכו'.

especially since "there is no righteous man upon the earth who does good" – always – "and does not sin" (Eccles. 7:20), **and charity atones and protects against retribution, and so on.**

That the righteous "does good" means that he fulfills the positive commandments that are incumbent on him, while "does not sin" refers to the prohibitions that he does not transgress. There is no person alive who is not somehow tainted by contact with *kelippa* and with evil, whether through committing sins or neglecting to do good deeds, or even merely by having negative thoughts or inadequacies. But charity can effect atonement, closing the breaches caused by these failings and preventing the negative consequences that might otherwise result.[5] In particular, charity atones for a person's failings in the realm of the performance of mitzvot, because charity is an addition to one's mitzva performance, especially when one gives beyond what is required of him.[6]

וְלָזֹאת הִיא רְפוּאַת הַגּוּף וְנֶפֶשׁ מַמָּשׁ, אֲשֶׁר "עוֹר בְּעַד עוֹר וְכֹל אֲשֶׁר לָאִישׁ יִתֵּן בְּעַד נַפְשׁוֹ" (איוב ב, ד).

As such, it is an actual remedy for the body and soul, because "skin for skin, everything that a man has he will give for his life" (Job 2:4).

---

4. The Lubavitcher Rebbe, Rabbi Menaḥem Mendel Schneerson, explains that the first reason pertains to the future, that a person will be the recipient of divine compassion as a result of one's own compassion toward another in the present. It is therefore delineated by the phrase "with you" in the verse "And your brother shall live with you," implying that in providing for the needy, they become equals. The second reason pertains to rectifying the past and therefore one must even give beyond one's means.

5. See *Bava Batra* 10a; *Devarim Rabba* 5:3.

6. See also *Iggeret HaTeshuva*, chap. 2, where it is explained that charity is like fasting and sacrificial offerings in that it causes a person's repentance to be viewed positively by God. See epistle 3 above, where charity is compared to protective armor that arrows cannot penetrate.

Since charity protects a person both physically and spiritually,[7] it is likened to medicine. A person would give anything to be cured of an illness, and he would not consult a rabbi to ascertain how much he is required to spend to obtain it. He would give not only all of his possessions, but even of his very body, "skin for skin."[8]

בְּשֶׁגַּם אָנוּ מַאֲמִינִים בְּנֵי מַאֲמִינִים כִּי הַצְּדָקָה אֵינָהּ רַק הַלְוָאָה לְהַקָּדוֹשׁ בָּרוּךְ הוּא, כְּדִכְתִיב: "מַלְוֵה ה' חוֹנֵן דָּל וּגְמוּלוֹ יְשַׁלֶּם לוֹ" (משלי יט, יז),

In addition, we are believers, descendants of believers, who believe **that charity is nothing other than a loan to the Holy One, blessed be He, as it is written, "He who cares for the poor lends to the Lord, and He will pay his reward"** (Prov. 19:17).

The verse that the author of the *Tanya* quotes here states explicitly that giving to the poor is like lending to God and that He will repay the debt.[9] Thus, not only is giving to the poor actually giving to oneself, in that it brings a person atonement and protection; it is like giving to God, as it were. Not only that, it is actually not really giving at all, but lending, and the lender is guaranteed to be repaid considerably more than he gave. ☞

BELIEVERS, DESCENDANTS OF BELIEVERS

☞ By employing this phrase, "believers, descendants of believers," the author of the *Tanya* implies that the fulfillment of this guarantee is not necessarily easily observed and self-understood, and one must believe in this principle in order for it to inform his actions. God does not repay the loan immediately, and in the meantime the giver of charity may find himself lacking. Also, God does not inform the giver what he is being repaid for at the time he is being repaid. God has many ways to bestow blessing, and one does not always recognize the gift. Thus, although this guarantee is stated in a verse and affirmed by the Sages, one must have a deeply ingrained level of belief, that of "a believer, a descendant of believers," to risk the little that he has and to act in accordance with this principle.

---

7. See *Iggeret HaTeshuva*, chap. 3.
8. Rashi comments regarding this verse that if a person sees a sword being swung at his head, he would try to protect himself even by blocking it with his arm, and certainly he would give all his money.
9. See *Bava Batra* 10a.

בְּכִפְלַיִים בָּעוֹלָם הַזֶּה, דִּשְׂכַר כָּל הַמִּצְוֹת לֵיכָּא בָּעוֹלָם הַזֶּה לְבַד מִצְּדָקָה, לְפִי שֶׁהוּא טוֹב לַבְּרִיּוֹת, כִּדְאִיתָא בְּקִדּוּשִׁין סוֹף פֶּרֶק קַמָּא (לט, ב–מ, א).

God will repay the person **double,** meaning a double reward, including **in this world, since there is no reward for all the mitzvot in this world apart from charity because it is beneficial for** other **people, as stated at the end of the first chapter of *Kiddushin*** (39b–40a).

The giver of charity will be paid back double: once in the World to Come, where he receives reward for all the mitzvot he performed, and once in this world, where he is repaid with material benefit. As a rule, the full reward for mitzvot is awarded only in the World to Come, in the world of souls in the Garden of Eden. One reason for this is that this world is simply incapable of containing such reward. By performing a mitzva, one connects in the deepest possible way to God, and there is no expression of that connection in this world other than the performance of mitzvot, which constitute the connection itself.[10] But the reward for that connection, which constitutes the awareness of that connection and the sublime satisfaction it brings, cannot be attained in this world, where it is impossible to comprehend the true nature of the connection.

It is possible to get a taste of this reward only in higher spiritual worlds, such as the world of *Yetzira*, which is the lower Garden of Eden, or the world of *Beria*, which is the higher Garden of Eden. These are spiritual worlds that are unbounded by physical limitations, where there is a higher level of spiritual awareness. Charity is an exception to this rule. Aside from the connection to God that it creates, like any other mitzva, it also brings material benefit to others in this world.[11]

10. This gives meaning to the statement of the mishnaic statement "The reward for a mitzva is a mitzva" (*Avot* 4:2).

11. The Lubavitcher Rebbe, Rabbi Menaḥem Mendel Schneerson, notes that the author of the *Tanya* uses the general term *beriyot*, "people," to refer to the others in this world who benefit from the charity because it includes everyone (see *Likkutei Amarim* chap. 32). This implies that one should give even if the recipient would not be considered a "brother" as implied in the verse "And your brother shall live with you." Similarly, just as one should not be too exacting regarding the

Consequently, the reward is received not only in the next world but also in this world, because the material benefit a person brings to others creates a tangible receptacle to receive reward from above here below.

וְגַם יֵשׁ לָחוּשׁ לְעוֹנֶשׁ חַס וְשָׁלוֹם כְּשֶׁחֲבֵרָיו נִמְנִים לִדְבַר מִצְוָה וְהוּא לֹא נִמְנֶה עִמָּהֶם, כַּנּוֹדָע מִמַּאֲמַר רַבּוֹתֵינוּ ז״ל.

One should also be concerned about punishment, God forbid, when one's colleagues reach a consensus regarding a mitzva matter and he is not part of their consensus, as the well-known statement of our Rabbis attests.

Commenting on the verse "That which is deficient cannot be counted [*lehimanot*]" (Eccles. 1:15), the Talmud states, "This refers to one whose friends reached a consensus [*nimnu*] to perform a mitzva, and he was not part of their consensus" (*Berakhot* 26a; *Ḥagiga* 9b). This means that beyond the reward that a person loses for neglecting to perform the mitzva, he may also incur a punishment.

In general, one is punished only for violating prohibitions but not for failing to fulfill positive commandments. This is because the point of a punishment is to correct the damage a person has caused through the sin.[12] When a person fails to fulfill a positive commandment, he does not cause damage but rather fails to bring a flow of vitality from higher worlds to this world,[13] and that flow can be obtained only through mitzvot, not through punishments. Charity, though, is an exception because its effects are felt in this world, and therefore failure to give charity also needs to be rectified in this world. Moreover, when one's friends join together to fulfill a mitzva and he does not join them, he is impairing something positive that was pertinent to him. This impairment may then be rectified through punishment.

---

implications of the word "brother," he should not be too exacting regarding "live" and "with you," and one should therefore give even if the recipient is not lacking basic essentials and even to cover needs that one might not have for himself.

12. See *Likkutei Torah*, Num. 86d.

13. See *Iggeret HaTeshuva*, chap. 1.

וְלַשּׁוֹמְעִים יוּנְעַם, וְתָבוֹא עֲלֵיהֶם בִּרְכַּת טוֹב, בְּכָל מִילֵּי דְּמֵיטַב, הֵטִיבָה ה׳ לַטּוֹבִים וְיִשָׁרִים כְּנַפְשָׁם וְנֶפֶשׁ הַדּוֹרֵשׁ שְׁלוֹמָם מִכָּל לֵב וָנֶפֶשׁ.

May those who give heed have a pleasant reward, **and may a blessing of goodness, of all sorts of goodness, be bestowed on them. May God be good to those who are good and those who are upright in accordance with their wishes and the wishes of he who seeks their welfare with all** his **heart and soul.**

Having warned that those who do not heed his instructions may be subject to punishment, the author of the *Tanya* concludes by wholeheartedly blessing those who do contribute despite the inherent financial difficulty.

This letter was written to encourage the giving of charity even when the giver is himself in need. It is one thing to give up luxuries or amenities for the sake of charity. It is quite another to give in a manner that endangers one's life and the life of his family members. In fact, when a choice must be made between one's own life or that of another individual, one's own life takes precedence. But the reality is more complex. One does not know the specific condition of the recipients of the funds, particularly if they are in the Land of Israel, and one must assume that their circumstances are extremely dire. On the other hand, one generally does know if he himself can extend himself, earn a little extra money, take another loan, and continue on for another day. Nonetheless, one might naturally hesitate to give, thinking, *Can I really sacrifice the little I have? Am I even permitted to do so?* It is here that the author of the *Tanya* comes, with the authority of a hasidic Rebbe, and urges his followers to give. It is precisely such giving, despite the hardship it entails, that will shower the giver with divine mercy and save him from his own predicament.

Furthermore, the case under discussion was not a new request for charity but a request to continue a preexisting pattern of giving.[14] When a person regularly gives charity, but his circumstances change and

14. See epistle 30 with regard to maintaining a regular practice of giving.

he endures financial hardship, he may decide that he is not required to continue giving at present. Yet, although conditions had changed and his followers have endured financial hardship, the author of the *Tanya* urges them to maintain their fixed pattern of giving, in particular because this was not merely a personal practice but a joint enterprise of all the hasidim. Stopping the ongoing practice of giving would therefore constitute not only a cessation of one's own good practice, but a failure to join one's friends in a mitzva and a departure from communal practice.[15]

15. The Lubavitcher Rebbe, Rabbi Menaḥem Mendel Schneerson, points out that this consideration itself is sufficient reason to give. Consequently, even if one had already given his standard contribution, he should give again when his fellow community members give. This is the most significant innovation of this letter.

Epistle 17

THIS EPISTLE, ONE OF THE LAST THAT THE AUTHOR OF the *Tanya* sent to his hasidim (in 1810), also discusses the mitzva of charity. Unlike the previous epistle, which was sent to the members of a specific community to appeal to them to conduct a collection to address a specific situation, this letter is one of the regularly scheduled epistles that the author of the *Tanya* would circulate through an emissary who traveled to various localities to collect the charity that they had raised. Following its opening words, which are omitted here,[1] this epistle discusses the reward a person receives for performing the mitzva of charity. Although other epistles in *Iggeret HaKodesh* also discuss the reward for charity, they do so principally in terms of the reward given in this world, with the twin purposes of encouraging people to give charity and bolstering their trust in God. The emphasis in this epistle is on the reward given in the World to Come.

In the next world, a person can no longer perform mitzvot, but he can receive the light that they generate and gain an understanding of the significance of the mitzvot that he performed in this world. In view of this, reward in the World to Come is reward in its true sense. It does not serve as a spur and encouragement to continue performing a mitzva, but it is a heavenly response to the fulfillment of a person's earthly deed, a revelation of the Divine and the infinite pleasure this brings that the limited physical world cannot contain.

As part of this discussion, the epistle speaks of the reward

1. These introductory words are printed in *Iggerot Kodesh*, letter 101.

in the World to Come in general and the overall levels of the World to Come, which include the Garden of Eden and the physical world at the time of the resurrection of the dead, as well as their connection to the mitzva of charity.

24 Elul
21 Elul (leap year)

נוֹדָע דְּבְאִתְעָרוּתָא דִּלְתַתָּא **It is known that** in response to **an awakening from below,**

An awakening refers to the inception of a movement or illumination.[2] In the higher world, the movement is a descent from above to below, and in the lower world, it entails an ascent from below to above. When an action or illumination originates down below, it ascends, and when it originates from on high, it descends. Generally speaking, a human being initiates an awakening from below, and God initiates an awakening from above. These two are interwoven and one brings about the other. Together, they constitute the movement of life in man and in the world. ☞

Though the author of the *Tanya* discusses these concepts elsewhere, here they are presented somewhat differently. He is not speaking about two sources of a person's actions in the world, but about an action and its reward: the person's action below and its reward from above. This reward is not presented as a lever that propels a person from one act of service to another, as in "the reward of a mitzva is a mitzva," but is presented as an entity in itself.

AN AWAKENING FROM BELOW AND AN AWAKENING FROM ABOVE

☞ In general, Hasidism applies the concepts of an awakening from below and an awakening from above to the way each of these is manifested in the human soul. When a person has a thought or feeling that something is worth doing and he carries out the impulse to bring it about, that is an awakening from below. The initial impulse may also come from above, from a heavenly will or expression of kindness that can manifest itself in an incident that occurs to a person, a scenario that he sees, or a feeling that has no apparent connection to what he was doing or thinking. This is an awakening from above. Although these two types of awakening are independent of each other, the ideal is where an awakening from below generates an awakening from above, where an initial awakening from below leads to an incomparably greater awakening and vitality from above.

2. See *Zohar* 1:88a; see also epistle 16.

שֶׁהָאָדָם מְעוֹרֵר בְּלִבּוֹ **when a person evokes in his heart**

The awakening from below begins with the arousal of a person's heart. The act of giving charity, which is what the author of the *Tanya* is talking about here, begins within the soul, where the person's feelings and desires are impacted to feel compassion for another person in need. ☞

מִדַּת הַחֶסֶד וְרַחֲמָנוּת עַל כָּל הַצְּרִיכִים לְרַחֲמִים, אִתְעֲרוּתָא דִּלְעֵילָּא לְעוֹרֵר עָלָיו רַחֲמִים רַבִּים מִמְּקוֹר הָרַחֲמִים, **the attribute of kindness and compassion for all those who are in need of compassion,** there is a consequent **awakening from above that elicits abundant compassion for him from the source of compassion,**

Even while a person's awakening from below is confined to his heart and has not yet actualized as deed, even when it has only evoked feelings of kindness and compassion on those who are in need, feelings that have not yet been translated into acts of charity, an awakening from above is initiated. The awakening from above reflects the awakening from below both in terms of the type of awakening entailed and in terms of the person whose awakening from below has prompted the awakening from above, the person who has now become a vehicle to receive from above. Therefore, even if a person is only spurred to have compassion on someone else without any further effort, he elicits God's compassion from above. ☞

THE AROUSAL OF THE HEART

☞ The essence of the awakening from below is the arousal of the heart. What is important to God and leads to an awakening from above is not how much charity a person gives or how much Torah he studies. To God, who is infinite and omnipotent, that is not what is important. What matters is what a person gives of himself, the effort he makes, the hardships and pain, and, despite all that, the victories. All of that takes place principally in the heart.

ABUNDANT COMPASSION FROM THE SOURCE OF COMPASSION

☞ The awakening from above is an awakening of infinite, abundant compassion from the source of compassion, which transcends even the attribute of supernal compassion (see *Likkutei Amarim*, chap. 45). The author of the *Tanya* explains that there are two levels of divine compassion (see *Torah Or* 24b, 63b). First, there is the attribute of compassion within the structure of the *sefirot* and their devolvement

לְהַשְׁפִּיעַ לוֹ הַפֵּירוֹת בָּעוֹלָם הַזֶּה וְהַקֶּרֶן לָעוֹלָם הַבָּא.

bestowing on him the fruits of his actions **in this world while the principal** reward remains **for the World to Come.**

The abundant compassion from above, from the source of compassion, manifests itself in two ways: as the "principal" and as "fruits." These are concepts from the field of finance. The principal is the value of a property, and the fruits are the profits that it generates, like the fruits of a tree, without the property itself being diminished. Similarly, the divine flow of abundant compassion has these two characteristics of the principal and the fruits. The bestowal of the "fruits," which does not cause any diminution of the principal (the source of divine light), is merely an illumination that enters a receptacle. This flow is therefore associated with our finite and lowly world, which serves as this receptacle. The principal, on the other hand, is not merely an illumination, but an expression of the essence of the One who bestows abundance and vitality. This flow is not limited by the receptacle of the recipient at all. Therefore, it relates to the World to Come, which is not subject to such limitations. ☞ ☞

through the worlds. This attribute manifests itself through the ten *sefirot*, and it is finite since it is constricted by the trait of judgment. Then there is "abundant compassion," also called "supernal compassion," which transcends the worlds and their constraints and so it has no measure or limitation whatsoever (see *Likkutei Torah*, Lev. 23a).

Why does the author of the *Tanya* here speak specifically of "abundant compassion"? An awakening from above always mirrors the awakening from below. This is because, in a sense, all compassion possesses something of the essence of *Ein Sof*. When a person has compassion on someone in need and gives charity, he does not give because it is mandatory, nor does he make calculations and apply limits to his giving. The compassion that comes from an arousal from below has no limitations at all. This is in contrast to a case in which a person's compassion has a source from above, such as one of the *sefirot*. That source may constrict the measure of compassion he feels. It follows that when an awakening from below precedes an awakening from above, the consequent awakening from above is that of abundant compassion from the infinite source of compassion.

THIS WORLD AND THE WORLD TO COME

☞ The difference between this world and the World to Come is not absolute and unequivocal. A simple understanding that relates to our present reality is that

פֵּירוּשׁ, הַ׳פֵּירוֹת׳ הִיא הַשְׁפָּעָה הַנִּשְׁפַּעַת מִמְּקוֹר הָרַחֲמִים וְחַיֵּי הַחַיִּים בָּרוּךְ הוּא, וְנִמְשֶׁכֶת לְמַטָּה מַטָּה בִּבְחִינַת הִשְׁתַּלְשְׁלוּת הָעוֹלָמוֹת מִלְמַעְלָה לְמַטָּה כו׳,

This means that the "fruits" refers to the divine **sustenance that flows from the source of compassion and the** infinite **source of life, blessed be He, and is drawn down to the bottommost reaches through the downward progression of the worlds, from top to bottom, and so on,**

Although the flow of sustenance that is termed the "fruits" is merely an illumination of the principal, an illumination that diminishes the principal, it is drawn all the way down from the loftiest plane. The phrase "downward progression of the worlds" indicates the realm where the divine light, and not divinity itself, gives those worlds life. It indicates the nature of the connection between the worlds, which is a connection of one world devolving into another, like links in a chain, with the top of a lower link inserted into the bottom of a higher link.

this world is a physical realm in which people live in bodies, whereas the realm of the Garden of Eden constitutes the next world, the realm that a person's soul reaches only after it has passed through a physical lifetime in this world. But in this epistle, which is based on a broader kabbalistic conception, "this world" encompasses all of the levels of the Garden of Eden, because even at present these realms exist for all souls that are not currently in a body. Essentially, the Garden of Eden is no different from this world, but rather it is a sort of spiritual reflection and outcome of the reality of this world. What exists in this world also exists in the Garden of Eden. That is what the author of the *Tanya* means here by the concept of the World to Come. By contrast, the future world that will come about after the resurrection of the dead, which may also be referred to as the World to Come, constitutes an entirely different realm.

REWARD IN THIS WORLD AND IN THE WORLD TO COME

☞ The distinction that the author of the *Tanya* makes regarding two types of reward for charity corresponds to the distinction between two levels of the divine light: the light that surrounds the worlds and the light that fills the worlds. The reward that is termed "fruits" is the flow of light that fills all the worlds. This is the flow of divine light and life force that is drawn through the worlds from one level to another, where a higher level pours down whatever it can pour down, and the lower level receives what it is able to receive, in accordance with the capacity of its vessels. The "principal," on the other hand, is divine light that surrounds all worlds, the light and life force that transcends all of existence, which encompasses all the worlds and beyond.

The lower link receives and apprehends all it can possibly contain. There is a relationship between the links: The higher world is the cause of the lower world, and the lower world necessarily can apprehend that cause. Therefore, the higher world, although loftier, is not entirely separate from the lower world.

עַד שֶׁמִּתְלַבֶּשֶׁת בָּעוֹלָם הַזֶּה הַגַּשְׁמִי, **until it becomes enclothed within this physical world,**

This physical reality is the lowest world in the entire progression of worlds. It is precisely the illumination that is drawn from the highest plane, from the most supernal source of compassion, that reaches the bottommost reaches, the very depths of physicality.

בִּבְנֵי חַיֵּי וּמְזוֹנֵי כו'. in one's **children, life, and livelihood, and so forth.**

Children, life, and livelihood encapsulate the totality of a person's concerns in this physical world. "Children" refers to a person's children, to their birth and growth. "Life" refers to a person's life span, health, and well-being. "Livelihood" refers to a person's income and sustenance. Every tangible resource in this world fits into one of these three categories. These resources, which each person receives in accordance with his needs and situation, are only the "fruits" of the principal. They do not express anything of the mitzva's intrinsic nature, nor do they constitute the actual reward for performing the mitzva, which is an expression of God's will.

וְהַקֶּרֶן הוּא כְּמוֹ שֶׁכָּתוּב: "רְחָבָה מִצְוָתְךָ מְאֹד" (תהלים קיט, צו). **The "principal" relates to the verse "Your commandments are exceedingly wide"** (Ps. 119:96).

The principal constitutes the essence of the divine vitality that no vessel or world can contain. Only one thing is sufficiently large and broad enough to receive it, and that is a mitzva itself. As the verse states, "Your commandments are exceedingly wide." The term *me'od*, "exceedingly," implies something infinite.[3] ☞

3. See *Torah Or* 53d; *Likkutei Torah*, Num. 42c. All the worlds and everything in them are by definition limited, since they conceal *Ein Sof*. By contrast, a mitzva

וַהֲוָה לֵיהּ לְמֵימַר "מִצְוֹתֶיךָ", לְשׁוֹן רַבִּים (וְגַם לְשׁוֹן "רְחָבָה" אֵינוֹ מוּבָן).

The verse **should have said,** ***mitzvotekha,*** **in the plural,** rather than *mitzvatekha*, which literally means "Your commandment," in the singular. (**Moreover, the term *reḥava*,** wide, **is incomprehensible.**)

Since the verse is presumably referring to all 613 commandments, why does it speak of a single commandment? Also, how does the word "wide," a concept taken from the physical world, apply to a mitzva? In addition, why specifically employ this term, as opposed to "long" or "high"?

אֶלָּא "מִצְוָתְךָ" דַּיְיקָא הִיא מִצְוַת הַצְּדָקָה, שֶׁהִיא מִצְוַת ה' מַמָּשׁ, מַה שֶּׁהַקָּדוֹשׁ בָּרוּךְ הוּא בִּכְבוֹדוֹ וּבְעַצְמוֹ

Rather, the term **"Your commandment" is precise** because **it refers to the mitzva of charity, which**

A RECEPTACLE FOR THE INFINITE

☞ The verse "I see an end to all great things, but Your commandments are exceedingly wide" can be applied to the connection between a mitzva act and the feeling referred to as the "pining of the soul" (see *Torah Or* 53d). This pining is that which the soul feels when it apprehends the Divine and a love and fear of God is evoked, whether in this world or in the World to Come, yet it is finite: "I see an end to all great things."

By contrast, the commandments are "exceedingly wide," without end. When a person studies the commandments and fulfills them, he becomes a receptacle for *me'od*, for that which is infinite (see *Torah Or* 53d and *Likkutei Torah*, Num. 42c, which state that the term *me'od* connotes something that is infinite). This is because as long as something exists in the world, even in the spiritual worlds, the Divine is concealed to some extent, sometimes more, sometimes less. Inasmuch as the soul pines for God and expresses love and fear of Him, its apprehension of God must be finite since the Divine is concealed from it. The mitzvot, on the other hand, are a revelation of God's will, which is intrinsically boundless.

Yet this epistle is referring not to the mitzva performance itself but rather to its reward. As the author of the *Tanya* explains below, in essence the reward for a mitzva, the principal, is as much an infinite divine flow as the mitzva itself.

---

is a revelation of God's intrinsic, infinite will. Since the infinite is revealed in the mitzva, it expresses that which is infinite within the finite vessels that constitute the worlds.

עוֹשֶׂה תָּמִיד לְהַחֲיוֹת הָעוֹלָמוֹת,

is literally God's commandment, that which the Holy One, blessed be He, Himself in His glory constantly performs to sustain the worlds,

God gives life to all the worlds as an act of charity. The mitzva of charity is unconditional giving. It is giving that is not limited by the recipient's merit or by what he will give back in return. This is the type of giving performed by God, who is infinite and besides whom there is no other. In relation to God, all the worlds are as nothing and without value. Nothing obligates Him to give. All of existence and life exist solely due to His infinite charity and kindness. Moreover, the author of the *Tanya* adds, God gives "constantly" because the life and existence of the world must be constantly renewed at every moment in order for reality to continue to exist. ☞

THE CHARITY OF GOD

☞ The charity that God performs in giving life to the worlds is referred to as a mitzva, a "commandment," although there is no one to command God. Perhaps the reason is that just as a mitzva is distinguished from other acts by the fact that it expresses God's deep, intrinsic will, so too the life force that God grants all worlds, all the way down to our lowly world, expresses His intrinsic will, because His essential, supernal will inheres in it.

It is true that our Sages state that God keeps not just the mitzva of charity but all the mitzvot (see, e.g., *Berakhot* 6a). But that statement refers only to God's inserting His inner will into the minutiae of existence, each mitzva occupying its own niche, with a unique root and essence. By contrast, God's charity sustains created reality itself. Also, regarding all other mitzvot, the descent of the Divine depends on a person's performance of the mitzva. In that sense, the mitzva is a bond – a *tzavta* – between God's actions and man's actions. But God's charity is different. It is an act of unconditional kindness that sustains and vivifies the lower worlds, and in that sense, it is uniquely and literally God's mitzva.

Moreover, a human being performs the mitzva of giving charity like God, when he awakens the attribute of kindness and compassion in his heart. For a human being too the mitzva of charity differs from the other mitzvot because charity constitutes the inner essence of all the mitzvot that a person performs. Regarding every non-mitzva act that a person performs, there is a mundane rationale: He needs it, he gains pleasure from it, and so forth. That is not the case regarding a mitzva, or, at least, when a person performs it with the proper intent, for the sake of Heaven. By definition, a mitzva has no mundane rationale, so it constitutes an act of charity in the sense that it is like an undeserved gift that the person gives to the world and to the Divine Presence.

וְיַעֲשֶׂה לֶעָתִיד בְּיֶתֶר שְׂאֵת וְעֹז, **and He will do so in the future with greater magnitude and greater power,**

At the time of the resurrection of the dead, there will be a mighty and powerful revelation of the divine life force in the worlds. At present, there is only sufficient life force to maintain the worlds as they are. Should that vitality increase, the worlds would be subsumed within the revelation of the Divine. But in the future, when the world, and man in particular, will be able to contain a greater magnitude of life force, there will be an immensely powerful revelation.

וּכְמוֹ שֶׁכָּתוּב: "וְשָׁמְרוּ דֶּרֶךְ ה' לַעֲשׂוֹת צְדָקָה כו'" (בראשית יח, יט). **as it is written, "And they will observe the way of the Lord, to perform charity** and justice..." (Gen. 18:19).

Charity is "the way of the Lord" – the path on which God Himself sets forth from the supernal hidden place of His might and pours forth lifegiving sustenance and is revealed in the world. This path opens up through the mitzvot in general, and through the mitzva of charity in particular.[4] In light of this, the verse "They will observe the way of the Lord" means that when a person performs the mitzvot, and when he gives charity in particular, he keeps and maintains the channel through which the flow and revelation of the Divine may pour forth. Moreover, they prepare and build the powerful and mighty channel through which God will one day be revealed. ☞

THE WAY OF GOD

☞ On a higher level, the "way of God" is the way in which the infinite, boundless, indefinable divine light descends to the name of *Havaya*. The name of *Havaya* is the beginning and root of reality, of all of existence, since the letters of the name represent the process of creation (the *yod* represents constriction, the *heh*, expansion, the *vav*, a drawing down; see *Torah Or* 41a, 61d; *Iggeret HaTeshuva*, chap. 4). Thus, the way of God is first and foremost the hidden path from the undefined

4. Elsewhere the mitzvot are called "the limbs of the King." Just as a person's limbs draw the life force of the soul into the body, so do the mitzvot draw the Divine life force into the world. See *Likkutei Amarim*, chap. 23; *Likkutei Torah*, Ex. 3b.

כְּמוֹ דֶּרֶךְ שֶׁהוֹלְכִים בָּהּ מֵעִיר לְעִיר עַל דֶּרֶךְ מָשָׁל, כָּךְ הַצְּדָקָה הִיא בְּחִינַת גִּילּוּי וְהֶאָרַת אוֹר אֵין סוֹף בָּרוּךְ הוּא, סוֹבֵב כָּל עָלְמִין, שֶׁיָּאִיר וְיִתְגַּלֶּה עַד עוֹלָם הַזֶּה,

Metaphorically speaking, like a road on which people **travel from one city to another, so too charity is the revelation and illumination of the light of *Ein Sof*, blessed be he, which encompasses all worlds so that it may shine and manifest itself** even **as far as this world**

In order to travel from one place to another, there is a road that one must take. Likewise, in the spiritual realm, there are stages and the manner in which something is brought about.

Charity makes it possible for the infinite divine light, a light that encompasses all worlds, to shine on this world and be revealed in it. It is therefore "the way of God" – the way in which the unlimited encompassing light of *Ein Sof* is drawn into this finite world. The entire world and its creations are literally nothingness in relation to the light of *Ein Sof*. But charity can leap over boundaries, so that it vivifies even the one who has nothing to give in return, whether that is a creation, a person, or the lowly world. Charity alone can cross that gap, can bind the light that encompasses all worlds with the light that fills all worlds.

Charity makes it clear that the road from above to below consists of giving and revealing. But that is not enough, because that which is below must be capable of receiving. How can the infinite light of *Ein Sof* be received and revealed in a world that is finite?

בְּאִתְעָרוּתָא דִלְתַתָּא בְּתוֹרַת צְדָקָה וְחֶסֶד חִנָּם,

through an awakening from below that evokes God's **charity and undeserved kindness,**

The author of the *Tanya* now returns to the statement he made at the beginning of the letter: that the giving that comes from the source of compassion in order to pour forth the "fruits" and "principal" flows

and unfathomable *Ein Sof* to the initial framework of creation, the name of *Havaya*, and from that name the flow descends to all the worlds in a cause-and-effect progression.

forth as a result of an awakening from below. Only when a person arouses the trait of kindness and compassion in his heart, when he extends himself and breaks through his own boundaries and gives charitably and kindly to someone in need, can he receive the illumination of *Ein Sof* in the manner of charity and undeserved kindness from above. ☞

לֶעָתִיד, בִּתְחִיַּית הַמֵּתִים בְּיֶתֶר שְׂאֵת וְיֶתֶר עָז לְאֵין קֵץ מִבְּחִינַת גִּילּוּי (הָאָרָה) [הַהֶאָרָה] בְּגַן עֵדֶן הַתַּחְתּוֹן וְהָעֶלְיוֹן.

in the future, at the time of the **resurrection of the dead, with infinitely greater magnitude and greater power than the illumination in the lower and higher Garden of Eden.**

The powerfully intense illumination of *Ein Sof* will occur only in the future. The present time is in essence a time of action, of performing the commandments, whereas the time to receive reward through the revelation of the Divine for the deeds that were performed is in the future. The present is not the proper time for such a revelation. On the contrary, proper deeds can be performed to perfection only out of concealment. Only when we do not appreciate a deed's greatness and significance can we perform it with pure intentions. In the future time of revelation, then, there will be no more mitzvah performance.

In this context, the term "future" generally has two meanings: the

THE ILLUMINATION OF *EIN SOF* THROUGH AN AWAKENING FROM BELOW

☞ This is apparently an internal contradiction. If the illumination of *Ein Sof* depends on an awakening from below, which entails doing acts of kindness and performing kindness, then the illumination could not be considered charity and undeserved kindness. Yet in order for *Ein Sof* to pour forth its abundance from above, it must do so specifically through charity and undeserved kindness, and in order for a person's soul to be able to receive that illumination, there must be a parallel awakening from below. Both these dynamics come about through an act of charity. The awakening from below is the charity that a person gives, particularly when he arouses in his heart the trait of compassion to give an undeserved gift. Yet any charity that a person gives is necessarily limited. Although God's charity was prompted by the awakening from below, its measure is far beyond the quantity that a person can possibly bestow. It is only at its essence, in its quality, that a person's act of charity can be compared at all to the charity of God.

future of an individual and the future of the world. The future of an individual refers to the stage that follows physical life in this world, when the body expires and the soul ascends to the Garden of Eden.[5] Once the soul is no longer in the body, it is not limited by the body's boundaries, and it can receive illumination and revelation beyond that which it could have received while in the body. Yet this revelation still remains intrinsically limited. While the Garden of Eden is in a loftier realm than our world of *Asiya,* while it exists in the worlds of *Yetzira* (as the lower Garden of Eden) and *Beria* (as the higher Garden of Eden), these worlds are not infinite, and neither is the revelation that these worlds can contain. The infinite revelation that the epistle speaks of here will occur only in the future of the entire world, at the time of the resurrection of the dead.

The existence of every soul in the Garden of Eden is intrinsically no different from its previous existence in this world. That which is revealed in the Garden of Eden is essentially that which exists in this world, except that in this world we cannot see it because of external limitations such as the physical body. The statement made in a number of texts that in the Garden of Eden the righteous rise from level to level, from the lower level of the Garden of Eden to the higher level of the Garden of Eden and onward, refers to the attainment of an increasingly profound and refined revelation.

In contrast to life after death, there is the time of the resurrection of the dead. Although it is apparently a return of a sort to the existence of this world, of the soul in the body, it will be an entirely different existence, a different world, where that which could not be revealed in the present world will be revealed in the next world, the world of the resurrection.

שֶׁהֲרֵי כָּל נִשְׁמוֹת הַצַּדִּיקִים וְהַתַּנָּאִים וְהַנְּבִיאִים, שֶׁהֵם עַתָּה בְּגַן עֵדֶן הָעֶלְיוֹן בְּרוּם הַמַּעֲלוֹת, יִתְלַבְּשׁוּ בְּגוּפוֹתֵיהֶם לֶעָתִיד וְיָקוּמוּ בִּזְמַן הַתְּחִיָּה לֵיהָנוֹת מִזִּיו הַשְּׁכִינָה.

That is **because all the souls of the righteous, the *tanna'im,* and the prophets, who are currently in the higher** level of the **Garden of Eden, in the most elevated heights, will in the future be clothed in their bodies and will rise at the time of the resurrection to enjoy the radiance of the Divine Presence.**

5. See Rambam, *Mishneh Torah, Sefer HaMadda, Hilkhot Teshuva* 8:8.

The proof for this is that the revelation and reward at the time of the resurrection of the dead will be loftier than that of the Garden of Eden. Not only those who are alive in this world but also the souls in the Garden of Eden, including souls on its highest level, will experience the resurrection. ☞

The resurrection will pertain to various types of souls, such as the souls of the righteous, the *tanna'im,* and the prophets, whose service and level in this world were very high.[6] Their spiritual level and service in this world resulted in a corresponding level of revelation in the Garden of Eden. In the future resurrection, they will be clothed once again in their bodies and rise to enjoy the radiance of God's presence. The level of revelation at the time of the resurrection of the dead that they will experience will be even higher than that of all of the levels of the Garden of Eden. ☞

THE TIME OF THE RESURRECTION

☞ According to Kabbala (see, e.g., Ramban, *Sha'ar HaGemul*), the World to Come is the state of reality that will come about after the resurrection of the dead, which will occur at the end of time. Souls will return to their bodies, not in the way they occupy the body in the present, but in a more refined manner; the common denominator will only be the connection between the body and the soul. According to this conception, the Garden of Eden is an intermediary stage in which souls that have completed a certain stage in this world wait, perfect themselves, and prepare for the future.

ENJOYING THE RADIANCE OF THE DIVINE PRESENCE

☞ This description of reward at the time of the resurrection, "to enjoy the radiance of the Divine Presence," applies in a certain sense to all reward, because the payment of reward is the benefit, physical or spiritual, that a person receives from the work that he has done. Reward is like the answer to a question, the response to a prior stage and its completion. This is always the stage of enjoyment and pleasure. In every creative endeavor, for instance, whether in the realm of music, literature, and other creations, there is an initial stage in which expectations are built and tension develops. This stage does not necessarily bring pleasure, and it even makes demands of a

---

6. The Lubavitcher Rebbe, Rabbi Menaḥem Mendel Schneerson, states that "the righteous" refers principally to the quality reached by keeping the commandments, "*tanna'im*" refers to the level reached by Torah study, and "prophets" refers to a revelation of the Divine.

לְפִי שֶׁהַהֶאָרָה וְהַגִּילּוּי שֶׁבְּגַן עֵדֶן הִיא בְּחִינַת 'מְמַלֵּא כָּל עָלְמִין',

This is **because the illumination and revelation of the Garden of Eden is that which fills all worlds,**

The principal difference between the divine revelation in the Garden of Eden and the revelation at the time of the resurrection of the dead is that the revelation in the Garden of Eden involves only the light that fills all worlds, whereas the revelation at the time of the resurrection involves the light that encompasses all worlds. ☞

שֶׁהוּא בְּחִינַת הִשְׁתַּלְשְׁלוּת מִמַּדְרֵגָה לְמַדְרֵגָה עַל יְדֵי צִמְצוּמִים עֲצוּמִים.

which descends **in a chain of progression from one level to another by means of immense constrictions.**

person. But this is followed by the fulfillment of the expectations, by a release of the tension. That stage reveals the pleasure in the creative process. Furthermore, this reward is drawn down from the loftiest plane through that effort. As in the soul, the deepest yet most transcendent aspect of anything is the intrinsic pleasure that results from all that effort and is manifest below.

THE LIGHT THAT FILLS ALL WORLDS AND THE LIGHT THAT ENCOMPASSES ALL WORLDS

☞ There are two levels of the divine light: that which fills all worlds and that which encompasses all worlds. The relationship between them is one of the most discussed topics in the writings of the author of the *Tanya*, and it is infused in almost every comparative analysis that he makes. Since all of existence constitutes a combination of lights and vessels, this classification describes the initial relationship of the light to the vessel: There is light that enters a vessel, which gives definition to the light, and there is light that does not enter a vessel and so is not defined by it. The light that fills all worlds is that which vivifies and sustains all of existence, and the light that encompasses all worlds transcends it.

The relationship between these lights also informs the dynamic of reality on all levels: between inside and outside, finite and infinite, hidden essence and illuminated revelation. This classification also expresses the essential difference between the revelation of the Garden of Eden and the revelation of the time of the resurrection: between the revelation of the light as it relates to the worlds and which is given definition in them, and the light that transcends the existence of the worlds and is presently concealed from them only to be revealed in the future, within the new reality that will exist after the resurrection of the dead.

The light that fills all worlds in the Garden of Eden descends progressively through the worlds from level to level as a result of immense constrictions. At its essence it is the divine light that originates in *Ein Sof*, powerful and immeasurably vast beyond anything that the worlds can contain or apprehend. In order for this light to fill the worlds, to enter into their parameters and limitations, it must undergo many powerful constrictions. This entails constrictions not only in the passage from *Ein Sof*, which is beyond all the worlds, to the worlds, but from one world to the next, from the high spiritual worlds, which are almost transparent to *Ein Sof*, to the physical world of action, where the Divine is totally concealed. There are many levels, and each one almost entirely conceals and constricts the one above it. The descent of the divine light from one world to another is described as "a descent in a chain of progression from one level to another by means of immense constrictions."

וּכְמַאֲמַר רַבּוֹתֵינוּ ז״ל (מנחות כט, ב): בְּיוּ״ד נִבְרָא עוֹלָם הַבָּא.

This is in keeping with our Rabbis' statement "The World to Come was created with the letter ***yod***" (*Menaḥot* 29b).

Our Sages' reference to the World to Come that was created with the letter *yod* refers to the Garden of Eden, where the light of *Ein Sof* is so constricted that if there is any greater constriction there would be no light at all. This constriction, then, is compared to the letter *yod*, which is no more than a point.

The letters are God's tool of creation, just as letters are our means of speech. Just as the letters that we speak create meaning and messages, so do the letters of divine speech create the existence of the worlds and their meaning. As described at length in *Sha'ar HaYiḥud VeHa'emunah*, there are foundational letters that set the parameters for the world. These are then divided into many letters and combinations of letters that create the minutiae of creations in the worlds. One of the descriptions of these foundational letters is the Sages' statement that the World to Come was created with the letter *yod*.

The letter *yod* signifies constriction, in keeping with the form of the letter *yod*, which is essentially a point. The point, unlike the other letters, which have length and breadth, connotes maximal constriction. If the World to Come was created with the letter *yod*, this means that the World to Come was created with maximal constriction. The World to Come is the world in which the divine light is revealed to us, yet due to the limitations of creation, this revelation constitutes the greatest constriction possible of that infinite light. The human soul does not have the capacity to handle anything more.

וְהִיא בְּחִינַת חָכְמָה עִילָּאָה, **This is the level of supernal wisdom,**

The letter *yod* represents the *sefira* of *Ḥokhma*.[7] Like the *yod*, it is a *sefira* without dimensions, without area, without a vessel. *Ḥokhma* is spoken of as a point, a spark, a pulse, a flash of light that intrinsically cannot be grasped and defined. Before the illumination of *Ḥokhma* is absorbed into the *sefirot* below it, it cannot be grasped, neither by the intellect nor by experience. It is only a beginning, the initiation of the process of progressive descent and revelation.

הַנִּקְרֵאת ׳עֵדֶן הָעֶלְיוֹן׳, **which is called "supernal Eden,"**

According to hasidic teachings,[8] "Eden," "garden," and "river" are not one and the same realm but rather represent different levels and stages of revelation. As the verse states, "A river emerged from Eden to water the garden" (Gen. 2:10). "Eden" is the point of *Ḥokhma*. The "river" alludes to the point of *Ḥokhma* being drawn forth and expanded, to *Bina*, which broadens and spreads out from the point of *Ḥokhma* and even splits into various paths and ways. The "garden" is *Malkhut*, the place of revelation. At any rate, the starting point, the kernel from which the revelation of the Garden of Eden on all levels begins, is the point of *Ḥokhma*, which is called "supernal Eden."

הַמִּשְׁתַּלְשֶׁלֶת וּמִתְלַבֶּשֶׁת בְּכָל הָעוֹלָמוֹת, **which is progressively clothed in all the worlds,**

---

7. In the name *Havaya*, the *yod* corresponds to *Ḥokhma*, the first *heh* corresponds to *Bina*, the *vav* corresponds to *Tiferet* (or *Zeir Anpin*, which encompasses the six emotive *sefirot*), and the final *heh* corresponds to *Malkhut*.

8. *Likkutei Torah*, Song 39b; see also *Sefer HaMa'amarim Melukat*, vol. 4, p. 185.

Ḥokhma is the transfer point between *Ein Sof* and the worlds; it transmits the light of *Ein Sof* to the worlds. Since *Ein Sof* is the sole source of life and existence, *Ḥokhma* is not only the initial point of the progressive descent of that light, but it exists and is clothed in every point in the worlds as the source of their existence and life force.

כְּמוֹ שֶׁכָּתוּב: ״כּוּלָּם בְּחָכְמָה עָשִׂיתָ כו׳״ (תהלים קד, כד), וְ״הַחָכְמָה תְּחַיֶּה כו׳״ (קהלת ז, יב).

as it is written, "With wisdom You have made them all…" (Ps. 104:24), **and "Wisdom grants life** to its possessors…" (Eccles. 7:12).

The beginning of everything, which comes from above, which exists and gives life to every world and every entity down to the lowest level, is the point of *Ḥokhma*.

The two verses quoted here express two ways of viewing *Ḥokhma*: one from above and one from below. "With wisdom You have made them all" is the perspective from above, from *Ein Sof*. In relation to *Ein Sof*, *Ḥokhma* is compared to an action.[9] Analogously, the faculty of action is the lowest faculty, in comparison to willpower, thoughts, or speech. The life force that a person's actions receives from his soul is extremely diminished and constricted, almost negligent when compared to the soul itself. So too *Ḥokhma*, as viewed from above, is like a constricted action in comparison to the levels that exist beyond *Ḥokhma*.

The second verse, "Wisdom grants life to its possessors," expresses the view from below. In relation to the worlds below, *Ḥokhma* is the supernal source that gives life to everything. ☞

וּבְגַן עֵדֶן הִיא בִּבְחִינַת גִּילּוּי הַהַשָּׂגָה

In the Garden of Eden, this wisdom **is manifestly comprehensible**

ḤOKHMA AS AN INTERMEDIARY

☞ Alternatively, it is possible to say that since *Ḥokhma* is the bond and intermediary between above and below, between the light that encompasses all worlds and

9. Note that the word *asita*, "you have made," from the verse and the word for action, *asiya*, share the same root.

Ḥokhma exists in everything, but in the Garden of Eden, it becomes comprehensible. The Garden of Eden is not necessarily a different place. At most, it is merely a spiritual plane. That is to say, it is a place where the soul exists like a scout in his outpost, seeing and comprehending everything that it could not see before. ☞

לְכָל חַד לְפוּם שִׁיעוּרָא דִילֵיהּ. **to each person according to his capacity.**

the light that fills all worlds, it is, like every intermediary, comprised of both planes. "With wisdom You have made them all" expresses the level of the light that encompasses all worlds, and "Wisdom grants life to its possessors" expresses the level of the light that fills all worlds, the divine light that is clothed in everything and gives life to everything.

THE MANIFEST COMPREHENSIBILITY OF THE GARDEN OF EDEN

☞ To comprehend anything, we need certain tools and implements. A person attains an insight in the same way that he digests food. Just as the food must first undergo physical and chemical changes before it can be absorbed and integrated into the body, spiritual concepts must undergo changes, to be broken down so that they will be in alignment with the faculties of his soul so that they may connect to it. In this world, the soul exists in the body with the body's perceptions. It lives in this world, sees this world's images, and hears the deafening voice of this multiplicitous world, which whispers, "I am reality!"

But in the Garden of Eden, when the soul is liberated from the body and distanced from this voice, it can see things more closely and more clearly. It no longer needs to apprehend everything as they are crushed and molded into the forms of this world, but as they are, at their essence: as divine light and revelation.

The atmosphere of the Garden of Eden actually hovers around every person at all times. All his good thoughts and speech as expressed through Torah study and mitzvot are impressed into that atmosphere (see epistle 27). But since a person exists in this world, he cannot absorb these matters. He cannot see, experience, or take delight in them. Although they are connected to him and relate to him and to his life, they encompass him, hovering around him, so that his soul is not aware of them nor does he sense them. Being in the Garden of Eden means being in a situation in which one can assimilate and experience these matters. But even while in this world and while in the body, a person's soul may become so sensitive and refined that he can experience something of his Garden of Eden.

Moreover, every time the soul rises from a lower level in the Garden of Eden to a higher level of the Garden of Eden, the soul moves to a different state, where it can then receive a higher level of insight and experience from the atmosphere of the Garden of Eden around him. All such ascents occur in his personal lower and higher Garden of Eden. Every ascent constitutes a more profound and more refined insight and internalization of those matters.

The insight gained in the Garden of Eden is not the same for everyone. Every person's experience in the Garden of Eden is in a manner and on a level unique to him. This is also the case in a physical place: Each person experiences it in a manner unique to him. Even more, if the Garden of Eden is a state of revelation, that revelation exists for each person in accordance with his capacity to perceive it, in accordance with his attributes, ability, background, circumstances, and so forth. In light of this, there is not a single Garden of Eden, but each person has his own personal Garden of Eden, which he attains in accordance with his ability and situation at that time, ascending one level after another.

כַּנּוֹדָע שֶׁעוֹנֶג הַנְּשָׁמוֹת בְּגַן עֵדֶן הוּא מֵהַשָּׂגַת סוֹדוֹת הַתּוֹרָה,

As is known, the pleasure of the souls in the Garden of Eden stems from the apprehension of the secrets of the Torah,

The delight and pleasure that is experienced in the Garden of Eden is the delight of apprehension. The soul's capacity for delight may be on a very high level, on the level of *Keter*, which is higher than the intellectual apprehension with which the Garden of Eden is associated. But it is manifest through the apprehension and senses of the internal faculties of the soul.[10] Delight in itself encompasses the soul. It is a mystical secret that does not reveal itself, but rather is revealed when this secret is apprehended, when a person understands something, when he acquires it intellectually and experientially. Then he experiences the delight that was concealed within it. Every time a person attains a secret that was hidden from him, he uncovers the delight that was hidden there, which constitutes a higher level of the Garden of Eden. ☞

THE SECRETS OF THE TORAH, THE SECRETS OF DIVINITY

☞ The author of the *Tanya* does not refer to trivial secrets but "the secrets of the Torah," which is the innermost, greatest secret that the world conceals: the Creator God Himself. The divine life force that gives life and existence to all things is hidden in everything, in every detail in the world. The revelation of this divine secret on all levels of the world results in pleasure that has no equal in this-worldly insights but exists only in the insights of the Garden of Eden.

10. See *Zohar* 3:178:2; *Torah Or* 11b.

שֶׁעָסַק בָּעוֹלָם הַזֶּה בְּנִגְלֶה, which comes from **the revealed** aspect of the Torah **that one studied in this world,**

How does a person attain the revelation of the secrets in the Garden of Eden? After all, it is explained that on all levels of the Garden of Eden, a person does not learn or understand anything new. He only apprehends on higher levels that which he had already understood before. But a person can attain that initial understanding of the Torah only in this world through his study of its revealed aspects. Even if a person studies the hidden aspects of the Torah, he does not have an actual idea of what he is studying. He recites the words and thinks about abstract concepts and relates them to each other, but he does not actually know what it all means. The only way a person can attain actual insight into divine matters is when they are clothed in matters of this world, in the revealed part of the Torah: trading a cow for a donkey, making fringes out of wool, and so on. Only when a person is in this world, when the soul is in the body living and experiencing this reality, can he grasp the divine intellect and will that are clothed in it. A person in this world knows exactly what a donkey and cow are, and when the Torah speaks about trading one for the other, he knows exactly what it is speaking about.

This apprehension in this reality only involves revealed matters, the infrastructures of this world that express the divine wisdom. It is not an apprehension of the deeper, internal aspects of things, of the Divine that is concealed within them. Such an apprehension cannot exist in a reality of action. It is impossible to both act and feel. A person who acts does not feel, and a person who feels cannot act. This also applies to the relationship between the life of this world and the life of the Garden of Eden. In this world, in which a person acts, where he studies and understands how to perform the mitzvot, he does not sense or understand the greatness and holiness of those actions. In the Garden of Eden, on the other hand, where he senses the greatness of the mitzvot he performed, he can no longer act. The only way a person can have an actual understanding and sense of the secrets of the Torah, then, is when he will be in the Garden of Eden. Then he will understand the secrets of the revealed parts of the Torah that he understood in this world. Only then will concrete understanding that came from the revealed aspects of Torah be connected to the divine secrets it contains and to the concealed delight that is now manifest. ☞

כִּדְאִיתָא בַּזֹּהַר הַקָּדוֹשׁ פָּרָשַׁת שְׁלַח (חלק ג קסג, א), וּבַגְּמָרָא (בבא מציעא פו, א) בְּעוּבְדָא דְּרַבָּה בַּר נַחְמָנִי.

as stated in the holy *Zohar, Parashat Shelaḥ* (1:163a), **and in the Talmud** (*Bava Metzia* 86a) **with regard to the incident involving Rabba bar Naḥmani.**

The *Zohar* describes souls studying Torah in the Garden of Eden, while the Talmud tells of a dispute in the heavenly yeshiva, in the Garden of Eden.[11] The dispute concerned the laws involving the identification of *tzara'at*, an affliction commonly translated as leprosy. If a person has a white spot on his skin in which a white hair subsequently grows, it is determined that he is afflicted with *tzara'at*, whereas if the white hair preceded the white spot, it is determined that he does not have *tzara'at*. But what if the matter is uncertain? What if it is not clear which came first, the spot or the hair? In that case, in the heavenly yeshiva God stated that it is not *tzara'at*, but the sages there disagreed and said that it is. The Talmud concludes that the heavenly yeshiva declared that the dispute would be decided by Rabba bar Naḥmani.

This episode indicates that the Torah is studied and understood in the Garden of Eden and that the topics studied there are the same as those studied in this world. Yet there Torah study is not the same as Torah study below. In Heaven, there is no body, no *tzara'at* of the body, no practical *halakha*, and no deeds. As stated in several hasidic

THE SECRET REVEALED IN THIS WORLD

☞ There is a principle that "their beginning is embedded in their end" (*Sefer Yetzira* 1:7). The loftiest secrets, which are not revealed in the intellect or the emotions, are clothed in deed. The roots of all of the secrets and revelations in all the worlds are embedded in the revealed aspects of the Torah, which involves the world of deed and physical matters. When a person studies the revealed aspects of the Torah in this world, he grasps both: the tangible understanding together with the deepest contents that are embedded in that understanding.

11. See *Torah Or* 81c.

teachings,[12] it appears that the study there concerns the lofty, spiritual aspect of these matters.

Every Torah matter devolves from the loftiest heights through all the worlds, until it reaches our low world. In each world, it has a reality and meaning congruent with the vessels and concepts of that world. The loftier the world, the loftier, more abstract, and more expansive the Torah study. But ultimately, when a decision must be reached, not only to experience these matters and understand them better, but to determine the practical *halakha*, to choose between dissenting opinions, one must descend to our world. One must ask Rabba bar Naḥmani, who is still living in this world and studying the revealed Torah and who therefore comprehends the tangibility of these matters, because they are relevant to him.

Revelation in the Garden of Eden is indeed revelation, but that revelation does not involve the matters themselves, only their manifestations, the light that fills all worlds: the constricted illumination that is grasped and revealed in the vessels and parameters of the worlds.

But the revelation of the light at the time of the **resurrection of the dead will be on the level of** the light that **encompasses all worlds,**

אֲבָל גִּילּוּי הַהֶאָרָה שֶׁבִּתְחִיַּית הַמֵּתִים יִהְיֶה מִבְּחִינַת 'סוֹבֵב כָּל עָלְמִין',

The revelation at the time of the resurrection of the dead will be a divine light that transcends and encompasses all the worlds. The revelation of this light cannot exist in this world or in any world but only in the other reality that will exist at the time of the resurrection of the dead.

which is not characterized by constriction, measure, and limit, but is unlimited and infinite,

שֶׁאֵינָהּ בִּבְחִינַת צִמְצוּם וְשִׁיעוּר וּגְבוּל אֶלָּא בְּלִי גְּבוּל וְתַכְלִית,

The illumination that will be revealed in the future will be loftier than all parameters and boundaries. It will come from the light that encompasses all worlds, prior to the constrictions that generated the parameters of the worlds. This means that this will be a totally

12. See *Likkutei Torah*, Lev. 22b.

different category of revelation that is nothing like what we know and comprehend in today's reality. Indeed, in our world, it is hard to fathom how there can be such a revelation. We do not even have a metaphor for it. Nevertheless, it is possible to think of it as roughly analogous to the soul's comprehension of itself, not of the functions of the soul or the faculties of the soul, but the essence of the soul. Such a revelation is not in keeping with what we presently know and understand, the knowledge of that which is outside ourselves, which must be clothed in the parameters of our comprehension. Instead, it will be roughly analogous to our comprehension and knowledge of ourselves.

כְּמוֹ שֶׁנִּתְבָּאֵר בְּלִקּוּטֵי אֲמָרִים פֶּרֶק מ״ח בֵּיאוּר עִנְיַן ׳סוֹבֵב כָּל עָלְמִין׳, שֶׁאֵינוֹ כְּמַשְׁמָעוֹ כְּמוֹ עִיגּוּל חַס וְשָׁלוֹם, אֶלָּא שֶׁאֵינוֹ בִּבְחִינַת הִתְלַבְּשׁוּת וכו׳, וְעַיֵּין שָׁם הֵיטֵב.

as explained in *Likkutei Amarim*, chapter 48, with regard to **the meaning of the concept** of the light that **encompasses all worlds, that this is not in accordance with its plain meaning,** that the worlds are **like a sphere, God forbid. Rather, it** means that this light **cannot be enclothed** in the apprehension of a person's thoughts and intellectual understanding, **and so on. See there in depth.**

Likkutei Amarim discusses the problem of misinterpreting the concept of the light that encompasses all worlds, which results from thinking of that light in terms of physical phenomena. One might think that it is a sort of physical entity that encircles from the outside and not from within (an error that may be supported by images of spheres that exist in some kabbalistic works). But a person who thinks only in such terms can by no means understand the spiritual concept of the light that encompasses all worlds.

The author of the *Tanya* goes on to explain the concepts of the light that encompasses all worlds and the light that fills all worlds in terms we can understand: The light that fills all worlds refers to that which is clothed within our receptacles and faculties of the soul, whereas the light that encompasses all worlds refers to that which is not clothed in them because it is beyond their ability to classify it, beyond any classification at all. But unlike the physical understanding of something that encompasses, this does not mean that the encompassing light does not exist within the worlds but rather only without.

That we do not see or sense the encompassing light does not mean that it is not present. On the contrary, the encompassing light is everywhere, and within every entity it is even more significant than the reality of the light that fills all worlds. The light that fills all worlds relates to particular characteristics, to parameters that one must contemplate in order to recognize and identify them. But the light that encompasses all worlds constitutes the essential existence of a thing. This light does not exist as a constricted light that can be comprehended, but it exists within the essence of entities, as something in itself. Yet at present, our intellect cannot grasp this light. It will only be able to do so in the future, with the resurrection of the dead, when there will be an intrinsic revelation of the soul in the body, as well as an intrinsic revelation of the light of *Ein Sof*, the light that encompasses all worlds. ☞

NOT LIKE A SPHERE

☞ The discussion in *Likkutei Amarim* is emblematic of the problem of abstracting kabbalistic concepts from their physicality, a problem that is addressed extensively in Chabad literature. The concepts we think, like the words we speak, are taken from physical reality or from what relates to physical reality. This is not to say that they do not apply at all to the spiritual realm, but that the way that they are understood there is different.

Our thinking begins in physical existence. That is the starting point in the development of most human beings. The more we think about abstract entities that are separate from physicality, the greater effort we require to disengage ourselves from the physical meaning of words and concepts. We must learn to relate to these concepts differently, to apply a different understanding and context.

This problem, which relates to all abstract thought, is especially acute with regard to Kabbala. Kabbala is not based on a logical development of thought starting from any known point, but on the acceptance of axiomatic assertions. It is expressed through its own conceptual frameworks. Although it uses the same words as those used to describe the physical world, and the relationship among the phenomena described by these words even reflects similar relationships in the physical world, they are entirely different. There is then a concern that the concepts will be misunderstood, that wrong conclusions will be reached. As long as a person's study of Kabbala is confined to abstract, self-enclosed structures of thought in their relationship with each other (as in a number of approaches to studying Kabbala), the likelihood of these matters being mis-

25 Elul

22 Elul (leap year)

וְזֶהוּ שֶׁאָמְרוּ רַבּוֹתֵינוּ ז"ל (ברכות יז, א): "וְעַטְרוֹתֵיהֶם בְּרָאשֵׁיהֶם וְנֶהֱנִין כו'". 'עֲטָרָה' הִיא בְּחִינַת מַקִּיף וְסוֹבֵב, וְנִקְרָא 'כֶּתֶר' מִלְּשׁוֹן כּוֹתֶרֶת.

This is the meaning of the Rabbis' statement regarding the World to Come: "The righteous sit **with their crowns upon their heads, enjoying** the splendor of the Divine Presence" (*Berakhot* 17a). **A crown is something that encompasses and surrounds, and it is called a *keter* in the same sense as a *koteret*,** the capital on top of a pillar.

The Sages' description of the righteous sitting with their crowns on their heads, enjoying the splendor of the Divine Presence, will occur in the future world, after the resurrection of the dead. A crown rests on top of the head, an analogy to the light that exists above and beyond the limited light that is revealed and clothed within the head. It is for this reason that the first *sefira* is called *Keter*, Crown, implying that it encompasses and encircles.[13] Just as the crown on a person's head is not one of his limbs and is not counted among his limbs, so too the *sefira* of *Keter* is separate from the other *sefirot*. Unlike *Keter*, the other *sefirot* are like vessels that contain the faculties of the intellect and the emotive attributes.

וְהוּא בְּחִינַת מְמוּצָּע הַמְחַבֵּר הֶאָרַת הַמַּאֲצִיל אֵין סוֹף בָּרוּךְ הוּא לְהַנֶּאֱצָלִים.

The crown **is the intermediary that connects the light of the Emanator, *Ein Sof,* blessed be He, to the emanated beings,**

Keter is always an intermediary between worlds. For instance, *Keter* of the world of *Beria* is also *Malkhut* of *Atzilut*. Beyond the worlds, *Keter*

understood is small, But as soon as a person attempts to understand these matters deeply and abstractly, and he attempts to reach practical and personal conclusions from them – as Hasidism does – he must be more careful and more cognizant that they may be misperceived.

13. Elsewhere, we find other reasons for the name *Keter*; see *Likkutei Torah*, Lev. 69a. The author of the *Tanya*, however, focuses on the connotation of encompassment since that is the focus of the discussion here.

is the intermediary between the Emanator and the emanated, between God Himself and the highest world, the world of *Atzilut*.

Every intermediary mediates between two sides. *Keter* too signifies two sides: above and below, that which relates to the Emanator and that which relates to the emanated. *Keter* is, on the one hand, that which encompasses and is separate from the other *sefirot*. In that sense, it relates to the Emanator. On the other hand, it is defined as something that encompasses and surrounds the specific *sefirot* of a particular soul, of a particular person, as indicated by the term "their crowns." In that way, it relates to emanated beings.

If *Keter* is the intermediary that connects the light of *Ein Sof* to creation, one could say that the light that is revealed though *Keter* stems from the essence of the Divine. It is not the constricted light manifest in His thought, speech, and deeds, nor even in His wisdom or understanding. This illumination cannot be clothed in any one of the soul's faculties, great though they may be. It can be contained only in the essence of a person's soul or in the unique expressions of the essence of his soul, such as pleasure and will.

וְלֶעָתִיד יָאִיר וְיִתְגַּלֶּה בָּעוֹלָם הַזֶּה לְכָל הַצַּדִּיקִים שֶׁיָּקוּמוּ בִּתְחִיָּה ("וְעַמֵּךְ כּוּלָּם צַדִּיקִים כו'" [ישעיה ס, כא]).

and in the future, that light **will shine and be revealed in this world for all the righteous who will rise with the resurrection** (and not only the righteous but every Jew, as it is written, **"And your people, they are all righteous;** they will inherit the land forever" [Isa. 60:21])

In the future, at the time of the resurrection, the revelation will be different. First, it will occur in this world and not in a spiritual world such as the Garden of Eden. It will occur in the place of the resurrection, where the souls will be restored to bodies. Furthermore, it will affect all souls of Israel, who will be resurrected. That is because not only the uniquely righteous will rise, but all Jews of all generations.[14] With the total rectification and culmination of the world, all divine souls will

14. See Mishna *Sanhedrin* 10:1. The Lubavitcher Rebbe, Rabbi Menaḥem Mendel Schneerson, comments, "This is the difference between the resurrection of the dead and the Garden of Eden. The entire nation does not merit the Garden of Eden."

return in a rectified state to the bodies in which they had existed, in which they had studied Torah and performed mitzvot in this world, and they will have achieved the loftiest level they could attain, so that the divine revelation will be manifest equally to all.

This is in contrast to the divine revelation that manifests in the Garden of Eden, which affects each individual differently, congruent with his deeds, comprehension, and way of life in this world. In the future, upon the resurrection of the dead, the divine revelation will be the same for everyone, and each individual will apprehend the divine essence in his particular state of perfection. ☞

וְזֶה שֶׁאָמְרוּ רַבּוֹתֵינוּ ז״ל (בבא בתרא עה, ב): ״עֲתִידִים צַדִּיקִים שֶׁיֹּאמְרוּ לִפְנֵיהֶם קָדוֹשׁ״.

That is the meaning of the Rabbis' statement "In the **future, the righteous will** have the name **Holy recited before them** by the angels" (*Bava Batra* 75b),

At the time of the resurrection, the stature of a soul in a body will be loftier than that of any other being. The angels, as the agents of creation who express the way the creation relates to God and praises Him, will relate to the souls in their bodies as holy.

כִּי קָדוֹשׁ הוּא בְּחִינַת מוּבְדָּל,

because holy signifies separate,

That which is holy is not only lofty, but it is so lofty that one cannot have a relationship with it. All one can say is that it is separate and beyond all that one could comprehend and express. The word "holy" thus expresses the praise of God Himself. Moreover, the angels will

ALL ARE RIGHTEOUS

☞ In hasidic teachings, this verse expresses the idea that a concept that applies at times to the righteous relates in a certain sense to the entire nation of Israel, and not only at the time of the resurrection but at all times (see *Torah Or* 80d). This is because every Jew possesses something of the tzaddik. The *beinoni* has the ability to be like the tzaddik, to be on the tzaddik's level, with the tzaddik's sensibilities. He possesses something of the powers that exist in the tzaddik. In the future, when all of existence will be rectified, the level of tzaddik will be manifest in each individual in actuality.

declare "holy" before the souls that are restored to their bodies, because these souls are loftier than the angels and separate from them, just as the Divine is loftier than the angels and all created beings.

שֶׁאֵינוֹ בְּגֶדֶר הַשָּׂגָה וָדַעַת,

meaning **that** holiness **is not within the realm of apprehension and knowledge,**

Something that can be comprehended and known is not separate. Intellectual apprehension, comprehending with wisdom and knowledge, is in the parameter of apprehension of light within a vessel: apprehension of reality within our limitations and parameters and a comprehension of the relationships between cause and effect, giver and recipient, and so forth. That which is holy and separate, on the other hand, is not within the parameters of apprehension and knowledge.

כִּי הוּא לְמַעְלָה מַעְלָה מִבְּחִינַת הַחָכְמָה וָדַעַת שֶׁבְּגַן עֵדֶן,

since it is above and beyond the wisdom and knowledge that can be attained **in the Garden of Eden,**

Apprehension in the Garden of Eden is apprehension with wisdom and knowledge, which is the apprehension of the light that fills all worlds. Just as supernal wisdom is the beginning of the penetration of this inner light into the worlds, wisdom enables the apprehension of this inner light within the soul, an apprehension that the soul attains in the Garden of Eden. There it comprehends everything that is related to the light that fills all worlds in accordance with its capacity to apprehend it, but nothing beyond that.

כִּי "הַחָכְמָה מֵאַיִן תִּמָּצֵא" כְּתִיב (איוב כח, יב).

as the verse states, "But wisdom, where will it be found?" (Job 28:12).

This verse can also be interpreted as saying that *Ḥokhma* comes from *ayin*, or nothingness,[15] the hidden source of *Ḥokhma*. *Ḥokhma* is "found" from *ayin*, not as a logical result of a completed process but as something that appears suddenly, not out of any rationale but out of

15. See *Zohar* 2:121a.

the nothingness. *Ḥokhma* is the beginning of the light's descent to this world. Above *Ḥokhma* is the hidden nothingness that has no cause.

הוּא בְּחִינַת כֶּתֶר עֶלְיוֹן הַנִּקְרָא 'אַיִן' בַּזּוֹהַר הַקָּדוֹשׁ.

This refers to supernal *Keter*, which is called *ayin*, nothingness, **in the holy *Zohar*.**

This *ayin*, this nothingness, that is beyond comprehension, is *Keter*. It is called nothingness, not because it is nonexistent, but because it is separate and cannot be apprehended and grasped by wisdom and the faculties of the soul.

Yet *Ḥokhma* is "found from *ayin*." *Ḥokhma* and what we can comprehend of it come from there, from the nothingness of *Keter*. In view of this, although *Keter* is hidden and separate from the soul's ability to apprehend it, it is nevertheless the source that pours forth the light and life force into the soul. The soul comprehends, though subconsciously and not with its conscious senses and faculties, that there is something hidden beyond its comprehension that is the source of what it comprehends with its wisdom and knowledge.

וְהַשְׁפָּעָתוֹ וְהֶאָרָתוֹ בִּבְחִינַת גִּילּוּי הוּא דַּוְקָא כְּשֶׁהַנְּשָׁמָה תִּתְלַבֵּשׁ בְּגוּף זַךְ וְצַח אַחַר הַתְּחִיָּיה,

The sustenance and light that flows through *Keter* **will be** manifest **in a revealed form specifically when the soul will be clothed in a pure, refined body after the resurrection,**

In the present, a person apprehends the Divine with the spiritual faculties of his soul, with his cognitive and emotive attributes. One cannot apprehend that which is beyond his intellect and his capacity for wisdom, the light of *Keter*, which encompasses all worlds. Yet what is stated here seems paradoxical, that only when the soul returns to the physical body will it comprehend that which is beyond even the soul's spiritual faculties.

But this is not really a paradox, as the author of the *Tanya* will explain below, but a deeper understanding of the body and materiality.

Notice that the author does not refer solely to the body but rather emphasizes that the body is "pure and refined," and it will happen "after the resurrection." At present, the body is coarse and impure. It only conceals and does not reveal the divine light at all. But after the resurrection, the fundamental reality of this world will change, and then the body, and the physical world as a whole, will be "pure and refined" to an extent that is hard for us to even imagine. There will be such an essential transformation that it is precisely what conceals the divine light in the present that will reveal it. What is presently impossible – the revelation of the encompassing light of *Ein Sof* – will be the new reality. ☞

THE RECTIFICATION OF THE SHATTERING OF THE VESSELS

☞ The resurrection of the dead and the fact that the body will be pure and refined, or rectified, are intrinsically connected. Hasidic teachings explain (see *Likkutei Torah*, Lev. 38c) that death is associated with sin, with the "shattering of the vessels" of the world of *tohu*, the world of chaos, whereas the resurrection is connected with the rectification of sin and of shattering in general. Death essentially constitutes a shattering of vessels (bodies), which can no longer hold and reveal the light (the soul). But when the vessels will be completely rectified, with the culmination of all this-worldly service of God, and the body will become pure and refined, revealing the light of the soul, the resurrection of the dead will occur. With the resurrection of the dead, the encompassing light of *Ein Sof* will be revealed (see *Torah Or* 53c; *Likkutei Torah*, Lev. 42b).

Originally, the vessels broke because they could not hold the vast light of the world of *tohu*, a spiritual realm that existed at the time of the Creation. The shattering of the vessels occurred as a result. But after the ultimate rectification, which will affect all of humanity and the entire world, the light that encompasses all worlds, which transcends the inner light that is clothed in the faculties of a person's soul, will shine and be revealed.

The revelation at the time of the resurrection of the dead will necessarily be a revelation of the light that encompasses all worlds. That is because the revelation will be that of the soul and body equally, and it is for this reason that they will be rejoined. The revelation that shines on both body and soul equally can only be that of the encompassing light. The inner light, which is revealed in the Garden of Eden and is manifest in this world, shines to different degrees in the different levels of the soul, and there is a difference in the way it is manifest in the body and the soul. There is a level of revelation that the soul can attain but the body cannot, as in the Garden of Eden. But the encompassing light is beyond and separate from all the levels of the worlds, and so when it is revealed, there is no difference between one level and another, between physicality and spirituality, between body and soul.

When a person receives the inner light, there is a relationship between giver and receiver. They are not separate from each other. That is not the case regarding the separate, encompassing light. There the relationship is necessarily one-sided in the sense that the vast and intense illumi-

כִּי נָעוּץ תְּחִלָּתָן בְּסוֹפָן (ספר יצירה פרק א משנה ז) דַּוְקָא,

because "their beginning is embedded in their end" (*Sefer Yetzira* 1:7), **specifically,**

We must still understand why the revelation of the encompassing light, a light whose existence preceded the beginning of the worlds, requires the soul to be contained in the body. Therefore, the author of the *Tanya* adds that "their beginning is embedded in their end" and not at the midway point. The beginning of everything, that which preceded all the worlds – which is *Keter*, that which encompasses all worlds – is connected to the end of all worlds, to the end of the present physical reality. In the language of Kabbala, this is the connection between *Keter* and *Malkhut*.[16] In terms of the soul, it is the connection between supernal will and deed.

Everything that occurs within a person begins in his abstract will, which has not yet clothed itself in any specific form; it cannot be explained and has no defined image. The will expresses itself through deed, which is the culmination of everything that occurs in the soul. The deed is always the end, the outcome, the reality that manifests at the culmination of everything.

Of course, this is not invariably the case in man. Not everything willed by a person reaches its culmination in a deed. There are impairments and errors and unrealized desires that prevent the deed from being carried out. There are deeds that do not express a person's initial will but evince a corruption that occurred on the way, resulting in a

nation is not made finite by the character of the recipient.

An analogy that parallels the revelation of the encompassing light in this world is what we call atmosphere. A person comes to a certain place and is affected by its special ambience. There is no particular intellectual message, information, or meaning that is absorbed and susceptible to critical analysis. Something abstract and ethereal is transmitted without any relationship to effort and preparation, completely unrelated to the ability of the receiver to receive. When something definite with specific meaning and parameters is transmitted, different people receive it in different ways. But when the encompassing light is transmitted, it makes no difference whether a recipient is more or less intelligent, whether he knows much or little, because the transmission does not pass through the recipient's vessels.

16. See epistle 20; *Torah Or* 3d.

debased love or fear, delusions of a particular aspect of reality and other such distorted outcomes. But for God, for whom everything in potential is also actual, for whom there is no "other" interpolating between His will and His deed, "their beginning is embedded in their end."

וְ"סוֹף מַעֲשֶׂה בְּמַחֲשָׁבָה תְּחִלָּה" כו' (׳לכה דודי׳) כַּנּוֹדָע.

and "last in deed, first in thought..." (*Lekha Dodi* liturgy), **as is known.**

This phrase, "last in deed, first in thought," is not just another way of saying "their beginning is embedded in their end." In a sense, it is the other side of the coin. On the one hand, the beginning is embedded in the end. On the other hand, the end is connected to the beginning. Not only is the beginning expressed and revealed in the end, but the end of the deed is intrinsically most fitting for revealing the beginning more than all the points in the middle.

This means that although the physical deed of a mitzva is coarse and conceals spirituality, which constitutes a revelation of the Divine, it is precisely the physical deed that expresses divinity that is loftier than spirituality. The spiritual worlds reveal the divine light within them, the divine light that gives them life, but they do not reveal the divine light itself, which transcends them and does not pass through them. On the other hand, it is in the material world of action, in which the divine light that gives it light and life is also concealed and where the reality above it cannot be revealed in it because the distance between them is too great, that the light of *Ein Sof* itself may be revealed – the light that exists above and beyond all these distances, that can leap across the unfathomably infinite distance and bring the physical world into existence.

אַךְ אִי אֶפְשָׁר לְהַגִּיעַ לְמַדְרֵגָה זוֹ עַד שֶׁיִּהְיֶה בְּגַן עֵדֶן תְּחִלָּה

Yet it is impossible to attain this level without first having been in the Garden of Eden

It is impossible to reach the level that will be attained at the time of the resurrection, when the encompassing light will be revealed, without first having been in the Garden of Eden.[17] The Garden of Eden is not

17. See *Torat Shmuel* (1869), p. 26.

only a waiting room in which souls pass the time until the resurrection of the dead. The Garden of Eden also prepares the soul for the ultimate, genuine, infinite revelation that is to come. Every revelation requires preparation, because the nature of revelation is to be received in vessels. Even if the light can flow forth from above, the vessels below must be prepared prior to the revelation to be able to contain it. Just as life in this world constitutes preparation for the revelation in the Garden of Eden, so too the Garden of Eden constitutes preparation for the revelation that will exist at the time of the resurrection. In the Garden of Eden, the soul rises without any barriers presented by the body. It apprehends more and more, rising level by level. It apprehends everything that can be apprehended with the light that fills all worlds, until it is capable of apprehending that which cannot be apprehended: the light that encompasses all worlds.

The ultimate knowledge associated with the light that fills all worlds is the knowledge of the existence of the light that encompasses all worlds, the knowledge of the vessels that prepare and prime a person to know the thing itself, that which is revealed in the light that encompasses all worlds. ☞

THE REVELATION OF THE LIGHT THAT ENCOMPASSES ALL WORLDS

☞ At present, the encompassing light cannot be apprehended. It encompasses everything and is the distillation of everything, yet transcends all recognizable, tangible entities. Analogously, the faculties in the soul that operate through the body are revealed in the various limbs of the body: in the eyes that see, in the feet that walk, in the mind that thinks. But the essence of life, and certainly the essence of the soul, cannot be revealed in any limb or specific faculty. In the same way, the encompassing light cannot be revealed in any level of any world. For this to happen, a change must take place not in one aspect of existence, but fundamentally in all of existence. Existence overall must be transformed into something else.

Such a change cannot happen on its own. Principally, it is a transformation that must come from above. But it must be preceded by preparation that thoroughly rectifies everything that can be rectified. In order to attain the impossible, we must first attain all that is possible. We must rectify everything that needs rectification, perfect every blemish, so that nothing will be left out, no detail will remain unfinished, no schism will remain unresolved. Only then, when everything is connected and brought together, can reality be overturned and transformed into something that never existed before, that once was impossible, that was previously unrealistic. This utter rectification and revelation within the faculties of the soul, within the emo-

לְהַשִּׂיג בְּחִינַת חָכְמָה עִילָּאָה (כו׳) [אֶפְשָׁר צָרִיךְ לוֹמַר: כָּל חַד] כְּפוּם שִׁיעוּרָא דִילֵיהּ.

so that one may attain supernal wisdom (and so on) [**perhaps** the text **is supposed to state "each individual"**] **according to his capacity.**

Supernal *Ḥokhma* is the inception of the divine revelation, just as it is the inception of every process in the soul, and its apprehension is the ultimate purpose and essence of what a person can comprehend.

Apparently, the parenthetical insertion "and so on," which seemingly has no meaning, should have said "each individual,"[18] meaning each person in accordance with his capacity. The revelation of supernal *Ḥokhma* in the Garden of Eden and the revelation of the light that fills all worlds in general is adapted to each person in keeping with his capacity, with his vessels' ability to contain it. This is the character of the light that fills all worlds: It fills and enters the vessels, and therefore its revelation and attainment are in keeping with each person's vessels that it fills, in keeping with the root of his soul and with the clarity of his intellect, his knowledge, and so on.

וּלְאַחֲרֵי כָּל זֶה יָקוּם בִּתְחִיַּית הַמֵּתִים עַל יְדֵי טַל תּוֹרָה, כְּמַאֲמַר רַבּוֹתֵינוּ ז״ל:

After all this, he will rise at the resurrection of the dead by means of the dew of Torah, in accord with our Rabbis' statement

This phrase appears to be missing from the published text of the epistle. The Lubavitcher Rebbe, Rabbi Menaḥem Mendel Schneerson, adds it at this point in the epistle, which shifts from discussing apprehension of the Divine in the Garden of Eden to apprehension of the Divine upon the resurrection of the dead.

"וְטַל תּוֹרָה מְחַיֵּיהוּ".

"The dew of Torah will revive him."

tive attributes and the intellect, in the life of this world and in the life of the Garden of Eden, must therefore precede the revelation of the encompassing light that will exist with the resurrection of the dead.

18. Based on a note of the Lubavitcher Rebbe, Rabbi Menaḥem Mendel Schneerson.

Here the author of the *Tanya* adds a new layer to the discussion. The supernal *Ḥokhma* that is revealed on all levels in all the worlds constitutes the Torah. Its revelation in the worlds comes about through Torah study, both in this world and in the Garden of Eden. Moreover, "whoever engages in the dew of the Torah, the dew of Torah will revive him."[19] Studying Torah in this world and in the Garden of Eden is not only a preparation for the resurrection of the dead, but it itself revives the dead.

The concept of the "dew of Torah" can also be explained in a different manner.[20] Dew, like rain, flows down from above. But unlike rain, dew does not cease, because it does not depend on the deeds of those below. In this sense, dew is the flow and illumination of the light that encompasses all worlds, which does not flow forth in accordance with the level of the recipient. From its perspective, physicality and spirituality, the body and the soul, heaven and earth, are all one. That illumination, which unites the opposing entities of body and soul, is what revives the dead.

Yet an aspect of this dew that will revive the dead in the future exists even now in the Torah. The Talmud recounts that when the Jewish people heard the Ten Commandments at Mount Sinai, their souls left their bodies, and God revived them with the dew that will revive the dead.[21] The giving of the Torah, and the Torah in general, thus possesses these two facets. On the one hand, it contains a revelation of the divine light that the soul cannot bear in its current state in this world, because the soul would expire and leave the body to be subsumed in the light. On the other hand, the Torah allows the body to hold on to the soul to receive the revelation without expiring.[22] ☞

THE REVIVAL OF THE SOUL WITH DEW

☞ These two aspects of the Torah constitute a concept called "running and returning" (see *Likkutei Torah*, Num. 56a, s.v. "*zot ḥukat*"). "Running" entails disconnecting from the world to cling to the Divine, while "returning" entails bring the Divine

19. *Yalkut Shimoni, Va'etḥanan* 824; *Tikkunei Zohar* 12a, 38b; see *Ketubot* 111b.
20. See *Likkutei Amarim*, chap. 36; *Likkutei Torah*, Lev. 49c.
21. *Shabbat* 88b.
22. It is for this reason that the Torah is called "might." See *Torah Or* 67a.

"וַהֲקִיצוֹתָ הִיא תְשִׂיחֶךָ כו'" (משלי ו, כב), וְדַי לַמֵּבִין.

Then, **"when you awaken, it will be your conversation…"** (Prov. 6:22). **This is sufficient** elaboration **for one who understands** the esoteric wisdom.

The author of the *Tanya* adds that after the resurrection of the dead, "when you awaken" in a soul and purified body, the Torah "will be your conversation."[23] A person's life force will stem from the Torah he studied in this world and in the Garden of Eden. Not only will the Torah raise the dead, but it will revive them, giving them their life force and sustenance through the light that encompasses all worlds.

After this analysis of the reward of a mitzva, the fruits of one's deeds in this world and the principal reward that remains for the World to Come, which is ultimately charity from God, the author of the *Tanya* returns to the topic with which he began: the mitzva of charity that a person performs. The charity that God performs is "the way of the Lord," the way in which God pours forth the infinite divine light and light force. The mitzva of charity that a person performs is the vessel in the world that can contain that light.

26 Elul וְזֶהוּ "רְחָבָה מִצְוָתְךָ מְאֹד" (תהלים קיט, צו) הִיא מִצְוַת הַצְּדָקָה,

This is the meaning of **"Your commandments are exceedingly wide"** (Ps. 119:96), that **it refers to the mitzva of charity**

The epistle began with two questions regarding this verse: Why is the word *mitzvatekha*, literally "Your commandment," in the singular, and

down to the world. Running involves apprehending the Torah in accordance with one's ability to apprehend, aspiring for higher and higher levels of apprehension. The return is the "dew" of Torah. Since the soul cannot attain a higher level without being subsumed, it returns and comes back down, drawing the divine light down with it. Therefore, it is specifically the return that provides the power and might that a person studying Torah receives in order to be able to receive divine revelation while his soul is still in his body in this world (see also *Torah Or* 66c, s.v. "*baḥodesh hashelishi*"). In the future as well, this power, which is called the dew of Torah, will revive the body and restore the soul upon the resurrection of the dead.

23. See *Torat Kohanim*, Lev. 18:4; Mishna *Avot* 6:9; *Sota* 21a; *Sifrei*, Deut. 34.

why is it described as "exceedingly wide"? The author of the *Tanya* addressed the first question at the beginning of the epistle, explaining that the verse refers specifically to the mitzva of charity. He now goes on to address the second question.

שֶׁהִיא כְּלִי וְשֶׁטַח רָחָב מְאֹד לְהִתְלַבֵּשׁ בָּהּ הֶאָרַת אוֹר אֵין סוֹף בָּרוּךְ הוּא (וּכְמוֹ שֶׁכָּתוּב: "לְבוּשׁוֹ צְדָקָה" [מפיוט לימים נוראים]),

which is an exceedingly wide vessel and space to contain the illumination of the light of *Ein Sof*, blessed be He (as it is written, "His garment is charity" [from the High Holidays liturgy]**),**

God's own garment is the mitzva of charity.[24] This is because only charity can be a garment broad enough for Him. Moreover, the word *me'od*, translated here as "exceedingly," connotes that which is infinite,[25] without boundaries. Charity is likewise without parameters. At its essence, charity is given without terms or conditions, and it is not limited by anything that one might receive for it in exchange. ☞

AN EXCEEDINGLY WIDE VESSEL

☞ The question that underlies everything here is, what vessel could contain the infinite? The author of the *Tanya* stated above that the worlds can only contain the light that fills all the worlds, while the principal reward that is set aside at the time of the resurrection is the encompassing light, which transcends the limits of all the worlds. If that is the case, what vessel can receive such a light? The problem is apparently unsolvable, because by definition all the worlds are measured and limited, while that which is boundless and infinite cannot be confined within the world at all.

It is true that creation cannot contain the infinite encompassing light, and anything that could contain it ceases to exist, since it is nullified and subsumed within the light and becomes a vehicle for the infinite. At present, such a transformation can occur in only one way: as a result of a person performing a mitzva, when God's will and wisdom descend and are clothed in this world, when His infinite will, which can desire to limit and constrict itself within limited parameters, clothes itself in the vessels and bounds of this world. Yet it is not enough for the will and wisdom to flow forth from above. Something from within the world must connect with the infinite and actualize this bond so that this flash of the infinite will illuminate all the worlds.

24. See Isa. 59:17, 61:10.

25. As explained in several places with regard to loving God *bekhol me'odekha*, "with all your might."

The penetration of the divine will into the worlds constitutes the mitzva that God performs, His act of giving, and when a person performs a mitzva here below, he attaches himself to God. Granted, God commanded the person to perform the mitzva, but it is the person who closes the circuit by exhibiting a desire to attach himself to the divine will with his deed that connects to the divine deed. At that moment, with the performance of that deed, the will, understanding, and feelings of the person has no significance, because what he understands and what he wants and what he feels about the deed makes no difference. By performing the mitzva, he is expressing his desire to carry out the divine will, and the only thing that matters is the divine will that is manifest in that place and that moment through this deed.

This is true of every mitzva. The infinite divine will exists within every mitzva. But the mitzva of charity has an additional facet: Not only is the divine will manifest through the performance of the mitzva of charity, but the reward for the mitzva of charity constitutes the flow of divine light and life force into the world, a tangible giving and creation within the parameters of this world. Charity not only creates a bond and connection with the Divine, but also brings down a flow of sustenance and initiates divine giving to the world. Just as giving charity entails giving something tangible and material to someone who is in need and is lacking, so too God's charity entails giving and sustaining the world in a tangible way. That which is tangible and material, which has dimension in this world, is what the verse "Your commandment is exceedingly wide" refers to: It refers to charity in this world, which has actual breadth, a breadth that is defined by the word *me'od* – that is infinite.

When it comes to the dimensions of length, breadth, and depth, Chabad Hasidism explains that they are analogous to the understanding of the intellect in the realm of spirituality (see *Torat Ḥayyim*, Gen. 46d, Ex. 292b). Length is the intellect's ability to extend into boundaries that grow increasingly constricted. It means breaking down a piece of information down to its smallest details. Therefore, the verse states that the Torah's "measure is longer than the earth" (Job 11:9), because it descends to the lowest places in the earth. The depth of an insight, on the other hand, is the ability to apprehend the essence and root of a concept beyond analogies and metaphors that are provided to make something understandable. Breadth is the dimension of infinite expansion in all directions. We speak of a breadth of understanding or a broad explanation. This refers to the ability to understand and explain something in many ways.

Breadth is like a flat surface, because it does not stretch upward or downward. It encompasses many pieces of knowledge on a broad scale. Length is by definition constricted since it breaks down a specific piece of information into small details and so it is confined to the specific boundaries of that piece of knowledge. Depth, on the other hand, transcends boundaries, and so it cannot be contained by any vessel or parameter. The depth of a piece of knowledge can be infinite and is limited only by a person's capacity to understand

For this reason, a mitzva is specifically described as broad. Breadth is a flat vessel that expresses endless additional explanations and facets that express the essence of the infinite within the world. Torah and wisdom are only Torah and wisdom when we understand them. When we speak of an insight, of an emotion and experience, even if the subject is related to the Divine and the infinite, it is necessarily personal and confined within the vessel of the soul. That is not the case with regard to a mitz-

אֲשֶׁר יָאִיר לֶעָתִיד, בִּבְחִינַת בְּלִי גְבוּל וְתַכְלִית בְּחֶסֶד חִנָּם

which will shine in the future, limitlessly and infinitely, with unconditional kindness

In the future, at the time of the resurrection of the dead, God's illumination and granting of reward will be on the level of the light that encompasses all worlds, transcending every boundary and limitation. It will constitute unconditional kindness, charity that demands nothing in return, because the worlds have nothing equal to it that could repay what is bestowed.

בְּאִתְעֲרוּתָא דִלְתַתָּא זוֹ, הַנִּקְרֵאת "דֶּרֶךְ ה'".

elicited by **this awakening from below, which is called "the way of the Lord."**

The awakening from below is the mitzva of charity that a person performs here below, which is by its nature gratuitous kindness: giving to someone without boundary, without conditions. It is called "the way of the Lord" because it is analogous to the way God gives: also without boundary and limitation and with gratuitous kindness. Since it is analogous to the way God performs the mitzva of charity, it elicits an awakening from above, where God Himself actually performs the mitzva of charity, bringing the divine, infinite light down into the world, passing from one place, from the light that encompasses all worlds. to another place, to manifesting as the light that fills all worlds.

וְזֶהוּ לְשׁוֹן "מְאֹד" שֶׁהוּא בְּלִי גְבוּל וְתַכְלִית.

This is the meaning of **the term** ***me'od,*** "exceedingly," **that it is without bounds or limitations.**

The Hebrew word *me'od* always connotes a lack of limitation.[26] The mitzva of charity is thus "exceedingly wide," without limitation. This

va. Its nature is that of performing God's will, of the nullification of the person's self in the face of the Divine. A mitzva, then, is infinitely broad. There is no intrinsic limit to the words a person can speak, to the deeds he can perform, to the ways in which he can perform them. The only boundaries are those of the physical world, of time, place, and body, but the mitzva itself has no limits.

26. See *Torah Or* 39c, 53d; *Likkutei Torah,* Lev. 32d. In the same vein, when a

is in contrast to the soul's apprehension of the Torah and knowledge of the Divine, which is necessarily limited.

אֲבָל "לְכָל תִּכְלָה רָאִיתִי קֵץ" (תהלים קיט, צו), "תִּכְלָה" הִיא מִלְּשׁוֹן כְּלוֹת הַנֶּפֶשׁ שֶׁבְּגַן עֵדֶן, שֶׁהִיא בִּבְחִינַת קֵץ וְתַכְלִית וְצִמְצוּם כַּנִּזְכָּר לְעֵיל.

But "I see an end [*tikhla*] **to all great things"** (Ps. 119:96). ***Tikhla*** **connotes the pining of the soul in** the **Garden of Eden, which is an end, culmination, and constriction, as stated above.**

These words, "I see an end to all great things," are the beginning of the verse that the author of the *Tanya* quoted above: "Your commandments are exceedingly wide." In the Garden of Eden, the soul attains an apprehension of the light that fills all worlds. With that attainment, it reaches a state called "*kelot hanefesh*," the pining of the soul. In this state, the soul reaches the limit of its ability to contain and sustain something, at which point it "expires" (the word *kelot* also connotes expiration): It ceases to exist in the same form and confines in which it existed until that point.[27] The soul reaches this state of expiration only when it attains an awareness that enters and fills its vessels and parameters so that they cannot contain any more. Precisely when that which it apprehends is constricted within the vessels and faculties of the soul, when it reaches the perimeter of its boundaries, the soul can no longer contain it and it reaches this state. In the Garden of Eden, where apprehension in itself has no external boundaries, the soul constantly experiences such a state.

וּ"לְכָל תִּכְלָה", הוּא לְפִי שֶׁיֵּשׁ כַּמָּה וְכַמָּה מַעֲלוֹת וּמַדְרֵגוֹת גַּן עֵדֶן, זֶה לְמַעְלָה מִזֶּה עַד רוּם הַמַּעֲלוֹת,

The phrase **"an end to all things" is used because there are numerous ranks and levels of the Garden of Eden, one higher than the next, to the loftiest heights,**

---

person serves God *bekhol me'odekha*, "with all his might," with unlimited love, he elicits revelation of the infinite illumination that will occur in the future.

27. This means that the soul feels potentially capable of truly expiring, that its will, attainments, and feelings will be totally subsumed, but it does not actually cease to exist.

The words "I see an end to all things" can also imply "I have seen many types and levels of 'ends,'" indicating that there are a number of types and levels of expiration. Every degree of apprehension, every level of the Garden of Eden, has its own level of the "pining of the soul," of the soul's pining so much for the Divine that it feels as if it will expire. What happens to a soul after it reaches a state of expiration in the Garden of Eden? It rises to a higher level in the Garden of Eden. In the Garden of Eden, the soul attains and apprehends more and more, as much as that level permits and as much as it is capable of receiving at that level, as much as the vessels with which it arrived in the Garden of Eden can contain, until those vessels are completely full. Then, when it reaches the state of expiration, it rises to a higher level in the Garden of Eden. In this way, it continues to rise from one state of expiration to another, from one Garden of Eden to another, higher and higher.

כְּמוֹ שֶׁכָּתַב בְּלִקּוּטֵי הַשַּׁ״ס מֵהָאֲרִיזַ״ל, בְּפֵירוּשׁ מַאֲמַר רַבּוֹתֵינוּ ז״ל: תַּלְמִידֵי חֲכָמִים אֵין לָהֶם מְנוּחָה כוּ׳ (ברכות סד, א), שֶׁעוֹלִים תָּמִיד מִמַּדְרֵגָה לְמַדְרֵגָה בְּהַשָּׂגַת הַתּוֹרָה שֶׁאֵין לָהּ סוֹף כוּ׳,

as it is written in *Likkutei HaShas* by the Arizal, in explanation of our Rabbis' statement "Torah scholars have no rest..." (*Berakhot* 64a), **that** these scholars **are constantly ascending from one level to the next in** their **apprehension of the Torah, which has no limit, and so on,**

Torah scholars who studied Torah in this world continue to study Torah in the Garden of Eden. There, where there are no boundaries to understanding, they attain more and apprehend more until they completely fill their vessels and reach a state of expiration. Then they rise to a higher level of the Garden of Eden, where they attain greater insight into the aggregate of a higher level of concepts. Since the Torah has no end, so too their ascent from level to level continues without rest, without end.

עַד אַחַר הַתְּחִיָּה שֶׁיִּהְיֶה לָהֶם מְנוּחָה כוּ׳.

until after the resurrection, when they will have rest, and so on.

As the soul ascends from level to level, its vessels receive and contain the light that fills all worlds; on each level, there is always more light for it to attain. But after the resurrection, when revelation will come from the light that encompasses all worlds, there will be no more ascents and levels, because the revelation of the encompassing light will be the light of *Ein Sof* that transcends all levels, where everything, large and small, is equal. The one who has no rest in the Garden of Eden sees that there is always something more to attain, that he is still lacking and he yearns to fulfill that lack, to rise ever higher and attain another level of enlightenment. He cannot rest because there is always farther to reach. But the revelation after the resurrection will incorporate all levels. That revelation will not enter the levels and souls, but rather everything will enter it. Everything will be within it. Then all of creation will experience the rest for eternity, which constitutes the Divine Presence enveloping everything and being present in everything. This is the infinite pleasure that requires nothing else because everything is already here, now, present and felt.

This letter discussed the reward that a person receives for performing the mitzva of charity. Though other letters also discuss the reward a person receives from above for the charity he gives here below, the reward is discussed in terms of a single act of charity for which there is a single instance of reward – the initial awakening from above that is caused by the awakening from below when a person gave charity. The other letters deal with the aspect of reward that relates to our lives in this world and which helps us serve God in this world. This epistle, on the other hand, discusses the topic of reward in general, in all its breadth. It does not refer only to reward that affects a person in the present, but that which will be granted in the future, both in the afterlife and at the end of days.

The reward for performing a mitzva is not only a onetime payment given for a mitzva that has been performed. Since the mitzva that a person performs remains forever because it is the fulfillment of God's inner will, which transcends place and time, its reward also lasts forever. Moreover, the reward for performing the mitzva shines within all the worlds: within this world and within the spiritual worlds, in the Garden of Eden.

These two aspects of the reward for performing a mitzva are compared to the "principal" and the "fruits." The principal is the reward for the mitzva itself. Like the mitzva, it transcends all worlds, too intense and broad to enter the confines of this world. The fruits allude to the reward that is manifest in this world, pouring forth abundant light and sustenance within the worlds as well.

Why is it important to know all this? We can understand why it is important for a person to know about the reward that affects him in this world, because that can inspire him to perform more mitzvot. But why is it necessary to describe the reward for mitzvot in the World to Come, in the Garden of Eden, and beyond that, at the time of the resurrection of the dead – a reward that is not relevant to the deeds of this world?

Perhaps the essential promise of such future reward can bolster a person's service of God in the present. But a deeper reason may be that the three stages that this epistle discusses, the performance of the mitzva, its reward in this world and in the Garden of Eden, and its reward in the future upon the resurrection of the dead, are in essence one and the same. Just as a person's soul is one, all its experiences throughout these stages are merely three different facets of one existence, each of which cannot exist without the other.

This epistle states that the common denominator in all these stages is the mitzva of charity. Charity is the secret of the existence of creation, the secret of the soul's service of God, and the secret of the soul's purpose. It is the secret of the existence of creation because the only way that a descent of divinity is possible, a descent of the cause and effect impelled by the will that leads to the existence of creation, is due to the charity that God performs for creation in giving it existence. It is the secret of the soul's service of God because it allows the soul to fulfill the mitzva of charity, to having compassion on another and give to a person who is lacking, even when one has no desire or pleasure in giving to him. It is the secret of the soul's purpose, because through a person's giving charity, God Himself, His intrinsic infinite essence, is revealed, and not through a constricted illumination with boundaries, concealment, and a devolvement that constricts the light of revelation.

In this limited world, in which the infinite is concealed, we cannot see the entirety of all that occurs. We do our part and look forward to salvation and anticipate our reward. But we must also know that it is occurring now as well. The mitzva and reward, this world and the World to Come, it is all one and the same. What connects and holds all these states of reality together is a person's knowledge of their essential unity. In a person's lifetime in this world, what connects his self of yesterday to his self of today is his awareness that that self is me and that other self is also me. In the greater scope of the existence of humanity and this world and the World to Come, what bonds them all together is man's knowledge that they are all essentially different facets of the same reality. Even if a person does not require this knowledge to perform every mitzva, that knowledge must exist for a person's service of God and for his understanding to be complete.

Glossary

alef First letter of the Hebrew alphabet

aliya Immigration to the Land of Israel

Amida Silent prayer recited three times daily

amora'im Sages of the Talmud who lived from approximately 200 to 500 CE

Arizal Rabbi Yitzḥak Luria of Tzefat (1534–1572), the most influential kabbalist of modern times

Ashkenazic A Jew who originated from northern and eastern Europe, primarily Germany and its environs

Asiya The world of Action, the fourth and lowest of the spiritual worlds

Atzilut The world of Emanation, the highest of the four spiritual worlds and closest to the source of creation

ayin Nothingness; the sixteenth letter of the Hebrew alphabet

Ba'al Shem Tov Rabbi Yisrael ben Eliezer (1698–1760), founder of the hasidic movement

beinonim Literally, "intermediates"; those who are on a level where he is neither wicked nor righteous

Beit Hillel Literally, "House of Hillel"; a school of thought named after the mishnaic Sage Hillel, who founded it

Beit Shammai Literally, "House of Shammai"; a school of thought named after the mishnaic Sage Shammai, who founded it

Beria The world of Creation, the second of the four spiritual worlds

bet The second letter of the Hebrew alphabet

Bina Understanding, one of the ten divine attributes known as *sefirot*

Chabad An acronym of the three cognitive attributes, *Ḥokhma, Bina,* and *Da'at*; the name attributed to Lubavitch Hasidism, founded by Rabbi Shneur Zalman of Liadi

Da'at Knowledge, one of the ten divine attributes known as *sefirot*

dalet The fourth letter of the Hebrew alphabet

Ein Sof God's infinite being

etrog Citron, one of the four species waved on the festival of Sukkot

gaon An outstanding Torah scholar

Gevura Restraint, one of the ten divine attributes known as *sefirot*

gimmel The third letter of the Hebrew alphabet

Haggada Book that tells the story of the Exodus to be related at the Seder on the first night of Passover

halakha (pl. halakhot) Jewish law

hasid (pl. hasidim) Literally, "pious individual"; a follower of Hasidism, the movement initiated by the Ba'al Shem Tov

Havaya A reference to the four-letter name of God known as the Tetragrammaton

ḥaya The second highest of the five soul levels

ḥayot Angelic creatures that appear in Ezekiel's mystical vision

heh The fifth letter of the Hebrew alphabet

Ḥesed Kindness, one of the ten divine attributes known as *sefirot*

ḥet The eighth letter of the Hebrew alphabet

Hod Splendor, one of the ten divine attributes known as *sefirot*

Ḥokhma Wisdom, one of the ten divine attributes known as *sefirot*

Ḥumash The five books of the Torah

Ibn Ezra Abraham ben Meir ibn Ezra (c. 1092–1167), a Spanish poet, grammarian, and biblical commentator

Kabbala The mystical teachings of the Torah

kaf (or khaf) The eleventh letter of the Hebrew alphabet

kelippa (pl. kelippot) Literally, "husk"; the aspect of the universe that is unholy and conceals the Divine

kelippat noga Literally, "glowing husk"; a form of *kelippa* that contains an element of goodness that can be elevated

Keter Crown, one of the ten divine attributes known as *sefirot*

Kislev The third month in the Jewish calendar, which falls out during winter

kof The nineteenth letter of the Hebrew alphabet

lamed The twelfth letter of the Hebrew alphabet

lulav Palm frond, one of the four species waved on the festival of Sukkot

Maggid of Mezeritch Rabbi Dovber (d. 1772), a disciple of the Ba'al Shem Tov and the teacher of Rabbi Shneur Zalman of Liadi, author of the *Tanya,* who strengthened the Hasidism of his master, anchoring it firmly in Jewish thought and practice

Maharal An acronym for Rabbi Yehudah Loew of Prague (1525–1609), one of the outstanding scholars and Jewish leaders of the sixteenth century

Malkhut Kingship, one of the ten divine attributes known as *sefirot*

mem The thirteenth letter of the Hebrew alphabet

menora Candelabrum with eight lights traditionally lit during the festival of Hanukkah, also known as a *ḥanukkiya*

mezuza A parchment scroll on which four portions from the Torah are inscribed and affixed to the doorpost of a Jewish home

Midrash Collection of homiletic interpretations of the Scriptures by the Sages of the Talmud

mikveh Bath used for ritual immersion

Mishna A concise summary of the teachings of the Sages on all topics of Torah, which was redacted in the beginning of the third century CE by Rabbi Yehuda HaNasi

mitzva (pl. mitzvot) A Torah commandment

moḥin Literally "brains"; the *sefirot* corresponding to the cognitive faculties

nefesh The soul; specifically, the lowest of the five levels of the soul

neshama The soul; specifically, the third of the five soul levels

Netzaḥ Dominance, one of the ten divine attributes known as *sefirot*

nun The fourteenth letter of the Hebrew alphabet

parasha (pl. parashiyot) Torah portion

partzuf (pl. partzufim) Literally, "divine countenance"; a particular arrangement of the ten *sefirot*

peh The seventeenth letter of the Hebrew alphabet

peruta Coin of a small denomination

Rabba Rabba bar Naḥmani (died c. 320 CE), a prominent third-generation talmudic Sage from Babylon

Rabbeinu Baḥya A rabbi and scholar (1255–1340), best known for his commentary on the Torah

Rambam Maimonides; Rabbi Moses ben Maimon (1138–1204), a leading halakhic authority and philosopher

Ramban Nachmanides; Rabbi Moses ben Naḥman (1194–1270), renowned for his commentary on the Torah and Talmud

Rashi Rabbi Shlomo Yitzḥaki (1040–1105), one of the foremost commentators of the Torah and Talmud

resh The twentieth letter of the Hebrew alphabet

Rosh HaShana Jewish New Year

ruaḥ Second of the five soul levels

samekh The fifteenth letter of the Hebrew alphabet

Sanhedrin A tribunal of sages consisting of seventy-one members

se'a A unit of volume measurement used in talmudic times

sefira (pl. sefirot) One of the ten divine attributes with which God creates, sustains, and directs the worlds

shamash Attendant

Shema Prayer recited three times daily in which one declares one's faith in the oneness of God

shin The twenty-first letter of the Hebrew alphabet

shofar Ram's horn sounded on the festival of Rosh HaShana

siddur Prayer book

sitra aḥara Literally, "the other side"; a general term for evil, including all aspects of the universe that counter the Divine

sukka Hut or shelter with a roof of branches and leaves used as a temporary residence during the festival of Sukkot

Sukkot The harvest festival celebrated in the fall during which Jews leave their houses to live in temporary shelters

tallit Prayer shawl

Tanakh An acronym for *Torah, Nevi'im, Ketuvim* (Torah, Prophets, Writings), comprising the twenty-four books of the Scriptures

tanna'im Sages who lived in the period spanning 332 BCE to 220 CE whose views were recorded in the Mishna

tav Twenty-second letter of the Hebrew alphabet

tefillin Leather boxes worn on the arm and forehead containing certain biblical passages that declare the unity of God and the miracles of the exodus from Egypt

tet Ninth letter of the Hebrew alphabet

Tiferet Beauty, one of the ten divine attributes known as *sefirot*

Tosafot Medieval commentators of the Talmud

tzaddik (pl. tzaddikim) Righteous individual; a person born with the extraordinary ability and brilliance to perceive God

Tzemaḥ Tzedek The third Lubavitcher Rebbe, Rabbi Menaḥem Mendel Schneerson (1789–1866), grandson of the author of the *Tanya*, Rabbi Shneur Zalman of Liadi

tzadi Eighteenth letter of the Hebrew alphabet

tzitzit Strings that are affixed to four-cornered garments

vav The sixth letter of the Hebrew alphabet

Vilna Gaon Rabbi Eliyahu of Vilna (1720–1797), a commentator and kabbalist who was known as a leader of the opponents of Hasidism

yeḥida The highest of the five soul levels

yesh Existence, substance, entity

yeshiva (pl. yeshivot) An academy dedicated to the study of Torah

Yesod Foundation, one of the ten divine attributes known as *sefirot*

Yetzira The world of Formation, the second of the four spiritual worlds

yod The tenth letter of the Hebrew alphabet

Yom Kippur The Day of Atonement, when the Jewish people engage in fasting, prayer, and repentance

zayin The seventh letter of the Hebrew alphabet

Works Cited in This Volume

Avodat HaKodesh A kabbalistic work by Rabbi Meir ibn Gabbai, a kabbalist born in Spain in 1480

Avot deRabbi Natan A commentary and exposition of the teachings of the *Pirkei Avot,* compiled during the geonic period (c. 700–900 CE)

Ba'al Shem Tov al HaTorah A compendium of teachings on the Torah and the festivals by the founder of the hasidic movement, anthologized by Shimon Menaḥem Mendel Vodnik

Beit Rebbe A biography of the author of the *Tanya,* Rabbi Shneur Zalman of Liadi (1745–1812), and his successors by Chaim Meir Heilman

Beit Yosef Written by Rabbi Yosef Karo (1488–1575), a commentary on the halakhic work *Arba'a Turim* by Rabbi Yaakov ben Asher

Bemidbar Rabba Midrash comprising a collection of homiletical interpretations of the book of Numbers

Bereshit Rabba Midrash comprising a collection of homiletical interpretations of the book of Genesis

Degel Maḥaneh Efrayim A work of hasidic teachings on the Torah by Rabbi Moshe Ḥayyim Efrayim of Sudilkov (c. 1748–1800)

Derekh Ḥayyim A work by the second Lubavitcher Rebbe, Rabbi Dovber Schneuri (1773–1827), on the subject of repentance

Derekh Mitzvotekha Hasidic discourses on the esoteric meaning of the mitzvot by the third Lubavitcher Rebbe, Rabbi Menaḥem Mendel Schneerson (1789–1866), also known as the Tzemaḥ Tzedek

Devarim Rabba Midrash comprising a collection of homiletical interpretations of the book of Deuteronomy

Eikha Rabba Midrash comprising a collection of homiletical interpretations of the book of Lamentations

Etz Ḥayyim The fundamental work of the Arizal's Kabbala, compiled by his disciple, Rabbi Ḥayyim Vital

Gevurot Hashem Commentary on the exodus from Egypt and the Passover Haggada by Rabbi Judah Loew, the Maharal of Prague (c. 1520–1609)

HaMa'asar HaRishon An account of the incarceration of the author of the *Tanya* by Rabbi Yehoshua Mondshein

HaYom Yom An anthology of hasidic aphorisms and customs arranged according to the days of the year, compiled by Rabbi Menaḥem Mendel Schneerson, the Lubavitcher Rebbe (1902–1994)

Hemshekh Samekh Vav Compilation of hasidic discourses by the fifth Lubavitcher Rebbe, Rabbi Shalom Dovber Schneerson, all of which were taught between 1905 and 1908

Hemshekh Ayin Bet Compilation of the hasidic treatises of the fifth Lubavitcher Rebbe, Rabbi Sholom Dovber Schneerson (1860–1920), from the Hebrew year 5672 to 5676 (1911–1916)

Ḥiddushei HaRim Work of hasidic teachings by Rabbi Yitzḥak Meir Rothenberg Alter (1799–1866), the first Rebbe of Gur

Hilkhot Talmud Torah Literally, "Laws of Torah Study," published anonymously by the author of the *Tanya* in 1794

Idra Rabba A section of the *Zohar* on *Parashat Naso*, in which kabbalistic mysteries that Rabbi Shimon bar Yoḥai revealed to nine of his students are transcribed

Iggeret HaTeshuva The third section of the *Tanya*

Iggerot Kodesh A comprehensive collection of correspondence written by the Rebbes of Chabad, including those of the fifth Lubavitcher Rebbe, Rabbi Shalom Dovber Schneerson (1860–1920), and seventh Lubavitcher Rebbe, Rabbi Menaḥem Mendel Schneerson (1902–1994)

Jerusalem Talmud Written in the Land of Israel, an extensive work built upon the foundation of the Mishna like its better-known counterpart, the Babylonian Talmud

Kad HaKemaḥ An encyclopedic work of ethical instruction and self-improvement written by Rabbeinu Baḥya ben Asher, the topics organized alphabetically according to the letters of the *alef-bet*

Kehillat Yaakov Kabbalistic dictionary by Rabbi Yaakov Tzvi Yalish of Dinov (1778–1825)

Kerem Chabad A journal founded and edited by Rabbi Yehoshua Mondshine, comprising articles on Chabad hasidic teachings and history, published between the years 1987 and 1992

Keter Shem Tov Collection of teachings of the Ba'al Shem Tov (c. 1698–1760), compiled from the works of his disciples, by Rabbi Aharon HaKohen

Kol Mevaser A collection of essays compiled from the works of the students of Rabbi Simḥa Bunim of Peshisḥa and published by Rabbi Yehuda Menaḥem Baum in 1991

Kol Sippurei HaBa'al Shem Tov A collection of stories and chronicles on the life of the Ba'al Shem Tov compiled and arranged according to topic by Rabbi Yisrael Yaakov Klapholtz

Kuntres Aḥaron The fifth and final section of the *Tanya*

Likkutei Amarim The first section of the *Tanya*

Likkutei Amarim Also known as *Maggid Devarav LeYaakov*, a collection of teachings of Rabbi Dov Ber, the Maggid of Mezeritch (c. 1700–1770), compiled by his disciple, Rabbi Shlomo of Lutzk)

Likkutei Biurim LaSefer HaTanya Explanations on the *Tanya* culled from other works of Chabad Hasidism, including the discourses of the seventh Lubavitcher Rebbe, Rabbi Menaḥem Mendel Schneerson (1902–1994), compiled by Rabbi Yehoshua Korf

Likkutei Dibburim A series of books containing the teachings of the sixth Lubavitcher Rebbe, Rabbi Yosef Yitzḥak Schneerson (1880–1950)

Likkutei HaShas A collection of the Arizal's writings on the Talmud

Likkutei Levi Yitzḥak A collection of marginalia from the *Tanya* of the kabbalist Rabbi Levi Yitzḥak Schneerson, the father of the Lubavitcher Rebbe, Rabbi Menaḥem Mendel Schneerson

Likkutei Siḥot The collected discourses of the seventh Lubavitcher Rebbe, Rabbi Menaḥem Mendel Schneerson (1902–1994) on the Torah and festivals

Likkutei Torah Hasidic discourses by the author of the *Tanya*, Rabbi Shneur Zalman of Liadi (1745–1812) on the last three books of the Torah and the festivals

Likkutei Torah Collection of mystical teachings of the Arizal (1534–1572) on the Torah (not to be confused with the work written by the author of the *Tanya* of the same name)

Ma'amar Bati LeGani The title of the last hasidic discourse of the sixth Lubavitcher Rebbe, Rabbi Yosef Yitzḥak Schneerson (1880–1950), and the first, as well as subsequent, discourses of his successor Rabbi Menaḥem Mendel Schneerson

Ma'or Einayim Hasidic teachings on the Torah by Rabbi Menaḥem Naḥum Twersky of Chernobyl (1730–1798)

Me'orei Or Kabbalistic reference book by Rabbi Meir Paprish (1624–1662)

Metzudat Zion A commentary on Prophets and Writings by Rabb David Altshuler that focuses on explaining difficult or unfamiliar words in the verses

Metzudot Referring to the commentaries of Metzudat Tzion and Metzudat David on Prophets and Writings by Rabbi David Altshuler, Metzudat Tzion focusing on unfamiliar and difficult words in the verses and Metzudat David delving into the meaning of the verses

Mevo She'arim An introduction to the wisdom of Kabbala from the writings of Rabbi Ḥayyim Vital

Midrash Shoḥer Tov Midrash comprising a collection of homiletic teachings expounding the Psalms; another name for *Midrash Tehillim*

Midrash Tanḥuma Midrash comprising a collection of homiletic teachings expounding the Torah

Midrash Tehillim Midrash comprising a collection of homiletic teachings expounding the Psalms

Mishneh Torah Code of Jewish law composed by Rambam (1138–1204), containing fourteen books, including *Sefer HaMadda* (the Book of Knowledge), which addresses fundamentals of Judaism

Olat Tamid A work on meditations in prayers by Rabbi Ḥayyim Vital based on the teachings of the Arizal

Or HaTorah Compilation of hasidic discourses on the *Tanakh* and festivals by the third Lubavitcher Rebbe, Rabbi Menaḥem Mendel Schneerson (1789–1866), also known as the Tzemaḥ Tzedek

Otzar HaMidrashim Collection of two hundred minor midrashim, compiled by Yehuda David Eisenstein

Pardes Rimmonim The primary exposition of the kabbalistic system of Rabbi Moshe Kordevero, famously known as the Ramak (1522–1570)

Pirkei Avot Literally, "Chapters of the Fathers"; a tractate of the Mishna dealing with ethics and piety

Pirkei deRabbi Eliezer Homiletic work on the Torah containing exegesis and retellings of biblical stories

Pri Etz Ḥayyim Mystical teachings of the Arizal on rituals and holidays as recorded by his disciple Rabbi Hayyim Vital

Raya Meheimna Subsection of the *Zohar* presenting a kabbalistic exposition of the commandments and prohibitions of the Torah

Sefer HaArakhim An encyclopedic work of hasidic concepts compiled by Rabbi Yoel Kahn and Rabbi Shalom Dovber Lipsker

Sefer HaBahir A kabbalistic work attributed to first-century talmudic Sage Rabbi Neḥunya ben HaKanah

Sefer HaIkkarim A fifteenth-century work on principles of Judaism by Rabbi Yosef Albo (1380–1444)

Sefer HaKen An anthology of articles on the life and work of the author of the *Tanya*, Rabbi Shneur Zalman of Liadi, compiled and edited by Rabbi Adin Even-Israel Steinsaltz at the behest of the Lubavitcher Rebbe, Rabbi Menaḥem Mendel Schneerson

Sefer HaMa'amarim A series of works containing the collected hasidic discourses of the Lubavitcher Rebbes, arranged by year

Sefer HaMa'amarim Melukat Selected discourses by the Lubavitcher Rebbe, Rabbi Menaḥem Mendel Schneerson, arranged according to the festivals

Sefer HaSihot A compilation of discourses delivered by the sixth Lubavitcher Rebbe, Rabbi Yosef Yitzchak Schneerson

Sefer Mitzvot Katan A halakhic work by Rabbi Yitzḥak of Corbeil (d. 1280) that is a summary of *Sefer Mitzvot Gadol* by thirteenth-century scholar Rabbi Moshe of Coucy, containing an enumeration of the 613 commandments

Sefer Yetzira Ancient mystical work attributed to the biblical Abraham

Sha'ar HaGemul Treatise on divine justice by Nachmanides

Sha'ar HaGilgulim A kabbalistic work based on the teachings of the Arizal on the topic of reincarnation and the nature of the soul

Sha'ar HaKavanot A kabbalistic work based on the teachings of the Arizal on the mystical underpinnings of daily rituals and the daily prayers

Sha'ar HaYiḥud VeHa'emuna The second section of the *Tanya*

Sha'ar Ruaḥ HaKodesh A kabbalistic work based on the teachings of the Arizal containing hundreds of meditations geared toward purifying the soul and attaining higher levels of consciousness

Sha'arei Kedushah Mystical work on piety by Rabbi Ḥayyim Vital (1542–1620)

She'eilat Ya'avetz Halakhic responsa by Rabbi Yaakov Emden (1697–1776)

Shemot Rabba Midrash comprising a collection of homiletic interpretations of the book of Exodus

Shir HaShirim Rabba Midrash comprising a collection of homiletical interpretations of the book of Song of Songs

Shivḥei HaBa'al Shem Tov Biographical stories of the Ba'al Shem Tov and his disciples

Shulḥan Arukh The most important and influential codification of Jewish law, compiled by Rabbi Yosef Karo of Tzefat (1488–1575)

Siddur Admor HaZaken Prayer book edited in accordance with the teachings of the author of the *Tanya*, Rabbi Shneur Zalman of Liadi (1745–1812)

Sifra Midrash containing halakhic exegesis on the book of Leviticus

Sifrei Midrash containing halakhic exegesis on the books of Numbers and Deuteronomy

Tanna deVei Eliyahu A compilation of midrashic teachings ascribed to the prophet Elijah

Targum Yerushalmi An Aramaic translation and commentary on the Torah

Targum Yonatan Aramaic translation and commentary on Prophets composed by Rabbi Yonatan ben Uziel

Tikkunei Zohar Also known as the *Tikkunim*, an appendix to the *Zohar* consisting of seventy commentaries on the opening word of the Torah, *bereshit*

Torah Or Hasidic discourses by the author of the *Tanya*, Rabbi Shneur Zalman of Liadi (1745–1812), on the books of Genesis and Exodus, as well as on Hanukkah and the book of Esther

Torat Ḥayyim The collected discourses of the second Lubavitcher Rebbe, Rabbi Dovber Schneuri (1773–1827), on the books of Genesis and Exodus

Torat Kohanim The halakhic Midrash to the book of Leviticus

Torat Menaḥem The comprehensive collection of discourses and speeches of the seventh Lubavitcher Rebbe, Rabbi Menaḥem Mendel Schneerson (1902–1994)

Torat Shmuel A collection of discourses by the fourth Lubavitcher Rebbe, Rabbi Shmuel Schneerson (1834–1882)

Vayikra Rabba Midrash comprising a collection of homiletical interpretations of the book of Leviticus

Ya'arot Devash Collection of the sermons of Rabbi Yehonatan Eibeshitz

Yalkut Shimoni Collection of homiletic teachings on the books of *Tanakh*, compiled between the eleventh and fourteenth centuries

Zohar One of the fundamental texts of Kabbala (Jewish mysticism) that consists of the teachings of Rabbi Shimon bar Yoḥai (second century CE), as recorded by his close disciples

אגרת הקודש

לכ״ק אדמו״ר הזקן

הרב רבי שניאור זלמן
מליאדי

בעל התניא והשו״ע

אגרות א-יז

אגרת א

ג באב פשוטה
ז באב מעוברת

פותחין בברכה לברך ולהודות לה' כי טוב. שמועה טובה שמעה ותחי נפשי. אין טוב אלא תורה. תורת ה' תמימה. זו השלמת כל הש"ס כולו ברוב עיירות ומניינים מאנ"ש. הודאה על העבר ובקשה על העתיד. כה יתן וכה יוסיף ה' לאמץ לבם בגבורים מדי שנה בשנה בגבורה של תורה. ולהודיע לבני אדם גבורתה של תורה שבע"פ וכחה עוז.

פי' שלמה המלך ע"ה חגרה בעוז מתניה כו' מתנים הם בחי' דבר המעמיד כל הגוף עם הראש הנצב ועומד עליהם. והם המוליכים ומביאים אותו למחוז חפצו. וכמו שהוא בגשמיות הגוף כך הוא בבחי' רוחניות נפש האלהית האמונה האמיתית בה' אחד א"ס ב"ה דאיהו ממכ"ע וסוכ"ע ולית אתר פנוי מיניה למעלה עד אין קץ ולמטה עד אין תכלי' וכן לד' סטרין בבחי' א"ס ממש וכן בבחי' שנה ונפש כנודע. הנה אמונה זו נק' בשם בחי' מתנים דבר המעמיד ומקיים את הראש הוא השכל המתבונן ומעמיק דעת בגדולת א"ס ב"ה בבחי' עולם שנה נפש. וברוב חסדו ונפלאותיו עמנו להיות עם קרובו ולדבקה בו ממש כנודע ממאמר יפה שעה אחת בתשובה ומע"ט בעוה"ז מכל חיי עוה"ב שהוא רק זיו והארה מבחי' הנק' שכינה השוכן כו' ונברא ביו"ד א' משמו ית' כו' אבל תשובה ומעשים טובים מקרבין ישראל לאביהם שבשמים ממש למהותו ועצמותו כביכול בחי' א"ס ממש וכמ"ש הודו על ארץ ושמים וירם קרן לעמו כו' אקב"ו כו' וכמים הפנים כו' להוליד מתבונה זו דו"ר שכליים או טבעיים להיות בחי' צעק לבם אל ה' או בחי' רשפי אש ושלהבת עזה בבחי' רצוא ואח"כ בבחי' שוב להיות פחד ה' בלבו וליבוש מגדולתו כו' והוא בחי' שמאל דוחה כמ"ש במ"ת וירא העם וינועו ויעמדו מרחוק כו' והן בחי' הזרועות והגוף שבנפש:

ד באב פשוטה
ח באב מעוברת

אך מי הוא הנותן כח ועוז לבחי' מתנים להעמיד ולקיים הראש והזרועות הוא עסק ולימוד הלכות בתורה שבע"פ שהיא בחי' גלוי רצון העליון דאורייתא מחכמה היא דנפקת אבל מקורה ושרשה הוא למעלה מעלה מבחי' חכמה והוא הנקרא בשם רצון העליון ב"ה וכמ"ש כצנה רצון תעטרנו כעטרה שהיא על המוחין שבראש וכנודע ממ"ש ע"פ אשת חיל עטרת בעלה. וכל השונה הלכות בכל יום כו'. וזהו חגרה בעוז מתניה אין עוז אלא תורה שהיא נותנת כח ועוז לבחי' מתנים החגורים ומלובשים בה לחזק ולאמץ זרועותיה הן דו"ר שכליים או טבעיים כל חד לפום שיעורא דיליה. (ועל העמדת וקיום בחי' הראש שבנפש הוא השכל המתבונן כו' אמר טעמה כי טוב סחרה כו' ומבואר במ"א): אך עת וזמן החיזוק ואימוץ

הזרועות והראש היא שעת תפלת השחר שהיא שעת רחמים ועת רצון העליון למעלה. ולזאת אותה אבקש ממבקשי ה׳ יבינו וישכילו יחדיו ולהיות לזכרון בין עיניהם כל מה שכתבתי אליהם אשתקד בכלל. ובפרט מענין כוונת התפלה מעומקא דלבא יום יום ידרשון ה׳ בכל לבם ובכל נפשם ונפשם תשתפך כמים נוכח פני ה׳ וכמארז״ל בספרי עד מיצוי הנפש כו׳:

ה באב פשוטה
ט באב מעוברת

ועתה הפעם הנני יוסיף שנית ידי בתוספת ביאור ובקשה כפולה שטוחה ופרושה לפני כל אנשי שלומים הקרובים והרחוקים לקיים עליהם שכל ימי החול לא ירדו לפני התיבה הבעלי עסקים שאין להם פנאי כ״כ. רק אותם שיש להם פנאי או המלמדים או הסמוכים על שולחן אביהם שיכולים להאריך בתפלת השחר ערך שעה ומחצה לפחות כל ימות החול מהם יהיה היורד לפני התיבה ע״פ הגורל או ע״פ ריצוי הרוב. והוא יאסוף אליו בסביב לו כל הסמוכים על שולחן אביהם או מלמדים שיוכלו להאריך כמוהו בבל ישונה נא ונא:

אך בשבתות וימים טובים שגם כל בעלי עסקים יש להם פנאי ושעת הכושר להאריך בתפלתם בכוונת לבם ונפשם לה׳. ואדרבה עליהם מוטל ביתר שאת ויתר עז כמ״ש בשולחן ערוך אורח חיים וכמ״ש בתורת משה ששת ימים תעבוד כו׳ ויום השביעי שבת לה׳ אלהיך דייקא כולו לה׳. ולזאת גם הם ירדו לפני התיבה בשבת ויום טוב על פי הגורל או בריצוי הרוב כמ״ש אשתקד:

וכגון דא צריך לאודועי שבדעתי אי״ה לשלוח לכל המנינים מרגלים בסתר לידע ולהודיע כל מי שאפשר לו וכל מי שיש לו פנאי להאריך ולעיין בתפלה ומתעצל יהי׳ נידון בריחוק מקום להיות נדחה בשתי ידים בבואו לפה לשמוע דא״ח ומכלל לאו אתה שומע הן ולשומעים יונעם ותבא עליהם ברכת טוב ואין טוב אלא תורה וכו׳:

אגרת ב

אחר ביאתו מפ״ב

ו באב פשוטה
י באב מעוברת

קטנתי מכל החסדים ומכל כו׳. פי׳ שבכל חסד וחסד שהקדוש ב״ה עושה לאדם צריך להיות שפל רוח במאד. כי חסד דרועא ימינא. וימינו תחבקני. שהיא בחי׳ קרבת אלהים ממש ביתר שאת מלפנים. וכל הקרוב אל ה׳ ביתר שאת והגבה למעלה מעלה. צריך להיות יותר שפל רוח למטה מטה כמ״ש מרחוק ה׳ נראה לי. וכנודע דכולא קמי׳ דווקא

כלא חשיב. וא"כ כל שהוא קמי' יותר הוא יותר כלא ואין ואפס וזו היא בחי' ימין שבקדושה וחסד לאברהם שאמר אנכי עפר ואפר. וזו היא ג"כ מדתו של יעקב. ובזאת התנצל על יראתו מפני עשו ולא די לו בהבטחתו והנה אנכי עמך כו'. מפני היות קטן יעקב במאד מאד בעיניו מחמת ריבוי החסדים כי במקלי כו'. ואינו ראוי וכדאי כלל להנצל כו'. וכמארז"ל שמא יגרום החטא שנדמה בעיניו שחטא. משא"כ בזלע"ז הוא ישמעאל חסד דקליפה. כל שהחסד גדול הוא הולך וגדל בגובה וגסות הרוח ורוחב לבו.

ולזאת באתי מן המודיעים מודעה רבה לכללות אנ"ש על ריבוי החסדים אשר הגדיל ה' לעשות עמנו לאחוז במדותיו של יעקב שאר עמו ושארית ישראל שמשים עצמו כשיריים ומותרות ממש שאין בו שום צורך. לבלתי רום לבבם מאחיהם כו' ולא להרחיב עליהם פה או לשרוק עליהם ח"ו. הס מלהזכיר באזהרה נוראה רק להשפיל רוחם ולבם במדת אמת ליעקב מפני כל אדם בנמיכות רוח ומענה רך משיב חימה. ורוח נכאה כו'. וכולי האי ואולי יתן ה' בלב אחיהם כמים הפנים וגו':

אגרת ג

ז באב פשוטה | יא באב מעוברת

וילבש צדקה כשריון וכובע ישועה בראשו. ודרשו רז"ל שריון זה כל קליפה וקליפה מצטרפת לשריון גדול אף צדקה כל פרוטה ופרוטה מצטרפת לחשבון גדול. פי' שהשריון עשוי קשקשים על נקבים והם מגינים שלא יכנס חץ בנקבים. וככה הוא מעשה הצדקה:

וביאור הענין כי גדולה צדקה מכל המצות שמהן נעשי' לבושי' להנשמה הנמשכי' מאור א"ס ב"ה מבחי' סובב כל עלמין (כמבואר הפי' ממכ"ע וסובב כ"ע בלק"א ע"ש) באתערותא דלתתא היא מצות ה' ורצון העליון ב"ה. ועיקר המשכה זו מאור א"ס ב"ה הוא לבוש ואור מקיף לי"ס דאבי"ע המשתלשלות מעילה לעילה וממדרגה למדרגה כו' הנקראות בשם ממלא כ"ע. פי' כי א"ס ב"ה מתלבש ומאיר בתוך כל השתלשלות הע"ס דאבי"ע והוא המאציל הע"ס דאצילות המשתלשלו' לבי"ע ע"י צמצום עצום המבואר בע"ח ונקרא אור פנימי. וע"י קיום המצות נמשך אור מקיף הנ"ל ומאיר תוך הע"ס דאבי"ע ומתייחד עם האור פנימי ונקרא יחוד קוב"ה ושכינתי' כמ"ש במ"א. ומהארה דהארה מאור מקיף הנ"ל ע"י צמצום רב נעשה לבוש לבחי' נר"ן של האדם בג"ע התחתון והעליון שיוכלו ליהנות ולהשיג איזה השגה והארה מאור א"ס ב"ה כמ"ש במ"א. וזה שאמרו רז"ל שכר מצוה בהאי עלמא ליכא. כי בעוה"ז הגשמי ובעל גבול וצמצום רב ועצום מאד מאד א"א להתלבש שום הארה מאור א"ס

ב"ה כ"א ע"י י"ס הנקראים גופא בזוה"ק. חסד דרועא ימינא כו'. לפי שכמו שאין ערוך לו להגוף הגשמי לגבי הנשמה כך אין ערוך כלל לי"ס דאצילות לגבי המאציל העליון א"ס ב"ה. כי אפי' ח"ע שהיא ראשיתן היא בבחי' עשיה גופנית לגבי א"ס ב"ה כמ"ש בלק"א. ואי לזאת במעשה הצדקה וגמ"ח שאדם אוכל מפירותיהן בעוה"ז יש נקבים עד"מ בלבוש העליון המקיף על גופא הם הכלים די"ס. להאיר מהם ולהשפיע אור ושפע מחסד דרועא ימינא אורך ימים בעוה"ז הגשמי ועושר וכבוד מדרועא שמאלא. וכן בתפארת. והוד והדר וחדוה וכו': אך כדי שלא ינקו החיצונים למעלה מאור ושפע המשתלשל ויורד למטה מטה עד עוה"ז הגשמי. וכן למטה להגין על האדם ולשמרו ולהצילו מכל דבר רע בגשמיות וברוחניות. לזאת חוזר ומאיר אור המקיף וסותם הנקב עד"מ. כי הוא מבחי' א"ס וסובב כ"ע כנ"ל. וזהו שאמרו רז"ל מצטרפת לחשבון גדול דייקא כי גדול ה' ומהולל מאד בלי סוף ותכלית וגבול [ח"ו]: אך מי הוא הגורם לירידת האור והשפע לעוה"ז הגשמי מי"ס הנקראים גופא הוא היחוד הנ"ל שהיא תוספת הארה והשפעה מבחי' אור א"ס המאציל העליון ב"ה ביתר שאת על ההארה וההשפעה שבתחילת האצילות וההשתלשלות וכו'. וראשית תוספת ההארה וההשפעה היא לראשית הי"ס וזה הוא וכובע ישועה בראשו ישועה הוא מלשון וישע ה' אל הבל ואל מנחתו. והוא ירידת האור והשפע דש"ע נהורין שבזוה"ק. וכמ"ש יאר ה' פניו אליך. יאר פניו אתנו סלה. אתנו הוא ע"י מעשה הצדקה. וזה הוא זורע צדקות מצמיח ישועות. וככה יאר ה' פניו אליהם צדקתם עומדת לעד וקרנם תרום בישועת מצמיח קרן ישועה צמח צדקה מהכובע ישועה הנ"ל. כנפש תדרשנו:

ח באב פשוטה
יב באב מעוברת

אגרת ד

ט באב פשוטה
יג באב מעוברת

אין ישראל נגאלין אלא בצדקה שנא' ושביה בצדקה. כתיב צדק לפניו יהלך והול"ל ילך. אך הענין עפ"י מ"ש לך אמר לבי בקשו פני פי' בקשו פנימית הלב כי הנה בלהב יסוד האש האלקית שבלב (נ"א הנה בהלב [יסוד האש האלקית שבלב]) יש ב' בחי'. בחי' חיצוניות ובחי' פנימיות. חיצוני' הלב היא התלהבות המתלהבת מבחי' הבינה והדעת בגדולת ה' א"ס ב"ה (להתבונן) [להתבונן] בגדולתו ולהוליד מתבונה זו אהבה עזה כרשפי אש וכו'. ופנימי' הלב היא הנקודה שבפנימיות הלב ועומקא דליבא שהיא למעלה מעלה מבחי' הדעת והתבונה שיוכל האדם להתבונן בלבו בגדולת ה'. וכמ"ש ממעמקים קראתיך ה' מעומקא דליבא (ועד"מ כמו במילי דעלמא לפעמים יש ענין גדול מאד מאד שכל חיות האדם תלוי בו ונוגע עד נקודת פנימיות הלב ועד בכלל וגורם לו לפעמים לעשות מעשים

ולדבר דברים שלא בדעת כלל) וזלע״ז ככה הוא ממש בעבודה שבלב. והיינו לפי שבחי׳ נקודת פנימית הלב היא למעלה מבחי׳ הדעת המתפשט ומתלבש במדות שנולדו מחב״ד כנודע. רק היא בחי׳ הארת חכמה עליונה שלמעלה מהבינה והדעת ובה מלובש וגנוז אור ה׳ ממש כמ״ש ה׳ בחכמה
כו׳ והיא היא בחי׳ ניצוץ אלקות שבכל נפש מישראל. ומה שאין כל אדם י באב פשוטה
זוכה למדרגה זו לעבודה שבלב מעומקא דלבא בבחי׳ פנימיות היינו לפי שבחינה זו היא אצלו בבחי׳ גלות ושביה והיא בחי׳ גלות השכינה ממש כי היא בחי׳ ניצוץ אלהות שבנפשו האלהית וסבת הגלות הוא מאמר רז״ל גלו לבבל שכינה עמהם דהיינו מפני שהלביש בחי׳ פנימית נקודת לבבו בזה לעומת זה דהיינו בלבושים צואים דמילי דעלמא ותאות עוה״ז הנקרא בשם בבל והיא בחי׳ ערלה המכסה על הברית ונקודה הפנימית שבלב ועל זה נאמר ומלתם את ערלת לבבכם. והנה במילה יש שני בחינות מילה ופריעה שהן ערלה גסה וקליפה דקה וכן בערלת הלב יש ג״כ תאות גסות ודקות מילה ופריעה ומל ולא פרע כאלו לא מל מפני שסוף סוף עדיין נקודת פנימית הלב היא מכוסה בלבוש שק דק בבחי׳ גלות ושביה. והנה על מילת הערלה ממש כתי׳ ומלתם את ערלת לבבכם אתם בעצמכם אך להסיר הקליפה הדקה זהו דבר הקשה על האדם וע״ז נא׳ בביאת המשיח ומל ה׳ אלהיך את לבבך כו׳ לאהבה את ה׳ אלהיך בכל לבבך ובכל נפשך למען חייך כלומר למען כי ה׳ לבדו הוא כל חייך ממש. שלכן אהבה זו היא מעומקא דלבא מנקודה פנימית ממש כנ״ל ולמעלה מבחי׳ הדעת ולכן משיח בא בהיסח הדעת לכללות ישראל והיא גילוי בחינת נקודה פנימית הכללית ויציאת השכינה הכללית מהגלות והשביה לעד ולעולמי עולמים וכן כל ניצוץ פרטי מהשכינה שבנפש כל אחד מישראל יוצאת מהגלות והשביה לפי שעה בחיי שעה זו תפלה ועבודה שבלב מעומקא דלבא מבחינת נקודה הפנימית הנגלית מהערלה ועולה למעלה לדבקה בו בתשוקה עזה בבחינת למען חייך והוא גם כן בבחי׳ היסח דעת האדם כי בחינה זו היא למעלה מדעת האדם והתבוננותו בגדולת ה׳ רק היא בחינת מתנה נתונה מאת ה׳ מן השמים מהארת בחי׳ פנים העליונים כמ״ש יאר ה׳ פניו אליך וכמ״ש
ומל ה׳ אלקיך כו׳. אך מודעת זאת כי אתערותא דלעילא היא באתערותא יא באב פשוטה
דלתתא דוקא בבחינת העלאת מ״נ כמשארז״ל אין טפה יורדת מלמעלה כו׳. ולכן צריך האדם לעשות בעצמו תחלת מילה זו להסיר ערלת הלב וקליפה הגסה ודקה המלבישות ומכסות על בחי׳ נקודת פנימית הלב שהיא בחינת אהבת ה׳ בחינת למען חייך שהיא בגלות בתאוות עוה״ז שהם ג״כ בבחי׳ למען חייך בזלע״ז כנ״ל והיינו ע״י נתינת הצדקה לה׳ מממונו שהוא חיותו ובפרט מי שמזונותיו מצומצמים ודחיקא ליה שעתא טובא שנותן

מחייו ממש ובפרטות אם נהנה מיגיע כפיו שא"א שלא עסק בהם פעמים רבות בבחי' נקודת פנימית הלב מעומקא דלבא כמנהג העולם בעסקיהם במו"מ וכה"ג והרי עתה הפעם כשמפזר מיגיעו ונותן לה' בשמחה ובטוב לבב הנה בזה פודה נפשו משחת דהיינו בחי' נקודת פנימית לבבו שהיתה בבחי' גלות ושביה בתוך הקליפה גסה או דקה כמ"ש מכל משמר נצור לבך משמר פי' בית האסורים ועתה נפדה מהחיצונים בצדקה זו וזה גם כן לשון פריעה ענין פריעת חוב שנתחייב ונשתעבד לחיצונים שמשלו בו על נקודת פנימיות לבבו וזהו ושביה בצדקה. וזהו צדק לפניו יהלך לפניו הוא מלשון פנימיות ויהלך הוא מלשון הולכה שמוליך את פנימית הלב לה' ואחר כך ישים לדרך ה' פעמיו כמ"ש והלכת בדרכיו אחרי ה' אלהיכם תלכו בכל מעשה המצות ות"ת כנגד כולן שכולן עולין לה' על ידי פנימית הלב ביתר שאת ומעלה מעלה מעלייתן לה' ע"י חיצונית הלב הנולד מהתבונה והדעת לבדן בלי הארת פנים מלמעלה אלא בבחינת הסתר פנים כי אין הפנים העליונים מאירים למטה אלא באתערותא דלתתא במעשה הצדקה הנקרא שלום. וז"ש פדה בשלום נפשי נפשי דייקא. וזהו ג"כ הטעם שנקרא הצדקה שלום לפי שנעשה שלום בין ישראל לאביהם שבשמים כמארז"ל דהיינו על ידי פדיון נפשותיהן הם חלק ה' ממש מידי החיצונים ובפרט צדקת א"י שהיא צדקת ה' ממש כמ"ש תמיד עיני ה' אלהיך בה והיו עיני ולבי שם כל הימים והיא שעמדה לנו לפדות חיי נפשנו מעצת החושבים לדחות פעמינו ותעמוד לנו לעד לשום נפשנו בחיים אמיתים מחיי החיים לאור באור החיים אשר יאר ה' פניו אתנו סלה אכי"ר:

יב באב פשוטה | יד באב מעוברת

אגרת ה

יג באב פשוטה | טו באב מעוברת

ויעש דוד שם ופי' בזוה"ק משום שנאמר ויהי דוד עושה משפט וצדקה לכל עמו כו' בכה ר"ש ואמר מאן עביד שמא קדישא בכל יומא מאן דיהיב צדקה למסכני כו'.

ויובן בהקדים מאמר רז"ל ע"פ כי ביה ה' צור עולמים בה' נברא עוה"ז ביו"ד נברא עוה"ב. פי' שהתענוג שמתענגים נשמות הצדיקים ונהנין מזיו השכינה המאיר בג"ע עליון ותחתון הוא שמתענגים בהשגתם והשכלתם שמשכילים ויודעים ומשיגים איזה השגה באור וחיות השופע שם מא"ס ב"ה בבחינת גילוי לנשמתם ורוח בינתם להבין ולהשיג איזה השגה כאו"א לפי מדרגתו ולפי מעשיו ולכן נקרא עולם הבא בשם בינה בזוה"ק והשפעה זו נמשכת מבחי' ח"ע שהוא מקור ההשכלה וההשגה הנקרא בשם בינה והוא קדמות השכל קודם שבא לכלל גילוי השגה והבנה רק עדיין הוא בבחי'

העלם והסתר רק שמעט מזעיר שם זעיר שם שופע ונמשך משם לבחינת בינה להבין ולהשיג שכל הנעלם ולכן נקרא בשם נקודה בהיכלא בזוה״ק וזו היא תמונת יו״ד של שם הוי׳ ב״ה ונקרא עדן אשר עליו נאמר עין לא ראתה כו׳ ונקרא אבא יסד ברתא.

פי׳ כי הנה התהוות אותיות הדבור היוצאות מה׳ מוצאות הפה אינן דבר מושכל ולא מוטבע בטבע מוצאות הללו להוציא מבטא האותיות ע״י ההבל והקול המכה בהן עפ״י דרך הטבע ולא על פי דרך השכל כגון השפתים עד״מ שאותיות בומ״פ יוצאות מהן אין הטבע ולא השכל נותן ליציאת מבטא ארבע חלקי שינויי ביטוי אותיות אלו על פי שינויי תנועת השפתים שמתנועעות בהבל אחד וקול אחד הפוגע בהן בשוה ואדרבה שינוי התנועות שבשפתים הוא לפי שינוי ביטוי האותיות שברצון הנפש לבטא בשפתים כרצונה לומר אות ב׳ או ו׳ או מ׳ או פ׳ ולא להיפך שיהיה רצון הנפש וכונתה לעשות שינוי תנועות השפתים כמו שהן מתנענעות עתה בביטויי ד׳ אותיות אלו. וכנראה בחוש שאין הנפש מתכוונת ויודעת לכוין כלל שינוי תנועות השפתים בשינויים אלו ויותר נראה כן בביטוי הנקודות שכשהנפש רצונה להוציא מפיה נקודת קמץ אזי ממילא נקמצים השפתים ובפתח נפתחים השפתים ולא שרצון הנפש לקמוץ ולא לפתוח כלל וכלל ואין להאריך בדבר הפשוט ומובן ומושכל לכל משכיל שמבטא האותיות והנקודות הוא למעלה מהשכל המושג ומובן אלא משכל הנעלם וקדמות השכל שבנפש המדברת ולכן אין התינוק יכול לדבר אף שמבין הכל:

אך האותיות הן בבחינת חומר וצורה הנקרא פנימית וחיצונית כי הגם שמקורן הוא מקדמות השכל ורצון הנפש זו היא בחינת צורת שינוי המבטא שבכ״ב אותיות אבל בחינת החומר וגוף התהוותן והוא בחי׳ חיצוניותן הוא ההבל היוצא מהלב שממנו מתהוה קול פשוט היוצא מהגרון ואח״כ נחלק לכ״ב הברות וביטוי כ״ב אותיות בה׳ מוצאות הידועות אחה״ע מהגרון גיכ״ק מהחיך כו׳ ומבטא ההבל הוא אות ה׳ אתא קלילא כו׳ והוא מקור החומר וגוף האותיות טרם התחלקותן לכ״ב ולכן ארז״ל שעוה״ז נברא בה׳: יד באב פשוטה טז באב מעוברת

והנה הגם שהיא ה׳ תתאה ה׳ אחרונה שבשם הוי׳ ורז״ל דרשו זה על פסוק כי ביה היינו לפי שמקורה וראשיתה לבא לבחי׳ גילוי מהעלם היו״ד הוא מושפע ונמשך מבחינת ה׳ עילאה שיש לה התפשטות אורך ורוחב להורות על בחינת בינה שהיא התפשטות השכל הנעלם בבחינת גילוי והשגה בהרחבת הדעת והשפעתה מסתיימת בלב וכמ״ש בתיקונים טו באב פשוטה

דבינה לבא ובה הלב מבין ומשם יוצא ההבל מקור גילוי גוף האותיות הדבור המתגלות בה׳ מוצאות מהעלם היו״ד ותמונת ה׳ תתאה בכתיבתה גם כן בהתפשטות אורך ורוחב מורה על התפשטות בחי׳ מלכותו יתברך מלכות כל עולמים למעלה ולמטה ולד׳ סטרין המתפשטות ונמשכות מאותיות דבר ה׳ כמ״ש בקהלת באשר דבר מלך שלטון כמ״ש במ״א. [ולהבין מעט מזעיר ענין ומהות אותיות הדבור באלהות שאין לו דמות הגוף ולא הנפש ח״ו כבר נתבאר בדרך ארוכה וקצרה (בלק״א ח״ב פי״א וי״ב ע״ש)]:

טז באב פשוטה

יז באב מעוברת

אך ביאור הענין למה אמרו רז״ל שעוה״ז דוקא נברא בה׳. הנה ידוע לכל חכמי לב כי ריבוי העולמות וההיכלות אשר אין להם מספר כמ״ש היש מספר לגדודיו ובכל היכל וגדוד אלף אלפין ורבוא רבבן מלאכים וכן נרנח״י מדרגות לאין קץ ובכל עולם והיכלות מריבוי היכלות שבאצי׳ בריאה יצירה הנה כל ריבויים אלו ריבוי אחר ריבוי עד אין קץ ממש הכל נמשך ונשפע מריבוי צירופי כ״ב אותיות דבר ה׳ המתחלקות ג״כ לצירופים רבים עד אין קץ ותכלית ממש כמ״ש בספר יצירה שבעה אבנים בונות חמשת אלפים וארבעים בתים מכאן ואילך צא וחשוב מה שאין הפה יכול לדבר כו׳ והגם שיש במעלות ומדריגות המלאכים ונשמות כמה וכמה מיני מעלות ומדריגות חלוקות לאין קץ גבוה על גבוה הנה הכל נמשך לפי חילופי הצירופים והתמורות בא״ת ב״ש כו׳ (וכמ״ש בפי״ב) אך דרך כלל הנה כולם בעלי חכמה ודעת ויודעים את בוראם מפני היות חיותם מפנימיות

יח באב מעוברת

האותיות הנמשכות מבחי׳ ח״ע וכנ״ל. אך העוה״ז השפל עם החיות שבתוכו קטן מהכיל ולסבול אור וחיות מבחי׳ צורת האותיות ופנימיותן להאיר ולהשפיע בו בלי לבוש והסתר כמו שמאירות ומשפיעות לנשמות ומלאכים רק ההארה וההשפעה באה ונשפע לעוה״ז מבחי׳ חומר וגוף האותיות והיצוניותם שהוא בחינת ההבל המתחלק לז׳ הבלים שבקהלת שעליהם העולם עומד כמ״ש בזוה״ק והוא מוצא פי ה׳ המתלבש בעולם הזה וכל צבאיו להחיותם ובתוכו מלובשת בחינת צורת אותיות הדבור והמחשבה ממדותיו הקדושות ורצונו וחכמתו וכו׳ המיוחדות בא״ס ב״ה בתכלית (וז״ש האר״י ז״ל שבחינת חיצוניות הכלים דמל׳ דאצילות המרומזות בה׳ של שם הוי׳ ב״ה הם ירדו ונעשו נשמה לעולם העשיה) וכ״כ בתקונים שהיו״ד הוא באצי׳ כו׳ וה׳ תתאה מקננת בעשיה:

יז באב פשוטה

יט באב מעוברת

והנה באדם התחתון למשל מי שהוא חכם גדול להשכיל נפלאות חכמה ומצמצם שכלו ומחשבתו באות אחד מדבורו הנה זה הוא צמצום עצום וירידה גדולה לחכמתו הנפלאה ככה ממש עד״מ ויתר מזה

לאין קץ הי׳ צמצום גדול עצום ורב כאשר בדבר ה׳ שמים נעשו בששת
ימ״ב וברוח פיו כל צבאם היא אות ה׳ של שם הוי׳ ב״ה אתא קלילא כמ״ש
בהבראם בה׳ בראם היא מקור הט׳ מאמרות שנמשכו ממאמר ראשון
בראשית דנמי מאמר הוא היא בחינת חכמה הנקראת ראשית אך אז
היתה המשכה וירידה זו בלי אתדל״ת כלל כי אדם אין לעבוד כו׳ רק כי
חפץ חסד הוא ועולם חסד יבנה וזהו בהבראם באברהם כי חסד לאברהם
כו׳. אך אחר בריאת האדם לעבדה כו׳ אזי כל אתדל״ע לעורר מדת חסד כ באב מעוברת
עליון הוא באתדל״ת בצדקה וחסד שישראל עושין בעולם הזה לכן אמרו
רז״ל כל האומר אין לו אלא תורה בלי גמ״ח אפילו תורה אין לו אלא
לעסוק בתורה ובגמ״ח כי הנה הגם דאורייתא מחכמה נפקת ובאורייתא
מתקיים עלמא ובאינון דלעאן בה כי בדבורם ממשיכים הארות והשפעות
(נ״א והשראות) ח״ע מקור התורה לבחינת אותיות הדבור שבהן נברא
העולם כמארז״ל א״ת בניך אלא בוניך הרי המשכה זו היא בחינת ירידה
גדולה ולזה צריך לעורר חסד עליון הנמשך כמים ממקום גבוה למקום נמוך
באתדל״ת בצדקה וחסד תתאה שממשיכי׳ חיים וחסד להחיות רוח שפלים
ונדכאים. וז״ש אל יתהלל חכם בחכמתו כו׳ כ״א בזאת יתהלל כו׳ כי אני ה׳
עושה חסד כו׳ כי החסד הוא הממשיך חיי החכמה למטה וא״ל הרי נקראת
חכמתו לבדו בלי המשכת חיים ממנה ח״ו. ובזה יובן מ״ש האריז״ל שיש ב׳ יח באב פשוטה
מיני נשמות בישראל נשמות ת״ח העוסקים בתורה כל ימיהם ונשמות בעלי
מצות העוסקים בצדקה וגמ״ח. דלכאורה הרי גם ת״ח צריכים לעסוק בגמ״ח
כמארז״ל שאפילו תורה אין לו אלא שהת״ח שתורתן עיקר ורוב ימיהם
בה ומיעוט ימיהם בגמ״ח הנה פעולת אתערותם דלתתא לעורר חסד עליון
להמשיך ולהוריד אוא״ס המלובש בחכ״ע מקור תורת ה׳ שבפיהם הוא רק
לעולם הנשמות שבבריאה ע״י עסק התלמוד ולמלאכים שביצירה ע״י לימוד
המשנה יען היות חיות הנשמות והמלאכים נשפעות מצירופי אותיות הדיבור
היא תורה שבע״פ ומקור האותיות הוא מח״ע כנ״ל אך להמשיך ולהוריד
הארה וחיות מבחינת הבל העליון ה׳ תתאה לעולם הזה השפל שהוא
צמצום גדול ביתר עז לא די באתעדל״ת של ת״ח העוסקים מיעוט ימיהם
בצדקה וגמ״ח אלא על ידי אתערותא דבעלי מצות העוסקים רוב ימיהם
בצדקה וגמ״ח (וכמ״ש בלק״א בח״א פל״ד) ולכן נקראו תמכי אורייתא והן
בחינות ומדרגות נו״ה להיותן ממשיכין אור התורה למטה לעולם העשיה.
ובזה יובן למה נקרא הצדקה בשם מעשה כמ״ש והיה מעשה הצדקה שלום
על שם שפעולתה להמשיך אור ה׳ לעולם העשיה. וזהו דקדוק לשון זוה״ק
מאן דעביד שמא קדישא דעביד דייקא כי באתערותא דלתתא בצדקה
וחסד תתאה מעורר חסד עליון להמשיך אור א״ס מבחינת חכמה עילאה

יו"ד של שם לה' של שם בחינת הדבור ורוח פיו יתברך כדי להשפיע לעולם העשי' ועד"מ להבדיל הבדלות אין קץ כמו שאדם אינו מדבר אלא לאחרים (ולא כשהוא בינו לבין עצמו) ואז מצמצם שכלו ומחשבתו בדבורו אליהם והמשכילים יבינו:

אגרת ו

יט באב פשוטה
כא באב מעוברת

זורע צדקה שכר אמת (במשלי י"א). פי' ששכר זריעת הצדקה היא מדת אמת וכתיב תתן אמת ליעקב ושבחא דקוב"ה מסדר נביא כו' כמ"ש בזוה"ק פירוש שהקב"ה הוא הנותן מדת אמת ליעקב וצריך להבין וכי אין אמת ביעקב ח"ו עד שהקב"ה יתן לו מלמעלה:

אך הנה מודעת זאת דמדת יעקב היא מדת רחמנות ועבודת ה' במדת רחמנות היא הבאה מהתעוררות רחמים רבים בלב האדם על ניצוץ אלקות שבנפשו הרחוקה מאור פני ה' כאשר הולך בחשך הבלי עולם והתעוררות רחמנות זו היא באה מהתבונה והדעת בגדולת ה' איך שאפילו העולמות העליונים למעלה מעלה עד אין קץ כלא ממש חשיבי קמיה כי כל שפעם וחיותם אינו רק מזיו והארה מאות אחד משמו יתברך כמאמר ביו"ד נברא עוה"ב כו'. והנה בזיו והארה זו שהוא התפשטות החיות משמו יתברך להחיות עליונים ותחתונים הוא שיש הבדל והפרש בין עליונים לתחתונים שעולם הזה נברא בה' וכו' וכן כל שינויי הפרטים שבכל עולם ועולם. הוא לפי שינויי צירופי האותיות וכן שינויי הזמנים בעבר הוה ועתיד ושינויי כל הקורות בחילופי הזמנים הכל משינויי צירופי האותיות שהן הן המשכת החיות ממדותיו ית"ש (כמ"ש בלק"א ח"ב פי"א) אבל לגבי מהותו ועצמותו יתברך כתיב אני ה' לא שניתי בין בבחינת שינויי ההשתלשלות מרום המעלות עד למטה מטה שכמו שהוא יתברך מצוי בעליונים כך הוא ממש בשוה בתחתונים (וכמ"ש בלק"א ח"א פנ"א) ובין בבחינת שינויי הזמן שכמו שהיה הוא לבדו הוא יחיד ומיוחד לפני ששת ימי בראשית כך הוא עתה אחר הבריאה והיינו משום שהכל כאין ואפס ממש לגבי מהותו ועצמותו וכמו אות אחד מדבורו של אדם או אפילו ממחשבתו לגבי כללות מהות הנפש השכלית ועצמותה עד"מ לשכך את האזן ובאמת אין ערוך אליך כתיב וכמ"ש במ"א (בלק"א ח"ב פ"ט) ע"ש. וזהו שאומרים המלך המרומם לבדו מאז פירוש כמו שמאז קודם הבריאה היה הוא לבדו הוא כך עתה הוא מרומם כו' ומתנשא מימות עולם פי' שהוא רם ונשא למעלה מעלה מבחינת זמן הנקרא בשם ימות עולם והיינו לפי שחיות כל ימות עולם הוא רק מבחינת המלך כו' וכמ"ש במ"א. ואי לזאת הרחמנות גדולה מאד

מאד על הניצוץ השוכן בגוף החשוך והאפל משכא דחויא העלול לקבל טומאה ולהתגאל בכל התאוות ר״ל לולי שהקב״ה מגן לו ונותן לו עוז ותעצומות ללחום עם הגוף ותאותיו ולנצחן וז״ש אדון עוזנו כו׳ מגן ישענו כו׳. והנה מודעת זאת דיש ב׳ מיני דו״ר הראשונות הן הנולדות מהתבונה והדעת בגדולת ה׳ ובדברים המביאין לידי אהבת ה׳ ויראתו והאחרונות הן הבאות אחר כך מלמעלה בבחי׳ מתנה וכמ״ש במ״א ע״פ עבודת מתנה אתן את כהונתכם שהיא מדת אהבה וכן הוא ג״כ ביראה. והנה ודאי אין ערוך כלל בין הראשונות שהן תולדות השכל הנברא לגבי האחרונות שהן מהבורא ית״ש. ולכן הן הן הנקראות בשם אמת כי חותמו של הקב״ה אמת שהוא אמת האמיתי וכל האמת שבנבראים כלא חשיבי קמיה אך איזה הדרך שיזכה האדם לאמת ה׳ הנה הוא על ידי שיעורר רחמים רבים לפני ה׳ על הניצוץ שבנפשו שהיא מדתו של יעקב מבריח מהקצה אל הקצה דהיינו מרום המעלות עד למטה מטה להמשיך אמת ה׳ לעולם השפל הזה החשוך וכמ״ש כי אשב בחשך ה׳ אור לי וזהו כי גבר עלינו חסדו כו׳. אך התעוררות ר״ר לפני ה׳ צ״ל ג״כ באמת וגם כשהוא באמת שלו איך יוכל על ידי אמת שלו לעורר רחמים עליונים מאמת ה׳. אך העצה לזה היא מדת הצדקה שהיא מדת הרחמים על מאן דלית ליה מגרמיה להחיות רוח שפלים כו׳ ובאתעדל״ת אתעדל״ע ה׳ מעורר ישנים ומקיץ נרדמים הם בחי׳ רחמים רבים וחסדים עליונים הנעלמים לצאת מההעלם אל הגילוי והארה רבה לאור באור החיים אמת ה׳ לעולם (וזה) [וזהו] לשון זריעה הנאמר בצדקה להצמיח אמת העליון אמת ה׳ ובפרט בצדקה וחסד של אמת שעושים עם אה״ק תובב״א לקיים מ״ש אמת מארץ תצמח על ידי זריעת הצדקה בה וחסד ור״ר הנאספים ונלקטים לתוכה הם מעוררים ג״כ חסדים עליונים הצפונים ונעלמים (בנ״א בה) כמ״ש אשר צפנת כו׳ לכוננה ולהקימה וז״ש בצדקה תכונני:

כ באב פשוטה

כב באב מעוברת

אגרת ז

אשרינו מה טוב חלקנו ומה נעים גורלנו כו׳ ה׳ מנת חלקי וכוסי וגו׳. חבלים נפלו לי וגו׳. להבין לשון חלקנו וגורלנו צריך לבאר היטב לשון השגור במארז״ל אין לו חלק באלהי ישראל כי הגם דלכאורה לא שייך לשון חלק כלל באלקות יתברך שאינו מתחלק לחלקים ח״ו. אך הענין כמ״ש ביעקב ויקרא לו אל אלהי ישראל פירוש כי הנה באמת הקב״ה כשמו כן הוא כי אף דאיהו ממכ״ע עליונים ותחתונים מרום המעלות עד מתחת לארץ הלזו החומרית כמ״ש הלא את השמים ואת הארץ אני מלא אני ממש דהיינו מהותו ועצמותו כביכול ולא כבודו לבד אעפ״כ הוא קדוש

כא באב פשוטה

כג באב מעוברת

ומובדל מעליונים ותחתונים ואינו נתפס כלל בתוכם ח"ו כתפיסת נשמת
האדם בגופו עד"מ כמ"ש במ"א באריכות. ולזאת לא היו יכולים לקבל
חיותם ממהותו ועצמותו לבדו כביכול רק התפשטות החיות אשר הקב"ה
מחיה עליונים ותחתונים הוא עד"מ כמו הארה מאירה משמו יתברך שהוא
ושמו אחד וכמ"ש כי נשגב שמו לבדו רק זיוו והודו על ארץ ושמים וגו'.
והארה זו מתלבשת ממש בעליונים ותחתונים להחיותם ונתפסת בתוכם על
ידי ממוצעים רבים וצמצומים רבים ועצומים בהשתלשלות המדרגות דרך
עלה ועלול וכו'. והנה הארה זו אף שלמעלה היא מאירה ומתפשטת בבחי' כב אב פשוטה
בלי גבול ותכלית להחיות עולמות נעלמים לאין קץ ותכלית כמ"ש באדרא כד באב מעוברת
רבא אעפ"כ בירדתה למטה ע"י צמצומים רבים להחיות הנבראים והיצורים
והנעשים היא נחלקת דרך כלל למספר תרי"ג כנגד תרי"ג מצות התורה
שהן הן תרי"ג מיני המשכות הארה זו מאור א"ס ב"ה להאיר לנשמת האדם
הכלולה מרמ"ח אברים ושס"ה גידים אשר בעבורה הוא עיקר תכלית ירידת
והמשכת הארה זו למטה לכל הנבראים והיצורים והנעשים שתכלית כולן
הוא האדם כנודע:

והנה מספר זה הוא בדרך כלל. אבל בדרך פרט הנה כל מצוה ומצוה
מתחלקת לפרטים רבים לאין קץ ותכלית והן הן גופי הלכות
פרטיות שבכל מצוה שאין להם מספר כמ"ש ששים המה מלכות הן ס'
מסכתות כו' ועלמות אין מספר הן ההלכות כו' שהן המשכת רצון העליון
כו' וכן הוא ממש בנשמת האדם כי הנה כל הנשמות שבעולם היו כלולות
באדה"ר ודרך כלל היתה נשמתו נחלקת למספר תרי"ג רמ"ח אברים
ושס"ה גידים אך דרך פרט נחלקת לניצוצות אין מספר שהן נשמות כל
ישראל מימות האבות והשבטים עד ביאת המשיח ועד בכלל שיקוים
אז מ"ש והיה מספר בנ"י כחול הים אשר לא ימד ולא יספר מרוב. והנה כג באב פשוטה
שופריה דיעקב מעין שופריה דאדה"ר שתיקן חטא אדה"ר והיתה נשמתו כה באב מעוברת
ג"כ כלולה מכל הנשמות שבישראל מעולם ועד עולם והיה מרכבה לתורה
שלמעלה שנק' בשם אדם כמ"ש ועל דמות הכסא דמות כמראה אדם וכו'
וכמ"ש וזאת לפנים בישראל כו' אין זאת אלא תורה כו' שהיתה כלולה
ומלובשת בנשמת ישראל סבא הכלולה מכל הנשמות וזהו ויקרא לו אל
אלקי ישראל. אל לשון המשכת ההארה מאור א"ס ב"ה מההעלם אל
הגילוי להאיר בבחי' גילוי בנשמתו וכמ"ש אל ה' ויאר לנו ואחריו כל
ישרי לב העוסקים בתורה ובמצות מאיר אור ה' א"ס ב"ה בבחינת גילוי
בנשמתם וזמן גילוי זה ביתר שאת ויתר עז ההארה במוחם ולבם הוא
בשעת התפלה כמ"ש במ"א. והנה אף שגילוי זה ע"י עסק התורה והמצות כד באב פשוטה
הוא שוה לכל נפש מישראל בדרך כלל כי תורה אחת ומשפט א' לכולנו כו באב מעוברת

אעפ״כ בדרך פרט אין כל הנפשות או הרוחות והנשמות שוות בענין זה לפי עת וזמן גלגולם ובואם בעוה״ז וכמארז״ל אבוך במאי הוי זהיר טפי א״ל בציצית כו׳ וכן אין כל הדורות שוין כי כמו שאברי האדם כל אבר יש לו פעולה פרטית ומיוחדת העין לראות והאזן לשמוע כך בכל מצוה מאיר אור פרטי ומיוחד מאור א״ס ב״ה ואף שכל נפש מישראל צריכה לבוא בגלגול לקיים כל תרי״ג מצות מ״מ לא נצרכה אלא להעדפה וזהירות וזריזות יתירה ביתר שאת ויתר עז כפולה ומכופלת למעלה מעלה מזהירות שאר המצות. וזהו שאמר במאי הוי זהיר טפי דייקא. והנה יתרון האור הזה הפרטי לנשמות פרטיות אינו בבחינת טעם ודעת מושג אלא למעלה מבחינת הדעת שכך עלה במחשבה לפניו יתברך ודוגמתו למטה הוא בחינת הגורל ממש:

אגרת ח

זורע צדקות מצמיח ישועות הנה מ״ש לשון זריעה במצות הצדקה וכמ״ש בפסוק זרעו לכם לצדקה כו׳. יובן ע״פ מה שארז״ל ר״א יהיב פרוטה לעני והדר מצלי דכתיב אני בצדק אחזה פניך פי׳ כי גילוי אלקותו יתברך המתגלה במחשבתו של אדם וכונתו בתפלתו כל חד לפום שיעורא דיליה הוא בתורת צדקה וחסד ה׳ מעולם ועד עולם על יראיו כו׳ כלומר שאור ה׳ א״ס ב״ה המאיר למעלה בעולמות עליונים בהארה רבה בבחי׳ גילוי רב ועצום עד שבאמת הן בטלין במציאות וכלא ממש חשיבי קמיה ונכללין באורו ית׳ והן הן ההיכלות עם המלאכים והנשמות שבהן המבוארים בזוה״ק בשמותם למקומותם בסדר התפלה שסדרו לנו אנשי כנה״ג הנה משם מאיר האור כי טוב לעולם השפל הזה על יראי ה׳ וחושבי שמו החפצים לעבדו בעבודה שבלב זו תפלה וכמ״ש וה׳ יגיה חשכי והנה ירידת הארה זו למטה לעוה״ז נקראת בשם חסד ה׳ המכונה בשם מים היורדים ממקום גבוה למקום נמוך כו׳: כה באב פשוטה / כז באב מעוברת

והנה מודעת זאת שיש למעלה גם כן מדת הגבורה והצמצום לצמצם ולהסתיר אורו יתברך לבל יתגלה לתחתונים אך הכל תלוי באתעדל״ת שאם האדם מתנהג בחסידות להשפיע חיים וחסד כו׳ כך מעורר למעלה כמשארז״ל במדה שאדם מודד בה מודדין לו אלא דלכאורה זו אינה מן המדה כ״א להשפיע לו חיי העוה״ב לבד כנגד מה שהוא משפיע חיי עוה״ז אבל לא להשפיע לו חיי הארת אור ה׳ [נ״א א״ס ב״ה] ממש שיאיר ויגיה חשכו בעבודה שבלב זו תפלה שהיא בחינת ומדרגת תשובה עילאה כנודע שהרי היא למעלה מעלה מכל חיי עוה״ב כמשארז״ל יפה כו באב פשוטה

שעה אחת בתשובה ומע"ט כו' וכמ"ש במ"א באריכות דעוה"ב אינו אלא זיו והארה וכו':

כז באב פשוטה **אך** הענין הוא עד"מ כמו שזורעין זרעים או נוטעין גרעין שהשבולת הצומחת מהזרע והאילן ופירותיו מהגרעין אינן מהותן ועצמותן של הזרע והגרעין כלל כי מהותם ועצמותם כלה ונרקב בארץ וכח הצומח שבארץ עצמה [נ"א עצמו] הוא המוציא והמגדל השבולת והאילן ופירותיו רק שאינו מוציא ומגלה כחו לחוץ מהכח אל הפועל כי אם על ידי הזרע והגרעין שנרקבין בארץ וכלה כל כחם בכח הצומח שבארץ ונתאחדו והיו לאחדים וע"י זה מוציא כח הצומח את כחו אל הפועל ומשפיע חיות לגדל שבולת כעין הזרע אבל בריבוי הרבה מאד בשבולת אחת וכן פירות הרבה על אילן א' וגם מהותן ועצמותן של הפירות מעולה בעילוי רב ועצום למעלה מעלה ממהותו ועצמותו של הגרעין הנטוע וכן כה"ג בפירות הארץ הגדלים מזרעונין כעין גרעינין כמו קשואים וכה"ג והכל הוא מפני שעיקר ושרש חיות הפירות נשפע מכח הצומח שבארץ הכולל חיות כל הפירות. והגרעינין הזרועים בארץ אינן אלא כעין אתערותא דלתתא הנקראת בשם העלאת מ"נ בכתבי האריז"ל:

כח באב פשוטה **וככה** ממש עד"מ כל מעשה הצדקה שעושין ישראל עולה למעלה בבחינת העלאת מ"נ לשורש נשמותיהן למעלה הנקרא בשם כנ"י ואימא תתאה בלשון הזהר ושכינה בלשון הגמרא הכלולה מכל מדותיו של הקב"ה ומיוחדת בהן בתכלית וראשיתן היא מדת החסד וע"י העלאה זו מתעורר חסד ה' ממש שהוא גילוי אורו יתברך לירד ולהאיר למטה לנשמות ישראל בבחי' גילוי רב ועצום בשעת התפלה עכ"פ כי אף שלגדולתו אין חקר עד דכולא קמיה כלא חשיבי הרי במקום שאתה מוצא גדולתו שם אתה מוצא ענותנותו כמים שיורדין כו'. וז"ש זרח בחשך אור לישרים חנון ורחום וצדיק דע"י שהאדם חנון ורחום וצדיק צדקות אהב גורם לאור ה' שיזרח לנשמתו המלובשת בגופו העומד בחשך שהוא משכא דחויא וזה נקרא בשם ישועה כד אתהפכא חשוכא לנהורא וזהו מצמיח ישועות שישועה זו צומחת מזריעת הצדקה שזורעין בארץ העליונה ארץ חפץ היא השכינה וכנ"י שנקראת כן ע"ש שמתלבשת בתחתונים להחיותם כמ"ש מלכותך מלכות כל עולמים ובפרט מן הפרט כשזורעין באה"ק התחתונה המכוונת כנגדה ממש שהזריעה נקלטת תיכף ומיד בארץ העליונה בלי שום מניעה ועיכוב בעולם מאחר שאין שום דבר חוצץ ומפסיק כלל בין ארצות החיים כי זה שער השמים משא"כ בחו"ל וד"ל:

אגרת ט

כט באב פשוטה
כח באב מעוברת

אהובי אחיי ורעיי אשר כנפשי באתי כמזכיר ומעורר ישנים בתרדמת הבלי הבלים ולפקוח עיני העורים יביטו לראות להיות כל ישעם וחפצם ומגמתם לכל בהם חיי רוחם במקור מים חיים חיי החיים כל ימי חייהם מנפש ועד בשר דהיינו כל מילי דעלמא ועסקי פרנסה לא יהיה כאלו דעבדין לגרמייהו ולא יהיה בית ישראל ככל הגוים דזנין ומפרנסין ומוקרין לנשייהו ובנייהו מאהבה כי מי כעמך ישראל גוי אחד בארץ כתיב דהיינו שגם בעניני ארץ לא יפרידו [נ״א יפרדו] מאחד האמת ח״ו להעיד עדות שקר ח״ו בקריאת שמע ערב ובוקר בעינים סגורות ה׳ אחד בד׳ רוחות ובשמים ממעל ובארץ מתחת ובפקוח עיני העורים התעיף עיניך בו ואיננו ח״ו אך בזאת יאות לנו להיות [נ״א בהיות] כל עסקינו במילי דעלמא לא לגרמייהו כי אם להחיות נפשות חלקי אלקות ולמלאות מחסוריהם בחסד חנם שבזה אנו מדמין הצורה ליוצרה ה׳ אחד אשר חסד אל כל היום חסד של אמת להחיות העולם ומלואו בכל רגע ורגע רק שאשתו ובניו של אדם קודמין לכל על פי התורה. חוץ מצדיקים שבדור שהן קודמין לבניו וצדיקים שבא״י קודמין לצדיקים שבחו״ל לבד מזאת שלא הניחו כמותן בחו״ל וד״ל.

ל באב פשוטה
כט באב מעוברת

ע״כ אהוביי אחיי שימו נא לבבכם לאלה הדברים הנאמרים בקצרה מאד (ואי״ה פא״פ אדבר בם בארוכה) איך היות כל עיקר עבודת ה׳ בעתים הללו בעקבות משיחא היא עבודת הצדקה כמ״ש רז״ל אין ישראל נגאלין אלא בצדקה ולא ארז״ל ת״ת שקול כנגד גמ״ח אלא בימיהם שת״ת היה עיקר העבודה אצלם וע״כ היו חכמים גדולים תנאים ואמוראים. משא״כ בעקבות משיחא שנפלה סוכת דוד עד בחי׳ רגלים ועקביים שהיא בחי׳ עשיה אין דרך לדבקה בה באמת ולהפכא חשוכא לנהורא דילה [נ״א דיליה] כ״א בבחי׳ עשיה ג״כ שהיא מעשה הצדקה כידוע למשכילים שבחי׳ עשיה באלקות היא בחי׳ השפעת והמשכת החיות למטה מטה למאן דלית ליה מגרמיה כלום וכל הזובח את יצרו בזה ופותח ידו ולבבו אתכפיא ס״א ומהפך חשוכא לאור השי״ת השוכן עלינו בבחי׳ עשיה בעקבות משיחא ויזכה לראות עין בעין בשוב ה׳ ציון כו׳:

אגרת י

א באלול פשוטה
ל באב מעוברת

אד״ש וחיים פתח דברי יעיר אזן שומעת תוכחת חיים אשר הוכיח ה׳ חיים ע״י נביאו ואמר חסדי ה׳ כי לא תמנו וגו׳ והל״ל כי לא תמו כמ״ש כי לא תמו חסדיך וגו׳. ויובן עפ״י מ״ש בזוה״ק אית חסד ואית חסד אית חסד עולם כו׳ ואית חסד עילאה דהוא רב חסד כו׳. כי הנה מודעת

זאת התורה נקראת עוז שהוא לשון גבורה וכמו שאמרו חז״ל תרי״ג מצות נאמרו למשה מסיני מפי הגבורה וכדכתיב מימינו אש דת למו פי׳ שהתורה מקורה ושרשה הוא רק חסדי ה׳ המכונים בשם ימין דהיינו המשכת בחי׳ אלהותו ית׳ והארה מאור א״ס ב״ה אל העולמות עליונים ותחתונים ע״י האדם הממשיך האור על עצמו בקיום רמ״ח מ״ע שהן רמ״ח אברים דמלכא. פי׳ רמ״ח כלים ולבושים להארה [נר׳ דצ״ל להההארה] מאור א״ס ב״ה המלובש בהן (ומאור זה יומשך לו דו״ר בכל מצוה כנודע) רק שהמשכה זו נתלבשה תחלה במדת גבורתו של הקב״ה המכונה בשם אש שהיא בחי׳ צמצום האור והחיות הנמשכות מאור אין סוף ב״ה כדי שתוכל להתלבש במעשה המצות שרובן ככולן הם בדברים חומריים כציצית ותפילין וקרבנות וצדקה ואף מצות שהן ברוחניות האדם כמו יראה ואהבה אעפ״כ הן בבחי׳ גבול ומדה ולא בבחי׳ א״ס כלל כי אהבה רבה לה׳ בלי קץ וגבול ומדה אין האדם יכול לסובלה בלבו ולהיות קיים בגופו אפילו רגע וכמארז״ל שבשעת מ״ת שהיתה התגלות אלהותו ית׳ ואא״ס ב״ה בבחי׳ דיבור והתגלות פרחה נשמתן כו׳:

והנה לפי שהמצות ניתנו לנו ע״י התלבשות במדת גבורה וצמצום ההארה כו׳ לכן רוב המצות יש להן שיעור מצומצם כמו אורך הציצית י״ב גודלין והתפילין אצבעים על אצבעים ומרובעות דוקא והלולב ד״ט והסוכה ז״ט והשופר טפח והמקוה מ׳ סאה וכן בקרבנות יש להן שיעור מצומצם לזמן כמו כבשים בני שנה ואילים בני שתים ופרים כו׳ וכן במעשה הצדקה וגמ״ח בממונו אף שהיא מהעמודים שהעולם עומד עליהם וכדכתיב עולם חסד יבנה אפ״ה יש לה שיעור קצוב חומש למצוה מן המובחר ומעשר למדה בינונית כו׳ וזה נק׳ חסד עולם פי׳ חסד אל כל היום המתלבש בעולמות עליונים ותחתונים ע״י אתערותא דלתתא היא מצות הצדקה וחסד שעושים בני אדם זה עם זה ולפי שהעולם הוא בבחי׳ גבול ומדה מהארץ עד לרקיע ת״ק שנה וכן מרקיע לרקיע כו׳ ושית אלפי שני הוי עלמא כו׳ לכן ניתן שיעור ומדה גם כן למצות הצדקה והחסד שבתורה כמו לשאר מצות התורה אך היינו דוקא לשומר התורה ולא סר ממנה ימין ושמאל אפילו כמלא נימא אבל מי שהעביר עליו הדרך ח״ו מאחר שהעוה דרכו לתת מגרעות בקדש העליון שגרע ערכו בחי׳ המשכתו מה שהיה יכול להמשיך מבחי׳ אלהותו והארת האור מאור א״ס ב״ה אילו היה שומר התורה ומקיימה כהלכתה הרי מעוות זה לא יוכל לתקן כ״א בהמשכת האור העליון שלמעלה מהעולמות ואינו מתלבש בהן הנק׳ חסד עילאה ורב חסד לפי שמאיר ומתפשט בבחי׳ א״ס בלי גבול ומדה מאחר שאיננו מצומצם תוך העולמות אלא בבחי׳ מקיף עליהן מלמעלה מריש

ב באלול פשוטה

א באלול מעוברת

ג באלול פשוטה

כל דרגין עד סוף וכו׳ וכשהאדם ממשיכו למטה במעשיו ואתעדל״ת אזי
אור עליון זה מאיר ומתפשט תוך העולמות ומתקן כל מעוות וכל מגרעות
שניתנו בקדש העליון ומחדש אורן וטובן ביתר שאת ויתר עז בבחי׳ אור
חדש ממש לכן אמרו במקום שבע״ת עומדין וכו׳. והנה עיקר התשובה הוא ד באלול פשוטה
בלב כי על ידי החרטה מעומקא דלבא מעורר עומק אור העליון הזה אך ב באלול מעוברת
כדי להמשיכו להאיר בעולמות עליונים ותחתונים צריך אתעדל״ת ממש
בבחי׳ מעשה דהיינו מעשה הצדקה וחסד בלי גבול ומדה דכמו שהאדם
משפיע רב חסד פי׳ ח״ס דלי״ת דהיינו לדל ואביון דלית ליה מגרמי׳ כלום
ואינו נותן גבול ומדה לנתינתו והשפעתו. כך הקב״ה משפיע אורו וטובו
בבחי׳ חסד עילאה הנק׳ רב חסד המאיר בבחי׳ א״ס בלי גבול ומדה תוך
העולמות עליונים ותחתונים שכולם הם בבחי׳ דלי״ת אצלו יתברך דלית
להון מגרמיהון כלום וכולא קמיה כלא חשיבי ועי״ז נתקנו כל הפגמים
שפגם האדם בעונותיו למעלה בעולמות עליונים ותחתונים. וז״ש עשה
צדקה ומשפט נבחר לה׳ מזבח לפי שהקרבנות הן בבחי׳ שיעור ומדה וגבול.
משא״כ בצדקה שיוכל לפזר בלי גבול לתקן עונותיו. ומ״ש המבזבז אל
יבזבז יותר מחומש היינו דוקא במי שלא חטא או שתקן חטאיו בסיגופים
ותעניות כראוי לתקן כל הפגמים למעלה. אבל מי שצריך לתקן נפשו עדיין
פשיטא דלא גרעה רפואת הנפש מרפואת הגוף שאין כסף נחשב וכל אשר
לאיש יתן בעד נפשו כתיב. והנה מדת חסד זו בלי גבול ומדה נקראת על ה באלול פשוטה
שמו של הקב״ה חסדי ה׳ כדכתיב וחסד ה׳ מעולם ועד עולם כו׳ כי הגם ג באלול מעוברת
שכל ישראל הם רחמנים וגומלי חסדים ברם יש גבול ומדה לרחמי האדם.
אבל הקב״ה נק׳ א״ס ב״ה ולמדותיו אין סוף כדכתיב כי לא כלו רחמיו
וכו׳. וז״ש הנביא אחר החורבן והגלות חסדי ה׳ כי לא תמנו וגו׳. פי׳ לפי
שלא תמנו שאין אנו תמימים ושלמים בלי שום חטא ופגם בנפש ובעולמות
עליונים ע״כ צריכין אנו להתנהג בחסדי ה׳ שהם בלי גבול ותכלית כדי
לעורר עלינו רחמים וחסד עילאה שהוא רב חסד ורחמים בלי גבול ותכלית
כמ״ש כי לא כלו רחמיו וגו׳. וזהו שארז״ל אין ישראל נגאלין אלא בצדקה
שיעשו גם אם יהיו פטורים מדינא כי אין בן דוד בא כו׳:

אגרת יא

להשכילך בינה כי לא זו הדרך ישכון אור ה׳ להיות חפץ בחיי בשרים ו באלול פשוטה
ובני ומזוני כי ע״ז ארז״ל בטל רצונך כו׳ דהיינו שיהי׳ רצונו ד באלול מעוברת
בטל במציאות ולא יהיה לו שום רצון כלל בעניני עולם הזה כולם הנכללים
בבני חיי ומזוני וכמארז״ל שע״כ אתה חי:

וביאור הענין הוא רק אמונה אמיתית ביוצר בראשית דהיינו שהבריאה יש מאין הנק׳ ראשית חכמה והיא חכמתו שאינה מושגת לשום נברא הבריאה הזאת היא בכל עת ורגע שמתהוים כל הברואים יש מאין מחכמתו ית׳ המחיה את הכל וכשיתבונן האדם בעומק הבנתו ויצייר בדעתו הווייתו מאין בכל רגע ורגע ממש האיך יעלה על דעתו כי רע לו או שום יסורים מבני חיי ומזוני או שארי יסורין בעולם הרי האין שהיא חכמתו יתברך הוא מקור החיים והטוב והעונג והוא העדן שלמעלה מעוה״ב רק מפני שאינו מושג לכן נדמה לו רע או יסורים אבל באמת אין רע יורד מלמעלה והכל טוב רק שאינו מושג לגודלו ורב טובו וזהו עיקר האמונה שבשבילה נברא האדם להאמין דלית אתר פנוי מיני׳ ובאור פני מלך חיים ועי״כ עוז וחדוה במקומו הואיל והוא רק טוב כל היום ועי״כ ראשית הכל שישמח האדם ויגל בכל עת ושעה ויחיה ממש באמונתו בה׳ המחיה ומטיב עמו בכל רגע ומי שמתעצב ומתאונן מראה בעצמו שיש לו מעט רע ויסורין וחסר לו איזה טובה והרי זה ככופר ח״ו ועי״כ הרחיקו מדת העצבות במאד חכמי האמת. אבל המאמין לא יחוש משום יסורין בעולם ובכל עניני העולם הן ולאו שוין אצלו בהשוואה אמיתית ומי שאין שוין לו מראה בעצמו שהוא מערב רב דלגרמייהו עבדין ואוהב א״ע לצאת מתחת יד ה׳ ולחיות בחיי הגויים בשביל אהבתו א״ע ועי״כ הוא חפץ בחיי בשרים ובני ומזוני כי זה טוב לו ונוח לו שלא נברא כי עיקר בריאת האדם בעוה״ז הוא בשביל לנסותו בנסיונות אלו ולדעת את אשר בלבבו אם יפנה לבבו אחרי אלהים אחרים שהם תאוות הגוף המשתלשלים מס״א ובהם הוא חפץ או אם חפצו ורצונו לחיות חיים אמיתים המשתלשלים מאלוקים חיים אף שאינו יכול (צ״ע. ובאיזה כת״י ליתא תיבות אלו [אף שאינו יכול] ובנוסחא אחרת מצאנו כך. ״או אם חפצו ורצונו אף שאינו יכול לחיות חיי אמיתים כו׳״. ולפי נוסחא זו נראה שתיבות [אף שאינו יכול] הוא מאמר מוסגר). ויאמין שבאמת הוא חי בהם וכל צרכיו וכל עניניו משתלשלים באמת בפרטי פרטיותיהם שלא מס״א כי מה׳ מצעדי גבר כוננו ואין מלה כו׳ ואם כן הכל טוב בתכלית רק שאינו מושג ובאמונה זו באמת נעשה הכל טוב גם בגלוי שבאמונה זו שמאמין שהרע הנדמה בגלוי כל חיותו הוא מטוב העליון שהיא חכמתו יתברך שאינה מושגת והיא העדן שלמעלה מעוה״ב הרי באמונה זו נכלל ומתעלה באמת הרע המדומה בטוב העליון הגנוז:

ז באלול פשוטה

אגרת יב

ח באלול פשוטה
ה באלול מעוברת

והיה מעשה הצדקה שלום ועבודת הצדקה השקט ובטח עד עולם. להבין ההפרש שבין מעשה לעבודה ובין שלום להשקט ובטח כו׳

ע"פ מה שארז"ל ע"פ עושה שלום במרומיו כי מיכאל שר של מים וגבריאל
שר של אש ואין מכבין זה את זה כלומר שמיכאל שר של חסד הנק' בשם
מים היורדים ממקום גבוה למקום נמוך והוא בחי' ההשפעה והתפשטות
החיות מעולמות עליונים לתחתונים ובחי' אש שטבעה לעלות למעלה היא
בחי' הגבורה והסתלקות השפעת החיים ממטה למעלה שלא להשפיע רק
בצמצום עצום ורב והן מדות נגדיות והפכיות זו לזו והיינו כשהן בבחי'
מדות לבדן. אך הקב"ה עושה שלום ביניהם דהיינו ע"י גילוי שמתגלה בהן ו באלול מעוברת
הארה רבה והשפעה עצומה מאד מאור א"ס ב"ה אשר כשמו כן הוא שאינו
בבחי' מדה ח"ו אלא למעלה מעלה עד אין קץ אפילו מבחי' חב"ד מקור
המדות ואזי המדות נגדיות של מיכאל וגבריאל נכללות במקורן ושרשן
והיו לאחדים ממש ובטלים באורו יתברך המאיר להם בבחי' גילוי ואזי
מתמזגים ומתמתקים הגבורות בחסדים ע"י בחי' ממוצעת קו המכריע ומטה
כלפי חסד היא מדת הרחמים הנק' בשם תפארת בדברי חכמי האמת לפי
שהיא כלולה מב' גוונין לובן ואודם המרמזים לחו"ג ולכן סתם שם הוי'
ב"ה שבכל התורה מורה על מדת התפארת כמ"ש בזוה"ק לפי שכאן הוא
בחי' גילוי אור א"ס ב"ה הארה רבה ביתר שאת משאר מדותיו הקדושות
יתברך. והנה אתערותא דלעילא לעורר גילוי הארה רבה והשפעה עצומה ט באלול פשוטה
הנ"ל מאור א"ס ב"ה לעשות שלום הנ"ל היא באתערותא דלתתא במעשה ז באלול מעוברת
הצדקה והשפעת חיים חן וחסד ורחמים למאן דלית ליה מגרמי' כלום
ולהחיות רוח שפלים כו'. ומודעת זאת מה שאמרו רז"ל על העוסק בתורה
לשמה משים שלום בפמליא של מעלה ובפמליא של מטה. פמליא של מעלה
הם השרים והמדות הנ"ל שהן ההיכלות עליונים בעולם הבריאה שבזוה"ק
ופמליא של מטה הן ההיכלות התחתונים ובפרט עוה"ז השפל המעורב טוב
ורע מחטא אדם הראשון והרע שולט על הטוב כמ"ש אשר שלט האדם
באדם כו' ולאום מלאום יאמץ וכנראה בחוש באדם התחתון הנקרא בשם
עולם קטן שלפעמים הטוב גובר ולפעמים להיפך ח"ו ואין שלום בעולם עד
עת קץ שיתברר הטוב מהרע לידבק בשרשו ומקורו מקור החיים ב"ה ואזי
יתפרדו כל פועלי און ורוח הטומאה יעבור מן הארץ כשיתברר מתוכו בחי'
הטוב המחייהו ובירור זה יהיה ג"כ ע"י גילוי אלקותו למטה בהארה רבה ח באלול מעוברת
והשפעה עצומה כמ"ש כי מלאה הארץ דעה את ה' ונגלה כבוד ה' כו'
וזהו בכללות העולם לעתיד אך באדם התחתון בכל עת מצוא זו תפלה או
שאר עתים מזומנים להתבודד עם קונו כ"א לפי מעשיו זוכה למעין בירור
זה ע"י עסק התורה לשמה וכן ע"י הצדקה כמ"ש ר"א יהיב פרוטה לעני
והדר מצלי דכתיב אני בצדק אחזה פניך היא בחי' גילוי הארה והשפעת
הדעת והתבונה להתבונן בגדולת ה' ולהוליד מזה דו"ר שכליים כנודע
ועי"ז נברר הטוב לה' ונפרד הרע כמ"ש מצרף לכסף וכור לזהב ואיש לפי

מהללו. פי׳ לפי הילולו את ה׳ בעומק הדעת להוליד דו״ר ככה נברר הטוב
ונפרד הרע כבירור ופירוד הסיגים מכסף וזהב במצרף וכור. והנה מודעת י באלול פשוטה
זאת שישראל בטבעם הם רחמנים וגומ״ח מפני היות נפשותיהם נמשכות ט באלול מעוברת
ממדותיו ית׳ אשר החסד גובר בהן על מדת הדין והגבורה והצמצום וכמ״ש גבר חסדו על יריאיו שלכן נקראת הנשמה בת כהן כמ״ש בזוה״ק. והנה הצדקה הנמשכת מבחי׳ זו נק׳ בשם מעשה הצדקה כי שם מעשה נופל על דבר שכבר נעשה או שנעשה תמיד ממילא והיא דבר ההווה ורגיל תמיד ואף כאן הרי מדת החסד והרחמנות הוטבעה בנפשות כל בית ישראל מכבר מעת בריאותן והשתלשלותן ממדותיו ית׳ כמ״ש ויפח באפיו כו׳ ואתה נפחת בי ומאן דנפח כו׳ וגם בכל יום ויום בטובו מחדש מעשה בראשית וחדשים לבקרים כו׳. אך לשון עבודה אינו נופל אלא על דבר שהאדם עושה ביגיעה עצומה נגד טבע נפשו רק שמבטל טבעו ורצונו מפני רצון העליון ב״ה כגון לייגע עצמו בתורה ובתפלה עד מיצוי הנפש כו׳. ואף כאן במצות הצדקה ליתן הרבה יותר מטבע רחמנותו ורצונו וכמ״ש רז״ל ע״פ נתן תתן
אפילו מאה פעמים וכו׳. וז״ש והיה מעשה הצדקה שגם הצדקה הנק׳ בשם יא באלול פשוטה
מעשה ולא בשם עבודה אעפ״כ באתעדל״ת אתערותא דלעילא מעורר י באלול מעוברת
גילוי אור א״ס ב״ה בהארה רבה והשפעה עצומה ונעשה שלום במרומיו וגם בפמליא של מטה רק שבעוה״ז השפל לא יתגלה השלום והבירור ופירוד הרע מהטוב עד עת קץ ולא בזמן הגלות כנ״ל רק בעולם קטן הוא האדם בכל עת מצוא זו תפלה כמ״ש בצדק אחזה פניך כנ״ל אך אחר התפלה יוכל להיות הרע חוזר וניעור בקל ולהתערב בטוב כאשר יתהלך בחשכת עוה״ז. אך הצדקה בבחי׳ עבודה הנה מאשר יקרה וגדלה מעלתה במאד מאד בהיותו מבטל טבעו ורצונו הגופני מפני רצון העליון ב״ה ואתכפיא ס״א ואזי אסתלק יקרא דקוב״ה כו׳ וכיתרון האור מן החשך דוקא כנודע. אי לזאת אין הרע יכול להיות עוד חוזר וניעור בקלות כ״כ מאליו רק אם האדם יעוררנו וימשיכנו ע״ע ח״ו. וז״ש השקט ובטח עד עולם. השקט הוא מלשון שוקט על שמריו דהיינו שהשמרים נפרדים לגמרי מן היין ונופלין למטה לגמרי והיין למעלה זך וצלול בתכלית. ועד״ז הוא בעבודת הצדקה השמרים הן בחי׳ תערובת רע שבנפשו נברר ונפרד מעט מעט עד שנופל למטה למקורו ושרשו וכמ״ש ותשליך במצולות ים כל חטאתם:

אגרת יג

מה רב טובך אשר צפנת ליראיך וגו׳. הנה בכלל עובדי ה׳ יש ב׳ בחי׳ יב באלול פשוטה
ומדרגות חלוקות מצד שורש נשמתם למעלה מבחי׳ ימין ושמאל יא באלול מעוברת
דהיינו שבחי׳ שמאל היא מדת הצמצום וההסתר בעבודת ה׳ כמ״ש והצנע

לכת כו׳ במסתרים תבכה כו׳ כל העוסק בתורה בסתר כו׳. והנה ממדה זו נמשכה ג״כ בחי׳ הצמצום והגבול בעבודת ה׳ כמו בצדקה להיות נידון בהשג יד והמבזבז אל יבזבז יותר מחומש וכה״ג בת״ת ושארי מצות די לו שיוצא י״ח מחיוב מפורש שחייבתו התורה בפי׳ לקבוע עתים כו׳. אך בחי׳ ימין היא מדת החסד וההתפשטות בעבודת ה׳ בהתרחבות בלי צמצום והסתר כלל כמ״ש ואתהלכה ברחבה כו׳ וממנה נמשך ג״כ מ״ש רז״ל זרוק מרה בתלמידים כו׳ (צ״ע. ונראה שצ״ל קודם אך בחי׳ ימין כו׳) וגם בלי צמצום וגבול כלל ואין מעצור לרוח נדבתו בין בצדקה ובין בת״ת ושארי מצות ולא די לו לצאת י״ח בלבד אלא עד בלי די כו׳:

והנה כל איש ישראל צ״ל כלול מב׳ בחי׳ אלו ואין לך דבר שאין לו מקום ולכן מצינו כמה דברים מקולי ב״ש ומחומרי ב״ה ללמדנו שאף ב״ש ששרש נשמתם מבחי׳ שמאל העליון ולכן היו דנין להחמיר תמיד בכל איסורי התורה. וב״ה שהיו מבחי׳ ימין העליון היו מלמדין זכות להקל ולהתיר איסורי ב״ש שיהיו מותרים מאיסורם ויוכלו לעלות למעלה אעפ״כ בכמה דברים היו ב״ש מקילין מפני התכללות שרש נשמתם שהוא כלול גם מימין וכן שורש נשמת ב״ה כלול גם משמאל כידוע דרך ומדות קדש העליון דלית תמן קיצוץ ופירוד ח״ו וכל המדות כלולות זו מזו. ולכן הם מיוחדות זו בזו כידוע לי״ח וכדכתיב באברהם שהוא מדת החסד והאהבה עתה ידעתי כי ירא אלהים אתה ע״י שלבש מדת הגבורה ויעקוד את יצחק בנו ויקח את המאכלת כו׳. ומה שאמר הכתוב אברהם אוהבי ופחד יצחק הנה ההפרש וההבדל הזה הוא בבחי׳ גילוי והעלם שבמדת יצחק הפחד הוא בבחי׳ גילוי והאהבה מסותרת בבחי׳ העלם והסתר וההיפך במדת א״א ע״ה וזהו שאמר דהע״ה מה רב טובך וגו׳ כלומר שמדת הטוב והחסד אשר היא בבחינת העלם והסתר אצל כל מי ששורש נשמתו מבחי׳ שמאל הנק׳ בשם יראיך כמדת ב״ש. הנה אף שהוא טוב הגנוז וצפון אעפ״כ הוא רב וגדול מאד כמו מדת הגדולה והחסד ממש שמבחי׳ ימין ושתיהן הן מבחי׳ גילוי בלי גבול ומדה ושיעור. וז״ש מה רב טובך כלומר בלי גבול ומדה בין הטוב אשר צפנת ליראיך ובין אשר פעלת לחוסים בך שהם בעלי הבטחון שמבחי׳ ימין וחסדם וטובם הוא ג״כ בבחי׳ גילוי והתפשטות נגד בני אדם ולא בבחינת צמצום והסתר כלל. (ומ״ש ליראיך ולא ביראיך היינו משום שכל מה שהוא בבחינת העלם בכל נשמה הנה בחי׳ זו אינה מלובשת תוך הגוף במוחו ולבו אלא הוא בבחינת מקיף מלמעלה ומשם היא מאירה למוחו ולבו לעתים הצריכים להתעוררות בחי׳ זו שתתעורר ותאיר למוחו ולבו כדי לבא לידי מעשה בפועל ממש). ואמר ע״כ אשר רב טוב לבית ישראל הצפון והגלוי הוא בבחי׳ בלי גבול ומדה לפי ערך נפשותם המלובשת בגוף לכן

יג באלול פשוטה

יד באלול פשוטה

גם אתה ה' תתנהג עמהם במדת חסדך הגדול בלי גבול ותכלית הנק' רב חסד. דאית חסד ואית חסד. אית חסד עולם שיש כנגדו ולעומתו מדה"ד ח"ו למעט ולצמצם חסדו וטובו. אבל חסד עליון הנק' רב חסד אין כנגדו מדה"ד למעט ולצמצם רוב חסדו מלהתפשט בלי גבול ותכלית כי הוא נמשך מבחי' סוכ"ע וטמירא דכל טמירין הנק' כתר עליון וז"ש תסתירם בסתר פניך וגו' תצפנם בסוכה וגו':

אגרת יד

טו באלול פשוטה

יב באלול מעוברת

לעורר את האהבה הישנה וחבת אה"ק להיות בוערת כרשפי אש מקרב איש ולב עמוק כאלו היום ממש נתן ה' רוחו עלינו רוח נדיבה בהתנדב עם למלאות ידם לה' ביד מלאה ורחבה בריבוי אחר ריבוי מדי שנה בשנה הולך ועולה למעלה ראש כמדת קדש העליון המאיר לאה"ק המתחדש ומתרבה תמיד כדכתיב תמיד עיני ה' אלהיך בה מרשית השנה ועד אחרית שנה דהאי ועד אחרית כו' אינו מובן לכאורה שהרי באחרית שנה זו מתחלת שנה שניה וא"כ הל"ל לעולם ועד:

אך הענין יובן ע"פ מ"ש ה' בחכמה יסד ארץ שיסוד הארץ העליונה היא בחי' ממלא כ"ע והתחתונה היא ארץ חפץ המכוונת כנגדה ממש ונק' על שמה ארץ החיים הנה הוא נמשך מהמשכת והארת חכמה עילאה מקור החיים העליונים כדכתיב החכמה תחיה בעליה וכו' והארה והמשכה זו היא מתחדשת באור חדש ממש בכל שנה ושנה כי הוא יתברך וחכמתו אחד בתכלית היחוד ונק' בשם אוא"ס ב"ה שאין סוף ואין קץ למעלת וגדולת האור והחיות הנמשך ממנו יתברך ומחכמתו בעילוי אחר עילוי
יג באלול מעוברת עד אין קץ ותכלית לרום המעלות למעלה מעלה ובכל שנה ושנה יורד ומאיר מחכמה עילאה אור חדש ומחודש שלא היה מאיר עדיין מעולם לארץ העליונה כי אור כל שנה ושנה מסתלק לשרשו בכל ער"ה כשהחדש מתכסה בו ואח"כ ע"י תקיעת שופר והתפלות נמשך אור חדש עליון מבחי' עליונה יותר שבמדרגת חכמה עילאה להאיר לארץ עליונה ולדרים עליה הם כל העולמות העליונים והתחתונים המקבלים חיותם ממנה דהיינו מן האור א"ס ב"ה וחכמתו המלובש בה כדכתיב כי עמך מקור חיים באורך נראה אור דהיינו אור המאיר מחכמה עילאה מקור החיים (וכנודע לי"ח שבכל ר"ה היא הנסירה ומקבלת מוחין חדשים עליונים יותר כו') ובפרטי פרטיות כן הוא בכל יום ויום נמשכין מוחין עליונים יותר בכל תפלת השחר ואינן מוחין הראשונים שנסתלקו אחר התפלה רק גבוהין יותר ודרך כלל
טז באלול פשוטה בכללות העולם בשית אלפי שנין כן הוא בכל ר"ה ור"ה. וז"ש תמיד עיני

ה׳ אלהיך בה שהעינים הם כינוים להמשכת והארת אור החכמה שלכן נקראו חכמים עיני העדה ואוירא דא״י מחכים והארה והמשכה זו אף שהיא תמידית אעפ״כ אינה בבחי׳ ומדרגה אחת לבדה מימי עולם אלא שבכל שנה ושנה הוא אור חדש עליון כי האור שנתחדש והאיר בר״ה זה הוא מסתלק בער״ה הבאה לשרשו. וז״ש מרשית השנה ועד אחרית שנה לבדה ולכן כתיב מרשית חסר א׳ רומז על הסתלקות האור שמסתלק בליל ר״ה עד אחר התקיעות שיורד אור חדש עליון יותר שלא היה מאיר עדיין מימי עולם אור עליון כזה והוא מתלבש ומסתתר בארץ החיים שלמעלה ושלמטה להחיות את כל העולמות כל משך שנה זו אך גילויו מההסתר הזה תלוי במעשה התחתונים וזכותם ותשובתם בעשי״ת וד״ל:

אגרת טו

להבין משל ומליצה דברי חכמים וחידותם בענין הספירות מודעת זאת בארץ מפי קדושי עליון נ״ע לקרב קצת אל השכל מאי דכתיב ומבשרי אחזה אלוה שהכוונה היא להבין קצת אלהותו יתברך מנפש מלובשת בבשר האדם וע״פ מארז״ל ע״פ ברכי נפשי וגו׳ מה הקב״ה כו׳ אף הנשמה כו׳ וע״פ מאמר הזהר ע״פ ויפח באפיו נשמת חיים מאן דנפח מתוכי׳ נפח ואפי׳ נפש דעשיה היא באה מזיווג זו״נ דעשיה והמוחין שלהם שהם בחי׳ חיה ונשמה דזו״נ שהן הן אחוריים דכלים דזו״נ דאצילות שהם אלהות ממש שבתוכם מאיר אור א״ס ב״ה המלובש וגנוז בחכמה דאצי׳ דאיהו וגרמוהי חד באצילות וע״כ גם בנשמת האדם מאיר אור א״ס ב״ה מלובש וגנוז באור החכמה שבה להחיות את האדם וממנה יוכל האדם להבין קצת בספירות העליונות שכולן מאירות בנשמתו הכלולה מהן. אך צריך להקדים מה ששמעתי ממורי ע״ה ע״פ ואנכי עפר ואפר שאמר אברהם אבינו ע״ה על הארת נשמתו המאירה בגופו מאור חסד עליון והיא מדתו מדת אהבה רבה (נ״א שבה הי׳) שהיה אוהב את הקב״ה אהבה גדולה ועליונה כ״כ עד שנעשה מרכבה להקב״ה וסד״א שבחי׳ חסד ואהבה שלמעלה בספירות העליונות היא מעין וסוג מהות מדת אהבה רבה של א״א ע״ה רק שהיא גדולה ונפלאה ממנה למעלה מעלה עד אין קץ ותכלית כנודע ממדות העליונות שאין להם [נ״א קץ] סוף ותכלית מצד עצמן כי אור א״ס ב״ה מאיר ומלובש בתוכם ממש ואיהו וגרמוהי חד. משא״כ בנשמת האדם המלובשת בחומר שיש למדותיה קץ וגבול. אבל מ״מ סד״א שמדותיה הן מעין וסוג מדות העליונות ולז״א ואנכי עפר ואפר דכמו שהאפר הוא מהותו ועצמותו של העץ הנשרף שהיה מורכב מד׳ יסודות ארמ״ע וג׳ יסודות אמ״ר חלפו והלכו להם וכלו בעשן המתהוה מהרכבתן כנודע ויסוד הד׳ שהיה

יז באלול פשוטה
יד באלול מעוברת

יח באלול פשוטה
טו באלול מעוברת

בעץ שהוא העפר שבו היורד למטה ואין האש שולטת בו הוא הנשאר קיים והוא האפר והנה כל מהות העץ וממשו וחומרו וצורתו באורך ורוחב ועובי שהיה נראה לעין קודם שנשרף עיקרו היה מיסוד העפר שבו רק שאמ"ר כלולים בו כי העפר הוא חומרי יותר מכולן ויש לו אורך ורוחב ועובי משא"כ באש ורוח וגם המים הם מעט מזעיר בעץ וכל ארכו ורחבו ועוביו הכל היה מן העפר והכל שב אל העפר שהוא האפר הנשאר אחרי שנפרדו ממנו אמ"ר והנה כמו שהאפר אין לו דמיון וערך אל מהות העץ הגדול באורך ורוחב ועובי קודם שנשרף לא בכמותו ולא באיכותו אף שהוא [הוא] מהותו ועצמותו וממנו נתהוה כך עד"מ אמר אאע"ה על מדתו מדת החסד והאהבה המאירה בו ומלובשת בגופו דאף שהיא [היא] מדת האהבה וחסד העליון שבאצילות המאיר בנשמתו שהיתה מרכבה עליונה אעפ"כ ברדתה למטה להתלבש בגופו ע"י השתלשלות העולמות ממדרגה למדרגה על ידי צמצומים רבים אין דמיון וערך מהות אור האהבה המאיר בו אל מהות אור אהבה וחסד עליון שבאצילות אלא כערך ודמיון מהות העפר שנעשה אפר אל מהותו ואיכותו כשהיה עץ נחמד למראה וטוב למאכל עד"מ ויותר מזה להבדיל באלפים הבדלות רק שדברה תורה כלשון בני אדם במשל ומליצה:

יט באלול פשוטה
טז באלול מעוברת

והנה כללות הי"ס שבנשמת האדם נודע לכל [בדרך כלל. בכ"י ליתא] שהמדות נחלקות בדרך כלל לז' מדות וכל פרטי המדות שבאדם באות מאחת מז' מדות אלו שהן שורש כל המדות וכללותן שהן מדת החסד להשפיע בלי גבול ומדת הגבורה לצמצם מלהשפיע כ"כ או שלא להשפיע [נ"א כל עיקר] כלל ומדת הרחמים לרחם על מי ששייך לשון רחמנות עליו והיא מדה ממוצעת בין גבורה לחסד שהיא להשפיע לכל גם למי שלא שייך לשון רחמנות עליו כלל מפני שאינו חסר כלום ואינו שרוי בצער כלל ולפי שהיא מדה ממוצעת נקראת תפארת כמו בגדי תפארת עד"מ שהוא בגד צבוע בגוונים הרבה מעורבי' [בו בכ"י ליתא] בדרך שהוא תפארת ונוי. משא"כ בגד הצבוע בגוון אחד לא שייך בו לשון תפארת ואח"כ בבוא ההשפעה לידי מעשה דהיינו בשעת ההשפעה ממש צריך להתיעץ איך להשפיע בדרך שיוכל המקבל לקבל ההשפעה כגון שרוצה להשפיע דבר חכמה ללמדה לבנו אם יאמרנה לו כולה כמו שהיא בשכלו לא יוכל הבן להבין ולקבל רק שצריך לסדר לו בסדר וענין אחר דבר דבור על אופניו מעט מעט ובחינת עצה זו נקראת נצח והוד שהן כליות יועצות וגם [נ"א והן] תרין ביעין המבשלים הזרע שהיא הטפה הנמשכת מהמוח דהיינו דבר חכמה ושכל הנמשך משכל האב שלא יומשך כמו שהוא שכל דק מאד במוחו ושכלו רק ישתנה קצת מדקות שכלו ויתהווה שכל שאינו דק כ"כ כדי שיוכל הבן לקבל במוחו והבנתו

והוא ממש עד"מ כטפה היורדת מהמוח שהיא דקה מאד [מאד] ונעשית גסה וחומרית ממש בכליות ותרין ביעין וגם נו"ה נקראים שחקים ורחיים ששוחקים מן לצדיקים כמו הטוחן [חטים] ברחיים עד"מ שמפרר החטים לחלקים דקים מאד כך צריך האב להקטין השכל ודבר חכמה שרוצה להשפיע לבנו ולחלקם לחלקים רבים ולומר לו מעט מעט במועצות ודעת וגם בכלל בחינת נצח הוא לנצח ולעמוד נגד כל מונע ההשפעה והלימוד מבנו מבית ומחוץ. מבית היינו להתחזק נגד מדת הגבורה והצמצום שבאב עצמו שהיא מעוררת דינים ברצונו על בנו לומר שאינו ראוי לכך עדיין (בכ"י נרשם חסר) ובחי' יסוד היא עד"מ ההתקשרות שמקשר האב שכלו בשכל בנו בשעת למודו עמו באהבה ורצון שרוצה שיבין בנו ובלעדי זה גם אם היה הבן שומע דבורים אלו עצמם מפי אביו [שמדבר בעדו ולומד לעצמו. בכי"ק אדמו"ר בעל צ"צ נ"ע (בדרוש כי ידעתיו סעי' י"ג שהועתק שם לשון זה) ליתא תיבות אלו] לא היה מבין כ"כ כמו עכשיו שאביו מקשר שכלו אליו ומדבר עמו פא"פ באהבה וחשק שחושק מאד שיבין בנו וכל מה שהחשק והתענוג גדול כך ההשפעה והלימוד גדול שהבן יוכל לקבל יותר והאב משפיע יותר כי ע"י החשק והתענוג מתרבה ומתגדל שכלו בהרחבת הדעת להשפיע וללמד לבנו (וכמו עד"מ בגשמיות ממש רבוי הזרע הוא מרוב החשק והתענוג ועי"ז ממשיך הרבה מהמוח ולכן המשילו חכמי האמת לזיווג גשמי כמו שית'). והנה מדות אלו הן בחי' חיצוניות יז באלול מעוברת
שבנפש ובתוכן מלובשות מדות פנימיות שהן בחי' אהוי"ר כו' דהיינו עד"מ באב המשפיע לבנו מחמת אהבתו ומונע השפעתו מפחדו ויראתו שלא יבא לידי מכשול ח"ו. ומקור ושרש מדות אלו הפנימיות והחיצוניות הוא מחב"ד שבנפשו כי לפי שכל האדם כך הן מדותיו כנראה בחוש שהקטן שהחב"ד שלו הן בבחי' קטנות כך כל מדותיו הן בדברים קטני הערך וגם בגדולים לפי שכלו יהולל איש כי לפי רוב חכמתו כך הוא רוב אהבתו וחסדו וכן שאר כל מדותיו פנימיות וחיצוניות מקורן הוא מחב"ד שבו והעיקר הוא הדעת שבו הנמשך מבחי' החו"ב שבו כנראה בחוש כי לפי שינוי דעות בני אדם זה מזה כך הוא שינוי מדותיהם. והנה כ"ז הוא רק עד"מ לבד כי כ"ז הוא בנפש כ באלול פשוטה
השכלית התחתונה שבאדם הבאה מקליפת נוגה אך באמת לאמיתו בנפש יח באלול מעוברת
העליונה האלהית שהיא חלק אלוה ממעל כל המדות פנימיות וחיצוניות הן לה' לבדו כי מחמת אהבת ה' ומרוב חפצו לדבקה בו הוא חפץ חסד כדי לידבק במדותיו כמארז"ל ע"פ ולדבקה בו הדבק במדותיו וכן במדת הגבורה להפרע מן הרשעים ולענשם בעונשי התורה וכן להתגבר על יצרו ולקדש א"ע במותר לו ולעשות גדר וסייג לתורה מפני פחד ה' ויראתו פן יבא לידי חטא ח"ו וכן לפאר את ה' ותורתו בכל מיני פאר ולדבקה בשבחיו בכל בחי' נפשו דהיינו בהתבוננות שכלו ומחשבתו גם בדיבורו וכן לעמוד בנצחון נגד כל מונע מעבודת ה' ומלדבקה בו ונגד כל מונע מלהיות כבוד ה' מלא את

כל הארץ כמלחמות ה׳ אשר נלחם דהע״ה וכן להשתחוות ולהודות לה׳ אשר מחיה ומהוה את הכל והכל בטל במציאות אצלו וכולא קמיה כלא חשיב וכאין ואפס ממש ואף שאין אנו משיגים איך הוא הכל אפס ממש קמיה אעפי״כ מודים אנחנו בהודאה אמיתית שכן הוא באמת לאמיתו ובכלל זה ג״כ להודות לה׳ על כל הטובות אשר גמלנו ולא להיות כפוי טובה ח״ו ובכלל זה להודות על כל שבחיו ומדותיו ופעולותיו באצי׳ ובריאות עליונים ותחתונים שהם משובחים עד אין תכלית [נ״א חקר] ונאים וראוים אליו ית׳ וית׳ והוא מלשון הוד והדר וכן במדת צדיק יסוד עולם להיות נפשו קשורה בה׳ חיי החיים ולדבקה בו בדביקה וחשיקה בחשק ותענוג נפלא ובמדת מל׳ לקבל עליו עול מלכותו ועבודתו כעבודת כל עבד לאדונו באימה וביראה ומקור ושורש כל המדות הן מחב״ד דהיינו החכמה היא מקור השכל המשיג את ה׳ וחכמתו וגדולתו ומדותיו הקדושות שמנהיג ומחיה בהן כל העולמות עליונים ותחתונים ובינה היא ההתבוננות בהשגה זו באורך ורוחב ועומק בינתו להבין דבר מתוך דבר ולהוליד מהשגה זו תולדותיה שהן מדות אהוי״ר ושארי מדות הנולדות בנפש האלהית המשכלת ומתבוננת בגדולת ה׳ כי לגדולתו אין חקר ויש בחי׳ גדולת ה׳ שע״י התבוננות הנפש האלהית בה תפול עליה אימתה ופחד שהיא יראה תתאה שהיא בחינת מלכות ויש בחי׳ גדולת ה׳ שממנה באה יראה עילאה יראה בושת ויש בחינה שממנה באה אהבה רבה ויש בחינה שממנה באה אהבה זוטא וכן במדות החיצוניות שהן חסד כו׳ ובכולן צריך להיות מלובש בהן בחינת הדעת שהוא בחינת התקשרות הנפש הקשורה ותקועה בהשגה זו שמשגת איזה ענין מגדולת ה׳ שממנה נולדה בה איזה מדה מהמדות כי בהיסח הדעת כרגע מהשגה זו מסתלקת ג״כ המדה הנולדה ממנה מהגילוי בנפש אל ההעלם להיות בה בכח ולא בפועל ולכן נקרא הזיווג בלשון דעת מפני שהוא לשון התקשרות וזהו בחי׳ דעת תחתון [נ״א הדעת התחתון] המתפשט במדות ומתלבש בהן להחיותן ולקיימן ויש בחינת דעת העליון שהוא בחינת התקשרות וחיבור מקור השכל המשיג עומק המושג שהוא כנקודה וכברק המבריק על שכלו שיתפשט למטה ויבא עומק המושג לידי הבנה בהרחבת הביאור באורך ורוחב שהיא בחינת בינה הנק׳ רחובות הנהר כמו שיתבאר במקומו:

כא באלול פשוטה

אגרת טז

לאנשי ק׳ וכו׳

כב באלול פשוטה

יט באלול מעוברת

אהובייי אחיי ורעיי אשר כנפשי הנה לא נעלם ממני צוק העתים אשר נתדלדלה הפרנסה ובפרט הידועים לי ממחניכם אשר מטה ידם בלי שום משען ומשענה וממש לווים ואוכלים ה׳ ירחם עליהם וירחיב להם

בצר בקרוב ועם כל זה לא טוב הם עושים לנפשם לפי הנשמע אשר קפצו ידם הפתוחה מעודם עד היום הזה ליתן ביד מלאה ועין יפה לכל הצטרכות ההכרחיים לדי מחסורי האביונים נקיים אשר עיניהם נשואות אלינו ואם אנו לא נרחם עליהם ח״ו מי ירחם עליהם וחי אחיך עמך כתיב ולא אמרו חייך קודמין אלא כשביד אחד קיתון של מים וכו׳ שהוא דבר השוה לשניהם בשוה לשתות להשיב נפשם בצמא. אבל אם העני צריך לחם לפי הטף ועצים וכסות בקרה וכה״ג כל דברים אלו קודמין לכל מלבושי כבוד וזבח משפחה בשר ודגים וכל מטעמים של האדם וכב״ב ולא שייך בזה חייך קודמין מאחר שאינן חיי נפש ממש כמו של העני שוה בשוה ממש כדאיתא בנדרים דף פ׳.

והנה זהו עפ״י שורת הדין גמור. אבל באמת גם אם הוא ענין דלא שייך כ״כ ה״ט ראוי לכל אדם שלא לדקדק להעמיד על הדין רק לדחוק חייו וליכנס לפני ולפנים משורת הדין ולדאוג לעצמו ממארז״ל שכל המדקדק בכך סוף בא לידי כך ח״ו וגם כי כולנו צריכים לרחמי שמים בכל עת באתערותא דלתתא דוקא בכל עת ובכל שעה לעורר רחמינו על הצריכים לרחמים וכל המאמץ לבבו וכובש רחמיו יהיה מאיזה טעם שיהיה גורם כך למעלה לכבוש וכו׳ ח״ו ומה גם כי אדם אין צדיק בארץ אשר יעשה טוב תמיד ולא יחטא והצדקה מכפרת ומגינה מן הפורענות וכו׳ ולזאת היא רפואת הגוף ונפש ממש אשר עור בעד עור וכל אשר לאיש יתן בעד נפשו בשגם אנו מאמינים בני מאמינים כי הצדקה אינה רק הלואה להקב״ה כדכתיב מלוה ה׳ חונן דל וגמולו ישלם לו בכפליים בעולם הזה דשכר כל המצות ליכא בעוה״ז לבד מצדקה לפי שהוא טוב לבריות כדאיתא בקדושין ס״פ קמא וגם יש לחוש לעונש ח״ו כשחבריו נמנים לדבר מצוה והוא לא נמנה עמהם כנודע ממארז״ל ולשומעים יונעם ותבוא עליהם ברכת טוב בכל מילי דמיטב הטיבה ה׳ לטובים וישרים כנפשם ונפש הדו״ש מכל לב ונפש:

בג באלול פשוטה

כ באלול מעוברת

אגרת יז

כד באלול פשוטה

כא באלול מעוברת

נודע דבאתערותא דלתתא שהאדם מעורר בלבו מדת החסד ורחמנות על כל הצריכים לרחמים אתערותא דלעילא לעורר עליו רחמים רבים ממקור הרחמים להשפיע לו הפירות בעוה״ז והקרן לעוה״ב. פי׳ הפירות היא השפעה הנשפעת ממקור הרחמים וחיי החיים ב״ה ונמשכת למטה מטה בבחינת השתלשלות העולמות מלמעלה למטה כו׳ עד שמתלבשת בעוה״ז הגשמי בבני חיי ומזוני כו׳ והקרן הוא כמ״ש רחבה מצותך מאד והל״ל מצותיך לשון רבים (וגם לשון רחבה אינו מובן) אלא מצותך דייקא היא מצות הצדקה שהיא מצות ה׳ ממש מה שהקב״ה בכבודו ובעצמו עושה תמיד להחיות העולמות ויעשה לעתיד ביתר שאת ועז וכמ״ש ושמרו דרך

ה׳ לעשות צדקה כו׳ כמו דרך שהולכים בה מעיר לעיר עד״מ. כך הצדקה היא בחי׳ גילוי והארת אור א״ס ב״ה סובב כל עלמין שיאיר ויתגלה עד עוה״ז באתערותא דלתתא בתורת צדקה וחסד חנם לעתיד בתחיית המתים ביתר שאת ויתר עז לאין קץ מבחינת גילוי (הארה) [ההארה] בג״ע התחתון והעליון שהרי כל נשמות הצדיקים והתנאים והנביאים שהם עתה בג״ע העליון ברום המעלות יתלבשו בגופותיהם לעתיד ויקומו בזמן התחייה ליהנות מזיו השכינה לפי שההארה והגילוי שבג״ע היא בחינת ממלא כל עלמין שהוא בחינת השתלשלות ממדרגה למדרגה ע״י צמצומים עצומים וכמארז״ל ביו״ד נברא עוה״ב והיא בחינת חכמה עילאה הנקראת עדן העליון המשתלשלת ומתלבשת בכל העולמות כמ״ש כולם בחכמה עשית כו׳ והחכמה תחי׳ כו׳ ובג״ע היא בבחינת גילוי ההשגה לכל חד לפום שיעורא דילי׳ כנודע שעונג הנשמות בג״ע הוא מהשגת סודות התורה שעסק בעוה״ז בנגלה כדאיתא בזוה״ק פ׳ שלח ובגמ׳ בעובדא דרבה בר נחמני. אבל גילוי ההארה שבתחה״מ יהי׳ מבחינת סובב כל עלמין שאינה בבחינת צמצום ושיעור וגבול אלא בלי גבול ותכלית כמ״ש בלק״א פמ״ח ביאור ענין סוכ״ע שאינו כמשמעו כמו עיגול ח״ו אלא שאינו בבחי׳ התלבשות וכו׳ וע״ש היטב. וזהו שארז״ל ועטרותיהם בראשיהם ונהנין כו׳ עטרה היא בחינת מקיף וסובב ונקרא כתר מלשון כותרת והוא בחי׳ ממוצע המחבר הארת המאציל א״ס ב״ה להנאצלים ולעתיד יאיר ויתגלה בעוה״ז לכל הצדיקים שיקומו בתחייה (ועמך כולם צדיקים כו׳). וזה שארז״ל עתידים צדיקים שיאמרו לפניהם קדוש כי קדוש הוא בחי׳ מובדל שאינו בגדר השגה ודעת כי הוא למעלה מעלה מבחינת החכמה ודעת שבג״ע כי החכמה מאין תמצא כתיב הוא בחינת כתר עליון הנקרא אין בזוה״ק והשפעתו והארתו בבחינת גילוי הוא דוקא כשהנשמה תתלבש בגוף זך וצח אחר התחי׳ כי נעוץ תחלתן בסופן דוקא וסוף מעשה במחשבה תחלה כו׳ כנודע. אך א״א להגיע למדרגה זו עד שיהא בג״ע תחלה להשיג בחינת חכמה עילאה (כו׳) [אפשר צ״ל כל חד] כפום שיעורא דיליה וטל תורה מחייהו והקיצות היא תשיחך כו׳ וד״ל. וזהו רחבה מצותך מאד היא מצות הצדקה שהיא כלי ושטח רחב מאד להתלבש בה הארת אור א״ס ב״ה (וכמ״ש לבושו צדקה) אשר יאיר לעתיד בבחינת בלי גבול ותכלית בחסד חנם באתערותא דלתתא זו הנק׳ דרך ה׳ וזהו לשון מאד שהוא בלי גבול ותכלית. אבל לכל תכלה ראיתי קץ תכלה היא מלשון כלות הנפש שבג״ע שהיא בבחי׳ קץ ותכלית וצמצום כנ״ל ולכל תכלה הוא לפי שיש כמה וכמה מעלות ומדרגות ג״ע זה למעלה מזה עד רום המעלות כמ״ש בלקוטי הש״ס מהאריז״ל בפי׳ מארז״ל ת״ח אין להם מנוחה כו׳ שעולים תמיד ממדרגה למדרגה בהשגת התורה שאין לה סוף כו׳ עד אחר התחי׳ שיהיה להם מנוחה כו׳:

כה באלול פשוטה
כב באלול מעוברת
כו באלול פשוטה